Geospatial Web Services:

Advances in Information Interoperability

Peisheng Zhao
George Mason University, USA

Liping Di
George Mason University, USA

INFORMATION SCIENCE REFERENCE

Hershey · New York

Senior Editorial Director: Kristin Klinger
Director of Book Publications: Julia Mosemann
Editorial Director: Lindsay Johnston
Acquisitions Editor: Erika Carter
Typesetters: Michael Brehm, Milan Vracarich, Jr., and Deanna Zombro
Production Coordinator: Jamie Snavely
Cover Design: Nick Newcomer

Published in the United States of America by
Information Science Reference (an imprint of IGI Global)
701 E. Chocolate Avenue
Hershey PA 17033
Tel: 717-533-8845
Fax: 717-533-8661
E-mail: cust@igi-global.com
Web site: http://www.igi-global.com/reference

Library of Congress Cataloging-in-Publication Data

Geospatial web services : advances in information interoperability / Peisheng
Zhao and Liping Di, Editors.
     p. cm.
  Includes bibliographical references and index.
  Summary: " This book highlights the strategic role of geospatial Web
services in a distributed heterogeneous environment and the life cycle of
geospatial Web services for building interoperable geospatial applications"--
Provided by publisher.
  ISBN 978-1-60960-192-8 (hardcover) -- ISBN 978-1-60960-194-2 (ebook) 1.
Geographic information systems. 2. Internet. I. Zhao, Peisheng, 1971- II.
Di, Liping.
  G70.212.G4789 2011
  910.285'67--dc22
                     2010051815

British Cataloguing in Publication Data
A Cataloguing in Publication record for this book is available from the British Library.

Table of Contents

Section 3
Registry and Discovery

Manil Maskey, The University of Alabama in Huntsville, USA
Helen Conover, The University of Alabama in Huntsville, USA
Ken Keiser, The University of Alabama in Huntsville, USA
Luis Bermudez, Southeastern Universities Research Association, USA
Sara Graves, The University of Alabama in Huntsville, USA

Fabio Gomes de Andrade, Federal Institute of Education, Science and Technology
    of Paraiba, Brazil
Fábio Luiz Leite Jr., Paraiba State University, Brazil
Cláudio de Souza Baptista, Federal University of Campina Grande, Brazil

Section 4
Semantic Web

Sven Schade, European Commission – Joint Research Centre, Institute for Environment and
Sustainability, Italy

Zhong-Ren Peng, University of Florida, USA & Tongji University, China
Tian Zhao, University of Wisconsin – Milwaukee, USA
Chuanrong Zhang, University of Connecticut, USA

Carlos Granell, Universitat Jaume I, Spain
Sven Schade, European Commission – Joint Research Centre, Institute for Environment and
Sustainability, Italy
Gobe Hobona, University of Nottingham, UK

Naijun Zhou, University of Maryland College Park, USA

Detailed Table of Contents

Section 1
Standards

Section 1 explores geospatial interoperability standards. The Open Geospatial Consortium (OGC) has developed a set of specifications aimed at the full integration of "geo-enabled" Web services into mainstream computing to make complex spatial information and services interoperable and useful with all kinds of applications. The OGC Web service specifications have been widely accepted by the geospatial communities. Some of them are becoming International Organization for Standardization (ISO) standards.

Chapter 1

Carl N. Reed, Open Geospatial Consortium, USA

Chapter 1 introduces the background of the OGC Web services and provides information on the OGC Reference Model and the importance of reference architecture for the successful deployment of applications using OGC and related standards. This chapter highlights the OGC Web service architecture and relevant key OGC Web services standards. It also discusses planned work on the OGC Web services standards baseline as well as reflections on the impact of current technology trends, such as the mobile internet and cloud computing.

Section 2
Design and Implementation

Section 2 discusses several basic aspects of service design and implementation that facilitate building a better geospatial Web service. Choices relating to granularity affect service interfaces, data storage and organization, and XML format design.

Chapter 2

Elias Z. K. Ioup, Naval Research Laboratory, USA
John T. Sample, Naval Research Laboratory, USA

Chapter 2 highlights the importance of analyzing usage and performance requirements when choosing granularity in the design of a geospatial Web service and provides common examples that explore the different approaches to granularity which are available.

Chapter 3

Richard Onchaga Moses, Kenya Polytechnic University College, Kenya

Chapter 3 identifies and elaborates quality concerns and uses data quality and quality of service to define a quality model for geospatial Web services. An ontology framework that explores ontologies to provide a consistent set of concepts to unambiguously define and reason about the quality of geospatial Web services is presented.

Chapter 4

Bastian Schäffer, University of Münster, Germany
Rüdiger Gartmann, Conterra GmbH, Germany

Chapter 4 presents an approach that goes beyond classical Role-Based Access Control models to support ad-hoc license agreements directly in process, without any prior offline negotiated agreements being necessary between service provider and service user for on-demand access.

Section 3
Registry and Discovery

Section 3 discusses how to use catalog services to facilitate the registry and discovery of geospatial Web services.

Chapter 5

Manil Maskey, The University of Alabama in Huntsville, USA
Helen Conover, The University of Alabama in Huntsville, USA
Ken Keiser, The University of Alabama in Huntsville, USA
Luis Bermudez, Southeastern Universities Research Association, USA
Sara Graves, The University of Alabama in Huntsville, USA

Chapter 5 presents a service registry compliant with the OGC Catalog Service for Web (CSW). It is developed as part of an OGC-sponsored interoperability experiment involving the ocean sciences community. A standards-compliant registry for this endeavor eliminates the need for discovering the services from ad-hoc registries and opens up avenues for the development of automated tools.

Chapter 6

Fabio Gomes de Andrade, Federal Institute of Education, Science and Technology
of Paraiba, Brazil
Fábio Luiz Leite Jr., Paraiba State University, Brazil
Cláudio de Souza Baptista, Federal University of Campina Grande, Brazil

Chapter 6 introduces a distributed catalog service that uses ontologies to describe the underlying information to provide a more accurate search. The proposed catalog service that is able to rewrite and propagate queries to other distributed catalogs allows the catalog services in different SDIs to cooperate and exchange information directly with each other without the traditional problems imposed by a centralized architecture.

Section 4
Semantic Web

With Semantic Web technologies, geospatial ontologies can capture the semantic network of the geospatial world. Intelligent applications can then take advantage of these built-in geospatial reasoning capabilities for achieving semantic interoperability. Section 4 discusses the infrastructure, interoperability, and application of the geospatial Semantic Web.

Chapter 7

Sven Schade, European Commission – Joint Research Centre, Institute for Environment and
Sustainability, Italy

Chapter 7 introduces the VIsionary Semantic service Infrastructure with ONtologies (VISION) to depict required components and highlight the most important services of geospatial semantics.

Chapter 8

Zhong-Ren Peng, University of Florida, USA & Tongji University, China
Tian Zhao, University of Wisconsin – Milwaukee, USA
Chuanrong Zhang, University of Connecticut, USA

Chapter 8 shows how to take advantage of geospatial semantic Web services to provide a unique approach to address semantic heterogeneity, through a case study of transportation road networks and transit networks for a transit trip planning system.

Chapter 9

Carlos Granell, Universitat Jaume I, Spain
Sven Schade, European Commission – Joint Research Centre, Institute for Environment and
Sustainability, Italy
Gobe Hobona, University of Nottingham, UK

The Linked Data enables data providers to use the existing links, tags and annotations to help users connect to other related geospatial data. Chapter 9 proposes a Linked Data approach to SDI and suggests it as a way to combine SDI with Volunteered Geographic Information (VGI).

Chapter 10

Naijun Zhou, University of Maryland College Park, USA

Chapter 10 provides an updated overview of geospatial portals followed by detailed discussion on how the ontological and semantic technologies are incorporated into geospatial portals. Three recent research and practice of geospatial portals are briefly introduced as the case studies of service-oriented portals.

Section 5
Distributed Computing

Many geospatial applications involve not only distributed heterogeneous data, but also special processing capabilities available at remote sites. With the advances in network bandwidth, computing platforms and the standardization of Geospatial Web Services, it is possible to implement distributed geospatial computing over the Web. Section 5 discusses the current state-of-the-art of approaches to distributed geospatial computing.

Chapter 11

Theodor Foerster, University of Münster, Germany
Bastian Schäffer, University of Münster, Germany
Bastian Baranski, University of Münster, Germany
Johannes Brauner, Technische Universität Dresden, Germany

Chapter 11 explores the current state-of-the-art approach to distributed geoprocessing. It discusses the OGC Web Processing Service, workflows, Quality of Service, and legacy system integration

Chapter 12

Gobe Hobona, University of Nottingham, UK
Mike Jackson, University of Nottingham, UK
Suchith Anand, University of Nottingham, UK

Chapter 12 examines the potential for offering capabilities of the Geographic Resources Analysis Support System (GRASS) as a service within a cloud computing.

Section 6
Workflows

Individual Geospatial Web services can be assembled into a workflow to represent a more complicated geospatial model and process flow to achieve desired results. The service-oriented workflow is essential for complex geospatial applications and knowledge discovery over the Web. Section 6 discusses some advanced aspects of building workflows.

Chapter 13

Peng Yue, Wuhan University, China
Lianlian He, Hubei University of Education, China
Liping Di, George Mason University, USA

Chapter 13 addresses key research issues for intelligent chaining of geoprocessing services using the Semantic Web. This chapter discusses a set of applicable solutions and provides a proof-of-concept prototype system and some use cases to prove the applicability of the presented approach.

Chapter 14

Tino Fleuren, University of Kaiserslautern, Germany
Paul Müller, University of Kaiserslautern, Germany

Chapter 14 discusses executing large-scale geospatial workflows in Grid environments. The chapter presents a workflow enactment system that maintains the robustness of centralized control, but is enhanced by distributed components that can communicate with each other to allow for efficient coupling between parallel tasks and avoiding of unnecessary data transfers in Grid environments.

Section 7
Applications

An increasing number of geospatial applications are implemented based on Web services. This increase significantly enhances the ability of users to collect, analyze and derive geospatial data, information, and knowledge. Sections 7 discusses some domain applications that highlight the promise of geospatial Web services for information interoperability.

Chapter 15

George Percivall, Open Geospatial Consortium, USA, UK and Australia

Chapter 15 presents an evolutionary development process and reusable architecture methods for applying Web services to a global scale system of systems for Earth observations. The GEOSS architecture, which is organized and documented in the ISO RM-ODP standard, is explored in this chapter.

Chapter 16

Chapter 16 examines the potential for operational and scalable delivery of on-demand personalized EO data using the interoperable OGC Web Coverage Service (WCS). The basic aspects of OGC WCS, such as standards, implementation, performance and scalability, and relevant data, are discussed in this chapter.

Chapter 17

Chapter 17 discusses how interoperable geospatial Web services, especially the ones standardized by the OGC, have been used in different phases of emergency management. This chapter highlights that a holistic approach with geospatial Web services will create more value for emergency management.

Chapter 18

Chapter 18 outlines the architecture and functionalities of a SOA-based system that integrates sensor data transmitted by a fleet of unmanned aircraft for territorial surveillance and protection from natural disasters.

Chapter 19

Chapter 19 introduces the GeoBrain Online Analysis System (GeOnAS): an SOA-based geospatial Web portal. This data-rich and service-centric portal provides the standards-based discovery, retrieval, visualization, and analysis of geospatial data and service.

Foreword

Two decades ago geospatial Web services, the subject of this book, would have been almost impossible to imagine. The first Web browser was still three years away, and while the Internet was among the most successful of the various competing electronic networks, it was by no means as dominant as it became five years later. Geospatial services were provided by geographic information system (GIS) software operating on stand-alone Unix machines or on minicomputers and delivered over local-area networks. The notion that one day it would be possible to invoke services from remote machines using simple interfaces would have seemed like an impossible dream.

How far we have come in two short decades. Geospatial Web services are proliferating rapidly, and are familiar to almost anyone blessed with a high speed Internet connection from a home computer, laptop, or third-generation phone. We rely on such services to find our way in strange cities, to locate businesses, to make hotel reservations, and a myriad of other daily tasks. Moreover most if not all of the more sophisticated GIS operations needed by planners, researchers, resource managers, utility companies, and virtually every other occupation of the 21st Century are also available from industrial-strength GIS servers.

This book comes at an appropriate time, and fills a niche that has emerged recently in the GIS bookshelf. It describes applications of geospatial Web services to many areas of human activity, from research on global environmental change to the planning of transit systems and to emergency management. The core concepts of Web portals, service-oriented architectures, and spatial data infrastructures are covered, and the book identifies and examines some of the fundamental issues, including the granularity of functions, semantics, and the standardization of functionality.

The book will be invaluable to anyone working in this rapidly developing area. Geospatial Web services are an increasingly important part of the education of any GIS professional, but often too new to be treated in any depth in the standard curricula and textbooks. The book will also be an excellent text for more specialized courses, at the upper undergraduate or graduate levels, and as reading matter for practitioners.

The editors and authors are to be congratulated for bringing together such a powerful collection, and for having the foresight to see the potential of this field. Much remains to be done, however, and the field is still in its infancy. It is still difficult, for example, to achieve the holy grail of the spatial join, because so many forms of uncertainty pervade geospatial data. We still do not have a clear, standard taxonomy or ontology of spatial functions, making a mockery of efforts to build systems for search and discovery of geospatial Web services. And while we have many technologies for supporting various aspects of geospatial Web services, it is still difficult for a novice to navigate through the numerous standards and software alternatives. We can be confident, however, that many of these issues will be resolved in time if the research community addresses them with imagination and vigor, and that the task of building a practical, operational application of chained geospatial Web services will become easier with time.

Michael F. Goodchild
University of California, Santa Barbara, USA

Michael F. Goodchild *is Professor of Geography at the University of California, Santa Barbara, and Director of UCSB's Center for Spatial Studies. He received his BA degree from Cambridge University in Physics in 1965 and his PhD in geography from McMaster University in 1969. He was elected member of the National Academy of Sciences and Foreign Member of the Royal Society of Canada in 2002, member of the American Academy of Arts and Sciences in 2006, and Foreign Fellow of the Royal Society in 2010; and in 2007 he received the Prix Vautrin Lud. He was editor of Geographical Analysis between 1987 and 1990 and editor of the Methods, Models, and Geographic Information Sciences section of the Annals of the Association of American Geographers from 2000 to 2006. He serves on the editorial boards of ten other journals and book series, and has published over 15 books and 400 articles. He was Chair of the National Research Council's Mapping Science Committee from 1997 to 1999, and currently chairs the Advisory Committee on Social, Behavioral, and Economic Sciences of the National Science Foundation. His current research interests center on geographic information science, spatial analysis, and uncertainty in geographic data.*

Preface

W3C defines a Web service as a software system designed to use standard protocols to support interoperable machine-to-machine interactions (publication, discovery, access, and orchestration) over a network. As Web services technology has matured in recent years, a new scalable Service-Oriented Architecture (SOA) is emerging as the basis for distributed computing and large networks of collaborating applications. Meanwhile, an increasing amount of geospatial content and capabilities are available online as Web services. This increase significantly enhances the ability of users to collect, analyze and derive geospatial data, information, and knowledge. Geospatial Web services are designed to use Web service technology to deal with spatial information over the network. They provide a promising approach to interoperability for distributed heterogeneous geospatial data and applications. SOA and geospatial Web services are changing the way in which spatial information applications and systems are designed, developed, and deployed. Therefore, the field of geospatial Web services is emerging as one of the most desirable research areas of geospatial information.

The term geospatial Web service involves not only service technology, but also domain-specific conceptual, methodological, technical, and managerial issues. Such issues include new geospatial SOA frameworks for building cutting-edge interoperable geospatial applications, the basic knowledge and recent progress of standards for interoperable geospatial Web services, the techniques for design, development, deployment, and operation of geospatial Web services, the mechanisms of geospatial Web service registration and discovery, the theories and applications of the geospatial Semantic Web, and the models, methods, languages, and tools of geospatial Web service orchestration. This book provides comprehensive and in-depth academic descriptions, empirical research findings and applications, and future challenges and emerging trends for geospatial Web services.

This book is organized in seven (7) distinct sections, each addressing a state-of-art topic in geospatial Web services: Standards, Design and Implementation, Registry and Discovery, the Semantic Web, Distributed Computing, Workflows, and Applications.

Interoperability is achieved by using standards. Section I explores geospatial interoperability standards. The Open Geospatial Consortium (OGC), a non-profit, international, voluntary consensus standards organization, has developed a set of specifications aimed at the full integration of "geo-enabled" Web services into mainstream computing to make complex spatial information and services interoperable and useful with all kinds of applications. The OGC Web service specifications have been widely accepted by the geospatial communities. Some of them are becoming International Organization for Standardization (ISO) standards. As seen in Chapter 1, Carl Reed introduces the background of the OGC Web services and provides information on the OGC Reference Model and the importance of reference architecture for the successful deployment of applications using OGC and related standards. This chapter highlights the

OGC Web service architecture and relevant key OGC Web services standards. It also discusses planned work on the OGC Web services standards baseline as well as reflections on the impact of current technology trends, such as the mobile internet and cloud computing.

Designing and implementing a geospatial Web service with high performance and better reliability presents developers and architects with an interesting set of problems. Approaching service development armed with just the underlying technologies, such as SOAP and WSDL, is not sufficient. Design issues and patterns related to the geospatial domain must also be studied. Section II, which consists of chapters 2-4, discusses several basic aspects of service design and implementation that facilitate building a better geospatial Web service.

Choices relating to granularity affect service interfaces, data storage and organization, and XML format design. Chapter 2, authored by Elias Ioup and John Sample, highlights the importance of analyzing usage and performance requirements when choosing granularity in the design of a geospatial Web service and provides common examples that explore the different approaches to granularity which are available.

Use of geospatial Web services in mission-critical applications and business processes nonetheless raises important quality concerns. Chapter 3, authored by Richard Onchaga Moses, identifies and elaborates quality concerns and uses data quality and quality of service to define a quality model for geospatial Web services. An ontology framework that explores ontologies to provide a consistent set of concepts to unambiguously define and reason about the quality of geospatial Web services is presented. The chapter also proposes domain middleware to facilitate efficient and cost-effective quality-aware chaining of geospatial web services.

Enabling the commercial use of geospatial Web services in an on demand and ad-hoc fashion highly depends on the efficient mechanisms of security and licensing. Chapter 4, authored by Bastian Schäffer and Rüdiger Gartmann, presents an approach that goes beyond classical Role-Based Access Control models to support ad-hoc license agreements directly in process, without any prior offline negotiated agreements being necessary between service provider and service user for on-demand access. In particular, this chapter focuses on state-of-the-art interface specifications from OGC and defines generic security extensions that are applicable to all OGC standards based on OGC Web Service Common. The static model with trust relationships between the different components of the architecture in heterogeneous security domains as well the dynamic structure is studied.

As the number and variety of geospatial Web services has increased rapidly, registration and discovery of a service, which involves domain knowledge, service metadata, and service interfaces, is becoming a major problem. A catalog service acts as an important "directory" role in SOA: service providers register the service availability by using meta-information, thereby allowing service consumers to discover the desired services by querying meta-information. Section III, which consists of chapters 5 and 6, discusses how to use catalog services to facilitate the registry and discovery of geospatial Web services.

Chapter 5, authored by Manil Maskey et al., presents a service registry compliant with the OGC Catalog Service for Web (CSW). It is developed as part of an OGC-sponsored interoperability experiment involving the ocean sciences community. A standards-compliant registry for this endeavor eliminates the need for discovering the services from ad-hoc registries and opens up avenues for the development of automated tools. The implemented catalog service supports OGC Sensor Observation Services (SOS) and additional functionality to minimize requirements on service providers and maximize the robustness of the registry.

One of great challenges in Spatial Data Infrastructures (SDI) is the provision of semantics for high precision searching for the underlying data and services. Chapter 6, authored by Fabio Gomes de

Andrade et al., introduces a distributed catalog service that uses ontologies to describe the underlying information to provide a more accurate search. The proposed catalog service that is able to rewrite and propagate queries to other distributed catalogs allows the catalog services in different SDIs to cooperate and exchange information directly with each other without the traditional problems imposed by a centralized architecture.

The lack of semantics in Web services makes it impossible to implement reliable and large-scale interoperation by computer programs or agents. With Semantic Web technologies, geospatial ontologies can capture the semantic network of the geospatial world. Intelligent applications can then take advantage of these built-in geospatial reasoning capabilities for achieving semantic interoperability. Section IV, which consists of chapters 7-10, discusses the infrastructure, interoperability, and application of the geospatial Semantic Web.

Sven Schade, in Chapter 7, introduces the VIsionary Semantic service Infrastructure with ONtologies (VISION) to depict required components and highlight the most important services of geospatial semantics. Model-as-a-Service (MaaS) is introduced as a central concept for encapsulating geospatial environmental models as services. The German-funded GDI-GRID project is discussed to illustrate the examples of MaaS, the need for different types of ontologies, interoperability challenges arising, and potential uses of grid technology.

Chapter 8, authored by Zhong-Ren Peng et al., shows how to take advantage of geospatial semantic Web services to provide a unique approach to address semantic heterogeneity, through a case study of transportation road networks and transit networks for a transit trip planning system. This approach takes advantages of ontology to provide semantic definitions for geospatial data, and uses spatial query functions of OGC Web Feature Service (WFS) for spatial data searches and relational database search functions for non-spatial data queries. The results show that this approach is more efficient than conventional methods of converting all data into ontology instances, as it avoids the costs and consistency problems of data replication.

The Linked Data enables data providers to use the existing links, tags and annotations to help users connect to other related geospatial data. Carlos Granell et al., in chapter 9, propose a Linked Data approach to SDI and suggest it as a way to combine SDI with Volunteered Geographic Information (VGI). This chapter details different implementing strategies, gives examples, and argues for the benefits of this method, while at the same time trying to outline possible fallbacks. The approach presented is a way towards a single shared information space.

A geospatial portal is a gateway of distributed geospatial data, tools and services. Ontology and semantics play an increasingly important role in geospatial portals due to the demand of interoperability. Chapter 10, authored by Naijun Zhou, provides an updated overview of geospatial portals followed by detailed discussion on how the ontological and semantic technologies are incorporated into geospatial portals. Three recent research and practice of geospatial portals are briefly introduced as the case studies of service-oriented portals.

Many geospatial applications involve not only distributed heterogeneous data, but also special processing capabilities available at remote sites. With the advances in network bandwidth, computing platforms and the standardization of Geospatial Web Services, it is possible to implement distributed geospatial computing over the Web. Section V, which consists of chapters 11 and 12, discusses the current state-of-the-art of approaches to distributed geospatial computing.

Enalbing geospatial processing over the Web is a key aspect of the requirements for distributed computing. Chapter 11, authored by Theodor Foerster, explores the current state-of-the-art approach to distributed geoprocessing. This chapter discusses the OGC Web Processing Service, workflows, Quality of Service, and legacy system integration. It uses two scenarios to introduce related concepts and demonstrates different applications for distributed geoprocessing.

Cloud computing is a new promising computing platform that delivers software, hardware, and infrastructure as services on demand. Gobe Hobnona et al., in chapter 12, examine the potential for offering capabilities of the Geographic Resources Analysis Support System (GRASS) as a service within a cloud computing. The chapter describes a prototype "Cloud" service that adopts the OGC WPS standard.

Individual Geospatial Web services can be assembled into a workflow to represent a more complicated geospatial model and process flow to achieve desired results. The service-oriented workflow is essential for complex geospatial applications and knowledge discovery over the Web. Section VI, which consists of chapters 13 and 14, discusses some advanced aspects of building workflows.

Chapter 13, authored by Peng Yue et al., addresses key research issues for intelligent chaining of geoprocessing services using the Semantic Web. This chapter discusses a set of applicable solutions, including a common data and service environment, semantic descriptions of geoprocessing services, and a general process for intelligent generation of geoprocessing workflows. A proof-of-concept prototype system and some use cases are demonstrated in this chapter to prove the applicability of the presented approach.

Tino Fleuren and Paul Müller, in chapter 14, discuss executing large-scale geospatial workflows in Grid environments. The chapter presents a workflow enactment system that maintains the robustness of centralized control, but is enhanced by distributed components called proxy services that can communicate with each other to allow for efficient coupling between parallel tasks and avoiding of unnecessary data transfers in Grid environments.

An increasing number of geospatial applications are implemented based on Web services. This increase significantly enhances the ability of users to collect, analyze and derive geospatial data, information, and knowledge. Sections VII, which consists of chapters 15-19, discusses some domain applications that highlight the promise of geospatial Web services for information interoperability.

The Global Earth Observation System of Systems (GEOSS) aims to provide comprehensive, coordinated, and sustained observations of the Earth system. George Percivall, in chapter 15, presents an evolutionary development process and reusable architecture methods for applying Web services to a global scale system of systems for Earth observations. The GEOSS architecture, which is organized and documented in the ISO RM-ODP standard, is explored in this chapter.

For the Earth Observation data to be fully utilized, one of the most important aspects is to adopt technologies that will enable users to easily find and obtain needed data in a form that can be readily used with little or no manipulation. Chapter 16, authored by Wenli Yang, examines the potential for operational and scalable delivery of on-demand personalized EO data using the interoperable OGC Web Coverage Service (WCS). The basic aspects of OGC WCS, such as standards, implementation, performance and scalability, and relevant data, are discussed in this chapter.

To confront the ever-growing volume and complexity of disasters, a highly interoperable, loosely coupled, dynamic, geospatially-enabled information platform with comprehensive situational awareness is required. Chapter 17, authored by Ning An et al., discusses how interoperable geospatial Web services, especially the ones standardized by the OGC, have been used in different phases of emergency management. This chapter highlights that a holistic approach with geospatial Web services will create more value for emergency management.

Elena Roglia and Rosa Meo, in chapter 18, outline the architecture and functionalities of a SOA-based system that integrates sensor data transmitted by a fleet of unmanned aircraft for territorial surveillance and protection from natural disasters. This chapter also addresses a service for the annotation of spatial objects of interest to exploit the on-line information sources continuously updated by the social network communities.

The geospatial Web portal is the gateway to integrating news, information, data, and applications from the geosciences communities. Chapter 19, authored by Weiguo Han et al., introduces the GeoBrain Online Analysis System (GeOnAS): an SOA-based geospatial Web portal. This data-rich and service-centric portal provides the standards-based discovery, retrieval, visualization, and analysis of geospatial data and service. It facilitates geoscience research and education around the world and helps decision-makers and analysts work more efficiently and effectively within an SOA runtime environment.

This book provides researchers, scholars, and other professionals with the most advanced research developments, solutions, and implementations of geospatial Web services. It is expected to provide a better understanding of the strategic role of geospatial Web services in a distributed heterogeneous environment and the life cycle of geospatial Web services for building interoperable SOA-based geospatial applications. The book is also expected to be used in advanced courses as supplemental course material on geospatial interoperability, advanced GIS, and e-Science education.

Peisheng Zhao
George Mason University, USA

Liping Di
George Mason University, USA

Section 1
Standards

Chapter 1
The Open Geospatial Consortium and Web Services Standards

Carl N. Reed
Open Geospatial Consortium, USA

ABSTRACT

This chapter discusses the role of Open Geospatial Consortium (OGC) geospatial standards as a key aspect in the development, deployment, and use of Geospatial Web Services. The OGC vision for web services is the complete integration of geographic (location) and time information into the very fabric of both the internet and the web. Today, the Geospatial Web Services encompasses applications ranging from as simple as geo-tagging a photograph to mobile driving directions to sophisticated spatial data infrastructure portal applications orchestrating workflows for complex scientific modeling applications. In all of these applications, location and usually time are required information elements. In many of these applications, standards are the "glue" that allow the easy and seamless integration of location and time in applications - whether simple mass market or integration into enterprise workflows. These standards may be very lightweight, such as GeoRSS, or more sophisticated such as the OGC Web Feature Service (WFS) and Geography Markup Language (GML).

INTRODUCTION

This chapter is structured from the perspective of a standards organization and the work activities of

DOI: 10.4018/978-1-60960-192-8.ch001

the OGC Membership. One of the key aspects of standards development is that the work activities are defined by the Membership and thus reflect market forces, business needs, and technology trends. Therefore, this chapter begins with an overview of the Open Geospatial Consortium

(OGC), our vision, and mission. This is followed by definitions of what the OGC means by "services", "web services", and services architectures. We then describe the history of OGC web services standards work. In order to provide context, the chapter then provides information on the OGC Reference Model and the importance of Reference Architecture for the successful deployment of applications using OGC and related standards. This discussion is followed by short descriptions and examples of the use of key OGC web services standards. The chapter concludes with statements regarding planned future work on the OGC web services standards baseline as well as reflections on the impacts of current technology trends, such as the mobile internet and cloud computing.

BACKGROUND

This section provides background on the OGC, OGC Web Services, and key terms and definitions.

What is the OGC?

Founded in 1994, the Open Geospatial Consortium (OGC) is a global industry consortium with a vision to "Achieve the full societal, economic and scientific benefits of integrating location resources into commercial and institutional processes worldwide". Inherent in this vision is the requirement for geospatial standards and strategies to be an integral part of business processes.

The OGC consists of 400+ members - geospatial technology software vendors, systems integrators, government agencies and universities - participating in a consensus process to develop, test, and document publicly available geospatial interface standards and encodings for use in information and communications industries.

Open interfaces and protocols defined in OGC standards are designed to support interoperable solutions that "geo-enable" the Web, wireless and location-based services, and mainstream IT, and to empower technology developers to make complex spatial information and services accessible and useful to all kinds of applications. As such, the mission of the OGC is to serve as a global forum for the development, promotion and harmonization of open and freely available geospatial standards. Therefore, the OGC also has a major commitment to collaborate with other Standards Development Organizations (SDOs) that have requirements for using location based content. These SDOs include such organizations as ISO[1], OASIS[2], the IETF[3], NENA[4], OMA[5] and the W3C[6].

OGC Web Services: A Short History

The OGC Membership began exploring the concept and implementation of web services back in 1997 (Gardels 1997, Doyle 1997). These early discussions led to a new type of activity in the OGC – interoperability test beds and the development of the first OGC web service standard. The Web Mapping Test bed Phase 1 (WMT-1) was OGC's first Interoperability Initiative and marks an important milestone in the history of geoprocessing. Results of the pilot projects were demonstrated in September 1999, and a second phase of pilot projects ended in April 2000.

WMT-1 yielded interface prototypes vendors used to enable users to immediately overlay and operate on views of thematic map data on the web from different online sources (subject to limitations of the data), regardless of which vendor's software was serving that data. These prototypes ultimately resulted in the OGC Web Map Server Standard (OGC 2000). Also, the Geography Markup Language (GML), OGC's standard system for XML encoding of geographic features, was prototyped in WMT-1.

Interestingly enough, the term "Web service" did not gain any extended usage until about the year 2000. The OGC Membership was quick to pick up the concept and developed an OGC white paper on the topic in 2001 (Doyle and Reed). In 2001 terms, this paper outlined the OGC consensus agreement on what a web service is, their value in the IT stack, and the role of standards. Back in 2000, SOAP[7] was not an official W3C standard until 2003 and REST was just a doctoral dissertation! The early OGC activity in web services predated the implementation of these activities by several years.

Building on this early OGC activity, each year the OGC has staged a major interoperability OGC Web Services test bed. These test bed activities are designed to quickly and effectively document use cases, requirements, and interoperability pain points and then to use a rapid engineering process to define, development, test, and demonstrate geospatial standards solutions that meet the stated requirements and resolve the documented interoperability issues[8]. OGC Web Services 7 is the 2010 activity (OWS 7 2009).

These test beds and the related OGC standards development activities have resulted in a robust, widely implemented set of OGC web service interface standards and related encodings. There are currently ten OGC web service interface standards as well as nine related encoding standards. In sum, OGC Web Services provide a vendor-neutral, interoperable framework for web-based discovery, access, integration, analysis, exploitation and visualization of multiple online geodata sources, sensor-derived information, and geoprocessing capabilities.

Before provided short summaries of each of these standards, some terms and definitions need to be provided. Further, the OGC Reference Model needs to be introduced.

Terms and Definitions Used in this Chapter

The following are key terms and definitions that will help provide the proper context in terms of understanding the development and use of OGC web service standards. Note: Many of the terms and definitions used in the work of the OGC are defined in the OGC glossary (OGC Glossary) and in the ISO TC 211 Terminology Database.

Encoding: The activity of converting data into code, such as a coordinate into XML. (ISO Terms and Definitions)

Interface: A named set of operations that characterize the behavior of an entity. For a given distributed computing technology, an interface is an implementation of one or more operations that include the syntax of the interaction between two functional entities. An interface shared boundary between two functional entities. (ISO 19119, 2005)

Operation: Specification of a transformation or query that a service may be called to execute. (ISO 19119, 2005)

Service: Distinct part of the functionality (as expressed in operations) that is provided by an entity through interfaces. (ISO 19119, 2005)

Standard: A document, established by consensus and approved by the OGC Membership, that provides, for common and repeated use, rules, guidelines or characteristics for activities or their results, aimed at the achievement of the optimum degree of order in a given context. (OGC TC P&P, 2009)

Web Service: The OGC follows a definition of a web service as originally proposed by IBM, Motorola and others (Vasudevan, 2001):

Web Services are self-contained, self-describing, modular applications that can be published, located, and invoked across the Web. Web services perform functions, which can be anything from simple requests to complicated business processes. Once a Web service is deployed, other applications (and other Web services) can discover and invoke the deployed service.

Please note that the OGC does not subscribe to the need of a web service to use SOAP – or any other protocol or implementing technology! This is a very important distinction – and one that does create some interesting standards development issues as will be discussed later in this chapter.

The OGC Reference Model (ORM)

The OGC Reference Model (ORM) describes the OGC Standards Baseline focusing on relationships between the OGC and ISO standards and related supporting best practices. (Percivall 2009) The OGC Standards Baseline (SB) consists of the approved OGC Abstract and Implementation Standards (Interface, Encoding, Profile, Application Schema, and Best Practice documents.

What is the purpose of the ORM?

- To provide an overview of OGC Standards Baseline;
- To provide insight into the current state of the work of the OGC;
- To serve as a basis for coordination and understanding of the documents in the OGC SB;
- To provide a useful resource for defining architectures for specific applications.

The ORM provides a technology neutral, open standards model as a reference for all of the work of the OGC, including OGC web services.

The Importance of Reference Architectures

Writing applications that use OGC standards without context or descriptions of how the OGC standards are to be implemented (guidance) greatly reduces the chance for success of the deployed application. Therefore, the OGC strongly encourages any organization that wishes to implement OGC standards first develop a reference architecture.

From the OASIS Reference Architecture Foundation for Service Oriented Architectures (OASIS 2009)

A reference architecture models the abstract architectural elements in the domain independent of the technologies, protocols, and products that are used to implement the domain.

Part of the reference architecture is to specify at an abstract level the interface and encoding requirements. A reference architecture can then be used as the foundation to derive operational or implementation architectures.

The OGC community typically uses ISO/IEC 107461 Reference Model for Open Distributed Processing (RM-ODP) as the pattern for all OGC reference architecture and modeling activities. RM-ODP specifies the use of multiple viewpoints: enterprise, information, computational, engineering, and technology. The first three view points are technology neutral. More detail on the enterprise, information, and computational viewpoints is provided:

- The *enterprise viewpoint* focuses on the purpose, scope and policies for the target system or application. In this viewpoint, the business requirements and how to meet them and described.
- The *information viewpoint* focuses on the semantics of the information and the information processing performed. The information viewpoint describes the information managed by the system and the structure and content type of the supporting data.
- The *computational viewpoint* enables distribution through functional decomposition on the system into objects that interact through interfaces and communicate via encodings and protocols. This viewpoint is used to describe the functionality provided by the system and its functional decomposition.

A key aspect of defining the computational viewpoint is specifying the interfaces and encoding payloads necessary to meet the business and information model objectives of the architecture. This description should include the version of the standard that needs to be implemented.

An excellent example of the use of the RM-ODP approach to defining a reference architecture and defining which standards and versions of standards to be implemented is the Reference Model for the ORCHESTRA Architecture – RM-OA (Uslander, 2007). This reference architecture is an extension of the OGC Reference Model and contains a specification framework for the design of geospatial service-oriented architectures and service networks. The RM-OA comprises the generic aspects of service-oriented architectures, i.e., those aspects that are independent of the risk management domain and thus applicable to other application domains. The ORCHESTRA Architecture is a platform-neutral (abstract) specification of the informational and functional aspects of service networks taking into account and evolving out of architectural standards and service specifications of ISO, OGC, W3C and OASIS. The target audience of the RM-OA comprise system architects, information modelers and system developers.

OGC WEB SERVICE STANDARDS

This section provides short descriptions with examples of key OGC web service interface and encoding standards. However, this section does not provide information on all of the OGC web services standards currently being implemented. A complete list may be found on the OGC web site. Note: The OGC community maintains an online directory of products that implement OGC standards. (OGC Implementing 2010). This directory is by no means complete as we rely on the community to provide the reference information. The directory can be searched by OGC standard.

We begin with a simple diagram that provides a simple architecture view as well as the context for how the various OGC Web Services are related.

OGC Web Services Architecture

The OGC Web Services (OWS) framework allows multiple services to be connected in sequence while at the same time allowing them to keep internal business logic independent – and if need be, proprietary. Figure 1 provides a general architectural schema for OWS. This schema identifies the generic classes of services that participate in various geoprocessing and location activities. Further, it identifies the properties that the services in those classes must have to connect them into useful applications.

Figure 1. 2010 July OGC Web Services

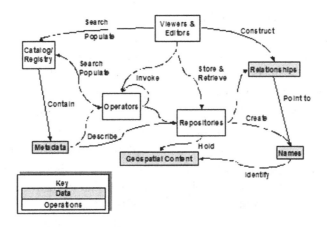

Viewers and Editors (Visualization)

The following OGC standards are best used in client applications for viewing and visualizing geospatial content stored in one or more distributed, heterogeneous repositories.

The OGC Web Map Service Interface Standard (WMS)

The OGC **WMS** standard defines a simple HTTP interface for requesting geo-registered map images from one or more distributed geospatial databases. A WMS request defines the geographic layer(s) and area of interest to be processed. The response to the request is one or more geo-registered map images (returned as JPEG, PNG, etc) that can be displayed in a browser application. The interface also supports the ability to specify whether the returned images should be transparent so that layers from multiple servers can be combined. A WMS falls in the "Viewer" category in the OWS architecture. A WMS can also invoke operations, such as Style Layer Descriptor (SLD).

WMS is perhaps the most widely implemented and used of the OGC Web Services standards baseline. From SDI portals to mobile internet applications, WMS provides interoperable access to hundreds of thousands of layers of geospatial content (repositories). There are many excellent examples of WMS implementations.

An excellent example of a portal (Spatial Data Infrastructure - SDI) applications is NC OneMap. "NC OneMap relies on Web Map Services (WMS) to bring data together from multiple hosts. NC OneMap partners establish a WMS from their servers. This OGC standard allows data to be created and stored in numerous proprietary software configurations (ESRI, MapInfo, Intergraph, etc), but is viewable by all."

Another very recent application is the use of WMS in a mobile internet application available on iPhones and Android phones. (WMS Mobile 2008 and 2009)

Search, Populate, Store, Retrieve, and Invoke

The following OGC standards are related to searching multiple distributed geospatial repositories and retrieving the specified content and/or updating specified content. Specific operations may also be invoked as part of the retrieval.

The OGC Web Feature Service Interface Standard

The **WFS** standard defines a data access service that enables features, such as roads or soils, from multiple repositories to be queried and managed using an HTTP based interface. The standard defines operations that enable clients to:

- Discover which feature collections in a given repository the service offers (GetCapabilities)
- Get a description of the properties of features (DescribeFeatureType)
- Query a collection for a subset of features that satisfy some filter
- expression (GetFeature)
- Execute transactions against feature collections (Transaction)

The mandatory encoding for input and output is the Geography Markup Language (GML). However, other encodings, such as GeoRSS, can be also provided.

While not as widely implemented as the WMS standard, WFS is a key standard interface available in many SDI portal applications. An excellent example of using a WFS service to provide open and interoperable access to large amounts of geospatial content via a government portal is the USGS Framework Web Feature Services offered in support of the development of the National Spatial Data Infrastructure (NSDI) (USGS WFS 2009). Selected US Framework data themes are available from their native database formats to services that conform to the Open Geospatial Consortium's (OGC) Web Feature Service (WFS) and Geography Markup Language for Simple Features (GML) standards and the FGDC/ANSI Geographic Information Framework Data Content Standards.

The OpenGIS Web Coverage Service Interface (WCS) Standard

The **WCS** standard defines a data access service that enables coverages, such as digital elevation models, from multiple repositories to be queried using an HTTP based interface. As such, OGC WCS standard specifies how client applications can request parts of grid coverages offered by a Web server. A coverage is a feature that associates positions within a bounded space (its spatio-temporal domain) to feature attribute values (its range). GIS coverages (including the special case of Earth images) are two- (and sometimes higher-) dimensional metaphors for phenomena found on or near a portion of the Earth's surface. The response to a WCS request includes coverage metadata and an output coverage whose pixels are encoded in a specified binary image format, such as GeoTIFF or NetCDF.

A client application can define the spatial-temporal domain of an identified grid coverage to be returned as well as the identified parts of the range of values for the coverage. A client application can also select the output format for the selected grid coverage part and the output grid coordinate reference system, allowing origin and scale changes and image georectification or orthorectification. The WCS primarily handles continuous coverages (such as a satellite image) but the grid coverages can be discrete such as a LIDAR point cloud.

As with other OGC standards, there are numerous excellent examples of deployed WCS implementations. One example is NDBC High Frequency (HF) Radar Web Coverage Service (WCS) developed and deployed by the US Na-

tional Ocean and Atmospheric Administration (NOAA) (NOAA WCS 2009). HF Radar is used to remotely measure ocean surface currents. Another is the National Aeronautical and Space Administration (NASA) WCS for accessing Atmospheric Infrared Sounder (AIRS) Data (NASA WCS 2009). This is one of the Goddard Earth Systems Data and Information Service Center's OGC WCS instances that provides Level 3 Gridded atmospheric data products derived from AIRS data as generated on board NASA's Aqua spacecraft.

The OGC Sensor Observation Service Interface (SOS) Standard

The OGC SOS standard defines an interface and operations that when implemented enable access to observations from sensors and sensor systems in a standard way that is consistent for all sensor systems including remote, in-situ, fixed and mobile sensors. The goal of SOS is to provide access to observations from sensors and sensor systems in a standard way that is consistent for all sensor systems including remote, in-situ, fixed and mobile sensors. SOS leverages the Observation and Measurements (O&M) specification for modeling sensor observations and the SensorML specification for modeling sensors and sensor systems.

The approach that has been taken in the development of SOS, and the SWE standards on which SOS depends, is to carefully model sensors, sensor systems, and observations in such a way that the model covers all varieties of sensors and supports the requirements of all users of sensor data. This is in contrast to the approach that was taken with the Web Feature Service (WFS). The SOS approach defines a common mod-el for all sensors, sensor systems and their observations. This model is not domain-specific and can be used without a-priori knowledge of domain-specific application schemas.

There are numerous excellent implementations of SOS. The OpenIOOS.org has thirteen organizations providing SOS service instances providing access to over 1400 oceans sensors (OpenIOOS 2010). This operational demonstration "represents an effort to develop a Web Services Architecture for Ocean Observing".

The OGC Web Processing Service Interface (WPS) Standard

The WPS standard provides rules for standardizing how inputs and outputs (requests and responses) the for way geospatial processing services, such as polygon overlays and their inputs and outputs are described. The standard also defines how a client (viewer) can request the execution of a process and geospatial data stored in one more repositories, and how the output from the process is handled. The standard defines an interface that facilitates the publishing of geospatial processes and clients' discovery of and binding to those processes. Processes include any algorithm, calculation or model that operates on spatially referenced vector or raster data. A WPS may offer calculations as simple as subtracting one set of spatially referenced numbers from another (e.g., determining the difference in influenza cases between two different seasons), or as complicated as a global climate change model. The data required by the WPS can be delivered across a network or they can be available on a server.

While the WPS standard is relatively new, there has been considerable implementation and research related to the use of this new OGC standard. For example, Wolf Bergenheim, Sarjakoski, and Sarjakoski (2009) describe an implementation of a real time generalization service that can be accessed over the Internet. They describe an experimental implementation of the WPS they call the "WPS PHP Server". The service is built over an existing GIS platform, the Geographic Resources Analysis Support System (GRASS). A case study is also presented showing how the WPS PHP Server to can be used to generalize roads on the fly. Another example is described by Gao, Mioc, Yi, Anton, and Oldfield (2009) in which

WPS is used to analyze spatial-temporal health data for health data. Finally, the Grid computing community has been a considerable amount of WPS implementation. (GIS Science 2009)

Catalog, Registries, Metadata, and Description

The following OGC standard is focused on the catalog/registry aspects of the OGC web services architecture.

The OGC Catalogue Service Interface - Web (CS-W) Standard

The ability to search for and discover geospatial resources, such as a service instance and a particular theme of map data, is critical to many applications, such as spatial data infrastructures. While lightweight approaches, such as simple web searches, can "discover" geospatial data, for many enterprise applications a more formal approach is required for consistent expression and maintenance of geospatial metadata and related search and discovery operations. Therefore, catalogue services are the key technology for locating, managing and maintaining distributed geo-resources (i.e. geospatial data, applications and services). Client applications must be capable of searching for geo-resources in a standardized way (i.e. through standardized interfaces and operations) and, ideally, they are based on a well-known information model, which includes spatial references and further descriptive (thematic) information that enables client applications to search for geo-resources in very efficient ways. This is the role of the OGC Catalogue Standard, especially the web profiles.

The OGC Catalogue interface standard specifies a design pattern for defining interfaces to publish and search collections of descriptive information (metadata) about geospatial data, services and related information objects. Providers of resources, such as content provides, use catalogues to register metadata that conform to the provider's choice of an information model; such models include descriptions of spatial references and thematic information. Client applications can then search for geospatial data and services in very efficient ways.

There are several profiles of the current OGC CS-W model. These include:

- ISO 19115/19139 Metadata profile (OGC CSW 19115, 2007). This standard this document specifies an application profile for ISO metadata with support for XML encoding per ISO 19139 (ISO/TS19139) and HTTP protocol binding. This CS-W profile is widely implemented in Europe, such as in the Spatial Data Infrastructure for North Rhine Westphalia (federal state of Germany).
- CSW-ebRIM Registry Service. (OGC CSW ebRIM, 2009) This profile applies the CSW interfaces to the OASIS ebXML registry information model (ebRIM 3.0) so as to provide a general and flexible web-based registry service that enables users— human or software agents—to locate, access, and make use of resources in an open, distributed system; it provides facilities for retrieving, storing, and managing many kinds of resource descriptions. An extension mechanism permits registry content to be tailored for more specialized application domains.
- CSW 39.50: The Z39.50 Protocol binding uses a message-based client server architecture implemented using the ANSI/NISO Z39.50 Application Service Definition and Protocol Specification (*ISO 23950*). This protocol binding maps each of the general model operations to a corresponding service specified in the ANSI/NISO/ISO standard http://lcweb.loc.gov/z3950/agency/document.html.

There is currently considerable work being done on the OGC catalogue standard as well as the various application profiles. Much of this work has to do with restructuring the catalogue standard so that there is a well defined, easy to implement core coupled with a well defined mechanism for expressing a variety of extensions (previously known as application profiles).

OGC Encoding Standards

The following are descriptions of the key OGC encoding standards. In the OGC, all encoding standards are based on an abstract information model, such as ISO 19107: Spatial Schema.

The OGC Sensor Markup Language (SensorML) Encoding Standard

SensorML describes an information model and XML encodings that enable discovery and tasking of Web-resident sensors as well as exploitation of sensor observations. Within this context, SensorML allows the developer to define models and XML Schema for describing any process, including measurement by a sensor system, as well as post-measurement processing.

More specifically, SensorML can:

- Provide descriptions of sensors and sensor systems for inventory management Provide sensor and process information in support of resource and observation discovery;
- Support the processing and analysis of the sensor observations;
- Support the geolocation of observed values (measured data);
- Provide performance characteristics (e.g., accuracy, threshold, etc.);
- Provide an explicit description of the process by which an observation was obtained (i.e., it's lineage);

- Provide an executable process chain for deriving new data products on demand (i.e., derivable observation);
- Archive fundamental properties and assumptions regarding sensor systems.

Individual SensorML schema describe a specific sensor or an array of sensors and can be stored in a registry.

There are numerous examples of SensorML implementations, such as the NASA MSFC SMART program (Connor et. al. 2008). In this project the team developed a sensor web-enabled processing workflow to intelligently assimilate Atmospheric Infrared Sounder (AIRS) satellite temperature and moisture retrievals into a regional configuration of the Weather Research and Forecast model over the southeastern United States.

The OGC Geography Markup Language (GML) Encoding Standard

One of the key encoding standards developed and maintained by the OGC Membership is the Geography Markup Language (GML). GML is an XML grammar defined to express and communicate geographical features. GML serves as a modeling language for geographic systems as well as an open interchange format for geographic transactions on the Internet. Note that the concept of feature in GML is a very general one and includes not only conventional "vector" or discrete objects, but also coverages[9] and some elements of sensor data[10]. The ability to integrate all forms of geographic information is key to the utility of GML.

OGC work on the GML standard began in 1998. GML was first formally approved as an OGC standard in 2001. GML became an ISO standard in 2007. GML 3.2.1[11] is the most current revision of the joint OGC-ISO standard. Versions 3.2.2 and 4.0 are currently in progress.

GML contains a rich set of primitives that are used to build application specific schemas or application languages. These primitives include:

- Feature
- Geometry
- Coordinate Reference System
- Topology
- Time
- Dynamic feature
- Coverage (including geographic images)
- Unit of measure
- Directions
- Observations
- Map presentation styling rules

Understanding the use of "Feature", "Geometry", and "CRS" is critical in the use and development of any GML based encoding.

GML is broadly implemented in a variety of information communities and domains. For example, consider GeoSciML. Back in 2003, the geoscience community recognized the importance of being able to query and exchange digital geoscientific information between data providers and users in a standardized way. Therefore, a meeting of international geoscience data providers, mainly geological surveys, was held in Edinburgh in 2003 to define a work plan. Following from this meeting, a working group under the auspices of the IUGS Commission for the Management and Application of Geoscience Information (CGI) was set up. The group was tasked with developing a conceptual geoscience data model, mapping this to a common interchange format, and demonstrating the use of this interchange format through the development of a testbed. Active participants in the working group are drawn from BGS (United Kingdom), BRGM (France), CSIRO (Australia), GA (Australia), GSC (Canada), GSV (Australia), APAT (Italy), JGS (Japan), SGU (Sweden) and the USGS (USA).

Once the conceptual model was defined, the model was mapped to an interchange format. The

GeoSciML application is a standards-based data format that provides a framework for application-neutral encoding of geoscience thematic data and related spatial data. GeoSciML is based on Geography Markup Language (GML – ISO DIS 19136) for representation of features and geometry, and the OGC Observations and Measurements standard for observational data.

The OGC KML Encoding Standard

KML is an XML language focused on geographic visualization, including annotation of maps and images. Geographic visualization includes not only the presentation of graphical data on the globe, but also the control of the user's navigation in the sense of where to go and where to look.

In 2006, Google submitted KML (formerly Keyhole Markup Language) to the OGC for consideration as a standard KML was the first instance of a de-facto standard being submitted into the OGC standards process and as such the OGC modified our standards approval process to accommodate standards that have been developed externally from the OGC and then submitted into the OGC process. There were four objectives for this standards work:

- That there be one international standard language for expressing geographic annotation and visualization on existing or future web-based online maps (2d) and earth browsers (3d).
- That KML be aligned with international best practices and standards, thereby enabling greater uptake and interoperability of earth browser implementations.
- That the OGC and KML community will work collaboratively to insure that the KML implementer community is properly engaged in the process and that the KML community is kept informed of progress and issues.

- That the OGC process will be used to insure proper life-cycle management of the KML candidate specification, including such issues as backwards compatibility.

KML was approved as an OGC standard in 2008 because the Membership believed that having KML as an OGC standard will encourage broader implementation and greater interoperability and sharing of earth browser content and context.

KML is complementary to most of the existing OGC specifications including key standards such as GML (Geography Markup Language), WFS (Web Feature Service) and WMS (Web Map Service). Currently, KML (v2.1) utilizes certain geometry elements derived from GML (version 2.1.2). These elements include point, line-string, linear-ring, and polygon.

WHAT IS THE CURRENT AND FUTURE WORK IN GEOSPATIAL STANDARDS?

The OGC community is working on a number of key activities related to the continued evolution of the OGC web service standards baseline. Several of the current major activities are described.

Geo-Syncronization

In today's spatial data infrastructure environment, many users and organizations are collaborating over the creation and on-going maintenance of geospatial data sets. Therefore of critical importance is the ability for all partners and constituents to be able to update and share geographic information in real time while at the same time making the costs associated with sharing—in labor and IT resources—negligible.

Some organizations approached solving this requirement from the database perspective by mandating the use of a single data store shared by all or by database replication technology for their geographic data sharing needs. This strategy cannot work in most cases because, most notably, every organization needs to work with a different information model. For example, a local jurisdiction often needs to maintain a large set of properties on their roads data, such as maintenance-related items like pavement quality and type. This information may not be required at a national level.

The single data store approach simply will not work in the majority of use cases. This is due to the facts that 1.) the data are never current and 2.) the processing overhead of translating all content from many jurisdictions into a single content model.

A key limitation of replication technology is that all parties must be using the same software. This is rarely the case in a multi-organization setting. Finally, replication involves reaching deep into another organization's IT infrastructure, requiring a level of trust between the parties which isn't always there.

In the web services world, a much more elegant approach has been vigorously pursued by the OGC Membership. Called "geo-syncronization", the process implies that a data provider may decide to keep their data store in synchronization with a portion of or all of the content of one or more other geospatial data sources at a particular time. If the initial process involves also copying the content of the source to the target data store then the geo-synchronization service may also be used for data replication.

This concept was initially explored in the OGC Pilot Loosely Coupled Synchronization of Geographic Databases in the Canadian Geospatial Data Infrastructure (OGC 08-001, 2008). The work is currently being expanded in the OGC Web Services 7.0 test bed. In OWS 7, the focus for geo-sync is web services and client components to support synchronization of geospatial data and updates across a hierarchical Spatial Data Infrastructure (SDI). The goal for this activity is an OGC best practice guidance on how to use OGC and related standards for federated or enterprise

wide synchronization of distributed geospatial repositories.

Information Models and XML Encodings

Coordination and development of community or domain specific information models. A number of domains, such as meteorology, hydrology, and oceans are using the OGC process as a collaborative environment to discuss information sharing requirements and then based on consensus agreements, working on editing existing information models for global use. From wikipedia, "An information model in software engineering is a representation of concepts, relationships, constraints, rules, and operations to specify data semantics for a chosen domain of discourse. It can provide sharable, stable, and organized structure of information requirements for the domain context." Once the information models are defined and agreed to, the next step is to encode that model in some XML grammar. In the OGC community, the encoding standard of choice is GML. We expect this type of activity to increase in the OGC.

Harmonization of the OGC Standards Baseline

The OGC standards baseline has developed over many years. As such, inconsistencies and ambiguities have developed that need to be resolved. There are currently (January 2010) 20 OGC standards in revision. Much of this work is related to harmonizing various elements in the standards baseline. Another aspect of this work is that in August 2009, the OGC approved a policy document on how to consistently structure and document an OGC standard (Herring 2009). This document also speaks to the design and development of modular OGC standards and promotes the use of the "core-extension" model. In a sense, core-extension is much like having a kernel for an operating system and then having many extensions that work from the kernel. The harmonization and core-extension activities will result in late 2010 through 2011 a series of revisions to OGC standards that will be better documented, more consistent, and easier to implement and test. This is a very large undertaking but is critically important to the long term use and utility of OGC standards.

Lightweight Interfaces and Encodings

Another area of web services standards development activity in the OGC is the definition and approval of "light-weight" encodings and interface standards. Many existing OGC standards could be considered "heavy-weight". For example, WFS allows for numerous operations, supports a detailed query language, and has numerous optional elements. WFS was designed to allow query and retrieval of geospatial features of any type from any repository. As such, there is a certain level of "degrees of freedom" in the interface definition that requires more effort by the implementation community to learn, understand, and implement.

Therefore, there is a vigorous effort in the OGC community to also define more lightweight, more highly constrained, and easier to implement interfaces and encodings. There are several examples of current work activities in this area, including the OpenSearch Geospatial extension, GeoSMS, and a "core" version of WFS that supports simple encodings such as GeoRSS. These more light-weight standards have broad applicability in the consumer or mass market development communities.

Sensor Web Enablement (SWE)

The OGC work on the suite of sensor interface and encoding standards continues at a vigorous pace. Given the considerable implementation experience over the last couple of years, the SWE community in the OGC is revising the entire suite of sensor standards. A major aspect of this effort

to define core components for each of the standards, such as SOS and to also define common elements so that a new SWE Common standard can be approved.

A related activity in the OGC is Sensor Fusion for decision support. For example, n OGC Web Service 7.0, the Sensor Fusion thread builds on the OGC Sensor Web Enablement (SWE) framework of standards to focus on integrating the SWE interfaces and encodings with workflow and web processing services to perform sensor fusion. A key emphasis for sensor fusion during OWS 7 is full Motion Video Fusion. This activity investigated the geo-location of motion video for display and processing. The work also includes change detection of motion video using the OGC Web Processing Service (WPS) with rules.

Security and Authentication

Now that OGC web services standards are deployed in numerous applications, the OGC Members are continuing to actively insure that OGC standards can operate properly in a variety of security and authentication environments. The result of such activities is typically Engineering Reports that the Members then approve as OGC Best Practices. A current example of OGC activity in authentication is the recently initiated OGC Authentication Interoperability Experiment. The Authentication Interoperability Experiment will test standard ways of transferring authentication information between OGC clients and OGC services by leveraging mechanisms already existing in the transport protocol (HTTP and SOAP). The following mechanisms will be tested: HTTP Authentication, HTTP Cookies, SSL/X509, SAML[12], Shibboleth, OpenID and WS-Security. The result will be a best practice document describing how OGC web services can work with any of these authentication technologies.

OGC COMPLIANCE TESTING

Two different applications implementing a given OGC standard, such as WMS, does not guarantee interoperability. There are also questions from the user community such as, "Does implementation XYZ of WMS actually comply with the OGC WMS standard?" To further advance interoperability and to help users and procurement officers validate that a specific OGC standard implementation actually complies with the standard, the OGC maintains and is extending the OGC Compliance Testing Program (OGC Compliance 2010).

The OGC Compliance Testing Program allows organizations that implement an OGC standard to test whether their implementation is compliant with the mandatory elements of that standard. The program provides a well-documented process for testing compliance of server implementations of OGC standards. Currently this Program only tests server products. In other words, the Program can only test whether server products generate compliant responses. The program does not presently offer capability to test compliance of client side products, although this capability is being considered for future compliance testing.

There is a very well structured process and related instructions for each available test. The program is designed so that the organization doing the implementation can self-test their implementation. Once they believe that their implementation passes the compliance test, they notify the OGC staff. Staff then validates the results of the test. If the implementation passes, then a registration fee is paid to cover the costs of maintaining the compliance testing capability and the organization receives a Brand and certificate stating compliance for a given version of a given OGC standard.

OGC compliance tests are available for some but not all OGC standards. The OGC is continually enhancing and expanding the Compliance Testing Program as resources allow. The current list of available tests includes WMS, WFS, WCS,

Simple Featyres, Catalogue and GML validation. Plans are to extend the available tests to include the OGC SWE standards.

A list of products and implementations that have passed compliance testing can be found on the OGC website (OGC Compliant 2010).

SUMMARY AND CONCLUSION

The OGC Web Services baseline of standards is mature and widely implemented. However, the work of the OGC on these standards is not complete. New requirements and change requests are continually being submitted into the OGC process. These requirements and change requests reflect experience gained in implementing OGC standards in deployed applications. The other aspect of the continued work of the OGC is the development of "profiles" of existing OGC standards as well as community consensus

REFERENCES

Bergenheim, W., Sarjakoski, L. T., & Sarjakoski, T. (2009). *A Web processing service for GRASS GIS to provide on-line generalisation.* Paper presented at the 12th AGILE International Conference on Geographic Information Science 2009.

Compliance, O. G. C. (2010). Retrieved from http://www.opengeospatial.org/compliance

Compliant, O. G. C. (2010). Retrieved from http://www.opengeospatial.org/resource/products/compliant

Conover, H., Goodman, H., Zavodsky, B., Regner, K., Maskey, M., Lu, J., et al. (2008). *Intelligent Assimilation of Satellite Data into a Forecast Model Using Sensor Web Processes and Protocols.*

Doyle, A. (1997). *WWW Mapping Framework.* OGC Project Document.

Doyle, A., & Reed, C. (May 2001). *Introduction to OGC Web Services*. OGC® White Paper. Retrieved from http://portal.opengeospatial.org/files/?artifact_id=14973&version=1&format=pdf

Gao, S., Mioc, D., Yi, X., Anton, F., and Oldfield, E. (2008), Geospatial services for decision support on public health. *The International Archives of the Photogrammetry, Remote Sensing and Spatial Information Sciences, 37*(B8).

Gardels, K. (1998). *A Web Mapping Scenario*. OGC Project document 98-068.

Herring, J. (Ed.). (2009). *The specification model: A standard for modular specifications*. OGC Document 08-131r3. Retrieved from https://portal.opengeospatial.org/files/?artifact_id=34762

ISO 19107. (2003). *Geographic Information – spatial schema*. International Organization for Standards. Retrieved from http://www.iso.org/iso/catalogue_detail.htm?csnumber=26012

ISO 19119. (2005). *Geographic information – services*. International Organization for Standards. Retrieved from http://www.iso.org/iso/iso_catalogue/catalogue_tc/catalogue_detail.htm?csnumber=39890

ISO 23950. (2003). Information Retrieval (Z39.50): Application Service Definition and Protocol Specification.

ISO TC 211. (2009) *Terms and definitions*. Retrieved from http://www.isotc211.org/Terminology.htm

ISO/TS19139. (2007). *Geographic information -- Metadata -- XML schema implementation*. Retrieved from: http://www.iso.org/iso/catalogue_detail.htm?csnumber=32557

NASA.(2009). WCS for accessing Atmospheric Infrared Sounder (AIRS) Data. Retrieved from http://idn.ceos.org/KeywordSearch/Metadata.do?Portal=webservices&KeywordPath=(Project%3A+Short_Name%3D%27EOS%27]&EntryId=NASA_GES_DISC_AIRS_Atmosphere_Data_Web_Coverage_Service&MetadataView=Full&MetadataType=1&lbnode=mdlb1

NC OneMap. (2008). *NC OneMap*. Retrieved from http://www.nconemap.com/Default.aspx?tabid=287

NOAA WCS. (2009). *HF radar Web Coverage Service (WCS)*. Retrieved from http://hfradar.ndbc.noaa.gov/

OASIS. (2009). *Service oriented architecture*.

OGC. (2000). *Web map service interface specification*, (version 1.0 Project Document 00-028). Retrieved from http://www.opengeospatial.org/standards/wms

OGC. (2007). *OGC Glossary*. Retrieved from http://www.opengeospatial.org/ogc/glossary

OGC. (2010). *Implementing Products*. Retrieved from http://www.opengeospatial.org/resource/products

OGC CSW ebRIM. (2009). *CSW-ebRIM Registry Service - part 1: ebRIM profile of CSW*. Retrieved from http://portal.opengeospatial.org/files/?artifact_id=31137

OGC CSW ISO 19115 (2007), *Catalogue services specification 2.0.2 - ISO metadata application profile*. Retrieved from http://portal.opengeospatial.org/files/?artifact_id=21460

OpenIOOS. (2010). Retrieved from http://www.openioos.org/real_time_data/gm_sos.html

OWS-7. (2010). *OGC Web Service Test Bed 7*. Retrieved from http://www.opengeospatial.org/projects/initiatives/ows-7

Percivall, G., Reed, C., Leinenweber, L., Tucker, C., and Cary, T. (2008). *The OGC Reference Model (ORM)*. OGC Document OGC 08-062r4.

Reed, C. (Ed.). (2009). *OGC technical committee policies and procedures*. OGC Document 09-020r14.

Science, G. I. S. (2009). *SDI and the GRID special issue*. Retrieved from http://portal.opengeospatial. org/files/?artifact_id=35975

Singh, R. (Ed.). (2008). *Loosely coupled synchronization of geographic databases in the Canadian geospatial data infrastructure*. OGC. Retrieved from http://portal.opengeospatial.org/files/?artifact_id=26609

USGS WFS. (2009). *USGS Framework Web Feature Services*. Retrieved from http://frameworkwfs.usgs.gov/

Uslander, T. (Ed.). (2007). *Reference Model for the ORCHESTRA Architecture (RM-OA) V2 (Rev 2.1)*. Retrieved from http://portal.opengeospatial. org/files/?artifact_id=23286.

Vasudevan, V. (April 2001). *A Web Services Primer*. Retrieved from http://webservices.xml.com/pub/a/ws/2001/04/04/webservices/index.html

WMS. (2008, 2009). *iPhone and Android WMS apps*. Retrieved from http://androidgps.blogspot. com/2008/09/simple-wms-client-for-android. html http://www.appstorehq.com/mapprowms-iphone-61560/app

ENDNOTES

[1] International Standards Organization Technical Committee 211 (http://www.isotc211. org/)

[2] Organization for the Advancement of Structured Information Standards (http://www. oasis-open.org/)

[3] Internet Engineering Task Force GeoPriv Working Group (http://datatracker.ietf.org/wg/geopriv/charter/)

[4] National Emergency Number Association Next Generation 911 (http://www.nena.org/ng911-project)

[5] Open Mobile Alliance

[6] World Wide Web Consortium

[7] SOAP: W3C Simple Object Access Protocol recommendation.

[8] Publicly available information on all OGC test bed activities can be found on the OGC web site: http://www.opengeospatial.org/ogc/programs/ip

[9] A coverage is a subtype of feature that has a coverage function with a spatio-temporal domain and a value set range of homogeneous 1- to n-dimensional tuples. A coverage may represent one feature or a collection of features —to model and make visible spatial relationships between, and the spatial distribution of, Earth phenomena.

[10] For an integrated approach to defining, tasking, modeling, and accessing sensors in a sensor network, the OGC recommends using the OGC Sensor Web Enablement framework of standards. http://www.ogc-network.net/SWE

[11] However, most existing GML applications are based on GML 3.1.1 and even 2.1. More on this later.

[12] SAML: OASIS Security Assertion Markup Language

Section 2
Design and Implementation

Chapter 2
Managing Granularity in Design and Implementation of Geospatial Web Services

Elias Z. K. Ioup
Naval Research Laboratory, USA

John T. Sample
Naval Research Laboratory, USA

ABSTRACT

Granularity is often ignored when designing geospatial Web services. Choices relating to granularity affect service interfaces, data storage and organization, and XML format design. This chapter highlights the importance of analyzing usage and performance requirements when deciding on granularity choices in the design of geospatial Web services. Often, instead of making design decisions based on these requirements, geospatial services are implemented using default, commonly used techniques which may reduce performance, increase complexity, or fail to fully meet user needs. This chapter discusses the importance of granularity in designing and implementing geospatial Web services and provides common examples that highlight the different approaches to granularity which are available.

INTRODUCTION

A common issue in the design of enterprise class geospatial Web services is that of granularity. Granularity refers to the fineness in which services and data are divided. For example, consider a mapping service which provides road data. If

coarsely defined, the service might just provide a single layer titled "Roads." This single layer makes the service easy to use for the average user. Alternatively, a GIS analyst may prefer to have the road data sub-divided into several layers, each representing different types of roads. The increased granularity provides technical benefits to the power user that a layperson would not

DOI: 10.4018/978-1-60960-192-8.ch002

value, all at additional cost to the computational requirements of the service.

There is no rule of thumb for the right amount of granularity to provide in the design of geospatial Web services. An analysis of the tradeoffs associated with different levels of granularity must be performed on a case-by-case basis. This analysis is necessary not only in the design of geospatial service data groupings, but also in the underlying storage of data and the XML encoding used for sharing data. A parallel exists in the design of database indexes. There is no one-size-fits-all index which will universally increase the performance of all queries for every dataset. Careful study must be made of a variety of parameters such as query frequencies, computational load, and result set sizes before an optimal indexing scheme may be chosen (Lewis 2001). Too often granularity is ignored as a design choice when creating geospatial services, leading to increased costs and decreased functionality when the service is deployed.

This chapter will outline the general issues relating to granularity in the design and deployment of geospatial web services. It will provide a discussion and analysis of the impact of granularity on three principal issues:

1.   Design of external interfaces for geospatial Web services
2.   Storage and organization of the underlying geospatial data
3.   Encoding of geospatial data in XML formats

The primary focus of the chapter will be the Open Geospatial Consortium (OGC) collection of geospatial service standards (OGC 2010). OGC services provide few highly structured access patterns that should be used to motivate the design of geospatial data storage systems and retrieval services.

BACKGROUND

Granularity in geospatial data is often dealt with as a resolution issue (Robinson et al. 1995). In mapping terms, resolution refers to the level of detail or accuracy of a data set. For example, satellite imagery can have pixel resolutions of anywhere from 500 meters per pixel to under 1 meter per pixel. Additionally, paper maps often have a nominal scale, like 1:10,000 or 1:100,000. In the context of map scale, granularity is a major issue. A paper map of a large area, like a state, might only depict major roads and larger cities, while a map of single city would include streets, alleys, parks and playgrounds. Within digital mapping, data sets are often designed with multiple scales. For example, a data set of roads at the 1:100,000 scale, might depict a road's path with 50 vertices, while the 1:10,000 version of the same road path might use 500 vertices. Consider the road paths shown in Figure 1. Both polylines represent the same path at different resolutions. The top path uses many more vertices than the bottom path. One might ask, why would the lower resolution bottom path ever be used, if a higher resolution version was available. First, the lower resolution path requires less storage space, allowing it to be retrieved and sent to user much faster. Additionally if both of these paths were viewed at a lower scale view, for example 1:100,000, they would look exactly the same. It is only at the higher scale view, 1:10,000, where their differences are apparent. Figure 2 shows the same two paths, but at a lower scale view. In this view, the differences between the paths are less visible.

Lastly, map resolution has a significant affect on precision. The following table relates map scales to precision in meters.

From Table 1, we can see that the resolution of a point on a 1:500,000 scale map is 250 meters. Thus, even though a point on the map may appear to be precise, its position can only be definitively placed within a circle with radius 250 meters centered on that point.

Figure 1. Two depictions of the same road path at different resolutions

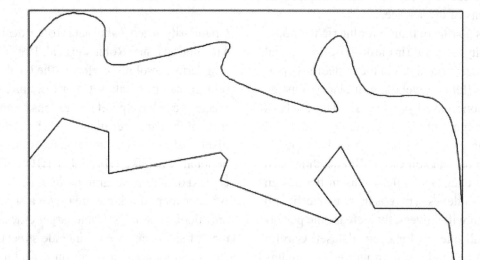

Figure 2. Small scale version of the two resolutions of the same road path

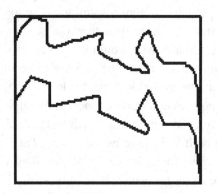

Table 1. Approximate relationships between scale and resolution, from (Robinson 1995)

Scale	Resolution (Precision)
1:1,000,000	500 meters
1:500,000	250 meters
1:250,000	125 meters
1:100,000	50 meters
1:50,000	25 meters
1:10,000	5 meters

Granularity as it relates to map resolution is separate from the issues of granularity that we are discussing in this chapter. When we discuss granularity, we mean the degree of fineness with which data and services are subdivided for the purposes of storage in a database or a file system, organized into Web services, and encoded in XML.

Discussions of granularity in this sense are limited. For the most part, geospatial services are created using a limited number of common design patterns without a serious analysis of usage requirements. Mitchell (2005) provides a good overview of the two most common patterns, native file and database-backed services. The former is a simple method of creating a geospatial Web service using data stored in native geospatial file formats on the file system along with a server such as Map Server (Lime 2008) which automatically creates the geospatial services. New data layers are created by dropping a geospatial file into a folder and linking it into the server. Often the file is automatically included in the service because the folder is constantly monitored by the system. Each file is made into a data layer. Queries are performed by scanning the relevant file for the queried layer, decoding it, and returning the relevant data from within. For example, an ESRI Shapefile named "parks" may be stored on the file system. A corresponding layer named "parks" would be made available from the geospatial service and queries would only search for data from within that particular Shapefile.

The second common pattern for creating geospatial services is the database pattern. Geospatial data is stored in a series of tables. Each feature is stored as a record in one table. Features may be added, updated, or deleted individually. Queries for data use the built-in database query solver. Usually, a database with geospatial query functionality is used such as Oracle with the Spatial Extension (Oracle 2010) or PostgreSQL with PostGIS (Chen & Xie 2008). Using this pattern, the "parks" Shapefile might be a single database table or it might be added to a larger table encompassing more features types which share the same schema (perhaps an "Entertainment Locales" table). Queries may be performed over one table or many table. The result is a system which is more complex but provides significantly more functionality out of the box (Mitchell 2005).

Haesen et al. (2008) discuss granularity from a Web service, rather than geospatial, perspective. They classify service granularity into three distinct types: functional granularity, data granularity, and business value granularity. Functional granularity is defined as the amount of functionality provided by a Web service. Data granularity is defined as the amount of data a service takes as input or provides as output. Business value granularity is a measure of the value a service has to a particular business. In their classification, coarse granularity refers to having more of a property and fine granularity less of a property. A service with coarse functional granularity provides more functionality than a service with fine-grained functional granularity (e.g. HandleClaimProcess() is more coarse

than IdentifyCustomer()). Their classification is designed to guide the creation of business Web services and generally promotes the use of coarse services. While their granularity classification is useful, it does not apply perfectly to the geospatial Web services we are interested in. Geospatial systems tend to have more complex data types, stricter functionality requirements, and different ways of assessing value. However, the premise of their work is to encourage an analysis of granularity in Web services, a goal that this chapter seeks to fulfill for geospatial Web services.

The purpose of this chapter is to shift the focus to design of geospatial service granularity motivated by usage rather than arbitrary choices. While both database and file-based architecture designs are useful in many circumstances, the discussion of the pros, cons, and alternatives to these patterns is lacking. The assumption is that the complexity of implementation will determine the desired solution, i.e. if the system architect is willing to implement a database-backed solution then that pattern should be used. Instead, implementers should be performing an analysis of the intended usage of their systems and determine the proper architecture from that analysis.

Geospatial Web Services

A clear understanding of how geospatial Web services are implemented and used is necessary to motivate proper choices about granularity in their design. Geospatial Web services have increased in popularity along with a set of design principles collectively called Service Oriented Architecture (SOA). The goal of SOA is to provide a loosely coupled collection of Web services that can be used together to achieve a unified purpose. Generally speaking, Web services are distributed systems designed to enable computer-to-computer interaction over a network and, in the non-geospatial community, usually refer to the World Wide Web Consortium (W3C) standards for XML communication. W3C Web Services use a communication protocol called SOAP (formerly Simple Object Access Protocol). The Web Service Description Language (WSDL) is used to describe the interface of a SOAP-compliant service. W3C services are a general purpose solution for implementing Web services to support any type of computer application or business domain. A key feature of SOAP/WSDL based Web services is their self-defining nature. The WSDL document defines the functions that a service provides and the data structures used for queries and responses. The data formats are XML encoded and formally defined with XML Schema.

In contrast to the general purpose W3C services, the geospatial services community has developed Web service standards specifically designed for geospatial applications. These Web service standards are maintained by the Open Geospatial Consortium (OGC). Each OGC standard is designed to disseminate a specific geospatial data type or provide a specific geospatial function. Additionally, OGC services are widely supported by GIS applications which allow off-the-shelf use by ordinary GIS users. Web Map Service (WMS), Web Feature Service (WFS) and Web Coverage Service (WCS) are three of the most commonly adopted standards for sharing geospatial data over networks. WMS is used to serve rendered maps and imagery (usually JPEG or PNG images), WFS is used to serve vector data encoded using XML, and WCS is used to serve coverages (generic non-image raster data) in a variety of native GIS or scientific formats.

OGC services have a different interaction model from SOAP/WSDL services. Since SOAP/WSDL services are general and self-describing, each service must be examined before it can be used. In contrast, the functions provided by an OGC service are defined in its standard and are fixed. For example, all WMS services must provide common set of functions: GetCapabilities, GetMap, and optionally GetFeatureInfo. The GetCapabilities document provides the list of available map layers. The GetMap request allows users to request map images over a specific geographic area. The optional GetFeatureInfo request allows users to request information on the features at a specific location on a rendered map. All mandatory functions must be implemented by a compliant WMS, and functions absent from the standard are disallowed.

OGC Service Usage Pattern

OGC services provide a baseline for use in modeling geospatial service usage patterns. Not only have OGC services become one of the most common methods of providing geospatial data over the Internet, their interaction model is similar to non-standard geospatial service implementations (e.g. proprietary Web-based maps). Usage of these three services has had a large impact on the design and implementation of geospatial data architectures. The following general usage patterns (which do have exceptions) apply to both OGC services as well as most other non-standard geospatial Web services:

- Services are read-only.
- Service queries operate over rectangular areas and query only the geometry component of features' attributes.
- Service queries access groups of features rather than individual features.
- Services are intensely performance sensitive.

The read-only nature of geospatial services is important to consider when designing the granularity of services. WMS and WCS are specified as strictly read-only. An extension to the WFS specification, called WFS-T (for transactions) allows updates to the underlying services data. In practice, WFS-T is rarely implemented due to the relative inefficiencies involved with uploading large GIS data sets via XML and HTTP. In general, geospatial services are used by organizations wishing to publish their data to a large third-party audience of consumers. Exceptions to the read-only geospatial service pattern do exist, and an example will be presented later in the chapter.

All three common OGC services; WMS, WFS, and WCS, include a bounding box a primary component in the query. For WMS, the bounding box is required as there is no other query parameter included in the query other than what data is desired. Other attributes may be used to determine how the features are rendered or symbolized as a result of a query, but not to determine which features are returned to the user. WFS does support complex queries over any attribute of a feature; however, support for this language is not required and frequently not implemented. In general, geospatial services are dominated by geospatial queries (Vretanos 2005).

The third usage pattern is a direct result of the second. Service queries usually operate over a geospatial region. That region will most likely have a number of features.

GIS users expect to move a map's view frequently, and require that supporting data services respond promptly. The desire for high performance and instantaneous response times from geospatial services is only heighted since examples such as Google Maps and Google Earth provide exactly this level of response. When WMS or WFS services are used to provide "background" maps for GIS applications users do not want to wait for maps to be rendered and refreshed.

Again, these usage patterns are not hard and fast rules. They are generalities that are common to many geospatial Web services. As a result, they provide a good baseline by which to drive decisions on how geospatial service interfaces are designed, geospatial data is stored and organized, and XML encodings are created.

Granularity of Geospatial Web Service Interfaces

Each of the three most common OGC services, and other geospatial services, are fundamentally

designed around the concept of a map "layer." Therefore, granularity in the design of geospatial service interfaces is focused primarily on the choices and organization of layers. Layers (or equivalent constructs) are the atomic unit for requesting map data from most OGC services. A map layer is a logical grouping of geospatial information. The term "layer" is used to convey the idea of multiple graphical layers stacked in some order in a visual display. In practice, layers are formed by logical groupings of geospatial data. For example, an "entertainment" map layer would include locations of movie theaters, parks, zoos, museums, etc.

WMS services provide a hierarchical list of layers in the GetCapabilities document (Beaujardière 2006). Figure 3 shows a pseudo-snippet from a WMS GetCapabilities document. This service offers five layers: Entertainment, Movie Theaters, Zoos, Parks and Museums and they are hierarchically organized. A user may request the Entertainment layer to get a single map image with all the data from the sub-layers, or a user can request individual map images from the sub-layers.

The WMS specification also allows for the definition of "abstract" layers in the capabilities document. Abstract layers appear as layers with a title, but not a name. They are only meant for organization or grouping of sub-layers, and cannot be queried directly or rendered as map images.

The Entertainment layers example demonstrates the two primary granularity-affecting actions which may be taken in the design of a geospatial service interface: combining data to form a layer, and partitioning data to form a layer. Combining and partitioning data is quite simple in the above example. Movie Theaters, Zoos, Parks, and Museums are easily chosen as distinct layers and the simple union of these datasets forms a perfect parent Entertainment layer.

A more complex example occurs when the underlying data becomes three or four dimensional. The WMS service is primarily designed to

Figure 3. XML snippet of WMS GetCapabilities document

```xml
<Layer>
    <Title>Entertainment</Title>
    <Name>Entertainment</Name>
    <Layer>
        <Title>Movie Theaters</Title>
        <Name>Entertainment:MovieTheaters</Name>
    </Layer>
    <Layer>
        <Title>Zoos</Title>
        <Name>Entertainment:Zoos</Name>
    </Layer>
    <Layer>
        <Title>Parks</Title>
        <Name>Entertainment:Parks</Name>
    </Layer>
    <Layer>
        <Title>Museums</Title>
        <Name>Entertainment:Museums</Name>
    </Layer>
</Layer>
```

support 2-dimensional layers. Queries are defined by a two-dimensional geographic rectangle that specifies the area to be visualized and return two-dimensional images. However, current versions of the WMS standard support optional time and elevation parameters, allowing a third and fourth dimension to be included in the query.

Consider a Weather Map service with temperature forecasts. The temperature forecasts are available at various times and elevations. A single integrated "temperature" layer in our WMS service would allow the service to be queried by geographic rectangle, time and elevation. However, some WMS client applications do not support time and elevation requests. To support those clients, separately named temperature layers would need to be generated for each combination of time and elevation. If we have 10 elevations and 10 times, we would have to list 100 layers in our capabilities document. What then is the best way to design the interface for the Weather Map service? In this case, the data does not directly indicate the proper design, but rather the target audience. If the target audience is a limited set of users with an application known to support the time and elevation query parameters then a single layer is the best option. However, if the target audience is wide and application support should be as flexible as possible, then the supporting separate layers for each time/elevation combination is probably the best choice. For the latter case, it is still advisable to create a single parent layer which supports the time and elevation query parameters to simplify use for supporting applications. Abstract layers (which essentially act as folders) should also be used to organize the time/elevation combinations so they are easier to find.

The final case study refers back to the Road layer example. In this example, a WMS returns road maps rendered dynamically from a vector roads dataset. Here there are three possible organizations for the WMS layer interface. The first is to provide a single layer containing all roads. The second option splits roads into separate layers by type. For example, there will be a layer for Interstates, one for Major Highways, one for Surface

Streets, etc. These two options mirror those for the Entertainment layers and a potential solution is to provide both the combined and separated layers to users. However, a third solution may provide a better option: a map scale aware, auto-switching road layer. Instead of providing a layer that displays all roads in a geographic area, the auto-switching layer will only show roads appropriate to the requested map scale. For small-scale map requests, the layer may only show data from the Interstates layer. For large-scale map requests, the layer will show all road data. Additionally, the rendering of the roads may change depending on the map scale. The WMS is easily able to determine the map scale based on the geographic area of the request and the requested image dimensions.

The auto-switching layer is important to discuss because it highlights another factor in determining the proper granularity of a geospatial service interface, performance. The performance of the all roads combined layer will be significantly worse than the performance of the auto-switching layer because at smaller map scales it will be required to draw most or all of the roads into one image. The same problem exists when partitioning the roads into separate layers for the Surface Streets and possibly the Major Highways layers. For a Roads layer it is obvious that performance will be a problem when users try to dynamically draw every road in a country at once. However, the same performance issues exist in many large geospatial datasets where the problem and solution is not so obvious. Directly converting a geospatial file or database table into a service layer is not always the best solution for geospatial interface granularity.

WFS and WCS services have similar problems and solutions to WMS services. An important difference is the lack of hierarchy in their layer structure. For WFS services layers are called "feature types" and for WCS services layers are called "coverages." Both only allow flat lists of layers, meaning that the hierarchy solution to the Entertainment WMS layers is not available for these other services.

For WFS there are several ways to replicate the functionality from our WMS service with 5 entertainment layers. Rather than returning a rendered image, the WFS service will return a document with the features encoded in XML. The four basic data types (zoos, parks, movie theaters, and museums) are similar enough to share a common XML schema. The different types of entertainment activities may be delineated in an attribute called "ActivityType." All the zoo features would have "Zoo" in the ActivityType attribute field, and likewise for the other types. In this case, our WFS service would only have one feature type, called "Entertainment". Queries to this feature type would return a mixture of all the types of activities. If users want only zoos or parks, they would use the query functionality built in to the WFS specification. The ability to support queries over feature attributes is not universal to WFS clients, so granularity choices must be based on target audience and application. By limiting the number of feature results returned to the client, the lack of attribute queries may not matter.

The same ideas on granularity also apply to WCS services. The major difference for WCS is its built-in support for serving and querying high dimensional data (Whiteside & Evans 2008). A common occurrence with WCS data is to map native files directly to WCS coverages. However, often this interface design ignores the inherent support for queries over all dimensions of a coverage. For example, suppose a WCS was serving the temperature data discussed above. Often, a new coverage will be made for each time when a forecast is available. However, native support for dimensionality in WCS means a better method of providing the data is with one temperature coverage which allows queries over space, elevation, and time. This design simplifies the interface and allows users to invoke the WCS native support for interpolation and re-gridding over any dimension. Interpolation is unavailable on the server-side when data is separated into multiple layers. Concerns over client support for

WCS functionality are less relevant because WCS clients tend to be custom and designed toward the particular service they are consuming.

As shown above, granularity decisions about geospatial service interfaces are rarely simple. Underlying data organization, intended audience, performance, and service capabilities must all be analyzed when designing a geospatial service interface. These same characteristics are important in making decisions about granularity in other part of geospatial service design.

Design of Geospatial Web Service Interfaces

The first choice in the design of a geospatial Web service is whether to implement an existing OGC standard. If the choice is made to implement an OGC standard, then in most cases the interface for the service is fixed. WMS, WFS, and WCS, the three most common OGC service standards, have a fixed interface. Implementers may choose what data is exposed, but they may not change the functions provided by the service.

On the other hand, when the interface is not fixed by a standard, either because no standard is being used or the standard is flexible (e.g. OGC Web Processing Service), there are many design decisions related to granularity which must be considered. Here is it useful to consider two of the classifications proposed by Haesen et al. (2008): functional granularity and data granularity. There is no single "correct" granularity when designing a geospatial Web service interface. An analysis of the service usage is necessary to determine the best granularity for the design.

Functional granularity defines how much functionality a service bundles into a single function or separates into multiple functions. For example, a Web service may have the task of providing a weather report for an area. A service which has three separate functions for retrieving a radar map, temperature ranges, and a precipitation forecast is a fine-grained Web service. On the other hand,

a service which has one function that creates an entire weather report document is a coarse-grained Web service. The coarse service is most effective when clients only are interested in the combined document whereas the fine-grained service is most effective when clients may only require portions of the weather report. A key point to notice is that neither option is mutually exclusive. One Web service could provide both the combined document function and the separate product functions. Often this will be the case with functional granularity.

Data granularity refers to the design of the input and output parameters. For example, a generic geospatial data service which outputs images, vector data, and grids has coarse output data granularity. A real example of coarse data granularity is the WMS SOAP interface. Retrieving data from the WMS via SOAP uses only a single GetMap() function. All variation in the service is controlled and realized in the input and output parameters. The Layers input parameter controls which map layers are returned and the output parameters changes based on those choices. A finer-grained alternative WMS SOAP binding creates a separate function for each data layer, e.g. GetStreetMap() and GetSatelliteMap(). The benefit of the fine-grained approach is that the capabilities of the Web service are clearly indicated in the WSDL description, making it easier for clients to discover and use functionality.

Another example is the Joint METOC Broker Language (JMBL) which defines a Web service interface for retrieving meteorological data (Katikaneni et al. 2004). A JMBL Web service has coarse granularity. A single function provides all the data for the service and a single query parameter controls the actions of the service. The single query parameter requires a complex query language to control the actions of the service. The effect of this design is to hide the functionality and usage of the service behind a custom query language rather than revealing it in the Web service interface. Generally, this is a bad idea. Hiding functionality in data parameters makes it difficult for clients to

Figure 4. Example point, line and area features with attributes

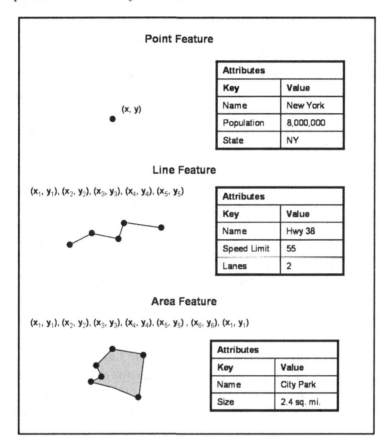

find and properly use a service. It is much easier to see the capabilities of a service when its functions are GetStreetMap() and GetSatelliteMap() instead of just GetMap(). Similarly, JMBL services are difficult to use because they require a custom query language to control functionality. A simpler service would be more fine-grained. The Web service would be controlled through multiple SOAP functions with multiple data parameters specific to those functions. The interface would assist in defining the proper usage of the service.

Storage and Organization of Geospatial Data

Granularity is immensely important when considering storage and organization of geospatial feature data. Specifically, we are interested in

where geospatial data is stored, how it is grouped together when stored, how fine queries results may be, and how data is indexed to increase query performance. For the purposes of this discussion, geospatial feature data consists of two components. The first component is one or more geometric primitives, like points, lines and polygons delineated with coordinates in a given coordinate system that represent features on the earth's surface. The second component is formed by the attributes attached to those geometric primitives. For example, a road feature might be represented as a series of line segments that trace the course of the road's paths, and the attached attributes would include the name of the road, the speed limit and the number of lanes. Figure 4 shows examples of point, line and area features with attached properties. Composite features can also be created that contain different types of geometries. Likewise, features with geometry dimensions greater than two are possible. Three and four dimensional features, those with elevation and time dimensions, are common. We refer to a feature's attribute names and types as its attribute schema.

Geospatial Features in Relational Database Management Systems

There are two common ways of storing geospatial feature data: in a relational database management system (RDBMS) or directly on a computer file system. Features stored in a RDBMS typically occupy one row per feature. Each attribute of the feature, including the geometry, occupies a column. This organization and storage scheme is the default paradigm used by most Geospatial Information Systems (GIS) and can be considered the lowest level of granularity given that each feature is individually accessible, for both queries and updates (Oracle 2010; Chen & Xie 2008). Additionally, this scheme reflects the traditional use of relational databases, and enables storage, retrieval and editing of geospatial features. One consequence of RDBMS storage is that separate tables are required for each type of feature.

Figure 4 shows three features of differing types. These features require three separate database tables since each has different attributes. In many GIS enabled RDBMS different types of geometries can be stored under the same column, but differing numbers and types of non-geospatial attributes always require separate tables.

An RDBMS storage system is useful when users are querying and editing the individual properties of individual features. These systems have built-in support for indexing of data, even geospatial data. Oracle Spatial and PostgreSQL/PostGIS support R-Tree geospatial indexes, which support efficient geospatial queries. Analysis queries are also possible. For example, a user may query the RDBMS for all city parks whose border is longer than 5 mi. PostGIS supports queries with functions on geometries, making development of analysis tasks simple.

Geospatial Features Stored Directly on the File System

Geospatial features may also be stored in files directly on a computer's file system. File system storage requires the system developer to manually design and implement a storage and organization scheme for the geospatial features. For example, one option would be to store each feature in a separate file. The overhead of computer file systems would make this an inefficient approach for all but the smallest data sets.

A common approach is to store all features sharing a single attribute schema in a single collection. This is the pattern used by the ESRI Shapefile format. As with a database, the attribute schema defines how features are organized. Feature classes with different attributes have to be stored in separate Shapefiles.

An alternative file storage approach is to store multiple feature classes in a single collection. This method comes at the cost of an increase in storage overhead, but provides an increase in flexibility. The increased storage overhead is generated by the requirement to store the feature attribute names and types along with the values, because unlike the Shapefile and database approaches, the attribute schema varies across all features in a collection.

File based storage methods also require the developer to create custom methods for data queries, updates, and indexes. This comes with an increase in development time, but provides greater flexibility. The data queries, updates, and indexes can be created to suit specific applications, and in many cases, will out-perform off the shelf solutions.

Data Storage and Organization Requirements

Granularity requirements for access to geospatial data should be of primary consideration when deciding on the data storage and organization design for a geospatial service. Often a data storage methodology is chosen strictly on the basis of ease of implementation or what is commonly used by others without analyzing specific application requirements. A simple file system organization scheme, where data is stored in its native geospatial files, is often used because it is easy to implement. An RDBMS may be implemented because that is how data is supposed to be stored when creating Web services. No single best methodology for storing geospatial data for Web services exists. Granularity requirements must be used when deciding how data will be stored.

For the purpose in analyzing geospatial service requirements, all operations on a geospatial dataset will be categorized as either an update or a query. Updates include adding new data, changing existing data, or deleting data. Queries include any action that results in the retrieval of data, including retrieving a single record, a number of records, or an entire dataset.

As discussed above, one property of geospatial services is that they are primarily read-only. For these services updates are in bulk. A significant number of features or perhaps the entire dataset is changed at once. Consider the Roads Web service discussed earlier. Commonly for these systems, road data is collected by a third-party which then gives the data to the application providers. A road data provider may be a commercial entity such as NAVTEQ or a government entity such as the US Census Bureau. The geospatial service provider renders the data into maps, either ahead of time or on the fly, and makes it available over the Web to a large number of users. Therefore, updates are infrequent and queries are frequent. Additionally, both updates and queries operate on a large amount of data. Updates occur infrequently enough that a large number of features have changed. Queries are for geospatial regions, usually with a significant number of roads in them. Updates and queries are not designed to operate on a single feature.

In contrast, the OpenStreetMap web-based mapping application allows users to update the underlying road map data of the system. Thus, the OpenStreetMap service does not follow our general rule about the read-only nature of geospatial Web services. It follows that there is no reason that the system should store data using the same methodology as a read-only system. As updates are made, the OpenStreetMap system pre-renders the roads into images. Creation of new pre-rendered images occurs approximately once an hour, if underlying updates to the road data warrant it. In contrast to the previous example, both updates and queries are frequent. Additionally, updates do operate on individual features whereas queries still operate on multiple features (OpenStreetMap 2010).

The OpenStreetMap service is an example of when a RDBMS is a perfect storage solution for geospatial data. Updates operate on individual features, meaning that efficient feature level access is necessary to the application. An RDBMS provides exactly this capability. In a database, features can be indexed by a unique ID. When updating a particular feature, an index on feature IDs may be used to make execution time for the operation negligible. An index over an ID is a built-in feature of all modern RDBMS. Additionally, a clustered geospatial index over the features will provide efficient access to the data for queries. However, given the size of the underlying dataset and the possible large query result sets, it is possible that queries will not execute instantaneously. The OpenStreetMap service is not sensitive to query costs because feature queries are only used to generate pre-rendered tiles, not to generate data presented to the user.

The first example is of more interest, since most geospatial services follow the read-only model. These geospatial services do not require access to individual features, whereas for OpenStreetMap such access is a major requirement. Despite the different requirements of these services, their geospatial data is often stored in a RDBMS as it is with the OpenStreetMap system. Below we will discuss some alternatives to the standard storage approaches which better fit the usage pattern common to geospatial Web services.

Feature Storage Granularity

A reevaluation is necessary of the granularity of feature storage. Normally each individual geospatial feature is a first order element. An analogy would that of the byte. In all modern computer systems the byte (8 bits) is the smallest atomic unit of memory that can be addresses and accessed. Accessing a single bit requires reading the byte containing that bit and then computationally extracting the single bit. The granularity of memory storage in a computer is a tradeoff. Many applications, such as compression algorithms, must address sub-byte units. These algorithms could potentially operate much more efficiently if they could directly address individual bits. However, this would be highly inefficient. In fact, while modern systems allow addressing of individual bytes, they read and write to disk in pages which can be several thousand bytes.

Similarly, it is often more efficient to bundle storage of geospatial features. While it may be more convenient to store individual features as first order elements, it significantly adds to the amount of space and effort needed to create indexes. Suppose there is a database of features for producing maps for ocean navigation. The feature classes are dividing into categories like Depth Contour Lines, Shipwreck Points, Restricted Areas, Fishery Areas, Buoys, and Beacon Points. Additionally, these features are already subdivided by area; there are individual sets for each major harbor and port in the United States. In actual usage, users load all the features for a specific port or harbor into an electronic chart display.

The standard approach would be to create a database table for each feature class, and then load all the features into those tables. However, storing individual features separately creates needless overhead. The individual features are never changed or accessed by themselves. Instead, all the features for a specific feature class and harbor or port may be bundled into a single Shapefile. A database table may hold records referring to entire Shapefiles instead of individual features. The binary contents of the Shapefile are stored as BLOBs (Binary Large Objects) in the database, and the table also includes columns for the metadata, including the feature class name, the harbor or port name, and a single bounding rectangle for all the features in the Shapefile. This organization reduces the number of database rows from millions to a few thousand. As a result queries run much faster and, since our feature BLOBs are stored in contiguous memory, reading them is as fast as possible.

File System Storage and Indexing

As an alternative to using a RDBMS, the file system may be used to store geospatial data and, in many cases, out perform more sophisticated database-driven solutions. Suppose we have several large sets of geospatial features over the whole world, such as roads in our example above. The goal is to provide a map rendering service which has the high query frequency and low update frequency usage pattern. Instead of using the RDBMS with an R-Tree index, a Quadtree index may be used to organize the geospatial features on the file system.

Why is the above file system storage method an improvement over an RDBMS? First, file system storage allows a level of customization which a database will not. An RDBMS must be created to support a wide range of usage characteristics. A file system storage scheme need only support one application. The result is a storage system whose granularity is designed and optimized for

Figure 5. Execution times for file and database feature queries

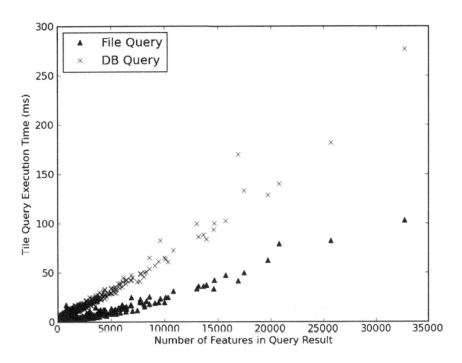

that application. Storage granularity refers to the number and size of the files used to store the data. For example, the file size for a quad may be chosen so that it is large enough to support most queries given the geospatial service but small enough to fit and load into memory. In contrast, an RDBMS will determine page sizes for an R-Tree automatically. All RDBMS systems support tuning, but this is complicated and difficult to get right. Often an RDBMS requires a dedicated administrator to ensure proper performance tuning (Ramakrishnan & Gehrke 2003). For a geospatial service implementer, it is often easier to design a custom storage methodology along with the rest of the service implementation. A basic file system storage scheme, as described above, will often perform as well as, or better, than a database, because a database has significant overhead in memory costs, transaction control, file locking, and the application/database interface. An RDBMS adds a significant amount of complexity to geospatial service design which is often not necessary given

the limited number of capabilities geospatial services actually require from the database.

A good example for comparing the performance of an RDBMS and file-based stored is the task of pre-rendering image tiles of infrequently updated road data. As an example experiment we stored commercially available NAVTEQ street data for the entire US in both a RDBMS and a tile based custom file format. We designed geographic queries at an appropriate scale, executed the series of queries, and compared the execution times for retrieving road data from a database and the file system. Each geospatial query is chosen to match the geospatial boundaries of image tiles. After features are loaded into memory, they are rendered into image tiles. The custom file storage scheme removes the need to search for features because queries are pre-computed when features are stored in files. Achieving this same cost savings with a database would be difficult. Figures 5 and 6 show the comparative query performance for the file based and database based methods.

Figure 6. Execution times for file and database features queries with 1000 or fewer features

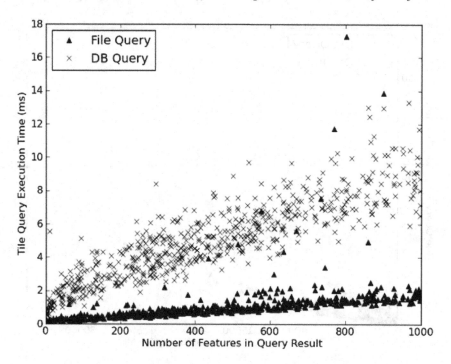

Figure 5 shows the execution time to retrieve 1 tile worth of features for both file and database queries. Execution times are ordered by the number of features retrieved per query. Figure 6 shows the execution time to retrieve 1 tile worth of features for only the tiles containing 1000 or fewer features.

Design of XML Based Geospatial Services and Features

Almost all geospatial web services use XML in some fashion. WFS, WMS and WCS all use XML to encode the services' capabilities. WFS uses XML to encode the actual data responses.

The GetFeature request of a WFS returns geospatial features in response to various types of allowed queries. These features are encoded using XML according to a defined schema. The client executes the DescribeFeatureType request to get an XML Schema Document (XSD) that provides the template for the actual features. The service specific XSD returned by DescribeFeatureType will define the geometry of features using the OGC standardized Geography Markup Language (GML). Only the geometry attribute of a feature follows the GML format. All other attributes as well as the overall structure of the geospatial feature are custom created for the geospatial service (or group of services if they agree on a common schema).

GML is a set of XML Schema documents that define a standardized vocabulary for communicating geospatial properties in XML. GML is quite broad and expressive. Practically any geospatial construct or property can be communicated with the aid of GML. However, GML is not a file format. It only provides templates that must be combined with application specific content to form a freestanding document format. This places a burden on WFS service providers and consumers. Providers must design the structure of their geospatial features, and consumers must be prepared to accept customized features.

Figure 7. XML snippet with point feature

```
<City>
    <gml:Geometry>
        <gml:Point>
            <gml:pos dimension="2 "> 39.3160 74.4963 </gml
        </gml:Point>
    </gml:Geometry>
    <Name>Detroit</Name>
    <Population>3,423,423</Population>
    <State>Michigan</State>
</City>
```

Figure 8. Alternative method for encoding parameters

```
<Feature type="City">
    <gml:Geometry>
        <gml:Point>
            <gml:pos dimension="2 "> 39.3160 74.4963 </gml:pos>
        </gml:Point>
    </gml:Geometry>
    <attribute name="Name">Detroit</Attribute>
    <attribute name="Population">3,423,423</Attribute>
    <attribute name="State">Michigan</Attribute>
</Feature>
```

Granularity in the Design of XML-Encoded Features

Definition granularity is the first design decision necessary when designing XML-encoded geospatial features. As stated earlier, most traditional geospatial data models provide for features with a geometry attribute and several other named attributes (see Figure 4). This flat structure is used primarily to align geospatial features with the storage model used by relational databases. Although it is not a requirement, many XML based geospatial encodings follow this pattern. Figure 7 shows a point feature encoded in XML with a GML compliant geometry attribute.

The above example has fine definition granularity because the definition of the feature is specific only to City features with Name, Population, and State attributes. Alternatively, coarse definition granularity will allow a number of different feature types to be stored in a single XSD. These different feature types may have different attributes. A single generic attribute element is used to encode all attributes. Figure 8 presents the same data as Figure 7 but with a generalized feature definition that does not require a City feature or Name, Population, and State attributes. The same underlying XML schema would support Country features or Restaurant features with completely different attributes.

Coarse granularity allows many features types to share a common XML Schema, however, not all generic WFS clients may properly handle the coarse granularity design.

Feature granularity must also be considered when designing XML-encoded geospatial features. Feature granularity refers to the actual construction of the feature, its attributes and geometry. XML allows complex, hierarchical features to be created which do not follow the standard database table or Shapefile data model. For example, a "City" feature might have both a point and an area geometry attribute. The point would be used to plot the location of the city at lower scales, and the area would be used to show the city's boundaries at higher scales.

Hierarchical attributes may also be added to a feature. For example, a WFS for Entertainment locations (similar to Figure 3) may organize all features according to city. The service would provide a City XML feature that has embedded in it parks, zoos, museums, etc. The granularity of this feature is coarser than the design discussed earlier that separates Entertainment locations into separate features. This design is perfect for a service intended to provide a map of cities points which may be selected to see available attractions. The number of queryable features is reduced. The coarse feature granularity will improve performance.

In addition to WFS, the Catalog Service for the Web (CSW) uses XML heavily. A CSW is a registry of geospatial information and services. Providers of Web based geospatial resources store records of their resources in a catalog service. The catalog service provides a queryable interface to those records. Though CSW provides multiple interfaces, its XML based interface is most relevant to this discussion. In this case, data providers can submit XML documents to the catalog for storage. While the records contain certain mandatory elements, a catalog service can be configured to accept XML documents that are almost freeform in nature (Nebert et al. 2007).

Feature granularity is also important in the design of a CSW. In this case, features are records of geospatial datasets and services. As with the design of other services, databases color the choice of feature granularity when a CSW is being created. Often a geospatial dataset is broken down into its most atomic components and each is turned into a record in a CSW. For example, a large dataset

of imagery may contain 5 million individual images. One design of a CSW will store 5 million individual records, one of each image. However, the images themselves are bundled into CD-size collections when they are created and distributed. Most metadata is shared between images in the same bundle. Additionally, users always download these bundles rather than the individual images. Thus, a better CSW design is to index the bundles rather than the individual images. Instead of 5 million records for each image in the CSW, there will only be approximately 10000 records for each bundle. The overall performance of the system will increase significantly, and it will more closely match the usage patterns of the data itself. A close analysis of the necessary granularity for this service will increase the overall performance of the services, and provide improved functionality.

CONCLUSION

There is no one size fits all solution to the design of geospatial Web services, especially when deciding on the various aspects of granularity of the system. Other aspects of computing encourage analysis of intended usage and performance requirements when designing system, databases being a prime example. Unfortunately, the designers of geospatial services often ignore this process and use default solutions which are not necessary optimal for the systems being created. Granularity of geospatial services, from data models to storage techniques, can have a large affect on performance and overall complexity of a geospatial service implementation. The techniques and examples discussed in this chapter are meant as a guide to the numerous design choices available when creating a geospatial Web service. While not exhaustive, hopefully this discussion on granularity as it relates to the design of services highlights the importance of proper analysis when designing a geospatial Web service.

ACKNOWLEDGMENT

This work was funded in large part by the Naval Research Laboratory Core Program, Program Element No. 0602435N.

REFERENCES

Chen, R., & Xie, J. (2008). Open source databases and their spatial extensions. In Hall, G. B., & Leahy, M. G. (Eds.), *Open Source Approaches in Spatial Data Handling* (pp. 105–129). Berlin: Springer-Verlag. doi:10.1007/978-3-540-74831-1_6

de la Beaujardière, J. (2006). *Web Map Server Implementation Specification (Version 1.3.0)*. Retrieved March 1, 2010, from http://portal.opengeospatial.org/files/index.php?artifact_id=14416.

Katikaneni, U., Ladner, R., & Petry, F. (2004). Internet delivery of meteorological and oceanographic data in wide area naval usage environments. In *Proceedings of the 13th international World Wide Web Conference Alternate* (pp. 84-88). New York: ACM.

Lewis, P. M., Bernstein, A., & Kifer, M. (2001). *Database systems: an application oriented approach*. Boston: Addison-Wesley.

Lime, S. (2008). Map server. In Hall, G. B., & Leahy, M. G. (Eds.), *Open Source Approaches in Spatial Data Handling* (pp. 65–85). Berlin: Springer-Verlag. doi:10.1007/978-3-540-74831-1_4

Mitchell, T. (2005). *Web Mapping Illustrated*. Sebastopol, CA: O'Reilly.

Nebert, D., Whiteside, A., & Vretanos, P. (2007). *OpenGIS catalogue services specification*, (Version 2.0.2). Retrieved March 1, 2010 from http://portal.opengeospatial.org/files/?artifact_id=20555

Open Geospatial Consortium. (2010). *Open Geospatial Consortium*. Retrieved March 1, 2010, from http://www.opengeospatial.org/.

OpenStreetMap. (2010). *OpenStreetMap FAQ*. Retrieved March 1, 2010, from http://wiki.openstreetmap.org/wiki/FAQ.

Oracle Corporation. (2010). *Oracle spatial datasheet*. Retrieved March 1, 2010, from http://www.oracle.com/technology/products/spatial/htdocs/data_sheet_9i/9iR2_spatial_ds.html

Ramakrishnan, R., & Gehrke, J. (2003). *Database management systems*. New York: McGraw Hill.

Robinson, A. H., Morrison, J. L., Muehrcke, P. C., Kimerling, A. J., & Guptill, S. C. (1995). *Elements of Cartography* (6th ed.). New York: Wiley.

Vretanos, P. (2005). *Web feature service implementation specification (Version 1.1.0)*. Retrieved March 1, 2020 from http://portal.opengeospatial.org/files/index.php?artifact_id=8339

Whiteside, A., & Evans, J. (2008). *Web Coverage Service Implementation Standard (Version 1.1.2)*. Retrieved March 1, 2020 from http://portal.opengeospatial.org/files/?artifact_id=27297

KEY TERMS AND DEFINITIONS

Application Programming Interface (API): An abstraction that describes an interface for the interaction with a set of functions used by components of a software system.

Coarse-Grained: Consisting of few, larger components.

Fine-Grained: Consisting of many, smaller components.

Granularity: The extent to which a system is broken down into smaller parts.

Web Service: Software component exposed to users via a Web-based interface with a standardized API.

Chapter 3
Enabling Quality of Geospatial Web Services

Richard Onchaga Moses
Kenya Polytechnic University College, Kenya

ABSTRACT

Following concerted efforts in service chaining and increased maturity of requisite technologies, the potential of geospatial web services in mission-critical applications and business processes is increasingly becoming apparent. Use of geospatial web services in mission-critical applications and business processes nonetheless raises important quality concerns for which guarantees should be provided. As a contribution to the subject of quality of geospatial web services, this chapter identifies and elaborates quality concerns pertinent to geospatial web services and their use in mission critical applications and business processes. The chapter defines a quality model for geospatial web services comprising data quality and quality of service. Quality propagation is outlined and the influence of quality of input data and that of component geospatial web services in a service chain on the quality deliverable end-to-end illustrated. Further, an ontology framework for quality of geospatial web services is presented. The framework comprises an upper ontology, two domain ontologies and potentially many application ontologies. Collectively, the ontologies provide a consistent set of concepts that can be used to unambiguously define and reason about quality of geospatial web services. The chapter also proposes a domain middleware to facilitate efficient and cost-effective quality-aware chaining of geospatial web services. The service design and high-level architecture for the middleware are presented.

DOI: 10.4018/978-1-60960-192-8.ch003

INTRODUCTION

Geospatial web services have emerged as a novel and promising framework for acquiring and disseminating geographic information (Yue, Di, Yang, Yu & Zhao (2007); Alameh, 2003). The services are not only enabling interoperability among disparate geographic information systems (GISs) but are also mainstreaming geographic information (GI) and GIS technology by integrating GIS with other enterprise information technology (IT) systems across technology and organizational boundaries (Onchaga, 2005). More fundamentally though, the services afford added flexibility in that autonomous but interoperable geospatial web services can be located and chained on-demand to create customized geoprocessing solutions (Alameh, 2003).

With maturity of requisite technologies, geospatial web services are increasingly being deployed and made available for exploitation; see for instance Tait (2005). Furthermore, it is anticipated that as the services proliferate, they will increasingly form part of mission-critical applications and business processes (Onchaga, 2006). Meanwhile, pioneering attempts at service chaining are yielding promising results; see for instance Alameh (2003), Poveda, Gould & Grannel (2004), Yue, Di, Yang, Yu & Zhao (2007) and Open Geospatial Consortium (OGC) web services interoperability demonstrations.

While expected and desirable, use of geospatial web services in mission-critical applications and business processes will nonetheless raise pertinent quality concerns – users are likely to be concerned about the performance, reliability and security of the services in addition to quality of the information delivered by the services (Herring, 2001; Tait, 2005; Subbiah, Alam, Khan & Thuraisingham, 2007; Umuhoza, Agbinya, Moodley & Vaheed, 2008).

In order to achieve and sustain user-satisfaction in the marketplace, there is a need to continuously guarantee acceptable levels of quality of geospatial web services for users. However, providing quality guarantees to individual users in a heterogeneous and increasingly dynamic geospatial web services environment is not a trivial challenge. The challenge becomes even more difficult when user requirements are addressed by locating and orchestrating two or more geospatial web services in a service chain. In the context of a service chain, given a set of (quality) requirements, an optimal set of geospatial services has to be located from a potentially large population of candidate services and subsequently orchestrated and their execution monitored so as to ensure delivery of required geospatial information while adhering to specified quality constraints.

In this chapter, we call a chaining process in which quality requirements of users and quality capabilities of candidate geospatial web services are considered as quality-aware service chaining. Quality-aware service chaining is a highly complex process fraught with many challenges. This is partly due to the distributed and dynamic nature of the computing environment for geospatial web services and partly due to the following factors (Onchaga, 2006):

- In an open geospatial web service marketplace, one is likely to find multiple services (from different providers) offering similar functionality but with rather different qualities;
- In a geospatial web service (chain), achievement of one quality will not necessarily contribute positively to the achievement of other qualities e.g. providing secure access to a service is likely to compromise its performance;
- In a service chain, quality deliverable end-to-end is not known a priori but can only be estimated;
- In an open competitive environment, it is possible to have same levels of quality being offered at different costs e.g. two providers can offer the same level of quality at

different prices thus yielding varying perceptions of value;

- In a multi-provider multi-user environment, there is likelihood that quality will be understood differently e.g. different communities will use different concepts to describe the same aspect of quality and therefore inhibiting sharing and reuse of quality specifications because of semantic heterogeneity;

- In a distributed geospatial web services environment, quality encompasses tangible aspects of data or information deliverable as well as intangible aspects related to its creation and access.

In addressing the above concerns, this chapter contributes to the subject of quality of geospatial web services in two prime ways. First, the chapter motivates and defines a novel quality model for geospatial web services comprising relevant aspects of data quality and quality of service (QoS) and embeds it a quality ontology framework as a means of addressing semantic heterogeneity. Second, the chapter motivates and proposes a domain-specific middleware to facilitate quality-aware chaining of geospatial web services. The middleware shields users and user-applications from the complex process of quality-aware chaining and therefore enable more efficient and cost-effective quality-aware chaining of geospatial web services. The service design of the middleware and a high-level architecture are presented.

The remainder of the chapter is organized as follows. In Section 2, we define quality in the context of distributed geospatial web services. In the section, we propose a quality model for geospatial web services. In Section 3, we address propagation behaviors of quality characteristics. Using examples, we demonstrate the influence of quality of input data and quality of component geospatial services on quality deliverable end-to-end in a service chain. In Section 4, we motivate and define an ontology framework for quality of

geospatial web services. In Section 5, we argue the case for a domain middleware to facilitate quality-aware chaining of geospatial web services. In the section, we identify the basic services the middleware provides and define a high-level architecture for the middleware. In Section 6, we review prior work related to the subject matter. In Section 7, we present a summary of the key issues raised in the chapter and point to open research areas on the subject.

QUALITY MODEL FOR GEOSPATIAL WEB SERVICES

Quality is a universal concept which nonetheless lacks a universal definition. Thus, multiple and often conflicting definitions of quality are in common use (Reeves & Bednar, 1994). Within the geospatial industry, concerted efforts towards engendering a common and shared understanding of quality have led to industry-specific international standards on data quality (ISO, 2002; ISO, 2003a). The standards notwithstanding, the emergence of geospatial web services has introduced new challenges on the subject of quality. The challenges can be attributed to the nature of geospatial web services.

On the one hand, geospatial web services are in principle web services and as such their quality should be defined using established quality models for web services. We consider this a service-centric view of geospatial web services. On the other hand, geospatial web services are information services (Lutz, 2006). This means that unlike generic web services, execution of a geospatial web service will not change the state of the real world but instead it will change the state of the information space. Furthermore, the pre-conditions and post-conditions of a geospatial web service directly refer to its inputs and outputs and not to some external real world state (Lutz, 2006). Notably, geospatial data are key inputs and outputs of geospatial web services and their quality thus constitutes important pre- and post-conditions for the services. We consider this a data-centric view of geospatial web services.

Whereas the data-centric view concerns tangible properties of data like accuracy and completeness, the service-centric view concerns intangible quality of service (QoS) properties like performance and security. Clearly, neither the data-centric nor the service-centric view of quality alone can adequately address quality concerns for geospatial web services (Bertolotto and Egenhofer, 2001; Yang, Wong, Yang, Kafatos and Li, 2005; Onchaga, 2006; Umuhoza, Agbinya, Moodley & Vaheed 2008; Subbiah, Alam, Khan & Thuraisingham, 2007). In principle therefore, concerns in both views should be considered concurrently.

The argument for both views of quality is further supported by Wang (1998). Wang (1998) considers information quality concerns as resulting from considering an information processing system, in this case a geospatial web service, as a service centre offering information products and services. From a product perspective, one considers the products i.e. data created or maintained by the system and its tangible properties like accuracy and completeness. From a service perspective however, one considers the services e.g. data access or the processing offered by an information processing system and their intangible QoS properties like performance and security.

The need to use both data-centric and service-centric views of quality for geospatial web services is illustrated with performance and security on the one hand and accuracy on the other hand. Performance in general is about how quickly the data can be accessed or retrieved. Data which are delivered with poor performance is difficult to access and is considered unavailable and therefore of little practical value to the user, its accuracy notwithstanding. On its part, security is about the protection accorded to data. Data which are not secured are vulnerable to malicious change, destruction or viewing which makes them suspect

and therefore of little added-value. In both cases, QoS shall be said to have impede data quality.

Data Quality Model for Geospatial Web Services

From foregoing discussions, a quality model resulting from a data-centric view of geospatial web services is an integral part of the quality model for geospatial web services. In view of progress already made in the geospatial information industry on the subject of quality, a data quality model for geospatial web service will necessarily encompass data quality elements defined in ISO 19113 (ISO, 2002) and subject to the provisions of ISO 19114 (ISO, 2003a) and ISO 19115 (ISO, 2003b). ISO 19113 identifies quality elements that can be applied to describe quality of geographic data, ISO 19114 specifies quality evaluation procedures for geographic data and ISO 19115 specifies the range of metadata elements applicable to geographic data of which quality presents one category.

Overall, ISO 19113 defines an extensible quality model for spatial data comprising five quantitative data quality elements and fifteen data quality sub-elements. The data quality elements and sub-elements are shown in Table 1. In addition, the standard defines three data quality overview elements which are not quantitative. The quality overview elements are purpose, usage and lineage of data. Data purpose specifies the purpose for which data is created. Data usage describes the application(s) for which a dataset has been used whereas lineage describes the history of a dataset i.e. it recounts the life cycle of a dataset from collection through compilation and derivation in its current form.

In addition to the elements and sub-elements defined in ISO 19113, we have identified volume of data as an additional data quality dimension for geospatial web services. Volume of data denotes the size of the digital dataset that is to be retrieved or transported over a communication network and this becomes an important concern

Table 1 Geospatial data quality elements and sub-elements (ISO, 2002)

Data Quality Element	Data Quality Sub-Element
Completeness	Error of commission, Error of omission
Logical consistency	Conceptual consistency, Domain consistency, Format consistency, Topological consistency
Positional accuracy	Absolute accuracy, Relative accuracy, Gridded accuracy
Temporal accuracy	Accuracy of time measurement, Temporal consistency, Temporal validity
Thematic accuracy	Classification accuracy, Quantitative attribute correctness, Non-quantitative attribute correctness

especially when using the public Internet and for mobile and wireless devices.

Quality of Service Model for Geospatial Web Services

The second component of the quality model for geospatial web services is the QoS model which results from a service-centric view of geospatial web services. We previously have stated that geospatial web services are a type of web services. Necessarily therefore, their quality should be described based on established quality models for web services.

Following the advent of web services, the subject of quality of web services has received considerable attention within the web services research community. As a result, several QoS models for web services have been proposed; see for example Zeng, Benatallah, Dumas, Kalagnanam & Sheng (2003) and Cardoso, Miller, Sheth, Arnold & Kochut (2004).

While individual models may define different sets of QoS dimensions, among themselves, the models have several QoS dimensions in common. For the QoS model for geospatial web services, we have identified dimensions common among existing QoS models for web services from literature. The models considered are defined in Zeng, Benatallah, Dumas, Kalagnanam & Sheng (2003), Cardoso, Miller, Sheth, Arnold & Kochut (2004) and Lee, Jeon, Lee, Jeong & Park (2003). The dimensions found to be common among those

models that were considered were performance, service reliability, service availability and security. For the purposes of this chapter, these dimensions shall constitute the minimal QoS model for geospatial web services.

Proposed Quality Model and Contemporary Data Quality Frameworks

In foregoing sections, we have argued for data quality and QoS as components of quality for geospatial web services. In this section we validate the resulting quality model using the quality framework defined in Wang & Strong (1996). This framework was used because it is widely cited in quality literature.

The quality framework in Wang & Strong (1996) identifies four broad data quality (DQ) categories with fifteen dimensions as shown in Table 2. In the framework, intrinsic data quality denotes quality which is internal to data; contextual data quality concerns the fitness for use of a dataset in a given context; accessibility data quality concerns how easily and securely data can be accessed; and, representational data quality concerns how correctly data are represented in the information system. Notably, access and representational quality categories are defined by explicitly considering the system in which data are created and maintained (Wang & Strong, 1996).

Table 3 shows the mapping between the dimensions in the quality model for geospatial services

Table 2 Data quality categories and dimensions (Wang & Strong, 1996)

Quality Category	Data Quality Dimension
Intrinsic	Accuracy, Objectivity, Believability, Reputation
Accessibility	Accessibility, Access security
Contextual	Relevance, Value-Added, Timeliness, Completeness, Amount of data
Representational	Interpretability, Ease of Understanding, Concise representation, Consistent representation

Table 3 Mapping between proposed quality model and quality categories from Wang & Strong (1996)

Quality Model For Geospatial Web Services		Quality Category
Data Quality Model	**QOS Model**	
Completeness		Contextual
Logical Consistency		Representational
Accuracy (positional, temporal & thematic)		Intrinsic
Volume of data		Contextual
	Performance	Accessibility
	Reliability	Accessibility
	Security	Accessibility
	Availability	Accessibility

to quality categories as defined in the quality framework of Wang & Strong (1996). The table shows that accuracy falls under intrinsic data quality category, logical consistency falls under representational category while completeness and volume of data fall under contextual data quality category. Table 3 also shows that all identified dimensions in the minimal QoS model fall under the accessibility data quality category.

Table 3 shows that the quality model defined for geospatial web services has dimensions in all quality categories defined in the quality framework used for validation. This is not the case when data quality and QoS are considered independently. We interpret this to mean that the proposed quality model is more reflective of quality concerns for geospatial web services than the classical data quality model for geospatial data and contemporary QoS models for web services on their own.

QUALITY PROPAGATION MODELS

In a geospatial service chain, autonomous component services are orchestrated following specified business logic to realize desired service for a user. In practice, each geospatial web service in the chain will achieve a certain level of QoS and end-to-end QoS deliverable is an aggregation of QoS for individual component services. Even for a service delivered by a single geospatial web service, the QoS of the service will compound with QoS of underlying communication network. For brevity, we do not consider network QoS.

Meanwhile, individual geospatial web services in the chain may process and transform input geospatial data to create new data. Where this is done, the data transformation activities are likely to modify errors in input data such that resulting data have rather different error characteristics from the input data (Veregin, 1995; 1996).

In quality-aware chaining of geospatial web services, the need to reliably predict quality deliverable by a service chain is paramount. This is particularly critical during service selection and planning and will require knowledge of propagation behavior of pertinent data and service qualities. Propagation behaviors for data and QoS outlined below under the sub-topics error propagation and QoS composition respectively.

Error Propagation

In practice, no data acquisition process is perfect. As a consequence, every dataset has inherent errors which degrade its quality (Veregin, 1995; 1996). During data processing operations, errors in source data can be transformed and transferred to derived data such that the derived data and source data have different error characteristics. The process of error transference is called error propagation.

Error propagation can significantly degrade the quality of a derived dataset, therefore diminishing its fitness for use. In a geospatial service chain, it is helpful to understand how errors propagate under processing operations in the service chain. This enables selection of optimal datasets for specified user requirements.

An error propagation model emulates the process of error propagation for a geoprocessing operation or sets thereof. Given error characteristics of input data, an error propagation model will enable estimation of the error characteristics of output data resulting from the (set of) processing operation(s). The model therefore offers a way of estimating important quality indices for geographic data delivered by a processing operation and evaluation of fitness-for-use of derived information for intended use. Error propagation is illustrated with the following example on area computation.

A key activity in surveying and mapping for title registration is to estimate the acreage for the land parcels surveyed. In surveying parlance this is called *area computation*. For area computa-

tion, coordinates for the corner points defining the boundary of a parcel are required. Consider the parcel of land shown in Figure 1 with the boundary corners as B1, B2, B3, and B4, and 2D coordinates (x_i, y_i), $i=1,2,3,4$.

The Area, A of the parcel is related to coordinates of the corner points as (Caspary & Scheuring, 1993):

$$A = \frac{1}{2} \sum_{i=1}^{4} (y_{i+1} - y_{i-1}) x_i$$

During the survey, coordinates (x_i, y_i) will be determined with a certain level of accuracy, say σ_i. For $\sigma_1 = \sigma_2 = \sigma_3 = \sigma_4 = \sigma_p$, the accuracy of the area derived for the parcel S_A is related to σ_p in the following way ():

$$S_A = \sqrt{2}\, \sigma_p \Big/ 4 \sqrt{\sum_{i=1}^{n} S_i^2} \text{ where}$$
$$S_i^2 = (y_{i+1} - y_{i-1})^2 + (x_{i+1} - x_{i-1})^2$$

Knowing the allowable value of S_A for a survey, typically this will be legally defined, acceptable values of σ_p can be determined using the error propagation model.

Literature points to a growing body of error propagation models see for instance (Veregin, 1995; 1996; Arbia, Griffith & Haining, 1998; 1999; Heuvelink, 1998). Nonetheless pragmatic error propagation models remain difficult to define for several reasons:

- multi-dimensional character of geospatial data quality;
- in principle, each type of geoprocessing operation and quality element require a unique error propagation model;
- contemporary research on error propagation has mainly focused on single operations whilst in practice e.g. in a geospatial web service chain data are processed

Figure 1. Parcel boundary

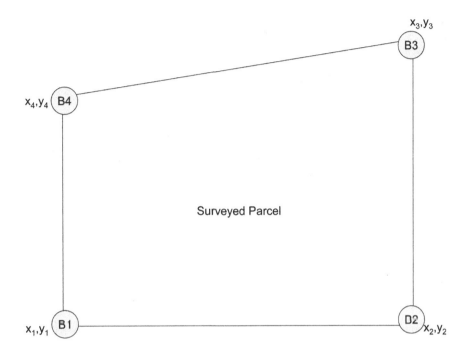

through several operations before output data are obtained;

- error propagation models are often defined assuming ideal conditions which makes them less appropriate for practical situation.

It is anticipated that error propagation will remain an active research area into the foreseeable future. Nonetheless, when pragmatic error propagation models become available and get applied in quality-aware data selection schemes, provision of guarantees on quality of data deliverable by geospatial service chains will increasingly become feasible.

QoS Composition

A geospatial service chain comprises multiple autonomous component services, each of which has distinct QoS capabilities. QoS deliverable end-to-end in the service chain is an aggregation of the QoS of individual component services in the service chain in addition to the QoS of the underlying transport and communication infrastructure. Although QoS of underlying transport and communication infrastructure is an important concern in distributed processing, it is beyond the scope of this chapter and shall not be elaborated. In this chapter, we solely focus on QoS due to component geospatial web services.

QoS composition refers to the aggregation of aspects of QoS in a service chain and a formal description of the aggregation behavior for a QoS aspect is called the QoS composition model for that aspect. Overall, a QoS composition model applicable depends on the QoS dimension(s) being considered and on how control is structured in the service chain.

For each combination of QoS dimension and flow control structure (e.g. sequence, split, split-and-join, unordered, choice and if-then-else), a QoS Composition Model can be defined. Zeng, Benatallah, Dumas, Kalagnanam & Sheng (2003)

Figure 2. Process model for disaster response

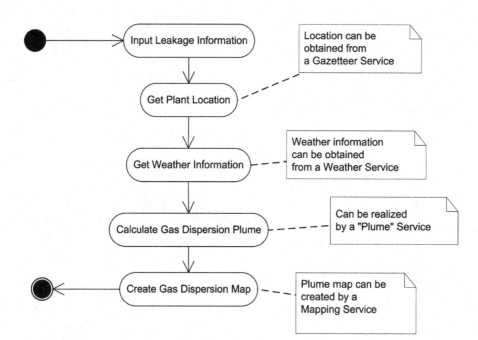

and Cardoso, Miller, Sheth, Arnold & Kochut (2004) define QoS composition models for common QoS dimensions and flow control structures. QoS composition for geospatial web services is illustrated by the following example.

Following an explosion at a facility handling toxic gas, emergency personnel require information indicating which populations are at risk. This information required is a ``plume map'' showing which region is enveloped by the toxic gas. An important QoS concern is time to create the required plum map, i.e., response time. Assuming that creating the plume map involves five operations which are sequentially executed as shown in Figure 2. Each operation executes in finite time t_i. The end-to-end response time for creating the plume map T_p is estimated as follows.

$$T_p = \sum_{i=1}^{5} t_i$$

This equation defines the QoS composition model for execution time. From the composition behavior of T_p, it is apparent that in order to minimize T_p, individual t_i should be minimized, i.e., each individual operation should be executed as fast as possible. Assuming that each operation in the process is executed by a different geospatial service, services that minimize T_p should be selected for chaining. It is assumed that candidate geospatial web services will advertise their T_p in their service metadata.

Although considerable progress on QoS composition has been made, QoS composition models for aggregate QoS dimensions have little been considered. We define an aggregate QoS dimension as a dimension which is derived by considering multiple QoS dimensions together. An example of aggregate QoS dimension is trust (Umuhoza, Agbinya, Moodley & Vaheed 2008).

Further, in a business context, it may prove useful to consider a set of relevant QoS dimensions and package designated service levels for dimensions in the set as distinct classes of service. A class of service provides assurances on service levels for a selected set of relevant quality dimensions. Different classes of service can be defined for the same set of dimensions, but typically each class will be offered at different costs.

AN ONTOLOGY FRAMEWORK FOR QUALITY OF GEOSPATIAL WEB SERVICES

Ideally, efficient quality-aware service chaining presumes automated service discovery and selection in which service offers from different providers are evaluated unambiguously with respect to user requirements. For this to happen, the semantics of service offers should be explicated. This creates need for quality ontologies. An ontology is an explicit specification of a conceptualization (Gruber, 1993). It can also be considered as an explicit account of a shared understanding in a subject area that serves to improve communication, promote greater reuse and information sharing, enhance interoperability and lead to development of more reliable software (Uschold & Gruninger, 1996).

A formal ontology enables automated reasoning and consequent formulation of inferences on the basis of the specified conceptualization. Ontology has been the subject of much study in the geospatial web services community in recent years e.g. (Lutz, 2007; Lemmens, Wytzisk, de By, Grannel, Gould & van Oosterom, 2006). In a geospatial web services environment, ontologies are required to explicate semantics of geographic data, geoprocessing operations and quality of data as well as quality of services.

Prior studies on ontology in the geospatial domain have largely been focused on aspects of data and geoprocessing operations with little attention to quality. The quality ontology framework proposed in this chapter aims at addressing this gap.

In a multi-user multi-provider open geospatial web services environment, there is likelihood that quality will be understood differently e.g. different communities will use different concepts to describe the same aspect of quality and therefore inhibiting sharing and reuse of information and services because of semantic heterogeneity. For instance, in one community the term *performance* may be used to refer to the time it takes a geospatial web service to respond to a user request while in another community the term *response time* may be used. Now, if there is no means of indicating that for the two communities performance and response time are synonyms, communication and exchange of information on the said quality aspect between parties in the two communities will be hampered. It can be anticipated that the problem will be acute in an open geospatial web services marketplace where diverse parties in different communities will be offering and exploiting geospatial web services (Onchaga, Widya, Morales & Nieuwenhuis, 2008).

Clearly, there is need for ontologies that will help mitigate negative effects of synonyms as well as homonyms in an open geospatial web services marketplace. The ontologies will explicate the semantics of quality specifications and therefore enable automated reasoning about quality aspects of service offerings and delivered information products and services. Effectively, service descriptions appropriately augmented with relevant quality ontologies will enable quality-aware service chaining and improve the prospects of user satisfaction.

Quality Ontology Framework

Towards addressing potential heterogeneity in quality specifications, this chapter proposes a comprehensive quality ontology framework. We conceive the ontology framework as comprising an Upper Quality Ontology, two Domain Ontologies and potentially many Application Quality Ontologies. Together, the ontologies offer concepts which

Figure 3. Geospatial quality ontology framework

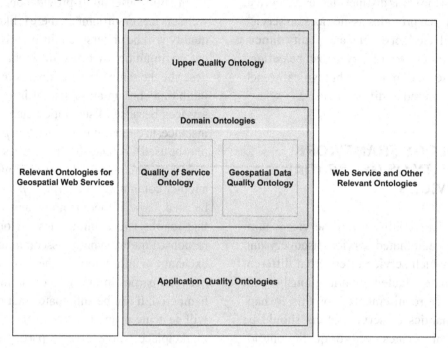

can be used to unambiguously define and reason about quality aspects of geospatial web services. The ontology framework is illustrated in Figure 3.

The Upper Quality Ontology explicates generic concepts and relations among them that are used to define quality independent of any domain or application context. In line with discussions on the extended quality model for geospatial web services, two domain ontologies are defined in the ontology framework i.e. the Geospatial Data Quality ontology and Quality of Service ontology. The ontologies specify relevant dimensions for geospatial data quality and QoS respectively. Lastly, Application Quality Ontologies define concepts and relations used to describe quality in specific applications. The ontologies specialize concepts and relations defined in the Upper Quality and Domain Ontologies.

In Figure 3, the geospatial quality ontology framework is shown to sit beside other geospatial web service ontologies, web service and other relevant ontologies. Among the other geospatial web service ontologies would be ontologies expli-

cating semantics of geospatial data and processing operations. Meanwhile, web service ontologies would include process ontologies. Other relevant ontologies would for instance be ontology for units of measurement that is necessary for defining quality measures.

The ontologies in our quality framework have been defined using Protégé ontology editor and checked for consistency using the RacerPro reasoner. Visualizations of the ontologies are provided below under respective paragraphs.

Upper Quality Ontology

The Upper Quality Ontology defines generic concepts that are used to describe quality. In an effort to limit ontological commitment, only the following concepts are defined: Quality dimension, Quality measure, Domain, Direction, Unit of Measure, Policy Constraint, Quality Profile and Service Offer. The concepts are outlined as follows.

Figure 4. A formal specification of quality dimension in description logics

$$
\begin{aligned}
\text{QualityDimension} \;\equiv\; & \text{QualityAttribute} \sqcap \\
& \exists\,hasDomain \cdot \text{Domain} \sqcap \\
& \forall\,hasDomain \cdot \text{Domain} \sqcap \\
& \forall\,hasUnitOfMeasure \cdot \text{UnitOfMeasure} \sqcap \\
& \exists\,hasDirection \cdot \text{Direction} \\
& \forall\,hasDirection \cdot \text{Direction}
\end{aligned}
$$

A quality dimension is a named aspect of quality that can be measured or evaluated e.g. response time or accuracy. Typically, a quality dimension will have a domain from which it will draw its values. A domain for a quality dimension may for instance be numeric, enumerated or a set. A dimension will also have a direction. The direction denotes how values for the dimension should be interpreted e.g. if large values for the dimension denote better quality then the direction is positive otherwise it is negative. Lastly, a quality dimension may have a unit of measure. A formal specification of a quality dimension in Description Logic is shown in Figure 4. For interested readers a detailed discussion of Description Logics is found in Baader & Nutt (2003).

A quality measure in the upper ontology may either be a constant quality measure (CQM) or a function quality measure (FQM). In principle, a CQM is a constraint which limits the values a quality dimension may take from its domain. It may therefore denote a predicate describing a result obtained after evaluating quality along a dimension of interest or it may also denote a quality requirement expressed over a dimension i.e. a desired level of quality along the dimension e.g. response time ≤ 10 seconds. Meanwhile, an FQM is a function which maps one or more CQM onto a single CQM. In this way, a FQM is said to aggregate CQMs. Examples of FQM are the error propagation models and QoS composition models previously discussed.

In practice, it may be necessary to specify additional constraints in addition to constant quality measures. The additional constraints will typically cover policy or business-level concerns which although they are not quality-related, have the effect of influencing quality achievable in a service chain. We call these constraints policy constraints. Examples of aspects which may be the subject of policy constraints include but are not limited to:

- conformance to standards e.g. a service user may specify that all resources to be used to create and deliver required information conform to relevant industry standards;
- copyright protection e.g. a data provider may require that it is explicitly acknowledged as the rightful owner of the data processed to create information products delivered to the consumer;
- privacy restrictions e.g. it may be necessary to explicitly specify applicable privacy or copyright protections to avoid liability;
- type of data or service provider e.g. a service consumer may require that preference is given to public data or service providers;
- cost of service e.g. a service consumer may specify a maximum cost that they are willing to pay for the service; and,
- the penalty to be applied when the agreed level of service is violated.

Using the concepts policy constraints and CQM, we define two new concepts in the upper ontology i.e. service offer and quality profile. A service offer is a specification of quality capabilities of a resource and pertinent policy concerns for the purposes of resource discovery, selection and exploitation. Essentially therefore, a service offer is metadata which declares quality capabilities of the service advertised and the applicable policy constraints. Meanwhile, a quality profile is a specification of quality constraints and policy constraints associated with a specific user e.g. a human end-user or an application system. The main distinction between a quality profile and a service offer is that whereas a quality profile refers to a user entity, a service offer refers to a provider entity.

Lastly, a quality dimension may be related to other quality dimensions in two possible ways. A dimension may positively satisfice another meaning that achievement of quality requirements along that dimension will contribute positively to the satisficing of requirements along the other dimension. Conversely, a quality dimension will be said to negatively satisfice another if positive achievement of requirements along the dimension will negatively contribute to the satisfaction of requirements along the other dimension. Thus, it shall be said that security negatively satisfices response time because increasing security negatively impacts response time.

It is notable that these relationships among quality dimensions are not necessarily commutative. Thus response time will not be said to negatively satisfice security although security negatively satisfices response time. The concepts in the upper ontology and the relations among them are shown in Figure 5.

Domain Quality Ontologies

Domain quality ontologies define concepts and relationships among them that are applied to describe quality in specific domains. More spe-cifically, domain ontology will identify quality dimensions used to define quality in a domain. For geospatial web services, two domains are of interest: geospatial data quality and quality of service (QoS) and we define two corresponding domain ontologies.

The geospatial data quality domain ontology identifies and defines quality dimensions used to describe quality of geospatial data. The main concepts in the geospatial data quality ontology are data quality measure, data quality dimension, error propagation model as well as specific data quality elements used to describe quality of geographic data e.g. positional accuracy, temporal accuracy, thematic accuracy, consistency, completeness and volume of data. The data quality ontology is illustrated in Figure 6.

On its part, the QoS domain ontology identifies and defines concepts that are used to describe QoS. The core concepts of ontology are QoS dimension, QoS measure, QoS composition model as well as the QoS dimensions used to describe quality of geospatial web services e.g. performance, availability, security and reliability. The QoS ontology is illustrated in Figure 7.

Application Quality Ontologies

An application quality ontology will specialize domain ontologies and other relevant ontologies to yield application specific quality dimensions for use in an application context. For instance, quality dimensions for a vehicle navigation service will be rather different from quality dimensions for an on-line orthophoto service because the type of information served and pertinent QoS concerns are different. In each case therefore, application specific data quality and QoS dimensions are identified and defined. In addition, pertinent error propagation or QoS composition models are also identified.

Figure 5. Upper quality ontology

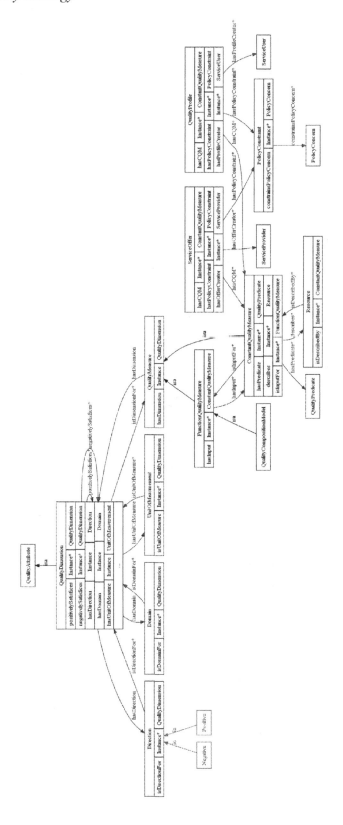

Figure 6. Geospatial data quality ontology

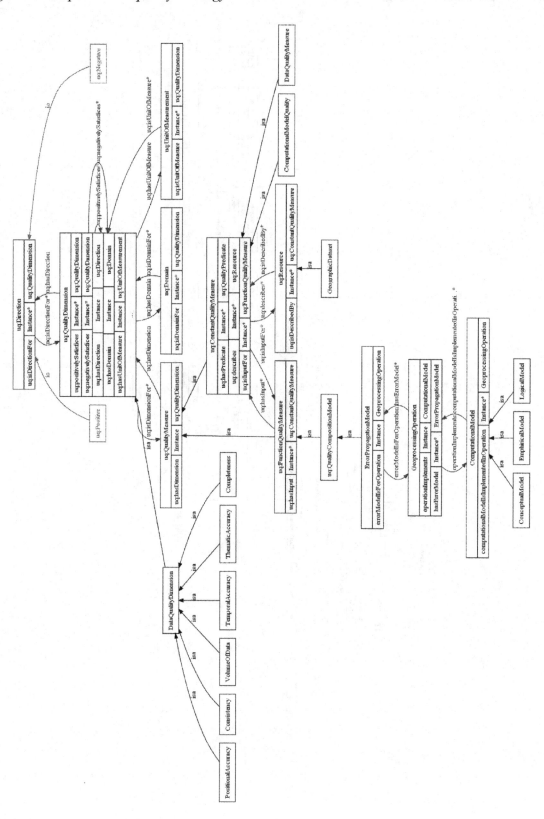

Figure 7. QoS ontology for geospatial web services

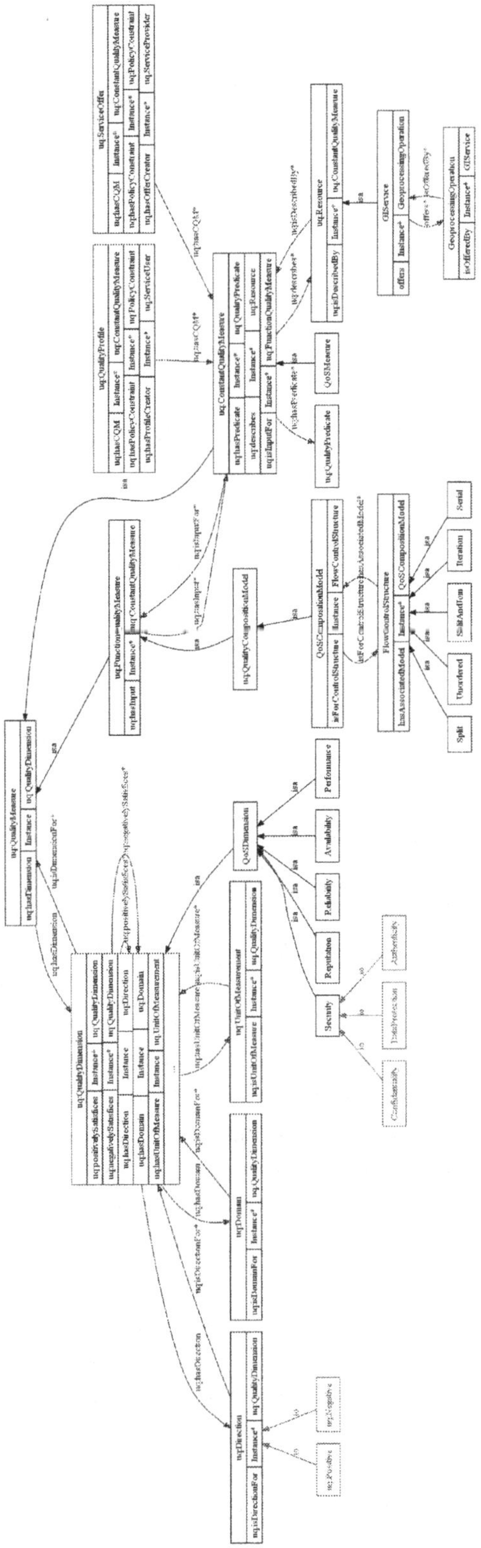

MIDDLEWARE FOR GEOSPATIAL WEB SERVICES

Presently, service composition is mainly performed by technical experts; see for example (Alameh, 2003). Given a set of requirements, the experts determine the appropriate types of geospatial services to be composed and subsequently locate and chain suitable service instances to realize desired behavior. This approach to service chaining, commonly called user-managed service chaining (ISO, 2005), is inherently expensive and inefficient and is therefore likely to negatively impact the appeal of dynamic service chaining in the enterprise. User-managed service chaining is expensive because it requires experts who are generally difficult to find and costly to retain and it is inefficient because service chains are manually configured and managed.

In order to foster acceptance of dynamic chaining, a more affordable and efficient approach to quality-aware service chaining is required. Ideally, such an approach should be automated so that direct involvement of the human end-user in the chaining process is minimized. We anticipate that automated, quality-aware service chaining will support a broader spectrum of users, including non-technical users, while offering acceptable levels of quality. The consequence of this will be increased confidence in services delivered (Herring, 2001).

An approach that is increasingly gaining appeal in web service chaining (see for e.g. Zeng, Benatallah, Dumas, Kalagnanam & Sheng (2003)) and which we adopt for quality-aware chaining of geospatial web services is the middleware-based approach. In this approach, a middleware system is used to achieve quality-aware service chaining on behalf of the user (application). As a result, in a middleware environment, designers of geospatial web services and user applications do not need to design functionality required to address quality-aware service chaining because these are provided as generic services by the middleware. The con-

Figure 8. The GI Middleware and its environment

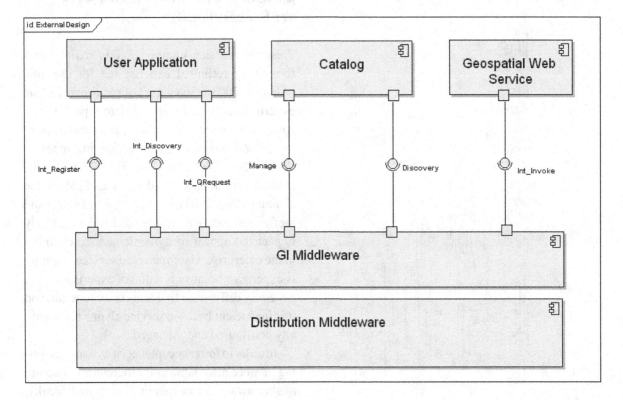

sequence, resulting designs for user applications and geospatial web services are simpler and the overall process of application development less costly. Besides, resulting applications are easier to maintain because they are less complex.

GI Middleware for Quality-Aware Chaining of Geospatial Web Services

For achieving quality-aware service chaining, we prescribe a domain-specific middleware herein called the GI Middleware. Architecturally, the GI Middleware sits between geospatial web services and user applications on the one side and distribution middleware on the other side. Figure 8 shows the GI Middleware and its environment.

As shown in Figure 8, the environment of the GI Middleware primarily comprises user applications, catalogs and geospatial web services.

- A user application is a (client) software system, typically with a user interface, which an end-user shall employ to request and receive geographic information in a networked environment. But we do not exclude applications running on servers.

- A Catalog is a software system which maintains metadata of geospatial resources including geospatial data, geospatial web services and sensor systems. Resource metadata provide information on the type and quality of a resource as well as information on how the resource can be accessed.

- A geospatial web service in this chapter denotes a web-enabled software component that provides access to geospatial data, geoprocessing functionality or sensor system.

Typically, a service consumer employs a user application e.g. a web-enabled GIS to interact with the GI Middleware which handles requests for service. Upon receipt of a request for service, the Middleware locates appropriate geospatial web services from a catalog and subsequently orchestrates then according to pre-defined business logic to create and deliver the required service. The interaction pattern for the GI Middleware follows the Publish-Find-Bind pattern prescribed for geospatial web services.

We note that descriptions of the GI Middleware we provide in this chapter are high level and will be without detailed interface specifications because the purpose of the chapter is to layout important concerns for enabling quality-aware service chaining and not to define the middleware system per se.

Service Design of the GI Middleware

The service or external design of the GI Middleware defines services which the GI Middleware offers to its environment. In our design, the GI Middleware offers three services to its environment i.e. quality-aware information service, geospatial resource registration service and resource discovery service.

With reference to Figure 8, the quality-aware information service is accessible at the Int_QRequest interface, the resource registration service is accessible at the Int_Register interface while the resource discovery service is accessible at the Int_Discovery interface. The Manage and Discover interfaces between the GI Middleware and the Catalog offer operations which the GI Middleware requires to manage resource metadata and transparently query the Catalog. Lastly, the Int_Invoke offers operations which the Middleware requires to remotely invoke selected geospatial web services. In the following sections we outline the services.

a) Quality-Aware Information Service

This is the definitive service offered by the GI Middleware. The service is a manifestation of the quality-awareness transparency provided by the GI Middleware. It enables GI applications, hence application users, to request and receive geospatial information with sufficient quality and within set QoS constraints. Given a valid request for a quality-aware information service, the GI Middleware performs internal actions and participates in selected interactions with its environment to create geographic information with sufficient quality and deliver it to the requesting application within specified QoS constraints.

The quality-aware information service is realized by three basic interactions between the GI middleware and its environment as illustrated in Figure 9. The interactions are the following:

- **request** – A user application employs the interaction to submit a request for service to the GI Middleware. The interaction establishes the type of information required by the user and quality constraints applicable to the information.
- **query** – The Middleware uses the interaction to query a selected Catalog for geospatial web services which satisfy specified quality criteria. The interaction establishes a query expression, which is executed by the catalog to locate required services. The query interaction occurs after request interaction has occurred.
- **invoke** – The Middleware uses the interaction to invoke a selected geospatial web service to execute desired tasks. The interaction establishes input parameters used by the geospatial web service to execute and return a result for the middleware.

In quality-aware service chaining, geospatial web services invoked are selected based on their quality capabilities. Typically, multiple instances

Figure 9. Top level architecture of the GI middleware

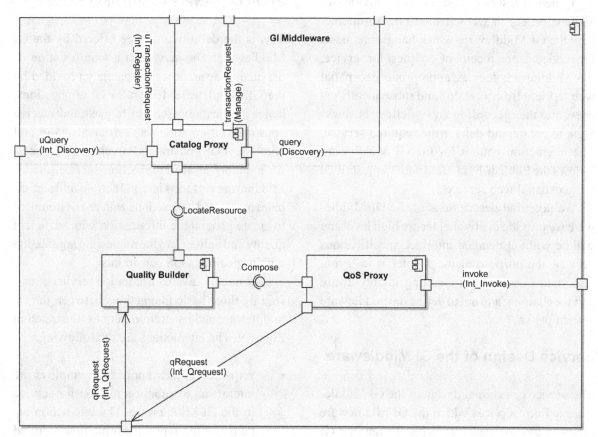

of each type of service will be discovered using metadata published in one or more distributed catalogs. Service selection entails selecting the set of resources, comprising one of each type that best meets specified quality requirements. Ideally, a resource is selected based on its influence on overall deliverable quality. Thus, a service is selected after its impact on end-to-end quality along relevant quality dimensions is considered. This service selection strategy has been called global resource selection strategy (Zeng et. al., 2003). In general, service selection is an optimization problem and appropriate optimization algorithms or heuristics for resource selection are needed.

b) Resource Registration Service

In a distributed multi-provider multi-user geospatial web services environment, before services can be discovered and chained, the resources have to be registered in a catalog. Resource registration entails publishing resource metadata in one or more catalogs. Only after resources are published can they be located by searching the catalog and exploited. The resource registration service adopted for our design of the GI Middleware is based on the "push" approach for resource registration. In the "push" approach resource providers actively publish their resources by "pushing" resource metadata to catalogs.

The alternative to the ``push'' approach is the ``pull'' approach. In the ``pull'' approach, the catalog actively harvests metadata from other catalogs, metadatabases of resource providers or the resources themselves. For instance, geospatial services which are compliant with the Open Geospatial Consortium (OGC) common service specification provide a getCapabilities operation which enables a user to query the geospatial service and obtain a description of its capabilities. A getCapabilities request returns a capabilities document which describes processing abilities of the GI service and its data holdings.

Although we prescribe here the push approach to resource registration, we make no assumptions on how service catalogs actually populate their registers – a catalog may employ one or both approaches.

The resource registration service is realized by two basic interactions as follows.

- **uTransactionRequest** – A resource provider uses the interaction to submit requests for metadata maintenance operations i.e. insert, update or delete metadata maintained in a catalog. This interaction occurs at the Int_Register interface (Figure 8).
- **transactionRequest** - GI Middleware uses the interaction to submit requests for insert, update or delete actions on metadata maintained in a catalog. This interaction takes place at the Manage interface (Figure 8).

Similar to the resource discovery service (see below), the role of the GI Middleware in resource registration is rather limited. The middleware simply relays transaction requests from resource providers to the catalog. It is notable that the operations uTransactionRequest and transactionRequest are essentially similar, only that they occur at different interfaces and are initiated by different entities.

c) Resource Discovery Service

The resource discovery service is an optional service that the GI Middleware may offer. Where offered, the service enables users to directly query remote service Catalogs and locate resources that meet specified criteria. The resource discovery service may prove beneficial especially to users with expertise in service chaining e.g. in user-managed service chaining. A knowledgeable user can use the service to locate GI resources and subsequently exploit the resources.

Resource discovery service is realized by two interactions; the uQuery and query interactions. The query interaction is similar to the one defined for the quality-aware information service. The uQuery interaction is used by a (user) application to query a selected catalog for resources that satisfy specified quality criteria. The interaction, which occurs at the Int_Discovery interface (Figure 8), establishes the query expression to be executed by the catalog to locate required resources. The query interaction is used by the GI Middleware to query a catalog during resource discovery. The interaction occurs at the Discovery interface (Figure 8). It is notable that in the resource discovery service, the middleware only serves to relay request and response messages between the (user) application and the catalog.

Architectural DESIGN of the GI Middleware

The architectural design captures the internal perspective of the GI Middleware. It specifies the internal structure which will realize services the GI Middleware offers to the environment. The architectural design depicts the GI Middleware as comprising parts, each of which may further comprise multiple sub-parts. For brevity, this chapter only presents the top-level architectural design of the GI Middleware. Before this top-level architecture is implemented, it will necessarily be decomposed through subsequent refinement phases to make it more concrete.

The top-level architecture of the GI Middleware consists of a Catalog Proxy, Quality Builder and QoS Proxy. The components are depicted in Figure 9. The components perform internal actions and interact with each other to realize services of the GI Middleware. In the following sections we define the behavior of each of the components and explain the interactions among them which are necessary to realize the overall behavior of the GI Middleware.

Catalog Proxy

The Catalog Proxy realizes resource discovery and resource registration services of the GI Middleware. In addition, the Catalog Proxy offers resource discovery services to the Quality Builder (see below).

Upon receipt of a request to insert, update or delete metadata records, the Catalog Proxy determines the target catalog and relays the request to it. Similarly, upon receipt of a request to locate resources that satisfy specified criteria from uQuery operation, the Catalog Proxy determines an appropriate target Catalog and relays the request to it. Requests to insert, delete or update metadata records in a catalog are received by the Catalog Proxy at the Int_Register interface (Figure 8) following invocation of uTransactionRequest operation and it relays the request to the appropriate catalog via the Manage interface. Requests for resource discovery are relayed at the Discovery interface.

In principle, the Catalog Proxy can route metadata registration, maintenance and discovery requests to one or more external catalogs. The decision to route a request to one or more external catalogs depends on the policies defined for the Catalog proxy. Where requests are sent to multiple catalogs, an incoming request may be broadcast to a set of selected catalogs. Alternatively, the request is submitted to a single catalog that subsequently distributes the request to other catalogs. In both approaches, all the Catalogs involved are peers.

The Catalog Proxy further supports the Quality Builder with resource discovery services. The Catalog Proxy offers a LocateResource interface (Figure 9) at which it receives requests from the Quality Builder. The interface offers an operation which the Quality Builder invokes to submit requests for service. In this way, the Proxy is said to support the Quality Builder with resource discovery services. Upon receipt of a request from the Quality Builder, the Proxy uses the data contained in the request to query an appropriate catalog. Notably, the LocateResource and Int_Discovery interfaces are similar in all respects except that the latter is visible to entities in the environment of the GI Middleware while the former is not.

Quality Builder

The Quality Builder collaborates with the QoS Proxy to realize quality-aware information services of the GI Middleware. Upon receipt of a request, the Quality Builder locates available geospatial services that can potentially address the request and from these selects a set of resources which optimally address quality requirements contained in the request.

The Quality Builder receives requests for quality-aware information services at the Int_QRequest interface (Figure 8). Following a request, the Quality Builder:

- determines an appropriate execution plan or for the request;
- uses the resource discovery service offered by the Catalog Proxy to locate geospatial services which potentially address specified quality requirements;
- where necessary, translates user requirements into quality requirements which are meaningful in the domain of resource providers and or distributed computing platform using domain quality ontologies;

Figure 10. Process model for example service chain

- from the potentially large collection of services discovered, selects a set of resources which optimally satisfy specified quality requirements;
- where necessary, determines level of QoS required at the transport or network level;
- uses the *process enactment service* offered by the QoS Proxy to initiate service chaining;
- where requested quality cannot be achieved, raises an appropriate exception.

The resource discovery service used by the Quality Builder to query remote catalogs is accessible at the LocateResource interface (Figure 9) offered by the Catalog Proxy. Meanwhile, the process enactment service used by the Quality Builder to initiate service composition is accessible at the Compose interface offered by the QoS Proxy as shown in Figure 9.

We illustrate the core functions of the Quality Builder with the following example. For brevity, we consider a service chain comprising two autonomous geospatial services which are to be sequentially executed as depicted in the state chart shown in Figure 10 and subject to the following quality constraint:

```
<rdf:description
rdf:ID="Constraint_1">

<qs:qualityDimension>Delay</
qs:qualityDimension>
          <qs:comparator>&le;</
qs:comparator>
          <qs:value>12</
qs:value>
```

```
<qs:unitsOfMeasure>second</
qs:unitsOfMeasure>
          </rdf:description>
```

The constraint specified states that the service should be delivered within no more than 12 seconds.

Upon receipt of the request for service, the Quality Builder queries the Catalog Proxy to locate potential instances of required services for S1 and S2 respectively. Now, consider that the Catalog Proxy returns the following set of metadata for S1. Again for brevity, consider only two sets of metadata for each type of service required.

```
<rdf:description rdf:ID="example1">
          <ex1:qualityDimension>
ResponseTime</ex1:qualityDimension>
          <ex1:comparator>&lt;</
ex1:comparator>
<ex1:value>6</ex1:value>
<ex1:unitsOfMeasure>second</
ex1:unitsOfMeasure>
</rdf:description>
<rdf:description rdf:ID="example2">
    <ex2:qualityDimension>Delay</
ex2:qualityDimension>
    <ex2:comparator>&lt;</
ex2:comparator>
    <ex2:value>10</ex2:value>
    <ex2:unitsOfMeasure>second</
ex2:unitsOfMeasure>
</rdf:description>
```

Further consider that Catalog Proxy returns the following set of metadata for S2.

```
<rdf:description rdf:ID="example3">
<ex3:qualityDimension>Throughp
utTime</ex3:qualityDimension>
<ex3:comparator>&lt;</ex3:comparator>
<ex3:value>4</ex3:value>
<ex3:unitsOfMeasure>second</
ex3:unitsOfMeasure>
</rdf:description>
<rdf:description rdf:ID="example4">
    <ex4:qualityDimension>Delay</
ex4:qualityDimension>
    <ex4:comparator>&lt;</
ex4:comparator>
    <ex4:value>8</ex4:value>
    <ex4:unitsOfMeasure>second</
ex4:unitsOfMeasure>
</rdf:description>
```

In order to service the request, the Quality Builder must among other things:

- Determine that the concepts Delay, Response Time and Throughput Time as used in the requirement and service metadata for examples 1 through 4 are semantically similar i.e. they refer to one and the same aspect of quality. This is achieved through semantic matching using domain quality ontologies as specified by the service providers respectively denoted by the namespaces qs: and ex1: through ex4:.
- Ensure that the service instances selected in each category realize an end-to-end quality of service that satisfies the stated requirement. In this case, selected service instances should deliver an end-to-end delay of no more than 12 seconds. The selection uses the composition behavior of the quality aspect in question which in this case is $D = \sum_i D_i$ where D is the end-to-end delay and D_i is the delay for individual service instances in the service chain. For

our example, $D \leq 12$ seconds. From the metadata results, only the combination of service instances *example1* and *example3* will sufficiently meet the specified requirements.

QoS Proxy

The QoS Proxy enacts the service chain and manages its end-to-end QoS. The QoS Proxy realizes the *process enactment service* which entails:

- scheduling selected geospatial services according to a designated process model;
- invoking selected geospatial we services according to an established schedule;
- where necessary, requesting appropriate network QoS;
- monitoring execution of scheduled GI services for ``QoS events'' e.g. service execution failure and upon the occurrence of an event, taking appropriate management actions; and,
- packaging information for delivery to the end user e.g. (de)compressing, formatting or encrypting data in compliance with user requirements.

To initiate the process enactment service, the Quality Builder invokes an appropriate operation of the Compose interface (Figure 9) and provides appropriate inputs including selected datasets and geospatial processing services as well as an appropriate process model that defines the pertinent business logic for the service chain.

RELATED WORK

Much work has been done on quality of web services and to a lesser degree on quality of geospatial web services. The works are briefly outlined below.

Quality of web services is extensively documented in literature and many important concerns which can be adopted for geospatial web services addressed. A significant amount of literature on techniques and tools for managing quality of web services is available. Menasce and Almeida (2000, 2002) for example, detail approaches to capacity planning and define performance and workload models that can be used to deploy and configure web services to provide predictable QoS. Within the framework of achieving web services with predictable QoS, Shan, Lin, Marinescu & Yang (2002) define and test dynamic load-balancing mechanisms in a web cluster environment. Overall, QoS mechanisms at the resource level are becoming commonplace.

Proposals for QoS model for web services are reported in literature. For instance, Zeng, Benatallah, Dumas, Kalagnanam & Sheng (2003), Lee, Jeon, Lee, Jeong & Park (2003) and Cardoso, Miller, Sheth, Arnold & Kochut (2004) have all proposed extensible QoS models for web services. Further, Dobson, Lock & Sommerville (2005) and Maximillien & Singh (2004) define QoS ontologies for web services. The ontologies are aimed at enabling quality-aware discovery of web services.

Many authors have also investigated QoS in the context of web service compositions. For example, Cardoso, Miller, Sheth, Arnold & Kochut (2004) have developed a predictive QoS model that makes it possible to compute the QoS for workflows automatically based on QoS attributes of atomic tasks. They also describe an algorithm to compute, analyze and monitor workflow QoS metrics. Similar work is reported by Zeng, Benatallah, Dumas, Kalagnanam & Sheng (2003) who advocate a global planning approach for optimal selection of component services for chaining in a process and formulate the service selection activity as an optimization problem.

The work reported in this chapter also benefited from the work of Chandrasekaran, Miller, Silver, Arpinar & Sheth (2003) who describe a service composition and execution tool (SCET) for dy-

namic composition of service processes. They also describe and test a simulation methodology that can be used to test the performance of a web process. Similar work is reported by Casati, Ilnicki, Jin & Krishnamoorthy (2000) who have developed a system called *eFlow* that support specification, enactment and management of composite e-services. The main goals of *eFlow* are to facilitate flexible and transparent adaptation of composite services in terms of QoS and also dynamic modification of web processes. These studies indicate a growing number of approaches and tools that facilitate automatic composition and management of web processes. These tools to different degrees realize QoS composition, control and management mechanisms which can be adapted and extended for use in the GI Middleware.

Work specifically related to quality of geospatial web services has also been reported. Bertolotto & Egenhofer (2001) and Yang, Wong, Yang, Kafatos & Li (2005) investigate performance of geospatial web services and propose mechanisms for performance improvement. However, the work of Bertolotto & Egenhofer (2001) and Yang, Wong, Yang, Kafatos & Li (2005) only focus on performance. Towards improved selection of geospatial web services, Subbiah, Alam, Khan & Thuraisingham (2007) advocate the extension of QoS models for web services with geospatial data qualities i.e. accuracy, completeness, resolution and data types. Further, Umuhoza, Agbinya, Moodley, & Vahed (2008) applied the work of Subbiah, Alam, Khan & Thuraisingham (2007) to define a reputation-based trust model and propose a trust ontology for geospatial web services. While Subbiah, Alam, Khan & Thuraisingham (2007) and Umuhoza, Agbinya, Moodley, & Vahed (2008) consider both QoS and data quality in an open geospatial web services environment, their work is not focused on service chains. Furthermore, they do not consider aspects of service monitoring which are necessary to guarantee deliverable quality.

CONCLUDING REMARKS

This chapter presented concepts and tools necessary to achieve quality-aware chaining of geospatial web services. Quality-aware chaining of geospatial web services is motivated by anticipated increased user demand for quality services as geospatial services become part of mission-critical systems and processes.

Summary

In a bid to address anticipated quality concerns, the chapter first proposes an extended quality model which addresses both data and quality of service (QoS) concerns pertinent to geospatial web services and service chains. Error propagation models and QoS composition models are also investigated as part of the extended quality model. Instances of both models prescribe the propagation behavior of quality that will manifest in geospatial service chains. In addition, in order to promote communication, sharing and re-use of quality information, the chapter proposes a layered quality ontology framework with multiple component ontologies. The framework comprises an upper quality ontology, two domain ontologies i.e. data quality and QoS ontology and potentially multiple application ontologies. The ontologies in the framework define concepts and relations to be used to unambiguously define, communicate and reason about quality of geospatial web services.

The work reported in this chapter is premised on an infrastructure for automated quality-aware chaining of geospatial web services herein called the GI Middleware. A detailed specification is available in a forthcoming PhD thesis to be published by the author of this chapter. The chapter motivates and prescribes a GI Middleware with functionality to enable automated quality-aware chaining of geospatial web services. A service design and a high level architectural design are specified. The service design defines services the GI Middleware offers to its environment. The services are a mandatory quality-aware information service and optional resource registration and discovery services. The architectural design specifies the GI Middleware as comprising of parts which cooperate and collaborate to realize the services of the GI Middleware. The parts identified are a Catalog Proxy which realizes resource registration service, a QoS Builder which realizes quality quality-aware service selection and planning and QoS Proxy which realize process enactment and monitoring to ensure attainment of end-to-end QoS.

Further Work and Open Research Issues

The work outlined in this chapter sketches a broad outline of pertinent concerns in quality-aware chaining of geospatial web services. In principle, quality-aware service chaining is predicated on a robust computing infrastructure that offers the necessary services and functions for quality-awareness.

A basic requirement for quality-awareness is that geospatial web services are self-describing both in terms of their functional and quality capabilities. As a prerequisite, geospatial services should be described and annotated with standardized metadata describing their functional as well quality capabilities. Ideally, the metadata should be semantically enriched to allow for automated quality-aware service discovery and chaining. To achieve this goal, application quality ontologies should be defined and published. Also, the GI Middleware architecture needs to be formally specified and made more concrete. This will entail formal specification, further refinement and translation into a platform-specific architecture.

Availability of proven error propagation models for geoprocessing operations of interest is fundamental for providing guarantees on quality of information deliverable by a service chain. Although considerable progress has been made in this area, error propagation models error propagation models remains an open research area. Further, quality-driven selection of geospatial to enact a service chain is essentially an optimization problem which may be np-hard. Algorithms and heuristics are therefore required for efficient geospatial resource selection.

REFERENCES

Agumya, A., & Hunter, G. J. (1997). Determining fitness for use of geographic information. *ITC Journal*, *2*(4), 109–113.

Alameh, N. S. (2003). Chaining geographic information Web Services. *IEEE Internet Computing*, *7*(5), 22–29. doi:10.1109/MIC.2003.1232514

Arbia, G., Griffith, D., & Haining, R. (1998). Error propagation modelling in raster GIS: overlay operations. *International Journal of Geographical Information Science*, *12*(2), 145–167. doi:10.1080/136588198241932

Arbia, G., Griffith, D., & Haining, R. (1999). Error propagation modelling in raster GIS: adding and ratioing operations. *Cartography and Geographic Information Science*, *26*(4), 297–315. doi:10.1559/152304099782294159

Baader, F., & Nutt, W. (2003). Basic description logics. In Baader, F., Calvanese, D., McGuinness, D., Nardi, D., & Patel-Scheider, P. F. (Eds.), *The description logic handbook: Theory, implementation and applications*. Cambridge, UK: Cambridge University Press.

Bertolotto, M., & Egenhofer, M. J. (2001). Progressive transmission of vector map data over the World Wide Web. *GeoInformatica*, *5*(4), 345–373. doi:10.1023/A:1012745819426

Cardoso, J., Miller, J., Sheth, A., Arnold, J., & Kochut, K. (2004). Modeling quality of service for workflows and web service processes. *Web Semantics: Science, Services, and Agents on the World Wide Web*, *1*(3), 281–308. doi:10.1016/j.websem.2004.03.001

Casati, F., Ilnicki, S., Jin, L., & Krishnamoorthy, V. (2000). *Adaptive and dynamic service composition in eFlow*. Technical Report HPL-2000-39, HP Laboratories, Palo Alto.

Caspary, W., & Scheuring, R. (1993). Positional accuracy in spatial databases. *Computers, Environment and Urban Systems*, *17*, 103–110. doi:10.1016/0198-9715(93)90040-C

Chandrasekaran, S., Miller, J. A., Silver, G. S., Arpinar, B., & Sheth, A. P. (2003). Performance analysis and simulation of composite web services. *EM–. Electronic Markets*, *13*(2), 120–132. doi:10.1080/1019678032000067217

Devillers, R., Bedard, Y., & Jeansoulin, R. (2005). Multidimensional management of geospatial data quality information for its dynamic use within GIS. *Photogrammetric Engineering and Remote Sensing*, *71*(2), 205–215.

Gruber, T. R. (1995). Towards principles for the design of ontologies used for knowledge sharing. *International Journal of Human-Computer Studies*, *43*(5), 907–928. doi:10.1006/ijhc.1995.1081

Herring, J. (2001). Quality is the future of geoprocessing. *GeoInformatica*, *5*(4), 323–325. doi:10.1023/A:1012711401679

Heuvelink, G. B. M. (1998). *Error propagation in environmental modelling with GIS*. London: Taylor & Francis.

ISO/TC211. (2002). *ISO 19113 Geographic information - quality principles*. Geneva: ISO.

ISO/TC211. (2003a). *ISO 19114 Geographic information - quality evaluation procedures*. Geneva: ISO.

ISO/TC211. (2003b). *ISO 19115 Geographic information – metadata*. Geneva: ISO.

ISO/TC211. (2005). *ISO 19119 Geographic information – services*. Geneva: ISO.

Lee, K., Jeon, J., Lee, W., Jeong, S.-H., & Park, S.-W. (2003). *QoS for Web services: requirements and possible approaches. W3C Working Group Note*. Retrieved on March 15, 2010, from http://www.w3c.or.kr/kr-office/TR/2003/ws-qos/

Lemmens, R., Wytzisk, A., de By, R., Grannel, C., Gould, M., & van Oosterom, P. (2006). Integrating semantic and syntactic descriptions to chain geographic services. *IEEE Internet Computing, 10*(5), 42–52. doi:10.1109/MIC.2006.106

Lutz, M. (2007). Ontology-based descriptions for semantic discovery and composition of geoprocessing services. *GeoInformatica, 11*(1), 1–36. doi:10.1007/s10707-006-7635-9

Masser, I. (2005). *GIS worlds: Creating Spatial Data Infrastructures*. Redlands, California: ESRI PRESS.

Menasce, A. D., & Almeida, A. F. V. (2000). *Scaling for e-business - technologies, models, performance, and capacity*. Upper Saddle River, NJ: Prentice Hall.

Menasce, A. D., & Almeida, A. F. V. (2002). *Capacity planning for Web Services: metrics, models, and methods*. Upper Saddle River, NJ: Prentice Hall.

Onchaga, R. (2005). *On quality of service and geo-service compositions*. Paper presented at the AGILE Conference on Geographic Information Science, Estoril, Portugal.

Onchaga, R. (2006). Quality of service management framework for dynamic chaining of geographic information services. *International Journal of Applied Earth Observation and Geoinformation, 8*(2), 137–148. doi:10.1016/j.jag.2005.06.012

Onchaga, R., Widya, I., Morales, J., & Nieuwenhuis, L. J. M. (2008, November). *An ontology framework for quality of geographical information services*. Paper presented at the ACM GIS conference, Irvine, CA.

Poveda, J., Gould, M., & Grannell, C. (2004, April). *ACE GIS project overview: adaptable and composable e-commerce and geographic information services*. Paper presented at the AGILE Conference on Geographic Information Science, Heraklion, Greece.

Reeves, A. C., & Bednar, D. A. (1994). Defining quality: alternatives and implications. *Academy of Management Review, 19*(3), 419–445. doi:10.2307/258934

Shan, C., Lin, C., Marinescu, D. C., & Yang, Y. (2002). Modeling and performance analysis of QoS-aware load balancing of Web-server clusters. *Computer Networks, 40*, 235–256. doi:10.1016/S1389-1286(02)00253-0

Strong, D. M., Lee, Y. W., & Wang, R. Y. (1997). Data quality in context. *Communications of the ACM, 40*(5), 103–110. doi:10.1145/253769.253804

Subbiah, G., Alam, A., Khan, L., & Thuraisingham, B. (2007, November). *Geospatial data qualities as web services performance metrics*. Paper presented at the ACM GIS conference, Seattle, Washington.

Tait, M. G. (2005). Implementing geoprotals: applications of distributed GIS. *Computers, Environment and Urban Systems, 29*, 33–47.

Umuhoza, D., Agbinya, J. I., Moodley, D., & Vahed, A. (2008). *A reputation based trust model for geospatial web services*. Paper presented at the 1st WSEAS International Conference on Environmental and Geological Science and Engineering, Malta.

Uschold, M., & Gruninger, M. (1996). Ontologies: principles, methods and applications. *The Knowledge Engineering Review, 11*(2), 95–155. doi:10.1017/S0269888900007797

Veregin, H. (1995). Developing and testing of an error propagation model for GIS overlay operations. *International Journal Geographical Information Systems, 9*(6), 595–619. doi:10.1080/02693799508902059

Veregin, H. (1996). Error propagation through the buffer operation for probability surfaces. *Photogrammetric Engineering and Remote Sensing, 62*(4), 419–428.

Wang, D. Y., & Strong, D. M. (1996). Beyond accuracy: what quality means to data consumers. *Journal of Management Information Systems, 12*(4), 5–34.

Wang, R. Y. (1998). A product perspective on total data quality management. *Communications of the ACM, 41*(2), 58–65. doi:10.1145/269012.269022

Yang, C., Wong, D. W., Yang, R., Kafatos, M., & Li, Q. (2005). Performance-improving techniques in web-based GIS. *International Journal of Geographical Information Science, 19*(3), 319–342. doi:10.1080/13658810412331280202

Yue, Y., Di, L., Yang, W., Yu, G., & Zhao, P. (2007). Semantic-based automatic composition of geospatial web service chains. *Computers & Geosciences, 33*(5), 649–665. doi:10.1016/j.cageo.2006.09.003

Zeng, L., Benatallah, B., Dumas, M., Kalagnanam, J., & Sheng, Z. (2003). *Quality driven web services composition.* Paper presented at 12th international conference on World Wide Web, Budapest, Hungary.

Zeng, L., Benatallah, B., Ngu, A. H. H., Dumas, M., Kalagnanam, J., & Chang, H. (2004). Qos-aware middleware for web services composition. *IEEE Transactions on Software Engineering, 30*(5), 311–327. doi:10.1109/TSE.2004.11

Chapter 4
Security and Licensing for Geospatial Web Services

Bastian Schäffer
University of Münster, Germany

Rüdiger Gartmann
Conterra GmbH, Germany

ABSTRACT

This paper presents an approach for enabling the commercial use of Geospatial Web Services in an on demand and ad-hoc fashion. The main goal is to go beyond classical Role-Based Access Control models in order to support ad-hoc license agreements directly in-process, without any prior offline negotiated agreements being necessary between georesource provider and geoprocessing user for on-demand access. Therefore, a general security and licensing architecture is defined as a transparent layer for Geospatial Web Services. In particular, this chapter focuses on state-of-the-art interface specifications from OGC and defines generic security extensions being applicable to all OGC standards based on OWS Common. The static model with trust relationships between the different components of the architecture in heterogeneous security domains as well the dynamic structure is studied. The presented ideas are verified by a proof-of-concept implementation following a real world scenario.

1 INTRODUCTION

Geospatial Web Services organized in a Spatial Data Infrastructures (SDIs) are designed for the purpose of providing and sharing georesources (data and models) across organizational and technical boundaries. The real potential lies in the agility of Geospatial Web Service via SDIs to access external georesources on-demand and to integrate them into business process on the fly (Groot & McLaughlin, 2000). This goal is mostly reached on a technical level by the provision of data encoding and service interface standards, such as established by the Open Geospatial Consortium (OGC).

DOI: 10.4018/978-1-60960-192-8.ch004

However, partners will only conduct business if their (geo)rights, trust and security requirements are met. Therefore, a general security architecture has to be defined as a transparent layer for Geospatial Web Services. In particular, this chapter will focus on state-of-the-art interface specifications from OGC and will define generic security extensions being applicable to all OGC standards based on OWS Common (OGC, 2006b). On an abstract level, such extensions should be independent of specific technology bindings, leading to a common abstract security architecture for OGC Web Services.

But besides the technical challenge, there is a legal barrier still in place, obstructing especially the commercial use of Geospatial Web Services. For commercial use, it is necessary to establish an agreement between georesource provider and georesource user regarding the terms and conditions of use regarding the specific georesource (OGC, 2006a). It is easily imaginable that this time-consuming way of licensing clearly contradicts the goal of seamless integration and agile interaction. This gap was also identified by IN-SPIRE (Infrastructure for Spatial Information in Europe), resulting in the demand for e-commerce services in the INSPIRE Directive, Article 14(4) (EU, 2007). Therefore we aim at going beyond classical Role-Based Access Control (see section 2.5) models in order to support ad-hoc license agreements directly in-process, without any prior offline negotiated agreements being necessary between georesource provider and geoprocessing user for on-demand access. This will give us the flexibility to support on-demand scenarios and fully support the SDI publish-find-bind pattern on an ad-hoc basis with prior unknown and untrusted entities.

This paper gives first a thorough overview of general security concepts such as authentication, authorization, cryptography and trust in a Geospatial Web Services context. This is followed by a two folded concept. At first, general security and licensing requirements for Geospatial Web Ser-vices are analyzed. This is followed by a specific security architecture, which includes a description of how standard SDIs can be enhanced in order to support ad-hoc license agreements directly in-process, without any a priory settled rights or trust relationships being necessary between data provider and data user. This also includes the aspects of license encodings, security to enforce license-conformant access to services, metadata extensions to inform about license- and security-related requirements of a certain service, protocol extensions to submit license and identity information between the communicating parties and federation concepts in order to establish trust between initially unknown parties.

Finally, these ideas are verified by a real world scenario, which serves as a proof-of-concept realization.

2 BACKGROUND

This section provides a review of basic concepts and related work in the context of rights management, security and licensing for Geospatial Web Services.

2.1 Web Service Security

The definition of computer security in general has been defined in multiple ways, as i.e. by (Gollmann, 1999) (Bishop, 2005). For this chapter we rely on ISO as an international accepted standardization body, which defines it as:

"Information held by IT products or systems is a critical resource that enables organisations to succeed in their mission. Additionally, individuals have a reasonable expectation that their personal information contained in IT products or systems remain private, be available to them as needed, and not be subject to unauthorised modification. IT products or systems should perform their functions while exercising proper control of the information to ensure it is protected against hazards such as unwanted or unwarranted dissemination, alteration, or loss. The term IT security is used to cover prevention and mitigation of these and similar hazards." (ISO, 1996).

In order to protect the exchange of information between secured systems and the management of the stored data, the standard states also that"[…] security services may apply to the communicating entities of systems as well as to data exchanged between systems, and to data managed by systems." (ISO, 1996).

Taking Web Services into account in this context (Hafner & Breu, 2009) defines Web Services security as"[…]the sum of all techniques, methods, procedures and activities employed to maintain an ideal state specified through a set of rules of what is authorized and what is not in a heterogeneous, decentralized and interconnected computing system", which is used as the definition for Web Service security in this chapter. The literature has no general definition for Web Service security and approach this term by defining Web Services and Security separately as for instance (Kanneganti & Chodavarapu, 2008) or (O'Neill, 2003).

2.2 Security Requirements

This section discusses the most relevant security requirements derived from literature review. Based on (Hafner & Breu, 2009; ISO, 1996; Kanneganti & Chodavarapu, 2008) Authentication, authorization, confidentiality, integrity, non-repudiation, protection and privacy are relevant aspects. These requirements only address message exchange, which is relevant when defining Web Service interfaces and protocols. There may be other requirements addressing physical or organizational protection as well as the protection of data, but this is out of scope for this chapter.

2.2.1 Authentication

Authentication is defined by (ISO, 1996) as "The provision of assurance of the claimed identity of

an entity." In other words, authentication describes the verification that a communication partner is what it pretends to be. In general authentication answers the question: "Who is accessing a resource". This differs from the concept of identification, which describes the process of providing an identity but not verifying it. The verification part is then referred to as authentication (Kanneganti & Chodavarapu, 2008).

In principle, there are three different way of authentication (Kanneganti & Chodavarapu, 2008):

- Authentication by knowledge
- Authentication by of possession
- Authentication by personal attributes

Authentication by knowledge uses secrets such as passwords or personal questions only known to the holder of that information. Many internet protocols such as HTTP, telnet, FTP or SMPT support this type of authentication. It has to be distinguished between simple passwords with an unlimited lifespan, one-time use passwords such as TANs and more complex challenge response protocols.

Authentication by possession typically uses digital signatures as described in section 2.3.2.2. Only the holder of a specific key (shared key in symmetric systems and private key in asymmetric systems, see section 2.3) is able to create a digital signature which can be verified by the receiver.

Authentication by personal attributes leverages biometric authentication. Fingerprints, irisscans, face, hand, voice or ear detection are common methods, but with limited adoption in Web Service environments.

2.2.2 Authorization

Authorization is not directly related to message exchange, but nevertheless it is one of the key security requirements. Authorization aims at controlling access to resources (Kanneganti & Chodavarapu, 2008). For access controlled services, incoming requests are matched against policies which define access rights to certain resources for certain subjects (requestors). If these access rights cover the requested action, access is permitted, otherwise access will be denied.

There are multiple access control models which apply the authorization principle (see section 2.5).

2.2.3 Confidentiality

Providing confidentiality means protecting messages against unauthorized reading (Kanneganti & Chodavarapu, 2008). It has to be ensured that only the designated communication partners (typically the sender and the receiver of a message) can access the content of a message and not a man-in-the-middle observing the communication. Encryption is a standard technique to ensure confidentiality (see section 2.3.2.1).

2.2.4 Integrity

Integrity protects messages against unnoticed modifications (Kanneganti & Chodavarapu, 2008). On the message level, integrity is typically provided by the use of digital signatures (see section 2.3.2.2). These signatures are tightly bound to the message to be protected. Whenever there has been a modification of a message after the signature was applied, a validation of this signature will fail. If security on transport level is provided, integrity is ensured once the secure communication session is established via e.g. SSL/TLS.

2.2.5 Non-Repudiation

Non-repudiation provides evidence to the receiver for the existence of a message (Kanneganti & Chodavarapu, 2008). This becomes important to prevent fraud claims against the message receiver. Non-repudiation is ensured by storing messages together with a valid signature of the sender. If a

sender denies having submitted a certain message afterwards, the receiver can expose the signed message. Since no one else but the sender would be able to generate the signature (see section 2.3.2.2), the stored message proves that the message was signed by the holder of the public key (see section 2.3.2) corresponding to his signature.

2.2.6 Protection

Protection against attacks in network environment is an elementary aspect. There are mainly three kinds of vulnerabilities which allow attacks according to (Kanneganti & Chodavarapu, 2008):

- Vulnerabilities on the application code level, which allow e.g. as SQL injection.
- Vulnerabilities on administration level, such as unchanged default passwords
- Vulnerabilities on the computing and network infrastructure, such as weaknesses in operating systems or underlying protocols i.e. TCP/IP.

Since this chapter focuses more on architectural aspects, protection is not further regarded but is included here for security requirements completeness reasons.

2.2.7 Privacy

Privacy deals with protecting confidential private/personal information to be disclosed to third parties. Legal issues play also a role in here as for instance shown by (Critchell-Ward & Landsborough-McDonald, 2007). In Web Service environments, user identities can be e.g. masked by pseudonyms coming from dedicated pseudonym services. A Policy Information Point (PIP, see section 3.4) can be used for this purposes. Since privacy is hard to enforce, this correlates strongly with trust (see Section 2.4)

2.3 Cryptography

Cryptography is a key technology to meet the security requirements described in section 2.1. According to (ISO, 1994), cryptography is "The discipline which embodies principles, means, and methods for the transformation of data in order to hide its information content, prevent its undetected modification and/or prevent its unauthorized use."

This section briefly discusses cryptographic methods used for encrypting and signing messages.

2.3.1 Symmetric Cryptography

Symmetric cryptography is sometimes called "secret-key cryptography" (versus public-key/asymmetric cryptography) because the entities that want to exchange a encrypted message, share a single key and therefore need to keep the key secret.

One classical example is for instance the Caesar cipher, which is a substitution cipher. Each letter in the plaintext is replaced by a letter, which is shifted a fixed number of positions in the alphabet. The shift number is therefore the shared secret key. For example, with a shift of 5, *A* would be replaced by *F*, *B* would become *G*, etc. The message sender and receiver need to know the same secret key (shift of 5 position to the right in this example) in order to encrypt/decrypt the message. Modern symmetric cryptography algorithms are i.e. AES (Daemen & Rijmen, 2002) or Twofish (Schneier, 1999).

Keeping the shared key secret entails both cost and risk when the key is distributed. In particular, for n partners, n/2*(n-1) keys must be exchanged (Schmeh, 2009). Thus, symmetric cryptography has a key management disadvantage compared to asymmetric cryptography.

2.3.2 Asymmetric Cryptography

Asymmetric cryptography (also known as Public Key Cryptography) uses a distinct pair of keys for any participant of a secure communication. One key has to be kept secret (private key), while the other key is public (public key) and has to be shared with the communication partners (Kanneganti & Chodavarapu, 2008) (for a review of Public-Key Infrastructure see section 2.3.4).

The basic principle of asymmetric cryptography is that plaintext encrypted with one key of this pair can only be decrypted with the other one. If a message is encrypted with a public key it can only be decrypted with the corresponding private key and vice versa. Mathematically, this concept can be expressed as:

$$c = e(a,m) \text{ and } m = d(x,c) \qquad (1)$$

as well as

$$c = e(x,m) \text{ and } m = d(a,c) \qquad (2)$$

where the sender has a public key *a* and a private key *x*, *m* is the message in plaintext, *c* the ciphertext, *e* the encryption function and the *d* the decryption function. In case (1), the sender has only to know the public key (*a*) of the receiver and both parties need to use the same cryptographic algorithm (encrypt function (*e*), decrypt function (*d*)). In case (2), the sender encrypts the message with its private key (x), which allows the receiver to verify with the senders public key (a) the authenticity of that message. A typical asymmetric cryptography algorithm is i.e. RSA, which is based on prime number multiplication (Adleman, Rivest, & Shamir, 1978).

Since the described mechanism works in both ways it can be used for encrypting and signing messages, as shown in following two subsections.

2.3.2.1 Encryption

Encryption is defined by (IETF, 2000) as a "cryptographic transformation of data (called "plaintext") into a form (called "ciphertext") that conceals the data's original meaning to prevent it from being known or used. If the transformation is reversible, the corresponding reversal process is called "decryption", which is a transformation that restores encrypted data to its original state."

For instance, if user *A* wants to send an encrypted message to user *B*, user *A* encrypts the message with *B's* public key using asymmetric cryptography, so only *B* is able to decrypt this message with his own private key.

Since asymmetric cryptography needs far more computation than symmetric encryption, both technologies are typically used in combination. First, the initiator of the communication creates a session key which is asymmetrically encrypted and sends it to the communication partner. Now, that a session key is securely exchanged, it can be used together with symmetric encryption for further communication between *A* and *B*. This hybrid encryption technique is for instance used in common TLS/SSL technologies.

In terms of Web Services, XML Encryption (Imamura, Dillaway, & Simon, 2002) is the most relevant standard also used in this chapter. It defines how to encrypt the contents of an XML document.

2.3.2.2 Digital Signatures

(IETF, 2000) defines Digital Signatures as "a value computed with a cryptographic algorithm and appended to a data object in such a way that any recipient of the data can use the signature to verify the data's origin and integrity."

In particular, digital signatures rely on asymmetric cryptography, which requires a pair of cryptographic keys for each participant involved in secure communication (Kanneganti & Chodavarapu, 2008). Therefore, sending a signed message requires asymmetric encryption of the message with the sender's private key. That allows anybody to decrypt the message with the sender's public key and thus proofs that nobody else could have encrypted this message but the owner of the corresponding private key.

For performance improvements, instead of encrypting the whole message, typically a hash value is computed out of the message and then this hash value is signed while the message itself is sent in plaintext.

Of course, encryption and signatures can also be used in combination, by first computing a signature with the sender's private key, and then encrypting the signed message with the recipient's public key.

For Web Service, XML Signature (Eastlake et al., 2002) is the most relevant standard. It specifies how an XML message can be digitally signed.

2.4 Trust

Trust and especially trustworthiness is a fundamental aspect of security in distributed systems. Basically, trust is an intrinsic part of all business transactions; over the internet or at the bank around the corner. On the one hand, customers must rely on that the seller really provides the service/good they advertise and does not disclose confidential information such as name, credit card number etc. On the other hand, sellers must rely on that e.g. customers are the person stated on their id card and i.e. are therefore old enough to buy a pack of cigarettes. Therefore, trust is an important factor for business decisions.

Especially in the context of this chapter, where business transactions span across enterprise and security domain boarders and when it comes to the dynamic conclusion of licenses of prior unknown entities, trust is obviously the decisive factor. Thus, this subchapter will deliver a definition and review extensively additional aspects of the concept of trust in the context of the general ideas of this chapter based on literature review.

2.4.1 Definition

In general, it can be distinguished between a *trustor*, an entity that trusts a target entity and *trustee*, an entity that is trusted. The concept of trusts involves multiple aspects like belief in truthfulness, reliability, reputation, risk etc. (Grandison,

2000). There is no general accepted definition of trust in the literature, however its importance has been recognized and multiple approaches could be found.

One of the first definitions came from Kini and Choobineh (Kini, 1998) from an socio-economical and social psychologist perspective. They define trust as "a belief that is influenced by the individual's opinion about certain critical system features." Their definition covers several aspects of human trust in computers but lack the definition of trust in e-commerce scenarios.

Grandison (Grandison, 2000) define trust after a survey of various definitions as " the firm belief in the competence of an entity to act dependably, securely and reliably within a specified context." (by assuming that dependability covers reliability and timeliness).

The Joint Research Centre (Jones and Morris, 1999) defined trust as: "The property of a business relationship, such that reliance can be placed on the business partners and the business transactions developed with them." The time variant and measurable notions were missing in these definitions and were added by Dimitrakos resulting in the definition, that "Trust of a party A in a party B for a service X is the measurable belief of A in B behaving dependably for a specific period within a specified context in relation to X" (Dimitrakos, 2003).

This definition also regards trust form a service oriented point of view. Therefore it can be used as the definition of trust in this paper.

2.4.2 General Aspects of Trust Relationships

Trust has to be regarded independently for every business transaction. However, there are some common aspects of all trust relationships according to (Grandison, 2000) and (Dimitrakos, 2003):

In principle, *trust is not absolute* and always bound to a specific action especially in the context of a business transaction. For instance, A trusts

B to be able to handle a car but not a gun. Even though there are approaches for a dual approach where a trustee is trusted or untrusted in general (Yahalom, 1993), this may result in an oversimplified view which cannot distinguish between the characteristics of different business tasks. It is interesting to note, that not even trust in oneself is absolute. For instance, protection against accidental overwriting files etc..

This leads to the proposition that *trust is measureable*. For instance, A trust B but A does not trust C for the same task. In the literature, no general metric can be found and has to be established for the specific domain and problem. However, it can be distinguished between a relative measurement and an absolute measurement.

Additionally, *trust is directed*, in other words not symmetric. For instance, A trust B but B does not necessarily has to trust A. Generalized: trust depends on the role of an entity in a transaction. Especially, when it comes to trust between groups, *trust is not necessarily distributed to the members of the group*. This means, that A can trust a collective $C := \{C_1 \ldots C_n\}$ but does not necessarily has to trust each member of C to the same degree. For instance, A trusts that C delivers a project in time, but does not trust C_i to the same degree to deliver because C_k may compensate the deficits of C_i.

By taking a closer look at the definition stated in 2.4.1 it is also important to note that *trust may be time-variant*. In other words, A trusted B in the past for a specific business transaction but A does not necessarily need to trust B in the future. For instance, if B has abused the trust given, trust may be revoked for the future.

2.4.3 Trust Management

The term *Trust Management* was firstly introduced by Blaze et al. (Blaze et al., 1996). It was defined as "a coherent intellectual framework [...] for the study of security policies, security credentials, and trust relationships." (Blaze et al., 1996). In other words, trust management is intended to determine the trustworthiness (or negatively expressed the risk) for A to interact with B in a specific context. Therefore, Trust Management always has to deal with a balance between increasing trust and thus exposing more vulnerabilities or decreasing the level of trust in favour of more security mechanisms leading to less efficiency and potential of making transactions between two entities virtually impossible.

During the decades, several solutions have been proposed such as PolicyMaker, KeyNote, REFEREE. The most influence in current internet application have public key certificates relying on Public-Key-Infrastructure as described in the following.

Public Key Infrastructure (PKI) Concept

The concept of asymmetric cryptography (public key cryptography) was already introduced in section 2.3.2. It allows arbitrary communication partners to exchange encrypted and/or signed messages, as long as the public keys of the communication partners are known.

This implies the need for a mechanism to securely exchange public keys between communication partners and to verify the validity of a received public key. Since the knowledge about these keys is a prerequisite to communicate securely, a secure way for the key exchange is needed. Sending a public key by email or downloading it from a web page via a potentially insecure communication channel such as the Internet does not fulfill these requirements. A potential man-in-the-middle could easily alter the key without leaving a trace.

Public Key Infrastructures (PKIs) solve this problem by introducing Certificate Authorities (CAs). These CAs are assumed to be trustworthy either per definition or within a certain security domain (Kanneganti & Chodavarapu, 2008). CAs issue digital certificates for owners of asymmetric key pairs, asserting that the actual public key belongs to a certain owner. Such a certificate is signed by the CA to ensure integrity (see sections 2.2.4).

Once a communication partner trusts a CA, it is assumed that he also trusts all certificates being issued by this CA. So for exchanging public keys, communication partners may now exchange their certificates including those public keys and the according identity information provided by the CA. If there is a valid signature of the CA on this certificate, the communication partners can be sure to have received the right public keys.

Of course, PKIs still need the public keys of the CAs to be known, but this affects only a very limited number of public keys (those of the CAs) instead of all keys of all communication partners. The so called root certificates, including the identity and the public key, of the most popular CAs are already included in many software components.

Besides the central CAs, a PKI has a Registration Authority (RA) in order to allow registration of new certificates. A Certificate Revocation List is also necessary to list all invalid certificates. Certificates become invalid if i.e. it expires or is actively revoked due to abuse. Additionally a Directory Service is needed to list and search for certificates.

Typical standards for PKIs are ITU-T X.509 (ITU-T, 2005). In this chapter only part 3 of the standard is used, which defines X.509 certificates, which is the most relevant standard is PKIX (Schmeh, 2009).

It is important to note, that certificates can be chained. For instance, a CA *rootCA* can issue a certificate for entity e_1. If an entity e_2 wants to access a resource r that trust only certificates from rootCA but no local certificates from e_2, e_2 can get a certificate either directly from *rootCA* or also let its certificate being signed by e_1. Entity r then has to go through the chain ($e_2 \rightarrow e_1 \rightarrow rootCA$) until it finds an entity that it trusts.

2.4.5 Trust Models

Trust is always needed for a secure communication between partners. Depending on the already existing trust relationships of the communication

Figure 1. Different trust relationship models

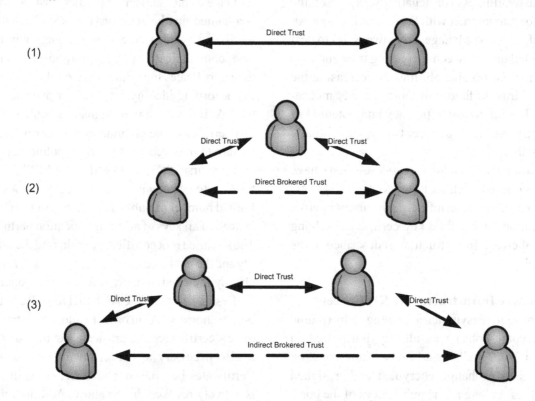

partners, it can be distinguished between different kinds of trust establishment on the basis of PKIs (see (OASIS, 2005c) as shown in Figure 1.

Direct Trust

Communication partners have a direct trust relationship, if there is a pre-established trust relationship between these partners. This already established trust relationship can be based on e.g. exchanged public keys. Because these two partners already trust each other there is no need to exchange any additional information as a prerequisite for secure communication. Thus, no CA is needed for establishing trust (see Figure 1).

Direct Brokered Trust

If two communication partners have no pre-established trust relationship, trust can be established by brokering. Trust brokers in PKIs are typically CAs, where a commonly accepted and trusted CA

vouches for the identity of both communication partners.

Indirect Brokered Trust

Indirect brokered trust is an extension of direct brokered trust, where there is no single CA which has a trust relationship to both communication partners. Thus, trust has to be brokered between several CAs, resulting in a trust chain between the communication partners.

2.5 Access Control Models

Authorization as described in the previous subsection must rely on specific access control models in order to take a decision. Most important are Protection Matrices, Discretionary, Mandatory and Role-Based Access Control.

2.5.1 Protection Matrices

Protection Matrices as introduced by (Harrison, Ruzzo, & Ullman, 1976), are abstract representations of access control policies as basis for an access control model. It is realized as a two dimensional array which holds subjects as rows and protected resources as columns. Therefore, each entry (s_i, r_j) defines what subject s_i is allowed to do with resource r_j.

Since many entries would be empty for a large set of subjects and resources, because not every subjects is usually allowed to perform an action on each resource, different structures have been developed as an optimization of Protection Matrices. The most important is the concept of Access Control Lists (ACL). ACLs store only the relevant entries and ignore empty entries. Therefore, an ACL is associated with a resource and defines for each subject which action the subject is allowed to perform on a given resource.

2.5.2 Discretionary Access Control

The Discretionary Access Control (DAC) model is based on the identity of subjects and ownership over objects (Sandhu & Samarati, 1994). Subjects are defined as owners over objects (resources) and have discretionary authority over who has access to that objects. This means that DAC is based on the administration of owner based access rights. Therefore, DAC allows the delegation of rights over an object to other subjects.

2.5.3 Mandatory Access Control

In Mandatory Access Control (MAC) system, the authorization decision is taken on the basis of a certain set of rules and polices enforced by a central authority. The most important implementation is the Bell-LaPadula model (Bell & Lapadula, 1973). This model defines a set of access control rules which define security labels on resources and clearances for subjects on resources. In detail, it defines a hierarchical order of security labels such as *Top Secret* at the top down to the least sensitive as e.g. *Unclassified*. Subjects are allowed to see all resources for their clearance level and below.

2.5.4 Role Based Access Control

Role Based Access Control centers on the idea of enforcing access control according to specific pre-defined policies, which assign certain rights to specific roles (Sandhu & Samarati, 1994).

Multiple subjects can be aggregated to a certain role and vice versa a subject can have multiple roles. Role hierarchies with inheritance are also possible which ease the administration overhead. Specific roles (e.g. administrator, fire-fighter, etc.) are granted all rights associated with this role such as access to specific resources.

2.5.5 Comparison to Licensing

Licensing, as used in this chapter, differs from the classical access control model briefly described in sections 2.5.1-2.5.4. There are mainly three distinctions:

At first, no central authority is needed such as required by ACL or MAC. Second, shared ownership in SDIs are sometimes hard to define and often given only temporarily. And third and most important a dynamic notion is added. Entities do not have to have a predefined business relationship with each other nor stored a-priori any passwords, roles or rights information. These relationships are established on-the-fly at runtime. A license has to be obtained and presented to the protected resources at runtime which describes all rights a requestor has. We want to stress that we do not focus on classical digital rights management, which deals with protecting the data (Rosenblatt, 2002). Our focus lays moreover on dynamic access control which is described in the following sections.

3 SECURITY ARCHITECTURE

A security and licensing architecture is never self-contained, rather to being an overlay to a domain-specific architecture. OGC defines such a service architecture, which is based on the OWS Common standard (OGC, 2006b) and reference model (OGC, 2003) and extended by other implementation standards, such as WMS (OGC, 2002).

3.1 General Requirements

In the OGC service architecture model, a security architecture should leverage the existing OGC specifications by defining generic security and licensing extensions being applicable to all OGC standards based on OWS Common (OGC, 2006b). On an abstract level, such extensions should be independent of specific technology bindings, leading to a common abstract security architecture for OGC Web Services.

To apply security and licensing to the existing OGC specification baseline, the following extensions are needed from a technical point of view:

- **R_1: Security metadata.** Services should be able to expose their security requirements to requesting clients as part of the technical service metadata. This may include
    - requiring certain security tokens (such as identity tokens or license tokens)
    - requiring the use of transport level security
    - requiring the use of message level encryption
    - requiring requests to be digitally signed

It is important to note, that these preconditions may vary for different georesources offered by the service (e.g. different layers may require different licenses offered by a specific WMS).

- **R_2: Protocol extensions.** To submit security-related information such as security tokens, extensions to the OGC service protocols should be defined, allowing such information to be submitted together with request and/or response messages.

- **R_3: Additional error definitions.** If a client fails to fulfill a service's security requirements or if access is denied to a certain request, the service may respond with an appropriate error message, indicating the reason for the failure of the request. Although error messages need to be specified, their use should be optional, since error messages may lead to undesired information leakage (e.g. a message indicating that access to a certain resource is denied nevertheless indicates i.e. that this resource actually exists).

3.2 Preconditions

In order to fulfill the first requirement, the secured OWS have to expose their security requirements to requesting clients, which we refer to as security preconditions as a common term in the security literature (see i.e. (IETF, 2007)

Preconditions play a key role in security enabled Web Services infrastructures and therefore as well for secured and licensing enabled OWS. In general, preconditions publicly announce a potential Web Service requestor, which conditions (in the context of security: which security model, tokens, encryption mechanism are required / supported) (Weerawarana, 2006). This concept ensures interoperability by allowing clients to be aware of and fulfill all required preconditions prior to service invocation. A general workflow should follow the following principle according to (Kanneganti and Ramarao, 2008):

A requestor fetches the service preconditions prior to invocation. These preconditions have to be intersected with the policies that the service can fulfill. If all preconditions can be met by the

Figure 2. Precondition extension of GetCapabilities metadata

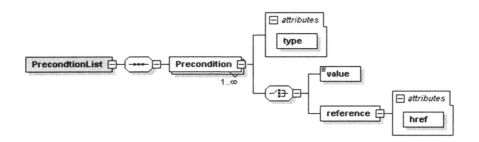

requestor and therefore an effective policy can be determined, the requestor can invoke the service according to the effective policy.

There are several ways to encode and expose preconditions. The most common solution in the context of Web Services in the mainstream IT world is WS-Policy (W3C, 2006a) in conjunction with WS-PolicyAttachment (W3C, 2006b) as a generic container to describe preconditions. However, in the OGC world, these standards have not been adopted yet but the basic workflow looks similar. In this particular case of OWS, the *fetch service's policy* part will return the capabilities document providing metadata about the service. To address preconditions, the returned ServiceMetadata has an *<AccessConstraints>* element as defined by OWS Common (OGC, 2006b). Unfortunately this implies two problems:

- The Element allows only plain text, which is not sufficient for machine readable use due to the lack of XML support (see (OGC, 2006b))
- The tight coupling of preconditions to the OGC specific *ServiceMetadata* does not permit the use in mainstream IT infrastructures

To overcome these limitations, a generic solution that fits both worlds has to be found and is presented in the following:

In order to anchor generic preconditions into a capabilities element, the current GetCapabilities response has to be extended and a new element one level below the root element level has to be created. In general, there are two options for this solution. Embed the preconditions directly in the GetCapabilities response or reference it. The proposed approach is held generic and thereby allows both options as shown in Figure 2.

The structure contains on the top level a *<PreconditionList>* element which serves as a container for 1..n *<Precondition>* elements. Each of these elements has a mandatory *type* attribute, which should contain a URN indicating the encoding of the precondition content given in either the value or reference element. Different encodings are possible which adds a great flexibility to this approach while maintaining interoperability at the same time due to the typed URN approach. The actual preconditions, as analyzed before, can be given either as value (using the *<Value>* element) or as reference by using the reference element with the corresponding *href* attribute for the URL.

A concrete example is given in listing 1

Listing 1. GetCapabitlites precondition extension.

```
<n1:PrecondtionList
xsi:schemaLocation="http://ogc.pre-
condtions Precondition.xsd"
xmlns:n1="http://ogc.precondtions"
```

```
xmlns:xsi="http://www.w3.org/2001/
XMLSchema-instance">
    <Precondition type="urn:ogc:geo-
policy">
        <reference href="http://
localhost:8080/preconditions/wps_pre-
conditions.xml"/>
    </Precondition>
</n1:PrecondtionList>
```

The example depicted in listing 1 uses as the precondition type the URN

```
urn:ogc:geo-policy
```

as indication for the encoding of the referenced document. This encoding is described in the following subsection.

3.2.1 GeoPolicy Encoding

As stated before, there are multiple ways and standards to encode preconditions and attach them to specific resources. As already mentioned, WS-Policy and WS-PolicyAttachment are the most prominent in this area. However, WS-Policy in combination with WS-PolicyAttachment can only be defined on the service and offered operations level (e.g. GetMap for a WMS) (Weerawarana, 2006). In contrast, OGC Services offer resources beyond the service and operations level, namely on the georesource level. For instance, the service level would be the whole service represented by the base URL, the operations level of a WMS would be the GetMap or GetFeatureInfo level. The georesource level would be the offered layers for the WMS example and as stated in requirement R_1, different layers for instance can have different preconditions, in other words may require different licenses. The proposed GeoPolicy preconditions encoding introduces a way of attaching preconditions to specific georesources offered by OGC Web Services and showing a way of indicating supporting services, where relevant tokens could

be fetched. For both contributions, WS-Policy and WS-PolicyAttachment are used and a standardized way is specified because this part is left open by these specifications.

To attach a georesource with a preconditions policy, it must be clear how georesources have to be identified. This is not defined yet in the OGC URN best practice yet. The OGC defines only URNs on the service level, but not on the georesource level[1]. For example, one operation (getMap (WMS) or execute (WPS)) can relate to multiple georesources such as different layers or geoprocesses. To uniquely identify a georesource with a precondition there are basically two options:

- define the relevant georesource in the policy, or
- define the relevant policy in the georesource description

Since we are aiming for a solution that extends the GetCapabilities response independently of the secured service, only the first option is suitable. The other option would have multiple extensions on the specification level while the first one can be introduced at a single point on the top-level common for all OGC Web Services.

To solve the first challenge of uniquely identifying georesources, the following grammar in EBNF form states for every OGC service type its georesource.

```
URN::= "urn:ogc:" OGCResourceType
OGCResourceType::= OGCDefintionType |
OGCSpecificationType | OGCServiceType
    OGCServiceType::= OGCService
OGCService::= WMS | WCS | WFS | SOS |
CSW | WPS | SPS | WCPS
WMS::=  "WMS:GetMap:"WMSResourceID":"
ResourceValue"
WMSResourceID::= "Layer"
WCS::= "WCS:GetCoverage:"WCSResourceI
D":"ResourceValue"
WCSResourceID::= "Coverage"
```

Figure 3. Extended policy attachment

```
WFS::= "WFS:"("DescribeFeatureType"|
"GetFeatures")":WFSResourceID:"Resou
rceValue
WFSResourceID::= "FeatureType"
SOS::= "SOS" ("DescribeSensor" |
"GetObservation")
SOSResourceID::=
Observation[":Feature"]
CSW::= CSW("DescribeRecord"
| "GetRecords")
":CSWResourceID:"ResourceValue
CSWResourceID::= "Typename"
WPS::= ("DescribeProcess" | "Exe-
cute") "WPSResourceID:"ResourceValue
WPSResourceID::= Process
SPS::= ("DescribeTasking" | "Submit")
"SPSResourceID:"ResourceValue
SPSResourceID::= "Sensor" [":Task"]
ResourceValue::= (letter | number |
other | reserved)+
letter::= upper | lower  upper::= "A"
| "B" | "C" | "D" | "E" | "F" | "G" |
"H" | "I" | "J" | "K" | "L" | "M" |
"N" | "O" | "P" | "Q" | "R" | "S" |
"T" | "U" | "V" | "W" | "X" | "Y" |
"Z"  lower::= "a" | "b" | "c" | "d" |
"e" | "f" | "g" | "h" | "i" | "j" |
"k" | "l" | "m" | "n" | "o" | "p" |
"q" | "r" | "s" | "t" | "u" | "v" |
"w" | "x" | "y" | "z"  number::= "0"
| "1" | "2" | "3" | "4" | "5" | "6" |
"7" | "8" | "9"  other::= "(" | ")"
| "+" | "," | "-" | "." | ":" | "=" 
| "@" | ";" | "$" | "_" | "!" | "*"
| "\" | " "  reserved::= "%" | "/" |
"?" | "#"
```

In detail, the grammar lists for every OGC type its mandatory operations and provided georesources through these operations. This allows the creation of a unique URN. For instance, a WPS URN would look like:

```
urn::ogc::WPS::Execute::Process
::buffer
```

for a process with the name/profile *buffer*.

Since we now have a methodology for identifying uniquely a georesource, we need a way for combining a georesource with a policy. In principle WS-PolicyAttachment can be used but it is very generic and the use is not further defined because the generic *any* ComplexType elements are used in its schemas. Therefore, a fully specified structure as a profile of the generic WS-PolicyAttachment schemas has to be created which clearly specifies each detail to foster interoperability. Figure 3 shows the schema representation snippet.

A <GeoPolicy> element is used as the root element and container for multiple WS-Policy-Attachment elements. This becomes necessary, because a precondition document can have multiple policies for different georesources as for example a process buffer has different preconditions (e.g. different license type) than a process intersect, but all are provided by the same service.

This is followed by a WS-Policy <AppliesTo> element, which holds a WS-Addressing W3C, 2004) <EndpointReference> element, which should have a WS-Addressing <Address> element to reference the services endpoint. Additionally, the Georesource is specified, wrapped in a WS-Addressing <ReferenceProperties> element. The <ReferenceProperties> element is then able to hold

Figure 4. Extended WS-policy

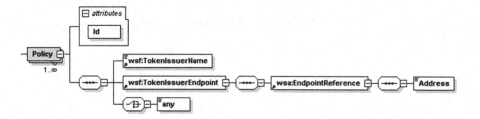

a URN constructed from the grammar constructed above. By using this mechanism, a georesource can be clearly identified and correlated to a policy created in the next step.

This policy is represented by the WS-Policy <Policy> element, which should be applied to the georesource from the <AppliesTo> branch. WS-Policy allows different combinations and ne nestings of policies, which are all valid here. The only constrain is, that on leaf level of the policy tree, a <TokenIssuerName> and 0....n <TokenIssuerEndpoint> both taken from the WS-Federation (W3C, 2003) namespace are used (see Figure 3). This extends the WS-Policy specification which is anticipated by WS-Policy (W3C, 2004) due to the use of generic ##any elements. The <TokenIssuerName> element should hold a URN following the created grammar to indicate a service type, where the required token can be obtained (e.g. a LicenseBroker (see section 3.4) for a license). The <TokenIssuerEndpoint> is also taken from the WS-Federation namespace and should hold an address, which indicated the URL of the service where the required token can be fetched. Since multiple <TokenIssuerEndpoint> elements are allowed, it is anticipated that it is possible to give a set of services where the client can chose from. This can improve service availability, because if one service is down, another equivalent can be taken. Additionally, if a trust relationship cannot be established with one service on the list, it might be possible to create a trust relationship with another service from the presented list (see section 3.5).

Besides, the <TokenIssuerName> and <TokenIssuerEndpoint> elements, a third element is needed. It has to be used for specifying the Token type, such as identity or license token indicated by the *any* type.

Figure 4 shows such an extended WS-Policy leaf element.

A concrete example can be seen in section 3.2.2.

3.2.2 Security Token precondition encoding

In this chapter, mainly two different token types are of relevance as identified in section 3.2.1. For Identity Token preconditions, existing standards like WS-SecurityPolicy can be used (OASIS, 2002b). But when it comes to licensing preconditions, no specific standard exist especially when georesources requirements have to be incorporated.

Therefore, for license preconditions, the following schema is proposed:

A <LicenseToken> element has the default attribute <usage> as defined by the WS-Policy specification for every token. It indicates, if the token is necessarily required or not. As technical guideline, which format is accepted, the <TokenType> element is used, which is also common to other tokens specified in (OASIS, 2002b). Anticipating workflow scenarios, an optional <AppliesTo> scheme as used for the general attachment of the precondition policy to a secured service

Figure 5. LicensePrecondition schema

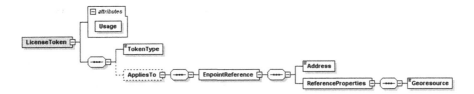

(see section 3.2.1) is employed here. In particular, the address and georesource should reference the service and georesource for which this license is ultimately required. If the license is for the same entity as indicated in the general <appliesTo> section, these elements are optional. An example can be seen in listing 2.

Listing 2. Complete Preconditions for a secured WPS.

```
<xyz:GeoPolicy xmlns:xsi="http://
www.w3.org/2001/XMLSchema-in-
stance" xmlns:wsa="http://schemas.
xmlsoap.org/ws/2004/08/address-
ing" xmlns:sp="http://schemas.
xmlsoap.org/ws/2005/07/securi-
typolicy" xmlns:wsp="http://
schemas.xmlsoap.org/ws/2004/09/
policy" xmlns:xyz="foo.bar"
xmlns:wsf="http://schemas.xmlsoap.
org/ws/2003/07/secext" x
si:schemaLocation="http://schemas.
xmlsoap.org/ws/2004/09/policy precon-
ditions_full.xsd">
    <wsp:PolicyAttachment>
        <wsp:AppliesTo>
            <wsa:EnpointReference>

<wsa:Address>http://localhost:8080/
wps/WebProcessingService/wsa:Address>

<wsa:ReferenceProperties>
                <xyz:Geore
source>urn:ogc:OGCGeoresouce:OGCSe
rvice:WPS:Execute:Process:Buffer</
```

```
xyz:Georesource>
                </
wsa:ReferenceProperties>
                </
wsa:EnpointReference>
        </wsp:AppliesTo>
        <wsp:Policy
Id="GeneralPrecondtion">
            <wsp:All>
                <wsp:Policy
Id="LicensePrecondtion">
                    <wsf-
:TokenIssuerName>urn:ogc:OGCGeore
souce:OGCService:LicenseBroker</
wsf:TokenIssuerName>

<wsf:TokenIssuerEndpoint>

<wsa:EndpointReference>

<wsa:Address>

http://localhost:8080/LicenseBroker
                    </
wsa:Address>
                    </
wsa:EndpointReference>
                    </
wsf:TokenIssuerEndpoint>

<xyz:LicenseToken
wsp:Usage="wsp:Required">
                    <xyz:To
kenType>urn:oasis:names:tc:SAML:1.1:X
ACML</xyz:TokenType>
```

```
                              </
xyz:LicenseToken>
                   </wsp:Policy>
                   <wsp:Policy
Id="IdentityPrecondtion">
                      <wsf:TokenIs
suerName>urn:ogc:OGCGeoresouce:OGCSer
vice:STS</wsf:TokenIssuerName>

<wsf:TokenIssuerEndpoint>

<wsa:EndpointReference>

<wsa:Address>

http://localhost:8080/STS
                              </
wsa:Address>
                              </
wsa:EndpointReference>
                           </
wsf:TokenIssuerEndpoint>

<xyz:IdentityToken
wsp:Usage="wsp:Required">
                           <xyz
:TokenType>"urn:oasis:names:tc:SA
ML:1.1</xyz:TokenType>
                           </
xyz:IdentityToken>
                   </wsp:Policy>
                </wsp:All>
             </wsp:Policy>
          </wsp:PolicyAttachment>
</xyz:GeoPolicy>
```

3.3 License Encoding

After presenting an interoperable way of how and where license tokens can be obtained, this leaves the question open, how such geo licenses can be expressed.

Following the OGC GeoDRM Abstract Specification (OGC, 2006a) a license consists

Table 1. OGC GeoDRM-OASIS mapping

OGC GeoDRM	OASIS/XACML
Grant	Policy
Principal	Subject
Right	Action
Resource	Resource
Condition	Condition
Signature	Signature

on a conceptual level of a *grant* element and an *issuer* element. The *grant* holds a *principal*, a *right*, a *resource* and an optional *condition*. The *issuer* has to sign the license to allow recipients to verify the validity of the license.

Since we expect additional license elements such as legal restrictions, disclaimers, etc., we regard this list as extensible.

On an encoding level, there a multiple rights expression languages (REL), such as ISO21000 (MPEG-21)(ISO, 2004), XrML(Wang et al., 2002), or XACML (OASIS, 2005a). This chapter focuses on the OASIS XACML specification as one possible solution. The advantage of XACML is the widespread use and therefore multiple implementations. Besides, it can be combined with OASIS SAML as a XACML SAML profile, which allows the seamless integration into the existing Web Service infrastructures.

In the OASIS/XACML terminology, *grants*, as defined in the GeoDRM Abstract Specification, represent policies. A mapping between GeoDRM and OASIS terminology would be the following:

In the remainder of this chapter the OASIS/XACML terminology will be used.

A license will be represented by a SAML 2.0 (OASIS, 2007) assertion, including a <XACML-PolicyStatement> element following the SAML 2.0 profile of XACML 1.1 (OASIS, 2005b).

In the proposed profile (see listing 5 for an example), the <XACMLPolicyStatement> is a specialization of the generic <saml:Statement> element. It is defined as <saml:Statement xsi:type="xacml-

Figure 6. Overview of the architecture

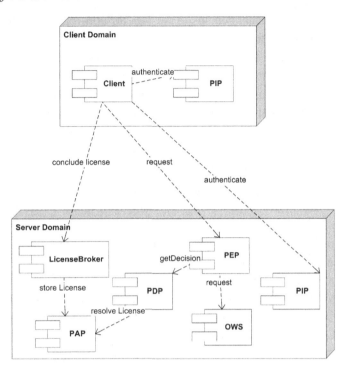

saml:XACMLPolicyStatementType"> and may include <xacml:Policy> and <xacml:PolicySet> elements as well as referenced policies. This is the anchor point to include XACML based licenses in SAML tokens.

In order to ensure integrity, the proposed license encoding includes a <ds:Signature> element to ensure the authenticity of a license via XML signature. Although the use of this element is not mandatory in the SAML specification, a signature is necessary to fulfill all requirements of the GeoRM abstract specification.

The signature has to be provided by the license issuing entity (License Manager, see section 3.4) being responsible for maintaining the license throughout its lifecycle.

3.4 Static Model

The static model describes the components of the proposed architecture. As depicted in Figure 6, two different domains exist. The client domain

consumes on-demand a previously unknown Geospatial Web Service from the server domain. Both domains are independent from each other. However, a (brokered) trust relationship must be established (see section 3.5). The general architecture is built on the well proven XACML security architecture (OASIS, 2005a).

The components of the client domain are a client component and a Policy Information Point (PIP) derived from the basic XACML architecture (OASIS, 2005a). The client component is responsible for invoking the secured Geospatial Web Service and gathering all required security tokens. A Policy Information Point (PIP), also called Authentication Service in other architecture such as KERBEROS (Neuman & Ts'o, 1994), issues, stores and manages user identities. In particular, this service allows requestors to obtain an *Identity Token*, which is understood and trusted by the requestor. Therefore, the requestor has to have a-priory established trust relationship with its PIP and an agreed authentication methods, such as

HTTP Basic Authentication aligned with a shared secret, i.e. a password. With this exchanged security secret (e.g. passwords), the client component can authenticate itself at the PIP in order to obtain an Identity Token. As we will see in section 3.5, the returned token might not be trusted by the targeted service. Therefore, additional authentication steps might be needed as described in section 3.5.

Besides, the PIP allows service providers to validate a received Identity Token. The interface can be adopted from WS-Trust (OASIS, 2005c), which defines a Security Token Service (STS) for this task. By leveraging mainstream IT standards, such as WS-Trust, a seamless integration outside of the geospatial domain will be guaranteed. Additionally, the Policy Information Point can issue different identity token encodings. In this paper we rely on SAML based identity tokens but other encodings are also possible.

The server domain consists of a standardized Geospatial Web Service, which provides the actual georesource. This service is secured by a Policy Enforcement Service (Policy Enforcement Point, PEP) adopted from the common XACML security model (OASIS, 2005a). A Policy Enforcement Point manages the access from and to a secured OWS. By applying this approach of separating the business logic from the security logic, flexibility is gained: Exiting service implementation do not have to be changed but could simply be wrapped by a PEP component serving as a transparent security proxy. In detail, the PEP analyzes incoming requests for completeness in terms of fulfilling the requirements stated in the preconditions. In general, a PEP requires:

- A license token for authorization purposes describing the granted rights issued by a License Broker.
- An identity token for authentication purposes issued by the PIP of the server's domain

- A digital signature of the request message for non-repudiation purposes.

Additionally, signatures have to be validated by e.g. going trough a certificate chain and/or validating a token by using the functionality from the PIP. Relevant information are extracted and forwarded to the PDP (Policy Decision Point). According to the returned decision, the secured OWS is requested or the initial requested is denied.

The standard Geospatial Web Service can be easily configured (e.g. by means of a firewall) to only allows access from its PEP's IP address. Thereby, any communication directed to the Geospatial Web Service has to go through the PEP security layer. Thus, the Policy Enforcement Point serves as a transparent proxy component securing the Geospatial Web Service without touching the implementation of it. To be transparent in regards to the client domain, the PEP has the same interface as the secured Geospatial Web Service, but adds additional security functionality, such as issuing preconditions and enforcing usage rights.

The decision (authorization) about the usage rights is made by the Policy Decision Point (PDP) coming also from the common security model (OASIS, 2005a). The Policy Decision Point (PDP) is in charge for deciding whether a certain request is allowed to access a service or not. Therefore, the tuple (Subject, Action, Resource, License Token) is fed into the service by the PEP. The License Token is resolved from the Policy Administration Point (PAP) and evaluated against the subject, action and resource from the request (see section 3.6 for details). As a result, a *accept* or *deny* decision will be issued. However, the PDP is also capable of issuing a decision with certain obligations such as requested granted but only if an administrator is informed, etc..

To manage the license, a Policy Administration Point (PAP) becomes necessary. A PAP is responsible for storing, resolving and revocation of a license. In detail, a license concluded e.g. by a License Broker could be stored on this service.

A reference to this license is returned back to the License Broker, which can further distribute it. Since only a reference is passed back, entities who want to validate the license have to resolve the license from the PAP first. This enables an easy to handle lifecycle management, due to the fact that in case e.g. a license is revoked by the creator, it could be easily propagated to the validating entity.

It is obvious that only authorized entities are allowed to create and revoke a license. Resolving of a license is not critical, since the license ID need to be known as well as a license is typically encrypted and therefore only readable to parties involved in the business transaction manifested in the license

In addition, a PIP is provided in the server domain as a trusted issuer for Identity Tokens in the server domain.

The common security XACML architecture is also extended by a License Broker. Such a License Broker Service is dedicated to negotiate and issue a license on behalf of the resource owner to the license consumer. In principle, three different assignment types have to be distinguished:

- Permanent and persistent assignment (leads to classical access control with pre-defined rights)
- Commercial Assignment (purchasing an assignment in an on demand fashion)
- Reconcilement assignment between issuer and consumer (agreement to terms-of-use)

In particular, the License Broker knows which license possibilities are available for certain products. On this basis, different options are offered to the client, which the client can choose from and conclude. The concluded licenses are stored at the PAP and a reference is provided to the license consumer. In general, the License Broker requires:

- An Identity Token from the servers domain
- A Signature of the request for non-repudiation purposes

A complete interface description for such a LicenseBroker has been described in (OGC, 2008).

3.5 Trust Relationships

This section analyzes which trust relationships have to be established between the different domains. A methodology is introduced which shows how to establish and validate these trust relationships especially between specific services described in section 3.6.

We can assume that inside of one domain such as client or server, static business and trust relationship exist. The interesting part is the ad-hoc formation of cross-organizational interactions which do not have necessarily established a trust relationship in advance.

According to section 3.4 (Figure 6), there are 3 cross-organizational interactions:

- Client ⟷ LicenseBroker (1)
- Client ⟷ Server PIP (2)
- Client ⟷ PEP (3)

Each relationship has to be regarded separately:

In the trust relationship (1), a LicenseBroker basically needs an Identity Token and a signature of the OrderLicense request as described in section 3.4. The Identity Token is required to extract the identity of the licensee and use it as the license subject, which is granted the specific rights. Therefore, a license broker needs to be able to trust the identity of the requestor. If the License-Broker does not trust the identity or respectively it's issuing authority, it cannot be sure if the real license requestor is the same entity as the entity that should be stated as the licensee. For instance, if an unauthorized man-the-middle attacker would replace the subject in the Identity Token and the OrderLicenseRequest with the attacker's one, the attacker would be the entitled entity of the license, while e.g. the payment information of the original requester is used. Therefore, a signature of the request message is required, which can be validated with the public key given in the Identity Token. If the issuer is trusted and the signature is valid, the license broker can be sure that the actual license requestor is the same entity as the license request issuer.

This is the reason why the LB states in its preconditions all directly trusted PIPs, where trusted Identity Tokens can be obtained. The <TokenIssuerEndpoint> element introduced in section 3.2 fulfills this role. This element allows to specify where a client can obtain a specific token that is trusted by the server domain.

To obtain such a trusted token, the client has to request the preconditions of the <TokenIssuerEndpoint> and evaluate if it can fulfill these requirements. If the client recognizes one of the identity token issuer endpoints e.g. by its URL, and a direct trust relationship exists between these two entities, the client is able to obtain a token from it. However, the client still has to verify that it can fulfill the preconditions and a direct trust relationship is still valid, e.g. by verifying the signature of the response.

We can therefore conclude, that trust between client and LicenseBroker relies on trust in the identity token and not directly between the client and the LicenseBroker.

This leads to trust relationship (2).

In the best case, the PIP in the client domain is listed as one of the trusted token issuers. This would follow a direct brokered trust model. However, we assume the worst case, where the client PIP is not in that list. An indirect brokered trust model has to be established (see section 2.4.5). Two models are proposed in the following to gather tokens from trusted identity token issuers.

Client Driven Trust Establishing Model

For a client driven approach, the client is responsible to evaluate and establish an indirect brokered trust relationship. At first, the metadata of the identity token issuing service has to be obtained (e.g. by a getCapabilities request) and

the preconditions extracted (see section 2.3). For the PIP, different authentication method might be stated. For instance, the acceptance of username password tokens, X.509 certificates or SAML Tokens. The trusted token issuers are also stated. The <TokenIssuerEndpoint> element introduced in section 2.3 fulfills this role. It allows to specify where a client can obtain a specific token that is trusted and understood by the server domain.

Therefore, the client has to check each token issuer with the same procedure as described above, to evaluate if it is either known (direct trust, e.g. accepts a pre-registered username and password) or accepts a token from a known client PIP, such as the one in the client domain. If such an intermediate PIP can be found, it would serve as trust broker between the client's PIP and the target PIP. It is obvious, that this procedure leads to a directed graph. It is important to note, that cycles are possible, as the following example shows:

Listing 3. Trust cycle

PIP_A trusts PIP_B
PIP_B trusts PIP_C
PIP_C trust PIP_A

Once such a service is found as the root of the graph, the client has to move to the next phase and actually establish trust. Therefore it needs to authenticate and obtain a token from its PIP as described above. This token has to be passed through the graph until the targeted server's PIP is reached as a graph leaf. The returned Identity Token from the targeted server's PIP can then be used for authentication in the server's domain.

In principle, WS-Federation (W3C, 2003) follows this approach but uses a more complex way of exchanging metadata and relies only on SOAP. Therefore, in the scenario described in 4, a manual and leaner way of establishing a directed trust tree is created as described above.

Server Driven Trust Establishing Model

In a server driven approach, the client is not responsible for evaluating the trust path and establishing trust. In this case, the client authenticates itself with its directly trusted PIP and sends this token to each PIP found on the precondition list of the LicenseBroker (<TokenIssuerEndpoint>). A PIP that receives this token does potentially not directly trust this token, because the signature cannot be verified due to any exchanged keys. However, instead of rejecting the token, the server tries to find an indirect brokered trust relationship. There are two possible options:

• One option is to lookup the signature of the issuer and if a certificate is included, the certificate chain (see section 2.4.3) can be gone through to find an entity that is trusted. If such an entity is found, the token can be trusted as explained in section 2.4.3. Therefore, the PIP can issue a token to the requestor. The requestor can than use it to authenticate at the target service that requires a token from that specific PIP.

• Another option is to follow the search algorithm described for the client driven approach. The PIP that receives an untrusted token requests all known and trusted PIPs. The preconditions have to be evaluated in terms of trusting the token issuer of the received untrusted token. If the token issuer of the untrusted token cannot be found on the trusted issuer list of the trusted PIPs, the search has to be continued with the trusted token issuers stated in the preconditions of the trusted PIPs.

(2) Client – PEP

Between the client and the PEP that is securing the OWS a trust relationship necessary is also necessary. At first, the PEP needs to trust the validity of the client's identity to ensure that the requestor is also the licensee. Second, the client needs to trust the issuers of the supplied tokens. All these trust relationships are established via the trusted token issuers that are announced in the preconditions. Therefore, the PEP trust relationship is established on the fly indirectly via the trusted supporting token issuers. No key needs to be shared between client and PEP.

An additional trust relationship needs to be established in case encryption is needed and if the client wants to validate the authenticity of the server responses. In both cases, the public key of the server part is required and the client needs to trust this key.

In terms of signature validation, if a certificate is attached to the signature (as possible with e.g. SAML tokens), the client can go through the certificate chain and evaluate if a trusted root element can be found to establish brokered trust.

In terms of encryption, the public key can be taken from e.g. signature validation or protocols like SSL can be used, which require that the server trusts the client's certificate (or a root issuer in the certificate chain).

3.6 Dynamic Model

The dynamic model shows the interactions between the different components presented in the static model.

By looking at the five business phases given by Hauswirth et al. (Hauswirth, Jazayeri, Schneider 2000), the *request* phase comes first. In the SOA world, this could be mapped to the *find* phase. Which means that in one way or the other, the client has to discover a potential service for a specific task and obtain initial information about the desired service. How the discovery is achieved is out of scope for this chapter. Standard means are the use of Catalogs (CSW) (OGC, 2007) or registries such as UDDI (OASIS, 2002a).

Instead, once a service has been discovered, the announcement of security related information is of interest. In general, WSDL documents could be leveraged for this purpose in the mainstream IT world to obtain metadata about a service. The OGC world traditionally uses the GetCapabilities operation common to all OGC Web Service (OWS) (OGC, 2006b) for this purpose.

In either case, resource offerings and security mechanisms have to be evaluated a-priori by the client in this phase, because the client has to check whether or not the georesource offerings are sufficient for the desired purpose and if the security requirements by the server could be satisfied.

Figure 7 shows this phase for the case, that a URL is already known.

At first the client uses the standard GetCapabilities operation, common to all OGC Web Services. As described in section 3.4, the PEP intercepts the request, because it acts a wrapper invisible to the caller.

The PEP evaluates and forwards the request to the secured OWS which responds accordingly with a complete metadata response. Based on the configuration of the PEP, it might be obliged to filter sensitive data, such as specific layers not visible to anonymous requestors.

The important part here is the attachment of preconditions to the metadata response to ensure interoperability in order to make the client aware what it has to provide to successful request the secured service. Section 3.2 shows how preconditions could be attached to a GetCapabilities response in a generic way. Once the preconditions are attached, URLs in the metadata response pointing to the original unsecured services have to be replaced in order to route all incoming requests to the PEP. After this step, the modified service metadata can be delivered back to the initial caller. To ensure the integrity of the message, the message can be digitally signed using e.g. XML Signature (see section 2.3.2.2). This technique allows the client to ensure, that the message has not been modified and e.g. a malicious URL to a LicenseBroker is inserted trying to phish sensitive

user information and payment information such as credit card numbers.

Upon retrieval, the client has to evaluate the service metadata, starting with validating the message signature based on a trust relationship (see section 3.5) and continuing in evaluating if the service offers the required resource. For instance, the client has to check if a WFS offers a layer in the desired spatial extend or topic or if a WPS offers a desired buffer process. Once this has been successfully achieved, the client needs to check if the preconditions match its own requirements such as encryption and capabilities in terms of delivering trusted tokens. As shown in section 3.2, licensing preconditions consist of the required token types, the trusted issuers and security means such as signature algorithms. By using the typed approach presented in section 3.2, interoperability is ensured because the client can evaluate the preconditions in the preferred encoding. In case all encodings are not understood by the client, the client is not able to evaluate the preconditions and has to reject the service. If a supported encoding is found, it is ensured that the client is able to compare the preconditions with its local requirements and capabilities.

The client has to verify that it understands the preconditions encoding and that it can fulfill the required preconditions indicated in the received metadata. In terms of licensing OWS, preconditions require three elements as described in section 3.4:

- A license token for authorization purposes describing the granted rights,
- an identity token for authentication purposes
- a digital signature of the requests for non-repudiation purposes.

Other security mechanisms such as encryption are optional.

Therefore, the first step for the client is to obtain a license token as shown in Figure 7. As

Figure 7. Dynamic model-license acquisition

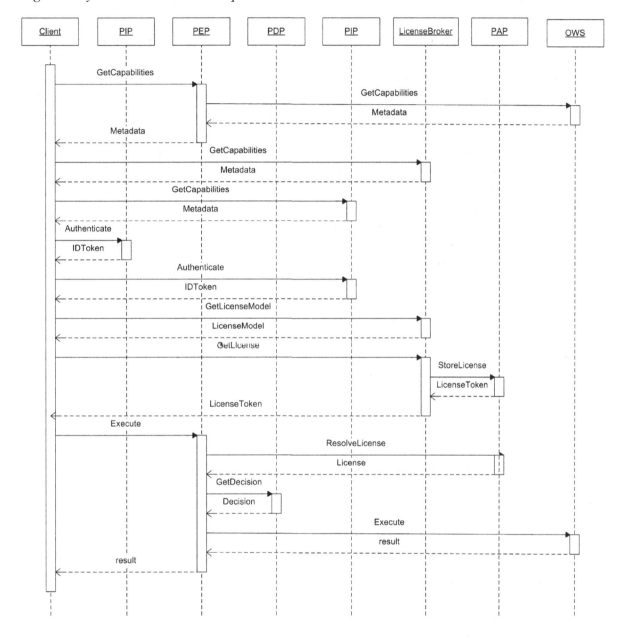

presented in section 3.4, license tokens can be negotiated. To negotiate a license, the client has to use the provided LicenseBroker URL indicated in the preconditions of the secured service. In the common WS-Policy encoding, the LicenseBroker URL will be encapsulated in the <TokenIssuerEndpoint> element as seen in listing 2.

Once the LicenseBroker URL is extracted from the preconditions, the GetCapabilities operation has to be invoked first as with every OWS.

The LicenseBroker metadata is also extended with preconditions following the same pattern as described above. It describes where the required identity token can be obtained from (e.g. the <TokenIssueEndpointr> element in a WS-Trust encoding). These preconditions have to be evaluated by the client. As described in section 3.4, the response of the license broker is digitally signed using XML-Signature to ensure the integrity of the message. Once the signature has been successfully validated, the preconditions describing additional security means and methods have to be evaluated as described above. For the LicenseBroker, especially the authentication of the user when concluding a license as well as signing the requests for non repudiation purposes is required in order to fulfil the preconditions stated in section 3.4. Taking the trust model described in section 3.5 into account, a trust relationship based only on the identity token has to be established between client and LicenseBroker to allow the LicenseBroker to trust the client.

Thus, an identity token has to be obtained first. Figure 7 shows that the client first gets the metadata from the trusted Identity Token issuer extracted from the LicenseBroker preconditions. As explained in section 3.5, different trust establishing models are possible. Figure 7 shows the client driven approach, where the client authenticates at its own PIP and then passes the obtained Identity Token as authentication information to the servers PIP, after evaluating that the server's PIP accepts Identity Tokens from the client's PIP.

The client details, such as public key information, are usually stored at the clients PIP in advance and it can authenticate itself via e.g. a predefined username and password using HTTP Basic Authentication.

Since the client observed from the server's PIP that it accepts Identity Tokens from the client's PIP as valid and trusted authentication information, the server's PIP returns with an Identity Token valid for the server's domain.

With this newly obtained Identity Token for the server's domain, the client can then negotiate and conclude the license with the LicenseBroker. As shown in Figure 7, at first a GetLicenseModel request can be sent to the server incorporating the newly obtained Identity Token. The license model

(see listing 4 for an example) can then be used as a template to negotiate the license. Parameters can be set and sent to the LicenseBroker via the TryLicenseOperation as specified in section 3.4. The returned result has to be evaluated and potentially further refined via another TryLicense request.

Listing 4. GetLicenseModel reponse showing a license model for a WPS DouglasPeuker algorithm with a maximal simplification value of 2.

```
<lbs:LBSGetLicenseModelR
esponse language="en-us"
xsi:schemaLocation="http://www.
conterra.de/lbs LicenseBroker_0_6.
xsd" xmlns:lbs="http://www.conter-
ra.de/lbs" xmlns:xsi="http://www.
w3.org/2001/XMLSchema-instance" xmlns
:saml="urn:oasis:names:tc:SAML:2.0:as
sertion">
    <lbs:LicenseModel ID="4c59b490-
dc08-11de-8a39-0800200c9a66">
        <lbs:Resource id="
urn::ogc::WPS::execute::Proc
ess::DouglasPeukerAlgorithm"
title="DouglasPeukerAlgorithm"
name="DouglasPeukerAlgorithm">
            <lbs:Abstract>DouglasP
eukerAlgorithm</lbs:Abstract>
            <lbs:ConfigParams>
                <lbs:Parameter
type="xs:float"
title="SimplificationRatio"
name="SimplificationRatio">

<lbs:MinValue>0.0</lbs:MinValue>

<lbs:MaxValue>2.0</lbs:MaxValue>
                </lbs:Parameter>
            </lbs:ConfigParams>
            <lbs:ProductAttribute
title="Product Info" name="info">
This is some information </
lbs:ProductAttribute>
        </lbs:Resource>
```

```
        <lbs:LicenseAttribute
title="Disclaimer"
name="disclaimer">This is a disclaim-
er!</lbs:LicenseAttribute>
        <lbs:Licensor
ID="conterra">
        <lbs:LicensorAddress>

<lbs:name>Rüdiger</lbs:name>

<lbs:forename>Gartmann</lbs:forename>

<lbs:street>Martin-Luther-King-Weg</
lbs:street>

<lbs:streetnum>24</lbs:streetnum>
        <lbs:zip>48155</
lbs:zip>

<lbs:city>Münster</lbs:city>

<lbs:country>Germany</lbs:country>
        <lbs:phone>+49
251 7474-301</lbs:phone>
        <lbs:email>r.
gartmann@conterra.de</lbs:email>
        </lbs:LicensorAddress>
        <saml:Subject>

<saml:NameID>ruedigergartmann</
saml:NameID>
        </saml:Subject>
        </lbs:Licensor>
    </lbs:LicenseModel>
</lbs:LBSGetLicenseModelResponse>
```

After negotiating the license terms, the actual license has to be concluded as also shown in Figure 10. The client has to check the already stored preconditions. For the OrderLicenseRequest, the already obtained identity token has to be attached to the request. This allows the client to authenticate and provide an identity for the licensee field in the license.

This electronic request is the legally binding act, which concludes the licenses. The request contains only the Identity Token and the agreed license model. The LicenseBroker stores the license at the PAP and retrieves a reference back. This reference is encapsulated in the LicenseBroker response. The response is also signed to ensure that the message has not been modified (see listing 5 for an example).

Listing 5. OrderLicense Response holding a reference to the licenseManager and a ID to obtain the full license from that service. The signature is kept separate, e.g. in a SOAP header.

```
<lbs:LBSOrderLicenseResponse
ID="ID_1" Version="0.5.0"
IssueInstant="2009-11-15T09:30:47.0Z"
xsi:schemaLocation="http://www.
conterra.de/lbs LicenseBroker_0_5.
xsd" xmlns:lbs="http://www.con-
terra.de/lbs" xmlns:ds="http://
www.w3.org/2000/09/xmldsig#"
xmlns:xsi="http://www.w3.org/2001/
XMLSchema-instance" xmlns:saml="urn:o
asis:names:tc:SAML:2.0:assertion">
    <saml:Issuer>http://conterra.de/
LB/PAP/saml:Issuer>
    <saml:Subject>

<saml:NameID>RuedigerGartmann</
saml:NameID>
    </saml:Subject>
    <saml:AttributeStatement>
        <saml:Attribute
Name="LicenseManagerURI">

<saml:AttributeValue>http://conterra.
de/LB/PAP/saml:AttributeValue>
        </saml:Attribute>
        <saml:Attribute
Name="LicenseID">

<saml:AttributeValue>916743582</
saml:AttributeValue>
```

```
            </saml:Attribute>
        </saml:AttributeStatement>
</lbs:LBSOrderLicenseResponse>
```

Once the required license is concluded, the other PEP preconditions have to be evaluated in order to request the secured OWS. The Identity Token already obtained for the LicenseBroker is also valid (if not expired) for the PEP, since both service reference the same PIP as trusted issuer. If different PIPs are used, an Identity Token has to be obtained again.

After all other preconditions can be fulfilled, the client is able to invoke the secured service. In a SOAP environment, the Identity and Licensing Tokens as well as the message signature can be put into the SOAP header by means of WS-Security. Other binding may handle this different, such as the base64 encoded in the HTTP header.

Conceptually, the request is sent to the secured service, which is encapsulated by it's PEP. The PEP, as described in section 3.4, intercepts the request and checks if all necessary tokens are present and extracts the tokens and requested georesource. Furthermore, the request message signature has to be checked against the provided public key in the identity token to ensure that the entity which belongs to the identity has send the request. The extracted information is then put into a PDP request.

The PDP extracts the information and resolves the license from the license reference. Therefore, it needs to access the PAP where the license has been stored by the LicenseBroker. Authentication means are here neglected since it is in the same domain. In an operative setting, the PAP also needs to be secured.

The PAP checks if the license is still valid and returns the full license.

The returned license is than evaluated on the basis of the requested georesources and given subject. In detail, the tuple <Subject, Action, Resource> of the license has to be checked if it matches the tuple <Subject, Action, Resource>

of the OWS request. The Subject comes from the identity token, the action is the operation and the resource the UUID constructed via the grammar presented in section 3.2.1.

If both tuples are identical, a accept message should be issued otherwise a deny message.

The PEP forwards the request to the secured service in case of an *accept* response and rejects it in any other case.

The results from the OWS are upon termination returned back to the client.

In case of an asynchronous request, which is supported e.g. by the WPS, only a reference encoded as a URL is returned back. This URL holds in that case a unique session key attached by the Policy Enforcement Point in order to only allow the dedicated recipient to resolve the correct georesource. Encryption is favourable in that case to ensure that no one can intercept the client server communication.

4 SCENARIO

This section presents a real-world scenario, which illustrates the presented ideas and acts as a proof-of-concept verification. The scenario is constructed around the ad-hoc acquisition of geoprocessing functionality coming from a Web Processing Service (WPS). The Douglas-Peucker simplification algorithm (Douglas & Peucker, 1973) is used in this case to simplify complex road geometries in the north-west of Spain. As described in Section 3, a client has to explore the existing functionality and security preconditions first. Since we will use OpenLayers as an OTS client, which does not come with any security capabilities, a proxy façade is used on the client side to first negotiate and conclude the license as well as obtaining Identity Tokens. The URL of the proxy façade is then presented as the actual endpoint to OpenLayers.

As presented in Section 3.3, different license types are possible. In this case, a licensemodel is

Figure 8. Open layers client showing the result of an execute request to a secured WPS

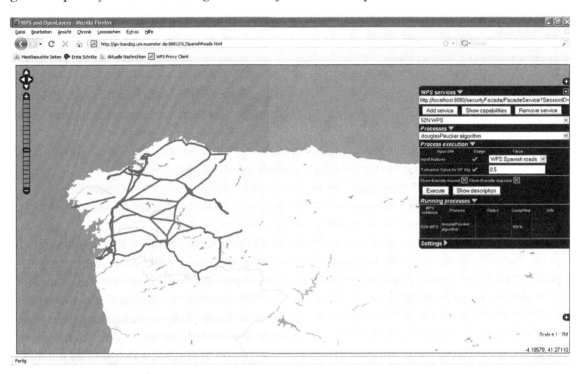

offered, which allows the client to accept certain conditions (see listing 4). Listing 5 shows a snippet of the full license describing the licensed simplification ratio encoded in XACML.

The algorithm has two inputs: a feature dataset and the simplification factor. After the license and an identity token are acquired by the proxy façade, the user can use OpenLayers to execute the process with an input layer and a specified simplification ratio following the protocol of Section 3.1.2.

Listing 6. Snippet of a License including Subject and resource section of license

```
<License xmlns="urn:n52:geoproces
sing:licence" xmlns:xsi="http://
www.w3.org/2001/XMLSchema-instance"
id="234932323894545423">
    <PolicySet xmlns="urn:oasis
:names:tc:xacml:1.0:policy" Pol
icyCombiningAlgId="urn:oasis:na
```

```
mes:tc:xacml:1.0:policy-combin-
ing-algorithm:first-applicable"
PolicySetId="234932323894545423"
xmlns:xsi="http://www.w3.org/2001/
XMLSchema-instance">
        <Description>WPS-Service
Douglas Peuker process license</De-
scription>
        <Target>
            <Subjects>
                <Subject>
                    <Subject-
Match MatchId="urn:oasis:names:tc:xac
ml:1.0:function:string-equal">
                        <At-
tributeValue DataType="http://
www.w3.org/2001/XMLSchema#string"
xmlns:xsi="http://www.
w3.org/2001/XMLSchema-
instance">RuedigerGartmann</Attrib-
uteValue>
```

91

```
                     <Sub-
jectAttributeDesignator Attrib
uteId="urn:conterra:names:sdi-
suite:policy:attribute:role-id"
DataType="http://www.w3.org/2001/
XMLSchema#string"/>
                </Subject-
Match>
                    </Subject>
                  </Subjects>
                  <!-- This License cov-
ers the following resources -->
                    <Resources>
                      <Resource>
                        <Resource-
Match MatchId="urn:oasis:names:tc:xac
ml:1.0:function:string-equal">
                        <At-
tributeValue DataType="..."
xmlns:xsi="...">http://giv-ban-
dog:8080/wps/WebProcessingService/At-
tributeValue>
                        <Re-
sourceAttributeDesignator Attribu-
teId="..." DataType="..."/>
                  </Resource-
Match>
                        <Resource-
Match MatchId="urn:oasis:names:tc:xac
ml:1.0:function:string-equal">
                        <At-
tributeValue DataType="..."
xmlns:xsi="..."> urn::ogc::WPS::Execu
te::Process:DouglasPeuker</Attribute-
Value>
                        <Re-
sourceAttributeDesignator AttributeId
="urn:oasis:names:tc:xacml:1.0:resour
ce:resource-type" DataType="..."/>
                  </Resource-
Match>
                        <Resource-
Match MatchId="urn:oasis:names:tc:xac
```

```
ml:1.0:function:double-less-than">
                      <At-
tributeValue DataType="..."
xmlns:xsi="...">0.5</AttributeValue>
                      <Re-
sourceAttributeDesignator AttributeId
="urn:oasis:names:tc:xacml:1.0:resour
ce:resource-type" DataType="..."/>
                  </Resource-
Match>
                    </Resource>
                  </Resources>
```

On the server side, the PDP has to verify that the request has a simplification ratio that matches the granted one in the license and that the identity of the requestor is identical to the subject in the license. Figure 9 shows the resulting geometries as a new layer (red) in OpenLayers. A simplification ratio of 0.5 was used, which yielded a reduction of the number of intermediate points compared to the original layer (yellow). *5 CONCLUSION* This paper describes an approach for enabling the commercial use of OGC Geospatial Web Services. An architecture is presented including the static components and their interactions. The requirement R1 (section 3.1) has been fulfilled by providing a standardized means to identify security preconditions and map them to georesources provided by Geospatial Web Services. R2 is also fulfilled by showing how protocols could be extended to supply this metadata. For sending additional tokens such as Identity or License Tokens, it was explained that optional message elements can be used such as SOAP Header, depending on the protocol. R3 has to be defined based on specific operational settings and thereby was not further elaborated in this chapter. In addition, trust relationships were analysed and two ways described of how to establish trust on the fly in Spatial Data Infrastructures. We have seen that trust between the different components can be reduced to trust only in the Identity Token providing a public key. Besides, these presented trust establishment concepts allow, at least from a conceptual perspective, the ad-hoc generation of geospatial models comprised of previously unknown Geospatial Web Services. On a technical level, is was shown, that only a license, identity token and a signature are necessary to enable licensing for Geospatial Web Services. Besides, the presented architecture can be applied to existing software without touching the non-security enabled backend services.

The introduced licenses are electronically established and are legally equivalent to paper-based licenses. They bridge the gap between the legal and the technical world by automatically defining aspects of licensing, such as access rights. Therefore, they present a foundation for on-demand use of georesources as the next evolution step in SDIs. Additionally, the presented concept is successfully validated via a proof-of-concept implementation for a secured Web Processing Service. However, the approach is designed to be extensible in order to combine different types of licenses, it is nevertheless out of scope for this paper to discuss specific price model. In general, the presented concept can be seen as an important step forward towards commercial applications in SDIs: Transition from the classical licensing model of GIS packages (e.g. ESRI AGD, AGS) and data storages (e.g. on CD) to commercial on-demand Geospatial Web Services. The presented concepts allow automated systems to negotiate licenses and to establish trustful Web Service interaction in an ad-hoc way. Thereby SDI will be enriched with a commercial dimension for sustainable use. This means that for the future, we can foresee, that no longer full GIS package are sold, but rather specific functionalities and datasets dynamically licensed in an on-demand fashion. For the future issues of delegating rights in Geospatial Environments become evident, if whole models comprised of different secured and licensed Geospatial Web Services are regarded. In addition, the introduced concept is also valid for the emerging trend of Software as a Service (SaaS) (Turner, Budgen, & Brereton, 2003) realized by Cloud Computing models (National Institute of Standards and Technology (NIST), 2009). In this context, GIS functions can be delivered in the SaaS way in an on demand fashion with a strong commercial perspective. This leads exactly to the definition of Cloud Computing as given by (National Institute of Standards and Technology (NIST), 2009). Therefore, the presented concepts can be seen as a foundation for commercial and sustainable use of Geospatial Web Services in the future and potentially cloud enabled SDIs.

REFERENCES

W3C. (2003). *Web services federation language (WS-federation)*.

W3C. (2004). *Web services addressing (WS-addressing)*.

W3C. (2006a). *Web service policy*.

W3C. (2006b). *Web services policy attachment (WS-Policy Attachment)*. W3C member submission.

Adleman, L., Rivest, R. L., & Shamir, A. (1978). A method for obtaining digital signature and public-key cryptosystems. *Communications of the ACM, 21*(2), 120–126. doi:10.1145/359340.359342

Bell, D., & Lapadula, J. (1973). *Secure computer systems: A mathematical model (Microfiche ed.)*.

Bishop, M. (2005). *Introduction to computer security*. Boston: Addison-Wesley.

Critchell-Ward, A., & Landsborough-McDonald, K. (2007). Data protection law in the European Union and the United Kingdom. In D. Campbell, & A. Alibekova (Eds.), *The comparative law yearbook of international business* (pp. 515-578). Alphen uan den Rhin: Kluwer Law International.

Daemen, J., & Rijmen, V. (2002). *The design of rijndael: AES - the advanced encryption standard with 17 tables*. Berlin: Springer.

Dimitrakos, T. (2003). A service-oriented trust management framework. In R. Falcone, S. Barber, L. Korba & M. Singh (Eds.), *Trust, Reputation, and Security: Theories and Practice*, (53-72). Bologne, Italy: AAMAS Selected papers.

Douglas, D. H., & Peuckcr, T. K. (1973). Algorithms for the reduction of the number of points required to represent a digitized line or its caricature. *Cartographica: The International Journal for Geographic Information and Geovisualization, 10*(2), 112–122. doi:10.3138/FM57-6770-U75U-7727

Eastlake, D., Reagle, J., Solo, D., Bartel, M., Boyer, J., Fox, B., et al. (2002). *XML-signature syntax and processing*. W3C Recommendation.

EU. (2007). Directive 2007/2/EC of the European parliament and of the council of 14 March, 2007 establishing an infrastructure for spatial information in the European community (INSPIRE). *Official Journal of the European Union*.

Ferraiolo, D. F. (2007). *Role-based access control* (2nd ed.). London: Artech House.

Gollmann, D. (1999). *Computer security*. New York: Wiley.

Grandison, T., & Sloman, M. (2000). A survey of trust in internet applications. *IEEE Communications Surveys and Tutorials, 3*(4), 2–16. doi:10.1109/COMST.2000.5340804

Groot, R., & McLaughlin, J. (2000). *Geospatial data infrastructure: Concepts, cases, and good practice*. Oxford: Oxford University Press.

Hafner, M., & Breu, R. (2009). *Security engineering for service-oriented architectures*. Berlin: Springer.

Harrison, M. A., Ruzzo, W. L., & Ullman, J. D. (1976). Protection in operating systems. *Communications of the ACM, 19*(8), 461–471. doi:10.1145/360303.360333

IETF (2000). *RFC 2828- internet security glossary*.

IETF (2007). *Security preconditions for session description protocol (SDP) media streams*. (RFC 5027).

Imamura, T., Dillaway, B., & Simon, E. (2002). *XML encryption syntax and processing*. W3C Recommendation.

ISO(1996). Information technology-open systems interconnection-security frameworks in open systems: access control framework.

ISO (2004). *MPEG-21 rights expression language (REL)*, ISO/IEC JTC - 21000-5.

ISO 7498-1. (1994). *Information technology–open systems interconnection–basic reference model*.

ITU-T. (2005)... *ITU-T RECOMMENDATION, X*, 509.

Jones, S., & Morris, P. (1999). *TRUST-EC: Requirements for trust and confidence in e-commerce. Technical Report EUR 18749 EN*. European Commission Joint Research Centre.

Kanneganti, R., & Chodavarapu, P. (2008). *SOA security*. Greenwich, CT: Manning.

National Institute of Standards and Technology (NIST). (2009). *Cloud computing*. Retrieved November 27, 2009, from http://csrc.nist.gov/groups/SNS/cloud-computing/cloud-def-v15.doc

Neuman, B., & Ts'o, T. (1994). Kerberos: An authentication service for computer networks. *IEEE Communications Magazine, 32*(9), 33–38. doi:10.1109/35.312841

O'Neill, M. (2003). *Web services security*. McGraw-Hill Osborne Media.

OASIS (2002a). UDDI version 3.0.

OASIS. (2002b). *Web services security policy language*. WS-SecurityPolicy.

OASIS (2005a). *eXtensible access control markup language 2.0.*

OASIS(2005b). Profiles for the OASIS security assertion markup language (SAML) V2.0.

OASIS (2005c). *Web services trust standard (WS-trust).*

OASIS(2007). Security Assertion Markup Language(v2. 0) technical overview.

OGC (2002). *Web map service implementation specification.*

OGC (2003). *OpenGIS reference model.*

OGC(2006a) Geospatial Digital Rights Mange ment Reference Model (GeoDRM RM).

OGC(2006b). OpenGIS Web Service common implementation specification (OWS-common).

OGC(2007). OpenGIS catalog service implementation specification.

OGC (2008). *License broker engineering report.*

Rosenblatt, W. (2002). *Digital rights management business and technology.* New York: M & T Books.

Sandhu, R. S., & Samarati, P. (1994). Access control: Principle and practice. *IEEE Communications Magazine, 32*(9), 40–48. doi:10.1109/35.312842

Schmeh, K. (2009). *Kryptografie (4th ed.).* Heidelberg: dpunkt-Verl.

Schneier, B. (1999). *The twofish encryption algorithm: A 128-bit block cipher.* New York: Wiley.

Turner, M., Budgen, D., & Brereton, P. (2003). Turning software into a service. *Computer, 36*(10), 38–44. doi:10.1109/MC.2003.1236470

Wang, X., Lao, G., DeMartini, T., Reddy, H., Nguyen, M., & Valenzuela, E. (2002). XrML-- eXtensible rights markup language. *Proceedings of the 2002 ACM Workshop on XML Security.* (pp. 71-79).

Weerawarana, S. (2006). *Web services platform architecture: SOAP, WSDL, WS-policy, WS-addressing, WS-BPEL, WS-reliable messaging and more* (4th ed.). Upper Saddle River, NJ: Prentice Hall/PTR.

Yahalom, R., Klein, B., & Beth, T. (1993). Trust relationships in secure systems-a distributed authentication perspective. *Proceedings from 1993 OEEE Computer Society Symposium on Research in Security and Privacy.* (pp. 150-164).

ENDNOTE

[1] see http://www.opengeospatial.org/ogcUrn-Policy

Section 3
Registry and Discovery

Chapter 5
OOSTethys/Oceans IE Service Registry Based on Catalog Service for Web

Manil Maskey
The University of Alabama in Huntsville, USA

Helen Conover
The University of Alabama in Huntsville, USA

Ken Keiser
The University of Alabama in Huntsville, USA

Luis Bermudez
Southeastern Universities Research Association, USA

Sara Graves
The University of Alabama in Huntsville, USA

ABSTRACT

Service registries can play a big role in helping developers, collaborators and agencies find deployed resources without difficulty. A service registry is especially useful if it follows a well-known, predefined specification that allows for automatic machine interactions and interoperability, such as the Open Geospatial Consortium (OGC) specification for Catalog Services for the Web (CSW). This chapter discusses a CSW-compliant registry developed as part of an OGC-sponsored interoperability experiment involving the ocean sciences community. The development approach for selecting, adapting and enhancing an open source implementation of the CSW is described. Implementation goals for the registry included support for OGC Sensor Observation Services (SOS) and additional functionality to minimize requirements on service providers and maximize the robustness of the registry. The registry's role in the OGC Ocean Science Interoperability Experiment is also discussed.

DOI: 10.4018/978-1-60960-192-8.ch005

INTRODUCTION

Geo-scientists today have access to unprecedented volumes of data collected by the many in-situ and remote sensing environmental sensors currently deployed. But in order to make use of the vast amounts of data available, scientists must address issues related to multiple data formats, discovery and access methods in use. Solutions across these issues, such as data format interchange and interoperable discovery and access services, would allow scientists to focus on science tasks rather than data technology. Data services supporting common standards specifications, such as community-accepted XML definitions, can provide the required information in a form understandable by machines, thus promoting data interoperability and inter-use. Web service specifications have provided new levels of interoperability, allowing users and applications to more easily discover and bind to available services. While interoperability is one of the main purposes behind the standardization of web services, in practice, it is sometimes difficult to obtain due to loose conformance to, or interpretation of, these specifications in actual implementations.

Standards development is a slow and difficult process that requires collaboration, iteration and consensus within the target community. Often the result can be large, complex specifications that attempt to satisfy everyone. Although the development of standards and specifications generally involves rigorous revision and approval processes, an accurate assessment of a standard's usefulness cannot be made until diverse teams of developers implement the standard in real systems. Standards often suffer from ambiguities and scalability issues. There are, however, tangible benefits to developing and using a standard, that are realized when interchangeable tools are developed that researchers can use and plug into their workflow as needed.

Hence, it is important that experienced developers identify such ambiguities as well as test the reliability and scalability of new or proposed standards in their areas of expertise. The Open Geospatial Consortium (OGC) conducts interoperability experiments to address the issue of interoperability for newly approved geospatial specifications (Percivall, 2009). OGC is an international organization consisting of various institutes and agencies with a common goal of developing standards for geospatial services and products. Thus, OGC is an ideal coordinator of the type of interoperability experiments needed. One such initiative is the Ocean Science Interoperability Experiment (Oceans IE http://www.opengeospatial.org/projects/initiatives/oceansie), which engages the marine science community to advance interoperability using OGC standards for data exchange. As part of Phase I of this experiment, the oceans community investigated the use of OGC Web Feature Services (WFS) and Sensor Observation Services (SOS), utilizing the reference implementations of the services produced by a related community activity, called OOSTethys. OOSTethys is a collaboration among software developers and marine scientists who develop open source tools in multiple languages, for use in the evolving Integrated Ocean Observing System (IOOS). Reference implementations and developer guides, such as the OOSTethys cookbooks for SOS standards (http://www.oostethys.org/best-practices), can be very helpful by providing implementation examples, usage tips and community specification profiles, for use by developers and system integrators – as was demonstrated in the Oceans IE project.

As an integral part of the Ocean IE, the authors developed a service registry compliant with the Catalog Service for Web (CSW) OGC standard for registries of data and services. The Oceans IE registry was created to index the growing number of data services (both SOS and WFS) that became difficult to track within the experiment. This registry supports easy registration of SOS and WFS, as well as discovery of the services using the CSW specifications. While CSW was a natural choice for an OGC service registry, it has other advantages as well, described in the CSW subsection later in the chapter.

This chapter describes the concepts and capabilities of an OGC service registry based on the CSW standard that delivers the value of a service registry in a heterogeneous environment. First, we discuss a variety of service metadata specifications and existing service registries. The next section describes the OGC CSW in some detail. Then we describe Oceans IE and its CSW service registry implementation, followed by a consideration of future research directions.

BACKGROUND: SERVICE-ORIENTED ARCHITECTURE AND OGC WEB SERVICES

Service Oriented Architecture (SOA) approaches offer increased interoperability, software reuse and reduced maintenance, as compared to more traditional software architectures. SOAs can transparently tie together services that provide different functions, are often distributed, and that communicate via standards. An SOA includes *producers* that offer specific functionality as a service and *consumers*, who make use of the services in the SOA framework. These architectures are typically built around web services, loosely coupled and often distributed services that are critical to creating workflows and problem solutions. Use of Extensible Markup Language (XML) has been key to attaining this goal. XML with a predefined schema (specification) has become the common way of storing and passing service information, especially because XML is able to provide precise machine-readable information about web services. Being machine-readable allows better automation, which eventually helps in development of supporting tools.

Geoscience tools can also take advantage of the SOA approach to implement flexible and easily adaptable workflows and processes. In such a scenario, consumers may be geospatial visualization, environmental data analysis or other tools that interface with the SOA framework using a standard protocol (usually HTTP) and messages that follow a certain specification. Embracing SOA for geoscience applications can enrich an organization's service offerings and provide value in overall efficiency, accuracy, and accessibility to organizational marketability. A geoscience SOA is supported by the efforts of geospatial professionals and environmental data scientists who use various industry proven software to configure, serve, and maintain science data and models. A complete geoscience SOA includes servers that provide web-accessible services along with supporting tools. OGC advocates use of its suite of web services along with supporting tools for almost all types of geospatial applications.

OGC Sensor Data Access Services

The Oceans Interoperability Experiment demonstrated the SOA approach using OGC data services. A primary focus of Oceans IE was the OGC Sensor Observation Service (SOS), a service protocol that provides a standard interface for requesting, filtering and retrieving sensor system information and observations. SOSs allow the user or calling program to select any number of the observation variables available from the data source, and to subset the data by spatial and temporal range, thereby significantly reducing data volume and transfer time. Sensor data is converted from its native format to the OGC Observations & Measurements encoding specification, and may be embedded directly into the SOS response or delivered as either ASCII or binary attachments, in order to foster data/application interoperability and reuse of multiple sensor data products. The mandatory operations for SOS are GetCapabilities, GetObservations, and DescribeSensor. Each of these operations is briefly described below.

- **GetCapabilities:** This operation returns the metadata about the SOS including descriptions of offered observations and links to description of the sensors being used.
- **GetObservation:** This operation returns observation data from sensors for the specified temporal and spatial range. GetObservation uses the *Observations & Measurements (O&M)* schema in its response. O&M is an OGC standard that provides models and XML specifications for encoding sensor observations and measurements. Using O&M, the SOS can define the data fields, data types, and structural organization in the data records. This allows for machine-readable responses for virtually any type of observation.
- **DescribeSensor:** This operation returns about a description of the sensor itself. The response is encoded in *Sensor Model Language (SensorML)*, an OGC standard that provides models and XML specifications for describing sensors and processes associated with measurements.

Used in conjunction with other OGC specifications such as CSW, the SOS provides a broad range of interoperable capability for discovering, binding to and interrogating individual sensors, sensor platforms, or network of sensors in real-time, archived or simulated environments.

Survey of Web Service Metadata Specifications

While web services and SOA are usually thought to be synonymous from a technical perspective, they are not. Web services are only one of the important aspects of SOA. Another equally pertinent component of SOA is the service registry. A *service registry* handles the management of service descriptions and serves as a record keeper of information on how to interface with the services. Usually the service registry uses ex-

tensive metadata to make services searchable and discoverable. Standards-based service registries expose service metadata for discovery by users or automated tools, fostering interoperability and promoting service reuse. Additional information about the functional capabilities and operational metadata can also be made searchable. Science data and analysis services have often been registered in ad hoc registries that are populated and maintained by the organizations that developed the services, and often contain only those services developed by the organization. Obviously, custom tools and interfaces would need to be developed to communicate with these proprietary registries. Thus, compatibility and interoperability are big issues and human interactions are almost certainly needed.

A solution is the use of standardized protocols for registering and discovering information about the services. The key questions when selecting a service registry specification should be what are the functional requirements and whether the registry is easy to use. By understanding which functions are needed to support an SOA approach, an appropriate registry solution can be selected. A simple service registry lifecycle is shown in Figure 1. For a viable registry, all three operations – publish, find, and invoke – follow defined specifications. Service providers *publish* their services into the service registry. Service consumers *find* services using search filter mechanisms. Once the service is located, the service consumers can *invoke* the service at the service provider using the protocols and descriptions defined in the service registry.

OGC web services serve geospatial content and capabilities. OGC has defined standard protocols for these services, including the required GetCapabilities operation for accessing service metadata. Hence, these services should be easily discovered and published using standard interfaces. Before we discuss CSW, we describe a few alternate approaches that have been used to tackle the service registry problem. We also dis-

Figure 1. Simple standard based service registry lifecycle

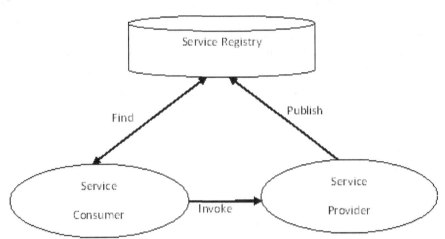

cuss the GEOSS interoperability registry that has the ability to interconnect the services using various service registries.

Universal Description, Discovery, and Integration (UDDI)

Universal Description, Discovery, and Integration (UDDI) is a specification for online directories to be used by both service providers and service consumers (OASIS, 2010). The UDDI specification complies with the Web Services Interoperability Organization (WS-I) standards of technical interoperability as a communication protocol for exchanging data. Service providers register their web services in a UDDI directory and service consumers search the service descriptions in this directory that will lead to the services that they are looking for. The drawback of UDDI is the use of high-level descriptions. The descriptions that are supported are very basic and generally are not machine-readable. Very few organizations are using the UDDI for service registry as a result. Even business registries provided by IBM and Microsoft have discontinued the use of UDDI (Microsoft, 2006).

Web Service Description Language (WSDL)

Web Service Description Language (WSDL) is an XML specification that describes a web service interface (W3C, 2001). WSDL is designed as an open content model so that it is extensible and flexible to be used with various web service bindings. Hence, the web service's interaction within an SOA framework is easily machine-readable. Without such standard description, one must rely on ad hoc documentation to communicate with the interfaces for SOA components. WSDLs have become a widely accepted standard since several industry-accepted WSDL tools have simplified the creation and usage of this standard. Lately, WSDLs have been critical to design and execution of scientific workflows.

ISO 19119

The International Organization for Standardization (ISO) sponsors geospatial community standards activities under Technical Committee 211 Geographic Information / Geoinformatics (ISO/TC 211). While much of the work of this committee deals with metadata for geographic data and information, ISO 19119 is a service standard developed with an intent to make geospatial resources available over a distributed environment (Percivall, 2002). A computational aspect of this standard is the ability to interlink data and services without prior knowledge about the data or service descriptions. ISO 19119 offers architectures exemplary of the different kinds of service chaining. Another feature is the description of a metadata model for service objects based on service instance, metadata and type. Models arc also provided for interoperability and service distribution.

Service Entry Resource Format (SERF)

National Aeronautics and Space Administration (NASA)'s Global Change Master Directory (GCMD) includes the Service Entry Resource Format (SERF), a specification intended to define information about geospatial data services relevant to the datasets cataloged in the GCMD. The SERF consists of both required and optional metadata fields and is intended to help users locate software tools and services for use with their data products, and to decide whether a particular service would be useful to them (Olsen and Stevens, 2008).

Survey of Web Service Registry Implementations

Several organizations have implemented service registries using one or more of these protocols. Some of these efforts are discussed here.

Global Change Master Directory (GCMD)

The primary purpose of National Aeronautics and Space Administration (NASA)'s Global Change Master Directory (GCMD) is to catalog the wealth of environmental datasets available from NASA and other data sources. In recent years, GCMD has also begun to catalog services relevant to its metadata holdings, using its SERF service metadata specification. Bai et al. (Bai, 2009), describe how service interoperability requirements are not fully met by well-known service registries like GCMD. GCMD is intended as a human search interface, allowing users to browse descriptions of services, often related to specific data products. GCMD allows consumers to search and access to the geospatial services using keywords that are too general to be referenced in a service instance level, preventing machine level interoperability.

Earth Observing System Clearinghouse (ECHO)

NASA's Earth Observing System Clearinghouse (ECHO) also supports the registration of Earth science data and related services, for use as an information resource by the science community. The ECHO service registry is primarily intended to provide reference to services that enhance the usability of the Earth science data sets and the integration of these data and services into service oriented architectures throughout the Earth science community. ECHO's registry is based on web services standards, as defined by W3C (Burnett, 2007), to include WSDL and UDDI. Registration of services with ECHO is dependent on multiple registration steps and multiple WSDL descriptions for each service. The registration process requires users to be formally registered as not only ECHO users, but also as ECHO service providers. Both steps involve interactions with ECHO administrators. The formal ECHO registry requires this level of accountability for registration submissions, but can be overly complex and intimidating for service providers seeking to share their functionality (Bai, 2007a). Though the barrier to entry is high, ultimately the ECHO support for web service standards should be instrumental in enabling service orchestration, the chaining of services together for programmatic solutions.

Geospatial One Stop (GOS)

The federal government mandated the management, interoperability and public access of all federally funded spatial datasets through a broad e-government initiative (OMB Circular A-16). For end-users, GOS provides a human-searchable catalog of metadata providing information about the type and location of datasets. The GOS registry is comprised of a network of interoperable catalogs and services that provide an interactive search capability across all registered resources. All spatial data collected by federal agencies (or their agents) are expected to be available through this registry. GOS uses the National Spatial Data Infrastructure (NSDI) as the underlying registry capability, following the Federal Geographic Data Committee (FGDC) metadata standards. Internally, GOS maintains a UDDI registry to track a list of data producers or sources. Metadata is subsequently harvested for specific data across the registered searchable registry services. To register a data source with GOS, the data producer must provide access to a registry that is compliant with GOS supported searches. GOS currently supports harvesting services for Z39.50, OGC CSW, WAF (web accessible folders), and OAI-PMH (Open Archive Initiative Protocol for Metadata Harvesting). The GOS portal provides a map viewer that can subsequently utilize a number of data access services to provide data displays to users, to include OGC WMS, WFS, and ArcIMS. Data producers may register their data sources through web-based forms at the GOS website (http://geodata.gov).

GEOSS

Global Earth Observation System of Systems (GEOSS; IEEE GEOSS, 2009) is an international infrastructure to connect users, producers and integrators of environmental information. One of the GEOSS goals is to make environmental information publicly available to a broad set of users. The core components of GEOSS are the "Components Registry" and the "Standards and Interoperability Registry". The Components Registry's main purpose is to provide a centralized place to register and access GEOSS components (e.g., web services, software, models). The Standards and Interoperability Registry's main purpose is to provide a centralized place to register and access standards, protocols and "special agreements". A special agreement could be a standard community profile or a non standard agreement among communities. As a "system of systems," GEOSS does not support a single registry protocol; rather multiple data and service registries will exist in the GEOSS framework, and will communicate each other via standardized protocols and interfaces.

THE OGC CSW STANDARD

Unlike UDDI and other high-level service registries, domain specific catalogs generally contain more detailed information. Where these catalogs are based on standards, this allows for supporting solutions based on automatic discovery of the services registered in the catalog. OGC has developed a standards-based registry specification for data and services, namely Catalog Service for Web (CSW). A CSW-compliant catalog allows stateless web/HTTP access with standard XML data being exchanged. The CSW specification allows for all properties in the metadata to be searchable, making service and data associations clearly traversable. CSW supports the ability to publish and search collections of descriptive information (metadata) about geospatial data, services and related resources (OGC, 2009). Providers of resources use catalogs to register metadata that conform to the information model that CSW supports. The information model includes detailed descriptions of data and services that are provided. Client applications can then efficiently search for geospatial data and services (OGC, 2009). CSW was recommended for implementation specification status in November 2005.

OGC specifies the interfaces, bindings, and a framework for defining *application profiles* required to publish and access a CSW that provides metadata for geospatial data, services, and related resource information. Metadata are represented as generalized properties that can be queried and returned through catalog services for resource evaluation and in many cases, invocation or retrieval of the referenced resource. The CSW standard and relevant application profiles are described in more detail in the next section.

CSW Information Structure and Semantics

OGC specifications allow for flexibility in the model for information exchange. In case of CSW, application profiles are allowed to be specific about what information content is to be communicated through the service. This information follows a particular syntax from the application profile. Thus an application profile should address the following items:

a) Identify information resource types that can be requested. In the case of a catalog service, the information resources being described by the metadata may include geographic data, imagery, services, controlled vocabularies, or schemas among a wide variety of possible types. This sub clause allows the community to specify or generalize the resource types being described in the metadata for their scope of application.

b) Identify a public reference for the information being returned by the service (e.g., ISO 19115:2003 "Geographic Information - Metadata"). Include any semantic resources such as data content model, dictionary, feature type catalog, code lists, authorities, taxonomies, etc.

c) Identify named groups of properties (element sets) that may be requested of the service (e.g. "brief," "summary," or "full") and the

valid format (syntax) for each element set. Identify valid schema(s) with respect to a given format to assist in the validation of response messages.

A service metadata schema must be defined for the purpose of interchange of information within an information community. This schema should provide a common vocabulary that supports search, retrieval, display, and association between the description and the object being described. Currently, the XML exchanges for CSW are based on two draft application profiles: ebRIM Registry Information Model Profile and the 19115/19119 Profile developed by ISO.

ISO 19119

The Catalog Application Profile (Senkler, 2004) definition, based on the CSW specification, takes advantage of both 19115 and 19119 for geospatial data and services, respectively. As ISO 19119 includes extensions that allow for the varying data/service binding described above, the profile uses the 19115 description with additional objects designed to include the necessary extensions. For example, 19119 includes a definition of CSW_CoupledResource, a class that regulates the interoperation of services and datasets. The profile excerpt shown in Figure 2 includes the object SV_ServiceIdentification that would suffice for the metadata functionality of 19115 but does not satisfy the service requirements of 19119.

The profile described uses an HTTP binding, but is also capable of using SOAP with XML binding. ISO 19119:2005 identifies and defines the architecture patterns for service interfaces used for geographic information, defines its relationship to the Open Systems Environment model, and presents a geographic services taxonomy and a list of example geographic services placed in the services taxonomy. It also prescribes how to create a platform-neutral service specification, how to derive conformant platform-specific

Figure 2. ISO 19119 profile excerpt

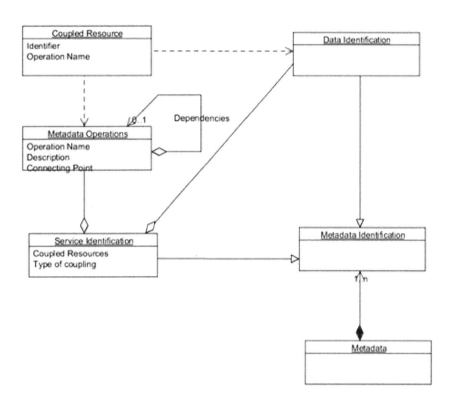

service specifications, and provides guidelines for the selection and specification of geographic services from both platform-neutral and platform-specific perspectives.

ebRIM

The ebXML Registry Information Model (ebRIM) (Nogueras-Iso, 2005; Chen 2009) has also been used as a profile for OGC CSW. The Model provides a format for ordering both the content and their connections (Martell, 2009) within the catalog, as shown below in Figure 3.

Extension packages can be used as needed to support application-specific functionality. Also, specific components, such as the RegistryObject, can be substituted where possible by similar elements. The slots can also be used if no conflicts are present with either extension packages or higher-level objects.

George Mason University's Center for Spatial Information Science and Systems (CSISS) (Bai, 2007b) uses an ebRIM-style catalog service designed to provide access to their Landsat images through a combination of geospatial data and geospatial services. The data and services are associated together, letting users tailor the data via the service interface. This specification is based on an OGC-compliant model, and thus is restricted to the same functions as the CSW, described below.

CSW Operations

The operations supported by CSW can be divided into three classes: *service operations* which are operations a client may use to question the service to determine its capabilities; *discovery operations* which a client may use to determine the information model of the catalog and to query catalog

Figure 3. ebXML registry information model

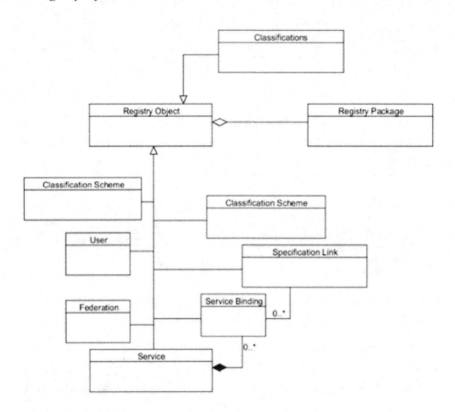

records; and *management operations* which are used to create or change records in the catalog.

Service Class Operation

GetCapabilities: Generate Capabilities document

Discovery Class Operations

DescribeRecord: Generate Record Schema

GetDomain: Determine value domain and generate response document

GetRecordById: Query repository for record with specified id and generate response

GetRecords: Execute query and generate response document containing result records

Management Class Operations

Transaction: Execute transaction and generate response document

Harvest: Generate response document that acknowledges receipt of request and execute request asynchronously.

In general, metadata consumers will invoke GetCapabilities, DescribeRecords, GetDomain, GetRecords, and GetRecordById operations whereas metadata producers will invoke Transaction and Harvest operations.

GetCapabilities Operation

Like all other OGC services, the CSW specification mandates the GetCapabilties operation. This operation allows clients to retrieve service metadata from a server. CSW servers allow the HTTP request for GetCapabilities to contain parameter and value pairs for Request, Service, Sections, AcceptVersions and AcceptFormats. The value of the Service parameter should be "CSW". The response to a GetCapabilities request is an XML document containing service metadata about the server. The document includes sections on ServiceIdentification, ServiceProvider, OperationsMetadata, and Filter_Capabilities. Of these sections, OperationsMetadata is the most important, as it lists all the operations supported by the CSW service.

DescribeRecord Operation

DescribeRecord is a mandatory operation that allows a client to discover elements of the information model supported by the catalog service. This method requires mandatory keyword-value pairs for parameters Request, Service, and Version. Other supported parameters are Namespace, TypeName, outputFormat, and schemaLanguage. The response for the DescribeRecord request contains SchemaComponent elements that describe each requested schema language.

GetDomain Operation

The GetDomain operation is optional. This operation returns a range of values for a metadata record element or request parameter.

GetRecords Operation

GetRecords is a mandatory operation that is used to search for records in the catalog. It uses the Query element to filter and identify the record. GetRecords also uses the outputSchema parameter to indicate which schema shall be used to generate the response to the GetRecords operation.

GetRecordById Operation

GetRecordById is a mandatory operation that retrieves a specified record from the catalog based on the provided identifier. This operation is generally used after executing another operation to get back the identifier for the record.

Transaction Operation

Transaction is an optional operation that provides mechanisms to create, modify, and delete catalog records. In particular, the Insert action allows one or more records to be inserted into the catalog. The Update action uses constraint elements to find the records to be updated. Similarly, the Delete action allows records to be deleted from the catalog in conjunction with the constraint element.

Harvest Operation

Harvest is an optional operation that references data to be inserted or updated in the catalog. The catalog itself will fetch the data and process into the catalog.

CSW Use Scenarios

In the context of SOA, Figure 4 illustrates an example sequence of operations performed by an SOS consumer. In this figure, the SOS consumer discovers two instances of SOSs using the GetRecords operation provided by CSW service catalog. Then, the consumer requests SOS capabilities documents for each service, using URLs from the CSW GetRecords response. The consumer can then make a choice of service by inspecting the observation offerings from both SOSs, and invoke the appropriate GetObservation from the selected SOS is invoked.

Again in the context of SOA, Figure 5 illustrates an example sequence of operations performed by two SOS providers (producers). The first producer discovers the second SOS from the CSW catalog. Whenever new sensors are discovered, the producers can register these sensors with their SOS. They will subsequently publish sensor observations that they are able to provide.

Figure 4. SOS consumer sequence diagram

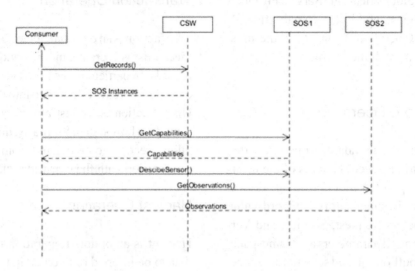

Figure 5. SOS sensor data publisher sequence diagram

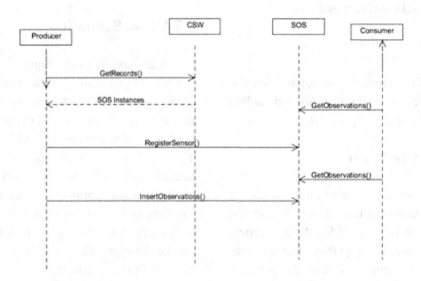

THE OGC OCEANS INTEROPERABILITY EXPERIMENT

Overview of Oceans IE

OOSTethys, the loose collaboration of software developers and marine scientists who worked with OGC to define and implement Oceans IE, was itself the product of several earlier collaborations: OpenIOOS, the SURA Coastal Ocean Observ- ing and Prediction (SCOOP) program, and the NSF-sponsored Marine Metadata Interoperability project. OpenIOOS has been demonstrating the concept that "standards enable innovation" for several years, thanks to data and service contri- butions from Ocean Observing Systems (OOSs) around the country. OpenIOOS.org, which is a proof of concept portal interface for the distributed participants, demonstrates a Service-Oriented Ar- chitecture (SOA) with heavy emphasis on Open

Geospatial Consortium (OGC) web-service specifications. With support from the NOAA Coastal Services Center and the Office of Naval Research, the Southeastern Universities Research Association (SURA) integrated OpenIOOS.org into the SCOOP program (http://scoop.sura.org). Through SCOOP and other programs, SURA has supported the vision of enabling a distributed laboratory for research and applications with broad participation from research institutions working in partnership with federal agencies and the private sector. The Marine Metadata Interoperability project, started in September 2004, now comprises more than 300 members, with a web site consisting of thousands of pages including guides and references about marine metadata issues (http://marinemetadata. org). One of the activities of MMI is an interoperability demonstration using an SOA, common use content standards, and semantic mediation via ontologies.

In 2005 MMI, OpenIOOS and SCOOP participants started working together on a single, combined interoperability test bed activity of a distributed, service-oriented architecture to share real time data. The combined team, which adopted the name OOSTethys, set up an initial set of metadata requirements such as geo-spatial location and platform type, and agreed on an interface to serve as a wrapper for each data system. OOSTethys members decided that working with standards organizations to select, exercise and advance appropriate standards was the logical path to move forward toward an integrated ocean observing system. With the OGC, OOSTethys members started the OGC Ocean Science Interoperability Experiment in 2007.

Through Oceans IE, a portion of the Ocean Observing community has reached consensus on its understanding of various OGC specifications, solidified demonstrations for Ocean Science application areas, hardened software implementations, and produced a candidate "OGC Best Practices" document that can be used to inform the broader ocean science community. To achieve these goals,

the Oceans IE engaged the OGC membership to assure that any community requirements coming from the Oceans group properly leveraged the OGC specifications. Change requests on the OGC specifications were provided to the OGC Technical Committee to influence the underlying specifications.

The Oceans IE Phase I, which ended in May 2008, investigated and compared the use of OGC Web Feature Services (WFS) and Sensor Observation Services (SOS) for representing and exchanging point data records from fixed in-situ marine platforms. This phase of Oceans IE produced an engineering best practices report and reference implementations for SOS. Phase I included a registry to record all the SOS that were developed. This ad hoc registry was a quick and temporary solution to the problem of cataloging and discovering the SOSs. Tools and interfaces that relied on the registry for SOS information had to use custom Representational State Transfer (REST) style services to communicate with the registry. We encountered a growing need for a standards-based service registry soon after completion of this initial service registry, as more participants began utilizing the registry from different applications. Research on available registry standards thus began during Phase I.

The Oceans IE Phase II ran from March 2009 to December 2009. The following topics were advanced: Automated instrument metadata/software installation via the PUCK protocol (MBARI, 2009), observation offerings of complex systems (e.g., observations systems containing other systems) such as collection of stations, linking data from SOS to out-of-band offerings, Semantic Registry and Services, CSW Registry, and IEEE-1451/OGC-SWE harmonization. During Phase II, CSW was investigated in depth along with other catalog standards. After CSW was selected, various open source reference implementations of the specification were also investigated. The *deegree* project was chosen as the base CSW implementation, and the authors developed various components to support additional Oceans IE needs and make the implementation more robust.

CSW Reference Implementations

Multiple organizations have implemented registries based on CSW. The Oceans IE community evaluated three such implementations, described below.

GeoNetwork

GeoNetwork is an open-source software project developed to provide the geospatial community a standards-based suite of applications and services (GeoNetwork, 2009). Geospatial standards developed by OGC and ISO are well supported by GeoNetwork. One of the functions offered is the cataloging of data and services. Although powerful in many aspects, the current development version of GeoNetwork at the time of evaluation did not support the latest version of the CSW specification. A number of ambiguities in the 2.0.1 specification have been clarified in 2.0.2 and should be reflected in the GeoNetwork implementation of CSW. In addition, at the time of our evaluation, the Transaction and Harvest operations were not supported by GeoNetwork implementation of CSW. These operations were critical to our experiment.

GI-cat

GI-cat is open source software developed by Earth and Space Science Informatics – Laboratory (ESSI-Lab) that provides implementations of the OGC CSW specification, along with a suite of other OGC standards (Nativi, 2007). GI-cat uses the ISO application profile information models for core operations and exposes standard query interfaces implemented by the profiler components. The software in developed using the Java Standard Edition that is capable of running under Apache Tomcat server. Although GI-cat is a

practical implementation of CSW, the installation procedures and other compatibility issues were deemed to be impractical for use in Oceans IE.

deegree

The deegree project is a Java implementation of an extensive suite of OGC service specifications. It also encompasses test clients for the suite of services. Deegree software is freely available as open-source software protected by the GNU Lesser General Public License (GNU LGPL) and is accessible at http://www.deegree.org/.

The deegree CSW implementation is designed in such a way that it is able to serve different metadata formats in parallel even with a single underlying relational database. This is possible because the deegree CSW implementation uses Extensible Stylesheet Language (XSL) (W3Schools, 2010) processing to transform requests as well as responses into the desired format. The deegree CSW does not contain a data access module of its own, rather it uses an OGC Web Feature Service (WFS), also implemented by deegree as a data source. It is possible to adjust the deegree CSW to almost any existing metadata profile without the need for replication. Because of its flexibility with respect to configuration and output formats, the deegree implementation was ideal for our purpose. It merely required modifying XML configuration files before installation.

The pros and cons of each of these CSW implementation are summarized in Table 1.

THE OCEANS IE CSW-COMPLIANT SERVICE REGISTRY

A primary goal of the Oceans Interoperability Experiment and the complementary OOSTethys project, is to dramatically reduce the time it takes to install, adopt and update standards-compliant web services, focusing on the OGC Sensor Observation Service (SOS). Open source Java,

Table 1. Summary of features of various CSW implementations

Features	Geonetwork	GI-cat	deegree
Open source	X	X	X
Latest version of CSW		X	X
Supports all CSW operations		X	X
Supports many OGC and ISO standards	X		
Can support multiple application profiles			X
Can serve multiple metadata formats in parallel			X
Easy installation and configuration			X
No compatibility issues			X

PERL, Python, PHP and ASP toolkits serving ocean observations from NetCDF-formatted files, THREDDS, various relational databases and even CSV (comma-separated value) text files have been developed. This matches the diverse data needs and software expertise of the Integrated Ocean Observing System community. In many cases data providers with limited software experience are able to install an SOS in mere minutes and configure it by editing a simple configuration file. This easy deployment has led to broad adoption of SOS by the marine science community. These successes were leveraged by developing an open source service registry and catalog based on the OGC's CSW which harvest metadata from the SOS GetCapabilities and DescribeSensor responses.

A real-time use of the CSW-compliant service registry is shown in Figure 6. Various SOSs deployed by the IOOS community can be discovered from the OOSTethys/Oceans IE registry. The observations from the registry are displayed in real-time at the website openioos.org. All of the source code developed for the experiment is available for the community to reuse at http://code. google.com/p/oostethys/. This architecture allows for reference implementations to be adapted and improved easily while keeping the overall usage as simple as possible.

The OOSTethys/Oceans IE SOS Service Registry was based on the deegree implementation of the CSW specification. This implementation allows communication using the ISO 19119 application profile. Other supporting components include the TEAM Engine Validator, a web-based user interface, a GetCapabilities metadata harvester, and SOS metadata to ISO metadata converter. Figure 7 illustrates the architecture of the entire system. Components of the system are described in the following subsections. This architecture is a specific case of SOA that we discussed earlier in the chapter. Service providers are responsible for storing and serving data collected from instruments and resulting derived products. In addition, they make their services available by simplified registration process exposed by CSW interface. End users and tools map to the service consumers in the SOA. The tools programmatically discover the services using the CSW interface. Once the services are discovered, the tools will invoke the services using the protocol described in the service metadata. OpenIOOS is an example of such tools used in OOSTethys/ Oceans IE.

Deegree CSW Registry Package

Deegree's CSW installation package is a web archive (WAR) file, which can be dropped easily into a web server. In our case, the Apache Tomcat web server suffices as a container to use for deployment of the deegree servlet module. It is also very convenient to use the bundled structured

Figure 6. OpenIOOS: real-time sos observations visualization

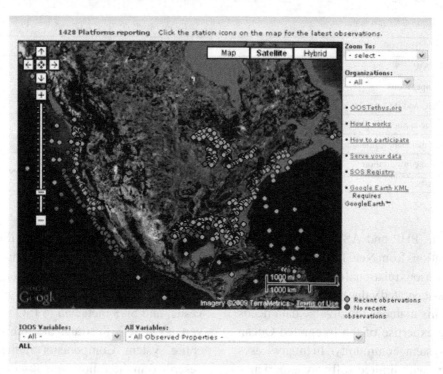

query language (SQL) scripts to create tables for the catalog. This implementation supports all of the operations defined for CSW and is compliant with the CSW 2.0.2 specifications. During Oceans IE, degree provided the solutions to any problems encountered via well supported online forums and user correspondence.

OGC and ISO geoinformatics standards played a vital role in development of deegree. In particular, deegree's CSW implementation supports the ISO 19119 standard, and is built on the deegree implementation of the OGC Web Feature Service (WFS) – see Figure 8. The WFS programming interface accepts WFS requests and replies with WFS responses for a particular data source. Therefore, the discovery and manager layers hide the WFS layer from the exposed API. These components transform incoming catalog requests into WFS requests and transform WFS responses into CSW responses.

TEAM Engine Validator

Compliance & Interoperability Testing & Evaluation (CITE) is an ongoing OGC initiative that develops tests for OGC standards, and makes those tests available for online access. An integral part of CITE is a test script interpreter, the Test, Evaluation, And Measurement (TEAM) Engine. It executes test scripts written in Compliance Test Language (CTL) to verify that a designated implementation complies with the specification.

Being an OGC member, we were able to obtain the source code for the TEAM Engine for use in the OOSTethys/Oceans IE Service Registry interface. The TEAM Engine test for SOS validation was adapted to integrate into the service registration process. The incorporation of most of the TEAM Engine open source code helped to create a complete and robust CSW registry. OOSTethys is able to distribute the TEAM Engine as a component of the Service Registry under the Mozilla 1.1 license.

Figure 7. OOSTethys/Oceans IE CSW registry system for SOS

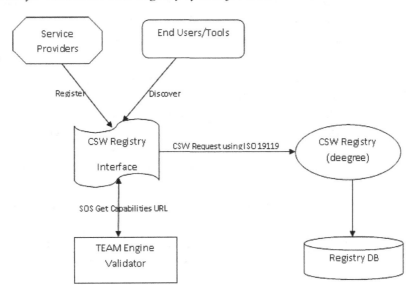

Figure 8. Dependency between deegree CSW and WFS

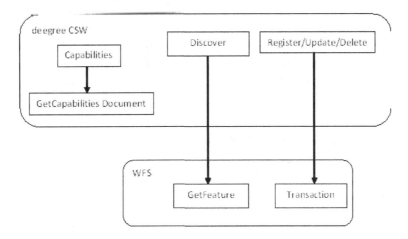

CSW Registry Web Interface

For Oceans IE, the authors developed a web-based user interface to the CSW registry for both producers and consumers of SOS. This user interface communicates with the CSW registry by generating the detailed XML request and response documents required by CSW operations, thus shielding users from these complex XML documents. The web interface for the OOSTethys/Oceans IE SOS Service Registry is available at: http://scoredev.

itsc.uah.edu/csw/. Two important operations that are offered through the web interface are service registration and service discovery.

Service Registration

All of the web service standards used for Oceans IE are developed and maintained by OGC. The CSW service registry leverages the fact that all OGC web services have commonalities in their design and interface, in particular the GetCapabilities operation. The response from a GetCapabilities request is an XML description of the service's information content and supported request parameters, and is therefore both machine- and human-readable. Since the XML-formatted response conforms to a predefined schema, clients can easily validate the response. GetCapabilities responses contain information on following sections:

- **ServiceIdentification**: Metadata about this specific server. The schema of this section is the same for all OGC web services.
- **ServiceProvider**: Metadata about the organization operating the server. The schema of this section is also the same for all OGC web services.
- **OperationsMetadata**: Metadata about the operations specified by this service and implemented by this server, including the URLs for operation requests. The basic contents and organization of this section is the same for all OGC web services, but individual services can add elements and/or change the use of optional elements.

Service providers merely need to provide a valid GetCapabilities URL to register their service in the registry. Automatic harvesting of service metadata is achieved by parsing the Get-Capabilities response from an SOS. The registry first validates the SOS using the TEAM Engine Validator. The provider is notified if the SOS is not in compliance with the OGC SOS specification. Once the SOS passes the TEAM Engine validation, the XSL transformation layer translates the SOS GetCapabilities service metadata to the ISO 19139 service metadata schema required by the deegree CSW registry package. For the service providers, all of these complex activities, such as the construction of valid XML insert request to register their services, are completely hidden. Service providers can enter an SOS GetCapabilities URL

and press the "Register" button for registration. Any error encountered during registration will be displayed to the registrant.

Service Discovery

The users of the registry can also bypass the creation of XML for discovery or transaction operations as the easy-to-use web interface builds the necessary XML from the specification of a few necessary query components by the user. Pressing "Get Record By Id" button in the web interface returns a CSW response for a GetRecordById request based on the provided identifier, currently "Service Title", and element set name. Pressing the "Get All Records" button returns ISO records for all the registered services. The underlying CSW web service can be accessed programmatically with a valid CSW request.

SOS Service Metadata to ISO 19119 Translator

Since the deegree registry interface accepts CSW requests that conform to the ISO 19119 profile, the SOS metadata harvested from the GetCapabilities response needs to be converted to an appropriate ISO record. The authors developed such a translator using an XSL transformation. This translator maps almost all available elements from the GetCapabilities response schema into the appropriate ISO 19119 schema. The translator is executed whenever providers register their service using the CSW interface. Figure 9 shows a portion of the XSL mapping from SOS service metadata to an ISO 19119 profile. In this subset of the XSL mapping, the ObservationOffering's id and description are translated into DataIdentification's title and identifier respectively. The CSW registry thus allows the services to be searched using these criteria.

Figure 9. Portion of XSLT mapping from SOS GetCapabilities to ISO 19119

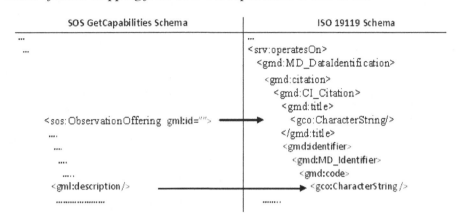

FUTURE RESEARCH DIRECTIONS

Since the evolution of web 3.0 technologies, the future of service registries also seems to moving towards the semantic-based service registry. Ocean community efforts related to semantic registries are available at http://oceanobservatories.org/spaces/display/CIDev/Metadata+Registry and http://oceanobservatories.org/spaces/display/CI-Dev/Harvester. The main difficulty with semantic registry is providing filtering by topics of large collections of metadata. If there is a thesaurus (terms with broader and narrower relations), it will be easier to navigate and discover the metadata records of interest. Furthermore, initial implementations of semantic-based service registries have suffered from performance issues. Much of the research is now focused on improving the performance of such registries. Currently, another research focus area is into ways to describe relationships between different web services so that such semantic relationships can be exploited in service discovery within the service registry.

CONCLUSION

As part of OGC Oceans Interoperability Experiment (Oceans IE), the authors developed a web service registry compliant with the OGC Catalog Service for Web (CSW) standard. The registry evolved with the need for a standards-based catalog to support a growing number of Sensor Observation Services (SOS). The resulting registry allows easy registration of SOSs via harvesting the service metadata from GetCapabilities responses, as well as easy discovery of these services using the CSW specifications. A standards-compliant registry for this endeavor was required to eliminate the need for discovering the services from ad-hoc registries. In addition, having a standard CSW registry opened up avenues for the development of automated tools. This open source registry uses Extensible Stylesheet Language (XSL) transformation to convert SOS metadata into the ISO metadata that is required by the CSW. Two plug-ins, the TEAM Engine Validator and CSW registry web interface, were also developed or enhanced and integrated to make the CSW registry more robust and easy to use. The authors believe that the availability of the OOSTethys/Oceans IE SOS CSW Registry will promote acceptance of SOS by the oceanographic community and facilitate service discovery and reuse. Furthermore, the OOSTethys/Oceans IE Registry is on schedule to be registered with GEOSS. This registration will allow creation of community registry that includes services from other organizations that are registered with GEOSS, and interconnected with OOSTethys/Oceans IE registry.

REFERENCES

W3C. (2001). *Web Services Description Language (WSDL 1.1)*. Retrieved from http://www.w3schools.com/xsl/

W3Schools. (2010). *XSLT Tutorial*. Retrieved from http://www.w3schools.com/xsl/

Bai, Y., Di, L., Chen, A., & Wei, Y. (2007b). Towards a geospatial catalogue federation service. *Photogrammetric Engineering and Remote Sensing, 73*, 699–708.

Bai, Y., Di, L., & Keiser, K. (2007a). *Review of NASA ECHO (version 8) Web service registration process*, Technical Whitepaper submitted to the Earth Science Data Systems' Technology Infusion Working Group.

Bai, Y., Di, L., & Wei, Y. (2009). A taxonomy of geospatial services for global service discovery and interoperability. *Computers & Geosciences, 35*, 783–790. doi:10.1016/j.cageo.2007.12.018

Burnett, M., Weinstein, B., & Mitchell, A. (2007). ECHO – enabling interoperability with NASA earth science data and services. *Proceedings from Geoscience and Remote Sensing Symposium and IGARSS 2007*.

Chen, N., Di, L., Yu, G., & Wei, Y. (2009). Use of ebRIM-based CSW with sensor observation services for registry and discovery of remote-sensing observations. *Computers & Geosciences, 35*, 360–372. doi:10.1016/j.cageo.2008.08.003

GeoNetwork. (2009). *GeoNetwork OpenSource community website*. Retrieved from http://geonetwork-opensource.org/

IEEE GEOSS. (2009). *IEEE Standards Association – GEOSS standards registry*. Retrieved from http://seabass.ieee.org/groups/geoss/

Martell, R. (2009). *CSW-ebRIM Registry Service - part 1: ebRIM profile of CSW*. Retrieved from http://portal.opengeospatial.org/modules/admin/license_agreement.php?suppressHeaders=0&access_license_id=3&target=http://portal.opengeospatial.org/files/index.php?artifact_id=31137

MBARI. (2009). *Marine plug-and-work consortium*. Retrieved from http://www.mbari.org/pw/puck.htm

Microsoft. (2006). *UBR Shutdown FAQ*. Retrieved from http://uddi.microsoft.com/about/FAQshutdown.htm

Nativi, S., Bigagli, L., Mazzetti, P., Mattia, U., & Boldrini, E. (2007). Discovery, query and access services for imagery, gridded and coverage data a clearinghouse solution. *Proceedings from Geoscience and Remote Sensing Symposium and IGARSS, 2007*, 4021–4024.

Nogueras-Iso, J., Zarazaga-Soria, F., Bejar, R., Alvarez, P., & Muro-Medrano, P. (2005). OGC Catalog Services: a key element for the development of Spatial Data Infrastructures. *Computers & Geosciences, 31*, 199–209. doi:10.1016/j.cageo.2004.05.015

OASIS. (2010). *Online community for the universal description, discovery, and integration*. Retrieved from http://uddi.xml.org/.

OGC. (2009) *Catalogue service*. Retrieved from http://www.opengeospatial.org/standards/cat

Olsen, L., & Stevens, T. (2008). *Service Entry Resource Format (SERF) standard*. (ESDS-RFC-013v0.1). Retrieved from http://www.esdswg.org/spg/rfc/esds-rfc-013/ESDS-RFC-013v0.1.pdf

Percivall, G. (2002). *ISO 19119 and OGC Service Architecture*. Presented at FIG XXII International Congress, Washington, D.C.

Percivall, G. (2009). *OGC Interoperability Program*. Retrieved from http://www.opengeospatial.org/ogc/programs/ip

Senkler, K., Voges, U., & Remke, A. (2004). *An ISO 19115/19119 profile for OGC catalogue services CSW 2.0*. Presented at the 10th EC GI & GIS Workshop, ESDI State of the Art, Warsaw, Poland.

ADDITIONAL READING

Chidambaram, C., Maskey, M., & Ramachandran, R. (2009). *Service Oriented Architecture for Data Mining at Data Centers and Computing Centers*. Poster presented at the Cloud Computing and Collaborative Technologies in Geosciences.

Conover, H., Berthiau, G., Botts, M., Goodman, M., Li, X., & Lu, Y. (2010). Using Sensor Web Protocols for Environmental Data Acquisition and Management. *Ecological Informatics*, 32–41. doi:10.1016/j.ecoinf.2009.08.009

Conover, H., Drewry, M., Graves, S., Keiser, K., Maskey, M., & Smith, M. (in press). SCOOP Data Management: A Standards-based Distributed Information System for Coastal Data Management. In Di, L., & Ramapriyan, H. K. (Eds.), *Standards-Based Data and Information Systems for Earth Observation*. Springer-Verlag.

Graves, S., Ramachandran, R., Movva, S., Conover, H., Fox, P., & McGuinness, D. (2008). *A distributed knowledge extraction framework based on semantic Web services*. AISR NASA Investigator Workshop, NASA, College Park, MD, 2008.

ISO 19119. (2008). *Geographic information services*. Fuger S., Najmi F., & Stojanovic, N. (2005). *ebXML Registry Information Model* (Version 3.0). OASIS Standard #OGC regrep-rim-3.0-os, May 2005.

Movva, S., Ramachandran, R., Maskey, M., & Li, X. (2009). *Building a semantic framework for e-science*. Paper presented at the American Geophysical Union Fall Meeting.

Shanming, W., & Jianjing, S. (2008). Ontology-Based Framework for Geospatial Web Services. *Information Science and Engineering.*, *2*, 107–110.

KEY TERMS AND DEFINITIONS

Application Profile: A metadata schema consisting of elements from one or more namespaces merged and optimized for use in a specific application area.

Catalog Service for Web (CSW): Specification that defines the schemas and interfaces to search, discover, register, and request geospatial data and services.

Catalog: A centralized location where information regarding the similar resources is stored, and where they can be searched for easily.

Interoperability: Capability of multiple software engineering components to communicate and exchange information.

Reference Implementation: A model or skeleton from which other similar implementations can be derived and customized easily.

Service Oriented Architecture (SOA): An approach to distributed computing using loosely coupled web services where communication and message exchanges are standards based.

Standard: A formal document that specifies a set of rules to be followed throughout a process.

Chapter 6
Using Distributed Semantic Catalogs for Information Discovery on Spatial Data Infrastructures

Fabio Gomes de Andrade
Federal Institute of Education, Science and Technology of Paraiba, Brazil

Fábio Luiz Leite Jr
Paraiba State University, Brazil

Cláudio de Souza Baptista
Federal University of Campina Grande, Brazil

ABSTRACT

Spatial data sharing among both private and public organizations is an old issue. Spatial Data Infrastructures (SDIs) have been proposed to solve data integration and discovery problems. Nonetheless, they can only partially work out these problems, as most of their catalog services are built on keyword based search. This approach always results in low precision on searching results. One of the greatest challenges in spatial integration is to provide the semantics for underlying data and services. This chapter describes a distributed catalog service that uses ontologies to describe underlying information so as to improve searching precision. The proposed catalog service can rewrite and propagate queries to other distributed catalogs to cooperate and exchange information directly without the traditional problems imposed by a centralized architecture.

1. INTRODUCTION

Spatial Data Infrastructures (SDIs) (Williamson, Rajabifard & Feeney, 2003) have become increas-

ingly popular in geospatial communities. These SDIs facilitates the access to and the sharing of geospatial data by providing retrieval mechanisms to integrate underlying data sets. As a result, several initiatives, at country and continental levels, were taken for the development of SDIs,

DOI: 10.4018/978-1-60960-192-8.ch006

including the USA NSDI ("National Spatial Data Infrastructure," 2010), the European INSPIRE ("Infrastructure for Spatial Information in the European Community," 2010), the Australian ASDI ("Australian Spatial Data Infrastructure," 2010) and GSDI ("Global Spatial Data Infrastructure," 2010). Some countries have been considering the implementation of nationwide SDIs, as it is the case of Brazil ("Infraestrutura Nacional de Dados Espaciais," 2010).

To design and develop a CDI one has to tackle several problems at the same time. This is due to the complexity inherent to spatial data. Currently, there exist standards for enhancing interoperability in SDI, particularly those provided by the Open Geospatial Consortium (OGC), such as the Web Map Service (WMS) ("Web Map Service Interface," 2004), the Web Feature Service (WFS) ("Web Features Service implementation specification," 2008) and the Web Coverage Service (WCS) ("Web Coverage Service implementation specification," 2008); helps to reduce the complexity regarding access to spatial data. However, many problems still call for effective and efficient information discovery.

Catalog services have been proposed as a way to deal with information discovery in SDI. These catalogs are used for storing and managing information available for both data and services provided by federation SDIs. A client may query these catalog services to discover where geospatial data or services are found. Generally, the information discovery process is based on keywords which relate to the syntax and structure of data sets; however, this process fails to explore the semantics inherent to either the query context or the application. This reduces the precision and the recall of the proposed overall SDI federation. Another important problem related to current SDI architectures is the centralization of catalog services. This centralization also entails some classical distributed system problems, including the existence of a single point of failure, a bottleneck for queries which reduces scalability, and the

complexity of maintaining an updated catalog in relation to dynamic SDI data sources.

This chapter presents the catalog service of the Semantic Web Services - GIS (SWS-GIS) (Leite, Baptista, Silva & Silva, 2007). The SWS-GIS is an architecture for information sharing among members of an SDI federation. The main contributions of this chapter are:

- the proposal of a semantic catalog service that uses inference to improve information discovery and facilitates spatial data integration among heterogeneous data sources; and
- the truly distributed catalog in which queries may be posed from any SDI client without the need of a central catalog. In our approach, each SDI has its own catalog. When a particular query is submitted to any SDI catalog, it is rewritten and propagated to other catalogs.

The remainder of the chapter is organized as follows: Section 2 discusses related works on information discovery in SDIs; Section 3 gives us a background on geospatial semantic web and spatial data infrastructures, focusing on the problems related to spatial data discovery; Section 4 presents the example used to demonstrate our approach; Section 5 highlights the proposed catalog service for the discovery of spatial data in SDIs; and finally, Section 6 presents the conclusions and future directions of this research.

2. RELATED WORKS

Many relevant research works have been proposed for the solution of spatial data discovery problems on SDIs via semantic web concepts. Nevertheless, most of these solutions focus on the use of semantics to get data from a single infrastructure. Such solutions do not consider the possibility of forwarding queries to other SDIs if when their catalog services fail to address a query posed by a user.

An important work has been proposed by Smits and Friis-Christensen (Smits & Friis-Christensen, 2007) for the discovery of resources in a European SDI. In their work, the terms used to describe resource metadata are processed by a software agent, after which each resource is linked to the semantic concepts defined by a thesaurus. Finally, users can locate resources by means of keywords or by browsing the thesaurus concepts. Stock et al (Stock, Atkinson, Higgins, Small, Woolf, Millard, et al, 2010) propose an approach based on a feature type catalog for describing the data offered by the infrastructure. In their work, they have defined features as classes by means of a set of attributes and operations that describe all the operations applicable to a feature type. Finally, the concrete implementation of these operations is linked to feature type specifications, which can be found by browsing for feature types. A disadvantage of these approaches is that they do not use ontologies, for the capacity of inferring new knowledge at execution time is limited.

Lutz and Kolas (Lutz & Kolas, 2007) have also proposed the use of ontologies for data discovery on SDIs. These authors use rules to map the concepts defined on a global ontology to concepts used by data sources one. In this case, when a query is posed to the infrastructure, its catalog service uses these rules to expand the query concepts. Thus, the system accesses and loads all features associated to query concepts on to a knowledge base. Finally, reasoning is carried out on this data in order to find spatial features that can be relevant to the user's query. In other work, Lutz et al (Lutz, Sprado, Klien, Schubert & Christ, 2008) use ontologies by means of description logic (Baader, Calvanese, McGuinness, Nardi, Patel-Schneider, 2003) for data discovery in SDIs. In their work, the WFS service features offered by the SDI are linked to the concepts described in the domain ontologies through mapping registers. When a user poses a query to the infrastructure, a reasoning based on

subsume relationships is applied to the ontology in order to establish concepts that are relevant to the user's query. Moreover, the catalog service retrieves the features linked to relevant concepts in order to find features which match the user's query. The SWING project (Roman & Klien, 2007) uses spatial data provided by OGC WFS services linked to concepts defined in the ontology through WSML. The project enables users to find spatial data by searching for concepts described in the domain ontologies. The main drawback of these approaches is that they do not include query propagation to other SDIs in case their catalogs do not fulfill the user's request.

Athanasis et al (Athanasis, Kalabokidis, Vaitis, Soulakellis, 2009) developed a method which uses semantics to describe resources on geographic portals. They use ontologies described in RDF-Schema to interpret semantic features of portal resources. In their method, when a data provider registers its resources, it offers some metadata, and links the resources to one or more concepts defined on the domain ontology. Users can formulate their queries based on ontology concepts. Then, the system generates an RQL query to find the resources that are relevant to the user. Lemmens et al (Lemmens, de By, Gould, Wytzisk, Grannel & van Oosterom, 2007) propose a framework to enable the semantic annotation of spatial services. This framework offers an ontology that defines various types of spatial services. However, their work focuses only on the discovery of service and service chains. Moreover, important issues, such as query propagation among catalog services, are not addressed.

The INSPIRE project proposes a catalog service (Senkler, Voges, Einspainer, Kanellopoulos, Millot & Luraschi, 2006) which can propagate queries to the underlying catalog of infrastructures. Nevertheless, this propagation only occurs if the query is submitted directly to the INSPIRE catalog. Furthermore, semantic mappings and query rewritings are not addressed, because all infrastructures use the standards defined by IN-

SPIRE. As there will be no communication with the catalog services that are not part of this SDI, this feature reduces data discovery. In another example, the SANY project (Havlik & Schimak, 2009) proposes a cascade service (Havlik, Bleier & Schimak, 2009) that permits access to sensors data provided by various services through a single point. However, the service presents the same limitations as in the case of the INSPIRE catalog, because propagation occurs only when the data are accessed from this service. Lassoued et al (Lassoued, Wright, Bermudez & Boucelda, 2008) implemented the Coastal Web Atlas, which offers a catalog service that offers a single access point to the spatial data of several catalogs, but it has also the limitations mentioned above.

These works' main drawbacks are that they focus on semantics to discovery data in a unique infrastructure. We believe that a complete solution to spatial data integration requires communication and cooperation among the various distributed infrastructures that are implemented today. In order to obtain this solution, semantic-enabled catalog services are required. These services should be capable of propagating users' queries to other catalog services offered by the infrastructures that lay outside the SDI where the query has been formulated.

3. BACKGROUND

This section offers a background to the technologies used to develop our work. It addresses issues concerning spatial data discovery based on ontologies, highlighting the main problems and challenges faced by the spatial data community.

3.1 Semantic Web and Ontologies

One of the main drawbacks of current web is that the semantics of its content cannot be understood by machines. This makes information exchange difficult among applications. The semantic web

(Berners-Lee, Hendler, Lassila, 2001) has been envisaged as one solution to overcome this limitation. It has been proposed as an extension of the current web where metadata are used to describe the semantics of published resources. Thus, various approaches have been proposed to implement the semantic web vision. The most popular approach is that of using ontologies to describe the semantics of such resources.

Ontologies (Guarino, 1995) are used to conceptualize knowledge domains. These domains are formally described through entities, properties and relationships. Entities represent the concepts which make the domain. Each entity can be a set of objects, which are called individuals. Properties are the features that characterize the domain entities. Finally, relationships are used to describe the relations that exist among the instances of each entity. Moreover, ontologies allow the definition of axioms to discover new knowledge related to the individuals' ontology during the search process. The main advantage of ontologies is that they make data semantics understandable by both humans and machines. Thus, software agents can apply reasoning on this semantics to develop more sophisticated search tools, and to improve the quality of their queries.

When a search process is based on ontologies, two types of knowledge are implied. The first type is called *intension*, which represents the knowledge obtained from the relationships among concepts. The second type is called *extension,* and it comes from the individuals that make up the ontology. This knowledge can also be inferred from the application of ontology inference rules. Several approaches have been proposed to describe ontologies. Among them, there is the description logic approach which has been used in many applications. Description logic is a logic–based language, where concepts can be defined by means of operators, including conjunction, disjunction, and existential quantifiers. Moreover, it defines two kinds of frameworks. The first is called TBox, which is used to tackle intentional knowledge, and the second is called ABox, used to deal with extensional knowledge. Ontology Web Language (OWL) ("OWL Web Ontology Language Guide", 2004) is recommended by the W3C to describe ontologies. It is created on top of Description Logic. Three versions of this language are defined: OWL-Lite, OWL-DL and OWL-Full. These versions vary according to expressivity power and computational decidability. The constructions offered by OWL allow both intentional and extensional knowledge.

3.2 Service Discovery

More recently, service-oriented architectures (SOA) (Erl, 2005) have gained growing popularity on the web. In SOA, providers offer small software applications as services that can be invoked by customers over the network. This type of architecture is basically composed of three kinds of components: providers, customers and registry services. Providers offer one or more services, which can be invoked by clients. Clients use the services offered by these providers. The registry service acts as a catalog that enables service discovery available in the network. Providers use this registry to advertise the services they offer, while customers use it to search for a desired service. Once the desired service is found, the client can invoke it directly on the web.

Web services technology (Alonso, Casati, Kuno, Machiraju, 2004) has been developed to enable SOA implementation. This technology defines a set of standards that can be used to implement SOA-based applications. The great advantage of web services technology is that it is entirely based on open standards. Moreover, these patterns are based on XML, which is widely used for information exchange among applications on the web. Examples of the standards proposed by this technology include SOAP and REST. These represent protocols for information exchange and service invocation: WSDL, which is used to describe the access information of services;

and UDDI, which is a directory service that can be used for the advertisement and discovery of web services.

Due to SOA and web services popularity, the number of services available on the network has increased in the last few years. However, this growth has been greeted by new information retrieval challenges. One of these challenges is to find the services which are already available on the web. Several factors account for this difficulty. Firstly, there is the current search tool developed for the discovery of documents and not for services. Secondly, there is the UDDI service which enables queries based only on keywords or, at most, on a classification of services via a defined taxonomy. These characteristics limit the ability of discovering these records. Finally, it is difficult for the user to express a desirable feature by means of mere keywords.

One solution to enhance service discovery is to use semantic web concepts to improve the description of these services. Basically, this is done by linking some features of service to the concepts defined in ontologies. This process is known as semantic annotation (or markup) of services, and the services recorded are called semantic web services (McIlraith, Son & Zeng, 2001). The information generated by the annotation process can then be used by search engines to improve service discovery.

3.3 Geospatial Semantic Web

Today, a plethora of geographic data is available on the web. However, the easy and most ample access to information still represents a big challenge to the spatial data community. This is so because geographic information is generally, heterogeneously provided. For example, data can be made available on different formats, organized through different data models, collected in different resolutions, and so on. The heterogeneity of spatial data makes it difficult to integrate and reuse data from different providers. Hence, spatial data producers must spend much effort and time in order to produce geographic data which are already available from other providers.

In order to achieve efficient spatial data integration, we need to locate the available spatial data on the web. Today, search tools are based on keywords, but they fail to explore the spatial features inherent to this kind of data. In order to overcome such limitation, the use of web semantic concepts has been recommended as the solution to improve spatial data discovery and, for that matter, data integration (Egenhofer, 2002), (Kuhn, 2005). Since then, several works have been proposed, in which semantic web concepts are used to solve problems related to spatial domain.

Besides geospatial semantic web, spatial data infrastructures have been proposed to facilitate the discovery and access to spatial data. These infrastructures offer the necessary support to the discovery, evaluation and retrieval of geographic data coming from various data sources. This support includes the solution of technical (data format, data models, service interfaces, etc) and non-technical issues (access rights, copyrights, pricing, etc). SDIs have gained increasing acceptance among spatial data providers, as evidenced by the various initiatives taken for SDI development throughout the world, mainly those initiatives taken by government agencies at different levels.

Spatial data infrastructures can be seen as a great development in spatial data discovery and integration. However, some important issues should still be addressed to solve the problems mentioned above. In the next subsection of this chapter, we will discuss the SDIs, the advances brought by them, and the challenges posed to the spatial data community.

3.4 Spatial Data Infrastructures

One of the main challenges concerning the reuse of spatial information is to efficiently find data and services which are already available on the web. These challenges are being addressed by

the geographic data community through spatial data infrastructures initiatives. A spatial data infrastructure can be viewed as a relevant base collection of technologies, policies and institutional arrangements to facilitate the availability and the access to spatial data (Nebert, 2004).

Spatial data infrastructures offer users a set of data and services. In order to make it easier for the user to discover and evaluate these resources, metadata are used to describe them. Several metadata standards have been proposed to describe geographic information. An important example is the Content Standard for Digital Geospatial Metadata (CS-DGM) ("Content Standard for Digital Geospatial Media," 2000) developed by the USA Federal Geographic Data Committee. In order to standardize geographic metadata descriptions, ISO TC 211 has developed the standard ISO 19115 ("Geographic information-metadata," 2003) to describe spatial resources. Another standard, the ISO 19139 ("Geographic information-metadata and XML schema implementation," 2007), defines how the information in ISO 19115 can be codified on to an XML file. The standards proposed by ISO have gained the immediate acceptance of spatial data providers. These standards have become the basis for SDI metadata description.

In order to publish and discover data and services, catalog services are provided by SDIs. These services give access to the information in the metadata which is found in the spatial data. A common interface for a catalog service was proposed by the OGC ("Open GIS Catalogue Services implementation," 2007) as a way to equalize access to this type of service. The interface defines a set of operations that a catalog service can offer to customers. This service is of fundamental importance for the implementation of SDIs, as it recommends metadata for both data and services provided by an infrastructure. Customers can then verify whether the underlying information fulfills their needs.

Although the catalog service proposed by the OGC has facilitated the implementation of and the access to catalogs, the problem of finding the available data efficiently has not been solved. The big flaw of current catalogs is that they base their searches entirely on keywords. Thus, the semantics of information used to describe the available data cannot be surveyed at the time of a query. This limitation leads to queries with low recall, since data described by synonyms or related terms cannot be retrieved by the search engine. Likewise, these queries end up by exhibiting low precision, since the irrelevant data that contains the keywords used in the request are eventually retrieved for the user.

Another major limitation of the current catalog services stems from the way spatial data infrastructures are developed. There are, at present, several initiatives of SDI development around the world. Each initiative proposes a catalog service to solve queries related only to the SDI to which it was deployed. Thus, when a catalog service does not have the information requested by the user, he/she must find a new SDI available, and resubmit his/her query until the information requested is found. This task, besides being time consuming, it is quite tedious as well.

We believe that to solve the problem of finding information in SDIs efficiently, we need to develop more sophisticated catalog services capable of exploiting the semantics of the underlying data in order to enable queries with greater recall and precision to be submitted. Moreover, mechanisms of communication and interoperability with other available catalog services for the propagation of queries are also required so as to make the discovery of spatial data a lot easier for the final user. The following sections of this chapter focus on a catalog service that addresses these two issues.

4. AN EXAMPLE

To explain it better, an example that monitors the floods in the São Francisco River is used throughout this chapter. The São Francisco River flows across several Brazilian states, and is managed by the WMA (Water Management Agency). Nearly every year, the overflow of the São Francisco River causes serious floods, affects coastal communities, destroys vegetation and kills animals. In an attempt to ameliorate the damages caused by the floods, an action plan is made to identify critical flooding points. The main flooded areas are clearly identified and quantified so that proper action can be taken to prevent future events. These actions are implemented at federal level by the Brazilian WMA, and at state level, by the Civil Defense and other agencies. After monitoring the river system, it is possible, with the help of the State Civil Defense, to identify the cities and the number of people who will be affected by the floods in the São Francisco Valley. Over two thousand miles of river area is periodically monitored throughout the year. It is very difficult for a single government agency to stores all the data gathered. Therefore, there needs a method of retrieving all decentralized information.

This example will be used to show a decentralized architecture in which the hierarchical catalogs of several SDIs can share information to resolve queries posed by users. Two SDIs that have hydrographic data will be introduced. One of them is at state level, and the other is at federal level. Both, however, use different ontologies to describe their data. Note that the catalog service proposed in this chapter can be applied to all distributed architecture. The type of architecture will influence only the implementation of the query forward module.

5. CATALOG SERVICE DESCRIPTION

The catalog service is the core of the proposed SDI architecture. This catalog is responsible for information discovery in the entire federation. The service descriptions contained in the catalogs are semantically enriched by ontologies. Figure 1 illustrates the architecture of the catalog service

Figure 1. The architecture of the catalogue service

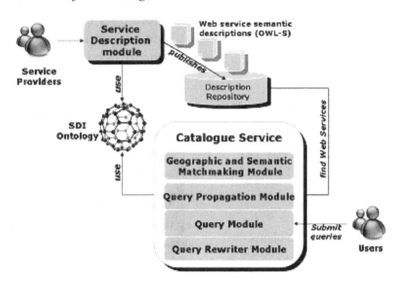

and its modules, which are further described in the following subsections.

5.1 The Service Description Module

One important feature of the catalog service proposed here is that it uses semantics to enrich the description of services offered by an SDI catalog. The semantics is described formally by means of ontologies, which allow the semantics of a field of application to be formally described in terms of classes, properties and relationships. Moreover, ontologies allow the definition of the axioms that will enable search engines to make inferences about the instances of these classes in order to discover new knowledge at the time of a query.

The proposed approach assumes that each infrastructure has a set of domain ontologies to describe data models. Domain ontologies describe specific fields of application, such as hydrography, topography, vegetation, transportation, etc. The greatest advantage obtained by the use of domain ontologies is that these will allow the development of software applications capable of identifying the meaning of the domain components and the semantic relationships between them. The

creation and maintenance of these ontologies can be easily carried out by one or more members of the organization responsible for infrastructure.

Figure 2 shows an excerpt of an ontology stub in which the concept *BodyOfWater*, which describes any kind of water reservoirs, is defined. This concept is characterized by the properties *hasName* and *hasGeometry*, which correspond, respectively, to the name of the reservoir and its geographical references. This concept has two subclasses: *Dam* and *River*, which represent the specialization of the reservoir concept. In addition to the attributes inherited from *BodyOfWater* class, each class has its specific attributes. The ontology also specifies that each instance of the class *Dam* has an instance of the class *River,* as its source.

However, the mere development of domain ontologies for describing data models does not solve the problem of service discovery. To find an efficient solution to this problem, we would need a mechanism that uses domain ontologies in order to improve the description of these services. The process of using ontologies to describe the properties of a service is called semantic markup (or annotation). This annotation is ob-

Figure 2. An ontology example

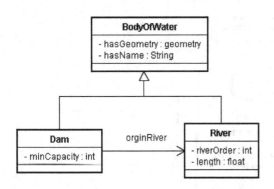

tained by linking some of the service characteristics to concepts defined in the domain ontologies.

Over the years, various solutions have been proposed to carry out the semantic annotation of services. Web Service Modeling Ontology (WSMO) (Brujin, Bussler, Fensel, Hepp, Keller, Kifer, et al, 2005) consists of a framework that uses four elements (ontologies, services, goals and mediators) to perform the semantic annotation of services. DAML-S (Ankolekar, Burnstein, Hobbs, Lassila, Martin, McIlraith, 2001) is an ontology created in DAML language in order to describe the semantics of web services. It describes each service by means of three models: the profile model, the process model, and the service grounding. In our solution, we used OWL-S (Martin, Paolucci, McIlraith, Burstein, McDermott, McGuinness, et al, 2005), which consists of service ontology similar to DAML-S, but described in OWL language. This has been chosen because it is based on OWL, the language recommended by W3C for the specification of ontologies. In OWL-S, a class Service is defined to describe the properties of each service. All instances of this class are described by these three models:

- ServiceProfile: it describes the general characteristics of the service, such as name and creator;
- ProcessModel: it describes the functional properties of the service, including input

and output parameters, the pre-conditions needed for the service, and the effects on their implementations. Moreover, this model offers constructs that can be used to describe either simple or composite services;

- ServiceGrounding: it describes the lower level features of a service, such as the location of its WSDL file, and the syntactic type of every input and output parameters.

In our catalog service, a process model for establishing the association between services and domain ontologies is used. In this model, all input and output parameters of the service are associated to a concept defined in the domain ontology. Through this association, a search engine can identify the meaning of each piece of information related to the service. In this case, the concept associated with each parameter of the service acts as a semantic type.

Figure 3 shows an example of ProcessModel used to perform the semantic annotation of a service. It describes the features of a gazetteer service. The description states that the service is called *ResolvePlaceNameService*, which receives the name of a particular location as input that refers to the concept *placename* of an ontology called SDIPE, and returns as an output, a water reservoir represented by the concept *BodyOfWater* of the same ontology.

In this proposed approach, the organization responsible for the SDI is the one that does both the semantic annotation of each service and the maintenance of this information. Once the task of annotation is accomplished, an OWL document is obtained. This document is stored in a relational database, and it is operated by the search module during the query process. The table, where this information is stored, also contains a spatial attribute, which refers to the bounding-box area of service coverage. The database of the catalog service is created by means of a spatial database. This allows the indexing of the spatial column,

Figure 3. Example of OWL-S process model

```
<profile:Profile rdf:about="#ResolvePlaceNameProfile">
        <profile:hasInput>
                <process:Input rdf:ID="placeName">
                        <process:parameterType
                        rdf:datatype="http://www.w3.org/2001/XMLSchema#anyURI">
        http://buchada.dsc.ufcg.edu.br/ontology/SDIPE.owl#PlaceName
                        </process:parameterType>
                        <rdfs:label>placeName</rdfs:label>
                </process:Input>
        </profile:hasInput>
<service:presentedBy rdf:resource="#ResolvePlaceNameService"/>
        <profile:hasOutput>
                <process:Output rdf:ID="BodyOfWaterResult">
                        <process:parameterType
                        rdf:datatype="http://www.w3.org/2001/XMLSchema#anyURI">
        http://buchada.dsc.ufcg.edu.br/ontology/SDIPE.owl#BodyOfWater
                        </process:parameterType>
                        <rdfs:label>BodyOfWaterResult</rdfs:label>
                </process:Output>
        </profile:hasOutput>
</profile:Profile>
```

accelerating query results; as the geographical matchmaking can be done faster.

The proposed catalog service renders each infrastructure free to use their own domain ontologies to describe their data models. Thus, the catalogs may route queries to one another. Because queries are based on concepts defined in the domain ontologies used by the catalog where they were made, a number of mechanisms are required for understanding the semantic relationships between the ontologies used by different infrastructures. For this purpose, we use another type of ontology called ontology mapping.

An ontology mapping resolves the association between concepts into different ontologies. Basically, this ontology contains two or more ontologies and should define equivalence relations between their concepts and properties. What is more, it should allow the specification of rules for the definition of more complex mappings. In this case, the catalog service database contains a set of mapping ontology, which is used to rewrite a query. Just like the domain ontologies and service descriptions, these domain ontologies need to be defined by one or more members of the organization responsible for the infrastructure.

Figure 4 shows an example of an ontology mapping created to define the relationships between the ontologies used by the Civil Defense and the state of Pernambuco SDIs, respectively. This example shows that the class *Body_Of_Water* in the Civil Defense ontology (right side on the Figure 4) is equivalent to the class *River* in the ontology of the state of Pernambuco (on the left side of Figure 4). The same relationship applies to the concepts *Body_Of_Water* and *Dam*. The ontology also offers a definition of equivalence relationships between properties. In this case, the properties of Geometry, which exists in the two ontologies, are equivalent.

5.1.1 The Hierarchical Architecture of the Example

In our approach, each data source has its own catalog service with a local ontology. To illustrate this approach, we adopted a federation-based architecture which is organized in a hierarchical form. As SDIs are related to a particular geographic area at different levels of granularity – for example at country-state-city levels – a hierarchy of ontologies is defined for each level. As a result, one can observe an implicit topologic relationship, and an explicit semantic relationship in between the ontologies involved in the SDI.

Therefore, a set of concepts need to be mapped on several SDIs through the communities formed by a semantic cluster, as illustrated in Figure 5.

Figure 4. Example of ontology mapping: (a) the ontology of the state of Pernambuco; (b) the civil defense ontology

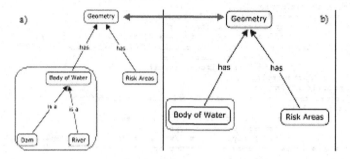

Figure 5. SDI semantic clusters

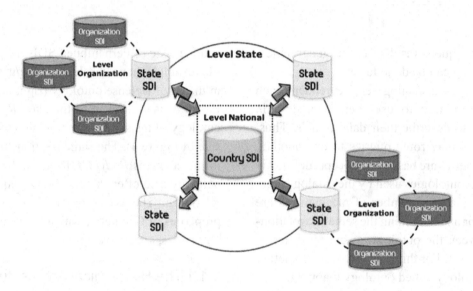

By using this hierarchy, the SDI catalogs may exchange information among them by using their respective domain ontologies and a set of mapping rules between the ontologies. Besides its own domain ontology, each catalog has the mapping rules for its parent ontology. The main advantage of this hierarchic approach is that the amount of mapping among source ontologies is reduced; hence, scalability is maximized. Furthermore, the storage of ontologies at local SDI facilitates the management, alignment and up-to-date maintenance of the ontologies.

5.1.2 A Query Example

Suppose an agent of the Civil Defense of the state of Pernambuco wants to identify the parcels that are likely to be damaged by flooding and compute the population that might be affected. To do this, the following information is required: a feature showing the São Francisco River within the state, the regions close to the river basin that are at risk of flooding, and a map of the houses located in these areas. Let us suppose also that the data required by the agent are spread along three SDIs; each one at a different level of governance, as depicted in Figure 6:

Figure 6. Hierarchical structure of an SDI

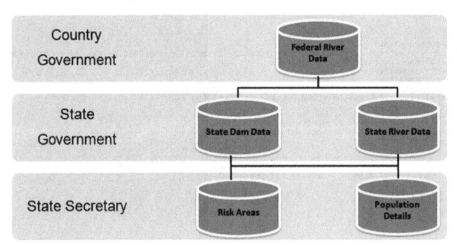

- the Civil Defense of the state of Pernambuco that provides a political map of the state, and maps showing the areas at risk of flooding (data described using the ontology of the SDI's own Department). Its catalog service is called CD-CAT;
- the Water Resources Department of the state of Pernambuco that provides maps containing the rivers and other water reservoirs in the state (data described using the ontology of Pernambuco SDI). Its catalog service is called WRD-CAT;
- the WNA that monitors the river at national level (data described using the ontology of the national SDI). Its catalog service is called WNA-CAT;
- the state of Pernambuco. This infrastructure does not have any of the data requested by the user. Nevertheless, it is responsible for propagating queries coming from the state SDIs to the SDI at federal level. Its catalog service is called PE-CAT.

The agent of the Civil Defense, who is in the Civil Defense office of the state of Pernambuco, submits a request to its SDI catalog in order to obtain the desired query result. This catalog is compliant to the OGC CS/W (Catalog Service for the Web) specification. Thus, the only action required here is to use the CS/W API to submit a query and get the desired information. The query uses the domain ontology that describes resources belonging to the Pernambuco SDI. Figure 4a shows part of this ontology.

5.2 The Query Module

The query module is responsible for processing users' queries, and it represents the communication interface between the catalog service and its clients. The catalog service can receive both queries posed directly to it, and requests from other infrastructure which have been propagated to it. In the catalog service, a query can be defined as a set $Q = <C, SC, FC>$, where:

- C represents a set of concepts defined in the domain ontologies used by the catalog. These concepts represent the types of features which the user is interested in. For example, the user can pose a query requesting information on the concept of *River* from the ontology shown in Figure 4;
- SC is the query spatial restriction. This restriction represents the bounding-box of the geographic region. For example, the

Figure 7. Initial query received by the query module

```
<ogc:Filter>
  <ogc:Or>
    <ogc:And>
      <PropertyIsEqualTo>
        <PropertyName>http://buchada.dsc.ufcg.edu.br/~lsi/ontology/SDIDFPE.owl#Name</PropertyName>
        <Literal>São Francisco River</Literal>
      </PropertyIsEqualTo>
      <PropertyIsEqualTo>
        <PropertyName>http://buchada.dsc.ufcg.edu.br/~lsi/ontology/SDIDFPE.owl#FeatureType</PropertyName>
        <Literal>http://buchada.dsc.ufcg.edu.br/~lsi/ontology/SDIDFPE.owl#River</Literal>
      </PropertyIsEqualTo>
      <Overlaps>
        <PropertyName>Geometry</PropertyName>
          <gml:Polygon srsName="urn:ogc:def:crs:EPSG:6.6:4618">
            <gml:exterior>
              <gml:LinearRing>
                <gml:posList>
                  -37.001821,-7.175744 -36.992499,-7.180127 -36.976542,-7.160474
                  ... -37.019035,-7.190465 -37.001821,-7.175744
                </gml:posList>
              </gml:LinearRing>
            </gml:exterior>
          </gml:Polygon>
      </Overlaps>
    </ogc:And>
    <ogc:And>
      <Dwithin>
        <PropertyName>http://buchada.dsc.ufcg.edu.br/~lsi/ontology/SDIDFPE.owl#Municipality</PropertyName>
        <gml:posList>
          -44.054321,-9.345744 -36.228347,-9.45332 -36.34556,-9.333456
          ... -40.3456345,-11.978677 -40.788965,-11.345564
        </gml:posList>
        <Distance units='km'>5</Distance>
      <Dwithin>
    </ogc:And>
  </ogc:Or>
</ogc:Filter>
```

user can submit a query to retrieve data related to the Northeast region of Brazil;

- FC represents a set of filter constraints. Restrictions in the filter can be applied to properties related to concepts defined in the set C. For example, the user can specify a restriction in a filter that indicates that he/she is only interested in rivers with lengths greater than 100 km.

The user specifies his/her query through an OGC Filter which is coded under the concepts defined in the domain ontologies used by the SDI to which the request is sent. Therefore, queries submitted directly to the catalog service are based on concepts defined in their domain ontologies, and can be directly routed to the semantic and geographic matchmaking module. Queries received through the propagation of other catalog services are based on concepts defined in the domain ontologies defined in the SDI where they were created. In this case, the query must be initially passed on to the query rewrite module, which will convert it into a format whose terms are used in the local domain ontologies, and then sent to the semantic and geographic matchmaking module.

Figure 7 shows an OGC filter on a query received by the catalog service as shown in the example above. This query is a search for cities that are located within a radius of 5 Km from a river called the *São Francisco River*. The query defines the bounding-box region of interest. The catalog service has also a gazetteer service which is used for extracting spatial footprints of places used on a request when its bounding-box is not informed at the time of the request. When the query is in accordance with the concepts used by the ontology for the catalog service, it is forwarded to the semantic and geographic matchmaking module.

5.3 The Semantic and Geographic Matchmaking Module

When the query is described in terms of local ontologies, it is sent to the semantic and geographic matchmaking module. Upon receiving the client's request, this module queries the SDI database and analyzes the semantic markup of the registered services to verify whether any of the services offered by the source fulfill, either partially or completely, the information requested by the client.

The matchmaking between the query received and the service descriptions stored in the database is made up of two steps. The first step is the geographical matchmaking where services are filtered according to their spatial extent. The second step is the semantic matchmaking where services are filtered according to the meaning of the output parameters offered to users.

The geographic matchmaking verifies whether the bounding-box of the service overlaps the bounding-box area defined in the user's query. The purpose of this is to reduce the number of services examined during the following step. To filter services in accordance with their geographic coverage, the matchmaking module analyzes the coverage area of existing services in the catalog service database. The matchmaking module makes a selection out of the services examined; those whose bounding-box of the coverage area intersects in the bounding-box region of the user's query interest.

The use of geographic matchmaking is important because it limits the amount of services that will have their semantic markup analyzed. The use of a spatial DBMS allows the indexing of spatial information, aiming at improving query performance. Then, a set of services is pre-selected.

The second stage of the matchmaking process selects, among the services retrieved in the previous step, those which provide the information requested by the user. This selection is done by checking whether the services output features and associated concepts are identical or semantically related to the concepts required by the query.

In this case, the catalog uses the local domain ontology to infer new knowledge through the relationship between the concepts of ontology and its axioms, and also to check whether the features offered by its services meet the search criteria defined in the query. Let $C = (C_1, C_2,..., Cn)$ be the set of concepts required by a user's query. The semantic matchmaking selects services, if they have any, in its output concepts:

- a concept similar to one defined in C;
- a concept which is synonymous with one of the concepts defined in C;
- a concept which is a subclass of one of the concepts defined in C;
- a concept which is related to one of the concepts defined in C, directly or indirectly, through one or more axioms of the ontology domain. By way of example, let us suppose there is, in the domain ontologies used by the catalog, a rule of reasoning which states that certain instances of a concept A, depending on the value of some properties, may be considered instances of concept B. In this case, if the concept B appears within the set C, any service that offers on its output the term A is also retrieved by the search engine, because its information may also be relevant for the user.

The great advantage of semantic matchmaking is that it allows semantic relationships between the concepts defined in ontologies as well as its reasoning rules to be used to expand the user's query concepts related to those used when the query was being formulated. This expansion provides greater recall at the time of query processing, since it allows the retrieval of services which were annotated with concepts related to those used in the request.

Following this step, the query module analyzes the services retrieved after spatial and semantic filtering. If a service offers all the requested data, it will mean that the service is included in the result list *t* and sent to the client. If one or more services partly meet the query, it means they will be included in the result collection, and the query

Figure 8. Algorithm for query rewrite

```
Let C = (C1, C2, ..., Cn) be the set of concepts requested by a user in its
original query:
For each Ci in C do
    Ontologies O = getOntolgies(Ci);
    For each Oi in O do
            EquivalentConcepts EC = oi.getSimilarConcepts(Ci);
            For each ECi in EC do
                    finalResult.add(ECi);
```

is forwarded to the query rewrite module. If the catalog does not offer any data requested by the user, it means that the query will be routed to the query rewrite module without any results in the result collection. The result of this module comprises a collection of services that will be sent to the client, in case the query has been fully satisfied, or otherwise sent to the query rewrite module.

5.4 The Query Rewrite Module

This module aims to translate semantic queries. Semantic query translations involve converting a filter made by the concepts of a particular ontology into another filter based on similar concepts defined in other ontologies. In the catalog service, the rewrite module can be used in two different situations:

- if a catalog service does not have all the requested data when the query is sent directly to it, the query will be forwarded to other catalog services. In this case, the original query based on a specific domain ontology needs to be translated into the vocabulary used by external ontologies before being transferred to the query propagation module; and
- if the query is sent by another catalog service, the original query is then based on some external ontology and must be translated into the vocabulary used by the local domain ontologies before being processed by the semantic matchmaking module.

To translate the request, the query rewrite module analyzes the set of concepts that make up the query and the mapping ontologies registered in the catalog database. In the first situation, the query is translated into concepts defined in the domain ontologies used by the infrastructure to which the query is gong to be forwarded. In this case, the new query is said to have a set of concepts 'C' formed by the algorithm shown in Figure 8.

According to this algorithm, the first step of query mapping is to locate, in the mapping ontologies, the concepts that are similar to the ones defined in the original query. Here, the similar concepts that have a relationship of equivalence with the concept used in the original query are discovered and used for the formulation of a new request. Once these concepts are found, the constraints used to filter the query are rewritten to the concepts described in C'. The mapping of these constraints is carried out according to the algorithm described in Figure 9.

According to this algorithm, the first step in filter constraints mapping is to locate, in the ontology mapping, the properties that are similar to the ones used for defining the filter constraints. In this step, all similar properties that have an equivalence relation with the one used in the specification of the restriction of the original filter are figured out, and a new filter constraint is generated. This one is identical to the original filter in the query, with the replacement of the original property by an equivalent property. The properties of filter constraint that cannot be mapped to any other property in the ontology

Figure 9. Constraint rewritten algorithm

```
Let us consider that the set FC corresponds to filter restrictions defined in the
original query.
For each FCi in FC
        Property P = FC[i].getProperty();
        Ontologies O = retrieveOntologies(P);
        For each Oi in O do
                EquivalentProperties EP = Oi.getSimilarConcepts(P);
                For each EPi in EP do
                        Constraint newFC = generateConstraint (FCi,EPi);
                        finalResult.add(newFC);
```

Figure 10. Rewritten query generated by the query rewrite module

```
<ogc:Filter>
  <ogc:Or>
    <ogc:And>
      <PropertyIsEqualTo>
        <PropertyName>http://buchada.dsc.ufcg.edu.br/~lsi/ontology/SDIFEDERAL.owl#FeatureName</PropertyName>
        <Literal>São Francisco River</Literal>
      </PropertyIsEqualTo>
      <Overlaps>
        <PropertyName>Geometry</PropertyName>
        <gml:Polygon srsName="urn:ogc:def:crs:EPSG:6.6:4618">
          <gml:exterior>
            <gml:LinearRing>
              <gml:posList>
                -37.001821,-7.175744 -36.992499,-7.180127 -36.976542,-7.160474
                ... -37.019035,-7.190465 -37.001821,-7.175744
              </gml:posList>
            </gml:LinearRing>
          </gml:exterior>
        </gml:Polygon>
      </Overlaps>
    </ogc:And>
    <ogc:And>
      <DWithin>
        <PropertyName>http://buchada.dsc.ufcg.edu.br/~lsi/ontology/SDIFEDERAL.owl#City</PropertyName>
        <gml:posList>
          -44.054321,-9.345744 -36.228347,-9.45332 -36.34556,-9.333456
          ... -40.3456345,-11.978677 -40.788965,-11.345564
        </gml:posList>
        <Distance units='km'>5</Distance>
      </DWithin>
    </ogc:And>
  </ogc:Or>
</ogc:Filter>
```

mapping are ignored and are not added to the final result.

Figure 10 shows an example of a new query generated by the query rewrite module, which shows the rewriting of the query presented in Figure 7 for further consultation through the mapping rules.

5.5 The Query Propagation Module

This module is responsible for forwarding the user's query to other sources in order to find one or more sources to provide the requested data. Where queries are propagated to, this will depend on the type of distributed architecture used to group the data sources. Following our approach, the archi-

tecture based on a federation of catalogs is chosen and implemented. However, the details about the mechanisms of how to identify these sources are outside the scope of this chapter and can be found in (Leite et al, 2007). It is also important to note that, while a federation-based architecture has been used to illustrate our examples, the proposed catalog service can be applied to any decentralized distributed architecture. In this case, the only change required would be on how the query should be propagated to other infrastructures.

5.6 The Query Processing Example

The resources needed to address the query in the proposed example may not be found exactly in the

Civil Defense SDI; nevertheless, the information on the national SDI and on the SDI of the State Department of Water Resources is still needed. Thus, as the results obtained do not satisfy the query completely, a process of query propagation to send the query to other catalogs in different SDIs is started. To make this possible, the CD-CAT uses the query rewrite module in order to create a new query to request the data that are still to be found. This new query uses the mapping between the local domain ontology and the domain ontology of the SDI that is the parent in the hierarchy, i.e. the ontology of the state of Pernambuco.

Figure 4 shows snippets of code with ontologies mapping. Note that the concepts of rivers and dams only exist in the ontology of the state of Pernambuco, as the concept of risk area exists only in the ontology of Civil Defense. Figure 10 shows a snippet of the rewritten query which retrieves only what is needed to complete the original query, and the areas where the highlighted concepts have already been mapped on to a higher level ontology. Finally, the new query is sent to the WRD-CAT and PE-CAT catalogs.

When it receives the query, the WRD-CAT maps the concepts used in the request for the concepts defined in the Department of Water Resources ontology, submitting this query to its service description database. Finally, it returns the result obtained with service descriptions WFS or WMS containing spatial information of state rivers and reservoirs.

One of the catalogs which have also received the propagated query sent by the CD-CAT is the PE-CAT. This catalog, on discovering it does not have the requested data (services for federal definition of rivers), it sends the query over to its parent, that is, the WNA-CAT. Thus, the query received by the PE-CAT is described by using its own ontology; and thus, before forwarding the query, the catalog maps the concepts on to its ontology and the federal ontology so as to generate a new query. Finally, the query is forwarded to the federal SDI (WNA).

Upon receiving the query generated by the PE-CAT, the WNA-CAT checks if it has the information requested. As the holder of the information (descriptions of services that provide data from Federal rivers domains), the WNA-CAT responds to the SDI of the state of Pernambuco as to the services requested. Then, the SDI of the state of Pernambuco returns the received references to the SDI catalog that started the whole process.

By using these services to solve the query, the CD-CAT sets up a service chain involving the following services (Figure 11 illustrates this service chain):

- WMS and WFS with state rivers and reservoirs (SDI field of the Water Resources Department of Pernambuco state),
- WMS and WFS with areas of risk and political maps of the state (SDI's own domain),
- WMS and WFS with data of Federal rivers (Federal SDI domain).

Finally, as the services returned images, considering that the outcome of the query is WMS services, one can see the outcome by means of a map rendering service. Thus, this map rendering service receives results from several WMS services, and exhibits the information on the screen. Figure 12 presents the result of query processing, where a map of the political division of municipalities, federal roads, a stretch of the São Francisco River and the area of risk are displayed.

6. CONCLUSION

The SDIs play an increasingly important role in the dissemination and sharing of spatial data among organizations of different levels of influence. However, the development of a catalog service capable of locating, most precisely, the information in each data source is still required.

Figure 11. Service chaining for the posed query

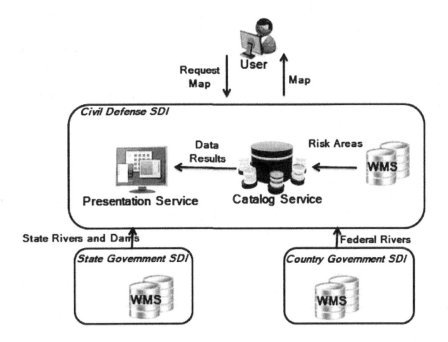

Figure 12. Query result

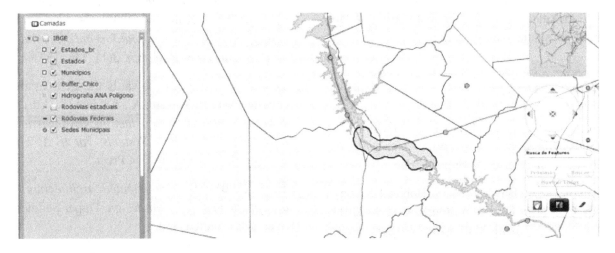

We propose here a catalog service that uses ontologies to provide more accurate searches. Moreover, such service is intended for use in distributed architecture without centralized control. This allows the catalog services in different SDIs to cooperate and exchange information directly, without the traditional problems imposed by a centralized architecture. While a federation-based architecture has been used to illustrate the application of our approach, the proposed catalog service can be employed in other decentralized architectures, for example, peer-to-peer systems.

A major problem concerning the use of ontologies in SDIs these days is the large amount of effort required by organizations to perform the semantic annotation of services. For future works, we propose the development of a tool to automate the process of annotation for these data services. Some important research works have already been developed in this area (Klien, 2007), (Scharl, Stern & Weichselbraun, 2008). The use of tools for the automatic annotation of spatial data and services may not be as precise as that used in manual annotation. However, the use of information provided by users who use catalog services can improve the accuracy of information, enriching the process of information retrieval.

The process that involves geographic information provided by the user is called Volunteered Geographic Information (VGI), and the benefits of its use for the annotation of geographic information have been already discussed in relevant research works (Craglia, Goodchild, Annoni, Camara, Gould, Kuhn et al, 2008), (Goodchild, 2007).

We have concluded that the use of an efficient solution for the discovery of available spatial data will facilitate the integration and sharing of data between spatial data sources.

REFERENCES

Alonso, G., Casati, F., Kuno, H., & Machiraju, V. (2004). *Web services: concepts, architectures and applications*. Berlin: Springer Verlag.

Ankolekar, A., Burstein, M. H., Hobbs, J. R., Lassila, O., Martin, D. L., McIlraith, S. A., et al. (2001). DAML-S: Semantic Markup for Web Services. In I. Cruz, F. Decker, S. Euzenat, & J. McGuinness (Ed.), *First Semantic Web Working Symposium, Vol. 75. SWWS* (pp. 411-430). IOS Press.

ANZLIC Spatial Information Council. (2010). *Australian Spatial Data Infrastructure*. Retrieved July 9, 2010 from http://www.anzlic.org.au/ASDI_quick.html

Athanasis, N., Kalabokidis, K., Vaitis, M., & Soulakellis, N. (2009). Towards a semantics-based approach in the development of geographic portals. *Computers & Geosciences*, *35*(2), 301–308. doi:10.1016/j.cageo.2008.01.014

Baader, F., Calvanese, D., McGuinness, D. L., Nardi, D., & Patel-Schneider, F. (2003). *The description logic handbook: theory, implementation, applications*. Cambridge, UK: Cambridge University Press.

Berners-Lee, T., Hendler, J., & Lassila, O. (2001). The Semantic Web. *Scientific American*, Retrieved July 9, 2010, from http://www.scientificamerican.com/article.cfm?id=the-semantic-web

Brujin, J., Bussler, C., Fensel, D., Hepp, M., Keller, U., Kifer, M., et al. (2005). Web Service Modelling Ontology (WSMO). *World Wide Web Consortium*, Retrieved July 9, 2010, from http://www.w3.org/Submission/WSMO/

Craglia, M., Goodchild, M., Annoni, A., Camara, G., Gould, M., & Kuhn, W. (2008). Next-generation digital Earth. *International Journal of Spatial Data Infrastructure Research*, *3*(1), 146–167.

Egenhofer, M. (2002). Towards the geospatial semantic Web. In Voisard, A., & Chen, S. (Ed.), *ACM International Symposium on Advances in Geographic Information Systems, Vol. 1. ACM 2002* (pp. 1-4). McLaen, CM Press.

Erl, T. (2005). *Service-oriented architecture: concepts, technology and design*. Upper Saddle River, NJ: Prentice Hall.

Federal Geographic Data Committee. (2000). *Content standard for digital geospatial metadata*. Metadata ad hoc working group. Retrieved July 9, 2010, from http://www.fgdc.gov/metadata/csdgm/

Federal Geographic Data Committee. (2010). *National Spatial Data Infrastructure*. Retrieved July 9, 2010, from http://www.fgdc.gov/nsdi/nsdi.html

Global Spatial Data Infrastructure Association. (2010). *Global Spatial Data Infrastructure*, Retrieved July 9, 2010, from http://www.gsdi.org/

Goodchild, M. (2007). Citizens as voluntary sensors: Spatial Data Infrastructure in the world of Web 2.0. *International Journal of Spatial Data Infrastructures Research*, *2*(1), 24–32.

Guarino, N. (1995). Formal ontology, conceptual analysis and knowledge representation. *International Journal of Human-Computer Studies*, *43*(5), 625–640. doi:10.1006/ijhc.1995.1066

Havlik, D., Bleier, T., & Schimak, G. (2009). Sharing sensor data with SensorSA and Cascading Sensor Observation Service. *Sensors (Basel, Switzerland)*, *9*(7), 5493–5502. doi:10.3390/s90705493

Havlik, D., & Schimak, G. (2009). Sensors anywhere – sensor Web enablement in risk management applications. *Ercim News*. Retrieved July 9, 2010, from http://ercim-news.ercim.eu/

Infraestrutura Nacional de Dados Espaciais. (2010). *Infraestrutura Nacional de Dados Espaciais*. Retrieved July 9, 2010, from: http://www.inde.gov.br/

International Organization for Standardization. (2003). *Geographic information – metadata*. Technical Committee 211. Retrieved July 9, 2010, from http://www.iso.org/iso/catalogue_detail.htm?csnumber=26020

International Organization for Standardization. (2007). *Geographic information: Metadata and XML schema implementation*. Technical Committee 211. Retrieved July 9, 2010, from http://www.iso.org/iso/catalogue_detail.htm?csnumber=32557

Joint Centre Research. (2010). *Infrastructure for spatial information in the European community*. Retrieved July 9, 2010, from http://inspire.jrc.ec.europa.eu/

Klien, E. (2007). A rule-based strategy for the semantic annotation of geodata. *Transactions in GIS*, *11*(3), 437–452. doi:10.1111/j.1467-9671.2007.01054.x

Kuhn, W. (2005). Geospatial semantics: why, of what, and how? In Spaccapietra, S., & Zimányi, E. (Eds.), *Journal of Data Semantics* (pp. 1–24). Berlin: Springer. doi:10.1007/11496168_1

Lassoued, Y., Wright, D., Bermudez, L., & Boucelma, O. (2008). Ontology-based mediation of OGC catalogue service for the Web – a virtual solution for integrating coastal Web atlases. In J. Cordeiro, S. Shishkov, A. Ranchordas, & M. Hrlfert (Eds.), *Third International Conference on Software and Data Technologies, Vol. I* (pp. 192-197). Porto, Portugal: INSTICC Press.

Leite, F. L. Jr, Baptista, C. S., Silva, P. A., & Silva, E. R. (2007). WS-GIS: towards a SOA-based SDI federation. In Davis, C. A. Jr, & Monteiro, V. M. (Eds.), *Advances in Geoinformatics* (pp. 199–214). Heidelberg, Germany: Springer.

Lemmens, R., de By, R. A., Gould, M., Wytzisk, A., Grannell, C., & van Oosterom, P. (2007). Enhancing geo-service chaining through deep service descriptions. *Transactions in GIS*, *11*(6), 849–871. doi:10.1111/j.1467-9671.2007.01079.x

Lutz, M., & Kolas, D. (2007). Rule-based in Spatial Data Infrastructure. *Transactions in GIS*, *11*(1), 317–336. doi:10.1111/j.1467-9671.2007.01048.x

Lutz, M., Sprado, J., Klien, E., Schubert, C., & Christ, I. (2008). Overcoming semantic heterogeneity in Spatial Data Infrastructures. *Computers & Geosciences*, *35*(4), 739–752. doi:10.1016/j.cageo.2007.09.017

Martin, D., Paolucci, M., McIlraith, S., Burstein, M., McDermott, D., & McGuinness, D. (2005). Bringing semantics to Web services: The OWL-S Approach. In Cardoso, J., & Sheth, A. (Eds.), *Semantic Web services and Web process composition* (pp. 26–42). Berlin: Springer. doi:10.1007/978-3-540-30581-1_4

McIlraith, S. A., Son, T. C., & Zeng, H. (2001). Semantic Web services. *IEEE Intelligent Systems, 16*(2), 46–53. doi:10.1109/5254.920599

Nebert, D. (Ed.). (2004). *Developing Spatial Data Infrastructures: The SDI Cookbook*. Global Spatial Data Infrastructure.

Open Geospatial Consortium. (2004). *Web map service interface*. Retrieved July 9, 2010, from http://www.opengeospatialorg./standards/wms

Open Geospatial Consortium. (2007). *Open GIS catalogue services specification*. Retrieved July 9, 2010, from http://www.opengeospatialorg./standards/csw

Open Geospatial Consortium. (2008). *Web coverage service implementation standard*. Retrieved July 9, 2010, from http://www.opengeospatialorg/standards/wcs

Open Geospatial Consortium. (2008). *Web feature service implementation specification*. Retrieved July 9, 2010, from http://www.opengeospatialorg./standards/wfs

Roman, D., & Klien, E. (2007). SWING – a semantic framework for geospatial Web services. In Scharl, A., & Tochtermann, K. (Eds.), *The Geospatial Web: how GeoBrowsers, social software and the Web 2.0 are shaping the network society* (pp. 229–234). London: Springer.

Scharl, A., Stern, H., & Weichselbraun, A. (2008) Annotating and visualizing location data in geospatial Web applications. In S. Boll, C. Jones, E. Kansa, P. Kishor, M. Naaman, R. Purvers, et al. (Eds.), *International Workshop on Location and the Web, ACM, New York, Vol. 1* (pp. 65-68). New York: ACM Press.

Senkler, K., Voges, U., Einspainer, U., Kanellopoulos, I., Millot, M., Luraschi, G., et al. (2006). *Software for distributed metadata catalogue services to support the EU portal*. Europe Commission – Joint Research Centre. Retrieved July 9, 2010, from http://inspire.jrc.ec.europa.eu

Smits, P., & Friis-Christensen, A. (2007). Resource discovery in a European Spatial Data Infrastructure. *IEEE Transactions on Knowledge and Data Engineering, 19*(1), 85–95. doi:10.1109/TKDE.2007.250587

Stock, K. M., Atkinson, R., Higgins, C., Small, M., Woolf, A., & Millard, K. (2010). A semantic registry using a feature type catalogue instead of ontologies to support Spatial Data Infrastructures. *International Journal of Geographical Information Science, 24*(2), 231–252. doi:10.1080/13658810802570291

Williamson, I., Rajabifard, A., & Feeney, M. F. (2003). *Developing Spatial Data Infrastructures: from concept to reality*. London: Taylor & Francis. doi:10.1201/9780203485774

World Wide Web Consortium. (2004). *OWL Web Ontology Language Guide*. Retrieved July 9, 2010, from http://www.w3.org/TR/owl-guide/

KEY TERMS AND DEFINITIONS

Catalog: Service that allows data discovery on SDIs.

Data Integration: Represents the problem of combining data provided by different local sources.

Distributed Databases: Database whose data are spread over several data sources.

Ontology: Formal conceptualization of application domain.

Semantic Web: Extension of the current web, which aims to describe the semantic of the resources published in the web.

Spatial Data Infrastructure: Framework that aims facilitates discovery and integration of spatial data.

Spatial Data: Data that owns a geospatial reference.

Section 4
Semantic Web

Chapter 7
VISION:
An Infrastructure for Semantic Geospatial Web Services

Sven Schade

European Commission – Joint Research Centre, Institute for Environment and Sustainability, Italy

ABSTRACT

Over the past years, many research projects and initiatives have provided heterogeneous building blocks for the so called Semantic Geospatial Web. The number of proposed architectures and developed components impede a definition of the state of the art, comparisons of existing solutions, and the identification of open research challenges. This chapter provides the missing generic specification of central building blocks. Focusing on service based solutions; VISION (VIsionary Semantic service Infrastructure with ONtologies) is introduced as a means to depict required components at a generalized level. The VISION architecture highlights the most important services for the Semantic Geospatial Web and brings structure to the numerous past and present partial solutions. Model-as-a-Service (MaaS) is introduced as a central concept for encapsulating environmental models. This has great potential to be a major part of future information infrastructures. The German-funded GDI-GRID project serves illustrating examples for MaaS and arising interoperability challenges. This paper will focus on VISION, and compare it with two other recent research projects and conclude by identifying major areas for future research on Semantic Geospatial Web Services and supporting infrastructures.

DOI: 10.4018/978-1-60960-192-8.ch007

INTRODUCTION

Envisioning a Semantic Spatial Web, Max Egenhofer coined the notion of the Semantic Geospatial Web as a step-stone, which is topic to the geospatial science community (Egenhofer 2002). The Semantic Web (Berners Lee et al. 2001) already provides means for re-organizing the data offerings of the World Wide Web (WWW). Solutions for sophisticated information retrieval are in place (Manning et al. 2008). Now the geospatial science community has to provide geospatial and temporal ontologies in conjunction with according query mechanisms and tools. Enabled reasoning should enhance information retrieval within and beyond geospatial information communities, as well as human computer interaction.

Many research projects address these challenges by using Web Service technology. In this context, basic data structures and interfaces of central services are standardized for the Semantic Web (W3C 2009, Turhan et al. 2006) and for spatial data infrastructures (SDI) (Nebert 2004). The combination of both provides well developed foundations for implementing the Semantic Geospatial Web (Janowicz et al. 2010, forthcoming). Still, it remains hard to coin the main benefits and drawbacks or to compare different solutions to geospatial decision support with each other. Arising research fields cannot be clearly identified. In order to proceed, we miss a generic functional specification of a Semantic Geospatial Web Service infrastructure.

In this chapter, we present such a description. We promote the VISION (VIsionary Semantic service Infrastructure with ONtologies) architecture, which generalizes over a literature review and applied research in combining Semantic Web, Geospatial Web and service oriented architectures. Core components of the Semantic Geospatial Web are identified and required functionality is grouped on a technology-independent level. The VISION architecture enables us to explain central building blocks of a Semantic Geospatial Web instead of

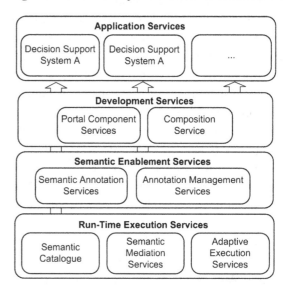

Figure 1. Overview of the VISION architecture

getting lost in implementation details and existing partial solutions. Figure 1 gives first insights.

Application Services, which are (geospatial) decision support systems (Densham 1991), make use of *Deployment Services* for building their required front-ends, services supporting semantic annotations of the required kinds, and execution services. A framework of frequently required components for portal development and a tool for composing basic services is provided at intermediate level. *Semantic Enablement Services* are divided into such tools that support annotating resources and visualizing annotations, and such, which manage annotations optionally including versioning. *(Run-Time) Execution Services* provide the foundation of the architecture, as they serve the most basic functionalities (access to data and processing), means for component retrieval, and execution environment(s) for service compositions.

In order to address the provision, retrieval and execution of environmental models, we integrate recently coined notion of Model-as-a-Service (MaaS) into the VISION architecture (Roman et al. 2009b). MaaS has evolved as a merge of the model web (Geller and Turner, 2007) and

Software as a Service (Bennett et al. 2000), a concept of being able to call-up re-usable, fine-grained software components across a network. It can be seen as a cutting edge concept for next generation SDIs. As MaaS includes mechanisms for encapsulating different means of encodings, it covers the use of independently managed data and processing centers, as well as the use of cloud computing (Chappell 2008) and grid computing (Foster and Kesselman 2003). However, in this chapter, semantic challenges are focused, while grid technologies are only included for completeness.

We introduce the GDI-GRID project for illustrations. GDI-GRID integrates SDI, Semantic Web, and grid computing in a working infrastructure and serves a demonstration of the complementarities of all three areas. Distributed geospatial data sets are put to use by processing and merging it with third-party data, creating standards-based, multi-functional, generic SDI services. Formal semantic descriptions facilitate interoperability between involved components. GDI-GRID can be seen as an instantiation of the VISION architecture and the scenarios as workflows for geospatial decision support. Once the architecture has been introduced, we illustrate its application for comparing GDI-GRID with two other projects (SWING and ENVISION) and for identifying areas for future work.

The remainder of this chapter is structured as follows. We present required background in section 2, where we focus on the GDI-GRID project and three related scenarios. We provide pointers to related work (section 3) and subsequently apply the GDI-GRID requirements to detail the building blocks of the VISION architecture (section 4). Here, we clarify the challenges related to data and service semantics and illustrate the need for introducing MaaS. In this section, we also relate VISION to our recent work considering standardization. The application of VISION to a comparison of research projects is given in section 5. The comparison allows identification of gaps in recent developments (section 6). The last section (section 7) includes a summary and our conclusions.

BACKGROUND AND EXAMPLE

Geospatial sciences faced semantic problems since their beginnings. These reached from philosophical questions like *what is location?* (Bittner 1997), *what is place?* (Casati, and Varzi 1999) or *what is measurement?* (Stevens 1946) to more technical questions, for example relating to data fusion (Goguen 2005). With the emergence of the WWW and related technologies, semantics related topics got even more attention (Wache et al. 2001, Lutz 2006, Andrei et al. 2008). The notion of the Semantic Web (Berners Lee et al. 2001) provided the illusion of an immediate solution for many open issues and efforts of connecting geospatial sciences with the Semantic Web emerged (Maué et al. 2008, Janowicz et al. 2010, forthcoming). In this section we briefly introduce background required to understand the potential and limits of the state of the art. We focus on the *Semantic Geospatial Web*, which by intention brings semantic technologies to the geospatial web community. Notably, this notion differs from approaches extending the Semantic Web with geospatial data and processing, i.e. from the *Geospatial Semantic Web*. As we consider services in the geospatial web, adding geospatial aspects to the Semantic Web community is out of scope of this work.

Geospatial Semantics

Although (geospatial) information communities always had to deal with semantics, related issues gain importance recently. At the beginnings, intended interpretations of data model (or schema) elements were known to the provider and user community. Experts developing flood simulations, for example, based their schemas on previously existing measurements or on results of own observations (Kurzback et al. 2009). This changed completely with the possibilities of the WWW and with the raising interest in information exchange (Bishr et al. 1997). Today, many third-party data is retrievable and can be re-used out of the initially intended context. Semantic interoperability, in the sense of the technical analogue to human communication and cooperation (Kuhn 2005), becomes a major issue and semantic engineering becomes a central task (Kuhn 2009). Numerous surveys illustrate semantic problems in interoperability. For an overview of challenges in the geospatial domain we recommend the following readings (Bishr et al. 1997), (Lutz et al. 2003) and (Kuhn 2005). In summary, all challenges relate to communication and cooperation among machines, or between humans and machines. Semantic aspects concern data and their schemas (Schade 2010), geospatial processing (Lutz 2007), and quality of information (Schade 2008).

Ontologies provide means for addressing the arising challenges. In the sense of engineering artifacts that specify the intended interpretation of a communities' vocabulary (Guarino 1998), ontologies became a common tool in the Semantic Web (Berners Lee et al. 2001). Underlying engineering approaches differ drastically. While community driven vocabularies are sometimes already considered ontologies (Mika 2005), more sophisticated approaches include philosophic notions into the engineering process (Massolo et al. 2003, Grenon and Smith 2004). The tool has been carried over into the geospatial community. Geospatial and temporal ontologies have to account for endurants (such as water bodies and reservoirs), perdurants, (such as precipitation and flooding), as well as abstract constructs (such as geospatial information items, environmental models, processing operations, and error characteristics). Some have already been developed over the past years and have been used in various settings (Frank 2003, Kuhn 2005, Schade et al. 2008).

Also ontologies are a central building block; they do not provide the complete solution to interoperability. Every ontology consists of building blocks, called primitives (Smith 1995). An ontology for floods for example, may be based on primitives like *water*, *reservoir*, and *precipitation*. Ensuring the correct interpretation of the conceptual structure provided by the ontology requires a clear definition of the intended interpretations of these primitives, which means symbol grounding (Harnad 1990). Interpretation rules for vocabularies used by information communities (to describe their schemas and processing operations) are defined by establishing a reference between the vocabulary and the ontology with grounded primitives. The process of establishing these links is called semantic referencing (Kuhn 2003) or semantic annotation (Maué et al. 2008). Once a vocabulary is semantically referenced/annotated, semantic transformation may be used to switch from one vocabulary to the other (Schade 2010). In the simplest case a semantic transformation is used to modify the units of a measurement. For example, precipitation described in millimeters per hour can be translated to a description using millimeters per day as the unit of measure. In order to establish a Semantic Geospatial Web, grounded ontologies must be provided, means for establishing and maintaining semantic references have to be available, and semantic transformation has to be supported in any form.

Service Oriented Approaches for a Semantic Geospatial Web

In this chapter, we focus on approaches for the Semantic Geospatial Web, which base on the notion of a service as defined for Service Oriented Architecture (SOA) (Bell 2008). In this context a service is a unit offering certain functionality, as for example access to geospatial data, or encapsulation of geospatial processing. In the context of the WWW, SOAs can be realized using Web Service technology (Alonso et al. 2004). We introduce services of Spatial Data Infrastructures (SDI) (Nebert 2004), as commonly used within the geospatial community in separation of services for the Semantic Web. The combination of both reveals the full potential.

To exchange data between SDI services, i.e. to make them interoperable, they have to share common schemas or transformation mechanisms have to be in place (Schade 2010). Standards of Open Geospatial Consortium (OGC)[1] and the Technical Committee 211 of International Organization for Standardization (ISO/TC211) [2] guarantee interoperability on a syntactic level. Services can exchange data, which is modeled in form of so called feature types (ISO/TC211 2001), if they agree on names and types for their inputs, outputs, and operations. Common encoding schemes for geospatial data are in place, Geography Markup Language (GML) (OGC 2007) is most frequently used in expert applications. The available specifications do not ensure whether data exchanged between services can be interpreted in a meaningful way. For example, a Web Processing Service (WPS) (Schut 2007) can be used to compute flood simulation scenarios based on hourly precipitation information delivered by a Sensor Observation Service (SOS) (Na and Priest 2007). Both services need to share a common understanding of precipitation measures to compute meaningful results (Bröring et al. 2009); otherwise the simulated flood would diverge from any realistic case. Similar cases apply to download services for geospatial object representations (Web Feature Service, WFS (OGC 2005)), download services for representations of geospatial fields (Web Coverage Service, WCS, (OGC 2006)), and visualization services (Web Map Service, WMS (OGC 2003)).

Infrastructure for Spatial Information in Europe (INSPIRE) provides a large-scale example (INSPIRE 2004). INSPIRE obliges the EU member states to provide their environmental data for 34 different themes in a harmonized manner. Matching national geospatial schemas with the specifica-

tions of INSPIRE requires formal specifications of the national schemas as well as the INSPIRE schema (Cai et al. 2010). GEOSS (Global Earth Observation System of Systems) [3] and SEIS (Shared Environmental Information System)[4] provide further practical cases on European and global level. So far, for each case the mappings between geospatial schemas have to be specified and tested outside the geospatial services (Andrei et al. 2008). It is impossible to evaluate on-the-fly whether a dataset has been consistently matched or whether it contains contradictions. To perform such tests, the schemas and the contained feature type definitions have to be downloaded manually in order to perform common reasoning tasks (Janowicz et al. 2009). This complicates communication in general and generation of geospatial workflows in particular (OGC 2009). Considering human and machine interaction, service and data retrieval is hampered, too (Manning et al. 2008, Lutz and Klien 2006). The challenge of establishing semantic interoperability between (web) services, i.e. the ability of services to exchange data in a meaningful way and with a minimum of human intervention (Harvey et al. 1999, Manso and Wachowicz 2009), remains.

Opposed to work on SDI, many services in the Semantic Web do not share common interfaces. Instead isolated solutions are provided, which lack a binding to each other (Janowicz et al. 2009). For instance, the SIM-DL server (Janowicz et al. 2007) can compute the similarity of geographic feature types. It uses an extended version of the Description Logics Interface Group (DIG) protocol (Turhan et al. 2006) for communication and the Web Ontology Language (OWL) (Bechhofer et al. 2003) for knowledge representation. Whereas OWL provides a formal language and encoding to exchange ontologies, DIG specifies a service interface for inference engines, i.e. reasoners. OWL and DIG are standardized, but these are two rare examples.

The GDI-GRID Project

For this work, we selected the German-founded GDI-GRID project[5] as a representative for Semantic Geospatial Web research. GDI-GRID focuses on the gridification of geospatial processing in an SDI environment and on related issues of interoperability. By using grid technology, a complex process, such as a simulation of a geospatial phenomenon is analyzed for possibilities of parallelization (Shen et al. 2004; Li et al. 2005). Identified sub-tasks are distributed among working nodes of the grid (Lee 2001). Gridification requires new functions to be added to the initial processing. First, tiling is used to separate independent working steps into a set of tasks; second, a process for joining the results of the separated steps is required (stitching). These functionalities are encapsulated in processing operations. Different operations use data spaces for exchange. Sensible communication between processing steps and valuable results can only achieved if:

- these data spaces follow a well-defined schema,
- the schemas are correctly mapped to processing inputs,
- processing outputs feed the subsequent data space correctly,
- processing operations are well defined (including the potential for parallelization), and
- quality information is continuously made transparent.

As GDI-GRID is a German-funded project, issues of multilingualism arise. Some of the involved components are described in German language, while others are specified in English. This situation adds complexity to the overall interoperability challenge.

In the following subsections we briefly introduce three scenarios, which were acquired from the GDI-GRID project. We illustrate all of the issues listed above, and identify central building blocks and related issues of semantic interoperability for each scenario. We separate basic input services, processing elements and their inputs, data spaces, and views on data spaces. Information flow is indicated by arrows. By comparing the results of this analysis with previous versions of the VISION architecture and components later in this chapter, we extracted a set of general functionalities for the Semantic Geospatial Web.

Scenario 1: Flood Simulation

Flood simulation provides us with a first scenario (Figure 2). It intersects several scientific disciplines; environmental science, water management, and urban and regional planning demand for flood simulation (Kurzbach et al. 2009). Complex tasks arise for all participating disciplines. These include prediction of flood events for rivers and sea, determination of flood areas and creation of flood risk maps. In this scenario, common applications are used as input for simulation tools based on current and dynamically integrated geospatial data. The required workflow is adapted to grid computing and distributed onto grid resources. Integration of sensor networks which deliver up-to-date data for disaster control is discussed.

In this scenario, process independent third-party inputs cover a digital elevation model (DEM), precipitation data, data on soil, demographic data (such as population) and more. At least four different data provision communities are involved. This means that the provided data (in terms of schemas and quality of data sets) has to be described in detail. Methods for matching these definitions with the affected processing inputs (of triangulation, flood simulation, and flood risk analysis) have to be in place. As floods may occur in various regions, discovery and retrieval mechanisms for suitable data have to be provided. The data spaces, which are shared between at least two processing steps, face similar

Figure 2. Flood simulation - workflow

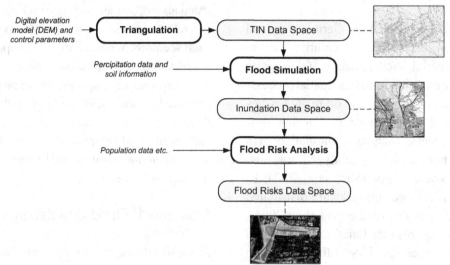

requirements, except the need for discovery. Those do not only include schemas for data exchange, but also rules for rendering, i.e. visualization. In these cases the process feeding a data space may impose semantics; for example, identified inundation zones strongly depend on the applied flood simulation. The three involved processes have to be annotated semantically, such that suitable implementing algorithms can be discovered. In respect to gridification, semantic descriptions have to include a specification of allowed tiling strategies. In cases of flood simulation, for example catchment areas could be used for geospatial-tiling. Parallel execution of algorithms can only be planned if allowed tiling strategies are defined. As indicated previously, the complete process must either follow a single methodology for quality propagation, or means for translating between quality models. In emergency cases related to flooding, probabilities of hazard scenarios are a prerequisite for valuable decision support.

Scenario 2: Noise Propagation in Urban Areas

Noise propagation in urban areas (Figure 3) is a scenario demanded by the EC (EC 2002). The directive mandates a quantification of environmental noise caused by noise emission. Required studies and simulations must be repeated periodically and require significant computation resources (Krüger and Kolbe 2008). The data basis consists of three dimensional environmental models aggregated and integrated from different sources. In applications, which are not grid-enabled, aggregation and integration is performed manually, based on file-based exchange formats. The actual computation of noise propagation is time-consuming. One such simulation can only be completed in a relatively short timeframe (within several weeks), if clusters of 200 computing nodes are available. Grid computing adds performance and offers the possibility to compute simulations with different levels of detail (Guercke et al. 2008).

Again, at least three third-party communities are involved in data providing. The community providing terrain data overlaps with the DEM community of the flood simulation scenario, but

Figure 3. Noise propagation - workflow

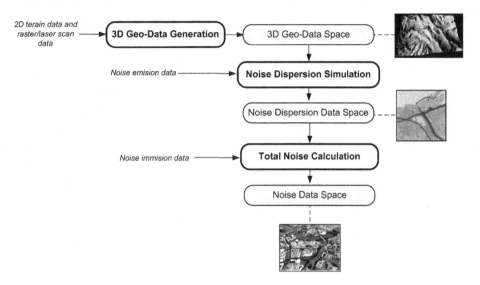

Figure 4. Emergency routing - workflow

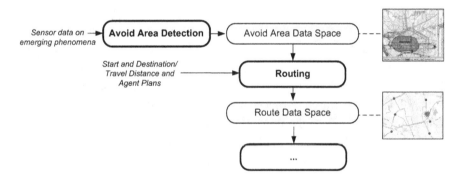

also involves, other raster and laser scanning communities. Communities providing noise emission data and noise immersion data may overlap, too. The remaining elements of the workflow face similar challenges as introduced for the flood simulation scenario.

Scenario 3: Emergency Routing

Emergency routing covers evacuation scenarios with simulation and optimization (Figure 4). Areas, which should be avoided in the route planning, are detected based on sensor measurements. Emerging phenomena and dynamic correlations increase complexity in developing and executing

simulations of evacuation. Agent-based simulation serves a solution, because they allow for individual modeling of behavior (Axelrod 1997). The required models involve large amounts of inputs and outputs, as for example complex street networks and agent specification plans. Within this scenario, we aim at a generic routing solution and therefore do neither restrict the measurement inputs to a specific observable (like a plum of toxic gas), nor to a specific application of the calculated routes. The developed components can be used to address many application specific problems, such as evacuation planning or coordination of relief units. Integration of previously existing algorithms and software components with grid infrastructures is a central objective.

This scenario is actually the smallest of the three. Still, many third-party communities may get involved. Avoid areas are not restricted to any specific phenomena; they include flooded zones, spreading plums of toxic gases and many more. Identification of relevant phenomena and according information retrieval is one of two central challenges in this scenario. Specifications of route start and destination are relatively straightforward and agent planning requires using a distinct ontology, which is specific to one applied routing algorithm. The second major challenge considers the connection of results with other applications, i.e. information communities. The content of the route data space has to be specified clearly and related quality (and trust) aspects have to be acknowledged.

Summary of Requirements

The GDI-GRID project with its applications serves a typical example of recent research projects with innovation in semantic and grid technology. Project needs can be summarized according to the main elements, which are required to implement the scenarios detailed above. The three scenarios request for three different spatial decision support systems, which all require the same building blocks: service discovery, service composition, and map visualization of final results. All have to facilitate explicit semantic descriptions for sensible communication between each other and towards human users. Aspects of data and service quality have to be included.

Components for providing services, data, and views could be re-used. When it comes to the integration of data sets, discovery has to overcome semantic heterogeneities between service and data set advertisements and search terms. Service composition requires content validation of involved components and their interplay. Last but not least, executing services have to be

developed and deployed. This includes highly specialized models of our environment. As this involves especially complex simulations and large data volumes, grid technology is required in order to achieve reasonably fast processing. In order to allow gridification, semantic process descriptions need to be connected with allowed tiling strategies. In order to overcome syntactic heterogeneities OGC standards should be applied. Semantic heterogeneities should be addressed by combining SDI and Semantic Web technologies. Geospatial and temporal ontologies have to support data generation, provision, access, and use; multilingualism has to be acknowledged by each.

RELATED WORK

Over the last years, several works focused on semantics and geospatial ontologies supporting SDI and OGC services. This includes work on semantics-based and context-aware retrieval of geographic information (Janowicz et al. 2007, Schade et al. 2008b, Keßler et al. 2009, Yue et al. 2009), ontology alignment (Cruz and Sunna, 2008), semantic annotation (Maué et al. 2009), ontology-driven data translation (Zhao et al. 2008, Schade 2010), as well as work on Semantic Geospatial Web services (Shi 2005, Roman and Klien 2007) and their composition into application specific workflows (Lemmens et al. 2006, Yue et al. 2007, Fitzner et al. 2009). This research has lead to a set of valuable tools such as ConceptVISTA[6] for ontology creation and visualization, the SWING Concept Repository[7], the Semantic Annotations API (sapience)[8], the SIM-DL similarity server and Protégé plug-in[9], the semantically-enabled Sensor Observation Service SemSOS (Henson et al. 2009), the sensor observable registry (Jirka and Bröring, 2009), or the OWL application profile for CSW (Stock et al. 2009). Even OGC itself has established test beds for researching the connection between Geospatial Web Services and the Semantic Web (Lieberman et al. 2006; OGC

2009). The World Wide Web Consortium (W3C) has launched an incubator group on Semantic Sensor Networks[10]. It became impossible to follow all recent developments, because a structured overview is missing. This is what we are going to provide in this chapter.

In addition, all existing approaches to enrich SDIs with semantics are coupled to a specific technology. The OWL-Profile for CSW suggested by Stock and colleagues (2009), for example, depends on implementations with Resource Description Framework (RDF) (W3C 2004) and is even restricted to the ontology language OWL. The registry proposal of Jirka and Bröring (2009) is even more restricted, namely to features observable by sensors. In contrast, we recently proposed an approach which abstracts from a particular inference engine and ontology language such as OWL, OWL 2.0 (W3C 2009), Web Service Modeling Language (WSML) (de Bruijn et al. 2006), or Topic Maps (ISO/IEC 2002). We suggested a semantic enablement layer for the integration of OGC services and semantic technology previously (Janowicz et al. 2010, forthcoming). This proposal will be re-visited later in this chapter.

We addressed the connection between the geospatial and the Semantic Web in numerous past and recent research projects. These includes GDI-GRID, SWING (Andrei et al. 2008), and ENVISION (Roman et al. 2009). All these works mainly address OGC and related standards. Feedback has been directly given (Maué et al. 2008; OGC 2009). In this chapter, we attempt generalization of existing solutions within geo-sciences and SDI. We will use the VISION architecture to compare the three above mentioned projects among each other in section 5.

SEMANTIC ENABLEMENT AND VISION

The requirements outlined for GDI-GRID are prototypical for many other research projects and initiatives. In this section, we define a generic VISION architecture that meets these requirements. By analyzing the GDI-GRID scenarios in relation to a previous version of the architecture (Roman et al. 2009), we extracted a set of general operations that possible instantiations should support. The MaaS concept is presented as a building block that connects environmental models with existing infrastructures. It is introduced in detail using the previously identified scenarios. Our recent work on semantic enablement for standard geospatial services (Janowicz et al. 2010), provides means to sharpen the functionalities underlying the separate VISION components. The resulting architecture can be used to map existing solutions to each other and to identify missing developments. We will approach both in later sections.

VISION in Detail

Figure 1 already provides first insides to VISION. We already introduced one layer per type of requirement. The Application Services, i.e. the decision support system, is based on a set of Development Services. Both layers make use of Semantic Enablement Services and all together rely on Execution Services. With the illustrating examples in mind we now add more details to these layers (Figure 5). In contrast to the previous version (Roman et al. 2009), we added a reasoning component and adopted naming of elements in order to underline its service-oriented nature. With both we concretize our initial approach.

At design time (left part of this figure), the VISION Deployment Services provide access to tools for generating application-specific content. An *Annotation Client* and an *Ontology Client* provide easy access to available ontologies and semantic descriptions of resources. The *Environmental Decision Support Services* offer interfaces for generating application-specific portal while the *MaaS Composition Services* offer functionality for visual specification of service compositions and their publication as MaaS. A *Se-*

Figure 5. Details about the VISION architecture (adapted from (Roman et al. 2009))

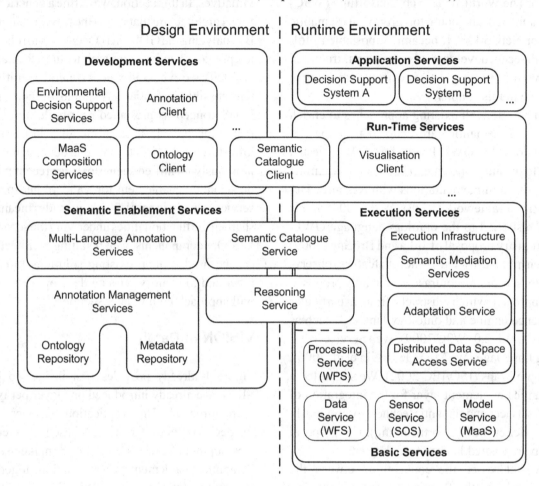

mantic Catalogue Client can be used for discovery of candidate services of a specific composition task. The *Multi-Language Annotation Services* provide functionality to the annotation and ontology clients as well as to the *Semantic Catalogue Service*. A *Reasoning Service* is separately available. The VISION Semantic Enablement Services also comprise tools which support ontology creation and the annotation of resources, and a component for multi-language annotation management. The *Annotation Management Services* require repositories for ontologies and for related metadata.

At run-time (right part of the figure), community specific decision support as requested by the flood simulation, noise, and emergency routing scenario and pilots has to be supported as *VISION Application Services*. They will directly apply a *(Semantic) Catalogue Client* and *Visualization Clients*, which are both provided by the VISION Run-time Services. Underneath, the VISON Execution Services provides the adaptive *Execution Infrastructure*. This incorporates mechanisms for data mediation and adaptation of service compositions. It provides access to a *Distributed Data Space*, which is fed by classical data services, such as WFS or SOS, or by MaaS (discussed below). Further resources, like processing functionality and environmental models are also provided as services (more details are given below). A *Semantic Catalogue* supports registration and discovery of semantically annotated resources. It thus provides the bridge between the executable components and the ontology infrastructure. Inferences on populated ontologies (knowledge bases) are enabled by the *Reasoning Service*.

MaaS in VISION

Model-as-a-Service (MaaS) serves as a connector between environmental models, such as flood simulations or noise propagation, and information infrastructures (Roman et al. 2009b). The notion evolved as a specialization of Software-as-a-Service (SaaS) concept for the model web. SaaS is defined as a model of software deployment whereby a provider licenses an application to customers for use as a service on demand (Bennett et al. 2000). The model web is defined as an approach to manage analytical models of geospatial phenomena on the Web (Geller and Melton 2008). MaaS is a specific type of SaaS, because it deploys software for the model web. It encapsulated environmental models. MaaS aims at providing the scientific community access to up to date geospatial research models through an automated request system for model runs, with up-to-date, online, visualization and analysis tools and through standard data. In this sense MaaS gives access to scientific geospatial workflows. At the first glance, it appears as a simple merge of ideas (SaaS and model web), but in this case the sum is more as its parts. On the one hand the specialization poses new demands to the SaaS, just because of the variety and complexity of models. On the other hand, the model web becomes equipped with a powerful tool. The provision of environmental models strongly depends on the flexibility, which should be allowed in respect to provided data and to changing model parameters. Many models are closely related to the underlying data and providers are often not willing to provide direct data access. Under the MaaS view several of these options can be enabled. Apart from the provision as service component, it has to be mentioned, that (ideally) clients should accompany the MaaS. These should

allow users to experience the MaaS, which allows fitness for purpose measures.

MaaS can be realized in different ways and on different platforms, from the use of independently managed geospatial data and processing centers through the use of cloud computing and geospatial-grid computing technologies (Shen et al. 2004; Li et al. 2005). An additional aspect of MaaS is the combination of technologies from cloud/grid computing with the use of Semantically Enabled Service Architectures (SESA) (Werthner et al. 2006) and Service Oriented Knowledge Utilities (SOKU) (de Roure 2006). SOKU captures three key notions. (i) *Service-orientation* leads to an architecture that comprises of services, which may be instantiated and assembled dynamically. Structure, behavior and location of software are changing at run-time. (ii) SOKU services are *knowledge-assisted* to facilitate automation and advanced functionality, the knowledge aspect is reinforced by the emphasis on delivering high level services to the user. (iii) *Utility* enforces directly and immediately useable service with established functionality, performance and dependability, illustrating the emphasis on user needs and issues such as trust. The convergence between grids and Web Services, grids and semantic technologies, and emerging service oriented architectures will enable the provision of computing, information and knowledge capabilities such as utility-like services in the future.

Notably, in the MaaS context, we consider models aiming at simulation, observation, and measurement. This excludes models in the broader sense. Accordingly we require functionality like sensor access and management and simulation. In VISION we focus initially on the basic infrastructure for semantic MaaS discovery and MaaS composition. At design time, the workflow of the environmental model is defined, existing resources are discovered, and the according MaaS is annotated and registered. At run-time, potential users discover the existing MaaS, connect them to relevant data sources, set additional parameters and execute scenarios of interest. In the end, each MaaS becomes part of the VISION Execution Services. It is in a sense a basic service, because it encapsulates simulations of (geospatial) phenomena. The simulations become a building block for potential, application-specific service compositions. Once these two functionalities (sensor access and simulation access) are defined, various technical solutions can be applied. Recently SOS and WPS were proposed to encapsulate environmental models. In the case of SOS, the same interface can be used for both functionalities (Na and Priest 2007).

Considering the previously introduced scenarios, basically all processing notes become MaaS. OGC services become the main providers for model inputs. In the following we revisit each of the three scenarios and identify involved MaaS and OGC services. In addition, each scenario can be directly encapsulated as a MaaS itself. The requirements for semantic interoperability (outlined above) become projected to MaaS. Input parameters and the out of a MaaS put have to be described including quality information, the encapsulated environmental model as such has to be described including assumptions, and possibilities for parallelization and tiling have to be clearly specified.

MaaS for Flood Simulation and Risk Assessment

Following service based modeling we identify three MaaS for the flood simulation case (Figure 6). Triangulation mechanisms are encapsulated and provided separately from flood simulation models and from models for flood risk analysis. Triangulations are only the front end to a complex workflow of optimizing DEMs for flood simulations. The DEM is provided via a WCS. In fact, this service exposes functionality to calculate a triangular irregular network (TIN) from high quality topographic data (Kurzbach et al. 2009). Point to raster conversion is applied to serve break

line detections, which are further generalized and converted to TIN (Rath 2007; Lanig and Zipf 2009). The results of the provided calculations fill the elevation TIN data space. Together with information on precipitation, which is provided via a SOS, and soil types, which are again provided using a WCS, this provides the input to the flood simulation MaaS. Here, water levels and flow velocities are approximated and flood maps are created. These maps fed the inundation data space. Also this is valuable information on its own; the inundation maps serve central input to the flood risk analysis (encapsulated as the third MaaS). In conjunction with support data, like data about population which may be provided in form of an OGC WFS, the maps are used to serve the flood risk data space. The flood hazard map is the most important outcome; it is officially requested by the 'flood directive' of the European Commission (EC) (EC 2007).

As water height and flow simulations are data and processing intense, they provide a good working case for parallelization and gridification inside a MaaS. Tiling and merging DEMs has already proven a powerful approach (Kurzback and Pasche 2009). It can be facilitated for the triangulation MaaS. The parallelization of flow simulations requires more sophisticated tiling and stitching strategies. Boundary conditions of connected model parts have to be detected in order to identify decomposable structures and global situations have to be reached in an iterative manner (Kurzbach et al. 2009). An according Flood Simulation Service is currently under development within the GDI-GRID project. The risk analysis required to generate the flood hazard map is currently not considered as a grid component, because required processing is not as crucial as in the other two cases.

The depicted workflow results in a highly specialized decision support document, the flood hazard map. Nevertheless, the overall approach is independent of the area of interest and of individual data sources and algorithms. Once

Figure 6. Flood simulation - service based modeling

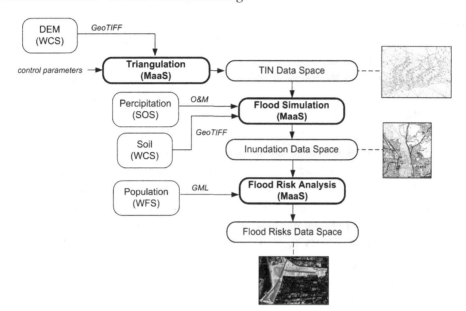

resources listed above are available as VISION Basic Services, the architecture (Figure 6) can be applied for goal-driven communication and cooperation. The complete composition can be defined using the VISION MaaS Composition Services and the VISION Semantic Catalogue Service for discovery. For this specific case, we at least require (grounded) ontologies describing geospatial entities and phenomena (earth surface, water bodies, bodies of soil, amount of people, as well as precipitation, flooding, and inundation), their characteristics (water level, flow velocity, duration, etc.), and related representations (for example TIN for elevation of the earth surface, demographic data tables, triangulation algorithms, encodings for height and velocity measurements, flood simulation, and risk maps). More general ontologies are required for common ways of tiling, representing error and uncertainty, as well as OGC services, such as WPS, WFS, SOS, and WCS and high-level data encoding in GML. Each process, input, and output has to be annotated with a subset of these ontologies. This is supported by the VISION Multi-Language Annotation Services,

the VISION Annotation Management Services, and according clients.

MaaS for Noise Propagation

For the second scenario, and again, with respect to service based modeling, several MaaS can be identified. This would add modifications to Figure 3. One MaaS generates three dimensional data from multiple inputs, a second simulating the dispersion of noise and a third, which integrated noise dispersion with immissions. In three-dimensional geospatial data generation, two-dimensional data from some data base with geospatial content is equipped with information about the third dimension. Additional information is gathered from raster and laser scan data. The two-dimensional data may be provided via an OGC WFS, while the raster data comes from a WCS. The 3D data space contains the resulting high dimensional objects. Among other purposes, these objects provide input to noise dispersion models. Here, reflections of noise are considered. Additionally required inputs include the noise emission data, which may be served via WFS. The results are offered in the noise dispersion data space. Together with data on noise immission (served by either a WFS or even as an image via a WMS) the final noise data space can be filled. It is this data space, which serves data as requested by the directive of the EC (EC 2002).

Taking gridification into account, tiling and stitching for generation of three-dimensional data can be established based on spatial location (Guercke et al. 2008). This is implemented inside the according MaaS. As for the case of flood simulation, gridifying noise dispersion underlies different constraints. Specific implementations are considered within the GDI-GRID project. Boundary conditions of the model parts have to be defined and common patterns have to be identified (Krüger and Kolbe 2008). As in previous scenarios, merging of data sets in not considered a practical case for required grid support. An according service can be established following common (non-grid) technology.

The VISION architecture can be applied as described for the previous scenario. Few more ontologies are required; especially for the three-dimensional representation of geospatial entities and conversion between two and three dimensions.

MaaS for Emergency Routing

Applying service based modeling, as advocated in this paper, to the emergency routing scenario results in two MaaS. The one encapsulates the detection of areas, which should be avoided for routing, the other performing the actual route calculations. The detection of avoid areas is based on measurement inputs from various OGC Sensor Observation Services (Na and Priest 2007), each of which encapsulates observation results gathered from a particular sensor network using the Observations and Measurements (O&M) standard of OGC (Cox 2007). The model results in a collection of polygon geometries. We call this collection the avoid area data space. In conjunction with a starting point and either a destination point or a

desired travel distance, this space provides input to the routing MaaS. This Maas serves input to the route data space, a space containing all possible routes given the conditions of avoid areas. It can be used as input for more specialized applications.

Given that sensor networks may cover various spatial extends, the avoid area detection MaaS can be implemented with grid technologies. The analysis of measurement results from each SOS can be distributed across working nodes. This only requires a tiling of measurements based on spatial distribution of sensor networks, and stitching by data merging. All this capabilities are encapsulated by the MaaS interface. In theory, parallelization could be applied to the routing MaaS, too. Single route calculations could be distributed among working notes of the grid. As non-parallelized routing algorithms already perform well, this option seems unnecessary.

Again, the VISION architecture can be applied as described above. Only the case-dependent ontologies have to be added. This basically covers routing algorithms, agent-based modeling, and O&M.

SEL Impacting VISION

In the following, we concretize the functionalities of the VISION Semantic Enablement Services, i.e. services that are required for supporting semantic aspects of interoperability in any form. This revision is based on our recent work on bridging the two worlds of Semantic Web and OGC; a discussion about semantic annotation of OGC services (Maué et al. 2008) and the introduction of a Semantic Enablement Layer (SEL) for OGC services (Janowicz et al. 2009b, Janowicz et al. 2010, forthcoming). Whereas we analyzed possible annotation possibilities in the former, we focused essential required functionalities in the latter. For the semantic enablement of OGC services we proposed a set of conformance classes. For further structuring, we initially categorized atomic functionalities into four classes. Here, we suggest a slight modification to five classes (we detail all in relation to the flood simulation scenario below):

- **Storage** aim at persistency of ontologies. It includes the operation *createOntology,* which can be used to create a new ontology with all its classes and relations inside a repository. The function *updateOntology* can be applied to register a new version of an ontology to the repository, while *getConcept, getRelation,* and *getOntology:* return different types of elements from a registered ontology.
- **Lookup** comprises a method to link elements of a vocabulary to an ontology, i.e. semantic annotation. The only contained operator (*getModelReference*) returns the appropriate ontology element ID for a given resource ID, e.g., GML Feature ID.
- **Reasoning** conformance class deals with everything related to inference. The basic operators are inspired by DIG. *loadOntology* loads a specific ontology into the reasoned, *releaseOntology* releases a specific ontology into the reasoned, *tell* Inserts a new fact into the knowledge base, and *ask* returns facts from the knowledge base.
- **Retrieval** provides the *achieveGoal* operator, which executes semantic matchmaking (Payne et al. 2002) between a goal/query and available web service advertisements.
- **Deployment** finally aid creating annotated vocabularies. The *createCapabilities* can be applied in order to create content-specific section of an OGC Capabilities Document; while *createFeatureTypeDescription* creates a GML feature type (created file may contain annotations).

The Storage conformance class groups functionalities which are required for ontology storage, evolution, and access. For the flood simulation scenario, this includes storage and access to flood simulation, and related ontologies about tiling. Opportunities for updating are included. The functionality to connect elements of a specific resource, e.g., a GML or RDF schema, with concepts or instances from an ontology is provided by Lookup functionality. This functionality can for example be used to provide the ontology fragment used to annotate the flood simulation MaaS. Reasoning groups operations about inferring hidden facts, while Retrieval supports discovery and access of data and services. Reasoning may reveal that information about canals (as they are a specific water body) should be included as sources for flood modeling. In contrast, retrieval can be used in order to retrieve any SOS which provides water level and flow velocity of any type of water body. Internally, retrieval may use reasoning to achieve desired discovery capabilities. In our initial proposal of SEL (Janowicz et al. 2010, forthcoming), we provided lookup and retrieval as a single conformance class. As both can be realized independent from each other, we now decide for separation. Deployment functionality supports the deployment of OGC services if their schemas have been encoded in ontologies. This aids annotation processes by injecting explicit ontology references into legacy documents. Such deployment includes the generation of a content description for an OGC web service which is advertised in its capabilities document as well as an automated creation of descriptions of resources such as feature type serializations. For example, a legacy WCS providing topographic data may be connected with an ontological definition of a DEM. This functionality ensures explicit linkages between services and content descriptions. In order to do so, it uses Lookup functionalities.

We proposed two profiles of existing OGC service as a technical solution to SEL (Janowicz et al. 2010, forthcoming). A Web Ontology Service (WOS) should profile the OWS specification of OGC and allows for ontology storage, lookup and retrieval. Reasoning can be brought to OGC using a Web Reasoning Service (WRS), which is a profile of the WPS.

The outcomes of this work cause an extension of VISION in respect to look-up and deployment, as well as to reasoning functionality. We suggest the following mapping of these functionalities to VISION:

- **Storage** is in fact part of the ontology and metadata repositories in semantic annotation management of VISION.
- **Lookup** should be a core functionality of VISION Annotation Management Services.
- **Reasoning** requests for an additional component, a reference service that can be used by the semantic catalogue during retrieval. It bridges semantic enablement services with execution services.
- **Retrieval**, as just stated, is a core functionality of the semantic catalogue.
- **Deployment** functionalities may be provided by annotation management services, too.

The resulting functional specification of VISION is detailed in the following section.

VISION Summary of Core Functionalities

With the MaaS and semantic extensions outlined above, we are now able to specify required functionality for each VISION building block. We structure these according deployment and run-time, as well as using the four layers of vision (Figure 1). In every layer, each previously identified component becomes a conformance class. With these distinctions, the functional elements of the extended version of VISION (Figure 5) can be summarized as follows:

- *Application Services* (run-time components)
  - Application specific functionalities per involved decision support system, which essentially interact with a set of domain relevant MaaS.
- *Run-Time Services* (run-time components)
  - *Visualization Client* renders geospatial data and can become embedded into various applications.
  - *Semantic Catalogue Client* provides a front-end for interactions with the Semantic Catalogue Service. For the geospatial domain this includes functionalities to describe geospatial, temporal and thematic parts of catalogue queries. The degree of which these three rely on ontologies may vary between implementations.
  - Execution Services
    - *Semantic Catalogue Service* provides retrieval functionalities for other Execution Services and data sets.
    - *Reasoning Service* encapsulates all reasoning, i.e. inferences on knowledge bases. This component may be applied by the Semantic Catalogue Service during semantic matchmaking and retrieval.
    - *Semantic Mediation Services* provides support in translation of queries to the catalogue service and of data. They may appear in various degrees of automation.
    - *Adaptation Service* provides means for the dynamic update of service compositions. Such may be required in cases of execution service failures. Implementation may facilitate semantic retrieval.
    - *Distributed Data Space Access Service* basically applies fusion

techniques (Giannecchini et al. 2006) to application-relevant data access services. They provide a single view, which may include added value during the fusion process.

- *Processing Service* (WPS) provides a basic service for accessing geospatial processing functionality. The OGC WPS interface may be applied.

- *Data Services* (WFS etc.) provides a basic service for accessing geospatial data. The OGC WFS interface may be applied.

- *Sensor Service* (SOS) provides a basic service for accessing geospatial sensors, observations, and measurements. The OGC SOS interface may be applied.

- *MaaS* provides a basic service for accessing analytical geospatial models. The OGC WPS or SOS interface may be applied.

- *Deployment Services* (deployment components)
    - *Environmental Decision Support Services* provide functionality, which can be re-used for deploying various geospatial decision support systems. These may include data modeling tools, support for graphical user interface (GUI) creation, or software for defining system architectures.
    - *MaaS Composition Services* provide functionality to generate workflows and to define service compositions, i.e. explicit bindings to workflow tasks.
    - *Ontology Client* provides possibilities to explore used ontologies from a user's perspective in any form, e.g. graph based or text based.

    - *Annotation Client* supports users in defining annotations of data elements and services. This includes semantic and multi-lingual annotation.

- *Semantic Enablement Services* (deployment components)
    - *Multi-Language Annotation Services* supports annotations in various languages. Functionalities may include language to language translations, identification of similar words, parsing of texts and suggesting for matching concepts from an ontology.
    - *Annotation Management Services* basically provide look-up and deployment functionalities.
        - *Ontology Repository* provides storage functionality for ontologies and potentially of knowledge bases. This may include versioning.
        - *Metadata Repository* provides storage for metadata, such as annotations. Again, this may include versioning.

In respect to all of the above, the general purpose of VISION should be acknowledged. Also in name, VISION does not depend on ontologies (as engineering artifacts). Any form of specification of vocabularies (including multi-lingual aspects) fit equally well. Reasoning has to be adjusted accordingly. Instead of using highly sophisticated ontologies and logic-based reasoning, repositories may serve thesauri, which might be interconnected, and reasoning services may facilitate such connections and similarity matching. According technologies are already in place. RDF can be used for encoding thesauri, Simple Knowledge Organization System (SKOS) (W3C 2009b) can be used for defining relations. Various similarity algorithms are available (Euzenatand and Shvaiko 2007). The notion of Linked Data (Bizer et al.

2008), an approach for connecting heterogeneous resources, may be analyzed in this context.

PROJECT COMPARISON USING VISION

The VISION architecture provides a high-level definition of the functions of an infrastructure for the Semantic Geospatial Web. Core components have been identified and their functionality has been specified above. In the following, we show how those can be applied to project comparison and gap analysis. As example we apply one already completed project (SWING[11], finished early 2009), one project that finishes soon (GDI-GRID, will be completed in 2010) and a recently started EU-founded project called ENVISION[12] (kicked-off in January 2010) (Table 1). Here, we relate each functional building block of VISION to the content of the three research projects. VISION-levels are indicated by bold text. The SWING and ENVISION instantiations were already introduced for an earlier version of the VISION architecture (Roman et al. 2009). Nevertheless, we add potential elements to ENVISION in order acknowledging the functionalities identified in this chapter.

Given the three projects, we observe a clear evolvement of concepts and technology. Whereas SWING initiated developments in semantic annotation and discovery for SDI, GDI-GRID emphasized workflows, grid technologies, and Semantic Web. It added management functionalities to ontologies and annotations. The recently started ENVISION project generalizes over both and focuses on facilitating collaborations between Semantic Geospatial Web Services and their user communities.

Notably, this approach cannot only be applied to a whole project dealing with semantics in SDI environments. The comparison table can also be used to relate existing solutions to the big (VISION) picture. For example, ConceptVISTA provides an ontology client for visualization

and creation of ontologies, the SWING Concept Repository is one approach of ontology repository. The SIM-DL similarity server is a reasoning service, while the SIM-DL Protégé plug-in is an annotation service. The semantically-enabled Sensor Observation Service SemSOS (Henson et al. 2009) can be seen as a SOS encapsulated reasoning service, which is connected to a fixed knowledge base. Sensor observable registries as well as the OWL-profile for CSW, are both approaches for semantic catalogues; the former specifically for observables, the later specifically using OWL-encoded ontologies.

FUTURE RESEARCH DIRECTIONS

VISION should not be seen as a static solution, but as a general view at the scenery, which may be further extended. Our recent considerations did not include security or e-commerce. The two are important in operational systems. Future extensions of VISION may include support for both. In addition, the use of Linked Data principles may be advocated.

The potential instantiation of ENVISION already provides directions for future research. For the moment, we see central needs in respect to vocabulary, ontology, and annotation maintenance, which should include user feedback. Versioning of ontologies is one issue, but versioning in annotations may be an even harder problem. Works on multi-lingual vocabularies and ontologies have to be connected instead of considering both as orthogonal tasks.

Ontology and annotation clients open further research fields for the Semantic Geospatial Web. User and machine interaction with ontologies has to be supported. GUIs are one central aspect, but also annotation supporting services require further research. The paradigm of user interaction in terms of ontologies and annotation has to be revisited. This holds especially for the use of such GUIs

Table 1. Comparison between GDI-GRID, SWING, and ENVISION

	GDI-GRID	SWING	Potentials for ENVISION
Application Services			
Application-specific function-alities	Algorithms for flood simulation, flood-risk analysis, noise dispersion, avoid area calculation, and routing. Application specific tilling and stitching	Components for the use case front end, called Mineral Resource Management System (MiMS)	Specific front-end for the two internal pilots in the areas of oil spill and land slide
Run-Time Services			
Visualization Client	Common OGC WMS client	Common OGC WMS client, and Java Applet inside MiMS	Common OGC WMS client
Semantic Catalogue Client	Not applied	Support for ontology- based queries on thematic aspects (space and time following OGC Catalogue Service Web (CSW) (Nebert et al. 2007))	Support for ontology- based queries on geospatial, temporal, and thematic aspects
Semantic Catalogue Service	Not applied	Support for ontology- based retrieval of WFS, semantically enabled CSW	Support for ontology- based retrieval of all Basic Services, (probably as semantically enabled CSW)
Reasoning Service	IRIS Reasoner (Bishop and Fisher 2008), built-in to the semantic validation of service compositions	IRIS Reasoner, built-in to the semantic discovery component	IRIS as separate reasoning service (potentially WRS)
Semantic Mediation Services	Non-semantic solution using WPS based data fusion	Only experimental as part of the reasoning process during discovery	Part of adaptive service composition.
Adaptation Service	Not applied	Not applied	For OGC service compositions
Distributed Data Space Access Service	Not applied, data is integrated stepwise into the workflows	Not applied, data is integrated stepwise into the workflows	Application specific fusion of relevant basic data services
Processing Service	Encapsulation of grid jobs implementing the processing steps of the three scenarios	Encapsulation of use case specific workflows	Only applied if processing steps should be re-used between MaaS
Data Services	Encapsulation of workflow inputs, basically as WFS	WFS for all geospatial data involved in the use cases	WFS and WCS planned
Sensor Service	Encapsulation of workflow inputs	Not applied	Use of OGC Sensor Web Enablement (SWE), especially SOS
MaaS	Not applied	Not applied	To be implemented as one objective of the proposal
Deployment Services			
Environmental Decision Support Services	Triangulation, 3D geospatial data generation, tilling and stitching by spatial extent	Generic web service for WFS manipulation, data merging functionalities	Common elements of the involved decision support systems may be provided here
MaaS Composition Services	Non-MaaS oriented composition using BPEL and executing on a grid (Fleuren and Müller 2008)	Non-MaaS oriented composition studio with WFS frontend	Extending the composition studio from SWIG for MaaS enablement
Ontology Client	CMapTools[13] for intermediate representation, WSMT (a toolkit for the WSML language)	CMapTools, WSMT, project internally developed ontology browser	CMapTools, WSMT, improved ontology browser

continued on the following page

Table 1. continued

	GDI-GRID	SWING	Potentials for ENVISION
Annotation Client	Annotations done manually inside WSML files	Project internal development	Advanced version of SWING annotation client
Semantic Enablement Services			
Multi-Language Annotation Services	Multilingualism is out of the scope of this project	Support as part of the annotation services (project internal development)	Aiming at a general solution for supporting multi-language vocabularies
Annotation Management Services	Open-source project sapience for lookup and retrieval based on the ontology repository	Implemented inside the catalogue component, separated between CSW and WSMX (an execution service for the WSML language)	Re-use of sapience and focusing on maintenance of ontologies and annotations
Ontology Repository	SWING Concept Repository	SWING Concept Repository (project internal development)	SWING Concept Repository including user feedback mechanisms
Metadata Repository	Support of look-up via a data base	Part of CSW and WSMX with project internal synchronization mechanism	Use of generalized interfaces and implementation back-end, including user feedback mechanisms

in connection with semantic catalogue clients. Here the where, when, and what parts of a query should be linked closed together. The following semantic discovery of data sets and services has been researched to some extend, but we still face the need of best practices.

Considering service composition, we reached a point of certainty that semantic technologies will not solve all arising problems, but realistic support functions can be defined. Now it is time to apply these notions in the MaaS context. Here, we will especially require ontologies dealing with dynamics. Events and processes have to be described in order to capture the semantics of change in our environment.

Executing services are obviously the right place for grid technology. Anyhow, current approaches foresee the encapsulation of such technology behind basic service interfaces, such as SOS or WPS (Baranski 2009). Grid technology as part of the execution infrastructure or as part of reasoning engines may be considered as alternative settings, especially if it comes to large knowledge bases, reasoning may benefit. INSPIRE, SEIS and GEOSS provide the use cases, now it is time for action.

CONCLUSION

Much past and present research already addresses the areas of reasoning, semantic discovery, transformation, and execution services. Separate, i.e. disconnected, tools for many other parts of the architecture exist, but their interplay has not been uniquely specified. First attempts towards management of annotations have been made, but they are rare. On the technological level, integration between the Semantic Web and common SDI standards are still missing. We proposed VISION (VIsionary Semantic service Infrastructure with ONtologies) as a solution (Roman et al. 2009).

In this chapter, an extended and more detailed version of VISION was developed based on a literature review, the analysis of the Semantic Enablement Layer (SEL), and project instantiation. Specifically the recently proposed notion of Model-as-a-Service (MaaS), reasoning capabilities and look-up functionality was added. We provided a detailed overview on the required functionality when developing service oriented architectures for the Semantic Geospatial Web. In contrast to the Geospatial Semantic Web, this intends to enhance the existing Geospatial Web with semantic services and not vice versa. Examples from the GDI-GRID project illustrated semantic challenges and the need of different types of ontologies, the requirement for MaaS, as well as potential uses of grid technology. We showed how VISION can be used to compare existing solutions and to identify gaps in current research by instating the VISION architecture with three recent research projects. Closing gaps may involve project internal affords, but also aims at identifying potential future collaborations. At the same time VISION provides analysis for new project proposals.

We intend using VISION for a detailed state of play analysis considering the Semantic Geospatial Web from the viewpoint of existing architectures and available technology support in near future. In this context, we will visit the various functionalities and identify available support tools. At the same time, we will focus currently existing instantiations in terms of conceptual solutions. This will result in a communality and comprehensibility analysis of existing approaches. We may include an analysis of approaches without explicit semantic support in order to propose a strategy for semantic enablement of well established architectures, such as RM-OA (Klopfer and Kanellopoulos 2008) or SensorSA (Klopfer and Simonis 2009). We intend to give feedback to and active involvement in relevant standardization bodies.

REFERENCES

W3C. (2004). *W3C working group note: Web service architecture.* Retrieved November 18, 2009, from http://www.w3.org/TR/ws-arch/

W3C. (2009a). *OWL 2 Web ontology language document overview-W3C recommendation.* Retrieved November 18, 2009, from http://www.w3.org/TR/owl2-overview/

W3C. (2009b). *SKOS Simple Knowledge Organization System reference - W3C OWL Working Group Recommendation.* Retrieved November 18, 2009, from http://www.w3.org/TR/2009/REC-skos-reference-20090818/

Alonso, G., Casati, F., Kuno, H., & Machiraju, V. (2004). *Web services: concepts, architectures and applications.* Berlin: Springer Verlag.

Andrei, M., Berre, A., Costa, L., Duchesne, P., Fitzner, D., Grcar, M., et al. (2008). *SWING: A Geospatial Semantic Web service environment.* Paper given at the Workshop on Semantic Web meets Geospatial Applications, and AGILE 2008.

Axelrod, R. (1997). *The complexity of cooperation: agent-based models of competition and collaboration.* Princeton, NJ: Princeton University Press.

Baranski, B. (Ed.). (2009). *OGC OWS-6 WPS grid processing profile engineering report.* (Version 1.0.0, 09-041r3).

Bechhofer, S., van Harmelen, F., Hendler, J., Horrocks, I., McGuinness, D. L., Patel-Schneider, P. F., et al. (2003). *OWL Web ontology language reference.* Retrieved November 18, 2009, from http://www.w3.org/TR/owl-ref/

Bell, M. (2008). *Introduction to service-oriented modeling. Service-oriented modeling: service analysis, design, and architecture.* Wiley & Sons.

Bennett, K., Layzell, P., Budgen, D., Brereton, P., Macaulay, L., & Munro, M. (2000). Service-based software: the future for flexible software. *APSEC, 2000,* 214–221.

Berners-Lee, T., Hendler, J., & Lassila, O. (2001). *The semantic Web.* Scientific American Magazine.

Bishop, B., & Fischer, F. (2008). IRIS - Integrated Rule Inference System. *Proceedings from the 1st Workshop on Advancing Reasoning on the Web: Scalability and Commonsense (ARea2008) at the 5th European Semantic Web Conference (ESWC'08), Tenerife, Spain.*

Bishr, Y., Pundt, H., Kuhn, W., Molenaar, M., & Radwan, M. (1997). Probing the concept of information communities - a first step toward semantic interoperability. In Goodchild, M. F. (Eds.), *Proceedings of Interop'97* (pp. 55–71). Interoperating Geographic Information Systems.

Bittner, T. (1997). A qualitative coordinate language of location of figures within the ground. *Proceedings from the International Conference on Spatial Information Theory: A Theoretical Basis for GIS table of contents*. Laurel Highlands, PEN.

Bizer, C., Heath, T., & Berners-Lee, T. (2008). Linked data: principles and state of the art. *Proceedings from the World Wide Web Conference, 2008*.

Bröring, A., Janowicz, K., Stasch, C., & Kuhn, W. (2009). Semantic challenges for sensor plug and play. In: *Web & Wireless Geographical Information Systems, 7 & 8*. Maynooth, Ireland.

Cai, C., Schade, S., & Gudiyangada, T. (2010). Schema mapping in INSPIRE - extensible components for translating geospatial data. *Proceedings from the 13th AGILE Conference on GIScience*.

Casati, R., & Varzi, A. C. (1999). *Parts and places. The Structures of Spatial Representation*. Cambridge, MA: MIT Press.

Chappell, D. (2008). *A short introduction to cloud platforms: an enterprise-oriented view*. Retrieved November 18, 2009, from http://www.davidchappell.com/CloudPlatforms-Chappell.pdf

Cox, S. (2007). OGC implementation specification 07-022r1: observations and measurements, part 1 – observation schema.

Cruz, I., & Sunna, W. (2008). Structural alignment methods with applications to geospatial ontologies. *Transactions in GIS, 12*(6), 683–711. doi:10.1111/j.1467-9671.2008.01126.x

De Bruijn, J., Lausen, H., Polleres, A., & Fensel, D. (2006). *The Web Service Modelling Language - WSML: An overview*. Berlin and Heidelberg, Germany: Springer.

De Roure, D. (2006). Vision and research directions 2010 and beyond - future for European Grids: Grids and service-oriented knowledge utilities. *Next Generation Grids Expert Group Report 3*.

Densham, P. J. (1991). *Spatial decision support systems. Geographical Information Systems: Principles and Applications*. London: Longman.

EC. (2002). *Directive 2002/49/EC of the European Parliament and of the Council of 25 June 2002 relating to the assessment and management of environmental noise*. Official Journal of the European Communities.

EC (2007). Directive 2007/60/EC of the European Parliament and of the Council of 23 October 2007 on the assessment and management of flood risks. *Official Journal of the European Union*.

Egenhofer, M. J. (2002) Toward the Semantic Geospatial Web. In *Proceedings of the Tenth ACM International Symposium on Advances in Geographic Information Systems*. McLean, Va.

Euzenatand, J., & Shvaiko, P. (2007). *Ontology matching*. Heidelberg, Germany: Springer.

Fitzner, D., Hoffmann, J., & Klien, E. (2009). Functional description of geoprocessing services as conjunctive datalog queries. *GeoInformatica*, (October): 2009.

Fleuren, T., & Müller, P. (2008). BPEL workflows combining standard OGC Web services and Grid-enabled OGC Web services. *Proceedings of the 34th Euromicro Conference on Software Engineering and Advanced Applications*. Parma, Italy.

Foster, I., & Kesselman, C. (2003). *The Grid 2: Blueprint for a New Computing Infrastructure*. Morgan Kaufmann Publishers.

Frank, A. U. (2003). *Ontology for spatio-temporal databases*. LCNS 2520, 9-77. Heidelberg, Germany: Springer.

Geller, G. N., & Melton, F. (2008). Looking forward: applying an ecological model Web to assess impacts of climate change. *Biodiversity, 9*(3 & 4), 79–83.

Geller, G. N., & Turner, W. (2007). The model Web: A concept for ecological forecasting. *IEEE International Geoscience and Remote Sensing Symposium.* (pp. 2469-2472), Barcelona, Spain.

Giannecchini, S., Spina, F., Nordgren, B., & Desruisseaux, M. (2006). Supporting interoperable geospatial data fusion by adopting OGC and ISO TC 211 standards. *From proceedings at FUSION 2006.* Florence, Italy.

Goguen (2005). Data, schema ontology and logic integration. *Logic Journal of the IGPL 13*(6), 685-715.

Grenon, P., & Smith, B. (2004). SNAP and SPAN: towards dynamic spatial ontology. *Spatial Cognition and Computation, 4*(1), 69–103. doi:10.1207/s15427633scc0401_5

Guarino, N. (1998). *Formal ontology and Information Systems. Formal Ontology in Information Systems.* Amsterdam: IOS Press.

Guercke, R. Brenner & Sester, M. (2008). Data integration and generalization for SDI in a Grid Computing Framework. *In proceedings from 2008 ISPRS Congress.* Beijing.

Harnad, S. (1990). The Symbol Grounding Problem. *Physica D. Nonlinear Phenomena, 42,* 335–346. doi:10.1016/0167-2789(90)90087-6

Harvey, F., Kuhn, W., Pundt, H., Bisher, Y., & Riedemann, C. (1999). Semantic interoperability: a central issue for sharing geographic information. *The Annals of Regional Science, 33,* 213–232. doi:10.1007/s001680050102

Henson, C. A., Pschorr, J. K., Sheth, A. P., & Thirunarayan, K. (2009). SemSOS: Semantic Sensor Observation Service. *International Symposium on Collaborative Technologies and Systems (CTS 2009).*

INSPIRE. (2004). *INSPIRE scoping paper.* Retrieved November 18, 2009, from http://www.ec-gis.org/inspire/reports/inspire scoping24mar04.pdf.

ISO/IEC. (2002). *ISO/IEC 13250 topic maps.* Information Technology Document Description and Processing Languages.

ISO/TC211 (2001). *19101 Geographic information - Reference model.* ISO/TC211 standard.

Janowicz, K. Schade, S., Bröring, A., Keßler, C., & Stasch, C. (2009, October). A transparent semantic enablement layer for the Geospatial Web. *In proceedings from the Terra Cognita 2009 Workshop, in conjunction with the 8th International Semantic Web Conference (ISWC2009).*

Janowicz, K., Keßler, C., Schwarz, M., Wilkes, M., Panov, I., Espeter, M., et al. (2007). Algorithm, implementation and application of the SIM-DL similarity server. In F.T. Fonseca, A. Rodriguez, & S. Levashkin (Eds.), *Second International Conference on GeoSpatial Semantics (GeoS 2007).* LCNS 4853, (pp. 128-145).

Janowicz, K., Schade, S., Bröring, A., Keßler, C., Maué, P. & Stasch, C. (2010). *Semantic enablement for Spatial Data Infrastructures.* Transactions in GIS 14(2).

Jirka, S., & Bröring, A. (2009). *OGC discussion paper 09-112 – sensor observable registry.* Technical report, Open Geospatial Consortium.

Keßler, C., Raubal, M., & Wosniok, C. (2009). Semantic rules for context-aware geographical information retrieval. In P. Barnaghi (Ed.), *European Conference on Smart Sensing and Context, EuroSSC 2009.* LNCS 5741, (pp. 77–92).

Klopfer, M., & Kanellopoulos, I. (Eds.). (2008). *ORCHESTRA-an open service architecture for risk management*.

Klopfer, M., & Simonis, I. (Eds.). (2009). *SANY-an open service architecture for sensors*.

Krüger, A., & Kolbe, T. H. (2008). Mapping Spatial Data Infrastructures to a GRID environment for optimised processing of large amounts of spatial data. In *Proceedings from the 2008 ISPRS Congress Beijing*.

Kuhn, W. (2003). Semantic Reference Systems. *International Journal of Geographical Information Science, 17*(5), 405–409. doi:10.1080/1365881031000114116

Kuhn, W. (2005). Geospatial semantics: why, of what, and how? *Journal on Data Semantics Special Issue on Semantic-based Geographical Information Systems. LNCS, 3534*, 1–24.

Kuhn, W. (2009). Semantic Engineering. In G. Navratil (Ed.), *Research Trends in Geographic Information Science*. LNGC, 63-74.

Kurzbach, S., Lanig, S., Pasche, E., & Zipf, A. (2009). Benefits of grid computing for flood modeling in service-oriented Spatial Data Infrastructures. *GIS.* [REMOVED HYPERLINK FIELD]. *Science, 3*, 89–97.

Kurzbach, S., & Pasche, E. (2009). A 3D terrain discretization grid service for hydrodynamic modeling. *Proceedings of the 8th International Conference on Hydroinformatics (HEIC)*, Concepción, Chile.

Lanig, S. & Zipf, A. (2009): Towards generalization processes of LiDAR data based on GRID and OGC Web Processing Services (WPS). From *Proceedings in Geoinformatik 2009*, Osnabrück, Germany.

Lee, C. A. (2001, November). Grid computing. *GRID 2001, Second International Workshop*. Denver, CO: Springer.

Lemmens, R., Wytzisk, A., deBy, R., Granell, C., Gould, M., & vanOosterom, P. (2006). Integrating semantic and syntactic descriptions to chain geographic services. *IEEE Internet Computing, 10*(5), 42–52. doi:10.1109/MIC.2006.106

Li, W., Li, Y., Liang, Z., Huang, C. & Wen, Y. (2005). *The design and implementation of GIS Grid Services*. LNCS 3795.

Lieberman, J., Pehle, T., Morris, C., Kolas, D., Dean, M., Lutz, M., et al. (2006). *Geospatial Semantic Web interoperability experiment report*.

Lutz, M. (2007). Ontology-based descriptions for semantic discovery and composition of geoprocessing services. *GeoInformatica, 11*(1), 1–36. doi:10.1007/s10707-006-7635-9

Lutz, M., & Klien, E. (2006). Ontology-based retrieval of geographic information. *International Journal of Geographical Information Science, 20*(3), 233–260. doi:10.1080/13658810500287107

Lutz, M., Riedemann, C., & Probst, F. (2003). A classification framework for approaches to achieving semantic interoperability between GI Web services. In *Proceedings from COSIT 2003*. 186-203.

Manning, C. D., Prabhakar, R., & Schütze, H. (2008). *Introduction to information retrieval*. Cambridge, UK: Cambridge University press.

Manso, M. A., & Wachowicz, M. (2009). GIS design: A review of current issues in interoperability. *Geography Compass, 3*(3), 1105–1124. doi:10.1111/j.1749-8198.2009.00241.x

Masolo, C., Borgo, S., Gangemi, A., Guarino, N., & Oltramari, A. (2003). *D18-ontology library*. Deliverable of the WonderWeb Project.

Maué, P., & Schade, S. (2009). *Data integrations in the Geospatial Semantic Web. Cases on semantic interoperability for Information Systems Integration: Practices and Applications* (pp. 100–122). Hershey, PA: IGI Global.

Maué, P., Schade, S., & Duchesne, P. (2008). *OGC discussion paper 08-167r1: semantic annotations in OGC standards.*

Mika, P. (2005). Ontologies are us: A unified model of social networks and semantics. In *Proceedings of the 4th International Semantic Web Conference (ISWC 2005).*

Na, A. & Priest, M. (2007). *OGC implementation specification 06-009r6: OpenGIS Sensor Observation Service (SOS).*

Nebert, D. (2004). The SDI Cookbook, Version 2.0. *Global Spatial Data Infrastructure Association, Technical Working Group Report.*

Nebert, D., Whiteside, A. & Vretanos, P. (2007). *OGC implementation specification 07-006r1: OpenGIS catalogue services specification.*

OGC. (2003). Open Geospatial Consortium Inc. Web Mapping Service Implementation Specification 1.1.

OGC. (2005). Open Geospatial Consortium Inc. Web Feature Service Implementation Specification 1.1.

OGC. (2006). Open Geospatial Consortium Inc. Web Coverage Service Implementation Specification 1.0.

OGC. (2007). OpenGIS Geography Markup Language (GML) Encoding Standard 3.2.1.

OGC. (2009). Open Geospatial Consortium Inc. *OWS-6 Geoprocessing Workflow Architecture Engineering Report.*

Payne, T., Paolucci, M., Kawmura, T., & Sycara, K. (2002). Semantic matching of Web service capabilities. *Proceedings of the International Semantic Web Conference.*

Rath, S. (2007): *Model discretization in 2D hydroinformatics based on high resolution remote sensing data and the feasibility of automated model parameterisation.* Unpublished doctoral dissertation, Hamburg University of Technology, Hamburg, Germany.

Roman, D., & Klien, E. (2007). SWING – a semantic framework for geospatial services. *Advanced Information and Knowledge Processing Series,* 227–237. Springer.

Roman, D., Schade, S., Berre, A. J., Rune Bodsberg, N., & Langlois, J. (2009). Environmental services infrastructure with ontologies – a decision support framework. *EnviroInfo 2009*, Berlin, Germany.

Roman, D., Schade, S., Berre, A. J., Rune Bodsberg, N., & Langlois, J. (2009b): Model as a Service (MaaS). *Proceedings from AGILE Workshop, Grid Technologies for Geospatial Applications*, Hannover, Germany.

Schade, S. (2008). *Semantic reference systems accounting for uncertainty. Quality aspects in Spatial Data Mining.* Boca Raton, FL: CRC Press.

Schade, S. (2010). *Ontology-driven translation of geospatial data. GISDIS.* Amsterdam: IOS Press BV.

Schade, S., Klien, E., Maué, P., Fitzner, D., & Kuhn, W. (2008b). Report on modelling approach and guideline. *Deliverable D3.2 of the SWING Project.* Retrieved November 18, 2009, from http://swing-project.org/deliverables.

Schade, S., Maué, P., & Langlois, J. (2008). Ontology engineering with domain experts-a field report. *Proceedings of the European Geosciences Union - General Assembly*, Vienna, Austria.

Schut, P. (2007). *OGC Implementation Specification 05-007r7: OpenGIS Web Processing Service.*

Shen, Z., Luo, J., Zhou, C., Cai, S., Zheng, J., & Chen, Q. (2004). Architecture design of Grid GIS and its applications of Image Processing based on LAN. *Information Sciences, 166,* 1–17. doi:10.1016/j.ins.2003.10.004

Shi, X. (2005). Removing syntactic barriers for Semantic Geospatial Web services. *UCGIS 2005.*

Smith, B. (1995). Formal ontology, common sense and cognitive science. *International Journal of Human-Computer Studies, 43,* 641–667. doi:10.1006/ijhc.1995.1067

Stevens, S. S. (1946). On the theory of measurement. *Science, 103*(2684), 677–680. doi:10.1126/science.103.2684.677

Stock, K., Small, M., Ou, Y., & Reitsma, F. (2009). *OGC discussion paper 09-010 – OWL application profile of CSW.*

Turhan, A., Bechhofer, S., Kaplunova, A., Liebig, T., Luther, M., Möller, et al. (2006, November). DIG 2.0 — towards a flexible interface for description logic reasoners. *Second international workshop OWL: Experiences and Directions.*

Wache, H., Vögele, T., Visser, U., Stuckenschmidt, H., Schuster, G., Neumann, H., et al. (2001). Ontology-based integration of information - a survey of existing approaches. *Proceedings from IJCAI-01 Workshop: Ontologies and Information Sharing, Seattle, WA.*

Werthner, H., Hepp, M., Fensel, D., & Dorn, J. (2006, June 14-16). Semantically-enabled service-oriented architectures: a catalyst for smart business networks. *Proceedings of the Smart Business Networks Initiative Discovery Session,* Rotterdam, *The Netherlands.*

Yue, P., Di, L., Yang, W., Yu, G., & Zhao, P. (2007). Semantics-based automatic composition of geospatial Web services chains. *Computers & Geosciences, 33*(5), 649–665. doi:10.1016/j.cageo.2006.09.003

Zhao, P., Di, L., Yue, P., Yu, G., & Yang, W. (2008). Semantic Web Based Geospatial Knowledge Transformation. *Computers & Geosciences, 35*(4), 798–808. doi:10.1016/j.cageo.2008.03.013

ADDITIONAL READING

Alam, A., Subbiah, G., Thuraisingam, B., & Khan, L. (2006). Reasoning with semantics-aware access control policies for geospatial web services. *3rd ACM Workshop on Secure Web Services.*

Andrei, M., Berre, A., Costa, L., Duchesne, P., Fitzner, D., Grcar, M., et al. (2008). SWING: An integrated environment for Geospatial Semantic Web services. Paper presented at *ESWC '08,* June 2008.

Bai, Y., Di, L., Chen, A., Liu, Y., & Wei, Y. (2007). Towards a geospatial catalogue federation service. *Photogrammetric Engineering and Remote Sensing, 73*(6), 699–708.

Granell, C., Schade, S., & Hobona, G. (in press). Spatial Data Infrastructures and Linked Data. Accepted as book chapter for: P. Zhao (Ed.), *Geospatial Web Services: Advances in Information Interoperability.* Hershey, PA: IGI Global.

Hilbring, D., & Usländer, T. (2006). Catalogue services enabling syntactical and semantic interoperability in environmental risk management architectures. *20th International Conference on Informatics for Environmental Protection (EnviroInfo 2006),* September 6–8, 2006, Graz, Austria.

Kiehle, C., Keuck, C. J., & Greve, K. (2008). *Integration of SDI-components into Grid-computing infrastructures. Angewandte Geoinformatik 2008.* Salzburg, Austria: AGIT-Symposium.

Kolas, D., Dean, M., & Hebeler, J. (2006). Geospatial Semantic Web: architecture of ontologies. *2006 IEEE Aerospace Conference. Big Sky. Montana,* (March): 4–11.

Lutz, M. & Kolas, D. (2007). Rule-based discovery in spatial data infrastructures. *Transactions in GIS, special issue on the geospatial Semantic Web 11*(3), 317–336.

Maué, P. (2008). An extensible semantic catalogue for geospatial web services. *International Journal of Spatial Data Infrastructures Research, 3*, 168–191.

Poveda, J., Gould, M., & Granell, C. (2004). ACE GIS project overview: adaptable and composable e-commerce and Geographic Information Services. *The 7th AGILE Conference on Geographic Information Science.*

Schade, S., & Cox, S. (2010). Linked data in SDI or how GML is not about trees. *The 13th AGILE Conference on Geographic Information Science.*

Semantic Community. (2009). *GeoSpatial Ontology Framework and Reference Model.* Retrieved March 24th 18, 2009, from http://semanticcommunity.wik.is/Spatial_Ontology_Community_of_Practice/Reference_Model

KEY TERMS AND DEFINITIONS

Interoperability: Interoperability is the capability of two or more components to communicate and cooperate with each other. Syntactic and semantic interoperability are most commonly distinguished. Syntactic interoperability describes the capability to encode and decode shared messages, while semantic interoperability implies the capability of interpreting message content as intended.

Ontology: An ontology is an engineering artifact, which is build to specify the intended interpretation (aka meaning) of a set of expressions (aka vocabulary).

SDI: A Spatial Data Infrastructure (SDI) is a type of information infrastructure for enhancing geospatial data sharing and access.

Semantic Geospatial Web: The Semantic Geospatial Web is a subset of the Geospatial Web (a web of geospatial information and services), in which the intended interpretation (aka meaning) of provided content is formally specified. Notably, this notion differs from a concept, which may be termed the *Geospatial Semantic Web*, which focuses geospatial information and services in the Semantic Web.

Semantic Heterogeneity: Semantic heterogeneity characterizes the relation between two resources. In the case of sets of expressions (aka vocabularies), semantic heterogeneity means different interpretation of shared expressions or different expressions for shared interpretations. In the case of services, semantic heterogeneity means limited semantic interoperability.

Semantic Web: The Semantic Web is the subset of the World Wide Web, in which the intended interpretation (aka meaning) of provided content is formally specified.

SOA: Service Oriented Architecture (SOA) is a design approach that is based on loosely coupled, reusable components (aka services) and their communication.

ENDNOTES

[1] The official web site of OGC is available from http://opengeospatial.org (last accessed, November 17th, 2009).

[2] The official web site of ISO TC211 is available from http://www.isotc211.org/ (last accessed, November 17th, 2009).

[3] The official GEOSS web site is available from http://earthobservations.org (last accessed 15th of October 2009).

[4] The official SEIS web site is available from http://ec.europa.eu/environment/seis (last accessed 15th of October 2009).

[5] Official web site available from http://www.gdi-grid.de/ (last accessed 15th of October 2009).

6   Official web site available from http://www. geovista.psu.edu/ConceptVISTA/ (last accessed 15th of October 2009).

7   Official web site available from http://purl. org/net/concepts/ (last accessed 15th of October 2009).

8   Official web site available from http://purl. org/net/sapience/docs/ (last accessed 15th of October 2009).

9   Official web site available from http://sim-dl.sourceforge.net/ (last accessed 15th of October 2009).

10   Official web site available from http://www. w3.org/2005/Incubator/ssn/ (last accessed 15th of October 2009).

11   Official web site available from http://www. swing-project.org/ (last accessed 15th of October 2009).

12   Official web site available from http://www. envision-project.eu/ (last accessed 25th of March 2010).

13   Official web site available from http://cmap. ihmc.us/ (last accessed 15th of October 2009).

Chapter 8
Geospatial Semantic Web Services:
A Case for Transit Trip Planning Systems

Zhong-Ren Peng
University of Florida, USA & Tongji University, China

Tian Zhao
University of Wisconsin-Milwaukee, USA

Chuanrong Zhang
University of Connecticut, USA

ABSTRACT

Semantic heterogeneity in diverse data sources is a major obstacle in real time data access, exchange and integration. This chapter provides a unique approach to address this issue by developing a framework and prototype for a geospatial semantic web service, through a case study of transportation road networks and transit networks for a transit trip planning system. The uniqueness of this approach is that it takes advantage of the merits of ontology, Web Feather Services (WFS) and relational database query functions. Ontological constructs provide semantic definitions for geospatial data, making use of the spatial query functions of WFS for spatial data searches, the WFS client library for feature rendering, and relational database search functions for non-spatial data queries. The results show that this approach is more efficient than conventional methods of converting all data into ontology instances, as it avoids the costs and consistency problems of data replication.

INTRODUCTION

In the age of ubiquitous data access empowered by smart mobile devices and mobile applications, users demand instant access to location-based

DOI: 10.4018/978-1-60960-192-8.ch008

information wherever they go. Data accessibility and reusability are some of the most important forces that drive geospatial information research and technology development. The initial research effort in this research area focused on data clearinghouses and data warehousing to make data available. The second stage focused on data interoperability and accessibility by developing standard data services. The third stage focused on application access and interoperability by providing web services for applications. Through this process, it was found that semantic differences among datasets and applications were major obstacles in advancing geospatial web services. Therefore, recent research has focused on geospatial semantic web services, rather than geospatial web services. This chapter provides an overview of recent studies in this research area and reports our efforts to develop a geospatial semantic web service for online transit trip planning services.

This chapter begins with an introduction of the concepts of semantics, web services, geospatial web services and geospatial semantic web services. It then describes the unique problems in transportation databases and transit trip planning systems, as well as the necessity of semantic interoperability. Next, the chapter outlines the general framework of a geospatial semantic web service, followed by an implementation of the framework

Describe the general perspective of the chapter. Toward the end, specifically state the objectives of the chapter.

BACKGROUND

Semantics, Geospatial Web Services, and Geospatial Semantic Web Services

Geospatial databases created from a variety of sources have syntactic (data formatting), structural (schemas), and semantic (meaning of terms in specific contexts) heterogeneity problems (Lutz and Klien 2006). Previous research focused on addressing accessing data with syntactic and structural heterogeneity in distributed locations. Web services are one of the important technologies that have been developed. Standards such as OGC web services have also been created to

facilitate the exchange and share of heterogeneous geospatial information (OGC White Paper 2001).

Web services are reusable software components that interact in a loosely coupled environment, and are designed to interoperate in a loosely-coupled manner. A web service can be used by other web services, applications, clients, or agents. Web services can be combined or chained to create new services. They can also be recombined, swapped or substituted, or replaced. Due to the fact that web services are based on XML standards, they are currently used by enterprises for interoperability. Web services provide interoperable capability of cross-platform and cross-language in distributed net environments (Anderson and Moreno 2003).

Geospatial web services are a special kind of web services that provide access to heterogeneous geographic information on the Internet. OGC has developed several web service specifications to standardize geospatial web services to access geospatial data and applications. The important geospatial web services include Web Feature Services (WFS), Web Map Services (WMS), Web Coverage Services (WCS), Catalogue Service (CS), and Web Processing Services (WPS), etc. The Web Feature Services allow users to retrieve, inquire, and manipulate feature-level geospatial data encoded in Geography Markup Language (GML) from multiple sources over the Internet (OGC document 04-094, 2005). The Web Map Services were developed to create and display maps that come simultaneously from multiple heterogeneous sources in a standard image format (OGC document 04-024, 2004). The Web Coverage Services provide access to detailed and rich sets of geospatial information in forms useful for users rendering and input into scientific models (OGC document 03-065r6, 2003). Web Processing Services provide standard interface for accessing geospatial processing services and geospatial models (OGC document 05-007r7, 2005). The Catalog services allow users to classify, maintain, register, describe and search for information about web services. The Catalog services provide catalogues for the OGC data services and processing services, supporting the ability to publish and search collections of descriptive information (metadata) for data, services, and related information objects (OGC document 04-021r2 2004). These OGC web service specifications have become de facto standards in the development of distributed data sharing systems (Peng 2005; Peng and Zhang 2004).

Limitations of Geospatial Web Services

Though the rapid development of OGC web service technologies has undoubtedly improved the sharing and synchronization of geospatial information across diverse venues by providing standards, there are limitations to the current implementation of OGC web services (Zhang et al. 2010a).

First, the OGC web service specifications emphasize only the technical interoperability via standard interfaces and cannot resolve semantic heterogeneity problems inside geospatial data and processing models. Difference in semantics between various data sources and geospatial processing models is one of the major problems in geospatial information sharing and interoperability (Bishr 1998, Fabrikant and Buttenfield 2001). The OGC web service description only allows for the syntax specification of contents such as metadata, and filter capabilities, and provides no semantic descriptions as to the meaning of its contents. Therefore, identical XML descriptions may mean very different things, depending on the context of their uses. Similarly, variables like "house" and "building" from different databases may actually refer to the same geographic feature. In addition, the OGC web service specifications of the outputs of each call to the service lack semantic definitions as well. Here, all defined search operations return results using the same data structure, regardless of the information requested. For example, the road feature in the OGC Web

Feature Service contains a field highway which is used to describe highways, and a field local-road which is used to describe local roads. Even if the type of road specified in a road file was clearly identified in a type field by the interface designer, the OGC web feature service description provides no uniform way of enabling interpretations of different type of roads. It is up to the client to recognize the values in these fields, which indicate whether it is a highway or a local road. The lack of specifications and details on the data is a major flaw of the current OGC web services.

Second, with currently implemented OGC web services it is only possible to search and access geospatial data by keywords in metadata. It is impossible to directly search and access geospatial data and services based on their content. While this is useful, metadata still have semantic heterogeneity problems. Different metadata creators may use different names for the same geospatial feature. The metadata heterogeneity problems may arise when terms are unknown, the meaning of elements is not intuitively clear, or the understanding of the information provider differs from that of the requestor (Schuster and Stuckenschmidt 2001). Even though natural language processing techniques can increase the semantic relevance of search results with respect to the search request (e.g. Richardson and Smeaton 1995), keyword-based techniques are inherently restricted by the ambiguities of natural language. As a result, keyword-based search can have low recall if different terminology is used and/or low precision if terms are homonymous (Bernstein and Klein 2002, Lutz 2007). Finally, the keywords search may sometimes bring an overwhelming number of search results, and users may have to spend unnecessary amounts of time sifting through undesirable query results before finding the desired data set (Wiegand and García 2007).

The third barrier speaks to the lack of formal semantic descriptions. Here, without a formal semantic description of OGC web services, it is difficult to allow users and applications to discover, deploy, compose and synthesize web services automatically. The lack of an explicit semantic in the XML-based standard OGC web service description proves to be a major limitation for automatic capability matching. It is unrealistic to expect advertisements and requests of OGC web services to be the same, or even that there exists a service that can fulfill exactly the needs of the requester. For example, an OGC WFS may advertize as a road data provider, while a requester may actually need a highway data service. Thus in order to make OGC web services more practically searchable and ubiquitously available, we need a semantic-based approach, which permits the automatic discovery and composition of web services. The OGC web services' lack of semantic descriptions makes it impossible to develop clients that can, without human assistance, dynamically find and successfully invoke web services and integrate semantically heterogeneous data and service together. The OGC web service descriptions must be interpreted by programmers, who interpret the names of keywords or Capabilities using other supporting documentations to integrate specific services with their client applications.

It can be seen that while the OGC web services provide valuable services, they still face problems in respect to data uniformity and search capabilities.

Geospatial Semantic Web Services

To overcome the aforementioned problems, the concept of Geospatial semantic web services has been developed (Sheth 1999, Goodchild et al. 1999, Egnehofer 2002, Fonseca and Sheth 2002). Geospatial semantic web services address the semantic heterogeneous problem found in geospatial web services.

Geospatial semantic web services define the geospatial data and processing services in terms of semantics by building upon the ontologies and then assigning a specific meaning to that ontology. By providing a semantic interpretation of the data

and services, geospatial semantic web services make web information more readily accessible so that computers can automatically process the information (W3C 2004). Ontologies contain rules that can perform certain types of runtime automatic reasoning. Thus, ontologies allow computers to automatically understand the structure and meaning of diverse information sources and conduct automatic knowledge inferring or reasoning from existing data and documents. Using geospatial semantic web services, it is therefore possible to automatically search and integrate semantically heterogeneous data and services and answer complex queries without having to consider how to access various systems (Duke et al. 2005). The purpose of the geospatial semantic web services is to provide geospatial data and service interoperability at the semantic level. Geospatial semantic web services adopt Semantic Web technologies, such as ontologies, to make the geospatial data and services both machine readable and comprehendible. Substantial work has been done in the context of Semantic web services, such as the efforts around OWL for Services (OWL-S) (Martin et al. 2004), the Web Services Modeling Ontology (WSMO) (WSMO working group 2004; Lausen et al. 2005), and WSDL-S (Akkiraju et al. 2005). OWL-S is an upper level ontology for describing web services. It uses a process model to describe services. The process model contains a number of atomic processes that can be invoked individually or as combined together. WSMO refines and extends the Web Service Modeling Framework (WSMF) (Fensel et al. 2002) to a meta-ontology for Semantic Web services. WSDL-S augments the expressivity of WSDL with semantics by employing concepts analogous to those in OWL-S while being agnostic to the semantic representation language (Akkiraju et al. 2005). The efforts of OWL-S, WSMO and WSDL-S are built on WSDL, rather than reinventing that part of the web service picture. This has resulted in several distinct yet ad hoc, styles of integration with WSDL. Recently, W3C produced a standard set of "Semantic Annotations for WSDL and XML Schema" (SAWSDL) (Farrell and Lausen 2007). SAWSDL, based primarily on the earlier work on WSDL-S, provides a standard means by which WSDL documents can be related to semantic descriptions, such as those provided by OWL-S and WSMO (Martin et al. 2007).

With Geospatial semantic web services, the discovery, query, and consumption of geospatial content are based on formal semantic specifications and intelligent discovery of geospatial data and services through knowledgebase reasoning. Geospatial semantic web services can achieve semantic interoperability by annotating proper semantics for geospatial web services.

Semantic web utilizes ontology languages, such as Resource Description Framework (RDF) and Web Ontology Language (OWL) provide semantics information inside databases based on ontology. Ontology allows for the identification of the structure of the database and for the same data items in different databases. It can also be used to infer further knowledge from the databases using reasoners, while checking data for inconsistencies (Zhang et al, 2007).

Unfortunately, in most cases, the use of ontology requires first transforming all legacy geospatial data to ontology. This process is inefficient and prone to errors. A better solution is to keep legacy data in its original form, while providing a translation service that links to queries in legacy databases, converting user requests into ontology. This is the approach used for the purpose of this study.

There is recent interest by researchers in exploiting the geospatial semantic web for automatic integration of semantically heterogeneous geospatial data (e.g. Kuhn 2005; Yue et al. 2007, Wiegand and Garcia 2007, Di and Zhao 2008, Li et al. 2008, Yang et al. 2008, Zhao et al. 2009). But only a few publications focus on extending OGC WFSs for feature-level geospatial data sharing (Lutz and Klien 2006; Zhang et al 2007; 2010a, b; Zhao et al. 2008).

The study aims to examine geospatial semantic web services to enable disparate geospatial data and geospatial processing services so as to share and integrate data at the semantic level. Thus, the systems built on these technologies can automatically search and access geospatial data and services by their contents, rather than by merely keywords in metadata. Specifically, we developed a framework for geospatial semantic web services to enable geospatial data interoperability at the semantic level and then implemented it in a distributed transit trip planning system.

For the purposes of this study, a model was developed to link user requests to the original database without modifications or replications of the existing databases. The model interface acts as a translation service between the user request and the database. It provides an ontology layer that links the original spatial data through WFS. Users of the interface can access and query spatial data through the ontology layers without specific knowledge of database structure or data definitions. The query is then rewritten to convert ontology query into WFS and SQL query (Peng, 2005; Zhao et al, 2008). This process allows for the creation of a service that provides a link currently missing in data processing and ontology.

GEOSPATIAL SEMANTIC WEB SERVICES: A CASE FOR TRANSIT TRIP PLANNING SYSTEMS

Defining Geospatial Semantic Web Services

Semantic Interoperability

In order to provide semantic interoperability, we use ontological constructs to provide semantic definitions for geospatial data. Ontology is a way to formally represent knowledge of a domain using concepts and roles, which describe the relationships between these concepts. We then use these concepts and roles to describe and explain the properties of a domain. Ontology has been used extensively in the areas of Artificial Intelligence, Semantic Web, and Software Engineering. In particular, it has been very useful in formally defining and reasoning data with complex structures, such as geospatial data. Ontology is commonly encoded in ontology languages. There are two popular languages: RDF (Resource Description Framework) and OWL (Web Ontology Language). OWL is derived from and a proper extension of the RDF language. OWL contains more constructs than RDF and one of its subset, OWL-DL, whose logical formalism is provided by Description Logics (DLs). DLs refer to a group of knowledge representation languages. Even though many DLs are not as expressive as first order predicate logic, they have decidable decision problems. In other words, there is a decidable problem within DLs so as to answer questions about concepts and instances based on the description of a set of concepts. Questions include:

1. if an instance belong to a given concept,
2. whether a relationship exists between two instances of some concepts,
3. if a concept can be a subset of another one, and
4. whether a concept is consistent (i.e. no contradiction of definitions involving the concept).

Many tools (called reasoners, such as Pellet and Racer) help to answer these kinds of questions about a domain of knowledge encoded in OWL or RDF. OWL represents concepts using classes and represents roles using properties, which include datatype property (whose domain is a class and range is a datatype) and object property (whose domain and range are classes). Instances of an OWL class are called individuals. We can define OWL classes by extending existing classes with restrictions. Properties may also be extended. We can represent OWL ontology in RDF using triples,

each of which consists of a subject, a predicate, and an object. The subjects are individuals of a class and predicates are usually properties while objects can be individuals or primitive data such as strings or integers.

Another benefit of ontological representation is that it is extensible. We can divide ontology into two groups: upper and domain ontology. Upper ontology models common objects applicable to many domains. There are standard upper ontology such as Dublin Core and CFO, which provide vocabularies to describe objects in domain ontology. Geospatial data should be described by domain ontology since it should include domain-specific concepts. Due to the advantages of automatic reasoning and extensibility, with the ontological modeling of geospatial data, we can enable the sharing of data with syntactical and semantic differences.

As an example of connecting geospatial data with ontology, consider a data set about a bus transit system, where bus stops, route segments (called links) are in ESRI shapefile format, route and pattern data are in a relational database. To connect the data, we define domain ontology with a Feature class at the top. The Feature class has subclasses including both a spatial feature class and a non-spatial feature class. The spatial feature class contains data with point and line geometry such as Stop and Link and the non-spatial feature class contains data such as Route, LinkSequence, and Patterns, which are closely related to the spatial features. Each instance of the Route class contains several instances of Link that make up the route through the ontology property route-link. Through this property, we can easily locate the links belong to a bus route. Therefore, when a user queries for the geometry of a bus route by the route name or number, we can use ontology query engine to determine the link geometries of a bus route and return the geometries as line strings, which can be rendered by a map client. Similarly, we can define ontology property route-stop to connect the stops of a bus route. Through this property, a user can query for the stops located on a bus route by the route name as well. In particular, user can specify some criteria to filter the returned bus stop such as the nearby facilities of the bus stop. To specify this filter, users can rely on properties of bus stop in formulating their query. In comparison to traditional database queries, ontology-based query hides the details of the specifics of accessing databases such as establishing connectivity, understanding database schema, and performing table joins. Sometimes, the relationship between instances of different ontology classes cannot be directly inferred in ontology. For example, we may not have information as to the nearby bus stops of a point-of-interests. In this case, we first convert OWL ontology into RDF triples and load them into the knowledge base. We then apply inference rules to the facts in the knowledge base to determine the relations. The inference rule can be simple logical implication or geospatial computation.

There are a number of challenges in converting geospatial data into ontological presentations. One problem is defining acceptable domain ontology for geospatial data. There should be such an ontology that serves as the basis of application-specific geospatial ontology. However, such ontology has yet to emerge. Even though it is possible to make similar, yet different, ontology compatible with extensions to existing ones, there are differences that cannot be fully reconciled. This adds to the programming difficulties facing application developers. In addition, performance is a problem. Ontology query is slow compared to traditional access to geospatial database. One cannot expect all spatial data be turned into native ontology data.

Other than performance advantages, relational database systems provide concurrency control, integrity, consistency, and security. The best way to address this problem is to provide an ontological proxy to the geospatial data stored in the original medium, such as web service servers or database servers. Here, the benefits of rich semantic descriptions of ontology definitions and the performance, concurrency, and other useful properties of underlying storage facilities are obtained. Ontology representation presents another issue in how to efficiently support data queries. Relational databases and web feature services have well-defined query languages and protocol. As long as the users understand the syntax, semantics of the query language and the definitions of the data tables or spatial features, they can formulate correct queries and obtain data efficiently.

Ontology query is flexible. It specifies ontology classes and properties instead of table names, feature names, and filter constraints. The relations between ontology classes are encoded by properties so that users do not need to know the names of the tables or their explicit relations in order to formulate a query. Ontological concepts and roles are easy to understand, since they can be made compatible with commonly accepted high-level ontology. Users need to learn only a few high level ontology classes and properties to be able to write semantic queries. In addition, ontology query is intelligent since we can add ontology reasoning tool to deduce information not explicitly stated in the data itself. The problem with ontology query is that it is slower than relational query or web feature service query. The amount of time it takes may be exponential compared to the size of the ontology. Therefore, the best way to perform ontology queries is to know its limitations and not submit a request that would take excessive amounts of time to compute. There is no general way to determining which queries would take this kind of time, but part of this involves taking advantage of the fact that most geospatial data is stored in a database or web feature service through translating ontology query into database query or web feature service query, which can be executed efficiently.

From Enabling Data Sharing to Providing Web Services

Using ontology representations, we can enable the sharing of geospatial data. As explained in previous sections, it is not practical to convert all geospatial data into ontology representation due to reasons such as performance, concurrency, and security, etc. Therefore, we advocate the use of semantically-enabled web services to provide access to geospatial data. We use Web Feature Services (WFS) to publish feature-level data and then connect these services to geospatial ontology. The WFS descriptions are mapped to geospatial ontology so as to provide a semantically-based view of the services, which span from abstract descriptions of the capabilities of the services to the actual feature data contents that exchange with other services. Because OWL is based on Description Logics, we use a DL-based reasoner and inference rules to collect a knowledge base for the automatic geospatial feature matching engine. We also develop an extended DL formalism for spatial relations reasoning. Ontology classes and properties are generated by automatically converting Web Feature types into corresponding ontology classes and converting properties of the feature types into ontology data type properties. The inter-relations of the Web Feature types are modeled as ontology object properties. This has to be specified externally via a configuration file. The generated ontology definitions are connected to geospatial domain ontology by introducing subclass constraints and subproperty constraints. Additional constraints may be added to the ontology based on application specific knowledge.

Once the WFS descriptions are mapped into ontology, we are able to support semantic discovery and composition of WFS to provide answers to semantic queries. The geospatial feature discovery algorithm allows for the matching of a request described with ontological concepts with that the atomic WFS provides. The provided WFS are also described in ontological concepts. However, to precisely fulfill the user queries, atomic WFS may not be sufficient and two or more WFSs may be needed to synthesize the required service. A WFS composition algorithm is developed to address these problems. The WFS composition algorithm

allows one to create a workflow of WFS by splitting and joining the available WFS choices. To increase efficiency of complex geospatial feature discovery, the algorithms in the framework adopt an index strategy that allows rapidly locating the provided feature data that matches the request. The major advantage of our approach is that the WFS are enhanced semantically using geospatial ontology. It not only allows technical data interoperability via standard interfaces but also resolves semantic heterogeneity problems in feature-level spatial data sharing. The reasoning capability and computer interpretable semantic markup does not restrict geospatial feature matching to simple string comparison, but permits more complex semantic matching such as subsumption of concepts.

A WFS feature is mapped to ontology in two aspects. One aspect is to create an ontology instance to represent the metadata of the feature such as its feature type, property list, geometry type, and bounding box. Another aspect is to create an ontology class and a set of ontology properties that correspond to the feature type and properties. As an example, consider a WFS feature Link, which is a segment in a bus route. It has line geometry type and has properties to describe its ID and route ID. To translate this WFS feature to ontology, we create an instance of the spatial feature class to describe the Link feature's metadata. Also, we create an ontology class called Link and properties hasGeometry, hasID, and hasRouteID. Some properties such as hasGeometry and hasID might already have been created from other WFS features so that we can just reuse the existing ones. Note that the actual data of the WFS feature Link is not yet converted to ontology instances. Only its corresponding definitions have been created. We delay the translation of WFS feature data to ontology data until user sends specific data query.

Geospatial Feature Discovery

In order to find feature-level geospatial data while it does not require users to be concerned with server

Table 1.

Search attributes	Symbol	Search criteria for a Web Feature X
An ontology class that corresponds to a feature type	T	The feature type of X corresponds to a subclass of T
A set of ontology properties, each corresponds to a feature property	P	For each property p in P, we can find a feature property of X that corresponds to a subproperty of p
A geometry type	G	The geometry type if X is the same as G
A bounding box	B	The bounding box of X must contain B

details, we consider Web Feature as a basic unit of service, rather than the entire WFS server. A query processing module should handle the task of joint query transparently. Therefore, requesters can search multiple sources that are able to provide the requested information. The discovery algorithm considers a Web Feature description as a consistent collection of restrictions over the named attributes of a Web Feature, such as URI of the WFS server, feature type name, feature property names, geometry type of the feature, and bounding box of the geometries.

Table 1 summarizes the retrieval criteria used in our discovery algorithm. A search key is a tuple of (T, P, G, B) where T is an ontology class correspond to a feature type, P is a set of ontology properties, each of which corresponds to a feature property, G is a geometry type, and B is a bounding box. For each Web Feature X we search, we check whether the feature type of X corresponds to a subclass of T, and for each property p in P, we can find a feature property of X that corresponds to a subproperty of p, the geometry type of X is the same as G, and the bounding box of X contains the area described by B.

Before the discovery process, we must index the available WFS features for a more efficient search, particularly when there is a large number of features. We generate indices for feature names, feature properties, and geometry types. We also create an index for the center points of the bounding boxes. A service broker maintains the index files with an entry for each WFS feature. We also map the feature type name and feature

properties of each Web Feature into an ontology class and properties. A user query consists of an ontology class that corresponds to a feature type, a set of ontology properties, each of which corresponds to a feature property, a geometry type, and a bounding box.

In the discovery process, the discovery engine finds the appropriate WFS features by matching the descriptions required to the descriptions of WFS features. The algorithm first uses the query Bounding Box of Geometry parameter to narrow down the list of services in the repository. It acquires all of the services that produce at least matched Bounding Box of Geometry (all WFSs that are located within the geography limitation). From these services, it further narrows down the list of by Geometry Type of Features, then by Feature Type names, and finally by Property names. All the description parameters provided by WFS must be equivalent to or they subsume the required description parameters in the query. Whenever an exactly equivalent match is found, it is recorded with the highest score. Otherwise, according to the degree of match detected, it is recorded with a lesser score.

The similarity score of a Web Feature X is a weighted function of the similarities between each of the four attributes between a user query and X. The similarity score of ontology classes is computed by the degree of matching of the classes. Exact match gives the score of 1 and otherwise, the score is between 0 and 1 and is an inverse function of the distance from the classes to the nearest common super-class. The similarity

Table 2.

Attributes of search request	Attributes of retrieved Web Features	Relation between the attributes of the search request and those of the retrieved Web Features
T	T1 ... Tn	T1 ... Tn are subclasses of T
P	P1 ... Pn	Each property p in P has a corresponding subproperty in the union of P1 ... Pn
G	G1 ... Gn	G is the same as G1 ... Gn
B	B1 ... Bn	B is contained by the union of B1 ... Bn

score of ontology properties is defined similarly. One difference is that the similarity score of properties is a function of the similarity scores between the ontology properties of the query and the feature properties of X. Another difference is that though all ontology classes have at least one common ancestor, the same is not true for ontology properties. So if two properties have no common super-property, then we set the similarity score to 0. The similarity score of a set of properties is simply the mean of the similarity scores for properties in the set. The similarity score of geometry types is either 0 or 1. That is, if they are the same type, the score is 1, otherwise 0. The similarity of bounding boxes can be decided a number of ways. We can set the score to 1 if the Web Feature's bounding box encloses the query bounding box. Otherwise, the score is the fraction of the area of the query bounding box covered by the Web Feature bounding box.

We can choose different functions for computing the similarity score of a Web Feature depending on our emphasis on one or more attributes of the Web Feature. For example, if all attributes are considered, we can set the similarity score as the weighted average of the score of the four attributes. If some attributes such as geometry type have to be matched, we can compute the similarity score by multiply the scores of the four attributes so that if the score for geometry is 0, the total score is 0 as well. Other variations can be considered as well using Boolean logic to consider different scenario. For example, we set the total similarity score to 1 if bounding box is matched and, either geometry type or feature type matched.

Geospatial Web Feature Service Composition

If the matching engine cannot find a single Web Feature that matches the user's query, it will search for a set of Web Features that can be composed to synthesize the required service using composition algorithms. Table 2 summarizes the relationship between the search request and the Web Features included in the composition for answering that request.

When no completely matched Web Feature is discovered that satisfies a user's objective, the existing partially matched Web Features may be combined in order to fulfill the user's request. The WFS composition is therefore the process of selecting and combining Web Features to achieve the user's request, which cannot be realized otherwise. To perform automated composition, we first obtain a list of partially matched Web Features. Suppose the attributes of user request is T', G', P', and B'. The discovery engine retrieves the Web Features with feature type T and the geometry type G such that corresponding ontology class of T is the same or a subclass of that of T' and G is the same as G'. This will result in a set of service S1. Second, from the set of service S1, we narrow down the subset S1 to a subset S2 under the condition that for each ontology property p in P', there exists a feature property in P that corresponds to the subproperty of p, where P is the union of the feature properties of the Web Features in S2,. Third, we further narrow down the subset S2 to a subset S3 under the condition that the bounding box B is contained in the query bounding box B′, where B is the union of the bounding box parameters of the Web Features in S3. Steps two and three are repeated until S3 is found or all possible S2 have been tested. Finally, we return the services in S3 as a composition of the split services. The result of the composition is a collection of Web Features that, when put together, provides the requested data. The composition must provide the correct feature type, geometry type, list of feature properties, and coverage. The comparison of feature types, geometry types, and feature properties are based on their corresponding ontology classes and properties. We can query each of the resulting set of Web Features in parallel, then compose the returned results and return to the user.

The following is a case study that applies the above concept of Geospatial Semantic Web Services to a transit trip planning system

A Framework of Geospatial Semantic Web Services for Transit Trip Planning Systems

The online trip itinerary planning systems have evolved as web technology advances, from the initial proprietary system to open and interoperable systems, and from independent systems for each single transit agency to an inter-dependent inter-jurisdictional system. The initial transit trip itinerary planning systems were developed for individual transit agencies by individual vendors, based on proprietary system architecture and technologies. This is a great advance from manual systems. However, these independent proprietary systems cannot be utilized by users to plan cross-transit agency trips, even in the same metropolitan area with multiple transit agencies, and each transit agency having its own trip itinerary planning system. If the passenger travels across the border of

two or more transit agencies, the passenger cannot use independent transit trip planners to plan his/her itinerary, even when different transit service providers serve the same area.

A simple method of integrating diverse trip planning systems is to compile the data from the different transit agencies. If trip itinerary planning systems are developed by the same vendor, this is possible, as they use the same data structure and search algorithms. For almost all existing "region-wide" trip itinerary planning systems, such as those in Chicago and Washington, D.C. regions in the United States and the Greater Montreal Area in Canada, this is how region-wide trips are planned (Tr´epanier, et al, 2002).

One of the primary problems with this data integration approach, besides the requirement of adopting the same trip planning systems, is the issue of data semantics. For the transit network, various transit agencies use different terminologies to describe the same transit feature. Similarly, the same linear feature is referred to by different terminology in transit networks and road networks. This semantic mismatch worsens as the network and scheduling data must to be updated by individual transit agencies, oftentimes this is performed quarterly, but more frequently in some instances. These updates have to be sent or uploaded to the regional transit information center to be processed and put online. This is a time consuming and potentially error-prone process. This problem aggravates as the number of transit agencies increases.

Therefore, a distributed trip planning system that involves transit networks from a variety of transit agencies and road networks from different sources is a relevant case to address semantic heterogeneity issues. We have been experimenting on this issue, trying to tackle it from two different perspectives using a region-wide cross-jurisdiction transit trip planning system as an example. This is done in the following ways. First, we addressed the issue of semantic heterogeneity by developing a semantic web service. Second, we addressed the

Figure 1. Architecture of geospatial semantic web service

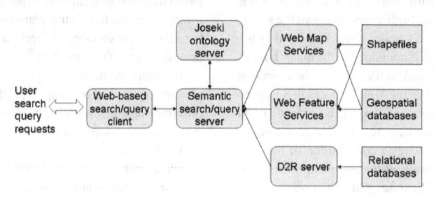

issue of cross-system coordination by creating a mediator system based on Web Services and XML technologies and the advanced traveler information systems (ATIS) standard developed by the Society of Automotive Engineers. Third, we addressed the issue of interoperable system design by developing an open and interoperable system using service-oriented design. (Peng and Tsou, 2003).

The "mediator system" developed to address cross-system coordination issue has been reported in Peng and Kim (2008). The "mediator" is created through a virtual server, connecting all transit trip planning servers by forwarding and collecting messages. For example, if a user asks for a trip that originates from service area A and ends at service area B, the mediator forwards the user request to both servers, receives partial results, and assembles the results into a set of final itineraries. The mediator does not have direct access to the path-finding algorithm inside the trip planning systems. Thus, this ensures the independence of and loose coupling between systems. The mediator has information on all transit trip planning servers. The message exchanges between the mediator and different trip planning systems (e.g., System A and System B in the above example) work through a standard or mutually agreeable XML schema, e.g., the ATIS XML schema. This system framework was implemented in the City of Waukesha and Milwaukee County Transit Systems (MCTS) in the Milwaukee Metropolitan area.

This chapter introduces a framework for creating a geospatial semantic web service to facilitate semantic interoperability among transportation network databases (e.g., transit networks and road networks) and non-spatial attribute databases. The framework is shown in Figure 1. It illustrates the architecture of the geospatial semantic web services, where geospatial data are in the format of shapefiles or other geospatial databases and are accessible through OGC web services (WFS and WMS), whereas non-spatial relational data is transformed to ontology format through D2R server application. The semantic search and query component uses an ontology server (i.e. Joseki server) to assist search and query of spatial data located in OGC web services or in other ontology servers (i.e. D2R server in this case).

In this architecture, spatial data in shapefiles is mapped to Web feature representation accessible through WFS/WMS servers while non-spatial data in relational databases is mapped to ontology representation accessible through D2R servers. The semantic search and query server processes a user query (in ontology query language such as SPARQL) in the following steps:

1. search the ontology server to locate the data sources (WFS and D2R servers),

2. create one or more sub-queries sent to WFS servers and D2R servers, and

3. integrate the answers from the sub-queries as solution to the original user query.

We use WMS server to obtain base maps when necessary.

Specifically, the architecture consists of:

- WFS servers, which are implemented using GeoServer application, which is a Java-based Web server program running in a Servlet container – Apache Tomcat.
- A geospatial ontology server, which is based on Joseki (http://www.joseki.org/) and provides HTTP services to answer semantic queries in SPARQL forms. The server uses a domain ontology for spatial features and application ontology for transportation network data. The ontology server stores ontology instances in files or databases;
- A spatial data query and transformation component, which was developed based on Jena library (http://jena.sourceforge.net/). This component extracts information from WFS servers, creates ontology definitions for the extracted web features, and it transforms feature instances into ontology format to store in the ontology server; and
- Web-based spatial query client programs, which are used to render the ontology queried results as maps. The clients use OpenLayers – a JavaScript library for spatial data.

A prototype has been developed based on the architecture framework to search and access semantically heterogeneous geospatial features for transportation data using the above described discovery and composition algorithms. The data used in the prototype come from the Waukesha Transit Trip Planning Project. Two WFS servers were created. The bus route WFS server pub-

lishes the bus route data using the feature name "wks:routes", while the bus stop WFS server publishes the bus stop data using the feature name "wksha:BusStops". Note that the namespace prefixes are different, which indicates that features are in different WFS servers that may use different naming conventions for bus stops and routes.

Implementation

The implementation includes the modules for maintaining domain ontology for transit data, indexing available WFS features, mapping WFS feature types to ontology definitions, and processing user query to return a list of WFS features.

We first create domain ontology for feature data in general and then application ontology for transit bus route and bus stop spatial data in particular. We created three domain ontology files used in transportation networks: transportation base, road networks, and transit networks. The domain ontology definitions are written in OWL and translated from existing UML data models for transportation applications. We developed algorithms to automatically transform these UML models into OWL ontology (Zhang et al. 2008). However, because of the differences between UML and OWL, we could not create all necessary ontology by the automatic transformation method. Therefore, we used the ontology editor tool Protégé to create those ontology definitions that could not be transformed from existing UML data models. Then, we integrated the three domain specific ontology files together. Since the ontology definitions are internally consistent, we successfully avoided typical integration difficulties that would arise from importing other transportation ontology into ours.

The application ontology in our prototype is divided into two parts: one part corresponds to WFS features and the other part corresponds to database tables that supplement the WFS features. To represent geospatial features as ontology instances, we used predefined OWL classes such as

Feature, Geometry (with subclasses *Point, Line,* and *Polygon*), *BoundingBox,* and *Area*. Relations between classes were often asserted with *owl:subClassOf* property. We introduced object properties, such as *has_geometry,* and datatype properties, such as *minx, maxx, miny, maxy* for the x, y coordinates of bounding boxes. Restrictions on properties were not used since it might prevent future extension. We also automatically generated OWL classes from WFS features such as *Route, Link,* and *Stop*. In addition, some OWL properties were auto-generated from feature properties. Because each OWL name is globally unique and name conflicts are not tolerated while WFS property names are locally scoped (i.e. the names are only unique with a particular feature type), we defined OWL properties to overwrite any previous definitions of the same names to resolve name clashes. To prevent any further conflicts, we did not place domain or range restriction on these properties. We related auto-generated OWL definitions with predefined ones through assertions such as *owl:subClassOf* and *owl:subPropertiesOf*. WFS feature instances were automatically translated into OWL individuals using the predefined and auto-generated classes and properties. To enable the WFS features search and discovery, we auto-generated an ontology individual for each feature type to include properties such as feature name, URL, bounding box, and name geometry type.

The application ontology corresponding to database tables is a virtual graph of RDF nodes created by a tool, D2R server (http://www4.wiwiss. fu-berlin.de/bizer/d2r-server/), from database tables in a separate server that contain spatial and non-spatial data. The RDF ontology was generated based on a mapping configuration file used by D2R server. The ontology is a straightforward mapping coming from database tables – one table maps to one ontology class and one column maps to one ontology property. Additional object properties were defined via inference rules based on existing datatype properties and classes. We defined inference rules to describe some object properties

to connect the two parts of application ontology to support the user query. For example, to find the geometry of the stops along a bus route, we need both the application ontology that corresponds to WFS features, which contains the geometries and the IDs of the stops, and the application ontology that corresponds to the database tables, which contains the correspondence between a route ID and the IDs of the stops in the route. Using the inference rules and the reasoning ability of OWL ontology, our prototype can support queries that cannot be answered by WFS or database alone.

We index the available WFS features with feature types, feature properties, geometry types, and bounding boxes of the features. The indices are instances of a special ontology class *Feature*. Each instance contains the detailed information about a WFS feature. When the user searches for features, the returned feature instances are used to locate the corresponding ontology classes, which are used to locate all the feature instances.

We also create mappings from WFS features, properties, and geometries to ontology classes and properties. This process was manual work so that the ontology classes generated from WFS features become subclasses of the domain and application ontology classes. If a generated ontology property is equivalent to an existing property, they are then merged. For example, we generated an ontology class *TransitRoute* corresponding to the feature *wks:routes*. We identify that this class is indeed a subclass of *TransitLink*, which describes a segment of a transit route. This information cannot be determined based on the names of the features alone since names can be misleading. Also, we generated an ontology property *the_geom* from a common feature property with the same name. A similar property *geom* has already been defined in our domain ontology to refer to the geometry of features. Therefore, we merged the two properties into one. After completing this process, we can automatically query for spatial data. For example, if we are to find out the geometry of a route by the name of "Summit", we can simply query for

Figure 2. A sample of query results: Bus routes and bus stops located within 1 km of the bus stop in Fox Run Shopping Center of downtown Waukesha

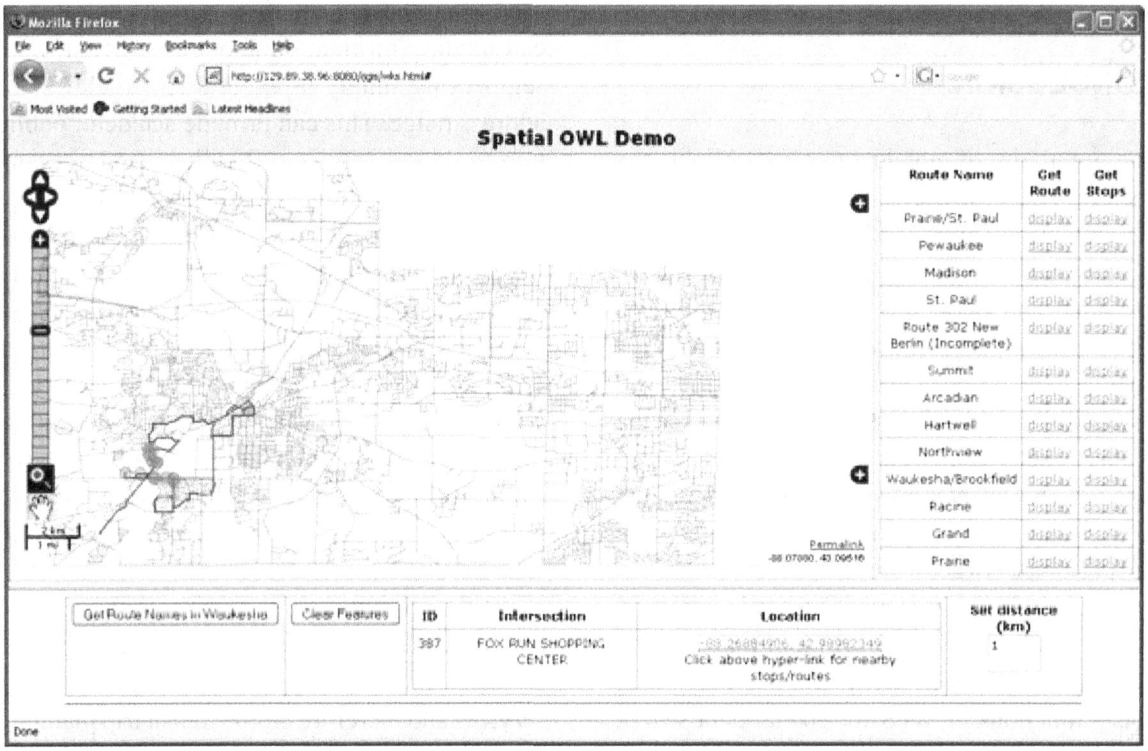

instances of *TransitRoute* with the name "Summit". The geometry of the route is the union of the geometries of the links on the route.

We also implemented a module to take a service query and return a list of WFS features that when combined can return data requested in the query. For example, to locate the requested bus route and bus stop features from the two separated WFS servers, two service queries are needed:

(TransitRoute, {geometry, description}, Line, B), and *(TransitStop, {geometry, intersection}, Point, B)*, where *B* is a bounding box. The first elements of the queries are the feature types *TransitRoute* or *TransitStop*. The second elements of the queries are the sets of feature properties such as *geometry*, *description*, and *intersection*. The third elements are the geometry types such as *line* and *point*. The last element of the queries is a bounding box *B*. Once a user supplies the two

queries, the system matches the ontology class *TransitRoute* to *wks:routes* and matches *TransitStop* to *wksha:BusStops*. Similarly, the property lists are matched against the properties of the two features. Finally, the system makes sure that geometry types are matched and the two feature services cover the bounding box *B*. If the system finds partial matches, it will compose the partially matched services. The resulting data can be parsed to present the needed results.

A screenshot of the prototype is shown in Figure 2, in which we locate the bus routes and stops in the vicinity of a particular location. The query is answered through an ontology server using integrated data from WFS servers located by searching known list of services. To improve performance, the retrieved feature instances were transformed into ontology individuals and were stored in the ontology server. This way, client does not have to repeatedly send requests to WFS servers for the same feature instances.

CONCLUSION

The popularity of mobile devices highlights the need for real-time access to location-based data. Unless data are provided from a single provider, it is unavoidable that the data must be accessed, extracted and integrated from diverse sources. The syntactic and structural heterogeneity of diverse data has been extensively addressed and successfully resolved over the years. However, the semantic heterogeneity is a more difficult issue to resolve. This chapter provides a unique approach to address this issue by developing a framework and prototype of a geospatial semantic web service.

The novelty of the approach taken in this study is that it takes advantage of the merits of both ontology and WFS. First, it can use the spatial query functions of WFS for spatial data search and use the existing WFS client library for feature rendering. Second, the interface can use relational databases as sources for non-spatial data searches to improve the performance of non-spatial data queries.

Empirical tests, using transportation road networks and transit data, show that this method is more efficient than converting all data to ontology instances, as it avoids the costs and consistency problems of data replication (Peng, 2005; Zhao et al 2008). The results demonstrate that user queries can be both more flexible and straightforward, based on the meaning of the data elements, rather than requiring specific knowledge of the data structure and elements. Consequently, this method may be further applied to both web service discovery and retrieval.

This approach is a huge departure from the conventional data sharing methods that rely on data downloading and integration. Users can make queries on a Web site using structured query language based on user needs without worrying about database structure, format and compatibility. Furthermore, this method allows users to make more complicated queries. For example, users can inquire information about a particular road segment by simply inputing a street address or address range. This can provide accident, public transportation services, flooding, land use and housing information that are associated with or within a certain distance from the street address from a diverse group of sources residing anywhere on the Internet without the conventional buffer operation inside GIS. Users can also search for information that meet certain criteria like locations with fatal accidents on a rainy day between 5:00 – 7:00 PM on any US Interstate highways, or search for all road segments that will be impacted by a 50-year flood. Users can then use this information to conduct a variety of analysis.

The next step in this process is to explore ways in which natural language searches for data services can be incorporated into semantic web services and therefore online transit trip planning systems. This contributes towards developing a user interface to mobile device users. If successful, this could be, for example, the next Google search. This would be at the database semantic level, which would enable researchers to address many research questions that we are not able to today, and enable mobile users to access any information from anywhere based on a common geographic location.

ACKNOWLEDGMENT

This research was supported in part by US National Science Foundation award BCS-0616957, National Natural Science Foundation of China award 50738004, China National High Technology Research and Development Program 863 award 2009AA11Z220. Any opinions, findings, and conclusions or recommendations expressed in this paper are those of the authors and do not necessarily reflect the views of the sponsors.

REFERENCES

W3C. (2004). *OWL Web ontology language overview*. Retrieved on May 21, 2010, from http://www.w3.org/TR/owl-features/

Akkiraju, R., Farrell, J., Miller, J., Nagarajan, M., Schmidt, T., Sheth, A., et al. (2005). *Web Service Semantics - WSDL-S*.

Bernstein, A., & Klein, M. (2002). Towards high-precision service retrieval. In I. Horrocks and J. Hendler (Eds.), *Proceedings from The First International Semantic Web Conference (ISWC 2002)*, (pp. 84-101). Sardinia, Italy: Springer.

Bishr, Y. (1998). Overcoming the semantic and other barriers to GIS interoperability. *International Journal of Geographical Information Science*, *12*, 299–314. doi:10.1080/136588198241806

Di, L., & Zhao, P. (2008). Geospatial Semantic Web interoperability. In Shekhar, S., & Xiong, H. (Eds.), *Encyclopedia of GIS* (pp. 70–77). Springer. doi:10.1007/978-0-387-35973-1_119

Duke, A., Davies, J., & Richardson, M. (2005). Enabling a scalable service-oriented architecture with semantic web services. *BT Technology Journal*, *23*(33), 191–201. doi:10.1007/s10550-005-0041-2

Egenhofer, M. (2002). Toward the Semantic Geospatial Web. *Proceedings from the Tenth ACM International Symposium on Advances in Geographic Information Systems*, 1-4. ACM Press.

Fabrikant, S. I., & Buttenfield, B. P. (2001). Formalizing semantic spaces for information access. *Annals of the Association of American Geographers. Association of American Geographers*, *91*, 263–280. doi:10.1111/0004-5608.00242

Farrell, J., & Lausen, H. (Eds.). (2007). *Semantic Annotations for WSDL and XML Schema, W3C Candidate Recommendation*. Retrieved May 21, 2010, from http://www.w3.org/TR/sawsdl/

Fensel, D., Bussler, C., Ding, Y., & Omelayenko, B. (2002). The Web Service Modeling Framework (WSMF). *Electronic Commerce Research and Applications*, *1*, 113–137. doi:10.1016/S1567-4223(02)00015-7

Fonsenka, F., & Sheth, A. (2002). *The Geospatial Semantic Web, UCGIS White Paper*. Retrieved May 21, 2010, from http://www.personal.psu.edu/faculty/f/u/fuf1/Fonseca-Sheth.pdf

Goodchild, M. F., Egenhofer, M. J., Fegeas, R., & Kottman, C. A. (Eds.). (1999). *Interoperating Geographic Information Systems*. New York: Kluwer.

Kuhn, W. (2005). Geospatial semantics: why, of what, and how? *Journal of Data Semantics*, *3*, 1–24. doi:10.1007/11496168_1

Lausen, H., Polleres, A., & Roman, D. (2005). *Web Service Modeling Ontology (WSMO)*. Retrieved May 21, 2010, from http://www.w3.org/Submission/WSMO/

Li, W., Yang, C., & Raskin, R. (2008). A semantic enhanced model for searching in spatial web portals. In: *AAAI Spring Symposium semantic scientific knowledge integration technical report SS-08-05*, 47-50. Palo Alto, CA.

Lutz, M. (2007). Ontology-based descriptions for semantic discovery and composition of geoprocessing services. *GeoInformatica*, *11*, 1–36. doi:10.1007/s10707-006-7635-9

Lutz, M., & Klien, E. (2006). Ontology-based retrieval of geographic information. *International Journal of Geographical Information Science*, *20*, 233–260. doi:10.1080/13658810500287107

Martin, D., Paolucci, M., & Wagner, M. (2007). *Toward semantic annotations of Web services: OWL-S from the SAWSDL Perspective*. Retrieved May 21, 2010, from http://www.ai.sri.com/OWL-S-2007/final-versions/OWL-S-2007-Martin-Final.pdf

OGC document 03-065r6. (2003). *Web coverage service (ver. 1.0.0)*. Retrieved May 21, 2010, from http://www.opengeospatial.org/standards/wcs

OGC document 04-021r2. (2004). *OpenGIS catalogue service specification*, Retrieved May 21, 2010, from http://www.opengeospatial.org/standards/cat

OGC document 04-024. (2004). *Web map service (ver. 1.3)*. Retrieved May 21, 2010, from http://www.opengeospatial.org/standards/wms

OGC document 04-094. (2005). *Web feature service implementation specification, version 1.1.0*. Retrieved May 21, 2010, from http://www.opengeospatial.org/standards/wfs

OGC document 05-007r7. (2005). *Web processing service*, Retrieved May 21, 2010, from http://www.opengeospatial.org/standards/wps

Peng, Z. R. (2005). A proposed framework for feature level geospatial data sharing: a case study for transportation network data. *International Journal of Geographical Information Science*, *19*(4), 459–481. doi:10.1080/13658810512331319127

Peng, Z.-R., & Kim, E. (2008). A standard-based integration framework of distributed transit trip planning systems. *Journal of the Intelligent Transportation Systems*, *12*(1), 13–19. doi:10.1080/15472450701849642

Peng, Z.-R., & Tsou, M.-H. (2003). *Internet GIS: distributed Geographic Information Services for the internet and wireless networks*. Hoboken, NJ: John Wiley & Sons.

Richardson, R., & Smeaton, A. (1995). *Using WordNet in a knowledge-based approach to information retrieval, technical, CA-0395*. Dublin, Ireland: Dublin City University, School of Computer Applications.

Schuster, G., & Stuckenschmidt, H. (2001). Building shared ontologies for terminology integration. Paper presented in *KI-01 Workshop on Ontologies*, Vienna, Austria.

Sheth, A. (1999). Changing focus on interoperability in Information Systems: from system, syntax, structure to semantics. In: M.F. Goodchild, M. J. Egenhofer, R. Fegeas, & C.A. Kottman (Eds.), *Interoperating Geographic Information Systems*, 5-30. New York: Kluwer.

Tr'epanier, M., Chapleau, R., & Allard, B. (2002). Transit user information system for transit itinerary calculation on the Web. *Journal of Public Transportation*, *5*(3), 13–32.

White Paper, O. G. C. (2001). *Introduction to OGC Web Services*. Retrieved May 21, 2010, from http://www.opengeospatial.org/pressroom/papers

Wiegand, N., & García, C. (2007). A task-based ontology approach to automated Geospatial Data Retrieval. *Transactions in GIS*, *11*(3), 355–376. doi:10.1111/j.1467-9671.2007.01050.x

WSMO working group. (2004). *WSMO*. Retrieved on May 21, 2010, from http://www.wsmo.org/

Yang, C., Li, W., Xie, J., & Zhou, B. (2008). Distributed geospatial information processing: sharing distributed geospatial resources to support Digital Earth. *International Journal of Digital Earth*, *1*, 259–278. doi:10.1080/17538940802037954

Yue, P., Di, L., Yang, W., Yu, G., & Zhao, P. (2007). Semantics-based automatic composition of geospatial web service chains. *Computers & Geosciences*, *33*, 649–665. doi:10.1016/j.cageo.2006.09.003

Zhang, C., Li, W., & Zhao, T. (2007). Geospatial data sharing based on geospatial semantic web technologies. *Journal of Spatial Science*, *52*(2), 35–49.

Zhang, C., Zhao, T., & Li, W. (2010b). A framework for Geospatial Semantic Web-based spatial decision support system. *International Journal of Digital Earth*, *3*, 111–134. doi:10.1080/17538940903373803

Zhang, C., Zhao, T., Li, W., & Osleeb, J. (2010a). Towards logic-based geospatial feature discovery and integration using web feature service and Geospatial Semantic Web. *International Journal of Geographical Information Science*, *24*, 903–923. doi:10.1080/13658810903240687

Zhao, P., Di, L., Yue, P., Wei, Y., & Yang, W. (2009). Semantic Web-based geospatial knowledge transformation. *Computers & Geosciences*, *35*, 798–808. doi:10.1016/j.cageo.2008.03.013

Zhao, T., Zhang, C., Wei, M., & Peng, Z.-R. (2008). Ontology-based geospatial data query and integration. In: Cova, T. J., Miller H. J, Beard K., Frank, A. U., and Goodchild, M. F. (Eds.), *Lecture Notes in Computer Science: Geographic Information Science,* 370-392. Springer.

ADDITIONAL READING

Benatallah, B., Dumas, M., & Sheng, Q. (2005). Facilitating the rapid development and scalable orchestration of composite Web services. *Distributed and Parallel Databases*, 5–37. doi:10.1023/B:DAPD.0000045366.15607.67

Brodie, M. (2007). Semantic technologies: realizing the services vision. *IEEE Intelligent Systems*, *22*(5), 13–17.

Duke, A., Davies, J., & Richardson, M. (2005). Enabling a scalable service-oriented architecture with semantic web services. *BT Technology Journal*, *23*(33), 191–201. doi:10.1007/s10550-005-0041-2

Fonseca, F. (2007). The double role of ontologies in information science research. *Journal of the American Society for Information Science and Technology*, *58*, 786–793. doi:10.1002/asi.20565

Fonseca, F. T., Egenhofer, M. J., Davis, C. A., & Camara, G. (2002). Semantic granularity in ontology-driven Geographic Information Systems. *Annals of Mathematics and Artificial Intelligence*, *36*(1–2), 121–151. doi:10.1023/A:1015808104769

Fonseca, F. T., & Martin, J. E. (2005). Toward an alternative notion of information systems ontologies: information engineering as a hermeneutic enterprise. *Journal of the American Society for Information Science and Technology*, *56*, 46–57. doi:10.1002/asi.20099

Grenon, P., & Smith, B. (2004). SNAP and SPAN: towards dynamic spatial ontology. *Spatial Cognition and Computation*, *4*(1), 69–104. doi:10.1207/s15427633scc0401_5

Huang, R., & Zhong, R.-P. (2008). A spatiotemporal data model for dynamic transit networks. *International Journal of Geographical Information Science*, *22*(5), 527–545. doi:10.1080/13658810701492399

Kavouras, M., & Kokla, M. (2002). A method for the formalization and integration of geographical categorizations. *International Journal of Geographical Information Science*, *16*, 439–453. doi:10.1080/13658810210129120

Peng, Z.-R., & Huang, R. (2000). Design and development of interactive trip planning for web-based transit information systems. *Transportation Research C. Emerging Technology*, *8*, 409–425. doi:10.1016/S0968-090X(00)00016-4

Zhang, C., & Li, W. (2005). The Roles of Web Feature Service and Web Map Service in real time Geospatial Data Sharing for time-critical applications. *Cartography and Geographic Information Science*, *32*(4), 269–283. doi:10.1559/152304005775194728

Zhang, C., Peng, Z.-R., Zhao, T., & Li, W. (2008). Transforming transportation data models from UML to OWL ontological representation. *Journal of the Transportation Research Board: Transportation Research Record, 2064*, 81–89. doi:10.3141/2064-11

KEY TERMS AND DEFINITIONS

Geospatial Semantic Web: Deals with geographic information that the basic Semantic Web research has not addressed to improve the results of queries looking for information stored in geographic databases.

Geospatial Semantic Web Services: Address the semantic heterogeneous problem found in geospatial web services. Geospatial semantic web services define the geospatial data and processing services in terms of semantics by building upon the ontologies and then assigning a specific meaning to that ontology.

Geospatial Web Services: Are a special kind of web services that provide access to heterogeneous geographic information on the Internet.

OGC has developed several web service specifications to standardize geospatial web services to access geospatial data and applications. The important geospatial web services include Web Feature Services (WFS), Web Map Services (WMS), Web Coverage Services (WCS), Catalogue Service (CS), and Web Processing Services (WPS), etc.

Ontology: Is a formal representation of the knowledge by a set of concepts within a domain and the relationships between those concepts. Ontologies contain rules that can perform certain types of runtime automatic reasoning.

Transit Trip Planner: Refers to an itinerary planning system for transit riders to plan trips on a transit network, based on the trip origin, destinations and the time of travel.

Web Ontology Language (OWL): Is a family of knowledge representation languages for authoring ontologies endorsed by the WWW consortium. They are characterized by formal semantics and RDF/XML-based serializations for the Semantic web.

Web Services: Are reusable software components that interact in a loosely coupled environment, and are designed to interoperate in a loosely-coupled manner.

Chapter 9
Linked Data:
Connecting Spatial Data Infrastructures and Volunteered Geographic Information

Carlos Granell
Universitat Jaume I, Spain

Sven Schade
European Commission – Joint Research Centre, Institute for Environment and Sustainability, Italy

Gobe Hobona
University of Nottingham, UK

ABSTRACT

A Spatial Data Infrastructure (SDI) is an information infrastructure for enhancing geospatial data sharing and access. At the moment, the service-oriented second generation of SDI is transitioning to a third generation, which is characterized by user-centric approaches. This new movement closes the gap between classical SDI and user contributed content, also known as Volunteered Geographic Information (VGI). Public use and acquisition of information provides additional challenges within and beyond the geospatial domain. Linked Data has been suggested recently as a possible overall solution. This notion refers to a best practice for exposing, sharing, and connecting resources in the (Semantic) Web. This chapter details the Linked Data approach to SDI and suggests it as a possibility to combine SDI with VGI. Thus, a Spatial Linked Data Infrastructure could apply solutions for Linked Data to classical SDI standards. The chapter highlights different implementing strategies, gives examples, and argues for benefits, while at the same time trying to outline possible fallbacks; hopeful this contribution will enlighten a way towards a single shared information space.

DOI: 10.4018/978-1-60960-192-8.ch009

1 INTRODUCTION

A Spatial Data Infrastructure (SDI) is an information infrastructure for enhancing geospatial data sharing and access (Nebert, 2004). An SDI embraces a set of rules, standards, procedures, guidelines, policies, institutions, data, networks, technology and human resources for enabling and coordinating the management and exchange of geospatial data between stakeholders in the spatial data community (Rajabifard et al., 2006; Masser, 2007). All involved resources (geospatial data sets, metadata, users, providers, organizations, etc.) are not static, i.e., they are dynamic over time. In addition, communication and information technologies have dramatically changed since 1990s, when first SDI projects took off (Masser, 1999). SDI is a live, adaptable entity by definition that needs to accommodate periodically to emerging technologies, user relationships, socio-economic contexts and other factors that have influence on SDI developments (Rajabijard et al., 2006; Masser, 2007; Budhathoki et al., 2008).

The web itself is evolving from the idea of an open, static repository (Callahan, 1985) to an application platform (Ackland, 2009). Recent advances in web technologies, such as social networks (Boyd and Ellison, 2007), enable new ways of participation, communication and creativity on the web. It is not surprising then that the web has changed the way in which we work nowadays. Citizens, experts and non-experts alike, are increasingly participating in the process of generating up-to-date information and collaborating with others in solving-problem tasks. This highlights the matter of a transition, changing role of users, from just mere data consumers to active consumers and producers. Consequently users interact, use and access information infrastructures in a different way.

The shift in the role of users has been also reflected in the geospatial domain, known as Volunteered Geographic Information (VGI) (Goodchild, 2007). VGI highlights that users are active producers of geographic information rather than passive recipients of geographic information by formal organizations. Budhathoki et al. (2008) have suggested a new generation of SDI, which is driven by user needs. However, some recent studies on how social networks are used to sharing data in SDI reveal that users are still poorly connected to data resources of their interest (Omran and van Etten, 2007; van Oort et al., 2010). Results also indicate that the position of individuals in a given organization (hierarchy of work relationships) has influences on their potential access to and sharing spatial data, i.e., most relationships are vertical, with few horizontal user-to-user connections between peers.

There is a need to establish connections among geospatial data sets, by linking users with other providers, users with users, and data sources with users and providers. Connecting resources in such a way would let stakeholders to find out who is actually using a particular data set. If someone is, for example, looking for information about the city of Nottingham (UK), any data set (reaching from geo-tagged photos to demographic data and related maps) should be connected to related data sources and users with similar interests. Such connections would enable seamless browsing and effective information retrieval. In this vision, Linked Data has been suggested as possible solution for creating such information spaces (Bizer et al., 2009). The notion of Linked Data refers to a best practice for exposing, sharing, and connecting data sources in the web[1]. In essence, Linked Data evolved from research on the semantic web (Berners-Lee et al., 2001) and is concerned with creating links between different data sources, to enable the discovery, navigation, analysis, and knowledge inference of data across disciplinary domains. We stick to the example of Nottingham (Section 3) throughout this chapter to exemplify the potential connections among SDI, VGI and Linked Data.

Given this context, the motivation of this chapter is two-fold:

- The idea of users as data producers is expanding the boundaries of SDI and creates new relationships between the traditional roles of consumer and providers. A network of consumers, producers and providers may benefit and enrich SDI developments, above all at local and regional level where the role of citizens is critical.

- In addition, providing multiple connections between resources helps to make explicit the actual links among stakeholders and at the same time affords alternative search strategies to locate useful content (Gahegan et al., 2009). This potentially alleviates the bottleneck of having just one traditional entry point in SDI, as the case of geoportals (Bernard et al., 2005), and also open up SDI resources to a wider audience. Without suitable provision for these needs, many useful resources will remain undiscovered to the user (Gahegan et al., 2009).

Linked Data has not yet been regarded in the context of SDI. We intend to explore the capabilities of Linked Data to the geospatial science community, with a special focus on the services in SDI. In a *Spatial Linked Data Infrastructure* resources can potentially connect to the vast repositories of structured geospatial data in a *Linked Data Space*, but also may benefit of establishing relationships not only with data sets but with other types of resources such as metadata, users, providers, organizations, etc. As SDI content expands, though, with user-generated content and Linked Data, it is necessary to consider whether traditional mechanisms are still useful for discovering interlinked resources, understanding these connections, and knowing how to use them appropriately.

The reminder of this chapter is structured as follows. Section 2 presents required technical background on SDI and geospatial web services, main projects supporting the Linked Data initiative, and also the most significant projects aligned to VGI. In Section 3, we illustrate how the three

notions relate to each other using the Nottingham example, which we already briefly introduced above. We include a comparison of the core concepts and outline related work. We introduce our projection of the Linked Data approach to classical SDI and VGI in Section 4. Here we also identify a set of challenging issues stemmed from the need of combining both approaches. Section 5 contains a solution together with three implementing strategies and an according discussion, before we subsequently outline future research directions (Section 6) and wrap-up (Section 7).

2 BACKGROUND

This section outlines the basic concepts underlying the topics tackled in this chapter: Spatial Data Infrastructure, Volunteered Geographic Information, and Linked Data. An illustration of combining the three notions and a summary table that compare all three fields is presented in the next chapter.

2.1 Architectural Styles

Geosciences research is a multidisciplinary field that demands not only heterogeneous data and models but also includes a multitude of expert profiles such as technologist, remote sensing specialist, and geoscientist (Granell et al., 2010). This scenario requires the use of new architectural styles which oppose centralized, isolated solutions, and instead support distributed processing capabilities and remote communications, necessary ingredients to successful collaborative and multidisciplinary research. Service-Oriented Architectures (SOA) and Resource-Oriented Architectures (ROA) are currently the architectural styles adopted in the development of collaborative, distributed Web systems and applications.

SOA is an architectural style to design applications based on a collection of best practices, principles, interfaces, and patterns related to the central concept of service (Bell, 2008). In SOA, services play a key role and become the basic computing unit to support development and composition of larger, more complex services, which in turn can be used to create flexible, ad hoc and dynamic applications. The main design principle behind SOA is that a service is a standards-based, loosely-coupled unit composed of a service interface and a service implementation. Service interface describes the functional capabilities of a service. Service implementation implements what a service should execute. This principle provides a clean separation of concerns especially between service interfaces (what services offer to the public community) and internal implementations (how services work). Essentially SOA introduces a new philosophy for building distributed applications, where services can be discovered, aggregated, published, reused, and invoked at the interface level, independently of the specific technology used internally to implement each service.

At the time of implementation SOA-based services must make use of concrete languages and protocols. Here is where web service technology gains importance because it increasingly is becoming the choice to implement SOA-based applications. Web services (Alonso et al., 2004) are, by definition, loosely coupled independent units and are well described (interface description contains functional properties), thereby promoting one of the goals of SOA: enabling interoperability or the ability of services to interact with minimal knowledge of the underlying structure of other services (Goodchild et al., 1999). Interoperability is achieved (or optimized) by using standard interfaces. Web service technology includes various standards such as Web Service Description Language (WSDL) for the description of service interfaces, Universal Description, Discovery and Integration registry (UDDI) for their advertisement and discovery, and Simple Object Application Protocol (SOAP) that enables communication among services (Curbera et al., 2002).

As opposed to SOA, focused on distributed capabilities and services, ROA is an architectural style devoted to manage distributed, heterogeneous domain resources. In SOA client applications interacts with a distributed Web applications through delegation, that is, by specifying the desired capability to a service component instead of directly acting on the resources themselves (Mazzetti et al., 2009). In ROA, through, client applications interact directly with the exposed resources.

The main constraints behind ROA-based applications are the set of architectural principles known as REpresentational State Transfer (REST) (Fielding, 2000):

- Resources should be identified properly using URI mechanism (Berners-Lee et al., 1998), that is, each resource must be addressable via a URI;
- Uniform interface through the use of HTTP as the unique application-level protocol. HTTP has a small, fixes of operational methods with specific purpose and meaning. For instance, the GET method is for retrieving representations of target resources, the POST method for creating new resources, PUT for updating resources, and finally, the DELETE method to eliminate a given resource.
- Resource are manipulated through representations since clients and servers exchange self-descriptive messages each another;
- Interaction stateless since servers only record and manage the state of their resources they exposes. Client sessions are not maintained in the server.
- Hypermedia as the engine of application state, that is the application state is built following hyperlinks according to the navigation paradigm.

As in the case of SOA-based services, ROA-based applications, such as Linked Data sources (Section 2.4), can be implemented in many different ways, such as RESTful web services (Richardson and Ruby, 2007) and Web Services Resource Framework (WSRF) (OASIS, 2006). Designing RESTful web services following the REST constraints described above has gained popularity within the Earth science, mobile and location based services community (Mazzetti et al, 2009). WSRF standardizes the representation of stateful resources within SOA architectures.

2.2 Spatial Data Infrastructures

The notion of Spatial Data Infrastructure (SDI) refers to the specialization of information infrastructures for the geospatial sciences (Nebert, 2004). President Clinton's executive order to establish a national (US) level SDI (Executive Office of the President, 1994) is one of earliest milestones in SDI development. Since then, dozens of SDIs have been developed across the globe, both on national-level and on international-level (Crompvoets and Bregt, 2007). In total, several billions of dollars are spent on SDI-related activities each year (Onsrud et al. 2004). These activities include technical developments and deployment of applications, but moreover work on institutional arrangements, acquisition and maintenance of geospatial data, and accessibility and usability of geospatial information (Masser, 2007).

The origins and objectives of the first generation of SDI are reported by Masser (1999). The first SDI initiatives promoted to make public data available to users (product- or data-driven) and engaged potential stakeholders in establishing institutional collaborations and data sharing policies. After the first generation, which last approximately until 2000, the second generation of SDIs is process-oriented (Rajabijard et al., 2006; Budhathoki et al., 2008). The approach of the second generation is driven by service-based data applications as opposed to the data themselves (Bernard and Craglia, 2005). The role of the SDI user slightly shifted from a passive data consumer to a service receipt (Budhathoki et al., 2008). Cur-

rent technical developments and growing interest in social aspects of geospatial information sharing indicate the transition to a third generation of SDI, which is way more user-based, i.e., VGI-oriented (Budhathoki et al., 2008).

Nowadays, SDIs describe the notion of service-oriented management, accessing, and processing of geospatial data; they are implemented using web services. In general, web services technology have facilitated data integration and promoted interoperability among heterogeneous distributed information sources. Indeed, the geospatial community has been at the forefront of the development of e-Infrastructure for the service-oriented sharing of data and computational capability. The application of e-Infrastructure in scientific research is sometimes referred to as e-Science (in Europe) and e-Research (in Australia and the US). SDI exemplify the adoption of the SOA paradigm (Section 2.1) in the geospatial domain and offer the possibility to access distributed, heterogeneous spatial data through a set of policies, common rules and standards that facilitate interconnecting spatial information users in an interoperable way. Interoperability is a basic requirement for distributed information systems and so it is also critical to SDI (Goodchild et al., 1999).

Geospatial web services allow users to access, manage, and process geospatial data in a distributed manner (Zhao et al., 2007). The demand for interoperability has boosted the development of standards and tools to facilitate data transformation and integration, mostly in terms of standard interfaces specified by Open Geospatial Consortium (OGC)[2] and Technical Committee 211 (TC211) of International Organization for Standardization (ISO)[3]. The Web Map Service (WMS), the Web Feature Service (WFS) and the Web Coverage Service (WCS) are some prominent examples of OGC interfaces for geospatial services. All appear in different versions, where WMS 1.3.0 (OGC, 2006a), WFS 1.1.0 (OGC, 2005a), and WCS 1.1.2 (OGC, 2008) are the most recent. Re-using the example from the introduction (Section 1), a

WMS could be used to provide a map of the city centre of Nottingham, a WFS may serve detailed transport network data, and a WCS may offer satellite imagery of the city and its surroundings. The central building-blocks for data, as well as service discovery, are provided by the Catalogue Services for the Web (CSW) (OGC, 2007b) and so called geo-portals (Bernard et al., 2005). The CSW provides one access point to users that search of data about Nottingham city. Linked to the SOA principle of service composition, many standards organizations, industry bodies, and the geospatial research community have paid attention to the effective composition and orchestration of geospatial web services; since geospatial web solutions continue to grow and increase in complexity (Alameh, 2003).

Information retrieval requires data and metadata exchange and processing. Numerous standards for related data (and metadata) and supporting services have been defined on conceptual and implementing level (Nebert, 2004). As SDIs target expert users, data models are complex (for example INSPIRE (2009)) and discovery supports sophisticated querying (OGC, 2005b). At the moment, data (and metadata) models are defined in UML (Rumbaugh et al., 1999) and encoded in XML Schema (W3C, 2001). An abstract structure for data modeling and encoding is provided in form of the Geographic Markup Language (GML) (OGC, 2007a). Concrete, domain specific data models are called GML application schema. GML already provides possibilities of including metadata, more sophisticated profiles (including information about providers, license, and sophisticated quality parameters) are provided separately (OGC, 2007b). The two ISO standards 19115 and 19139 provide the most common examples (ISO, 2003; ISO, 2007). A more visualization-centric, less-complex data structure has been standardized in form of KML (formerly Keyhole Markup

Language) (OGC, 2007c). GeoRSS, a way for adding information about geospatial location to RSS (Really Simple Syndication) feeds, has been acknowledged by OGC, too (OGC, 2006b).

One example of an SDI initiative that adopts geospatial web service standards is the Infrastructure for Spatial Information in the European Community (INSPIRE) Directive of the European Commission (European Parliament and Council, 2007). During the shaping of INSPIRE, one of the goals of the SDI research agenda was to focus on the importance of SDIs versus other information infrastructures. Context has dramatically changed since then. Not only are information technologies and computing infrastructures constantly evolving, but most importantly how communication and collaboration among geospatial scientists, researchers, and users in general have changed (Goodchild, 2009). The 2009 PAREDE[4] white paper for European Data infrastructure —a European effort to promote an e-infrastructure for long-term data preservation and common cross-disciplinary data services—, estimates almost 200 European research and social infrastructures, from bioinformatics, physics and environmental science to social sciences to even YouTube videos. SDI remain still a small community and needs to open its resources (data, services, standards, specifications, etc.) to other bigger communities to tackle multidisciplinary problems that go beyond the boundaries of geospatial information. Disciplines rely on different infrastructures, as for example bioinformatics projects that use grid computing extensively for their distributed processing tasks. In this sense, the geospatial community is already responding to these needs at service level, putting to work together geospatial processing services in grid infrastructures (Lee and Percivall, 2008; Hobona et al., 2010). However, a need for a 'universal' approach for indentifying and linking data from different disciplines remains.

2.3 Volunteered Geographic Information

In the previous section, SDIs were described as having evolved over two generations. Crompvoets and Bregt (2007) suggest that data were the key driver for SDI development in the first generation of SDI. However, in the second generation of SDI the use of data and the needs of users are the driving force for the development of SDI. Indeed, the user of geographic information now plays a greater role in the creation of geographic information through enabling technologies such as GPS-enabled mobile phones, geotagging cameras and Web 2.0 applications. The information created through these technologies has led to a concept referred to as Volunteered Geographic Information (VGI) (Goodchild, 2007) as a form of user-generated content.

VGI can be defined as geographic information generated through the widespread engagement of large numbers of citizens, each with the ability to add, review and revise the contributed information. One of the motivating factors of VGI is self-promotion (Goodchild, 2007). An example of a service that offers self-promotion is the MyMaps feature within Google Maps and the Google 3D Warehouse where users can upload their own generated 2D and 3D maps. Similar to open source software, another motivating factor is the potential economic benefit of a free and open product (Riehle, 2007). An example service that offers clear economic benefits through cost-saving is OpenStreetMap. However, for services such as Wikimapia[5] where contributors are anonymous, an additional benefit could be self-satisfaction. Some examples of services based on volunteered geographic information are:

- *OpenStreetMap* (Haklay and Weber, 2008) is a free interactive map of the whole world, developed and maintained by the general public. Users are able to view and edit the map online. Alternatively, users may up-load GPS tracks from their handheld devices. Developers are able to download the complete map for free and integrate it into their own GIS, if they have adequate data storage facilities.

- *Flickr*[6] is a website for sharing pictures and videos online. The website allows users to upload, publish, search and download images and video. The website also offers a web map that enables users to geotag photographs, i.e., users annotate their pictures via simple text tags. An indicator of the popularity of geotagging in Flickr, is that over three million photographs were geotagged within the first two weeks of Flickr natively supporting the Geo microformat, which exploits specific HTML attributes to put in place metadata to indicate the location of data, for geotagging (Suda, 2006). Flickr is provided by Yahoo!

- *Panoramio*[7] is a location-oriented website for sharing geotagged photographs. Some of its key features include a gazetteer that allows users to search by place name. It also offers a web map that presents photographs in their tagged locations. The web map is provided through the Google Maps API. Panoramio is provided by Google.

- *YouTube*[8], another service offered by Google, allows videos to be also geotagged on upload. This feature enables the videos to be linked to from geo-located pop-ups within Google Earth.

- The *MyMaps*[9] feature offered by Google Maps enables users to digitize points, lines and polygons over aerial imagery and cartographic maps presented by Google Maps. Users are also able to add unstructured attributive information to the digitized geometries, thereby creating geospatial features. The features can be collaboratively edited between multiple users and may also be published for viewing by anyone. The service allows users to export the created data to popular formats such as KML and GeoRSS.

- The *Google Sketchup 3D Warehouse* offers an archiving facility for 3D models created using Google Sketchup. The 3D models can also be imported into Google Earth for viewing in their modelled geo-location. The service also engages volunteers to contribute models towards creating 3D models of cities around the world.

- *Blogs* are online journals that allow maintainers to enter posts and visitors to comment on the posts. The posts are presented in reverse chronological order. Popular blogging services such as Wordpress geo-tagg posts through addition of geographic coordinates in metadata or through the Geo microformat (Suda, 2006). Posts can then be disseminated through GeoRSS.

- *Twitter*[10] is a micro-blogging service that allows maintainers to send posts as text messages from mobile phones. Posts in Twitter terminology are referred to as 'tweets'. The service offers an API that allows developers to geo-tag tweets. One of its main attractions is that it allows users to 'follow' a particular account. This means that the users are alerted when a new entry is posted.

The geographic information offered by these services is not centrally managed in the same way as traditional geographic information products offered by National Mapping Agencies (NMA) and the like. VGI is maintained through iterative revision by volunteers. This suggests that the accuracy of VGI is not consistent across complete data sets, for example, locations with more contributors receive more frequent updates. This also suggests that the accuracy of VGI is not as high as that of professionally created data. The likelihood of errors in VGI does not appear to be affecting the uptake of VGI, as implied by the ranking of

Wikimapia and OpenStreetMap at 1,152 and 12,823 respectively out of 16 million websites crawled by the Alexa information service[11] offered by Amazon, Inc. Whether to trust VGI or not, depends on the user and the application to which the VGI is required. For example, to find out information about social events nearby, users would likely adopt VGI. However, to find out where to construct a new road, a user is likely to adopt professionally acquired data. The accuracy of VGI continues to affect the perceived trustworthiness of VGI and has been examined recently (Bishr, 2008).

It should be noted that although some of the aforementioned services were developed initially outside the domain of geoinformatics, for example Flickr only adopted geo-tagging after its launch, it has become evident that location is a key part of the metadata associated with the user generated content. To this end, it is necessary to acknowledge the part played by advances in hardware in making geographically referenced user generated content available. An example of such hardware developments, include the lowering cost of GPS-enabled mobile phones and cameras (Goodchild, 2009).

Similarly, advances in web technology have made it possible implement web mapping toolkits. Web mapping Application Programming Interfaces (APIs), based on Web 2.0 technologies, have made it easier for developers to integrate interactive maps into most websites (Platt, 2007). Users find it easier to identify locations on a map than to recall the geographic coordinates of a location. Even with such significant developments in VGI services and technologies, there are indications that new innovations are emerging. An example of such innovations is the growing number of location based applications on smart phones. Location-aware applications such as Layar[12] and NearestWiki[13] augment maps and camera previews with VGI (Hill, 2006).

2.4 Linked Data

The basic pillars of Linked Data are essentially traditional web technologies and the usage of light-weight techniques for data model representation. The former resides on the use of Uniform Resource Identifiers (URIs) (W3C, 2001b) as reference points. A URI is used to uniquely identify an abstract of physical entity, i.e. a piece of data, as well as a person (Berners-Lee et al., 1998). In this context, the entity is called resource. For example, the URI 'http://dbpedia.org/resource/Nottingham' identifies a place description for the city of Nottingham. So-called resolvers can be used to decode a URI to the physical location of the according resource. The Domain Name System (DNS)[14] is most commonly used for this purpose.

Linked Data relies on the Resource Description Framework (RDF) (Lassila and Swick, 1999) as basic structure for any form of description. RDF provides means to describe any kind of resource in form of triples (subject-predicate-object) (Klyne and Carroll, 2004). In the triple, 'Nottingham memberOf EnglishCoreCitiesGroup' for example, 'Nottingham' is the subject, 'memberOf' the predicate, and 'EnglishCoreCitiesGroup' the object. A basic typing system for subjects, predicates and objects has been proposed as RDF-Schema (RDF-S) (Brickley and Guha, 2004). RDF-S allows for extensions in order to specify domain-dependent subtypes. It provides one way to describe domain vocabularies with its own namespace. For example, the 'foaf' namespace provides a vocabulary for social web sites and people, also known as Friend of a Friend (FOAF)[15], Simple Knowledge Organization System (SKOS) (Miles and Bechhofer, 2009), a standard way to represent knowledge organization systems, is provided using the 'skos' namespace, and the 'owl' namespace is used for the Web Ontology Language (OWL) (Bechhofer et al., 2003). Relationships built upon VGI vocabularies, such as FOAF and SKOS are a first attempt to connect Linked Data and VGI. Relationships such as *foaf:based_near* and *foaf:*

depiction permit links but still in a limited, punctual sense. At the end, RDF is used for implementing the Linked Data, as a single global model for all data sources. The most common query language for RDF is SPARQL (W3C, 2008). SPARQL is a query language similar those used for relational data bases, but optimized for the querying of RDF triple stores, which are databases optimized for the storage and retrieval of RDF data.

Content negotiation, allowing a client to specify an acceptable representation of a data set (Holtman and Mutz, 1998), builds the third and last pillar of the Linked Data principle. While connecting to a data source, the client may specify the desired representation. This may be plain RDF, or an HTML representation with increased readability for the human user.

Figure 1 provides a visual overview of data sets in the current Linked Data Space and their connections. The size of the circles corresponds to the number of triples in each data set. The direction of the arrows refers to the data set that contains the links, for example, an arrow from 'DBpedia' to 'LinkedGeoData' means that the data source DBpedia contains RDF triples that use identifiers from the data source LinkedGeoData. Bidirectional arrows mean incoming and outcoming links between both data sources.

Data sets are interlinked across several domains. For example, scientific papers and publications are represented by open repositories such as CiteSeer, ACM, DBLP, IEEE, e-prints and so forth. Media content (audio, video, music, etc) comprises a list of data sources, such as BBC, Musicbrainz, and Audio-Scrobbler. Also, there exists a useful bunch of data sources concerned mainly with the geospatial domain, which the most representative are the following:

- *Geonames*[16] is a huge gazetteer with nearly eight millions of place names that cover the whole planet. It collects and fusion data from dozens of data sources.

Figure 1. Linked Open Data community project (http://linkeddata.org/)

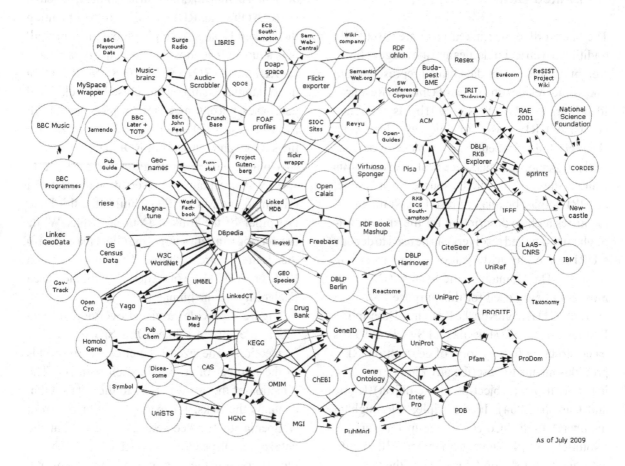

As of July 2009

- *LinkedGeoData*[17] uses the information collected by the OpenStreetMap project and makes it available as an RDF knowledge base according to the Linked Data principles. It interlinks this data with other data sources in the Linked Data Space (Figure 1).

- *US Census Data*[18] exposes data about population statistics at various geographic levels, from the U.S. as a whole, down through states, counties, sub-counties (roughly, cities and incorporated towns).

- *MONDIAL database*[19] contains mainly geopolitics data compiled from existing data sources with geographical and global

statistics content, such as the CIA World Factbook[20] and GeoHive[21].

- *Riese*[22] is a Linked Data effort to interlinking Eurostat[23] data sets, European Statistical Information Service that provides a large amount of data on a wide variety of European statistics.

- *British Ordnance Survey*[24] has recently released the Ordnance Survey Linked Data project that includes identifiers and names for the administrative and voting areas of UK, and topological relationships between these regions.

- *Telegraphis Linked Open Data*[25] exposes data about countries, capitals and currencies collected from Geonames and Wikipedia data sources.

- *Linked Railway Data Project*[26] brings together data on the UK railway network under Linked Data principles.

- *GEMET*[27] stands for GEneral Multilingual Environmental Thesaurus. It is the thesaurus recommended by INSPIRE to classify data sets in metadata records, and contains terms related to the environment and environmental data in more than 20 languages.

According to a July 2009 study about the amount of Linked Data available with each thematic domain (life science, geographic data, publications, media, etc) and the number of established links between data sets (Bizer, 2009), there exists great deal of geospatial data sources in RDF format (nearly 50%) but still poorly connected (scarcely 3%).

3 INTERPLAY OF THE THREE NOTIONS

In this section, we give first insights to the relations between the three notions of SDI, VGI and Linked Data. We elaborate on a detailed example, compare underlying principles with each other, and list related work on combining the three. On this basis, we will identify arising challenges in the next section and subsequently indicate possible solutions.

3.1 Illustrating Example

To illustrate the potentials of combining SDI and VGI with Linked Data and how this approach helps to open up SDI to a broader non-expert community, we examine the following scenario as a running example throughout the chapter.

A user plans a short trip to the city of Nottingham (UK) and wishes to get as much as possible informed about this city. She may start off using a semantic web search engine, such as the Falcons[28] search engine and simply types 'Nottingham' in the search text box. The Falcon engine provides related information about this term, such as the corresponding resource for the city of Nottingham in DBpedia[29] (http://dbpedia.org/resource/Nottingham). By following the link, she is prompted with a great amount of RDF-based data about the city of Nottingham rendered in HTML format. Rather than scrolling down a long HTML page, she may use some Linked Data browsers available, such as OpenLink Data Explorer[30] that helps users in navigating and inspecting structured content, as illustrated in Figure 2.

The DBpedia data source covers almost 3 million of things including any sort of (real world) resources, including people, places and organizations (Bizer et al., 2009b). Well-known resources, such as the city of Nottingham may be connected to a great deal of RDF triples, as shown in Figure 2. Some of the properties contain an implicit geographic connotation like *dbpedia_owl:twincity*, *dbpedia_owl: coordinates*, *dbproop: subdivisionName*, and *dpprob:location*. Connections to the same resource between different data sources are also available mostly by means of the *owl:sameAs* predicate, which is commonly used to indicate that two features actually refer to the same real-world entity.

From the current resource in DBpedia, she may leap to other data sources in a transparent way just by following the typed links. Figure 3 illustrates some existing connections between the Nottingham resource in DBpedia and other Linked Data sources. In particular, we focus here on data sources that have to do with geospatial contents, such as places, locations, regions, boundaries, etc. For instance, one of the *owl:sameAs* typed links brings her to Geonames data source. The counterpart Geonames resource for Nottingham city is reachable by dereferencing the (target resource) object property 'http://sws.geonames.org/26411170' for the predicate *owl:sameAs*. From this point, it is also possible both to navigate to

Figure 2. Linked Data browser displaying structured content of the resource Nottingham in DBpedia

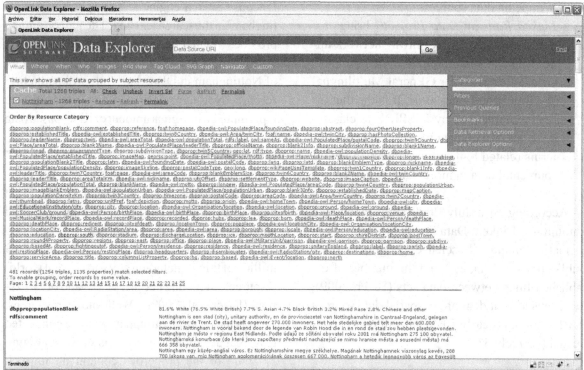

Figure 3.SDI, VGI and Linked Data sources interrelated around the resource 'Nottingham'

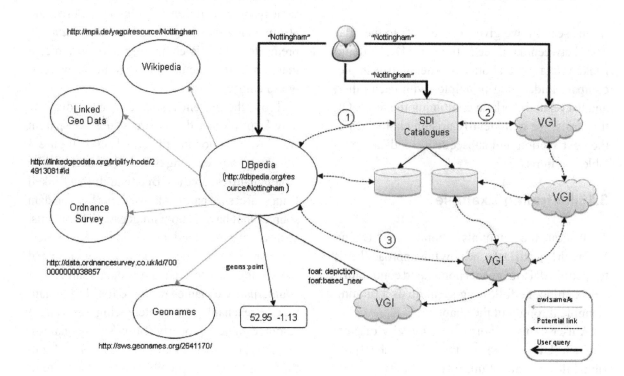

other services linked to the current Geonames resource as for instance a Google map viewer centered on the city and to access to other geo relationships belonging to the Geonames ontology[31], such as administrative hierarchy for countries (*geoNames:parentFeature*), neighbouring countries (*geoName:neighbour*) and nearby features (*geoName:nearby*). Accessing to other related Linked Data sources like the VGI-based LinkedGeoData and a data store of the British Ordnance Survey happens on the same basis.

Alternatively to Falcons, she may choose another searching path to discover data of her interest by using an SDI catalogue services (such as an OGC CSW) with 'Nottingham' as keyword or place name. Through a catalogue service, she is able to locate thematic data sets, ortofotos and SDI services that cover the area of Nottingham. In addition, she may turn into social networks and VGI service to search for Flickr images tagged with the term 'Nottingham' (http://www.flickr.com/search/?q=Nottingham).

This example highlights that structured geospatial data is available to be crawled by eager users. However, connections are seldom specified between data sources offered by SDI, VGI and Linked Data. This is illustrated in Figure 3 which presents a conceptual view of connections between Linked Data and SDI (1); SDI and VGI (2); Linked Data and VGI (3). The DBpedia resource of city of Nottingham contains no links (dotted line numbered with 1 in Figure 3) to data catalogues with metadata about Nottingham, WMSs that serve maps covering the Nottingham area, according data sets provided by a WFS, or at least a list of SDI services located in the UK. Suppose now, the same user queries a catalogue using 'Nottingham' as keyword. Resulting metadata records would contain Linked Data with typed links to other catalogues and third-party data sources.

It seems obvious that linked structured data has lots of benefits of a wide range of users. Taking DBpedia as an entry point, users would be able to:

- go through SDI catalogues to find WFS services of their interest,
- access a geoportal and reach Geonames data sources by following links,
- scan Flickr feeds (search results) and find out more about the location they are interested in, or,
- visit the BBC[32] website to find out about news and events in Nottingham

In essence, alternative search paths would enhance the discovery, access, and browsing of SDI data and services to a border community to exploit conveniently SDI, VGI and Linked Data to enrich geospatial applications. In the following we analyze arising challenges derived from the Nottingham example.

3.2 Comparison of the Three Notions

In Table 1 we compare SDI, VGI and Linked Data approaches (columns) with regard to a set of parameters (rows) that fall into the following categories: data model, data access, discovery and publishing. Data model refers to the model used to represent data sets and resources. The second group, data access, is concerned with the strategy adopted to retrieve resources. Discovery comprises the strategy and methods to perform searching. Finally, publishing refers basically to mechanisms to make new resources available. Each category contains some comparison parameters (rows in Table 1) that basically represent divergences and current open issues for these approaches.

In principle, all three approaches are not disjoint but complementary. This means that strengthening connections among them may lead to enriched, valuable, and useful information. However, some open issues and differences for each parameter analyzed in the Table 1 still remain and should be addressed to enable such collaboration. In the next section (Section 4) we discuss in detail some critical issues that fall into the data model category. Concerns like differences in the

Table 1. Comparison of intensions/capabilities of SDI, VGI, and Linked Data approaches

Parameters	SDI	VGI	Linked Data
DATA MODEL			
Rationale	Distributed community data sources (in possible cooperation)	Great deal of distributed, heterogeneous community data sources	A single global data space
Abstraction unit	Service	Service	Resource
Identification	Service endpoints	Service endpoints	URIs
Representation	• Some but detailed data models (GML, etc.) • Mainly machine readable • Metadata and data separated	• Several but simple data models (Atom, RSS, GeoRSS, geotags, simple annotation, micro-formats etc.) • Human readable • Flat metadata (as tags) and data together	• RDF model • Machine readable • Data and metadata together
DATA ACCESS			
Rationale	Metadata access through catalogue services and registries; data access via specialised services	Data and metadata access via services	Resource access via unique identifier
Mechanism	• Not so simple but standard access • Detailed service access mechanisms with several parameters • Standard connection bindings: HTTP GET, POST-XML, SOAP	• Simple but non-standard access. • Multiple APIs depending on concrete service • Multiple mechanisms depending on service: HTTP GET, POST, SOAP, Restful, proprietary protocol, etc.	• Simple and standard access. • Uniform interface: HTTP GET/POST/PUT/DELETE • URL dereferencing, just use HTTP and URIs
Clients	Multiple clients (desktop, web, mash-ups, mobile, etc.)	Multiple services in Web 2.0/ Social Web; mash-ups, programmatically	A few semantic web clients and browsers (not much user-friendly yet)
Is it 'linked'?	• No explicit links among SDI sources • Metadata and resource are linked by 'Online Resource' metadata descriptor (if exist) • GML allows for linking elements of the geospatial data model using 'xlink' (rarely used yet)	• No explicit links among VGI sources • No explicitly. Content is just geo-referenced	• Resource representation explicitly describes links to related resources
DISCOVERY			
Rationale	Data and service metadata on centralized repositories	Searchable resources in the web or via services	Searchable resources (data) on the very web
Mechanism	• Spatial queries via OGC Filter against catalogue services • Simple (keywords, titles) and advanced (complex) search • Distributed queries and harvesting expand over remote catalogues	• Diverse discovery methods based often on tag queries • Simple • Not cross-source queries, applied to one source at a time	• SPARQL-based queries, a language for querying RDF databases • Complex, high expert level required • Queries expand over several, distributed data sources taking benefit of the RDF graph structure

continued on the following page

Table 1. Comparison

Parameters	SDI	VGI	Linked Data
Clients	Several catalogs clients available	Simple interface (tag queries) via services	Proprietary GUIs for direct SPARQL queries
Is it 'linked'?	• Data and services isolated. Only links between data access services and associated data sets • Common keywords are potentially a means of 'linkage'	• Data sets isolated. • Knowledge structures may be derived from folksonomy as a potential means of 'linkage'	• Data sources linked. • SPARQL queries exploit in a natural way the notion of link over data sources
PUBLISHING			
Rationale	Populate metadata on catalogue and exposing (legacy) data via services. Complex tuning	Uploading, tag and ready	Transforming (legacy) source data into RDF triples
Mechanism	• Complex metadata editors and publishing tools (still disconnected) • Expert level required	• Very simple, intuitive: just tags annotation. • Expert and non-expert alike	• 'RDFising': proprietary solutions on content negotiation translate legacy data to RDF models • Complex tuning, expert usage
Clients	Front end to geospatial catalogues, sometimes embedded into metadata editors	Mainly embedded in web pages with few inputs required	Clients for establishing links required in the first place
Is it 'linked'?	Not explicit typed links	Not explicitly typed links	Publishers have to explicit link their structured data sources with others

basic abstraction unit and identification methods as well as links representation and semantics are priority and should be addressed in first term before attempting others regarding access, discovery and publishing. While some potential solutions are discussed in Section 5, those latter issues are treated in Section 6.

3.3 Related Work

The two main areas of related work concern (1) relations between SDI and Linked Data and (2) techniques and approaches for linking heterogeneous repositories, are overviewed in this section.

In our view that both approaches (SDI and Linked Data) do not exclude each other, Janowicz et al. (2010) share a similar vision with the notion of micro-SDI, as lightweight Linked Data applications that still keep the established OGC services for more complex applications. The authors suggest that such a micro-SDI should consist

of simplified and lightweight OGC services which can be directly embedded into web pages and applications. Examples towards establishing such a micro-SDI include recent work on next generation gazetteers (Janowicz and Keßler, 2008), a Linked Data serialization of the OpenStreet Map database (Auer et al., 2009), the work of the British Ordnance Survey mentioned above (Section 2.4), and JavaScript reasoners such as JSExplicit[33], which can be directly embedded into web pages to generate context and user-aware information, from RDF data on-the-fly.

Florczyk et al. (2010) are exploiting semantic linkages to services in SDIs. The authors propose a linked ontology of administrative units for referencing the same geographic concept to the corresponding instances form multiple WFS services. Similar examples come from the Ordnance Survey, with the publication of the Administrative Geography of Great Britain, an initiative to

Figure 4. Connections between addressable resources for the Nottingham example

publish administrative units as linked data sources (Goodwin et al., 2009).

We spotted that linking (geospatial) data is a philosophy of usage and not a technical matter and that GML could be characterized as 'premature Linked Data', it just uses other encodings for linkages (Schade and Cox, 2010). Also GML and RDF are quasi isomorphic to each other, practical SDI implementations rarely make use of the capabilities. Anyway, both (GML and RDF) are optimized for different purposes. While RDF allows for sophisticated querying, numerous SDI clients and services process GML. We will elaborate on this issue in Section 5.

Hummann-Haidvogel et al. (2009) propose the usage of multiple coordinated views for searching and navigating web content repositories. The authors collect information regarding a given domain using a web crawler and enrich the local content repository with geospatial, semantic and temporal annotations. Users may visualize annotated content in the local repository via a browser application with multiple coordinated views where any user action (selection, searching, etc.) in one view leads to contextualized updates in the remaining views.

An approach for discovering, describing and understanding resources based on the notion that meaning is carried in the interconnections between resources (data, services, tools, and ontology) and users in the cyberinfrastructure has been provided by Gahegan et al. (2009). Navigation around this universe is achieved by implementing the idea of perspectives as dynamic, conceptual views defined

by SPARQL-like queries against a knowledge collection. The authors describe a means to represent a wide variety of interactions between resources using the notion of a knowledge nexus.

Becker and Bizer (2009) have recently proposed DBPedia Mobile, a location –aware semantic web client for mobile devices. This application makes use of the current user location to extract geo-related data sets that have been published and interlinked in the context of the Linked Data Space.

4 CENTRAL CHALLENGES FOR SPATIAL LINKED DATA INFRASTRUCTURES

In this section, we identify related challenges and potentials in connecting geospatial web services and SDI content with emerging Linked Data and VGI communities. Table 1 (Section 3.2) highlights some divergences among these approaches grouped in four categories (data model, data access, discovery, and publishing). In this section, we look especially into the first category, the data model to focus our analysis mainly on the concerns of how to establish links among data sources that have different data models.

The current impediments and challenges for data model discussed in this section are (1) How to deal with the problem of identifying resources in these three approaches? (2) How to represent and where to place links among data sources? (3) How to interpret the semantic of these links?

Figure 5. Connections between service points for the Nottingham example

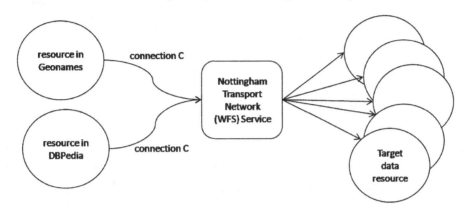

4.1 Challenge 1: Resource Identification

This section examines the issue on how to address resources univocally. In the Linked Data context, a connection takes place between a source resource and a target resource, as shown in Figure 4. A source resource, such as the Nottingham city resource in Geonames, is referenced by a unique URI (http://sws.geonames.org/2641170). A target resource, like the same resource in DBpedia, has also its own URL (http://dbpedia. org/resource/Nottingham). As both resources are identified properly, it is straightforward to connect them through a typed relationship (C1), such as *owl:sameAs*. Similarly, the Nottingham resource in LinkedGeoData (http://linkedgeodata. org/triplify/node/24913081) also may link (C2) to the same target resource in DBpedia. Creating links is a matter of identifying unambiguously the both edges of the link, the source (subject) and the target (object) resource.

Setting a connection then requires first to respond to a couple of questions: what is considered a resource itself (abstraction unit parameter in Table 1) and how to identify it (identification parameter in Table 1)? As aforementioned, from the Linked Data viewpoint, the first question is straightforward addressed since a resource can be anything that it is worth sharing with the community. For instance, looking at DBpedia one can encounter movies, films, actors, songs, musicians, cities, institutions, individuals, football teams, and so forth. Indeed, the web itself functions in this way since it contains a great deal of heterogeneous resources (web page, doc, image, video, etc). Every single web resource is univocally identified by its URI. Linked Data also relies on the URI mechanisms to identify any resource. Every single resource that might be of interest for the community should be identified unambiguously so that a user using its URI is able to access it. These simple tenets drive the foundations of Linked Data sources and support the existence of connections.

In contrast to Linked Data, in the SDI context the basic abstraction unit is the notion of service. Geospatial data sets are discovered, accessed, and shared though services. In this sense, the exercise of comparing Linked Data and SDI is similar to compare service-oriented and resource-oriented architectural styles (Section 2.1). The former is based on the service abstraction, while the latter is rooted by the resource abstraction. SDI provides a single, directly accessible service abstraction that often represents multiple different potential resources from the resource-oriented viewpoint. For instance, features representing roads offered by a WFS that contains the transport network of Nottingham might be regarded as candidate resources from a resource-oriented perspective.

At the moment, SDIs do not provide an explicit, univocally resource identification as Linked Data does, or at least such identifiers are not commonly used. Figure 5 shows how a source resource establishes a connection with an SDI service, addressable with a URI that refers to a service endpoint. Conceptually, the service acts as a proxy, receiving all incoming connections and bypassing access to the internal data sets. In the Nottingham example, the roads denoted as target data resources have always the same URL of the WFS service point, which hides and centrally manages various resources through service operations, such as *getCapabilities*, *describeFeatureType*, and *getFeature*. In practice, all target data sets at the backend are hidden to external entities and thus connections can be only established between source resources, such as the Nottingham resource in Geonames and DBpedia, and the proxy service exemplified by the Nottingham Transport Network WFS. This suggests that direct connections between resources within Linked Data and data sets in SDI cannot be set.

The divergence on the basic unit —resource abstraction versus service abstraction— and on the meaning of the URI in each case remains challenging issues. First it is necessary to determine clearly what is considered a resource in the SDI landscape: feature, data set, a collection of data set, metadata files, a collection of metadata files, an image file, etc. For example, each road, collections of connected roads, and the different types of roads may be suitable resources. Second, every single resource should be addressed unambiguously in such a way that referencing its URL lets access to the very resource. WFS already provides a mechanism to identify each feature with a unique URL via a *getFeature* query (Florczyk et al., 2010), however this approach only covers the case of considering each feature as a resource. Greater or lesser levels of granularity of resources (for example collections of roads)

cannot be addressable using current WFS methods. Adopting a resource-oriented architecture would help to add context and intelligibility to the SDI content (Lucchi et al., 2008). An alternative solution to overcome this issue would be to augment SDI services with URI resolvers, capable of decoding and creating valid URIs at request-time to the data resources they offer.

4.2 Challenge 2: Link Representation

This section examines the (metadata) issue of where to place a link representation. Resources may have multiple representations. When dereferencing a non-informational resource (real-world entities, such as a person, the city of Nottingham.) one does not get the resource itself, but a representation of the resource as a description in a certain format. In the scenario of Figure 3, the action of dereferencing the resource identifier http://dbpedia.org/resource/Nottingham in a browser renders the resource description in RDF/XML format. Such a description contains links to other resources.

In SDI, data and services are anyway equipped with metadata. So, metadata descriptions are *a priori* the best place where links representations and pointers to external resources should be. This implies a need to analyze the capabilities of metadata descriptions in SDI to contain pointers to other SDI resources, such as metadata records, data sets and services. In the following we deal with questions on how metadata records contain links to related resources within the SDI and/or to external resources.

Do Metadata Records Contain Links To Other SDI Resources?

Metadata descriptions are stored according to the international standard for geographic information metadata ISO19115 (ISO, 2003). Metadata based on ISO19115 can be presented in a variety of human readable formats such as HTML and

Table 2. Core metadata ISO 19115

Data set title (M) (MD_Metadata>MD_Identification.citation>CI_Citation.title)	Spatial representation type (O) (MD_Metadata>MD_DataIdentification.spatialRepresentation)
Data set reference date (M) (MD_Metadata>MD_Identification.citation>CI_Citation.date)	Reference system (O) (MD_Metadata>MD_ReferenceSystem)
Data set responsible party (O) (MD_Metadata>MD_Identification.pointOfContact>CI_ResponsibleParty)	Lineage (O) (MD_Metadata>DQ_DataQuality.lineage>LI_Lineage)
Geographic location of the data set (by four coordinates or by geographic identifier) (O) (MD_Metadata>MD_DataIdentification.extent>EX_Extent>EX_GeographicExtent>EX_GeographicBoudingBox or EX_GeographicDescription)	On-line resource (O) (MD_Metadata>MD_Distribution>MD_DigitalTransferOption.online>CI_OnlineResource)
Data set language (M) (MD_Metadata>MD_DataIdentification.language)	Metadata file identifier (O) (MD_Metadata.fileIdentifier)
Data set character set (C) (MD_Metadata>MD_DataIdentification.characterSet)	Metadata standard name (O) (MD_Metadata.metadataStandardName)
Data set topic category (M) (MD_Metadata>MD_DataIdentification.topicCategory)	Metadata standard version (O) (MD_Metadata.metadataStandardVersion)
Spatial resolution of the data set (O) (MD_Metadata>MD_DataIdentification.spatialResolution>MD_Resolution.equivalentScale or MD_Resolution.distance)	Metadata language (C) (MD_Metadata.language)
Abstract describing the data set (M) (MD_Metadata>MD_Identification.abstract)	Metadata character set (C) (MD_Metadata.characterSet)
Distribution format (O) (MD_Metadata>MD_Distribution.MD_Format.name and MD_Format.version)	Metadata point of contact (M) (MD_Metadata.contact>CI_ResponsibleParty)
Additional extent information for the data set (vertical and temporal) (O) (MD_Metadata>MD_DataIdentification.extent>EX_Extent>EX_>TemporalExtent or EXVerticalExtent)	Metadata data stamp (M) (MD_Metadata.dateStamp)

plain text. To support the structured encoding of metadata, ISO19139 (ISO, 2007) was developed to offer an XML schema for metadata based on ISO19115. The XML schema offered by ISO19139 makes it easier for applications to identify metadata elements because it formalizes the names and structure of the metadata elements. Where appropriate, restricted values for metadata elements are also enforced as 'enumerations' for example the *topicCategory* field in ISO19115. Whereas, the historic use of metadata has been to describe data, the uptake of services as key resources within SDI has led to the development of an international standard for geographic information services, ISO19119 (ISO, 2005), which includes metadata for describing services. It should be noted that

both the ISO19119 and the ISO19139 reference the ISO19115 as the base standard for metadata. Therefore, unless otherwise stated, the metadata elements described in the rest of this section are found in ISO19115.

In the ISO19115 metadata model numerous fields are offered. However, as acknowledged in the standard 'typically only a subset of the full number of elements is used' (ISO 19115, 2003). The standard identifies a minimum set of metadata elements that should be maintained for a data set. This minimum set of metadata elements is referred to as the core metadata for geographic data sets (Table 2). The table presents the name of each core metadata element in bold and identifies whether that particular element is mandatory (M), optional

(O) or Conditional (C). The hierarchical structure of the parent packages of the elements are also presented in descending order with a '>' sign, for example, the temporal extent is part of the extent package, which is part of the *dataIdentification* package and so on. The two-letter abbreviations before the name of the element identify which package that element belongs in, for example *CI* is the *Citation* package and *MD* is the *Metadata* package.

ISO19115 contemplates some metadata descriptors to provide the context necessary to reference a metadata (catalogue) record to the corresponding data or service:

- Filling the *MD_Distribution->transfer Options->MD_DigitalTransferOptions->onLine-> CI_OnlineResource* definition,
- setting the *MD_Metadata.fileIdentifier* and *MD_Metadata.parentIdentifier* attribute values, or
- setting the *MD_Metadata.dataSetURI* attribute value (not listed in Table 2).

The first option for linking to a resource is the *CI_OnlineResource* class defined in ISO19115 as the element in charge of containing information about online sources from which the data set, specification, or community profile name and extended metadata elements can be obtained. The *CI_OnlineResource* class permits to augment a URL in the *linkage* mandatory element with optional values for service definition in *protocol* and *applicationProfile* elements, providing thus a way to link data metadata records to the service. The values contained in this metadata descriptor provide the link to associated data sets in terms of query parameters to the appropriate service. This descriptor is crucial to avoid broken links among SDI resources. The *CI_OnlineResource* metadata descriptor has the following inner elements:

- *linkage* (mandatory) points to the URL from which the data set or service endpoint

can be accessed. In some instances, the linkage may point to the *GetCapabilities* document of a service, which itself presents the service endpoint and additional information.
- *name* (optional) presents the title of the resource (Coverage, FeatureType, Observation, etc.) in free text.
- *protocol* identifies the network binding for connecting to the resource (for example HTTP), specified in free text.
- *applicationProfile* (optional), describes a name of an application profile that can be used with the online resource, also in free text.
- *description* (optional) of what the online resource does, also in free text.
- *function* (optional) is a controlled list of the online resource's actions.

Apart from the linkage and function attributes of the *CI_OnlineResource* class, all other attributes are defined as free text, meaning that the values are not from a controlled vocabulary or format. Whereas 'free text' values ensure flexibility in the types of values that can be assigned to a metadata element, applications are not able to trace the resources to which 'free text' values point. The following example is adapted from ISO19139 as demonstrating how to reference a data set in-line (Listing 1). Line 04 in Listing 1 shows the service endpoint used in the Nottingham example.

Listing 1. ISO 10139 in-line reference to a data set in XML.

```
01  <onlineResource>
02  <CI_OnlineResource id="ID00004">
03   <linkage>
04    <URL>http://www.nottingham.org/
URL>
05   </linkage>
06   <protocol>
07    <gco:CharacterString>http</
```

```
gco:CharacterString>
08    </protocol>
09    </CI_OnlineResource>
10  </onlineResource>
```

For services it is not enough to offer the URL of the service endpoint. It is necessary to also provide a description of the standard and version supported by the service, for example, WFS version 1.0.0 offers fewer capabilities than version 1.1.0 of the same standard. The following example is adapted from the WFS specification (OGC, 2005a) as demonstrating how to describe a service in ISO19119 metadata presented in the *GetCapabilities* document of a service (Listing 2). Lines 03 and 04 in Listing 2 identify the service type and version respectively.

Listing 2. Extract of GetCapabilities document in XML.

```
01 <ows:ServiceIdentification>
02  <ows:Title>WFS</ows:Title>
03   <ows:ServiceType>WFS</
ows:ServiceType>
04    <ows:ServiceTypeVersion>1.1.0</
ows:ServiceTypeVersion>
05    <ows:ServiceIdentification>
06 …
07    <ows:Operation
name="GetFeature">
08     <ows:DCP>
09     <ows:HTTP>
10     <ows:Get xlink:href="http://
www.nottingham.org/transport/wfs.
cgi?"/>
11     <ows:Post xlink:href="http://
www.nottingham.org/transport/wfs.
cgi"/>
12    </ows:HTTP>
13   </ows:DCP>
14 …
15 </ows:Operation>
```

The preceding examples of metadata suggest that for the *CI_OnlineResource* class to provide enough information to bind to a service, it is necessary to include information about the service name, type and version in the protocol attribute of the class. This would allow a client application to bind to a service, if the client supports the specified service type and version. An approach for specifying the service type and version in the protocol attribute of the *CI_OnlineResource* class using a Uniform Resource Name (URN) (W3C, 2001b) as identifier is as follows (Listing 3). In this case, lines 08-09 in Listing 3 provide the URN of the WFS service of the Nottingham example.

Listing 3. Use of CI_OnlineResource in XML.

```
01 <onlineResource>
02  <CI_OnlineResource id="ID00001">
03   <name>WFS</name>
04   <linkage>
05    <URL> http://www.nottingham.
org/transport/wfs.cgi?service=WFS&req
uest=GetCapabilities/URL>
06    </linkage>
07   <protocol>
08    <gco:CharacterString>urn:ogc:se
rviceType:WebFeatureService:1.1.0
09    </gco:CharacterString>
11   </protocol>
11  </CI_OnlineResource>
12 </onlineResource>
```

URN refers to the subset of Uniform Resource Identifier (URI) 'required to remain globally unique and persistent even when the resource ceases to exist or becomes unavailable.' (Berners-Lee et al., 1998). Therefore, a URN does not need to be linked to an existing resource online. An example of the application of URN in SDI is presented by the OGC Best Practice document on the 'Definition identifier URNs in OGC namespace'[34]. For linking to resources online, the *linkage* attribute of the *CI_OnlineResource* class adopts URL as values. URL are a subset of URI 'that identify resources via a representation of their primary access mechanism (for example, their network 'location'), rather than identifying the resource by name or by some other attribute(s) of that resource.' (Berners-Lee et al., 1998). An application can automatically bind to a service if both the linkage and protocol attributes of the *CI_OnlineResource* class are filled with URL and URN values respectively, as for example in Listing 3. However, if 'free text' is used for the protocol, then a human is required to interpret the metadata and build an HTTP query to the concrete service serving the actual data set. OGC has a legacy of using URNs for resources identification, but has recently adopted an http URI scheme (Schade and Cox, 2010).

As the *CI_OnlineResource* entity is optional it may be empty and then there is no way from the user perspective to locate the data sets described by the associated metadata record. The current trend is that users obtain the requested core data set metadata record from the service catalogue but often fail to visualize the actual data set because the *CI_OnlineResource* metadata descriptor is missing or badly documented. Users are often prompted with an alert window that current data set is not accessible.

Another option for referencing resources in metadata is through the optional *dataSetURI* attribute of the main *MD_Metadata* class. The URI value of an *MD_Metadata.dataSetURI* attribute is typically a URL (service endpoint) to link to the service. This simple but direct approach may hold linking representations in a variety of formats (RSS, RDF/XML) since, according to the ISO 19115 specification, the data type of the attribute is again free text. It is however, necessary to highlight that a URL would need to be augmented with a description of the protocol needed to bind to the described service. In this group also fall the ISO 19115 *MD_Metadata.fileIdentifier* attribute for identifying the particular metadata record and the *MD_Metadata.parentIdentifier* attribute

for identifying the metadata record from which the source metadata is a subset. Filling both the *MD_Metadata.parentIdentifier* and *MD_Metadata.fileIdentifier* attributes enable a user to link metadata records that are related through a set-subset relationship.

The early generations of SDI placed particular significance on documenting metadata for data sets. The evolution of SDI and the key role played by geospatial web services suggests that the *CI_OnlineResource* metadata element should no longer be 'optional'. Instead, if a data set is not available through a service but through physical transfer (for example by courier), a specific URI could be associated with that transfer mechanism (for example 'urn:royalmail:parcelforce:samed ay'). We note that the version 3 of the INSPIRE implementation rules for metadata specify that the resource locator is 'mandatory if linkage to the service is available' (page 14). It is therefore necessary for metadata creation tools to enforce the filling of the *CI_OnlineResource* automatically or to support the service provider in doing so.

Talking about these options, the ability to find and access appropriate information within SDIs relies basically on having up-to-date metadata. Rajabifard et al. (2009) have suggested the use of integrated metadata directories to automatically generate metadata that would be maintained also dynamically. In this case, metadata descriptions would mirror continuously the evolution of spatial data sets and keep track of service link updates. The maintenance of links becomes a central issue.

Do Metadata Records Contain Links to External Resources?

Looking at the core metadata description (see Table 2), there are a lot of potential links that could be established to improve connectiveness to external data resources, such as the people responsible for data sets or keywords in a common thesaurus. In the following, we examine carefully some of such descriptors.

The *CI_ResponsibleParty* class belonging to the *MD_Identification.pointOfContact* entity contains the identification of people and institutions associated with the resource. The *CI_Contact* class offers attributes for the phone number, address, online resource, hours of service and contact instructions for the person or organization responsible for a resource. The *onlineResource* attribute of the *CI_Contact* class accepts values based on the *CI_OnlineResource* class, therefore, the attribute allows for referencing by URL. A first attempt is that these metadata descriptions may be related to people and institutions using the FOAF vocabulary (Section 2.4), which is encoded in RDF. Primary predicates, such as *foaf:Person* and *foaf:organization* may be used to designate relationships to physical people and institutions and the corresponding data set metadata record. Other secondary predicates can also be used as for example *foaf:homepage*, *foaf:name*, *foaf:depiction*, and *foaf:page*, to provide more connections. By virtue of supporting URL values, persons represented in FOAF can be referenced in the linkage attribute of the *CI_OnlineResouce* class.

However, not only FOAF data sources are suitable. Attribute values within the *CI_Address* class entity such as *city*, *country*, *postalCode* and *administrativeArea* are good candidate to be linked to external resources in target data sources, such as DBpedia, Geonames and LinkedGeoData.

INSPIRE recommends the use of the GEMET taxonomy (Section 2.4) for categorizing metadata records through the *topicCategory* attribute in *MD_DataIdentification* entity class. Indeed, the GEMET terms fit nicely with data sources in life science domain (see Figure 1). Similarly, the *MD_Keywords.keyword* attribute can be used as a 'linkage tag' to connect related items in VGI services, such as Flickr and Panoramio. Linkage can be enhanced by using keywords from a commonly used thesaurus such as GEMET or Semantic Web for Earth and Environmental Terminology (SWEET) (Raskin and Pan, 2005). SWEET is a unilingual (OWL) ontology defin-

ing environmental concepts and their properties. The *type* and *thesaurusName* attributes of the *MD_Keyword* class allows for the referencing of concepts in GEMET or SWEET.

In addition to the aforementioned thematic metadata elements, the geographic extent of the data set described by the metadata is specified in the *EX_GeographicDescription* element. The extent can be expressed as an identifier in the *geographicIdentifier* attribute of the *EX_GeographicDescription* class. The geographic identifier is defined as 'free text' therefore a URI could be used to reference a location.

The challenge for linking metadata to external resources is to increase the set of metadata elements that adopt URI whilst reducing those that use 'free text'. This will make metadata more machine readable, thereby enabling for links to be made from user needs, to services, to data and then to geographic features contained within the data. VGI services, such as Flickr and YouTube, already maintain persistent identifiers for resources they offer. Therefore, metadata creation tools should be enabled to support the referencing of resources offered by VGI where appropriate.

A further challenge for metadata publishers however, will be to ensure that the references remain valid even though the external resources are maintained by private citizens. For example, a metadata record of satellite imagery of the Nottingham region could be extended with references to road data that is available from some WFS, and to Flickr photographs taken by citizen or tourists. Whereas the metadata record is typically maintained by professionals, there is no guarantee that the Flickr photographs referenced by the metadata record will remain available. Therefore, it will be a challenge for SDI to adapt changes in references to resources in VGI. However, the significant amount of information offered by VGI makes this challenge worthwhile.

4.3 Challenge 3: Link Semantic and Context

Describing the model used to encode the range of data links is a general concern of the Linked Data paradigm. Linking data does not specify the meaning of elements, which are pointed to. Connections make only sense if linking to data in cases where the intended interpretation is well known. For example, a text may contain the term 'Nottingham', which is subject to a set of links (see also Figure 3). One linked may be termed 'description' and points to a Wikipedia article about the city. Another predicate uses the GeoRSS vocabulary and as object the according point. Another may use the predicate *os:feature* to point to some resource with the id 'http://data.ordnancesurvey. co.uk/id/7000000000038857', a fourth link may use a vocabulary called 'MyApplicationSpecificSchema', which points to an instance of a very complex GML data model for storing the transport network of the city of Nottingham. It depends on the information consumer, which of these links can be processed in a meaningful way.

With RDF, as well as GML, the structures used to represent the flexible content have to be communicated. This may either happen in a pre-deployment phase, i.e. the meaning of used data structures is fixed and well known before accessing the resource, or at run-time. Well known meaning can be defined as part of user requirements, as for example in the domain of reporting, or by detailed specifications using the context of the used links. One example for the reporting issues for geospatial science considers the environment in Europe. It is known as SEIS (Shared Environmental Information System)[35]. Here, required content is pre-defined in form of legal documents and obligations. Otherwise, in the case of RDF, the range of a link can be defined according to the types provided in the vocabulary (defined in RDF-S). Yet, the type system has to be documented outside the given model. The documentation of GeoRSS provides

one example (http://www.georss.org/Main_Page): 'A point contains a single latitude-longitude pair'. The ambiguity in interpretation and the need for human intervention remains challenging. GeoRSS does not specify what the point represents. We do not know if the point associated with Nottingham represents the centroid of the administrative area, the location of the town hall, or any arbitrary point. Adding ontologies, i.e. rich vocabularies, which allow for logical specification of intended interpretations of terms, addresses this issue only to some extent (Guarino, 1998). While the set of possible interpretations becomes reduced, the problem of defining intended interpretations of ontological primitives remains (Harnad, 1990).

Considering GML and its capabilities of using 'xlink', as alternative to RDF, such typing possibilities are not given by the current specifications. Here, the type of used GML property may define the data model for the range (or target) of the link. For example, if a link is embedded in the point property, the referred URI should follow the definition of a GML point data type. Such an approach requires validation mechanisms and powerful data parsing capabilities. Enabling run-time exploitation of data structures (or models) is even more challenging. It requires inclusion of data model information inside the link itself or to the range of the link. Solutions may include extended use of MIME times or explicit additional links to data models. Re-visiting the example from above, the subject 'Nottingham' may be linked via the predicate *myApplication SpecificSchema:transportNetwork* to a object of type *XML:GML: MyApplicationSpecificSchema*. This indicates that the range of the link is an *XML* element, following the general rules of *GML* and a more specialized encoding, which is defined as *MyApplicationSpecificSchema*. Depending on client capabilities the link range can be processed, i.e. parsed and analyzed, to a certain extent. The use of MIME types implies a need of management and introduction of types per application specific data model. Obviously this solution faces a large

Figure 6. All strategies considered in one figure

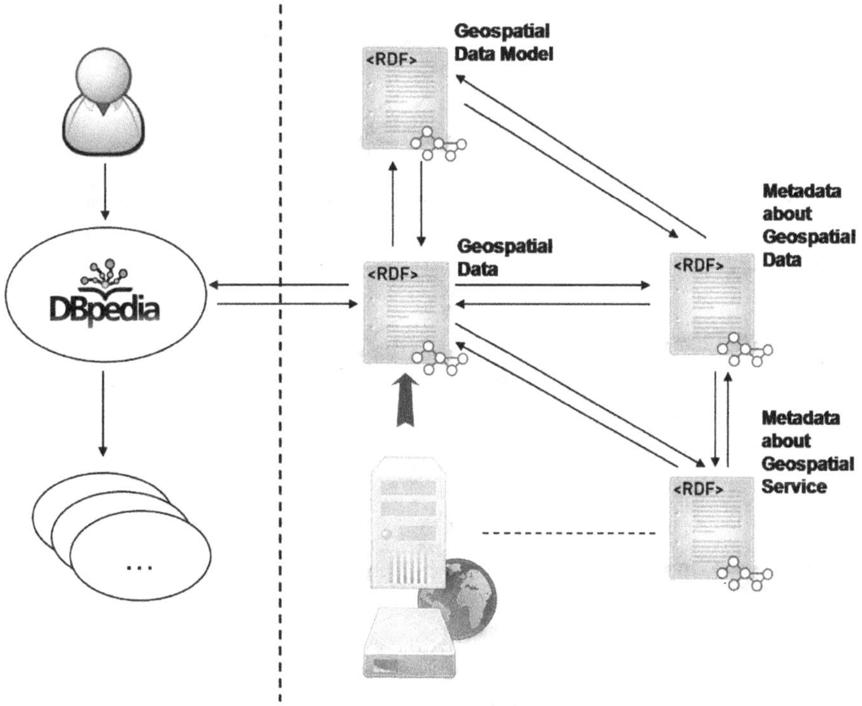

overhead. Using links (annotations) to the used model is another approach, which still has to be explored (Maué et al., 2009).

Overall, data can be linked at will, but it can only be handled properly, if the used vocabularies are (1) known beforehand, or (2) intended interpretations can be inferred at run-time. In the later case, either current GML specifications required extension, or a purely RDF-based solution have to be developed. Final decisions and best practices are not (yet) available.

5 USING LINKED DATA TO COMBINE SDI WITH VGI

In our opinion, the Linked Data approach can be projected to SDI and it can be used as a possibility to combine SDI with VGI. In this work we advocate the support of Linked Data within SDI. In this section we successively suggest some solutions for Linked Data to classical SDI standards, and give examples of novel ways of data usage, detail the relation to VGI, and argue for benefits.

In general we foresee a projection of the principle of Linked Data (and related technology) to SDI (right side of Figure 6). An SDI consists of several elements including people, data sets, technologies, standards and policies facilitating the sharing of data. If an SDI component is now considered to be a 'resource' then relationships between resources should become more visible. Once achieved, data provided by an SDI can be easily connected to other sources (left side of Figure 6). We will describe the overall approach, alternative strategies for applying the approach and its impacts on SDI in the following section. The proposed solution considers the application of RDF, which by definition is a standard for encoding definitions and relationships between resources. In this section we propose three strategies, which differ in the degree of resource orientation:

Figure 7. Turning SDI data and metadata into native RDF repositories

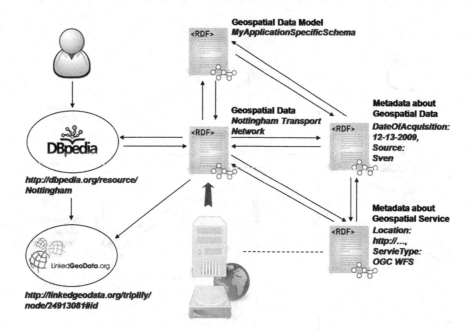

(1)   Full resource orientation through native RDF repositories (Section 5.1).

(2)   Semi-resource orientation through augmentation (Section 5.2).

(3)   Semi-resource orientation through mediator services (Section 5.3).

We subsequently argue for possible adaptation of classical data provision paradigm and for required changes in the use of services.

5.1 Full Resource Orientation through Native RDF Repositories

The direct application of Linked Data to SDI attempts to drastically convert all (meta) data models and data sets available in SDI into a single data structure. In parallel the naming schema in SDI is shifted from URNs to URIs. Services will be adopted accordingly. At the end, this means GML application schemas and metadata profiles will be encoded in RDF-S, and data and metadata sets will be directly represented in RDF. We present this approach in Figure 7, where examples are included in italic font. RDF will include additional links to other data, as for example links from DBpedia or to LinkedGeoData resources.

Once VGI is also represented in RDF, data from SDI and VGI can be linked and queried for relations. This solution may end the long-time discussion on distinguishing data from metadata as currently reflected in the use of GML and separate metadata documents, which for example use ISO 19115 and ISO 19139. Still, links have to be established in the first place and maintained thereafter. Continuation of resources and links poses new challenges, because the joined data is not gathered by a small and well-known community any more. An unknown number of sources become connected in unpredictable ways. In a sense this supports the transition of the classical, cathedral-style of SDI to the bazaar-style that has been imposed by VGI (Budhathoki et al., 2008).

In our opinion this scenario is optimal in terms of linking available elements, but unrealistic in terms of pure data load. Storage is a central concern of this approach. It remains unclear where links between data from various sources should be stored and how distributed data can be queried in a semantic web fashion. Also, solutions for describing the intended interpretation of elements still have to be included. Current Linked Data publishers and providers represent data entities in the form of RDF triples. The predicate in a RDF triple determines the type of the links by using common vocabularies (such as FOAF and SKOS), which define semantically the links among data entities. Although these typed relationships may span multiple data sources by just navigating across these explicit links, it seems to be an insufficient means to abstract (model) large scale issues like environmental sustainability that requires complex relationships among its components instead of just using the subject-object-predicate pattern in RDF models. The real impediment, however, stems from the social, policies, collaborative aspects that are part of an SDI. While this approach would be technically plausible, in terms of policies, collaborations and arrangements would be an endless process. We therefore consider the following two strategies for more realistic.

5.2 Semi – Resource Orientation through Augmentation

An alternative strategy is the augmentation of existing elements of SDI with references to external resources. Following this approach, the SDI community actually opens up to new horizons and provides native service interfaces that suit the Linked Data needs. This will be achievable if we consider an extended representation for geospatial data and services that include Linked Data, as well as references to other Linked Data sources. Logically we are talking about serving RDF, cross-referenced with established geospatial data formats such as GML and disseminated through current geospatial service interfaces. The resource 'http://linkedgeodata.org/triplify/node/24913081#id' would point to 'http://dbpedia.org/resource/ Nottingham', to related WFSs,

and vice versa. This approach implies mixing the current geospatial service architecture (defined by ISO19119) with a resource oriented architecture where appropriate. Candidates for resource oriented architectures include ROA-based technologies such as RESTful services and WSRF (Section 2.1). Mazzeti et al. (2009) discuss the benefits and limitations of exposing WCS services as RESTful services in Earth science applications settings. Other related studies have explored the integration of geospatial and grid computing through the import of geospatial data schema into WSRF service descriptions (Hobona et al, 2010; Woolf and Shaon, 2009).

This suggestion leads to multiple benefits. First, Linked Data sets are no longer static but dynamic, since structured content is generated on-the-fly, in a request basis. This allows user to access and discover up-to-date content. This approach also enables to convert VGI data into structured data where possible. In addition, navigating or browsing capabilities present in Linked Data are greatly affected with dynamic structured content. Describing explicitly structured data in advance makes it possible to use sophisticated query capabilities as those provided by SPARQL query language.

5.3 Semi – Resource Orientation through Mediator Services

Another alternative strategy is the use of mediators in applying resource orientation in SDI. Mediators offer content negotiation through the transformation of data to make it suitable for use in other applications (Wiederhold, 1992). Mediators have been applied in content negotiation for taxonomy-based information sources (Tzitzikas et al., 2005), therefore they could provide a 'bridge' between Linked Data and SDI if elements of SDI are uniquely identifiable. Current web services transparently make use of some capabilities for content negotiation in HTTP (Holtman and Mutz, 1998) to allow client applications (such as browsers) to negotiate various aspects of input and output data, for example media type, compression, character set and the language of a requested web page. A recent implementation of the open-source initiative 52n gives a first idea[36]. Here sensor data is offered in standard encoding, KML, or a diagram.

Assuming that a given resource has multiple representations associated with it, content negotiation would allow a client to make preferences about which resource representation to retrieve from a transparently negotiable resource for the corresponding service with content negotiation. Notably, within this approach classical SDIs can remain intact. Following the Linked Data approach, desired data encodings can be requested at runtime. Hence, clients may request geospatial data in (classical) GML and may retrieve (with little modification of the request) the same data encoded in RDF, or any other format (Figure 8). This is a direct application of the notion of content negotiation, as already common in the web context (Holtman and Mutz, 1998). While working on this chapter, first related applications and services were put into place. The data service of the British Ordnance Survey (Section 2.4) provides a good example. Additionally, the OGC Naming Authority[37] released a first set of dictionaries in GML, HTML, and RDF. In fact, exposing data, which is initially stored in GML, as RDF already provides many links within one data space (Schade and Cox, 2010). This high degree of connection goes far beyond any non-geospatial cases of linked data.

A recent study by van de Sompel et al. (2009) proposed a novel application, called Memento, to add a time dimension on preservation and curation of data. The authors exploit the content negotiation characteristics to let users retrieve past versions of current web sites, envisioning somehow a time traveler for the web. This gives an idea of the potentials of content negotiation if were applied to services with content negotiation in SDI.

Figure 8. Mediation Service for content negotiation (examples in italic font)

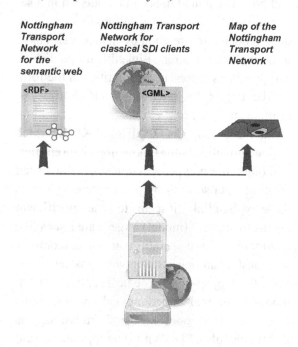

The primary difference between this approach and the augmentation approach (Section 5.2) is that augmentation would require extension of current geospatial information models to include references to external resources. In contrast, mediators do not need the information models to be modified in advance. Instead, mediators would require an additional 'catalogue' for cross-referencing between geospatial data (or services) and external resources. The recently presented work on the OGC Table Joining Service (OGC, 2010) may be useful in this context. It suggests means to join attribute data stored in different databases.

5.4 Discussion

Connecting conveniently data and metadata is a must to exploit the potential of current SDI catalogues and to link resources within SDI. In the SDI community, data and services are searchable by putting their metadata description in centralized catalogues. This strategy is appropriate for expert users because they perform elaborate queries using formalized metadata descriptors over a handful of well-documented repositories. Populating data catalogues in this way is a time-consuming task and it also requires experts in the concrete domain since the creation of metadata is still a manual, error-prone process, disconnected from the geospatial data assembly-line. Consequently, references to the physical location of data sets are often either missing or erroneously encoded. This limitation derives from the physical separation of data and metadata. Further, current geospatial data and metadata standards do not offer sufficient mechanisms for linking to external resources such as content from VGI sites. The previous section proposed some approaches for linking geospatial data and metadata to VGI through resource-oriented strategies. The envisioned result could be termed *Spatial Linked Data Infrastructure*. We used the Nottingham example for illustrations.

Applying the notion of Linked Data to currently existing concepts on SDI metadata raises two concerns. First, should metadata contain links to other resources of the same SDI? Second, should metadata contain links to external resources (including elements of third-party SDIs)? Both concerns apply to metadata about a data set, but also to service metadata. Technically neither of these issues causes any problems, because recent metadata standards (ISO, 2003; ISO, 2005; ISO, 2007; OGC, 2005b) allow for links using 'xlink' to connect to external resources. The primary difference to the Linked Data approach is the encoding language (Schade and Cox, 2010). On the conceptual level, however, it becomes a question to the information community. Such community is usually defined as a group of people, which share a common interest and use a shared vocabulary, in which intended interpretations have been clarified within the community (Bish et al., 1997). In such cases, the SDI requires a component for resolving the identifiers of resources, to which pointers exist. Following the recent Linked Data suggestion of using URIs, such resolvers are provided by DNS (Section 2.4).

Once clarified, how should we link from external resources to SDIs and especially to content managed within classical SDI catalogues? This concern does not directly affect the information community of the SDI, but the policy of making their content available to the outside. Again, resources within the SDI require identifiers and a common resolver has to be provided. Already there are indications of initiatives establishing registries for content other than data, for example, the INSPIRE Registry[38] offers a feature concept dictionary and the Global Earth Observation System of Systems (GEOSS) offers a Standards Registry[39]. A common resolver of identifiers across these initiatives could help to address the linking of VGI as well. Any other activities are topic to the outer-SDI environment. Either pointers to clearly retrievable resources are used, or catalogue clients have to be established. A best practice, established by the international geospatial community, is currently missing.

So far, we considered the classical setting of SDI. With the Linked Data notion, we may even revolutionize this common setting by breaking the (anyway fuzzy) separation between data and metadata. Once we acknowledge the Linked Data principles, they can be directly applied to the current way of using the OGC and ISO standards for geospatial information. Each XML document, being GML, a metadata record following the ISO profile offered by a catalogue service, or any other element of SDI can make use of the 'xlink' to connect to another resource inside the SDI. This way, data values can point to information about uncertainty, previous processing steps (also known as lineage) and any other piece of information in a unique manner. Of course, this suggests considering all elements of an SDI to be a resource. However, we contend that most, if not all, elements of SDI can be assigned unique identifiers such as URL (if they are accessible on the web) or URN (if they are not accessible on the web).

A much more general concern that applies to the overall Linked Data paradigm considers the data model used to encode the range of data links. Linking data does not specify the meaning of elements, which are pointed to. It makes only sense to link data in cases where we know the intended interpretation. The Nottingham example provides already a rich set of examples. With GML, as well as RDF, links may point to anything. Structures used to represent this flexible content have to be communicated. This may either happen in a pre-deployment face, i.e. the meaning of used data structures is fixed and well known, or at run-time. Well known meaning can be defined by user requirements, or by detailed specifications using the context of the used links. Enabling run-time exploitation of data structures (or models) requires inclusion of data model information inside the link itself or to the range of the link. Approaches for developing a *Spatial Linked Data Infrastructure* may apply full resource orientation by using native RDF repositories as the only option for resource presentation. We already argue that this approach seems unrealistic. Instead we suggest semi-resource-oriented approaches, and favor mediation services that implement content negotiation. The recent developments mentioned above already indicate feasibility of required components. We are on the cutting edge of connecting semantic and geospatial web. The final decisions have not been taken and reference implementations are still required. We list open issues in the next section.

6 FUTURE RESEARCH DIRECTIONS

Having reviewed some open issued concerned with resource identification and representation and semantics of links, this section identifies future challenges and research directions that must be addressed to achieve the goal of connecting geospatial web services and SDI with Linked Data and VGI communities. Main areas of research include data population, discovery, access, and maintenance.

Publishing classical geo-data and services is currently covered by the CSW specification of OGC and geoportals (Section 2.2). Moving to Spatial Linked Data Infrastructures requires revisiting at least the following core questions: How to publish resources? How to publish links? How to ensure links are valid? How to propagate link updates?

As in the case of service interoperability between distributed infrastructures, as for instance SDI-Grid (Lee and Percivall, 2008), Linked Data poses new challenges for data services that the geospatial community should immediately address. Consuming Linked Data sets are, or should be, based on customized regrouping and restructuring the spectrum of data sources over the Linked Data Space, according to specific user's perspective and needs. Relating the needs of the user to a data set by considering the resources referenced by that data set could offer a new and innovative approach for geographic data discovery. Further, the approaches in 'link analysis' could offer mechanisms for evaluating the relevance of linked geospatial data sets to the needs of a user (Borodin et al., 2005). One of the most successful applications of link analysis is the PageRank algorithm applied in Google (Brin and Page, 1998). Furthermore, in a previous section we proposed the establishment of a common resolver for identifiers. This presents a challenge for the SDI community to develop a service specification, conformant to ISO 19119, for resolving identifiers in support of both data and service discovery. Research questions for discovery in Spatial Linked Data Infrastructures would include: How to discover resources and services together? How to discover links? How to perform filtering capabilities? How to provide concrete views or perspectives of the whole Linked Data for specific user needs?

Future work will also have to consider the uniform access to heterogeneous sources from both SDI and VGI. This suggests a vision where geospatial data does not only offer the information it contains but also acts as a pointer towards other sources of information. Within service oriented architecture, a RESTful approach could help to implement this vision. However, it is necessary for the SDI community to consider how SDI and OGC web services will be able to access the heterogeneous data sources offered by VGI through a uniform and standardized mechanism. Again, we highlight that a solution would have to be developed through consensus, at an international level, in order to guarantee that the full potential of linked geospatial data is harnessed.

Establishing links between SDI and VGI resources could be a highly valuable capability. However, some of the safety critical applications of geospatial data will require the connections between Linked Data to be maintained through approaches such as versioning and caching. Versioning would allow changes in a referenced resource to be reported back to the data set referencing the resource. The URN approach used by the OGC already includes an element for 'version numbers'. Nevertheless, it is not yet clear whether a similar versioning approach could be extended to URLs of VGI content. Caching would allow for previous versions of resources to be stored and persisted, in case, they are required in the future (van de Sompel et al., 2009). In summary, the challenges involved in the management of linked geospatial data will require additional research on how to propagate and report changes to links.

7 CONCLUSION

The purpose of metadata in SDI is to help users (such as scientists, decision-makers, analysts, etc.) to fully understand a resource in order to assess its usefulness or applicability in their daily tasks. In contrast, the aim of metadata in Linked Data (at the current stage) and above all in VGI content is to describe something that can be discovered and browsed easily. For instance, with regards to VGI content, people share videos, photos, and such types of resources, by tagging a resource with minimal descriptors: a title, key words or tags, a pointer to the very resource and, in some cases, a location reference. Simple metadata mechanisms like tagging are often sufficient for general discovery purposes, but clearly lack of suitable mechanisms for filtering information, setting query criteria and interpreting the search results, necessary for specific discovery tasks.

Geospatial data from Linked Data sources, VGI and SDI is addressed to different audience since they have different needs and requirements. This implies that metadata techniques are also quite different, since describing something that can be discovered easily is different from describing something that can be fully understood. However, this does not mean that these worlds need to remain separated since data providers can use the existing links, tags and annotations to help users connect to other related geospatial data. In this sense, SDI content needs to exploit the vast amount of geospatial data present in social networks as for example, people who are interested in Geonames place names around the city of Nottingham might also like to inspect street and elevation layers of this city from SDI catalogues services. Conversely, people who have accessed some residential parcel data for Nottingham might also like to know some Flickr pictures from locals in such areas. Similarly, knowing the network of users and organizations that have interest in common data sets could help in reinforcing social and professional ties among peer stakeholders.

As the technology has been identified and a solution has been outlined, we moved closer to the third generation of SDI. We are aware of the existing practical and research challenges, and the foundations for reference implementations are set. Recent implementations indicate feasibility of various components, now it is up to us and the all other members of the community to implement a shared Spatial Linked Data Infrastructure.

REFERENCES

W3C. (2001). *XML Schema Part 0: Primer.* Retrieved from http://www.w3.org/TR/xmlschema-0/

W3C. (2001b). *URIs, URLs, and URNs: Clarifications and Recommendations 1.0.* Retrieved from http://www.w3.org/TR/uri-clarification/

W3C. (2008). *SPARQL query language for RDF.* Retrieved from http://www.w3.org/TR/xmlschema-0/

Ackland, R. (2009). Social network services as data sources and platforms for e-researching social Networks. *Social Science Computer Review, 27,* 481–492. doi:10.1177/0894439309332291

Alameh, N. (2003). Chaining geographic information Web services. *IEEE Internet Computing, 7*(5), 22–29. doi:10.1109/MIC.2003.1232514

Alonso, G., Casati, F., Harumi, K., & Machiraju, V. (2004). *Web services: concepts, architectures and applications.* Heidelberg: Springer.

Auer, S., Lehmann, J., & Hellmann, S. (2009). LinkedGeoData: adding a spatial dimension to the Web of data. In *Proceedings of the ISWC 2009,* LNCS 5823, 731-746.

Bechhofer, S., van Harmelen, F., Hendler, J., Horrocks, I., McGuinness, D.L., Patel-Schneider, P.F., et al. (2003). *OWL Web Ontology Language Reference.*

Becker, C., & Bizer, C. (2009). Exploring the Geospatial Semantic Web with DBpedia Mobile. *Journal of Web Semantics: Science. Services and Agents on the World Wide Web, 7*(4), 278–286. doi:10.1016/j.websem.2009.09.004

Bell, M. (2008). *Service-Oriented Modeling (SOA): service analysis, design, and architecture.* Hoboken, New Jersey: Wiley & Sons.

Bernard, L., & Craglia, M. (2005). *SDI—from spatial data infrastructure to service-driven infrastructure, research workshop on cross-learning between SDI and II. First research workshop on cross-learning on spatial data infrastructures (SDI) and information infrastructures (II).* International Institute for Geo-Information Science and Earth Observation.

Bernard, L., Kanellopoulos, L., Annoni, A., & Smits, P. (2005). The European Geoportal—one step towards the establishment of a European spatial data infrastructure. *Computers, Environment and Urban Systems, 29*(1), 15–31.

Berners-Lee, T., Fielding, R., & Masinter, L. (1998). Uniform Resource Identifiers (URI): Generic syntax. *Internet Engineering Task Force (IETF) Memo – RFC 2396.*

Berners-Lee, T., Hendler, J., & Lassila, O. (2001). The Semantic Web. *Scientific American Magazine, 284*(5), 34–43. doi:10.1038/scientificamerican0501-34

Bishr, M., & Mantelas, L. (2008). A trust and reputation model for filtering and classifying knowledge about urban growth. *GeoJournal, 72*(3-4), 229–237. doi:10.1007/s10708-008-9182-4

Bishr, Y., Pundt, H., Kuhn, W., Molenaar, M., & Radwan, M. (1997). Probing the concept of information communities-a first step toward semantic interoperability. M.F. Goodchild, et al (Eds.), *Proceedings of Interop '97-Interoperating Geographic Information Systems,* 55-71. Kluwer.

Bizer, C. (2009). The emerging Web of linked data. *IEEE Intelligent Systems, 24*(5), 87–92. doi:10.1109/MIS.2009.102

Bizer, C., Heath, T., & Berners-Lee, T. (2009a). Linked data - the story so far. *International Journal on Semantic Web and Information Systems, 5*(3), 1–22.

Bizer, C., Lehmann, J., Kobilarov, G., Auer, S., Becker, C., & Cyganiak, R. (2009b). DBpedia - A crystallization point for the Web of data. *Web Semantics: Science. Services and Agents on the World Wide Web, 7*(3), 154–165. doi:10.1016/j.websem.2009.07.002

Borodin, A., Roberts, G. O., Rosenthal, J. S., & Tsaparas, P. (2005). Link analysis ranking: algorithms, theory, and experiments. *ACM Transactions on Internet Technology, 5*(1), 231–297. doi:10.1145/1052934.1052942

Boyd, D., & Ellison, N. (2007). Social network sites: definition, history, and scholarship. *Journal of Computer-Mediated Communication, 13*(1).

Brickley, D., & Guha, R.V. (2004). *RDF vocabulary description language 1.0.*

Brin, S., & Page, L. (1998). The anatomy of a large-scale hypertextual Web search engine, *7th International World Wide Web Conference, 30,* 107-117.

Budhathoki, N. R., Bruce, B., & Nedovic-Budic, Z. (2008). Reconceptualizing the role of the user of spatial data infrastructure. *GeoJournal: An International Journal on Geography, 72,* 149–160.

Callahan, K. M. (1985). Social science research in the information age: online databases for social scientists. *Social Science Computer Review, 3,* 28–44. doi:10.1177/089443938500300104

Crompvoets, J., & Bregt, A. (2007). National spatial data clearinghouses, 2000–2005. In Onsrud, H. (Ed.), *Research and theory in advancing spatial data infrastructure* (pp. 133–146). Redlands, CA: ESRI Press.

Curbera, F., Duftler, M., Khalaf, R., Nagy, W., Mukhi, N., & Weerawarana, S. (2002). Unravelling the Web services web: an introduction to SOAP, WSDL, and UDDI. *IEEE Internet Computing, 6*(2), 86–93. doi:10.1109/4236.991449

European Parliament and Council. (2007). *Directive 2007/2/EC of the European Parliament and of the Council of 14, March 2007, establishing an Infrastructure for Spatial Information in the European Community (INSPIRE).* Official Journal on the European Parliament and of the Council.

Executive Office of the President. (1994). Coordinating geographic data acquisition and access: the national spatial data infrastructure. *Executive order 12906. Federal Register,* 59.

Fielding, R. (2000). *Architectural styles and the design of network-based software architectures.* Unpublished doctoral dissertation, University of California, Irvine.

Florczyk, A., Lopez-Pellicer, F. J., Béjar, R., Nogueras-Iso, J., & Zarazaga-Soria, F. J. (2010). *Applying semantic linkage in the Geospatial Web.* M. Painho, et al (Eds.), *Geospatial Thinking,* 201-220. *Springer.*

Gahegan, M., Luo, J., Weaver, S. D., Pike, W., & Banchuen, T. (2009). Connecting GEON: making sense of the myriad resources, researchers and concepts that comprise a geoscience cyberinfrastructure. *Computers & Geosciences, 35*(4), 836–854. doi:10.1016/j.cageo.2008.09.006

Goodchild, M. F. (2007). Citizens as voluntary sensors: spatial data infrastructure in the world of Web 2.0. *International Journal of Spatial Data Infrastructures Research, 2,* 24–32.

Goodchild, M. F. (2009). NeoGeography and the nature of geographic expertise. *Journal of Location Based Services, 3*(2), 82–96. doi:10.1080/17489720902950374

Goodchild, M. F., Egenhofer, M., Fegeas, R., & Kottman, C. (1999). *Interoperating Geographic Information Systems.* Norwell, MA: Kluwer Academic Publishers.

Goodwin, J., Dolbear, C., & Hart, G. (2008). Geographical linked data: the administrative geography of Great Britain on the Semantic Web. *Transactions in GIS, 12*(1), 19–30. doi:10.1111/j.1467-9671.2008.01133.x

Granell, C., Díaz, L., & Gould, M. (2010). Service-oriented applications for environmental models: reusable geospatial services. *Environmental Modelling & Software, 25*(2), 182–198. doi:10.1016/j.envsoft.2009.08.005

Guarino, N. (1998). Formal Ontology and Information Systems. N. Guarino (Ed.), *Formal Ontology in Information Systems (FOIS'98)*.

Haklay, M., & Weber, P. (2008). OpenStreetMap: User-Generated Street Maps. *IEEE Pervasive Computing / IEEE Computer Society [and] IEEE Communications Society, 7*(4), 12–18. doi:10.1109/MPRV.2008.80

Harnad, S. (1990). The symbol grounding problem. *Physica D. Nonlinear Phenomena, 42,* 335–346. doi:10.1016/0167-2789(90)90087-6

Hill, L. L. (2006). *Georeferencing: The Geographic Associations of information: digital libraries and electronic publishing.* Cambridge, MA: The MIT Press.

Hobona, G., Fairbairn, D., Hiden, H., & James, P. (2010). Orchestration of grid-enabled Geospatial Web Services in geoscientific workflows. *IEEE Transactions on Automation Science and Engineering, 7*(2), 407–411. doi:10.1109/TASE.2008.2010626

Holtman, K., & Mutz, A. (1998). Transparent content negotiation in HTTP. *Internet Engineering Task Force (IETF) Memo – RFC 2295.*

Hubmann-Haidvogel, A., Scharl, A., & Weichselbraun, A. (2009). Multiple coordinated views for searching and navigating Web content repositories. *Information Sciences, 179,* 1813–1021. doi:10.1016/j.ins.2009.01.030

INSPIRE. (2009). *INSPIRE data specification transport networks (Version 3.0).* INSPIRE Thematic Working Group on Transport Networks.

ISO (2003). 19115 Geographic information - metadata. *ISO/TC211 standard.*

ISO (2005). 19119 Geographic information - services. *ISO/TC211 standard.*

ISO (2007). 19139 Geographic information - metadata - XML schema implementation. *ISO/TC211 standard.*

Janowicz, K., & Keßler, C. (2008). The Role of ontology in improving gazetteer interaction. *International Journal of Geographical Information Science, 22*(10), 1129–1157. doi:10.1080/13658810701851461

Janowicz, K., Schade, S., Bröring, A., Keßler, C., Maue, P., & Stasch, C. (2010). Semantic Enablement for Spatial Data Infrastructures. *Transactions in GIS, 14*(2), 111–129. doi:10.1111/j.1467-9671.2010.01186.x

Klyne, G., & Carroll, J.J. (2004). *Resource Description Framework (RDF): concepts and abstract syntax.*

Lassila, O., & Swick, R. (1999). *Resource Description Framework (RDF) model and syntax specification.* Retrieved from http://www.w3.org/TR/PR-rdf-syntax/

Lee, C., & Percivall, G. (2008). Standards-based computing capabilities for distributed geospatial applications. *Computer, 41*(11), 50–57. doi:10.1109/MC.2008.468

Lucchi, R., Millot, M., & Elfers, C. (2008). Resource oriented architecture and REST: Assessment of impact and advantages on INSPIRE. *JCR Scientific and Technical Report.* EUR 23397.

Masser, I. (1999). All shapes and sizes: The first generation of national spatial data infrastructures. *International Journal of Geographical Information Science, 13*(1), 67–84. doi:10.1080/136588199241463

Masser, I. (2007). *Building European spatial data infrastructures*. Redlands, CA: ESRI Press.

Maué, P., Schade, S., & Duchesne, P. (2009). OGC discussion paper 08-167r1: semantic annotations in OGC standards. *Technical report, OGC, 2009*.

Mazzetti, P., Nativi, S., & Caron, J. (2009). RESTful implementation of geospatial services for Earth and Space Science applications. *International Journal of Digital Earth*, *2*(1), 40–61. doi:10.1080/17538940902866153

Miles, A., & Bechhofer, S. (2009). *SKOS Simple Knowledge Organization System Namespace Document - HTML Variant*.

Nebert, D. (2004). *SDI Cookbook*, Version 2.0.

OASIS. (2006). *Web Service Resource 1.2 (WS-Resource)*. OASIS Standard.

OGC. (2005a). Open Geospatial Consortium Inc. Web feature service implementation specification (version 1.1.0).

OGC. (2005b). OpenGIS® filter encoding implementation specification (version 1.1).

OGC. (2006a). Open Geospatial Consortium Inc. Web map service implementation specification (version 1.3.0).

OGC. *(2006b)*. OGC White Paper - an introduction to GeoRSS: a standards based approach for geo-enabling RSS feeds.

OGC. (2007a). OpenGIS® Geography Markup Language (GML) encoding standard (version 3.2.1).

OGC. (2007b). OpenGIS® catalogue service implementation specification (version 2.0.2).

OGC. (2007c). *OGC® KML (version 2.2)*.

OGC. (2008). Open Geospatial Consortium Inc. Web coverage service implementation specification (version 1.1.2).

OGC. (2010). OpenGIS® table joining service implementation standard (10-070).

Omran, E. L. E., & van Etten, J. (2007). Spatial-data sharing: applying social-network analysis to study individual and collective behaviour. *International Journal of Geographical Information Science*, *21*(6), 699–714. doi:10.1080/13658810601135726

Onsrud, H., Poore, B., Rugg, R. T., & Wiggins, L. (2004). The future of the spatial information infrastructure. In McMaster, R. B., & Usery, E. L. (Eds.), *A research agenda for Geographic Information Science* (pp. 225–255). Boca Raton: CRC Press. doi:10.1201/9781420038330.ch8

Platt, M. (2007). Geospatial Data and Web 2.0 - a MapMart perspective. *Directions Magazine*, July 26, 2007.

Rajabifard, A., Binns, A., Masser, I., & Williamson, I. (2006). The role of sub-national government and the private sector in future spatial data infrastructures. *International Journal of Geographical Information Science*, *20*(7), 727–741. doi:10.1080/13658810500432224

Rajabifard, A., Kalantari, M., & Binns, A. (2009). SDI and metadata entry and updating tools. In van Loenen, B., Besemer, J. W. J., & Zevenbergen, J. A. (Eds.), *SDI convergence: research, emerging tools, and critical assessment* (pp. 121–135). Rotterdam: Netherlands Geodetic Commission.

Raskin, R. G., & Pan, M. J. (2005). Knowledge representation in the Semantic Web for Earth and Environmental Terminology (SWEET). *Computers & Geosciences*, *31*(9), 1119–1125. doi:10.1016/j.cageo.2004.12.004

Richardson, L., & Ruby, S. (2007). *RESTful Web Services*. Sebastopol, CA: O'Reilly Media.

Riehle, D. (2007). The economic motivation of open source software: stakeholder perspectives. *IEEE Computer*, *40*(4), 25–32.

Rumbaugh, J., Jacobson, I., & Booch, G. (1999). *UML Reference Manual*. Boston, MA: Addison-Wesley.

Schade, S., & Cox, S. (2010). Linked data in SDI or how GML is not about trees. M. Painho et al. (Eds), *Proceedings of AGILE Conference 2010*.

Suda, B. (2006). *Using microformats*. Sebastopol, CA: O'Reilly Media.

Tzitzikas, Y., Spyratos, N., & Constantopoulos, P. (2005). Mediators over taxonomy-based information sources. *The International Journal on Very Large Data Bases*, *14*(1), 112–136. doi:10.1007/s00778-003-0119-8

van de Sompel, H., Nelson, M. L., Sanderson, R., Balakireva, L. L., Ainsworth, S., & Shankar, H. (2009). *Memento: Time travel for the Web*. Retrieved from http://www.arXiv.org

van Oort, P. A. J., Hazeu, G. W., Kramer, H., Bregt, A. K., & Rip, F. I. (2010). Social networks in spatial data infrastructures. *GeoJournal*, *75*(1), 105–118. doi:10.1007/s10708-009-9294-5

Wiederhold, G. (1992). Mediators in the architecture of future Information Systems. *IEEE Computer Magazine*, *25*(3), 38–49.

Woolf, A., & Shaon, A. (2009). An approach to encapsulation of grid processing within an OGC Web processing service. *GIS. Science*, *3*, 82–88.

Zhao, P., Yu, G., & Di, L. (2007). Geospatial Web services. In Hilton, B. N. (Ed.), *Emerging Spatial Information Systems and applications* (pp. 1–35). Hershey, PA: IDEA Group.

ADDITIONAL READING

W3C. (2001). URIs, URLs, and URNs: clarifications and recommendations (version 1.0). *Report from the joint W3C/IETF URI Planning Interest Group*.

Abdelmoty, A. I., Smart, P. D., Jones, C. B., Fu, G., & Finch, D. (2005). A critical evaluation of ontology languages for geographic information retrieval on the Internet. *Journal of Visual Languages and Computing*, *16*(4), 269–382. doi:10.1016/j.jvlc.2004.11.001

Andrei, M., & Berre, A. J. (2008) Swing: an integrated environment for geospatial semantic web services. In S. Bechhofer, M. Hauswirth, et al. (Eds.), *5th European Semantic Web Conference (ESWC2008)*, LNCS5021, 767-771. Springer.

de Longueville, B., & Ostlander, N. (2009). Addressing vagueness in Volunteered Geographic Information (VGI) - a case study. *11th International GSDI Conference*. Rotterdam, the Netherlands.

Egenhofer, M. J. (2002). Toward the semantic geospatial web. *Proceedings of the 10th ACM international symposium on advances in Geographic Information Systems*, 1-4. Virginia, USA.

Goodchild, M. F. (2007). Citizens as sensors: the world of volunteered geography. *GeoJournal*, *69*(4), 211–221. doi:10.1007/s10708-007-9111-y

Goodchild, M. F., Fu, P., & Rich, P. (2007). Sharing geographic information: an assessment of the geospatial one-stop. *Annals of the Association of American Geographers. Association of American Geographers*, *97*(2), 250–266. doi:10.1111/j.1467-8306.2007.00534.x

Lemmens, R., Wytzisk, A., de By, R., Granell, C., Gould, M., & van Oosterom, P. (2006). Integrating semantic and syntactic descriptions to chain geographic services. *IEEE Internet Computing*, *10*(5), 42–52. doi:10.1109/MIC.2006.106

Lieberman, J., & Pehle, T. (2006). *Geospatial Semantic Web interoperability experiment report. Technical report*. Open Geospatial Consortium.

Probst, F., & Lutz, M. (2004). Giving meaning to GI Web Service descriptions. *In 2nd International Workshop on Web Services: Modeling, Architecture and Infrastructure (WSMAI2004)*. Porto, Portugal.

Vickery, G. & Wunsch-Vincent, S. (2007). Participative Web and user-created content: Web 2.0 wikis and social networking. *Organization for Economic Co-operation and Development.*

Weets, G. (2006). *Toward a single European information space for environment. ESA - DG INFSO Interoperability workshop: Architecture workshop in support of GEO and GMES.* Italy: Frascati.

Yue, P., Gong, J., Di, L., He, L., & Wei, Y. (in press). Integrating Semantic Web technologies and geospatial catalog services for geospatial information discovery and processing in cyber-infrastructure. *GeoInformatica.*

KEY TERMS AND DEFINITIONS

Discovery: The action or task of searching or finding for geospatial data sets, metadata, services and resources in general.

Linked Data: Represents a set of structured data sources over the Internet connected via typed relationships.

Metadata: A set of information descriptors used to describe the characteristics (format, quality, use, proprietary, etc.) of geospatial data sets, services and resources in general.

Retrieval: The action or task of gathering or accessing to geospatial data sets, services and resources in general.

Spatial data: Data sets that refer explicitly to a geospatial connotation and/or are georeferenced.

Spatial Data Infrastructure (SDI): Is a type of information infrastructure for enhancing geospatial data sharing and access.

Spatial Linked Data Infrastructure: The idea of projecting Linked Data principles to SDI architecture and standards so that SDI and VGI content can be easily combined.

Spatial Web Service: Is a software component that delivers and processes any geospatial data over the Internet.

Volunteered Geographic Information (VGI): Is the harnessing of tools to create, assemble, and disseminate geographic data provided voluntarily by individuals (Goodchild, 2007).

ENDNOTES

[1] http://www.w3.org/DesignIssues/Linked-Data.html

[2] http://www.opengeospatial.org

[3] http://www.isotc211.org

[4] http://www.csc.fi/english/pages/parade

[5] http://www.wikimapia.org

[6] http://www.flickr.com

[7] http://www.panoramio.com

[8] http://www.youtube.com

[9] http://maps.google.com

[10] http://twitter.com/

[11] http://www.alexa.com

[12] http://layar.com

[13] http://www.acrossair.com

[14] http://tools.ietf.org/html/rfc1034

[15] http://www.foaf-project.org/

[16] http://www.geonames.org

[17] http://linkedgeodata.org

[18] http://www.rdfabout.com/demo/census/

[19] http://www.dbis.informatik.uni-goettingen.de/Mondial/

[20] https://www.cia.gov/library/publications/the-world-factbook/

[21] http://www.xist.org/

[22] http://riese.joanneum.at/

[23] http://europa.eu/estatref/download/everybody/

[24] http://data.ordnancesurvey.co.uk

[25] http://telegraphis.net/data/

26 http://ontologi.es/rail/

27 http://www.eionet.europa.eu/gemet/ rdf?langcode=en

28 http://iws.seu.edu.cn/services/falcons/ objectsearch/index.jsp (accessed 10th November 2009).

29 http://dbpedia.org (accessed 10th November, 2009).

30 http://ode.openlinksw.com/ (accessed 10th November, 2009)

31 http://www.geonames.org/ontology/ (accessed 11th November, 2009)

32 http://www.bbc.co.uk/blogs/radiola-bs/2008/07/music_beta_and_linked_data. shtml

33 http://jsexplicit.sourceforge.net

34 http://portal.opengeospatial.org/ files/?artifact_id=24045

35 http://ec.europa.eu/environment/seis

36 http://v-swe.uni-muenster.de:8080/52n-OXF-WS/RESTful/sos/OWS-5_SOS

37 http://www.opengeospatial.org/ogcna

38 http://inspire-registry.jrc.ec.europa.eu

39 http://www.earthobservations.org/gci_ sr.shtml

Chapter 10
Ontological and Semantic Technologies for Geospatial Portals

Naijun Zhou
University of Maryland College Park, USA

ABSTRACT

A geospatial portal is a repository of distributed geospatial data, tools and services, and supports the publishing, management, search, use and sharing of the resources. Geospatial portals have been developed as clearinghouses, metadata portals, data warehousing, and recently geospatial portals incorporated the Service Oriented Architecture and distributed computing to make service-oriented portals. In addition to software and computational challenges, ontology and semantics play an increasingly important role in geospatial portals due to the demand of interoperability. The interoperation and communication of data, tools and services become critical when heterogeneous resources are consolidated and exchanged on geospatial portals. This chapter provides an updated overview of geospatial portals followed by detailed discussion on how the ontological and semantic technologies are incorporated into geospatial portals. Three recent research and practice of geospatial portals are briefly introduced as the case studies of service-oriented portals.

INTRODUCTION

With advanced methods of geospatial data collection and increasing demands of georeferenced data and geoprocessing, sharing and interoperating geospatial resources (data, tools and services) becomes critical and useful. Geospatial portals support the publishing, delivering and thus sharing of geospatial resources. There have been several review articles of geospatial portals in terms of

DOI: 10.4018/978-1-60960-192-8.ch010

their software architecture and applications (Goodchild, Fu, & Rich, 2007; Tang, Selwood, 2005). This chapter starts with an updated overview of the concept and practice of geospatial portals, and introduces how the ontological and semantic technologies influence geospatial portals.

GEOSPATIAL PORTALS

The terms Web-based *portal* and *geospatial portal* have been overused leading to much confusion. A Web portal is a gateway to the distributed Internet-based resources, including Web pages, data, tools, Web Services, etc. Geospatial portals, also called geoportals, may be understood from their architecture as a Web-based system and from their functions.

- The Web system view. A geospatial portal is a Web site that assembles Internet-based resources and provides an entry point to these resources (Tait, 2005; Tang & Selwood, 2005, p. 13).
- The function view. A geospatial portal "organize[s] content and services such as directories, search tools, community information, support resources, data and applications" (Maguire and Longley, 2005), and provides functions such as the "search, evaluation, and downloading, and in some cases licensing or purchase" of geographic information (Goodchild, Fu, & Rich, 2007).

A geospatial portal is a repository of distributed geospatial data, tools and services, and supports the publishing, management, search, use and sharing of the resources. The output of geospatial portals may be the links to downloadable data, Web Services to be integrated into other applications, or just the contact information of resource providers. According to this definition, many client-server Web-based systems that facilitate data storage,

browse and query may not be considered as fully functioning geospatial portals in this paper.

The development of geospatial portals was driven by declined cost of data collection and data application, technical development and governmental initiatives. The major technical contributions may include database warehousing, Service Oriented Architecture (SOA), XML and Web Services, etc. Specifically, in geographic information community, the wide adoption of Geography Markup Language (GML), OGC Web Services, ISO geospatial standards, and distributed geographic information systems have significantly influenced the system architecture and the application of geospatial portals. On the other hand, geospatial portals have been promoted by two governmental initiatives: Spatial Data Infrastructures (SDI) and electronic government (or, e-government) (Homburg, 2008; Mayer-Schonberger & Lazer, 2007). Both initiatives, implemented by a majority of the countries in the world, encourage the sharing of (geospatial) data, information and knowledge in order to support transparent and effective decision making.

THE CLASSIFICTION OF GEOSPATIAL PORTALS

Since 1990s, geospatial portals have been developed at different stages as clearinghouses, metadata portals, and data warehousing. Recently, geospatial portals start to incorporate SOA and distributed computing to make service-oriented portals. This classification is not clear cut and some portals may be a hybrid of several categories of portals. In fact, a newer type of portal usually includes the functions of the older ones, and some portals continue to evolve by augmenting new advanced technologies on the top of current portals.

Initially designed as the major component of the U.S. National SDI (NSDI), a data clearinghouse is defined as "a distributed network of geospatial data producers, managers, and users linked elec-

Figure 1. Architecture of GeoSpatial One-Stop. (Source: Goodchild et al. 2007)

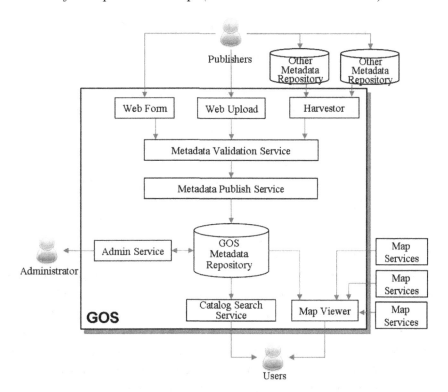

tronically" (U.S. Government Executive Order 12906). As an early stage of geospatial portals, a clearinghouse is primarily a framework that promotes the idea of data sharing among a collection of institutions. A clearinghouse is basically a catalogue of a variety of data sets organized and indexed by data themes (e.g., land use, hydrology, etc.) and by geographic locations (e.g., bounding box, jurisdiction, etc.). This catalogue is presented as a Web page that allows users to browse a list of themes and regions, and/or draw a box on a map to make selections.

Metadata portals have been successfully developed to fulfill the clearinghouse framework. Most of current geospatial portals belong to metadata portals. This category of portals supports the creation and storage of metadata as a catalogue on a centralized metadata server, the search and discovering of metadata entries, and the downloading of georeferenced data (ESRI,

2007, p. 2). A metadata portal only contains a catalogue of metadata records, while actual data are stored at distributed sources maintained by individual data providers. The most successful metadata portal would be the world largest portal, Geospatial One Stop (GOS) that is implemented by USGS as a component of NSDI (Figure 1). GOS allows data providers to register their metadata manually assisted by computer tools. As an option, GOS also offers computer programs to harvest metadata information from other metadata repositories via five metadata protocols including Z39.50, ArcIMS, Web-Accessible Folder, Open Archive Initiative and OGC Catalogue Service for Web (CSW). Additionally, NSDI was proposed to rely on standards for sharing. Therefore, GOS developed and adopted a standard format to encode metadata, i.e., the FGDC metadata. GOS constructs a Web-based user interface to search the metadata elements such as creator, topic, location,

Figure 2. Spatial ETL tools (Source: Murray, 2009)

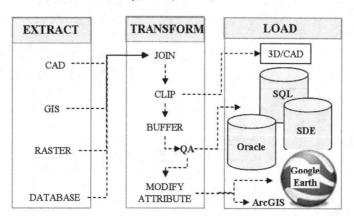

time, etc. The result of a GOS search can be a list of metadata records, downloadable data, offline data and document, and recently more options are added such as live data and map, and geographic services, etc.

A data warehousing aims to provide a federated database of diverse data sources. The schemas of diverse databases are merged into a global database schema using database integration methods (Doan & Halevy, 2005). A global view of data is presented to users based on which a database query is posed. Recently, to achieve "true" interoperability of data no matters where the data are stored and how the data are defined in terms of their formats and definitions, the tools of geospatial data extract, transform and load (ETL) have been made available (Murrary, 2009) (Figure 2). For a specific application, a spatial ETL system can extract data from multiple data sources, transform and consolidate data into a form that fit specific needs, and load data into the end targets. Here, the term *interoperability* is the capability of integrating multiple geospatial data, tools, services into a single application, and *interoperation* means the process of achieving interoperability.

The newest type of geospatial portals is service-oriented portals enabled by SOA and Web Services. Service-oriented portals integrate distribute data, tools and services. These geospatial recourses can be directly transferred and plugged in a user application without or with minimal human involvement. Portal requests and responses are processed by computers such that machine-to-machine interaction is made possible. Such portals have advantages over metadata portals on replacing human-oriented searching and integration with machines. In this way, service-oriented portals may be considered as a hub of an intelligent distributed system. The enabling technologies of service-oriented portals my include portlet, Web Services for Remote Portlets, Java Specification Request, and OGC Web Services (Yang, Evans, Cole, Marley, Alameh, & Bambacus, 2007). Zhao et al. (2008) proposed a service-oriented architecture to include components of user portal, data management, data analysis, workflow and data visualization. Metadata portals can be augmented to service-oriented portals with resources (data and tools) published as services, and with an additional interface for machine-to-machine communication. A distributed portal may still maintain a catalog of resources as metadata portals do, but the catalogue itself can act as a Web Service (e.g., OGC CSW) and distributed portal data may be served via Web Services (e.g., WMS and WFS).

Figure 3. OGC reference model (Adapted from OGC, 2008)

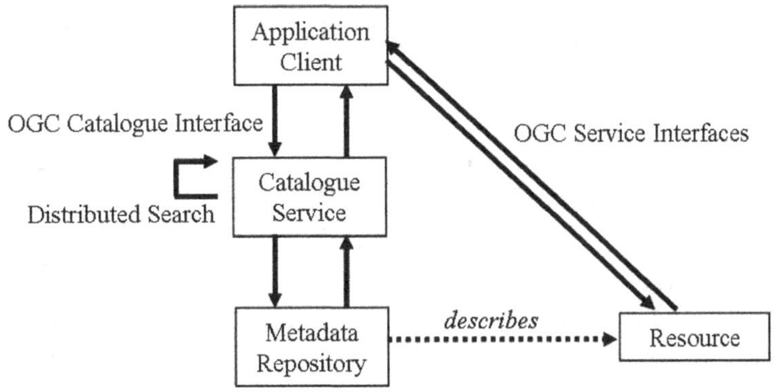

OGC specifications have played an important role in metadata portals and service-oriented portals. OGC employs a consensus process to allow geospatial creators, vendors and users to discuss, standardize and adopt a set of standard data models and protocols. On the top of a metadata repository, OGC CSW is added between users and the repository (Figure 3). The catalogue stores the definitions and descriptions of feature types, feature attributes and their relations, and all data are recorded such that they conform to the type definitions found in the feature catalogue (OGC, 2008).

Currently, geospatial portals are in the transitional stage from metadata to service-oriented portals. This transition may be expedited by a new computing vision, cyberinfrastructure. Based on the U.S. National Science Foundation (NSF), cyberinfrastructure integrates "hardware for computing, data and networks, ... and an interoperable suite of software and middleware services and tools" (NSF, 2007, p.5). In response to this vision, Zhang and Tsou (2009) suggested a framework for grid-enabled service-oriented geospatial portals. This framework includes four tiers: presentation, logic, service and grid, where the service tier includes services of visualization, geoprocessing and data that can be distributed over the Internet.

ONTOLOGY, SEMANTICS AND INTEROPERABILITY

In addition to the computational challenges, ontology and semantics are under investigation in geographic information science in order to achieve accurate and efficient interoperability. For all types of geospatial portals, interoperation is also needed when heterogeneous data, tools and services are consolidated and exchanged. Originally discussed for geospatial data integration, there are three levels of interoperability: system level for different file formats and software platforms, syntax level for different database schema, and semantics level for different data content models (Bisher, 1998). Interoperability becomes a more serious issue for geospatial portals when the portals often store or catalog a huge amount of data, tools and services, which are more likely heterogeneous in many aspects. Additionally, the heterogeneity problem is preferably to be solved by machines as required by the SOA-enabled service-oriented portals.

The three levels of interoperability may be extended and deployed for geospatial portals. System-level interoperability may not be critical when information is encoded as Web Services in the formats of XML, GML or other protocols. Syntax level interoperability aims to achieve the similar task of data warehousing by integrating the attributes in schemas. Semantic level interoperability can help understand the meanings and

Table 1. Tasks of interoperability for different types of geospatial portals

Type of portals	Search Criteria	Interoperability Tasks	Example Solutions
Clearinghouse	Find a data set.	Categorize data sets into a list of themes.	A controlled list of themes and topics; or Geographic locations are used as the unique index of data.
Data warehousing	Select an attribute to pose queries.	Integrate database schemas.	Database schema integration.
Metadata portals	Find metadata records based on the user-defined value(s) of metadata element(s).	Consolidate the representation of metadata elements.	Standard metadata such as the FGDC metadata.
Service-oriented portals	Find a service based on the description of the service.	Exchange metadata element definitions, parameter definitions of geoprocessing tools, service definitions and communication protocols.	Standard metadata, tool parameters, and service protocols; or Semantic integration algorithms of database attribute domain values, tool parameters and service descriptions.

thus exchange information encoded in different resources: database schemas (e.g., attribute definition), data (e.g., domain values), tools (e.g., parameters) and services (e.g., descriptions of services). The tasks of interoperability for different types of portals are summarized in Table 1, where a newer type of portals contains all the criteria, tasks and solutions in an older type. Note that semantic issue also resides in the other two levels because semantics study the meaning of representations (such as text and graph) appearing in the system and syntax levels as well. For example the schema level interoperability may need to recognize the text of database attributes *land use* and *land use type* as the same attributes. Apparently, geospatial portals should investigate the semantics of a piece of information even the information is represented in a same form.

The level of interoperability also determines the publishing, storage and functions of a geospatial portal. System level interoperation may support users to download data with different file formats, which may result in a clearinghouse. Syntax level interoperation can support searching data sets based on their integrated schema and standardized metadata elements, which may lead to a data warehousing or a metadata portal. Semantic level interoperation, together with the

other two types, may provide the most powerful functions of locating data sets, querying data content, and exchanging services and tools. Service-oriented portals need semantic level interoperation.

Ontology can be utilized as the mediator to facilitate the communication among geospatial portal resources, data providers, and users. In artificial intelligence and information science, ontology is a "logical theory accounting for the intended meaning of a formal vocabulary" (Guarino, 1998). Ontologies and spatial ontologies have been designed to provide rules of defining and representing geospatial objects with semantic integration as one of the applications (Agarwal 2005). Geospatial semantics, as the result of humans' conceptualization, indicate the representations of the geospatial world. Semantic integration of geospatial databases aims to provide "a global view of diverse terms in different data sources" (Zhou, 2005); and broadly, semantic integration aims to measure and identify resources (data, tools, services, etc.) with the same and similar meanings.

The ontological and semantic technologies are able to enhance every component of geospatial portals, particularly, the service-oriented portals. Ontology enables the understanding of human concepts given the context and knowledge of conceptualization. An example of ontology for understanding human conceptualization follows. By posing a query *find restaurants near to my home* may, one may mean ten miles or one mile depending on one's perception of the geographic concept *near*. An example of semantic integration can be illustrated in a search *find all datasets that have cropland in California*. After a user typed *cropland* as the keyword and selected California as the geographic extent, a metadata portal (e.g., GOS) will return a list of geospatial datasets together with their metadata. However, the user will find it difficult to explore each individual dataset to learn the meaning of *cropland* in order to decide which datasets to download. This exploration will become more time consuming (and most likely less accurate) when a huge amount of candidate datasets are available. In addition, the search is based on the theme level metadata (title, theme, abstract, etc.) instead of attribute domain values thus may ignore datasets that have *cropland* objects but have not recorded *cropland* in the metadata. Additionally, returning the actual query result (e.g., database records) instead of a whole data set either is more desired because it eliminates further data manipulation or is required by Web Services (e.g., WFS). Finally, the search is primarily based on string matching and advanced method without a consideration of the geographical semantics. That is, what *cropland* really means by the user? Does the user also want *grain land*, *pasture land*, *agricultural land*, etc. if *croplands* do not exist in a portal? Without a method of semantic integration, such semantically similar terms will not be returned to the user.

ONTOLOGICAL AND SEMANTIC CONSIDERATIONS IN GEOSPATIAL PORTALS

This section will discuss how ontological and semantic technologies have been incorporated into geospatial portals, and also introduce the potentials

of these technologies to improve interoperability. As stated early, because the interoperation of tools and services also involve the semantic and ontological methods, this section will focus on semantic data integration that can be applied to tools and services as well.

Common Data Models

There are two approaches to data interoperability on geospatial portals: common data model and algorithm-based automated semantic integration. A common data model may employ one or a set of standards to regulate the definitions of data, which all portal participants are required to adopt. Therefore, a common data model is a top-down approach to interoperability. Here, the data model means the representation of geometry and attributes elements of geospatial data. OGC defines an "essential model" as an *open* and *universal* geospatial data model for understanding geographical information representation and transformation. The essential model specifically defined *points*, *geometry*, *feature* and *feature collections*, *spatial reference systems, transformations, shapes*, etc. (OGC, 2008). OGC also develops GML to represent and transfer geospatial data over the Internet.

A "good" data model is expected to express every aspect of geospatial data. However, the representation, storage, retrieval and application of the model might be too complicated. Defining a common model may raise cultural, political and administrative issues. A "consensus" might never be realized. In fact, "the more you want to get people to agree, the more differences will be found." (Harvey, Kuhn, Pundt, & Bishr, 1999). This is particularly true for the Internet-based geospatial portals. It is not uncommon to see potential data providers are not willing to participate in a portal because there are too many requirements and standards to follow.

Due to the complexity and difficulty of semantic level heterogeneity, most standards and common data models are for system and syntax level interoperation. The FGDC metadata has standardized metadata elements to support the search of metadata elements; however data providers can use their own values of FGDC metadata elements even they agree to use the metadata, which likely result in semantic heterogeneity in data content.

Sometimes a simple and minimal common data model is employed. Users are allowed to add their own details in data content and to decide relations between their data and the common models. For example, GOS offers nineteen broad ISO standard data categories given below. Data providers can decide which categories their data belong to.

Agriculture and Farming
Biology and Ecology
Administrative and Political Boundaries
Atmospheric and Climatic
Business and Economic
Elevation and Derived Products
Environment and Conservation
Geological and Geophysical
Human Health and Disease
Imagery and Base Maps
Military
Inland Water Resources
Locations and Geodetic Networks
Oceans and Estuaries
Cadastral
Cultural, Society, and Demographics
Facilities and Structures
Transportation Networks
Utilities and Communication

Since common data models are agreed and employed by information communities, most of the interoperability tasks are achieved by registering data to the common models by human experts manually. On the other hand, automated semantic integration, which is a bottom-up approach by integrating actual data in portals, releases both providers and portals from making standards. Computer algorithm based automated semantic integration may take four consecutive steps:

semantic normalization, similarity discovery, similarity representation and semantic integration (Kalfoglou, Hu, Reynolds, & Shadbolt, 2005). Research has been conducted to automate one or few steps of semantic integration. Using individual data as a local ontology, the semantics of data can be integrated into a global ontology (upper ontology) with methods of ontology integration and ontology alignment (Cruz and Suna, 2008; Fonseca, Egenhofer, Davis, & Camara, 2002). Another group of research, called feature-based similarity measurement, employs a common set of features to define real-world objects and the semantics of the objects can be compared and integrated based on the features (Feng & Flewelling, 2004; Rodriguez & Egenhofer, 2000). Using document classification methods, Zhou (2004) extracted the semantic definitions of land categories and classified the semantics (based on the definitions) into different groups, from which the degree of semantic similarities are produced by the classification process. Note that some automated methods may use a common data model for the semantic normalization step of semantic integration, while the other three steps are executed by computer algorithms.

Ontology- and Semantic-Enabled System Architecture

Ontologies together with semantic integration methods can sit between the portal catalogue and the user interface. The common data model is indeed an ontology of all the data stored on a geospatial portal. Figure 4 shows the proposed OGC architecture using information community for semantic interoperability among different communities. Every community can provide OGC-compliant data and a semantic mediator (translator) between every pair of communities. The semantic translators are created such that data are mapped to other information communities.

Figure 5 depicts a framework of enhancing geospatial portals with the bottom-up semantic

Figure 4. OGC data interoperability

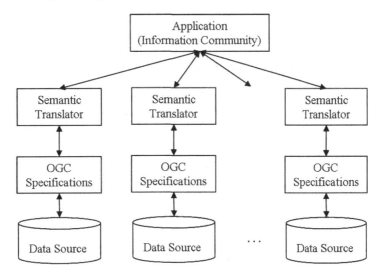

integration approach. With land categories as a case study, this framework addresses the above-mentioned example *find all datasets that have cropland in California*. First of all, the semantic definitions for individual categories are constructed from metadata. Computer algorithms are executed to measure the semantic similarities among geospatial categories (as numerical values and as qualitative relations). Then the land categories are merged into higher level categories (as an upper ontology) based on the semantic similarity measures. Semantic similarities and definitions are stored in OWL made available as Web Services. After the semantic integration process, users are provided an overview of all land categories on a single interface. Portal queries are primarily based on this global view of diverse land categories.

Semantic-Enabled Data Publishing, Discovering and Searching

Semantic-enabled geospatial portals require data providers to include semantic annotations to be used in semantic integration. Unfortunately, a large portion of current portal data does not explicitly include such semantic information. The data

publishing process may employ a common data model, or use automated integration algorithms to investigate semantic relations between data. Once data are integrated, a global view of diverse data is constructed. Semantic-enabled data discovering and search will significantly improve the usability of geospatial portals. In Figure 5, the global view of diverse data not only makes data search more efficient and accurate, but also provides knowledge of the data on geospatial portals so that the portals are transparent to users.

Software Agents for Geospatial Portals

Software agents play a central role in Semantic Web and ontological engineering. An agent can consult ontologies and be executed to facilitate data and service integration. Therefore, intelligent agents can automate the process of interoperation. Zhou and Li (2005) proposed a framework of using multi-agents for semantic-based data search using five types of agents (query agent, discovery agent, metadata agent, schema agent, and semantic agent). Figure 6 depicts the example to find *cropland* which may be finally converted

Figure 5. The architecture of a semantic-enabled geospatial portal

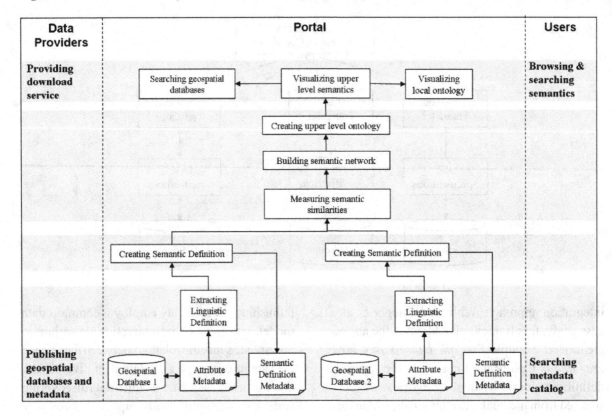

to *cropland/pasture* in semantics and *Land Use Type* in schema for a particular data set (Figure 6).

CASE STUDIES

This section briefly introduces three recent research and practice of geospatial portals with a special focus on the service-oriented portals. GOS is evolving from a metadata portal to a service-oriented portal, but will not be included here. The detailed discussion of GOS can be found in Goodchild et al. (2007) and Tang and Selwood (2005).

Semantic-Enabled SDI

Similar to the idea introduced in Figure 6 but in the form of OGC Web Services, Janowicz et

al. (2010) proposed a transparent Semantic Enablement Layer (SEL) based on OGC services (Figure 7). Although presented for SDI, SEL can be employed in geospatial portals because geospatial portals is a major component of SDI. SEL consists of a Web Ontology Service (WOS) to create, update and retrieve appropriate ontologies, and a Web Reasoning Service (WRS) to facilitate knowledge-based reasoning. WOS is developed as a profile of OGC CSW and the WRS as a profile of Web Processing Service (WPS). This approach requires semantic annotations to link data or services to predefined ontologies. WOS contains the definitions of different geospatial features, processes, etc. such as *Factory, NaturalReserve* and *InhabitedPlace*. In order to find all *natural reserves* in a certain area defined by a bounding box, WOS and WRS execute algorithms of semantic similarity measurement to look up all

Figure 6. Using multi-agent technology for semantic-based data search and query (Source: Zhou & Li 2005)

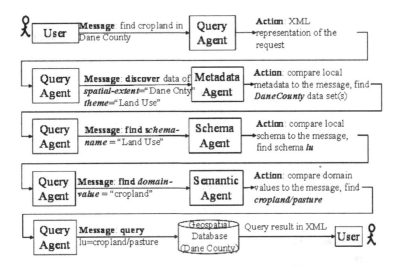

Figure 7. Using WOS and WRS to find natural reserve within a bounding box (Source: Janowicz et al. 2010)

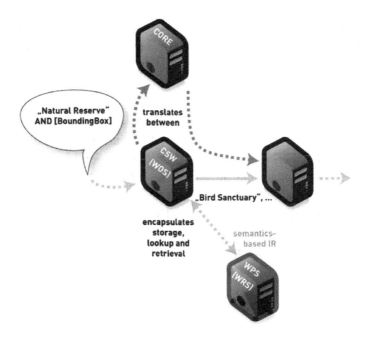

features that are semantically similar with *natural reserves* within the bounding box. This look up process is called reasoning. The result of query would include features such as *Bird Sanctuary* in a specific region.

Ocean Observing System

The Ocean Observing System (OOS) is developed by the OOSTethys community as a service-oriented portal of real time marine data (Figure

Figure 8. The architecture of OOS (Source: OOSTethys, http://www.oostethys.org/)

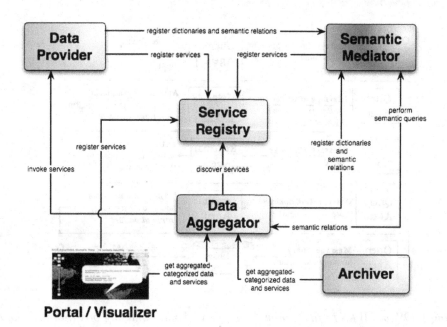

8). Local ocean observation systems collect ocean data (temperature, water level, etc.) and participate in the OOS portal using the SOA architecture. OOS consists of six components including data provider, service registry, semantic mediator, data aggregator, visualizer and archiver. Data providers serve their data and models as services of SOAP, WMS, WFS or WCS. The semantic mediator is in charge of the management of a controlled vocabulary, the registration and mapping of terms to the vocabulary. The semantic issue is addressed within the semantic mediator; for example, by consulting the stored mappings the relation *upward_sea-water_velocity* will be converted to *Ocean Currents*.

Semantic Integration and Visualization

Zhou and Wei (2008) developed natural language processing (NLP) methods to automate the semantic integration of diverse land categories in GOS sample data. Following the framework illustrated in Figure 5 and the bottom-up approach, computer algorithms can compute the semantic similarity of land use categories assisted by WordNet. Land categories are merged into an upper ontology. The ontology is modeled as a semantic network and a taxonomy with semantic relations between categories represented explicitly. In the network and the taxonomy each category is linked to related categories and corresponding metadata as well. Web-based visual tools are provided to browse and select categories in the ontology. These algorithms and tools are developed as a standalone application that can be plugged into different geospatial portals. Figure 9 illustrates an application of the above-mentioned tools to find certain land categories in data content. This example uses three heterogeneous land cover data sets, Washington, D.C., Maryland and Virginia. When a user wants to search and map *high density residential* lands within one mile to the Chesapeake Bay costal line, he or she may find that there are *high intensity residential* lands in Maryland dataset, *residential* lands in Washington, DC dataset, and *developed, high intensity* lands in Virginia datasets. Without a semantic solution,

Figure 9. Visualizing and querying semantically integrated land categories on geospatial portals: semantic network (upper right), ontology (lower right) (Adapted from Zhou and Wei 2008)

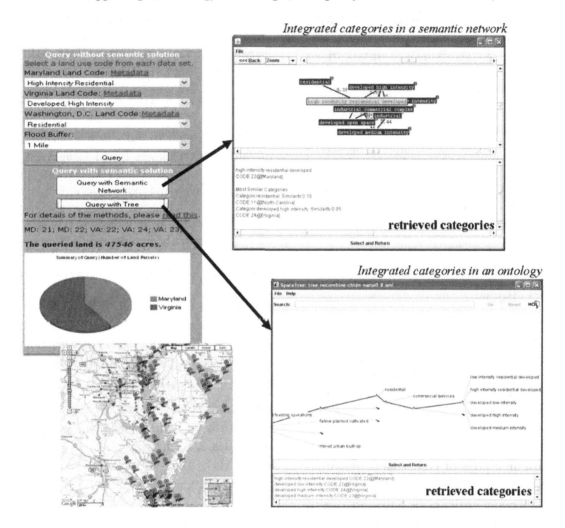

the user needs to study the metadata of each data set to identify these similar terms and pose three queries to the data. Instead, all the categories in the three data sets are visually presented to users together with their semantic relations. Users can select one or few categories and all related categories will be returned and queried.

FUTURE RESEARCH DIRECTIONS

Ontology and semantic technologies are being investigated in geographic information science

and are far from success. Geospatial portals have not fully incorporated these technologies either. Future research directions may include constructing widely accepted ontologies of geospatial data, tools and other services, developing automated and intelligent integration methods for multiple ontologies, and fully implementing the Semantic Web and the Geospatial Web (Scharl, 2007). Building services of ontologies and semantic integration methods will be at the core of service-oriented portals and related research is still in its early stage. Semantic Web Services (SWS) may be the solution to enabling ontological and semantic technologies into Web Services, which is defined as "self-contained, self-describing, semantically marked-up software resources that can be published, discovered, composed and executed across the Web in a task driven automatic way" (Arroyo et al., 2004). Enabled by the research of ontology, semantics and Web Services, software agents should be developed to make intelligent geospatial portals. Finally, the emerging cyberinfrastructure is proposed to provide high performance computing capability and bring more resources into geospatial portals. If this new vision of computing is fulfilled, it will significantly affect the architecture, capability and application of geospatial portals.

CONCLUSION

This chapter provides an overview of geospatial portals, and discusses the issues and potentials of the ontological and semantic technologies for geospatial portals. Geospatial portals is able to meet the increasing demands of geospatial data and geoprocessing tasks. However, the heterogeneity in system, syntax and semantics that exist in almost all aspects of geospatial portals from their construction, operation and applications, becomes a major barrier to the further success of geospatial portals. The standardization of data models, geoprocessing and service protocols has achieved a significant degree of interoperability. Unfortunately, the semantic and ontological issues may not be fully addressed by standards because of the nature and the complexity of the question. Research of semantic interoperability and ontological engineering are needed to construct intelligent and service-oriented geospatial portals and hence to further promote Internet-based sharing of data, tools and services.

REFERENCES

Agarwal, P. (2005). Ontological considerations in GIScience. *International Journal of Geographical Information Science, 19*(5), 501–536. doi:10.1080/13658810500032321

Arroyo, S., Lara, R., Gómez, J., Berka, D., Ding, Y., & Fensel, D. (2004). Semantic aspects of Web services. In Singh, M. (Ed.), *Practical Handbook of Internet Computing*. Baton Rouge, LA and New York, NY: Chapman & Hall and CRC Press. doi:10.1201/9780203507223.ch31

Bishr, Y. (1998). Overcoming the semantic and other barriers to GIS interoperability. *International Journal of Geographical Information Science, 12*(4), 299–314. doi:10.1080/136588198241806

Buehler, K., & McKee, L. (Eds.). (1996). *The OpenGIS Guide: introduction to interoperable geoprocessing and the OpenGIS specification.* OGIS TC Document 96-001, OGIS Project 6 Technical Committee of the OpenGIS Consortium, Inc.

Cruz, I., & Sunna, W. (2008). Structural alignment methods with applications to geospatial ontologies. *Transactions in GIS, 12*(6), 683–711. doi:10.1111/j.1467-9671.2008.01126.x

ESRI. (2007). *ESRI geospatial portal technology.* Retrieved July 13, 2010, from http://www.esri.com/library/whitepapers/pdfs/geospatial-portal-technology.pdf

Feng, C., & Flewelling, D. M. (2004). Assessment of semantic similarity between land use/land cover classification systems. *Computers, Environment and Urban Systems, 28,* 229–246. doi:10.1016/S0198-9715(03)00020-6

Fonseca, F., Egenhofer, M., Davis, C., & Camara, G. (2002). Semantic granularity in ontology-driven geographic information systems. *Annals of Mathematics and Artificial Intelligence, 36,* 121–151. doi:10.1023/A:1015808104769

GeoSpatial One-Stop. Retrieved July 13, 2010, from http://gos2.geodata.gov/wps/portal/gos

Goodchild, M., Fu, P., & Rich, P. (2007). Sharing geographic information: an assessment of the Geospatial One-Stop. *Annals of the Association of American Geographers. Association of American Geographers, 97*(2), 250–266. doi:10.1111/j.1467-8306.2007.00534.x

Guarino, N. (1998). Formal ontology and information systems. In Guarino, N. (Ed.), *Formal ontology in information systems* (pp. 3–15). Amsterdam: IOS Press.

Harvey, F., Kuhn, W., Pundt, H., & Bishr, Y. (1999). Semantic interoperability: a central issue for sharing geographic information. *The Annals of Regional Science, 33*(2), 213–232. doi:10.1007/s001680050102

Hipkiss, R. (1995). *Semantics: defining the discipline.* Mahwah, NJ: Lawrence Erlbaum Associates.

Homburg, V. (2008). *Understanding e-government: Information systems in public administration.* New York, NY: Routledge.

Janowicz, J., Broring, A., Maue, P., Schade, S., Kebler, C., & Stasch, C. (2010). Semantic enablement for Spatial Data Infrastructures. *Transactions in GIS, 14*(2), 111–129. doi:10.1111/j.1467-9671.2010.01186.x

Kalfoglou, Y., Hu, B., Reynolds, D., & Shadbolt, N. (2005). *Semantic integration technologies survey. Technical report, e-print #10842.* University of Southampton.

Maguire, D., & Longley, P. (2005). The emergence of geoportals and their role in spatial data infrastructures. *Computers, Environment and Urban Systems, 29,* 3–14.

Mayer-Schonberger, V., & Lazer, D. (Eds.). (2007). *Governance and information technology: from electronic government to information government.* Cambridge, MA: MIT Press.

Murray, D. (2009). True spatial data interoperability: new tools are turning a dream into reality. *GeoWorld.* March 2009, 24-26.

National Center for Geographic Information and Analysis. (2004). *Specialist meeting on Spatial Webs and Data Integration.* December 2-4, Santa Barbara, CA.

National Research Council. (2003). *IT Roadmap to a geospatial future.* Washington, D.C.: National Academies Press.

National Science Foundation (NSF). (2007). *Cyberinfrastructure vision for 21st century discovery.* Retrieved July 13, 2010, from http://www.nsf.gov/pubs/2007/nsf0728/nsf0728.pdf

OGC. (2008). *Open GIS Reference Model.* Retrieved July 13, 2010, from http://www.opengeospatial.org/standards/orm

Rodriguez, M., Egenhofer, M., & Rugg, R. (2004). Comparing geospatial entity classes: an asymmetric and context-dependent similarity measure. *International Journal of Geographical Information Science, 18,* 229–256. doi:10.1080/13658810310001629592

Scharl, A. (2007). Towards the geospatial Web: media platforms for managing geotagged knowledge repositories. In Scharl, A., & Tochtermann, K. (Eds.), *The Geospatial Web: how geobrowsers, social software and the Web 2.0 are shaping the network society* (pp. 3–14). London: Springer.

Su, Y., Jin, Z., & Peng, J. (2010). Building service oriented sharing platform for emergency management – an earthquake damage assessment example. In Luo, Q. (Ed.), *Advancing computing, communication, control and management, lecture notes in electrical engineering* (*Vol. 56,* pp. 247–255). London: Springer. doi:10.1007/978-3-642-05173-9_32

Tait, M. (2005). Implementing geoportals: applications of distributed GIS. *Computers, Environment and Urban Systems, 29,* 33–47.

Tang, W., & Selwood, J. (2005). *Spatial portals: gateways to geographic information.* Redland, CA: ESRI Press.

U.S. Executive Order 12906. (1994). Coordinating geographic data acquisition and access: the national Spatial Data Infrastructure. Retrieved July 11, 2010, from http://www.fgdc.gov/nsdi/policyandplanning/executive_order

Yang, C., Evans, J., Cole, M., Marley, S., Alameh, N., & Bambacus, M. (2007). The emerging concepts and applications of the spatial Web portal. *Photogrammetric Engineering and Remote Sensing, 73*(6), 691–698.

Zhang, T., & Tsou, M. (2009). Developing a grid-enabled spatial Web portal for Internet GIServices and geospatial cyberinfrastructure. *International Journal of Geographical Information Science, 23*(5), 605–630. doi:10.1080/13658810802698571

Zhao, P., Di, L., Han, W., Wei, Y., & Li, X. (2008, June). *Building service-oriented architecture based geospatial web portal.* Paper presented at the 2008 Geoinformatics Conference, Potsdam, Germany.

Zhou, N. (2003). A study on automatic ontology mapping of categorical information. In *Proceedings of national conference on digital government research.* 401-404.

Zhou, N. (2008). Geospatial semantic integration. In S. Shekhar, & H. Xiong (Eds.), *Encyclopedia of GIS.* 386-388. New York: Springer.

Zhou, N., & Wei, H. (2008). Semantic integration and visualization for geospatial data portals. In *Proceedings of the 2008 international Conference on Digital Government Research.* 417-418. Digital Government Society of North America.

ADDITIONAL READING

Agarwal, P. (2005). Ontological considerations in GIScience. *International Journal of Geographical Information Science, 19*(5), 501–536. doi:10.1080/13658810500032321

Bishr, Y. (1998). Overcoming the semantic and other barriers to GIS interoperability. *International Journal of Geographical Information Science, 12*(4), 299–314. doi:10.1080/136588198241806

Doan, A., & Halevy, A. (2005). Semantic integration research in the database community: a brief survey. *AI Magazine, 26*(1), 83–94.

Goodchild, M., Fu, P., & Rich, P. (2007). Sharing geographic information: an assessment of the geospatial one-stop. *Annals of the Association of American Geographers. Association of American Geographers, 97*(2), 250–266. doi:10.1111/j.1467-8306.2007.00534.x

Guarino, N. (1998). Formal ontology and information systems. In N. Guarino (Ed.), *Formal ontology in information systems.* 3-15. Amsterdam: IOS Press.

Harvey, F., Kuhn, W., Pundt, H., & Bishr, Y. (1999). Semantic interoperability: a central issue for sharing geographic information. *The Annals of Regional Science, 33*, 213–232. doi:10.1007/s001680050102

Homburg, V. (2008). *Understanding e-government: Information Systems in public administration.* New York, NY: Routledge.

Maguire, D., & Longley, P. (2005). The emergence of geoportals and their role in spatial data infrastructures. *Computers, Environment and Urban Systems, 29*, 3–14.

Murray, D. (2009). True spatial data interoperability: new tools are turning a dream into reality. *GeoWorld.* March 2009, 24-26.

National Science Foundation (NSF). (2007). *Cyberinfrastructure vision for 21st Century discovery*. Retrieved July 13, 2010, from http://www.nsf.gov/pubs/2007/nsf0728/nsf0728.pdf

OGC. (2008). *Open GIS reference model*. Retrieved July 13, 2010, from http://www.opengeo-spatial.org/standards/orm

Scharl, A. (2007). Towards the Geospatial Web: media platforms for managing geotagged knowledge repositories. In A. Scharl & K. Tochtermann (Eds.), *The Geospatial Web: How geobrowsers, social software and the Web 2.0 are shaping the network society*. 3-14. London: Springer.

Tait, M. (2005). Implementing geoportals: Applications of distributed GIS. *Computers, Environment and Urban Systems*, *29*, 33–47.

Tang, W., & Selwood, J. (2005). *Spatial portals: gateways to geographic information*. Redland, CA: ESRI Press.

U.S. Executive Order 12906. (1994). Coordinating geographic data acquisition and access: the national Spatial Data Infrastructure. Retrieved July 11, 2010, from http://www.fgdc.gov/nsdi/policyandplanning/executive_order

Yang, C., Evans, J., Cole, M., Marley, S., Alameh, N., & Bambacus, M. (2007). The emerging concepts and applications of the spatial Web portal. *Photogrammetric Engineering and Remote Sensing*, *73*(6), 691–698.

Zhou, N., & Wei, H. (2008). Semantic integration and visualization for geospatial data portals. In *Proceedings of the 2008 international Conference on Digital Government Research*. 417-418. Digital Government Society of North America.

KEY TERMS AND DEFINITIONS

Clearinghouse: An electronically linked distributed network of geospatial data producers, managers, and users.

Geospatial Portal: A portal of distributed geospatial data, tools and services that supports the management, search, and use of the resources.

Metadata: Data about data. A metadata record is a file of information, which captures the basic characteristics of a data or information resource. It represents the *who, what, when, where, why* and how of the resource.

Ontology: A formal and explicit specification of a shared conceptualization.

Portal: The gateway to the distributed Internet-based resources, including Web pages, data, Web services, etc.

Semantic Integration: A task to measure and merge multiple information based on their semantic relations.

Semantic: The meaning of symbols such as words, graph, and other representations that are employed to describe real-world objects.

Section 5
Distributed Computing

Chapter 11
Geospatial Web Services for Distributed Processing:
Applications and Scenarios

Theodor Foerster
University of Münster, Germany

Bastian Schäffer
University of Münster, Germany

Bastian Baranski
University of Münster, Germany

Johannes Brauner
Technische Universität Dresden, Germany

ABSTRACT

Processing and modeling of geodata are essential parts of the daily work of GIS technology experts. Domain experts often need to perform sophisticated GIS analysis of complex data. Currently, capturing, storing and requesting data are embedded in Spatial Data Infrastructures using Service-Oriented Architectures. GIS analysis is performed locally by first downloading geodata such as from SDIs. With the advancements in network bandwidth, processing power and the standardization of Web technology and Geospatial Web Services, distributed geoprocessing is the next step of realizing GIS analysis on the Web. Geoprocessing Services are considered to be a key aspect of meeting the requirements for distributed geoprocessing on the web.

This chapter provides an overview of the current state-of-the-art approach of distributed geoprocessing by describing the related concepts, such as the OGC Web Processing Service, workflows, Quality of Service and legacy system integration. Furthermore, the chapter demonstrates different applications for distributed geoprocessing. Finally, this chapter examines the introduced concepts by two scenarios.

DOI: 10.4018/978-1-60960-192-8.ch011

1 INTRODUCTION

Geospatial data and maps have become increasingly accessible remotely in a distributed fashion through standardized Geospatial Web Services using Service-Oriented Architectures (SOA) (Lake & Farley, 2007). SOAs are a technical foundation for implementing Spatial Data Infrastructures (SDIs). SDIs focus especially on providing access to and sharing of geospatial data by defining the technical and organizational framework. The technical framework is often based on common data models and a set of standard Geospatial Web Service interfaces integrated using the SOA paradigm. A number of Geopatial Web Service interfaces are specified as open standards by the Open Geospatial Consortium (OGC) and the International Organization for Standardization (ISO). Currently SDIs address data delivery and web mapping, but the requirement for real-time geoinformation (extracted by GIS analysis based on most recent geodata in real-time) is not yet met by current SDI implementations. The need for near real-time geodata and geoprocessing increases for many geographic applications, such as emergency services, risk management and alerting, in which data from different sources have to be integrated to support decision making with real-time geoinformation. Geoinformation is generated from geodata using geoprocess models (i.e. models of real-world geoprocesses). Thus, embedding geoprocess models into the web, which facilitate distributed Geospatial Web Services for providing geospatial data in real-time, is a prerequisite to achieve web-based geoinformation. In this chapter, creating and performing geoprocess models that are encapsulated as Web Services and access remote resources (i.e. Geoprocessing Services or Data Services) to generate geoinformation is called *distributed geoprocessing*.

The aim of this chapter is to give an overview about the current approaches for distributed geoprocessing. The chapter will introduce the basic concepts (Section 2) for distributed geoprocessing

by using the OGC Web Processing Service (WPS), establishing geoprocessing workflows, ensuring Quality of Service (Grid and Cloud Computing) and integrating functionality of legacy systems. Based on these concepts the chapter describes applications (Section 3), in which distributed geoprocessing on the web is utilized to provide real-time geoinformation. In particular, it will demonstrate how geoinformation extracted from web-based geospatial data can be integrated into mass-market applications. Two scenarios are described based on the introduced concepts to illustrate the full potential of distributed geoprocessing on the Web (Section 4). Section 5 will conclude the described approaches and will provide an outlook about future challenges. All the examples mentioned in this chapter are implemented as Open Source software at the 52°North Geoprocessing Community[1].

As this chapter focuses on distributed geoprocessing, the reader may refer to other chapters of the book for getting specific information on related topics such as Geospatial Web Services, data services (e.g. WFS, WCS).

2 RELEVANT CONCEPTS FOR DISTRIBUTED GEOPROCESSING

Geoprocesses are real-world processes that are modeled in computer systems to simulate and analyze real-world phenomena. For this chapter geoprocessing is defined as the application of a model representing a real-world geoprocess. As a result, geoprocessing is the transformation of geodata to geoinformation. The definitions of geodata and geoinformation are closely related to the definitions of data and information besides their specific geospatial focus. Geodata and geoinformation describe geospatial phenomena at different levels of abstraction. The terms data and information are not clearly defined in literature. This chapter follows the definitions of Ackoff (1989) and Chen et al. (2009). Ackoff (1989) defines data as a set of symbols and information as data which is processed to answer specific questions. Chen et al. (2009) applied these definitions to the computational domain by defining data as computational representations of models and attributes of real world or simulated entities (i.e. geospatial phenomena). Whereas information is data which have meaning attached and is thereby understandable by computational systems or human users.

Consequently, a geoprocess model handles geodata in a geospatial context. The input and the output contain geodata or its interpretation (e.g. a Boolean value to answer, if two geometries intersect each other) and the applied calculation takes the geospatial context into account. Examples of such models are simple buffer computations, geostatistical analysis or large-scale simulations of noise distribution.

A Web Service can be defined as a software component that provides functionality including access to data sources through a web-accessible interface in a programming language- and platform-independent manner (Vaughan-Nichols, 2002). The Web Service interface is described in a machine-understandable way, which is a fundamental requirement for interoperability. Based on these interfaces Web Services connect readily available software components on the Web in a loosely coupled way (Alonso, Casati, Kuno, & Machiraju, 2004). Loosely coupled means that the service interaction is established during runtime and the services do not know each other in advance. This enables to reuse software components in different applications. Moreover, as Web Services communicate based on platform-independent protocols (i.e. Hypertext Transfer Protocol) and exchange formats (i.e. XML), they can be reused by any application written in any programming language and/or running on any operating system. Additionally, Web Services are stateless software components that do not expose a specific state to the client and remain stateless before and after client interaction. This is a central

design characteristic to keep the architecture scalable and flexible for many different applications.

Establishing and performing geoprocess models over a network was initially achieved in the 1980s, when clients were able to trigger computations performed on remote computers. Since the advent of the Web and Web Services, it is possible to establish distributed architectures. Distributed architectures involve more than two remote nodes communicating with each other in a loosely-coupled way. This loosely-coupled communication is a characteristic of the web and is reflected for instance by the Publish-Find-Bind paradigm of SOA, in which the binding between the different nodes is established during runtime (Alonso et al., 2004).

Consequently, an architecture is termed distributed if it consists of more than two entities not located on the same node. Thereby several mechanisms are required to establish distributed geoprocessing:

- Standardization of the single nodes (i.e. Data Services, Registries and Geoprocessing Services)
- Managing the communication between multiple nodes through geoprocessing workflows
- Ensuring a Quality of Service (operational level)
- Incorporating existing geoprocess models (functional level).

Establishing single (OGC WPS) and complex geoprocess models (geoprocessing workflows) is the foundation for realizing distributed geoprocessing. Further, distributed geoprocessing can be enhanced once these geoprocess models are established on an operational level and on a functional level.

A requirement for establishing distributed architectures is interoperability. Interoperability is defined as the capability of two services to communicate at runtime to meet a common goal (Alonso et al., 2004). Web Services ensure interoperability by common service interfaces and standardized message encodings.

Interoperability can be established on two levels: the syntactic level and the semantic level. Syntactic interoperability is ensured by common service interfaces (i.e. syntax of input and output parameters). Semantic interoperability is established by meaningful interpretation of the interfaces and the exchanged messages.

One of the research challenges for Geoprocessing Services is semantic descriptions, which are the means to enable semantic interoperability of Web Services (Brauner, Foerster, Bastian Schaeffer, & Baranski, 2009). Other research challenges are:

- Service orchestration
- Strategies to improve performance.

This section will introduce the OGC Web Processing Service (OGC WPS) as the building block for establishing geoprocess models on the Web. Based on OGC's specification baseline, the WPS defines a way of publishing and performing geoprocess models on the web. As geoinformation is typically generated using some geoprocess models that are composed of single Geoprocessing Services, geoprocessing workflows play a major role (Section 2.2). In this respect this section also introduces an OGC compliant way of publishing workflows on the web based on the WPS interface specification (WPS-Transactional). To improve distributed geoprocessing on the operational level in terms of reliability and performance, Grid and Cloud Computing and corresponding Quality of Service (QoS) guarantees will be described in Section 2.3. Finally, to enable the reuse of existing GIS functionality (incorporated in so-called legacy systems) and improve the functional level of distributed geoprocessing, Section 2.4 demonstrates an approach for wrapping existing functionaliy of legacy systems with a standard interface for distributed geoprocessing. Further usage of existing functionality contributes to the sustainability of SDIs.

2.1 OGC Web Processing Service

In 2007, the OGC approved version 1.0.0 of the OGC Web Processing Service interface specification. The WPS interface specification describes a standardized method to publish and execute web-based geoprocess models of any type (OGC, 2007). According to the WPS interface specification, a geoprocess model is defined as any calculation operating on geodata.

In detail, the WPS interface specification describes three operations, which are all handled in a stateless manner: GetCapabilities, DescribeProcess and Execute. GetCapabilities is common to any type of OGC Web Service and returns service metadata. In case of WPS it also returns a brief description of the geoprocess models offered by the specific service instance. To get more information about the hosted geoprocess models, the WPS provides metadata about the geoprocess model through the DescribeProcess operation. This operation describes all input and output parameters of the geoprocess model. Based on this information the client can perform the Execute operation with the specific input parameters upon the designated geoprocess model. This course of action is depicted in Figure 1. Section 2.1.1 illustrates this course of action by request examples performing desired generalization functionality.

Figure 1. Basic WPS communication

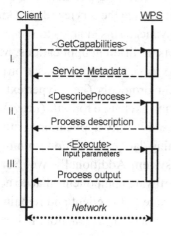

Section 2.1.2 describes how semantic interoperability is currently addressed by the WPS interface specification.

For the remainder of this chapter, geoprocess models provided by WPS are called *WPS-based geoprocess models*.

2.1.1 OGC WPS in Action

To illustrate a workflow sequence that triggers a WPS-based geoprocess model, this section describes the basic communication. In this example, a WPS instance is queried for a Douglas-Peucker algorithm (Douglas & Peucker, 1973) to simplify a set of road geometries. The listed XML messages are in most cases generated by client applications, which guide the user during Web Services interaction by harvesting user input and performing the requests accordingly. Such a client application is presented in Section 3.3. The listed examples are all based on the current version 1.0.0 of the WPS interface specification (OGC, 2007).

For reasons of simplicity it is assumed that the user knows the entry point of the WPS instance in advance. In real-world scenarios such entry points can be retrieved from catalog services. To get more information about the service the user queries the service metadata using a GetCapabilities request (Listing 1). The response of the WPS instance is depicted in Listing 2. From this response document the user can retrieve the service metadata, such as entry points for further communication (OperationsMetadata) or individual information about the provider (ServiceProvider). Also the provided geoprocess models are listed in the (ProcessOfferings). One of these geoprocess models listed is the Douglas-Peucker algorithm, which is briefly described with identifier, title and abstract. The identifier of the geoprocess model can be used to retrieve further metadata.

DescribeProcess provides this metadata based on the identifier of the designated geoprocess model (e.g. DouglasPeuckerAlgorithm). The DescribeProcess request (Listing 3) queries the WPS instance for further metadata on the specific geoprocess model such as input and output parameters. This information is important to trigger the specific geoprocess model appropriately. In the given example (Listing 4), the Douglas-Peucker algorithm requires complex data for the geometries to be processed and literal data (of type double) to indicate the tolerance value the algorithm has to apply to the data.

Based on these metadata, the client knows where (entry points in service metadata, Listing 2) and how (process metadata, Listing 4) to trigger the designated geoprocess model. The client performs the Execute request (Listing 5) with the designated parameters (geometries and tolerance value). The complex data (i.e. the geometries to be simplified) are included in the request as a reference to a WFS instance. The WPS has to retrieve the data from this location and process them accordingly. This is beneficial to limit the communication overhead between client and WPS instance, as the WPS instance can retrieve the data directly. Additionally, this enables the WPS instance to apply caching strategies, as the service can decide if and when to retrieve the data. Finally, the WPS instance returns the simplified geometries (Listing 6).

This basic sequence of actions can be extended by requesting asynchronous processing or storing of process results on the server side.

Listing 1. Example GetCapabilities request for WPS.

```
http://geoserver.itc.nl:8080/wps/WebProcessingService?REQUEST=GetCapabilities&
Service=WWP;
```

Listing 2. Example GetCapabilities response for WPS.

```
<?xml version="1.0" encoding="UTF-8"?>
<wps:Capabilities service="WPS" version="1.0.0" xml:lang="en-US"
xsi:schemaLocation="http://www.opengis.net/wps/1.0.0http://geoserver.itc.
nl:8080/wps/schemas/wps/1.0.0/wpsGetCapabilities_response.xsd" updateSe-
quence="1" xmlns:xlink="http://www.w3.org/1999/xlink" xmlns:wps="http://
www.opengis.net/wps/1.0.0" xmlns:ows="http://www.opengis.net/ows/1.1"
xmlns:xsi="http://www.w3.org/2001/XMLSchema-instance">
     <ows:ServiceIdentification>
          <ows:Title>My WPS</ows:Title>
          <ows:Abstract>Service based on the 52north implementation of WPS
1.0.0</ows:Abstract>
          <ows:Keywords>
               <ows:Keyword>generalization</ows:Keyword>
               <ows:Keyword>geoprocessing</ows:Keyword>
          </ows:Keywords>
          <ows:ServiceType>WPS</ows:ServiceType>
          <ows:ServiceTypeVersion>1.0.0</ows:ServiceTypeVersion>
          ...
     </ows:ServiceIdentification>
     <ows:ServiceProvider>
          <ows:ProviderName>52North</ows:ProviderName>
          <ows:ProviderSite xlink:href="http://www.52north.org/"/>
          ...
     </ows:ServiceProvider>
     <ows:OperationsMetadata>
          <ows:Operation name="GetCapabilities">
               <ows:DCP>
                    <ows:HTTP>
                         <ows:Get xlink:href="http://geoserver.itc.nl:8080/
wps/WebProcessingService"/>
                    </ows:HTTP>
               </ows:DCP>
          </ows:Operation>
          <ows:Operation name="DescribeProcess">
               <ows:DCP>
                    <ows:HTTP>
                         <ows:Get xlink:href="http://geoserver.itc.nl:8080/
wps/WebProcessingService"/>
                    </ows:HTTP>
               </ows:DCP>
```

continued on the following page

Listing 2. continued

```
        </ows:Operation>
        <ows:Operation name="Execute">
            <ows:DCP>
                <ows:HTTP>
                    <ows:Get xlink:href="http://geoserver.itc.nl:8080/
wps/WebProcessingService"/>
                    <ows:Post xlink:href="http://geoserver.itc.nl:8080/
wps/WebProcessingService"/>
                </ows:HTTP>
            </ows:DCP>
        </ows:Operation>
    </ows:OperationsMetadata>
    <wps:ProcessOfferings>
        <wps:Process wps:processVersion="2">
            <ows:Identifier>DouglasPeuckerAlgorithm</ows:Identifier>
            <ows:Title>douglasPeucker algorithm</ows:Title>
        </wps:Process>
        ...
    </wps:ProcessOfferings>
    ...
</wps:Capabilities>
```

Listing 3. Example DescribeProcess request retrieving metadata about Douglas-Peucker algorithm.

```
http://geoserver.itc.nl:8080/wps/WebProcessingService?REQUEST=DescribeProcess&
Service=WPS&Identifier=DouglasPeuckerAlgorithm;
```

Listing 4. Example DescribeProcess response describing the interface for the Douglas-Peucker algorithm. <?xml version="1.0" encoding="UTF-8"?>

```
<ns:ProcessDescriptions xmlns:ns="http://www.opengis.net/
wps/1.0.0" xmlns:xsi="http://www.w3.org/2001/XMLSchema-instance"
xsi:schemaLocation="http://www.opengis.net/wps/1.0.0http://schemas.opengis.net/
wps/1.0.0/wpsDescribeProcess_response.xsd" xml:lang="en-US" service="WPS" ver
sion="1.0.0"><ProcessDescription xmlns:wps="http://www.opengis.net/wps/1.0.0"
xmlns:ows="http://www.opengis.net/ows/1.1" xmlns:xlink="http://www.w3.org/1999/
xlink" wps:processVersion="2" storeSupported="true" statusSupported="false">
        <ows:Identifier>DouglasPeuckerAlgorithm</ows:Identifier>
        <ows:Title>douglasPeucker algorithm</ows:Title>
```

continued on the following page

Listing 4. continued

```
        <ows:Abstract>Uses JTS implementation. Does not support topological
awareness</ows:Abstract>
        <ows:Metadata xlink:title="douglas peucker"/>
        <DataInputs>
            <Input minOccurs="1" maxOccurs="1">
                <ows:Identifier>FEATURES</ows:Identifier>
                <ows:Title>input features</ows:Title>
                <ows:Abstract>Just features</ows:Abstract>
                <ComplexData>
                <Default>
                    <Format>
                        <MimeType>text/XML</MimeType>
                        <Schema>http://schemas.opengis.net/gml/2.1.2/
feature.xsd/Schema>
                    </Format>
                </Default>
                </ComplexData>
            </Input>
            <Input minOccurs="1" maxOccurs="1">
                <ows:Identifier>TOLERANCE</ows:Identifier>
                <ows:Title>Tolerance Value for DP Alg</ows:Title>
                <ows:Abstract/>
                <LiteralData>
                <ows:DataType ows:reference="xs:double"/>
                ...
                </LiteralData>
            </Input>
        </DataInputs>
        <ProcessOutputs>
            <Output>
                <ows:Identifier>SIMPLIFIED_FEATURES</ows:Identifier>
                <ows:Title>smooth geometries</ows:Title>
                <ows:Abstract>GML stream describing the smooth feature.</
ows:Abstract>
                <ComplexOutput>
                <Default>
                <Format>
                    <MimeType>text/XML</MimeType>
                    <Schema>http://schemas.opengis.net/gml/2.1.2/feature.
xsd/Schema>
```

continued on the following page

Listing 4. continued

```
            </Format>
            </Default>
            </ComplexOutput>
        </Output>
      </ProcessOutputs>
    </ProcessDescription>
</ns:ProcessDescriptions>
```

Listing 5. Example Execute request for Douglas-Peucker algorithm.

```
<?xml version="1.0" encoding="UTF-8" standalone="yes"?>
<wps:Execute service="WPS" version="1.0.0" xmlns:wps="http://www.opengis.net/
wps/1.0.0" xmlns:ows="http://www.opengis.net/ows/1.1" xmlns:xlink="http://
www.w3.org/1999/xlink" xmlns:xsi="http://www.w3.org/2001/XMLSchema-instance"
xsi:schemaLocation="http://www.opengis.net/wps/1.0.0http://geoserver.itc.
nl:8080/wps/schemas/wps/1.0.0/wpsExecute_request.xsd">
    <ows:Identifier>DouglasPeuckerAlgorithm</ows:Identifier>
    <wps:DataInputs>
        <wps:Input>
            <ows:Identifier>FEATURES</ows:Identifier>
            <wps:Reference schema="http://schemas.opengis.net/
gml/2.1.2/feature.xsd" xlink:href="http://geoserver.itc.nl:8080/ge-
oserver/wfs?REQUEST=GetFeature&amp;typename=topp:states&amp;BB
OX=-75.102613,40.212597,-72.361859,41.512517">
            </wps:Reference>
        </wps:Input>
        <wps:Input>
            <ows:Identifier>TOLERANCE</ows:Identifier>
            <wps:Data>
                <wps:LiteralData>2</wps:LiteralData>
            </wps:Data>
        </wps:Input>
    </wps:DataInputs>
    <wps:ResponseForm>
    <wps:ResponseDocument storeExecuteResponse="false">
        <wps:Output asReference="false">
            <ows:Identifier>SIMPLIFIED_FEATURES</ows:Identifier>
        </wps:Output>
    </wps:ResponseDocument>
    </wps:ResponseForm>
</wps:Execute>
```

Listing 6. Example Execute response for Douglas-Peucker algorithm including process information and simplified geometries.

```
<?xml version="1.0" encoding="UTF-8"?>
<ns:ExecuteResponse xmlns:ns="http://www.opengis.net/
wps/1.0.0" xmlns:xsi="http://www.w3.org/2001/XMLSchema-instance"
xsi:schemaLocation="http://www.opengis.net/wps/1.0.0http://geoserver.itc.
nl:8080/wps/schemas/wps/1.0.0/wpsExecute_response.xsd" serviceInstance="http://
localhost:8080/wps/WebProcessingService?SERVICE=GetCapabilities&amp;SERVICE=W
PS" xml:lang="en-US" service="WPS" version="1.0.0">
    <ns:Process ns:processVersion="2">
        <ns1:Identifier xmlns:ns1="http://www.opengis.net/ows/1.1">org.n52.
wps.server.algorithm.simplify.DouglasPeuckerAlgorithm</ns1:Identifier>
        <ows:Title xmlns:wps="http://www.opengis.net/wps/1.0.0"
xmlns:ows="http://www.opengis.net/ows/1.1" xmlns:xlink="http://www.w3.org/1999/
xlink">douglasPeucker algorithm</ows:Title>
    </ns:Process>
    <ns:Status creationTime="2009-11-16T17:24:14.809+01:00">
        <ns:ProcessSucceeded>The service succesfully processed the request.</
ns:ProcessSucceeded>
    </ns:Status>
    <ns:ProcessOutputs>
        <ns:Output>
            <ns1:Identifier xmlns:ns1="http://www.opengis.net/
ows/1.1">SIMPLIFIED_FEATURES</ns1:Identifier>
            <ows:Title xmlns:wps="http://www.opengis.net/wps/1.0.0"
xmlns:ows="http://www.opengis.net/ows/1.1" xmlns:xlink="http://www.w3.org/1999/
xlink">smooth geometries</ows:Title>
            <ns:Data>
                <ns:ComplexData schema="http://schemas.opengis.net/
gml/2.1.2/feature.xsd" mimeType="text/XML">
                    <wfs:FeatureCollection xmlns="http://www.opengis.net/
wfs" xmlns:gml="http://www.opengis.net/gml" xmlns:states="http://www.openplans.
org/topp" xmlns:wfs="http://www.opengis.net/wfs" xsi:schemaLocation="http://
www.openplans.org/topphttp://geoserver.itc.nl:8080/geoserver/wfs/DescribeFea
tureType?typeName=topp:stateshttp://www.opengis.net/wfshttp://geoserver.itc.
nl:8080/geoserver/schemas/wfs/1.0.0/WFS-basic.xsd">
                        <gml:boundedBy>
                            <gml:Box srsName="http://www.opengis.net/
gml/srs/epsg.xml#4326">
                                <gml:coordinates cs="," decimal="."
ts=" ">-80.5208,39.7195 -73.3451,45.0061</gml:coordinates>
                            </gml:Box>
                        </gml:boundedBy>
```

continued on the following page

Listing 6. continued

```
                            <gml:featureMember>
                                <states:states fid="states.39">
                                    <states:the_geom>
                                        <gml:MultiPolygon srsName="http://
www.opengis.net/gml/srs/epsg.xml#4326">
                                                <gml:polygonMember>
                                                    <gml:Polygon>

<gml:outerBoundaryIs>

<gml:LinearRing>

<gml:coordinates cs="," decimal="." ts=" ">-79.7635,42.2673 -73.3451,45.0061
-74.0066,40.7039 -79.7635,42.2673</gml:coordinates>
                                                                        </
gml:LinearRing>

                                                                    </
gml:outerBoundaryIs>

                                                    </gml:Polygon>
                                                </gml:polygonMember>
                                        </gml:MultiPolygon>
                                    </states:the_geom>
                                    ...
                            </gml:featureMember>
                        </wfs:FeatureCollection>
                    </ns:ComplexData>
                </ns:Data>
            </ns:Output>
        </ns:ProcessOutputs>
</ns:ExecuteResponse>
```

The depicted examples of request and response documents are based on 52°North WPS framework (Section 3.1). Nevertheless, the presented workflow should perform successfully on any OGC-compliant implementation of WPS 1.0.0 specification that offers the exercised processes in such a manner.

2.1.2 Semantic Interoperability of WPS

Semantic interoperability is a key requirement to perform geoprocess models meaningfully on the web. The semantics of a geoprocess model such as provided by WPS are unknown, due to the loosely-coupled nature of the Web and the distributed architecture. The links between the Web Services are established during runtime, based on the descriptions of the Web Services. WPS functionality is described through GetCapabilities and DescribeProcess response documents in particular. The syntax is described in the DescribeProcess documents (exemplified Listing 4), but the semantics of the input and output parameters are missing. Geoprocess models offered by WPS instances can only be described on an abstract level. To overcome this problem, one solution is to predefine specific geoprocess models, which are mandatory for any WPS instance. This solution has specific obstacles, as it is hard to determine a set of fixed geoprocess models, which should be offered by WPS instances.

Another solution is *WPS profiles*. These WPS profiles allow the client to identify syntactically and semantically equal geoprocess models provided by WPS instances. WPS profiles are referenced by process descriptions and describe the input and output parameters of a geoprocess model. The WPS profiles provide a common definition of geoprocess models and can be referenced by other WPS instances, which provide a similar geoprocess or a similar set of geoprocesses (syntactically and semantically). To give an example, let us assume there are two different implementations of a buffer algorithm and both published as WPS-based geoprocess models sharing the same interface (i.e. same input and output parameters). As both geoprocess models refer to the same WPS profile, they become interoperable (i.e. sharing the same interface) but also their functionality becomes comparable to the client. The client can select the appropriate WPS-based geoprocess model based on the quality of the process output and the performance of the geoprocess model. However, matching the semantics of the offered geoprocess model with the WPS profile is the responsibility of the service provider. From a technical perspective, WPS profiles are descriptions of WPS-based geoprocess model (i.e. defining input and output parameters), which

are web-accessible and are identified by an OGC Uniform Resource Name (URN).

Nash (2008) specified an initial set of these WPS profiles describing the most common GIS operations. Ostlaender (2009) also used WPS profiles to describe WPS-based geoprocess models in an SDI for spatial decision support.

WPS profiles are still a subject to research, as it is hard to determine if two geoprocess models are equal and if they can be matched to the same WPS profile. A geoprocess might appear equal for instance to the service provider, but not to the user. Nash (2008) and Bucher & Jolivet (2008) conclude that for meaningful WPS profiles the geoprocessing functionality has to be classified by a commonly agreed taxonomy of geoprocess models which is currently lacking. Finally, an agreed classification of functionality formalized as ontologies is required to enable semantic interoperability and semantic reasoning. Ontologies of such geoprocesses can be built in a coarse grain (Lemmens, 2006) or a fine grain (Lutz, 2007) manner.

2.2 Geoprocessing Workflows

The complexity of geodata and the complexity of the problem domain often require geoprocess models consisting of multiple steps. These complex geoprocess models can be implemented by chaining multiple WPS instances to create a value-added geoprocessing workflow.

In particular, we aim at enabling the full potential of OGC Web Services as an integration platform. This will be achieved when applications and business processes can be composed to perform complex interactions using a standardized process integration approach. Therefore, Geoprocessing Workflows regarded as service chains are one of the key concepts in enabling value-added chains in SDIs (Alameh, 2003).

A *workflow* is defined by ISO as an "automation of a business process, in whole or part, during which documents, information or tasks are passed from one participant to another for action, according to a set of procedural rules" (ISO/TC 211, 2005). For this chapter, the workflow participants are understood as Web Services, which pass information from one workflow participant (i.e. Web Service) to another especially across enterprise boundaries.

A *geoprocessing workflow* combines the concept of geoprocessing (defined in Section 2) and the concept of workflows. This chapter defines geoprocessing workflow as an automation of a geoprocess model, in whole or part, during which information is passed from one Geoprocessing Service to another according to a set of procedural rules using standardized interfaces.

In other words, geoprocessing workflows integrate data and services in an interoperable way, where each part of the workflow is responsible for only a specific task, without being aware of the general purpose of the workflow. Due to the distributed nature of geographic data and by using the presented definition, geoprocessing workflows provide a flexible means of processing highly distributed and complex data for a wide variety of uses across enterprise borders.

Section 2.2.1 will describe how geoprocessing workflows are modeled as service chains in SOAs and will introduce the different patterns of chaining. Moreover, the technologies for realizing such service chains are introduced (Section 2.2.2).

2.2.1 Realizing Geoprocessing Workflows as Service Chains

Workflows implemented as service chains are one of the key concepts in enabling value-added chains in SDIs (Alameh, 2003). The ISO19119/ Service Architecture standard defines service chaining as: "A sequence of services where, for each adjacent pair of services, occurrence of the first action is necessary for the occurrence of the second action" (ISO/TC 211, 2005).

A service chain is a directed graph, since the input of one service depends on the output of another service. A directed graph is defined as a set K of ordered nodes and a set E of edges, where each edge $e(u,v) \in E$ has a direction and consists of a node pair (u,v) where $u,v \in K$.

The nodes in a directed graph represent service entities and the arcs represent the service interactions. Directed acyclic graphs (DAG) are special types of directed graphs. The definition of a directed graph from above has to be extended with the constraint that for any node t, there is always an empty directed path that starts and ends on t.

However, some service chains require iterations and for this reason the graph has to be cyclic and therefore has to make use of conditions in the control function to address convergence.

In addition, there are four more characteristics of a service chain according to ISO19119 (ISO/TC 211, 2005):

- Parallel or serial sequences
- Variations in the links between nodes reflecting different methods of transporting data or invoking the service
- Parameters in nodes
- Pull processing vs. push processing.

Besides, there are three different architectural patterns for service chains defined as a foundation for geoprocessing workflows according to Alameh (2003) and ISO19119 (ISO/TC 211, 2005):

- Transparent chaining
- Translucent chaining
- Opaque chaining.

In the transparent chaining pattern, the knowledgeable user defines a service chain by specifying the different participants of the service chain and by defining the specific sequence of interaction. In particular, the user is responsible for discovering and evaluating available services as well as

Figure 2. Transparent chaining pattern

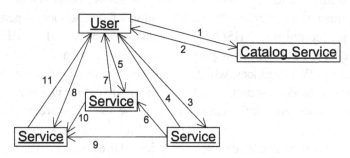

for defining the execution order, invoking the services and pass around process results as inputs. Furthermore, the user has to make sure that input and output messages have to be compatible and all required resources are available. Since all service details are visible to the user, this pattern is called transparent chaining. Figure 2 presents this pattern as an UML collaboration diagram.

In Step 1, the user sends a search request to a catalog service in order to discover service availability. The catalog service returns metadata about services fulfilling the search request. The user creates an execution order and invokes the first service in Step 3. The processed results (or a reference) are returned back to the user in Step 4. These results (or a reference) are passed in the second service in Step 5. If the user supplies a reference, the service has to obtain the actual data in Step 6 from the previous service. Again, the processed results (or a reference) are returned back to the user as can be seen in Step 7. In Step 8, the user invokes the third service with the results from the two previous services. If a reference to actual data is delivered, the third service requests the actual data from the corresponding in Step 9 and Step 10. After processing, the final results are returned to the user in Step 11.

The translucent chaining pattern allows a user to execute a predefined service chain managed by a workflow service. In this pattern, the service chain is already abstractly predefined and stored on a workflow engine. The user is aware of all participants of the service chain, but does

not have to deal with the execution order or with passing around processing results. But since the user knows all participating services, he is able to poll the current status of each participating service (if supported by the service). Figure 3 gives an overview of this pattern.

In Step 1, the user invokes an existing chain on the workflow service. The workflow service starts now the predefined execution order. The first service is invoked in Step 2. Since the user knows, that this service is invoked first, he/she can poll the current processing status of the service (Step 3). The processed results (or a reference) are returned back to the workflow service in Step 4. These results (or a reference) are passed in the second service in Step 5. If the workflow service supplies a reference, the service has to obtain the actual data in Step 6 from the previous service. Again, the user can poll the status in Step 7 and after processing, the results (or a reference) are returned back to the workflow service as can be seen in Step 8. In Step 9, the workflow service invokes the third service with the results from the two previous services. If a reference to actual data is delivered, the third service requests the actual data from the corresponding in Step 10 and Step 11. As seen before, the user is enabled to poll the current service status in Step 12. After processing, the final results are returned to the workflow service in Step 13 and from there back to the user in Step 14.

The opaque chaining pattern exposes a service chain and thereby a geoprocessing workflow as a

Figure 3. Translucent chaining pattern

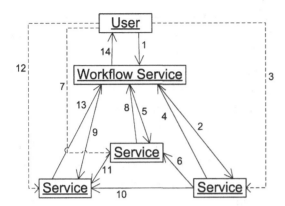

Figure 4. The opaque chaining pattern

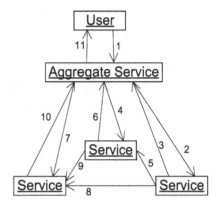

single service and hides all details from the user. The user is not even aware of the fact that the aggregate service hides a chain nor is the user aware of the types of services being used. Therefore, the aggregate service is responsible for all service coordination. Figure 4 describes this pattern.

In Step 1, the user invokes an aggregate service unaware of the implementation details (e.g. if the aggregate service uses a service chain and what kind of services are involved). The aggregate service starts now the predefined execution order at this point, so the first service is invoked in Step 2. The processed results (or a reference) are returned back to the aggregate engine in Step 3. These results (or a reference) are passed in the second service in Step 4. If the aggregate service supplies a reference, the service has to obtain the actual data in Step 5 from the previous service. Again, after processing, the results (or a reference) are returned back to the aggregate service as can be seen in Step 6. In Step 7, the aggregate service invokes the third service with the results from the two previous services. In case a reference to actual data is delivered, the third service requests the actual data from the corresponding service as presented in Step 8 and Step 9. After processing, the final results are returned to the aggregate service in Step 10 and from there back to the user in Step 11.

2.2.2 Technology for Service Chaining

As defined above, a geoprocessing workflow can be seen as a geoprocess model. Typically a geoprocess model incorporates different functionality. If such a geoprocess model is implemented as a SOA, this functionality is provided by different Web Services. Thus to realize such geoprocess models as geoprocessing workflows, the principles of a SOA play an important role.

Web Service Composition and *Web Service Orchestration* describe workflows from a SOA perspective and are therefore relevant concepts for geoprocessing workflows. According to Alonso et al. (2004) Web Service Composition combines several Web Services to one workflow to represent a desired business process. Alonso et al. (2004) define a composite service following the opaque chaining pattern and entitle the act of combining Web Services as *Web Service Composition*. The interaction of the Web Service in the workflow can be handled by *Web Service Orchestration*, which is a description of how combined Web Services interact on the message level (Peltz, 2003). This description includes the business-logic and execution order. *Web Service Orchestration* is often realized by a central orchestration engine coordinating the Web Service interaction according to a predefined workflow description and thereby falls into the opaque architecture pattern. In particular, this approach allows the Web Services to be held loosely coupled (Weerawarana, Curbera, Leymann, Storey, & Ferguson, 2005).

Several orchestration languages are available (Staab et al., 2003). XPDL as a Workflow Management Coalition workflow language, YAWL as a popular open source language (van der Aalst and Hofstede, 2005) and the Business Process Execution Language (BPEL) (Andrews et al., 2003) are the most relevant. In particular BPEL has advanced to a de-facto standard in the mainstream IT-world (van der Aalst et al., 2005). It is an OASIS standard for describing workflows based on elementary tasks implemented as Web Services using an XML-encoding. In particular, these so-called BPEL scripts describe the roles involved in the message exchange, supported port types and orchestration information of a process. Therefore, BPEL seems to be an appropriate candidate to create Geoprocessing Workflows in SOAs, as it enables the composition of workflows based on loosely coupled services.

2.2.3 Current Research & Future Challenges in Geoprocessing Workflows

Designing and realizing geoprocessing workflows are still a subject to current research and also remain future challenges. Leaving the semantic aspect out of scope (as for example addressed by Cardoso & Sheth (2003) and from a geo-related perspective addressed in Roman & Klien (2007)), some research regarding geoprocessing workflows has been accomplished recently. Kiehle, Greve, & Heier (2006) describe a rule-based approach and theoretical foundations for the orchestration of Geoprocessing Services. Granell, Gould, & Ramos (2005) as well as Friis-Christensen et al. (2006) provided conceptual foundations, such as elementary workflow patterns for Geospatial Web Services. Friis-Christensen, Lucchi, Lutz, & Ostlaender (2009) introduced the term *Distributed Geographic Information Processing* (DGIP)

and presented different architectural patterns for chaining of Geoprocessing Services. Besides, Weiser & Zipf (2007) focused on the application side by utilizing BPEL. Schaeffer (2008) showed an application of the opaque chaining pattern to geoprocessing workflows, by extending the WPS with a transactional interface (WPS-T). WPS-T provides a mechanism to deploy geoprocessing workflows, which are modeled as a service chain, as single WPS-based geoprocess models at run-time. Consequently, geoprocessing workflows are encapsulated as WPS-based geoprocess models and can be triggered using OGC-compliant messaging. The approach is based on BPEL but extensible through profiling the deployment procedure for different workflow languages.

On the standardization level, the OGC Interoperability and Specification Programs have also produced a significant body of knowledge and experience in designing, implementing and deploying Web Services (Keens, 2007; B. Schaeffer, 2009; Werling, 2008).

Besides the current research, still some challenges remain open, which can be categorized in three types. At first, performance is an issue in geoprocessing workflows. The orchestration of services and distributing data across a SOA comes always with an overhead. Suitable workflow patterns and efficient data encodings have to be found. Use of reference data might be one solution for centralized workflow approaches. Friis-Christensen, Lucchi, Lutz, & Ostlaender (2009) investigated several patterns, which are promising to be elaborated in the future such as efficient encoding of data for geoprocessing workflows.

At second, to improve the sustainability and the commercial potential of SDIs, security and licensing of specific geoprocessing workflows might become an issue as also foreseen by IN-SPIRE (2007). Consequently, to chain secured and licensed service, challenges regarding the delegation of rights between user and workflow engines and workflow partners arise. One solution to solve this issue in an interoperable way using open standards has been presented by Schaeffer (2009) for opaque workflows, but has to be extended to other workflow patterns.

Finally, the semantic annotation of Geoprocessing Services and thereby improving the semantic interoperability is also one major challenge for the future. Therefore, semantic annotations for geoprocessing workflows are promising to enable the automated creation of geoprocessing workflows.

2.3 Quality of Service in Distributed Geoprocessing

In legally mandated SDIs such as the Infrastructure for Spatial Information in the European Community (INSPIRE) (legally binding since 2007 (INSPIRE, 2007a)) several performance requirements are defined for the so called *network services* (INSPIRE, 2008, 2007b). For example, search queries need to be answered within 3 seconds and services must be able to handle up to 30 of these queries at the same time. To meet such performance requirements in peak times, scalable solutions have to be found which have not been implemented in SDIs yet. Furthermore, monitoring the performance of loosely coupled Web Services in a distributed architecture and the ability to react quickly on service quality fluctuations is overall an essential skill for service consumers and service providers in future business models. However, existing OGC specifications and standards do not support any kind of service quality enforcement functionality on a specification level.

Quality of Service (QoS) is defined by the International Telecommunications Union (ITU-T) as "the collective effect of service performances, which determine the degree of satisfaction of a user of the service" (ITU-T, 2001) and it "is characterized by the combined aspects of service support performance, service operability performance, service integrity and other factors specific to each service" (ITU-T, 1994). Performing geoprocess models over the web raises

serious QoS issues that did not occur in case of desktop-based geoprocessing. Firstly, the service quality is strongly affected by general service and network performance characteristics. Secondly, the overall performance of a geoprocess model is implementation and algorithm specific and depends on the amount of involved data as well as the complexity of the input data and the available computational resources.

Following the argumentation of Ran (2003), J. Lee, Jeon, W. Lee, Jeong, & Park (2003) and Geraci (1991), the reliability and performance of a Web Service can be identified as the two major issues of QoS in the context of a SOA. Additionally, several other quantifiable service properties can be identified like transaction-, security-, costs- and functionality-related QoS. The remainder of this section will describe the major QoS issues in more detail.

2.3.1 Ensuring Reliability

Reliability is the ability of a service to process service requests and to perform its required functions under stated conditions for a specified time interval. The reliability can be quantified in terms of availability, accessibility, capacity, scalability, robustness, flexibility and accuracy of a Web Service.

Among other things, common Server Load Balancing (SLB) and failover mechanisms can be utilized to increase the different aspects of reliability (such as availability and capacity of a Web Service). For example in so-called high-availability clusters redundant or standby computers are used for the purpose of providing high availability of Web Services. All these mechanisms and technologies are common in the mainstream IT world to improve reliability-related QoS and could be applied for Geoprocessing Services as well.

However, especially when processing large amounts of data or performing large-scale simulations the highest impact on the degree of satisfaction of the user of the Geoprocessing Service is caused by the duration of the geoprocess model itself.

2.3.2 Ensuring Performance

The performance describes the speed at which service requests are completed. Performance can be measured in combination of throughput, latency, response-, execution- and transaction-time. Several reliability and performance related parameters are strongly related and define the same quality aspect of a Web Service but with other measuring units.

Performance is reported to be crucial in the context of Geoprocessing Services (Baranski, 2008; Bernard, Craglia, Gould, & Kuhn, 2005; Di, A. Chen, Yang, & Zhao, 2003; Kiehle, Heier, & Greve, 2007; Scholten, Klamma, & Kiehle, 2006; Tu et al., 2004). The performance of a Geoprocessing Service heavily depends on the availability of sufficient computational resources, that are primary responsible for the speed in completing a single geoprocess in a convenient period of time. The resource requirements of computational jobs for submission to Grid Computing infrastructures are described in Anjomashoaa et al. (2005). The defined resource requirements and therefore the corresponding performance-related QoS parameters also apply to Geoprocessing Services, such as the provision of three CPUs and 20 GB storage in a specific time frame. As mentioned in Section 2.3, beside the availability of computational resources the overall performance of a geoprocess model is also implementation and algorithm specific and depends on the amount of involved data as well as the complexity of the input data.

In the context of Geoprocessing Services some research has been carried out to address the performance of large-scale computations by Grid Computing and Cloud Computing. Grid Computing overlaps with some concepts of Cloud Computing (Hartig, 2009). Both, Grid and Cloud Computing infrastructures provide a distributed network infrastructure for scaling applications by

sufficient storage and computational capabilities. However, Grid Computing is typically applied by the scientific community for large-scale computations (e.g. a global climate change model or the aerodynamic design of engine components). Whereas Cloud Computing enables small and medium-sized companies to deploy their web-based applications in an instant scalable fashion without the need to invest in large computational infrastructures for storing large amounts of data and/or performing complex processes (Myerson, 2008). As a consequence, national and international Grid Computing infrastructures (for example the Worldwide LHC Computing Grid) are typically funded by the government and operated by international joint research projects, whereas cloud infrastructures are operated by large-sized enterprises under economic aspects, such as Amazon or Google, enabling smaller companies to use their infrastructure.

Baranski (2008) and Lanig, Schilling, Stollberg, & Zipf (2008) extended the work of Di et al. (2003) and accomplished first experiments using Grid Computing technology for improving computational performance by distribution and parallel execution of processes. In the OGC Web Services, Phase 6 (OWS-6) initiative of the OGC Interoperability Program (Baranski, 2009), a WPS profile for accessing applications in Grid Computing infrastructures has been reviewed. Baranski, Schaeffer, & Redweik (2009) presented and tested an approach of bringing the OGC Web Processing Service to a Cloud Computing infrastructure. The SLA4D-GRID research project[2] is designing and realizing a Service Level Agreement (SLA) layer for the Germany's national Grid infrastructure D-Grid. SLAs are negotiated business contracts between service consumers and providers defining service qualities (beside other contractual elements like costs and penalties) that will be guaranteed by a service provider. The integration of SLA in mature grid middleware and the application of advanced resource reservation mechanisms in Grid Computing infrastructures will enable providers to guarantee promised service qualities. Providing sufficient computational resources for Geoprocessing Services (namely the WPS) is one important use case within the SLA4D-Grid project.

2.4 Legacy System Integration

Legacy systems encapsulate existing functionality, which performs well and is tested thoroughly. In particular they incorporate an exhaustive variety of geoprocess models, which is mostly available in desktop-based GIS or web-accessible in a proprietary (i.e. non-standardized) way. However, standardized Geoprocessing Services (e.g. OGC WPS implementations) still lack manifold functionality. To prevent a reimplementation and enable further usage of existing functionality in a sustainable way, an approach from mainstream SOA called *wrapping* (Papazoglou & Heuvel, 2007; Erl, 2005) can be used for Geoprocessing Services as well. A wrapper translates incoming requests to commands in such a way, that the wrapped legacy system understands them and performs accordingly. It is important to note that the standardized Web Service interface remains unchanged and therefore interoperability is ensured.

In the following the requirements for such wrapping will be analyzed and an architecture will be developed to extend a WPS implementation for wrapping the GIS functionality of a legacy system. In particular, creating descriptions for WPS-based geoprocess models automatically for functionality of a legacy system will be discussed. An implementation based on the 52°North WPS framework (as a wrapper) and GRASS GIS (as a legacy system) will be described. Besides, disadvantages will be pointed out and solutions to tackle theses problems will be proposed.

2.4.1 Wrapping Requirements

To successfully wrap existing functionality as WPS-based geoprocess models, several requirements have to be met by the legacy system. One

essential and mandatory requirement for the legacy system is the ability to invoke its functionality unsupervised for two reasons. At first, machine-to-machine communication and automatic service invocation are required by SOA and its Web Service environment (Erl, 2005). This is not ensured if human interaction is required to invoke specific functionality. At second, the stateless communication pattern of a SOA (Erl, 2005) requires that all parameters necessary for successful processing are sent by the time of invocation. All further interactive communication would break the stateless communication.

This capability is surprisingly frequent for legacy GIS systems, although originally mostly intended for batch processing (e.g. do the same raster classify for the satellite images of a whole year without entering the same input parameters for each single image). It is implemented differently among legacy GIS ranging from simple scripting interfaces like Linux shell or DOS batch programming to high-level programming APIs like Python or JAVA.

Another requirement is that the functionality of a legacy system has to be described by a WPS ProcessDescription document (Section 2.1). Creating process descriptions manually can become a tedious task, especially regarding the variety of functionalities offered by a Desktop GIS. For example, GRASS combines approximately 400 modules, which each can be offered as a geoprocess model (Neteler & Mitasova, 2008). If the legacy system offers structured and therefore machine-readable process descriptions, a semi-automatic transformation into the XML-based WPS DescribeProcess documents is generally possible (see details for this transformation later on). The wrapping approach is applicable nevertheless, if the legacy system does not provide structured process descriptions.

To improve the performance of the wrapping architecture (i.e. accessing a WPS-based geoprocess model based on functionality provided by a legacy system), the legacy system and the WPS may perform processes concurrently. Running processes concurrently requires a fine granular modularization with independent multiple executable modules. This improves the performance in contrast to legacy systems which can only be instantiated once at the same time (such as desktop-based GIS). Nevertheless, the execution of parallel incoming requests can be prevented by refusing requests (e.g. 'server busy') or by sequentially processing them.

2.4.2 Creating Process Descriptions for Legacy System Integration

To supply the wrapped functionality of the legacy system with applicable data, process descriptions have to be created. These process descriptions specify the syntax of the specific geoprocess model and allow the client to configure the geoprocess model accordingly. As mentioned above an automated approach for creating process descriptions might be feasible if the legacy system already offers structured information (i.e. encoded in XML format). In this case an Extensible Stylesheet Language Transformation (XSLT) document can be designed to transform the legacy descriptions into DescribeProcess documents. Creating such an XSLT filter might appear as a huge effort to publish a single functionality of the legacy system, but considering wrapping the functionality of a complete legacy system (incorporating 100 processes or more) such a XSLT filter might be the applicable solution.

This XSLT-based approach does not work out-of-the-box. Several aspects have to be considered carefully. First, not all functionality offered by a legacy system is applicable as a WPS-based geoprocess model. For instance, desktop-based functionality for visualization is not suitable as a WPS-based geoprocess model and is considered to be a client task. Assuming a structured description of the functionality offered by the legacy system is available (e.g. encoded in XML), the XSLT filter is not able to identify which functional-

ity is applicable to be published as WPS-based geoprocess model. The semantics of the specific functionality of the legacy system is not available. Consequently, inappropriate functionality has to be excluded manually, before the DescribeProcess documents are generated.

Second, the WPS distinguishes between simple and complex input parameters, whereas most legacy systems have a single type of input parameter. Complex input parameters for WPS incorporate geodata which are encoded in a data format, using a specific mime type and in case of XML a specific schema. Input parameters for legacy systems are usually described by a single String. No further information is necessary for processing as it can be assumed that it is already imported into the workspace in a legacy system internal data format. The name is sufficient to identify the input dataset and therefore it is ready to use without taking care of further data format related issues. Again, the XSLT filter is not capable of identifying which parameter is complex and needs to be described in greater detail. Listing 7 and Listing 8 show the different complexities between legacy system functionality (in this case GRASS) and WPS DescribeProcess documents.

Finally, it can be concluded that a fully automated approach for creating process descriptions is not feasible at the moment. The required semantics cannot be extracted from the description of the legacy system and interpreted by the XSLT filter. Nevertheless, a semi-automated approach using a manual selection of applicable geoprocess models and performing a XSLT filter on the specific process description is less time-consuming than creating all descriptions manual from scratch.

2.4.3 Wrapping Architecture

This section describes the conceptual architecture incorporating functionality of a legacy system in a WPS. To successfully wrap such functionality, one aspect has to be considered, which is specific to distributed architectures. As stated before, the

Figure 5. Architecture for wrapping functionality of legacy systems inside WPS

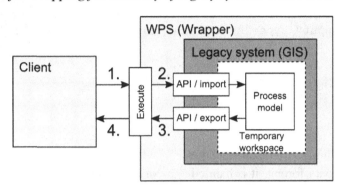

communication between Web Services is stateless (Erl, 2005), whereas legacy systems are able to maintain a certain state during several processing tasks. In case of legacy systems it is possible to store intermediate and final results inside the legacy system using a workspace-based concept incorporating also for instance information about the applicable Coordinate Reference Systems (CRS).

Hence, for accessing functionality of a legacy system inside a WPS, a workspace has to be created for each WPS Execute request. A workspace encompasses a CRS definition for the data to be imported and the data itself. Importing data into the workspace normally includes a transformation from the provided common format (such as GML or shape file format) into the internal data structure required by the legacy system. For providing the user with a result (mostly in a common data format again) the data has to be transformed again and exported to the requested data format. Additionally, if this response represents an intermediate result which has to be further processed on the same WPS, it nevertheless has to be sent back to the client and then sent back to the server and imported again. Creating workspaces and importing and exporting data is always required as already mentioned. This creates an overhead on the architecture regarding data transfer and processing time, which cannot be avoided without harming the interoperability (e.g. by introducing

additional parameters, which keep track of processing sessions). Some legacy systems require no data import for certain formats and work directly on the available data by referencing it into the workspace (e.g. GRASS for most vector and raster data). Still a workspace has to be created, however this limits the effort of importing, which in most cases is beneficial to improve performance.

Based on the mentioned implication of stateless Web Service communication and the requirements outlined in the previous section the following architecture is proposed (Figure 5).

All necessary parameters and the data to be processed or a reference to the data (e.g. URL) are incorporated in the Execute request which is sent by the client (Step 1). The data can be read directly from the request or retrieved from a reference incorporated in the request. Although it is possible to download such referenced data by functionality of legacy systems (e.g. a WFS connector) it should not be used due to security reasons. This prevents the uncontrolled infiltration of malicious code directly into the hosting environment. The WPS which runs autonomously as a Web Service has no direct access to the hosting environment. Unfortunately, this approach requires an additional import step whereas a WFS connector could import the data directly into the created workspace. After creating and importing the provided data (Step 2), the designated functionality of the legacy system is invoked and the

Listing 7. Example of a complex input parameter (geodata) in GRASS GIS process descriptions.

```
<parameter name="input" type="string" requires="yes" multiple="no">
        <description>
                    Name of input vector map
        </description>
</parameter>
```

data is processed accordingly. After exporting the result in the requested data format, it is handed back to the WPS (Step 3), which sends it back to the client (Step 4). Alternatively, the WPS directly understands the result's data format and is able to transform it into the requested format (e.g. in the case of SEXTANTE as legacy system).

2.4.4 Implementing the Wrapping Architecture

To demonstrate the approach of wrapping existing functionality as WPS-based geoprocess models, this section illustrates this approach by the example of two legacy systems:

- GRASS (Brauner & Bastian Schaeffer, 2008)
- SEXTANTE (see Diaz et al. 2008 for details).

Both legacy systems are incorporated in the 52°North WPS framework (Section 3.1). Additionally, the 52°North WPS framework is able to provide a subset of ESRI's ArcGIS Server functionality, as demonstrated by Müller, Vogel, & Bernard (2009).

GRASS

GRASS is an Open Source Desktop GIS for vector and raster analysis whose beginnings date back to the 1980ies. An exhaustive overview of GRASS' history is provided in Neteler & Mitasova (2008). Functionality in GRASS is grouped in modules

which can be invoked using command line tools or the desktop application of GRASS.

GRASS provides structured process descriptions in XML, which can be created by invoking a GRASS module with the '--interface-description' parameter. These descriptions can be transformed by an XSLT filter operation into WPS DescribeProcess documents (as described in Section GHM). GRASS modules group different functionality. It is therefore easy to exclude specific functionality by restricting the wrapper to specific modules which are not applicable in SDI (like visualization modules which all starts with a 'd.'). As long as GRASS modules require only a single complex input parameter (the geodata) they are labeled as 'input' and the XSLT filter is able to identify them as complex parameter and adds additional data format information. Modules with more than one complex input (like an overlay of two data sets) require manual adoptions. Listing 7 and Listing 8 show excerpts of process descriptions for GRASS and the WPS; the different complexities are highlighted in grey.

Wrapping of GRASS by the 52°North WPS framework is illustrated in the architecture depicted in Figure 6.

After receiving the WPS Execute request from a client (Step 1), the WPS downloads the appropriate input data and saves it as a temporary file on the hard disk or as a binary input stream in the main memory depending on the size and the type of data. The WPS then creates a console script (Step 2) with the appropriate GRASS commands to create a workspace, imports or references the complex input data into the workspace and pro-

Listing 8. Example of a complex input parameter (geodata) in a WPS DescribeProcess document.

```
<Input minOccurs="1" maxOccurs="1">
        <ows:Identifier>input</ows:Identifier>
        <ows:Title>Polygon to be buffered</ows:Title>
        <ows:Abstract>The geometries to buffer</ows:Abstract>
        <ComplexData>
                <Default>
                        <Format>
                                <MimeType>text/XML</MimeType>
                                <Schema>http://schemas.opengis.net/
gml/2.1.2/feature.xsd/Schema>
                        </Format>
                </Default>
                <Supported>
                        <Format>
                                <MimeType>text/XML</MimeType>
                                <Schema>http://schemas.opengis.net/
gml/2.1.2/feature.xsd/Schema>
                        </Format>
                </Supported>
        </ComplexData>
</Input>
```

Figure 6. Wrapping the NDVI calculation of GRASS by the 52°North WPS framework

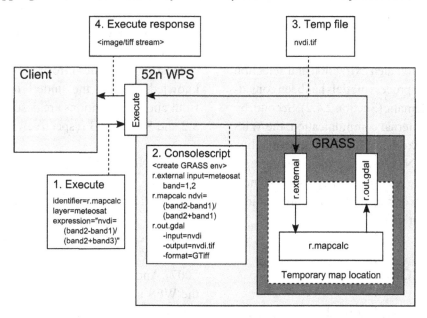

cesses the data. Finally, the WPS exports the process result in the requested data format into a temporary file (Step 3) and provides the client with the result (Step 4). GRASS offers modules to request data from external Web Services. Nevertheless, they are not used here due to the security reasons described in the architecture section.

SEXTANTE

SEXTANTE is a JAVA-based library incorporating over 200 different geoprocess models (ranging from simple buffer calculations to complex slope analysis). The integration into the 52°North WPS framework follows the same core architectural principles for wrapping as described above, but is nevertheless easier due to the following reasons. First, for creating of the DescribeProcess documents of the SEXTANTE functionality no XSLT filter is necessary. This is due to the fact, that SEXTANTE and 52°North WPS framework can communicate internally as they are both implemented in JAVA. JAVA allows the 52°North WPS framework to inspect the syntax of the SEXTANTE functionality using reflection. Thereby these DescribeProcess documents can be created at runtime and no manual interaction is required. This is also due to the fact, that SEXTANTE is only designed to provide processing functionality and no visualization for instance. This was one of the reasons, why automated extraction and selection of applicable geoprocess models has been considered to be problematic (Section 2.4.2). Second, by using Java for internal communication, the WPS can directly invoke the SEXTANTE functionality. Finally, SEXTANTE uses common data formats compatible to the ones used for the WPS. Hence, no workspaces or data transformation are required for successful wrapping.

3 APPLICATIONS

Distributed geoprocessing is addressed in many projects. It is the backbone to provide informa-

tion based on distributed geospatial data using geoprocess models. To illustrate the wide range of projects using distributed geoprocessing based on WPS Table 1 provides an overview of relevant projects. Brauner et al. (2009) provide a comprehensive overview about ongoing and finished applications and projects dealing with geoprocess models in an SDI context. Table 1 groups these projects according to their aim.

This section presents different applications, which are applied in some of these projects to realize distributed geoprocessing. The foundation for such projects is an implementation of the WPS interface specification to publish the geoprocess models on the Web. Section 3.1 describes the architecture of such a WPS implementation by the example of the 52°North WPS framework. To access the available geoprocess models client applications are necessary. The geoprocess models can be accessed in different ways using a common desktop-based GIS such as *User-friendly Desktop Internet GIS* (uDig[3]) or mass market applications such as Google Earth. Both applications have a different set of functionality to access and configure these geoprocess models. The WPS client application based on uDig allows expert users to thoroughly configure the specific geoprocess model. Whereas mass market applications such as Google Earth only aim ordinary users requesting specific information without any knowledge about the underlying architecture. Both client applications are described in Section 3.2 and Section 3.3 respectively.

3.1 52°North WPS Framework

This section describes the architecture of the 52°North WPS framework. This framework exemplifies the design challenges of implementing the OGC WPS interface specification (OGC, 2007). Another example of an implementation of the WPS interface specification version 1.0.0 is PyWPS (Cepicky & Becchi, 2007).

Table 1. Overview of current geoprocessing projects (Brauner et al. (2009))

Category	Project Name	Website	Selected literature
Raster-based processing	AWARE	www.aware-project.net	Granell, Diaz, & Gould (2007)
Grid computing	GDI-Grid	www.gdi-grid.de	Baranski; Lanig et al. (2008)
	SEE-GEO	edina.ac.uk/projects/seesaw/seegeo	Koutroumpas and Higgins 2008
	ESDISP		Di et al. (2003)
Automated Generalization	DURP ondergronden	www.durpondergronden.nl	Foerster & Stoter (2006)
	WebGen	webgen.geo.uzh.ch	Foerster et al.; Neun, Burghardt, & Weibel (2008)
Schema Translation in INSPIRE			Lehto (2007)
Wrapping existing (desktop) GIS			(Brauner, 2008; Brauner & Bastian Schaeffer, 2008; Diaz, Costa, Granell, & Gould, 2007)
Spatial statistics	INTAMap	www.intamap.org	Henneboehl & Pebesma; de Jesus, Hiemstra, & Dubois (2008)
Spatial Decision Support Systems (SDSS)	OK-GIS	www.ok-gis.de	Stollberg & Zipf (2007)
	ORCHESTRA	www.eu-orchestra.org	(Friis-Christensen, Ostlander, Lutz, & Bernard, 2007)
	AWARE	www.aware-project.net	Diaz et al. (2007)
	ImmoSDSS_RLP	www.i3mainz.fh-mainz.de/Article300.html	Stollberg & Zipf (2008)
SDSS / Multicriteria Evaluation	SoKNOS	www.soknos.de	Müller et al. (2009)

The development of 52°North WPS framework has been started in 2006, when the WPS interface specification was released under version 0.4.0. With the advancement of the specification the implementation has matured and is compliant to the most recent version 1.0.0 of the specification. The 52°North WPS framework is available as Open Source under the GNU General Public License at the 52°North Open Source initiative. The implementation is based on Open Source libraries such as GeoTools (Turton, 2008) and XMLBeans (xmlbeans.apache.org). The 52°North WPS framework is designed as a JAVA servlet application, which can be deployed for instance on an Apache Tomcat server.

The design goal of the 52°North WPS framework was to be extensible and pluggable in terms of geoprocess models and data handlers. Service providers are able to incorporate their own geoprocess models and to distribute the results regarding in their own data format using customized data handlers during runtime. The layout of the architecture is depicted in Figure 7.

To enable this extensible and pluggable architecture, three major entry points are defined:

*   Algorithm Repository
*   Repository Manager
*   Data Handler Repository.

These entry points are initialized based on a configuration file, which can be changed by the service administrator of the WPS using a graphical configuration tool. Whenever the configuration changes, the entry points are re-initialized to realize the pluggable notion of the architecture. The architecture takes care, that each of the entry points is triggered to serve the request accord-

Figure 7. Architecture of the 52°North WPS framework

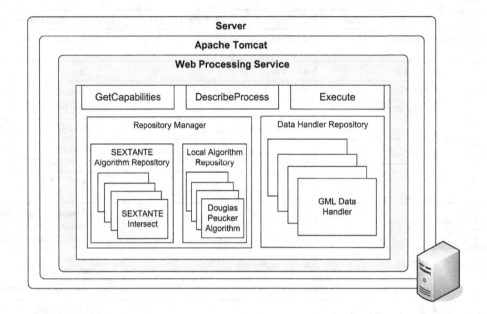

ingly. This so-called *inversion of control* limits the effort of the service provider implementing the specific geoprocess model and ensures that the added functionality (data handler or algorithm) is performed sufficiently.

An Algorithm Repository provides a list of available geoprocess models hosted by the WPS instance. It updates the GetCapabilities response document and DescribeProcess response documents. Additionally, it forwards any Execute request to the specific algorithm. The Algorithm Repository is managed by the Repository Manager, which creates different Algorithm Repositories for different legacy systems. To manage built-in algorithms, the Local Algorithm Repository is installed by default.

The Repository Manager is designed to incorporate different legacy systems such as GRASS or SEXTANTE (see Section 2.4). It initializes for each of the legacy systems an Algorithm Repository and forwards the calls accordingly. Thereby it is possible to incorporate the full set of functionality of a specific legacy system without incorporating the functionality on an individual basis (i.e. per single geoprocess model).

The Data Handler Repository lists all available data handlers and forwards any input and output parameter containing geodata to the applicable data handler. The data handler has to convert the geodata from the external format to an internal object representation. The object representations of geodata are based on the GeoTools library.

3.2 Example of a WPS Client Application

Client applications to configure and perform distributed geoprocessing are required to enable user-friendly interaction with such kind of services. Several client applications have been developed as extensions of GvSIG, OpenLayers, JUMP and uDig. For this chapter, we will illustrate the WPS client application realized as a plug-in for uDig. This plug-in is used throughout the chapter (e.g. Section 3.3 and Section 4.1), as a reference implementation. uDig has been chosen to be the suitable candidate for extending it with capabilities for communicating with WPS, as it already allows users to integrate distributed data available through Web Services.

The client is realized as a plug-in in uDig, which is organized as a set of plug-ins on top of the eclipse rich client platform (Clayberg & Rubel, 2008). The eclipse RCP implements the concept of inversion of control and allows thereby only specific parts of the workflow to be customized. The customization within the eclipse RCP is achieved via so called extension points, at which the intended functionality can be inserted into the RCP framework. The concept of extension points is inherited by uDig to insert intended functionality at designated points of the uDig workflow.

To the user, the WPS client plug-in appears to be a Wizard, in which the user can inspect, configure and perform the geoprocess model. During the configuration, all the data which is available to the client may serve as input to the specific geoprocess model. Like all the data available in uDig, the final result of the geoprocess model is available as a layer and can serve as input for further processing.

The user interaction with the wizard is depicted in Figure 8. In the given example, a road data set served by WFS needs to be simplified using Douglas-Peucker algorithm. First the designated type of service has to be chosen - in this case WPS (Step I.). The user is now able to register the entry point of the WPS instance (i.e. URL) (Step II). Based on this URL, the client is able to retrieve the GetCapabilities document of the specific WPS instance automatically and retrieves all the available process descriptions, which the user can inspect in Step III. The user is now able to select the designated geoprocess model (i.e. Douglas-Peucker algorithm). Based on the selected geoprocess model and its process description, the wizard generates a form with the required parameters, which have to be supplied by the user (Step IV.). For every required literal input, the user is presented with a corresponding text box. Additionally, for every complex input, the user can choose from a drop down list containing currently available layers (i.e. registered geodata) inside of uDig. If the user chooses a WFS layer,

the layer can be send by reference according to the general wizard configuration. This allows the WPS to fetch the data and saves up time, since not the whole data has to be prepared on the client-side and transferred to the service. In the given example, the user provides a tolerance value for the Douglas-Peucker algorithm and a road dataset, which is sent by reference to the WPS, as it is provided through a remote WFS instance. As a geoprocess model might provide multiple results, the user can select the appropriate ones, which need to be added as layers in uDig (Step V.).

The final result is presented as a separate layer in uDig as shown in Figure 11 (left).

3.3 Geoprocessing Services and Geospatial Mass-market Applications

Geospatial mass-market applications such as Google Earth allow ordinary user to access and share geospatial information over the web in an intuitive way. Mass-market applications provide full coverage of satellite base data and mechanisms to integrate geospatial information available on the web.

Geoprocessing Services provide real-time geoinformation and users demand real-time geoinformation especially in cases of emergency (e.g. flooding or forest fires). Thereby, the integration of such web-based information is promising for current geospatial mass-market applications to provide the users comprehensive access to up-to-date information.

The basic way, how geospatial information is described and exchanged in mass-market applications, is KML. KML is widely used in applications such as Google Maps and Google Earth and became an official OGC standard (OGC, 2008). KML is unique in the family of OGC data encodings, as it combines data encoding, styling and the special network facilities, which are called *NetworkLinks* and are also known as dynamic KML. These NetworkLinks are espe-

Figure 8. User interaction with wizard to perform Douglas-Peucker algorithm hosted by WPS (Foerster & Schaeffer, 2007)

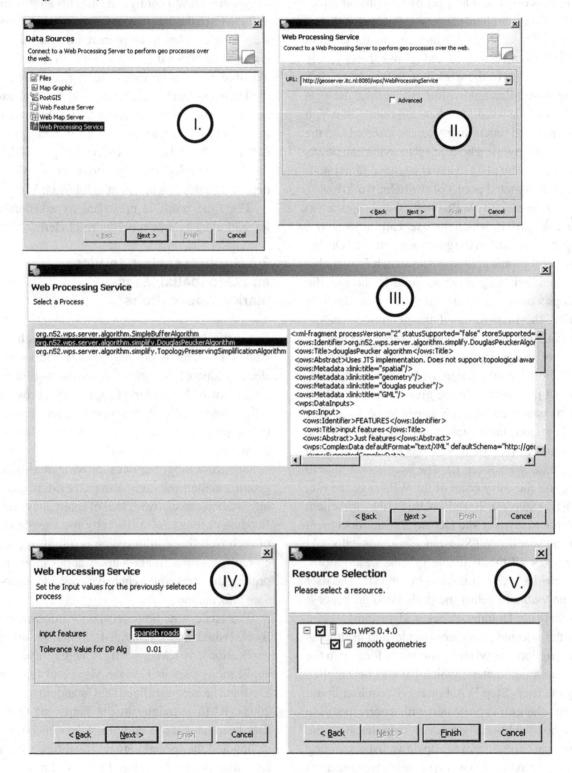

cially interesting for web-based geoinformation, as they allow the dynamic integration of remote resources (e.g. provided by WPS). Therefore, the content of a KML file might become dynamic and provide temporal data (e.g. from sensors). As NetworkLinks use URLs, KML is not only bound to file-based access, but can link any Web Service, as long as it operates via HTTP-GET and serves KML. NetworkLinks provide additional properties such as update, scheduling etc.

This section will describe the approach to integrate web-based geoinformation generated by WPS-based geoprocess models into such geospatial mass-market applications. Finally, the chapter will demonstrate the applicability of the proposed approach by a fire threat use case. This use case demonstrates how ordinary users can access the most current information through their geospatial mass-market application and take actions accordingly.

3.3.1 The Approach of Integrating WPS and Geospatial Mass-market Applications

To integrate WPS-based geoprocess models, several requirements of the geospatial mass-market applications have to be met. The major requirement is that the communication pattern (REST architecture & KML encoding) of the geospatial mass-market applications does not have to be changed. Thereby, the WPS-based geoprocess models become capable of being seamlessly integrated into such applications. This requirement is met by the WPS interface specification, as it supports the invocation of geoprocess models via HTTP-GET, which is a common approach of REST-architectures. Additionally, the WPS interface specification does not foresee any data encoding for its input and output parameters, thus KML is a valid format for the WPS. Finally, as the WPS is able to return process results as raw data without any WPS-specific message overhead it is

Figure 9. Approach to integrate WPS-based geoprocess models in mass-market applications such as Google Earth

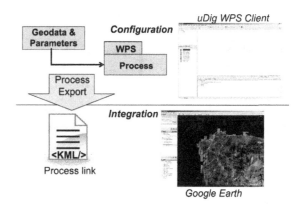

highly applicable for an integration into geospatial mass-market applications.

However, as the configuration of such process models is highly complex and not supported by current geospatial mass-market applications, a twofold approach is proposed. At first, the expert user selects and configures the geoprocess model through an expert user interface, most-likely a GIS. At second, the user integrates the pre-configured geoprocess model into his/her geospatial mass-market application of choice. This integration is possible, as the WPS interface meets the requirements of geospatial mass-market applications, as explained in the previous paragraph. The pre-configuration eases the integration of such geoprocess models and thereby the integration of web-based geoinformation in Google Earth for a non-expert user and is thereby not a drawback. Moreover, it prevents from false configuration of the geoprocess model through the non-expert user. This sequence of action is also depicted in Figure 9.

In particular, the WPS-based geoprocess models are configured through uDig (Section 3.2). For this approach, uDig has been enhanced to export these configured WPS-based geoprocess models as KML.

Figure 10. User interface to export the configured geoprocess model in uDig as KML

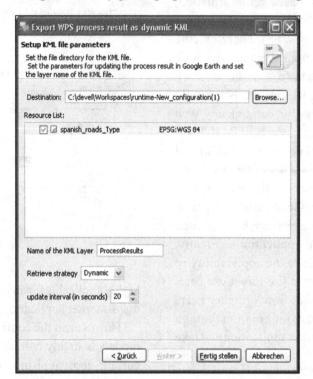

The export of the configured geoprocess model from uDig to KML can be configured in two ways:

1. Export the KML file as a link to a stored process result. This is the *static* option, in which no geoprocess model will be triggered when visualizing the KML file in Google Earth. This uses the store functionality of the WPS interface specification.
2. Export the KML file as a link, which triggers the WPS-based geoprocess model. This is the *dynamic* option and enables to trigger the geoprocess model in real-time, when incorporating the file in Google Earth. This allows one also to set a refresh rate to initiate performing the geoprocess model on the server again. It is important to note, that in this case, the WPS-based geoprocess model is triggered and if any WPS input data is defined as reference, the (updated) data is fetched and used as the basis for the calcula-

tion. This approach allows the processing of the latest available data and thus visualizing the latest results in mainstream applications.

In both cases the files incorporate the links using the *NetworkLink* functionality of KML. Figure 10 depicts the GUI dialog in uDig to configure the KML file referencing the configured geoprocess model (regarding the applied process strategy).

Listing 9 shows the generated NetworkLink using the dynamic option in the KML export of uDig (option 2). The generated KML includes an Execute request via HTTP-GET to a Douglas-Peucker algorithm for simplification, which is also used in the scenario described in Section 3.3.2. The request references remote WFS data.

By supporting these two options (dynamic vs. static), the integration is well-scalable and applicable to scenarios requiring dynamic or even static process results.

Listing 9. KML NetworkLink with a WPS-Execute request via HTTP-GET. The request references remote data hosted on WFS

```
<?xml version="1.0" encoding="UTF-8"?>
<kml xmlns="http://earth.google.com/kml/2.2">
    <Folder>
        <name>smooth geometries</name>
     <visibility>0</visibility>
     <open>0</open>
     <description>WPS Layer</description>
        <NetworkLink>
            <name>WPS Layer</name>
            ...
            <description>WPS Layer</description>
            <refreshVisibility>0</refreshVisibility>
            <Link>
            <href>http://geoserver:8080/wps/WebProcessingService?request=exe
cute&amp;service=WPS&amp;version=1.0.0&amp;Identifier=org.n52.wps.server.algo-
rithm.simplify.DouglasPeuckerAlgorithm&amp;DataInputs=FEATURES=@mimeType=text/
xml@href=http%3A%2F%2Fgeoserver%3A8080%2Fgeoserver%2Fwfs%3FSERVICE%3DWFS%2
6VERSION%3D1.0.0%26REQUEST%3DGetFeature%26typename%3Dtopp%3Aspanish_roads@
Schema=http://schemas.opengis.net/gml/2.1.2/feature.xsd;TOLERANCE=1&amp;RawDa
taOutput=SIMPLIFIED_FEATURES@mimeType=application/vnd.google-earth.kml%2Bxml@
schema=http://www.opengis.net/kml/2.2/href>
     <refreshMode>onInterval</refreshMode>
     <refreshInterval>20</refreshInterval>
    ...
</kml>
```

Finally the exported KML files are loaded into Google Earth. The result of the geoprocess model is then displayed directly with imagery and other content available in Google Earth.

It is important to note, that the client application (uDig) is able to perform and export single and chained geoprocess models and geoprocessing workflows. This task of chaining is performed locally at the client side and does not involve any central processing engine. A more sophisticated approach for geoprocessing workflows by the means of BPEL is described in Section 2.2.

3.3.2 Integrating Mass-market Applications for a Risk Management Scenario

The scenario is settled in the context of a risk management use case, in which in-situ-sensor data has to be analyzed for assessing a fictive fire threat in Northern Spain. The scenario and the involved services have been extensively presented in (Foerster & Bastian Schaeffer, 2007). In this example, the services and data are taken from the ORCHESTRA project, which addresses a similar fire risk management scenario (Friis-Christensen et al., 2006).

In the given scenario the expert configures the geoprocess model in the WPS client plug-in for uDig by buffering the fire threat areas and intersecting them with the road data. The buffering operation and the intersection operation are single WPS-based geoprocess models. The road data has been additionally simplified to improve the process performance and to improve portrayal at smaller scales. Overall, this allows the expert to assess which parts of the road infrastructure are at risk by a fire threat. The expert user exports the configured geoprocess model as a KML file and links it on the national portal site. The citizen (i.e. non-expert user) is now able to visualize the latest analysis results regarding the affected roads in his/her geospatial mass-market application by loading the KML file from the portal site. He/she can inspect the latest geoinformation (as calculated by a specific WPS-based geoprocess model) with underlying base information from areal imagery and/or topography and other content such as available in Google Earth. In the given scenario the specific citizen can inspect the current status of the road infrastructure and is able to perform appropriate actions. Figure 11 depicts the result of the configured geoprocess model in uDig and the same geoprocess model accessed through Google Earth.

4 SCENARIOS

This section examines two different scenarios to demonstrate the concepts of WPS, geoprocessing workflows, QoS and legacy systems as introduced in Section 2. One scenario focuses on an analysis of particulate matter distribution in Germany for air quality monitoring. This scenario involves different types of geoprocess models combined into a workflow. The other scenario presents the applicability of Grid and Cloud Computing as an application for increasing processing power for a risk management scenario in Taiwan.

4.1 Air Quality Monitoring in Germany

This section presents a real-world scenario, which illustrates the presented concepts (Section 2). Ambient air quality has been identified by the European Commission as one of the most critical environmental aspects. Therefore, it is one of the major objectives in the Sixth Environmental Action Programme[4]. Through legislation, the European Union has also been active in this field for several decades. With the Council Directives 1999/30/EC and 1996/62/EC strict air quality limits for several air quality parameters were

Figure 11. Screenshots of the configured geoprocess model in uDig (left) and exported to Google Earth (right) – simplified roads & affected road infrastructure (red)

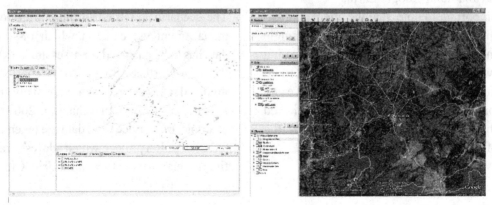

specified, which have to be adapted by national law by all member states.

This scenario addresses Particulate Matter (PM10) as one of the most hazardous aerosols. Several studies have researched the correlation of PM10 and health effects. For instance, Pope et al. (2002) found that for each rise of 10 $\mu g/m^3$ the lung cancer rate increases by 4-8%. Hence, the real-time monitoring of PM10 is a crucial task to support decision makers in protecting public health and to comply with the EU regulations. To automate this business process, a model realized as a geoprocessing workflow will be developed to monitor real-time spatial distributions of PM10 by applying the concepts of distributed geoprocessing.

Figure 12 presents the deployed workflow. It was modeled with the 52°North Workflow Modeler, which automatically creates WSDL documents for the workflow partners and describes the workflow via BPEL (Bastian Schaeffer & Foerster, 2008). While for instance Weiser & Zipf (2007) also showed the orchestration of OGC

Web Services with BPEL, they had to build the WSDL manually. Our approach goes beyond that and exposes the deployed workflow as a simple WPS-based geoprocess model using the WPS-T approach (Section 2.2). The client on the left-hand side (Figure 12) is now capable to invoke the workflow like any other WPS-based geoprocess model (Step 1). Only the reference to the sensor data has to be included in the request. In our case, the 52°North WPS uDig client application (Section 3.2) can be used to invoke the service and visualize the results (Figure 13).

After invoking the workflow represented by a WPS-based geoprocess model, hosted on the WPS-T, the underlying workflow engine is triggered in the backend (Step 2). Upon then, the workflow engine orchestrates the workflow and invokes each of the workflow partners. At first, a WPS-based filter process, which takes a URL from an OGC Sensor Observation Service (SOS) as input (Step 3) is triggered. The SOS instance is located on top of a sensor network and allows the client to query the observed phenomena in a

Figure 12. Deployed workflow for the described scenario

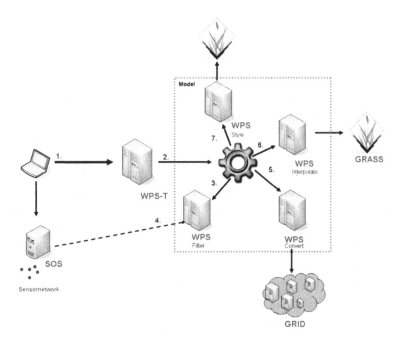

Figure 13. Workflow results visualized with states boundary of North-Rhine Westphalia and the sensor location. The red colored areas imply a high amount of PM10 (40 μg PM10 /m³ air), which violates current EU regulations

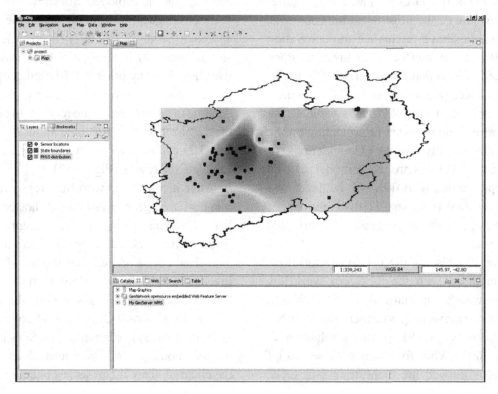

standardized format. In this scenario real-time air quality data from the state of North-Rhine West-phalia, located in the western part of Germany, is available through the SOS instance. The SOS instance provides up-to-date data of 56 monitoring stations distributed throughout this region. Internally, the WPS queries the SOS for its latest available sensor data regarding this specific region (Step 4). Next, the retrieved sensor data is converted into the common Geography Markup Language (GML) format (Step 5), which can be used for further processing. In particular, the geometry and observed values are extracted and new GML point features are created. This geoprocess model is performed by a Grid Computing enabled WPS, which delegates the conversion task to its underlying grid middleware due to high computational complexity. The following step (Step 6) takes the resulting point data from the

second geoprocess model as input and interpolates them with the GRASS Inverse Distance Weighting (IDW) method to a resulting GeoTIFF raster. In the last step (Step 7) the GeoTIFF raster becomes visualized according to the GRASS color scheme for air pollution is applied, in which the color red represents values above a specific threshold (40 μg PM10 /m³ air as the current EU legislation limit). The output is visualized as a new layer in uDig (Figure 13).

As the workflow analyses latest data in (almost) real-time and can be triggered on-demand, it allows the decision makers to monitor the current air quality and thereby to take actions accordingly based on the latest information. Additionally, it is possible to compare the phenomena over time and thereby get analyze its behavior more thoroughly.

Figure 14. An overview about the OWS-6 GPW Debris Flow demonstration scenario workflow

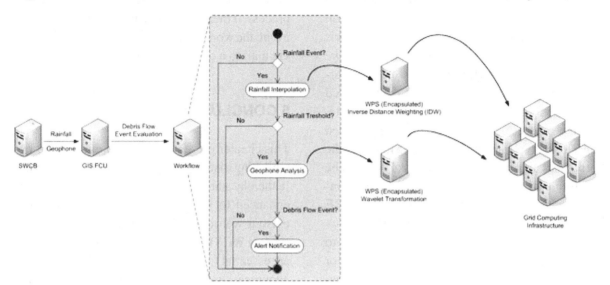

4.2 Grid Computing for Risk Management in Taiwan

Taiwan is located at the collision boundary of the Philippine Sea plate and the Eurasian plate. The mountain terrain is precipitous and the region, on the whole, is characterized by fragile rocks and frequent seismic activity. In addition, the concentrated torrential rainfall brought by typhoons causes extensive disasters. A debris flow, the most serious disaster caused by torrential rainfall, leads to very heavy casualties in recent years. Since 2002, the Soil and Water Conservation Bureau, which is responsible for the conservation and administrative management of hillside in Taiwan, has been cooperated with the Feng Chia University to build up a national debris flow monitoring system. Together they have successively carried out the establishment and maintenance of 13 fixed debris flow monitoring stations over the island. The main concept of the debris flow monitoring system is to connect various sensors (e.g. satellites, fixed and mobile monitoring stations, remotely operated aircrafts, etc.) to establish a network of ubiquitous monitoring to command, control, communicate,

survey and reconnoiter to give intelligence to decision makers.

However, the whole architecture was designed in late 2000 and implemented by traditional monolithic and proprietary methodologies. Since then, several interoperability issues have been unveiled in the recent years. An open standards-based architecture for debris flow monitoring following the SDI paradigm was presented in Chung, Fang, Chou, B. Lee, & Baranski (2009). The architecture applies OGC standards such as the specification of the Sensor Web Enablement (SWE) to connect to the deployed sensors and the WPS interface specification for processing the delivered sensor information.

During typhoon season, the debris flow monitoring system operates under full load and a lot of data from many sensors is produced and must be analyzed. In the OWS-6 testbed a proof of concept was developed, that utilizes a Grid Computing infrastructure for increasing the performance of processing the large amounts of live sensor data streams. An overview about the OWS-6 debris flow demonstration scenario workflow is given in Figure 14. The developed *Rainfall Interpolation* process implements an Inverse Distance Weighting (IDW) algorithm and calculates the rainfall distribution in a specific region depending on several rain gauges deployed at a fixed debris flow monitoring station. The developed *Geophone Analysis* process implements a wavelet transformation algorithm and calculates if the measured ground vibration reaches a specific threshold. Both processes use the Grid Computing enabled 52°North WPS framework (Figure 15) and split the processes task into smaller sub-tasks that will be performed distributed in a Grid Computing infrastructure based on the grid middleware UNICORE (Huber, 2001) (http://www.unicore.eu/).

If it begins to rain, a decision maker has to analyze if a debris flow event will be happen or not. The decision maker sends a request to a pre-defined workflow engine (realized through BPEL). The workflow engine requests the database for the measured rain gauge and earth vibration data. Afterwards, the workflow invokes the Rainfall Interpolation process, which runs in parallel on a Grid Computing enabled WPS to increase the computational performance. If the rainfall reaches a specific threshold, the workflow invokes the

(also distributed and parallel) Geophone Analysis process. If the computation indicates a debris flow event, the workflow will send an alert notification via mail to a decision maker.

5 CONCLUSION

This chapter presents current approaches for establishing distributed geoprocessing on the Web. It thereby shows how SDIs can be technically enhanced to provide geoinformation using the existing web-based data sources (e.g. provided by WFS or WCS). SOA and Geospatial Web Services are essential for the interoperability of web-based geoprocess models in SDIs. The WPS interface specification is presented as the OGC-compliant approach enabling single geoprocess models in SOAs. Single geoprocess models can be chained to complex ones using geoprocessing workflows. Further, these geoprocessing workflows can be deployed as single geoprocess models using WPS-T (Section 2.2.2). This approach in particular combines the expressiveness of existing workflow

Figure 15. Architecture of the Grid Computing enabled 52°North WPS framework

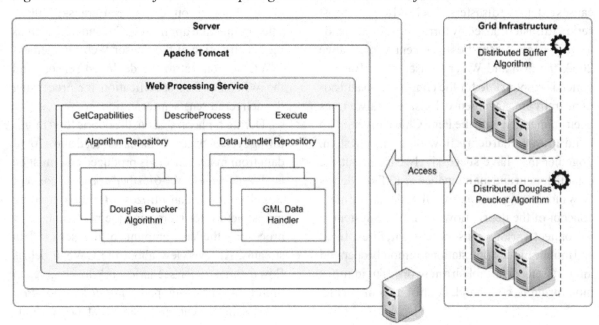

technologies of mainstream IT (e.g. BPEL) and existing OGC interface specifications (i.e. WPS). The presented approaches to ensure QoS within SOAs support distributed geoprocessing on an operational level. The integration of legacy systems contributes to its functional level.

Many projects are dedicated to distributed geoprocessing for geo-related decision support. Based on distributed geoprocessing, decisions can benefit from the most current data retrieved from different locations and transformed to suitable geoinformation using various complex geoprocess models. Specific applications are necessary to publish and access the geoprocess models. For a framework implementing the WPS interface specification, it is important to be extensible to limit the effort of integrating and adopting it into existing SOAs. This is demonstrated by the example of 52°North WPS framework. The client applications have to meet specific user requirements, as examined by the WPS plug-in for uDig and the mass-market application. In the latter case, the architecture had to meet the requirements of the mass-market application (i.e. KML and NetworkLinks) for integrating geoprocess models (i.e. the generated geoinformation).

To demonstrate the introduced concepts and applications, Section 4 illustrates how real-world scenarios can be addressed. As already mentioned throughout the chapter, some research challenges still remain.

The automation of distributed geoprocessing and its performance are still unsolved. The automated creation of geoprocessing workflows is still lacking due to missing semantics. These semantics need to be included in the description of the geoprocess models and the geoprocessing workflows itself. Therefore thorough classifications are required, which might be modeled as ontologies. Based on these semantics it will be possible to enable reasoning for automatically selecting single geoprocess models and chaining them to geoprocessing workflows.

Reliability and performance of distributed geoprocessing also require further concepts. For example, the current WPS specification does not offer any possibility to list the running geoprocess models at a WPS instance, to prioritize geoprocess models, to interactively pause and resume, nor to stop and restart geoprocess models. Furthermore, the current WPS specification does not give the users of a WPS any enhanced control over the computational resources in the backend (e.g. for advanced resource reservation and corresponding guaranteed provision of requested resources). However, not only standardization is important, but also research on the specific geoprocess model is required by optimizing the implementation or finding new algorithms.

Finally, solving the problems regarding the automation, reliability and performance of distributed geoprocessing will increase its applicability and will show the benefit of integrating functionality and data from distributed resources to efficiently support decision making and thereby support the future vision of SDI as stated for instance in Williamson, Rajabifard, & Feeney (2003).

REFERENCES

Ackoff, R. (1989). From data to wisdom. *Journal of Applied System Analysis, 16*, 3–9.

Alameh, N. (2003). Chaining geographic information Web Services. *IEEE Internet Computing, 07*(5), 22–29. doi:10.1109/MIC.2003.1232514

Alonso, G., Casati, F., Kuno, H., & Machiraju, V. (2004). *Web Services*. Springer Verlag.

Andrews, T., Curbera, F., Dholakia, H., Goland, Y., Klein, J., Leymann, F., et al. (2003). *Business process execution language for Web Services (version 1.1)*. 136. OASIS. Retrieved from http://download.boulder.ibm.com/ibmdl/pub/software/dw/specs/ws-bpel/ws-bpel.pdf

Anjomashoaa, A., Brisard, F., Drescher, M., Fellows, D., Ly, A., & McGough, S. (2005). *Job Submission Description Language (JSDL) (Specification No. GFD-R.056)*. Global Grid Forum.

Baranski, B. (2008). Grid computing enabled Web processing service. In E. Pebesma, M. Bishr, & T. Bartoschek (Eds.), *Proceedings of the 6th Geographic Information Days*, IfGI prints (Vol. 32, pp. 243-256). Presented at the GI-days 2008, Muenster, Germany: Institute for Geoinformatics. Retrieved from http://www.gi-tage.de/ archive/2008/ downloads/accepted Papers/Papers/ Baranski.pdf

Baranski, B. (2009). *OWS-6 WPS Grid Processing Profile Engineering Report* (OGC Public Engineering Report No. 09-041r3) (p. 101). OGC.

Baranski, B., Schaeffer, B., & Redweik, R. (2009). Geoprocessing in the clouds. In *Proceedings of Free and Open Source Software for Geospatial Conference*. Presented at the Foss4g 2009, Sydney: OSGeo.

Bernard, L., Craglia, M., Gould, M., & Kuhn, W. (2005). Towards an SDI research agenda. In *Proceedings of the 11th EC GIS Conference* (pp. 147-151). Presented at the 11th EC GIS & GIS Workshop and ESDI: Setting the Framework, Sardinia, Italy.

Brauner, J. (2008). Providing GRASS with a Web processing service interface. In E. Pebesma, M. Bishr, & T. Bartoschek (Eds.), *Proceedings of the 6th Geographic Information Days*, IfGI prints (Vol. 32, pp. 91-116). Presented at the GI-days 2008, Muenster, Germany: Institute for Geoinformatics.

Brauner, J., Foerster, T., Schaeffer, B., & Baranski, B. (2009). Towards a research agenda for geoprocessing services. In J. Haunert, B. Kieler, & J. Milde (Eds.), *12th AGILE International Conference on Geographic Information Science*. Presented at the AGILE 2009, Hanover, Germany: IKG, Leibniz University of Hanover. Retrieved from http://www.ikg.uni-hannover. de/agile/file admin/agile/ paper/124.pdf

Brauner, J., & Schaeffer, B. (2008). *Integration of GRASS functionality in Web based SDI service chains*. (pp. 420-429). Presented at the FOSS4G 2008, Cape Town, South Africa. Retrieved from http://www.osgeo.org/ ocs/index. php/foss4g/ 2008/paper/ view/133

Bucher, B., & Jolivet, L. (2008). Acquiring service oriented descriptions of GI processing software from experts . In Bernard, L., Friis-Christensen, A., Pundt, H., & Compte, I. (Eds.), *AGILE 2008*.

Cardoso, J., & Sheth, A. (2003). Semantic e-workflow composition. *Journal of Intelligent Information Systems, 21*(3), 191–225. doi:10.1023/A:1025542915514

Cepicky, J., & Becchi, L. (2007). Geospatial processing via Internet on remote servers - PyWPS. *OSGeo Journal, 1*, 5p.

Chen, M., Ebert, D., Hagen, H., Laramee, R., van Liere, R., & Ma, K. (2009). Data, information, and knowledge in visualization. *Computer Graphics and Applications, IEEE, 29*(1), 12–19. doi:10.1109/MCG.2009.6

Chung, L., Fang, Y., Chou, T., Lee, B., & Baranski, B. (2009). A SOA based debris flow monitoring system. Architecture and proof-of-concept implementation. In *17th International Conference on Geoinformatics* (pp. 1-6). Presented at the Geoinformatics 2009, Washington, USA: IEEE.

Clayberg, E., & Rubel, D. (2008). *Eclipse Plug-ins* (3rd ed.). Addison-Wesley Professional.

de Jesus, J., Hiemstra, P., & Dubois, G. (2008). Web-based geostatistics using WPS. In *Proceedings of GI-days 2008*. Institute for Geoinformatics.

Di, L., Chen, A., Yang, W., & Zhao, P. (2003). *The integration of Grid technology with OGC Web Services (OWS) in NWGISS for NASA EOS Data*. (pp. 24-27). Presented at the GGF8 & HPDC12 2003. Seattle: Science Press.

Diaz, L., Costa, S., Granell, C., & Gould, M. (2007). Migrating geoprocessing routines to Web services for water resource management applications. In M. Wachowicz & L. Bodum (Eds.), *10th AGILE International Conference on Geographic Information Science*. Aalborg University, Denmark.

Douglas, D. H., & Peucker, T. K. (1973). Algorithms for the reduction of the number of points required to represent a digitized line or its caricature. *The Canadian Cartographer, 10*(2), 112–122.

Erl, T. (2005). *Service-Oriented Architecture: concepts, technology, and design*. Prentice Hall PTR.

Foerster, T., Burghardt, D., Neun, M., Regnauld, N., Swan, J., & Weibel, R. (2008). Towards an interoperable Web generalisation services framework. In *Proceedings of the 11th ICA Workshop on Generalization and Multiple Representation*. Montpellier, France.

Foerster, T., & Schaeffer, B. (2007). A client for distributed geo-processing on the web. In G. Tayler & M. Ware (Eds.), *W2GIS*. LCNS 4857, 252-263. Springer.

Foerster, T., & Stoter, J. E. (2006). Establishing an OGC Web processing service for generalization processes. In *Proceedings from ICA workshop on Generalization and Multiple Representation*, Portland, OR. Retrieved from http://aci.ign.fr/Portland/paper/ ICA2006-foerster_ stoter.pdf

Friis-Christensen, A., Bernard, L., Kanellopoulos, I., Nogueras-Iso, J., & Peedell, S. Schade, S. et al. (2006). Building service oriented application on top of a Spatial Data Infrastructure - a forest fire assessment example. In *Proceedings of the 9th Agile Conference on Geographic Information Science* (pp. 119-127). Visegrad, Hungary.

Friis-Christensen, A., Lucchi, R., Lutz, M., & Ostlaender, N. (2009). Service chaining architectures for applications implementing distributed geographic information processing. *International Journal of Geographical Information Science, 23*(5), 561–580. doi:10.1080/13658810802665570

Friis-Christensen, A., Ostlander, N., Lutz, M., & Bernard, L. (2007). Designing service architectures for distributed geoprocessing: challenges and future directions. *Transactions in GIS, 11*(6), 799–818. doi:10.1111/j.1467-9671.2007.01075.x

Geraci, A. (1991). *IEEE standard computer dictionary: compilation of IEEE standard computer glossaries* (Katki, F., McMonegal, L., Meyer, B., Lane, J., Wilson, P., & Radatz, J., Eds.). The Institute of Electrical and Electronics Engineers, Inc.

Granell, C., Diaz, L., & Gould, M. (2007). Managing Earth observation data with distributed geoprocessing services. In *Proceedings from Geoscience and Remote Sensing Symposium* (pp. 4777 - 4780). Presented at the IGARSS 2007, IEEE.

Granell, C., Gould, M., & Ramos, F. (2005). Service composition for SDIs: integrated components creation. In *Proceedings of Sixteenth International Workshop on Database and Expert Systems Applications* (pp. 475-479). Presented at the Workshop on Geographic Information Management (DEXXA 05), Copenhagen: IEEE.

Hartig, K. (2009). *What is cloud computing? Cloud Computing Journal*. SYS-CON Media Inc.

Henneboehl, K., & Pebesma, E. (2008). *Providing R functionality through the OGC Web Processing Service*. Paper presented at the The R user conference, Technische Universitaet Dortmund.

Huber, V. (2001). UNICORE: A Grid computing environment for distributed and parallel computing. In V. Malyshkin (Ed.), *Proceedings of the 6th International Conference on Parallel Computing Technologies* (Vol. 2127, pp. 258-265). Presented at the PaCT 01, Novosibirsk, Russia: Springer.

INSPIRE. (2007a). Directive 2007/2/EC of the European Parliament and of the Council of 14 March 2007 establishing an infrastructure for spatial information in the European community. *Official Journal of the European Union. L&C*, 18.

INSPIRE. (2007b). *INSPIRE Network Services Performance Guidelines* (p. 22). INSPIRE Consolidation Team.

INSPIRE. (2008). *INSPIRE Network Services Architecture* (p. 30). European Commission.

ISO/TC 211. (2005). *Geographic information - Services (ISO Standard 19119)*. 67. International Organization for Standardization.

ITU-T. (1994). *Telephone network and ISDN - quality of service, network management and traffic engineering. International Telecommunication Union*. ITU.

ITU-T. (2001). *Transmission systems and media, digital systems and networks. International Telecommunication Union*. ITU.

Keens, S. (2007). *OWS-4 Workflow IPR (OGC IPR No. 06-187)*. OGC.

Kiehle, C., Greve, K., & Heier, C. (2006). Standardized geoprocessing - taking spatial data infrastructures one step further. In *9th AGILE International Conference on Geographic Information Science* (pp. 273-282). Visegrad, Hungary.

Kiehle, C., Heier, C., & Greve, K. (2007). Requirements for next generation Spatial Data Infrastructures-standardized Web Based geoprocessing and Web Service orchestration. *Transactions in GIS, 11*(6), 819–834. doi:10.1111/j.1467-9671.2007.01076.x

Lake, R., & Farley, J. (2007). Infrastructure for the geospatial Web. In Scharl, A., & Tochtermann, K. (Eds.), *The Geospatial Web, Advanced Information and Knowledge Processing Series* (pp. 15–26). London, UK: Springer.

Lanig, S., Schilling, A., Stollberg, B., & Zipf, A. (2008). Towards standards-based processing of digital elevation models for Grid computing through Web Processing Service (WPS). In *ICCSA*, LCNS 5073. (pp. 191-203). Presented at the Computational Science and Its Applications (ICCSA 2008), Perugia, Italy: Springer Verlag.

Lee, J., Jeon, W., Lee, W., Jeong, S., & Park, S. (2003). *QoS for web services: Requirements and possible approaches*. W3C. Retrieved from http://www.w3c.or.kr/ kr-office/TR/ 2003/ws-qos/

Lehto, L. (2007). Schema translations in a Web service based SDI. In M. Wachowicz & L. Bodum (Eds.), *10th Agile International Conference on Geographic Information Science 2007*. Aalborg University, Denmark.

Lemmens, R. (2006). *Semantic interoperability of distributed geo-services* (Doctoral dissertation, Delft University of Technology). Retrieved from http://www.ncg.knaw.nl/ Publicaties/Geodesy/pdf/63Lem mens.pdf

Lutz, M. (2007). Ontology-based descriptions for semantic discovery and composition of geoprocessing services. *GeoInformatica, 11*(1), 1–36. doi:10.1007/s10707-006-7635-9

Müller, M., Vogel, R., & Bernard, L. (2009). Multi-criteria evaluation for emergency management in a Web service environment. In M. Konecny, S. Zlatanova, T. Bandrova, & L. Friedmannova (Eds.), *Cartography and Geoinformatics for early warning and emergency management: towards better solutions* (pp. 439-446). Presented at the Joint Symposium of ICA Working Group on CEWaCM and JBGIS Gi4DM, Prague: Masaryk University Brno.

Myerson, J. (2008). *Cloud computing versus grid computing* (p. 9). IBM Corporation. Retrieved from http://www.ibm.com/ developer works/web/library/wa- cloudgrid/

Nash, E. (2008). WPS application profiles for generic and specialised processes. In E. Pebesma, M. Bishr, & T. Bartoschek (Eds.), *Proceedings of the 6th Geographic Information Days*, IfGI prints (Vol. 32, pp. 69-79). Presented at the GI-days 2008, Muenster, Germany: Institute for Geoinformatics.

Neteler, M., & Mitasova, H. (2008). Open source GIS: A GRASS GIS approach (3rd ed.). *The International Series in Engineering and Computer Science, 773*. New York: Springer.

Neun, M., Burghardt, D., & Weibel, R. (2008). Automated processing for map generalization using web services. *GeoInformatica*.

OGC. (2007). *OpenGIS Web Processing Service* (OGC implementation specification No. OGC 05-007r7). Open Geospatial Consortium. Retrieved from http://www.open geospatial.org/ standards/ wps

OGC. (2008). *OGC KML* (specification No. OGC 07-147r2). OGC Standard (p. 251). Open Geospatial Consortium. Retrieved from https://portal. open geospatial.org/ files/?artifact_ id=27810

Ostlaender, N. (2009). *Creating specific spatial decision support Systems in Spatial Data Infrastructures*. Unpublished doctoral dissertation, University of Muenster, Germany.

Papazoglou, M. P., & Heuvel, W. (2007). Service oriented architectures: approaches, technologies and research issues. *The International Journal on Very Large Data Bases, 16*(3), 389–415. doi:10.1007/s00778-007-0044-3

Peltz, C. (2003). Web services orchestration and choreography. *Computer, 36*(10), 46–52. doi:10.1109/MC.2003.1236471

Ran, S. (2003). A model for web services discovery with QoS. *SIGecom Exchanges, 4*(1), 1–10. doi:10.1145/844357.844360

Roman, D., & Klien, E. (2007). SWING - a semantic framework for geospatial services . In Scharl, A., & Tochtermann, K. (Eds.), *The Geospatial Web, Advanced Information and Knowledge Processing Series* (pp. 229–234). London: Springer.

Schaeffer, B. (2009). *OGC® OWS-6 geoprocessing workflow architecture engineering Report* (OGC Public Engineering Report No. 09-053r5) (p. 78). OGC.

Schaeffer, B., & Foerster, T. (2008). A client for distributed geo-processing and workflow design. *Journal for Location Based Services, 2*(3), 194–210. doi:10.1080/17489720802558491

Scholten, M., Klamma, R., & Kiehle, C. (2006). Evaluating performance in spatial data infrastructures for geoprocessing. *IEEE Internet Computing, 10*(5), 34–41. doi:10.1109/MIC.2006.97

Staab, S., van der Aalst, W., Benjamins, R., Sheth, A., Miller, J., & Bussler, C. (2003). Web Services: been there, done that? *IEEE Intelligent Systems, 18*(1), 72–85. doi:10.1109/MIS.2003.1179197

Stollberg, B., & Zipf, A. (2007). OGC Web processing service interface for Web service orchestration - aggregating geo-processing services in a bomb threat scenario . In *Proceedings of Web and Wireless Geographical Information Systems, LNCS* (pp. 239–251). Heidelberg, Germany: Springer-Verlag. doi:10.1007/978-3-540-76925-5_18

Stollberg, B., & Zipf, A. (2008). *Geoprocessing services for spatial decision support in the domain of housing market analyses - experiences from applying the OGC Web processing service interface in practice*. Paper presented at the AGILE 2008, Girona, Spain.

Tu, S., Flanagin, M., Wu, Y., Abdelguerfi, A., Normand, E., Mahadevan, V., et al. (2004). Design strategies to improve performance of GIS Web services. *Proceedings of the International Conference on Information Technology: Coding and Computing (ITCC 04), 2*.

Turton, I. (2008). GeoTools . In Hall, G. B., & Leahy, M. G. (Eds.), *Open source approaches in spatial data handling, advances in geographic information* (pp. 153–167). Berlin: Springer Verlag. doi:10.1007/978-3-540-74831-1_8

van der Aalst, W., Dumas, M., Hofstede, A. T., Russell, N., Verbeek, H., & Wohed, P. (2005). Life after BPEL? In *Formal Techniques for Computer Systems and Business Processes*, LCNS 3670, 35-50. Berlin: Springer.

Vaughan-Nichols, S. (2002). Web services: Beyond the hype. *IEEE Computer, 35*(2), 18–21.

Weerawarana, S., Curbera, F., Leymann, F., Storey, T., & Ferguson, D. (2005). *Web services platform architecture: SOAP, WSDL, WS-policy, WS-addressing, WS-BPEL, WS-reliable messaging, and more*. Prentice Hall PTR.

Weiser, A., & Zipf, A. (2007). Web service orchestration of OGC Web services for disaster management . In Li, J., Zlatanova, S., & Fabbri, A. (Eds.), *Geomatics Solutions for Disaster Management, LNGC* (pp. 239–254). Berlin: Springer Verlag. doi:10.1007/978-3-540-72108-6_16

Werling, M. (2008). *OGC® OWS-5 GeoProcessing workflow architecture engineering report* (Discussion paper no. 07-138r1) (p. 34). OGC.

Williamson, I., Rajabifard, A., & Feeney, M. F. (2003). Future directions in SDI development . In *Developing Spatial Data Infrastructures: From concept to reality* (pp. 301–312). Taylor & Francis.

KEY TERMS AND DEFINITIONS

Distributed Geoprocessing: The approach to realize complex geoprocess models (mostly modelled as geoprocessing workflows) on the web by the means of distributed resources Geoprocessing Services.

Geoprocess Model: Handles geodata in a geospatial context for representing real-world processes (such as simulations). In particular such geoprocess models are based on GIS analysis.

Geoprocessing Workflows: Complex geoprocess models consisting of multiple analysis steps, which are again geoprocess models. In a distributed service architecture this geoprocessing workflow is realized as a sequence of chained services.

OGC WPS: The OGC WPS interface specification describes a standardized method to publish and execute web-based geoprocess models of any type.

SOA: Service oriented architectures consist of distributed resources, which can be integrated into existing workflows using the publish find bind pattern.

WPS Client Application: An application allowing users to communicate with distributed WPS instances and integrate the WPS-based geoprocess models into their workflows.

ENDNOTES

[1] 52°North Geoprocessing Community website: www.52north.org/wps.

[2] SLA4D-GRID project website: http://www.sla4d-grid.de/.

[3] uDig website: http://udig.refractions.net.

[4] The Sixth Environment Action Programme of the European Community: http://ec.europa.eu/environment/newprg/index.htm.

Chapter 12
Implementing Geospatial Web Services for Cloud Computing

Gobe Hobona
University of Nottingham, UK

Mike Jackson
University of Nottingham, UK

Suchith Anand
University of Nottingham, UK

ABSTRACT

Cloud computing is concerned with the provision of hardware, infrastructure, software and data as services on the internet. A key attraction of cloud computing is that the infrastructure from which services are offered is able to scale upwards automatically as the load on the services increases. This chapter examines the potential for offering capabilities of the Geographic Resources Analysis Support System (GRASS) as a service within a compute cloud. GRASS is a free and open source desktop Geographic Information System (GIS). The chapter describes a prototype service that adopts the Web Processing Service (WPS) standard of the Open Geospatial Consortium (OGC). A case study is presented applying the prototype in the analysis of satellite imagery. The chapter concludes that the WPS standard can facilitate the provision of geospatial capability in compute clouds.

INTRODUCTION

It is estimated that approximately 80% of all digital information is referenced to a location, for example, any addressed document has a post code/zip code that can be referenced to a geographic space(MacEachren & Kraak, 2001). Geographically-referenced information is a fundamental aspect of operations in aviation, disaster management, e-government, environmental management, public administration, town planning, weather forecasting, security and policing. Further, most events reported in the news (such as football matches, floods, elections) happen at a spatially-referenced location. The growing availability of data through advances in Earth observation systems is expected to result in an increase in the need for geospatial processing capability. For example, former US

DOI: 10.4018/978-1-60960-192-8.ch012

Under Secretary of Commerce for Oceans and Atmosphere, Condrad Lautenbacher (2006: pp. 10) cautioned that "new observation systems will lead to a 100-fold increase in Earth observation data. Only by viewing observations as part of an end-to-end process will we fully maximize their utility". Further, mobile phones with built-in positioning devices now offer home users the ability to determine the geographic coordinates of any location and potentially map the location using web-based applications such as Google Maps, Google Earth or Microsoft Bing Maps. Although such mobile phones make it easier for home users to map locations, additional services are needed for processing collected data and integrating the data with other existing datasets; cloud computing offers a framework through which such processing and integration could be provided(NIST, 2009).

Cloud computing is concerned with the provision of hardware, infrastructure, software and data as services on the internet. Users interact with the services through thin clients such as web browsers. Wang et al (2008) identify three primary functionalities of cloud computing: Hardware as a Service (HaaS), Software as a Service (SaaS) and Data as a Service (DaaS). Recent studies have referred to HaaS as Infrastructure as a Service (IaaS) with recognition that virtualization offers more than just hardware (Vaquero, Rodero-Merino, Caceres, & Lindner, 2009). IaaS offer on-demand computational resources in the form of virtual machines, hosted in a cloud service provider's infrastructure. An example of IaaS is Amazon's Elastic Compute Cloud (EC2). Cloud computing also offers platforms on which systems can run, this is referred to as Platform as a Service (PaaS). An example is the Google App Engine (GAE), which does not offer direct access to a virtual machine but instead offers deployment in a running application server. Consistent with Vaquero et al (2009: pp.51), this book Chapter defines compute clouds as a "large pool of easily usable and accessible virtualized resources (such as hardware, development platforms and/

or services). These resources can be dynamically re-configured to adjust to a variable load (scale), allowing also for an optimum resource utilization. This pool of resources is typically exploited by a pay-per-use model in which guarantees are offered by the Infrastructure Provider by means of customized SLAs".

Within a geospatial context IaaS could offer a virtualization environment where users could deploy Geographic Information Systems (GIS) software to run computationally intensive tasks. DaaS could offer storage and retrieval of the petabytes of data that Earth Observing satellites produce every year. SaaS, as this paper will demonstrate, could offer geospatial functionality remotely hosted on third party machines. This paper will describe a specialization of SaaS involving the provision of geospatial capability; we shall refer to the approach as Geospatial SaaS (GeoSaaS). Approaches for distributed and parallel processing within cloud computing are inherited from web services and Grid computing. This often leads to confusion between cloud and grid computing as Vaquero et al (2009) observe. However, Vaquero et al (2009) also identify areas such as security and interoperability where there is a clear distinction between the cloud and grid computing. We contend that lessons learnt in the integration of Grid computing and geospatial web services(Lee & Percivall, 2008) provide a foundation for the development of GeoSaaS. One such lesson is the provision of geospatial capability in distributed platforms through the Geographic Resources Analysis Support System (GRASS).

This Chapter will address the question "**can a compute cloud offer geospatial processing capability as a service using a standardized interface?**". The Chapter shall discuss the implementation of a prototype GeoSaaS and its deployment in a compute cloud. The prototype service is a wrapping of the free and open source GRASS in a web service compliant to standards of the Open Geospatial Consortium (OGC), which is a group of over 300 private, public and academic organizations that promote interoperability between geospatial technologies through education, standards, testbeds and other initiatives. A Case Study is presented that uses the GRASS-supported web services to process satellite imagery using raster arithmetic (similar to matrix algebra). The discussion section of the Chapter considers the role of open source software on cloud-based virtualization infrastructure. With the potential for data to be processed on third-party resources, the Chapter also discusses implications for security and privacy, when processing geospatial data in clouds. To ensure a direct relation to spatial data infrastructure, a discussion on the relevance of cloud computing in spatial data infrastructure is offered.

GEOSPATIAL WEB SERVICES

Hayes suggests that a cloud computing system "must be able to coordinate information coming from multiple sources, not all which are under the control of the same organization"(Hayes, 2008: pp. 11). Therefore, for cloud computing services to be able to process the multitude of geospatial data types and integrate the various types of geospatial data sources, interoperability is essential. Interoperability specifications for geospatial web services are standardized by the OGC. The OGC Service Architecture described in the international standard ISO 19119, offers an abstract specification for geospatial web services. Interoperability between these web services is facilitated through standardization of common geographic data types such as coordinate systems, vector data models, raster data models, service interfaces and others.

In this section we introduce a few of the popular web service standards developed by the OGC. The web service specifications are based on the ISO19119. The services disseminate, process and portray geospatial information. Web Map Services (WMS) offer an interface for accessing dynamically rendered portrayals (maps). Web Feature Services (WFS) offer an interface for disseminating vector geospatial data. Web Coverage Services (WCS) offer an interface for disseminating raster geospatial data. WMS can obtain data from WFS and WCS, as well as from Database Management Systems (DBMS) such as Oracle Spatial[1]. WFS and WCS can also obtain data from a DBMS. Web Processing Services (WPS) offer an interface for publishing geocomputational algorithms such as constructive area geometry or climate models. Catalogue Services for the Web (CSW) offer an interface for discovery and retrieval of metadata about geospatial data and services. The OGC has a close relationship with other standardization bodies such as the Organization for the Advancement of Structured Information Systems (OASIS), which has led to the adoption of OASIS standards in OGC activities, for example there is now a CSW profile of the OASIS ebRIM standard.

The OGC has standardized web service operations for discovery, description and retrieval of resources. All OGC web services offer a getCapabilities operation for retrieving the list of resources available through the services. WFS offers a describeFeatureType operation that presents a schema definition of vector data offered by the web service. WCS offer a describeCoverage operation that presents a description of raster datasets, including for example, a list of supported formats and maximum permissible pixel dimensions. WPS offer a describeProcess operation that lists and describes input and output parameters of algorithms offered by the service. CSW offer a describeRecord operation that presents the information model adopted by the metadata offered by the service. For retrieving resources, WFS offer a getFeature operation that returns features encoded in Geography Markup Language (GML), an application schema of XML. WCS offer a getCoverage operation that returns a raster dataset in a variety of formats, for example JPEG, GeoTIFF and ArcGRID (encoded in ASCII text). CSW offer a getRecord operation that returns metadata based on a set of search parameters. WPS offer an Execute operation that invokes an algorithm and returns the results of the algorithm.

BACKGROUND: GRASS GIS ON THE WEB

GRASS was originally developed by the US Army Corp of Engineers (Goran & Finney, 1991). The system adopts a modular architecture where all functions are implemented as separate, though tightly coupled, programs. The architecture supports both vector and raster geospatial data models. Vector geospatial datasets model individual entities as points, lines and polygons. Raster geospatial datasets model the continuous variation of phenomenon as regular grids similar to matrices (e.g. TIFF images showing temperature over location). The raster data architecture implemented in GRASS is implemented on top of the Geospatial Data Abstraction Library (GDAL)—an open source library for reading and writing geospatial data formats. The vector data architecture comprises of geometry and attribute management sections. The geometry section offers support for reading and writing to PostgreSQL/ PostGIS, ESRI shapefiles and native GRASS files. ESRI Shapefiles are the historic de-facto standard for GIS. A single shapefile includes a DBF, SHP and SHX file. Geometry is stored in the SHP file; the attributes are stored in the Dbase DBF file; an index for accessing the geometries quickly is stored in the SHX file. PostGIS is the spatial extension of the PostgreSQL database. The native GRASS vector files are used for storing geometries as flat files. A mediator, called the Database Management Interface (DBMI), between the source database and the GRASS modules handles access to attributes in the vector datasets.Several studies have produced research on the web-enabling of GRASS for environmental information management. This section will describe some of the related key studies. Other

studies discussing the web-enabling of GRASS are reflected on by Mitasova and Neteler (2004).

Raghavan et al (2002) implemented an online landslide information system for Japan. Their system offers a spatial query option that allows the user to retrieve data from a relational database engine through spatial predicates. The user is able to select GRASS data layers through a menu on a web page. The system allows the user to select vector data layers to overlay on top of the raster data layers. The system also allows the user to view 3D models in Virtual Reality Modeling Language (VRML). The authors acknowledge that one of the main limitations of the system is the lack of support for geospatial interoperability standards. One of the implications of insufficient interoperability is that the system is limited to only GRASS data formats. They however, acknowledge the significant benefit of adopting international standards for enabling the system to offer seamless access to geospatial data. They concluded that the system could be easily adapted in a distributed database environment because of its use of open source software.

Hess(2002) describes a study wrapping GRASS in a PHP-based web application. The prototype was composed of a PHP interpreter and GRASS daemon. The PHP interpreter creates two separate files in a communication directory, one file for GRASS commands and another for Unix commands. The GRASS daemon continuously scans the communication directory and if it finds a command file (with a.sh extension) it executes the commands in the file; thereafter the command file is deleted. Their prototype offered a wrapping of the GRASS sunmask function that uses a sun position algorithm to compute shadow regions. The user interface is an HTML form that allows the user to enter their email address and parameters for the sunmask function (i.e. month, day, hour and minute). When the function is invoked, the GRASS commands are executed together with the input parameters. After invocation is completed the results of the sunmask function are converted to a jpeg and emailed back to the user. They argue that concurrency and asynchronous invocation are two important issues in the wrapping of standalone applications as web applications. Their prototype offers asynchronous invocation through a post-processing emailing mechanism.

Another study exploring the wrapping of GRASS GIS as a service is presented by Di et al (2007). Their paper describes the GeoBrain system developed at George Mason University (GMU). The system is part of a geospatial Grid system developed by GMU for processing, archiving, managing and distributing NASA Earth Observing System (EOS) data. The system addresses difficulties encountered by scientists in accessing or analyzing large volumes of EOS data. NASA archives EOS data in HDF-EOS format however, only a few analysis software packages can completely support the format. Further, EOS produces very large global datasets that exceed the hardware and software capabilities of most scientific computing laboratories. Di et al (2007) note that NASA EOS data pools offer approximately 1 Petabyte of data. GeoBrain offers geospatial web services based on standards of the OGC. The grid web service components are implemented using the Globus Toolkit. The geospatial functionality is provided through an installation of the GRASS GIS, accessed through a SOAP-web service interface. The system offers more than 50 operations, developed on top of GRASS, by extending an implementation of the 52°North WPS. The GMU implementation is possibly the earliest example of a GRASS-supported WPS and was successfully demonstrated during the fourth phase of the OGC interoperability testbed (OWS-4) in 2006(OGC, 2006). The Integrated Multiple-protocol Geoinformation Client (MPGC) offers a user interface for the data sources and the workflow management system. Through the MPGC a user can build a geoprocessing workflow, then submit it to the virtual data manager and the workflow execution manager for enactment.

Bergenheim et al (2009) presented an implementation of a GRASS-supported WPS. The implementation offers a generalisation service supported by the GRASS module v.generalize. The generalisation module allows for simplification and smoothing of linear geometries using the Douglas-Peucker algorithm (Douglas & Peucker, 1973). The WPS was implementation in PHP, which is an HTML-embedded scripting language, developed to run through a PHP module associated with a web server. The WPS initializes itself when an incoming request is received by the PHP module. During initialization, the WPS reads in a configuration file that specifies the environment properties (for example, the working directory, GRASS GIS configuration and so on). Bergenheim et al (2009) implemented a mechanism that enables new GRASS-supported processes to be added to the WPS through specification in an XML file. However, for complex processes requiring multiple GRASS GIS modules, a scripted program is required. The WPS distinguishes between GRASS-supported processes and native processes. The GRASS-supported processes typically require a single GRASS GIS module to work but could also involve chaining multiple modules together. In contrast, native processes do not require GRASS to work. This distinction is made because GRASS-supported processes in the generalisation service require additional steps in order to execute. These additional steps include transfer of imported data into a database before execution and export of the resulting data out of the GRASS GIS database into a format suitable for return to the service requestor. Our implementation differs from that of Bergenheim et al (2009) because ours is implemented in an enterprise Java environment instead of PHP. However, we acknowledge their implementation as a possible alternative to our approach.

Brauner & Schäffer (2008) presented an approach for integrating a GRASS-supported WPS in a service chain. They applied the WPS within a workflow for calculating the Normalised Differenced Vegetation Index (NDVI). Taking the pixel values of near infrared (N) and visible red (V) bands of a satellite image, NDVI is calculated by dividing the difference between values of N and V pixels by their sum. In developing the GRASS-supported WPS, they employed an XSLT filter for automatically transforming descriptions of GRASS functionality to WPS process descriptions. The filter significantly assisted the creation interfacing of GRASS functionality with WPS process. However, the filter still required human input in order to identify which processes are feasible and which inputs are complex. Their implementation employed a shell script for creating a workspace, importing data, processing the data and exporting the data. The processing capability within the WPS leveraged the *r.mapcalc* operation of GRASS. The *r.mapcalc* operation offers arithmetic calculations on pixels between different raster datasets. They implemented a service chain that involved clipping a dataset, calculating the NDVI and then applying a classification scheme in order to render the resulting dataset. Their study also extended the 52°North WPS to provide GRASS-supported processes.

Yue et al (2009) present a web service toolkit for geoprocessing called GeoPW. The geoprocessing services offered by the toolkit are developed by extending the 52°North WPS to offer a wrapper over GRASS and GeoStar software. GeoStar is an enterprise GIS software package. It offers functional components for feature and image data management, processing, and visualization. Whereas the 52°North WPS invokes GRASS functions through an instance of the GRASS command interface, the GeoStar functions are invoked via Windows Console applications. The Windows console applications invoke GeoStar through a dynamic link library (DLL). Similar to implementations by Di et al(2007) and Brauner & Schaeffer (2008), the GeoPW employs shell scripts to invoke GRASS commands. The sequence of internal commands that are needed to complete a GeoPW process are described in a

configuration file. An example process, made up of GRASS functions, could include importing, processing and exporting data. The configuration files could also describe the data bindings between input and output parameters of a process. The WPS generates executable scripts based on these configuration files.

It should be noted that although Yue et al (2009), Brauner & Schäffer (2008) and Di et al (2007) all extended the 52°North WPS to provide GRASS-supported processes, their implementations are different and implemented independently from one another. The 52°North open source software community intends to implement built-in support for GRASS within the WPS; however, as at March 14th 2010 the capability is still a work-in-progress(52°North, 2010b) and is not yet included in the source code distribution(52°North, 2010a). Considering that multiple studies have implemented independent versions of GRASS-supported WPS, it can be expected that future versions of the 52°North WPS will offer some standardizations of the implementations.

Considering some of the origins of cloud computing as coming from grid computing(Vaquero et al., 2009), we highlight that previous studies have examined the application of OGC web services in grid computing, as presented in a recent special issue of the GIS.Science journal[2]. Based on the example of the 2005 Hurricane Katrina, Lee and Percivall(2009) identify steps for future advancement of grid-enabled geospatial technologies in order to better predict such catastrophic weather events. They argue that to effectively predict and mitigate such events as Hurricane Katrina, advancements are needed in computational science and operational infrastructure. They highlight that advances in computational science are needed to create the necessary models and codes to accurately predict environmental disasters. They also highlight that advances in operational infrastructure and geographic information systems are needed to enable the necessary resources to be allocated on-demand to support decision makers and first responders. Another study examining the integration of grid and geospatial technologies is presented by Woolf and Shaon (2009). Their article describes use of geoprocessing technologies with grid-based standards such as Job Submission Description Language (JSDL). The potential for applying another grid-based standard, the Web Services Resource Framework (WSRF), within geospatial applications is explored by Kurzbach et al (2009). Collectively these studies highlight the beginnings of convergence between grid and geospatial standards. However, none of the aforementioned studies examines the role of cloud computing within future geospatial data infrastructure.

A related study that examined the deployment of the 52 North WPS within a compute cloud is presented by Baranski et al (2009a). Their study tested the potential for the 52 North WPS to be deployed in Google App Engine(GAE). They stress tested the WPS by sending up to 200 requests simultaneously to an instance of the WPS deployed locally and another deployed remotely(in GAE). They observed that response time of the remote WPS remains almost constant for up to 200 simultaneous requests; whereas the response time of the locally deployed WPS gradually increases as the number of requests increase. Their results give an indication of the elasticity of GAE in comparison to local servers. They concluded that by using GAE, "response times could be held almost constant in contrast to a non-cloud approach"(Baranski et al., 2009a). In a follow-on study they deployed the WPS in both GAE and Amazon EC2(Baranski, Schaeffer, & Redweik, 2009b). Similarly they observed that for up to 200 simultaneous requests, the response time remained almost constant in Amazon EC2. They suggested that the slight increase in response time in both GAE and Amazon EC2 could be due to "bottlenecks concerning the data allocation from an external server, laborious internal processing steps in the performance testing tool, and high traffic at the local machine and in the local sub-

network when running the performance testing tool" (Baranski et al., 2009b: pp. 26). There are similarities between their approach and ours, specifically, both studies deploy the 52 North WPS within Amazon EC2. However, our research examines the role of GRASS in supporting a WPS within the cloud whereas their study does not. We contend therefore that the two studies are complementary and together provide motivation for closer integration between geospatial and cloud computing.

CLOUD COMPUTING

In a comprehensive 2-page definition of cloud computing, the United States National Institute of Standards and Technology (NIST) offers the following summary "cloud computing is a model for enabling convenient, on-demand network access to a shared pool of configurable computing resources (e.g., networks, servers, storage, applications, and services) that can be rapidly provisioned and released with minimal management effort or service provider interaction"(Mell & Grance, 2009b). NIST also acknowledges that cloud computing is still an evolving paradigm, therefore, its definitions and characteristics will change over time. Summaries of the essential characteristics identified by NIST and illustrated in Figure 2 are:

- On-demand self-service: Users are able to access and consume computing capabilities, such as compute or storage resources, at anytime without human interaction with service providers.
- Broad network access: Compute and storage resources are available over the Internet and can be accessed through a variety of conventional clients (e.g. web browsers, mobile phones and terminal clients).

- Resource pooling: The resources offered within a cloud are shared to serve multiple consumers through a multi-tenant model.
- Rapid elasticity: Resources can be created, consumed and disposed of rapidly and elastically, in some cases automatically, to provide scalability on demand.
- Measured Service: Resource usage can be transparently monitored and controlled in order to ensure a reasonable quality of service for users of the cloud and also to bill subscribers for resources consumed.

We contend that the following characteristics are essential for a geospatial compute cloud:

- Geographic Information Systems (GIS): Applications offering geographic algorithms, environmental models, and other geospatial functions are needed to enable rapid creation and provision of geospatial capabilities within the Cloud.
- Interoperability Standards: Adoption of standardized interfaces by resources offered within the Cloud is needed for achieving interoperability between compute clouds and existing geospatial service infrastructure.

The rest of this section describes the delivery models, illustrated in Figure 2, through examples from related studies. The delivery models include Data as a Service (DaaS), Software as a Service (SaaS), Platform as a Service (PaaS), and Infrastructure as a Service (IaaS).

An example of DaaS was presented by Zhu et al (2006). They presented a study on enabling organisations to share resources by making data available as a service. The application was developed for a federated infrastructure, wherein several data sources are managed by autonomous entities. The named the concept DaaS and acknowledged its origins in SaaS. They proposed a service oriented data integration architecture

(SODIA) that provides a dynamically unified view of data on demand from various heterogeneous and distributed data sources. The architecture allows service providers to publish data through a data intensive service they refered to as a Data Access Service (DAS). Through the DAS, the consumer is able to discover the data input, out, format, security policy, cost and quality of service. The consumer is also able to discover the domain and functionality related to the data. The DAS is supported by an ontology, which is a formal representation of concepts(Agarwal, 2005). Ontologies have been used widely within information systems to improve semantic interoperability between heterogeneous applications(Fonseca, Egenhofer, Agouris, & Camara, 2002). Zhu et al (2006) presented a prototype implementation of SODIA that included a Federated Schema Service (FSS) and a Federated Query Service (FQS). The FSS maintains the federated schema and all the mappings between the local export schema and the global federated schema. The FQS contained a query decomposer that consults with the FSS in order to extract multiple local queries from a federated query. The FQS also receives the set of local results and combines them into a federated record. Zhu et al (2006) reported that a Security service is being implemented within a revised version of the prototype. The Security service provides dynamic enforcement of access control policies of the DASs. Through their implementation of DAS, FQS and FSS to offer DaaS, they concluded that although web services provide a good infrastructure layer, integration demands a higher level broker layer. We observe that access control through a security service, semantic interoperability through ontologies and dynamic data integration through data views generated on-demand are key characteristics of DaaS as presented by Zhu et al (2006).

IaaS involves making infrastructure such as a virtualization platform available as a service. Virtualization services allow for the creation of virtual machines that offer the same operating systems as physical machines. An example of an IaaS service that offers virtualization services is Amazon EC2, which enables users to create instances of a variety of operating systems including Windows Server, Fedora and Ubuntu Linux. Alternatively, a compute cloud may offer a platform for deployment of web applications such as those based on enterprise Java. Where a platform is offered instead of infrastructure, the service is referred to as PaaS. An example of PaaS is Google App Engine. For obvious commercial reasons, the architecture of Amazon EC2 and Google App Engine are not public, however, open source communities have developed software for establishing compute clouds. The "Intel Cloud Builder Guide to Cloud Design and Deployment on Intel Platforms" (hereinafter refered to as the Intel Whitepaper) describes a reference implementation of a cloud using the free and open source Eucalyptus and Ubuntu Enterprise Cloud (Intel Corporation, Canonical Ltd., & Eucalyptus Systems, 2010). These open source products enable organisations to establish 'clouds' using the same API and interfaces that are offered by Amazon EC2. Adopting an API based on that of Amazon EC2 offers smaller enterprise clouds the possibility of scaling to leverage larger clouds such as Amazon EC2. An illustration of the logical architecture of the reference implementation of the Eucalyptus cloud is presented in Figure 1. The Intel Whitepaper describes an implementation that included 12 servers, allowing for the creation of 128 virtual machines with associated storage of 1.4TB in size. Each virtual machine could be started and stopped, from a Secure Shell (SSH) command tool, without affecting the other virtual machines running in the same cloud. The architecture included a Cloud Controller which virtualizes the servers, storage, network and other underlying resources. The architecture also includes Cluster Controllers that offer a front-end for each cluster defined in the cloud. The Node Controllers are the machines on which instances of virtual machines run. Storage for each cluster is offered by the

Storage Controller, whereas the storage for the complete cloud is offered by a dedicated Storage service. A Management Platform provides various interfaces for cloud administration and configuration.

SaaS enables software functionality to be provided as a set of distributed services on the World Wide Web, thereby allowing for the separation of possession and ownership of the software from its use. Turner et al (2003) proposed a SaaS model that configures, executes and disengages one or more services based on user-defined requirements. They highlighted the role of a service integration layer within a SaaS model, offering service description, discovery, delivery and composition functionality. They identified various web service standards that offer these functions including for example, the Business Process Execution Language (BPEL) which allows for composition of service chains and their publishing as a service. Other example web service standards identified as key to the service integration layer included Web Service Description Language (WSDL) for describing the required bindings of services and the Simple Object Access Protocol (SOAP) for encoding messages transmitted between a service requestor and service provider. They argued that a key part of the SaaS model is the service negotiation which allows the client and requestor to negotiate the terms and conditions of service delivery. We observe that OGC web services already offer operations for service description, discovery and delivery. These are the Describe*Resource*, GetCapabilities and Get*Resource* operations respectively (where resource may be a feature type, coverage or observation for example). These OGC operations have the potential to support service negotiation within a SaaS context. We also observe that since 2006, new OGC web service standards or revisions of existing ones are supposed to offer optional support for SOAP/WSDL[3]. Turner et al (2003) observed that in the SaaS model it will be possible to dynamically compose services, when needed,

Figure 1. Eucalyptus reference cloud architecture

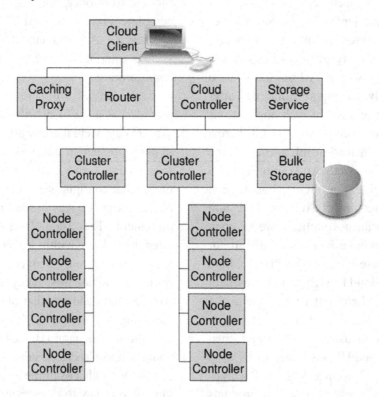

DESIGN AND IMPLEMENTATION

by binding several other lower-level services. There are currently several SaaS applications available for end users, for example, Gmail, Google Talk, Google Calendar, Google Docs (documents, spreadsheets, presentations, collaboration), Zoho Office, Microsoft Windows Live and so on(Kim, 2009). Morevover, many startup SaaS vendors provide their services on Amazon Web Services, which includes Amazon EC2 (Kim, 2009). As related studies have already demonstrated dynamic chaining of OGC web services using BPEL (Hobona, Fairbairn, & James, 2007; Yue, Di, Yang, Yu, & Zhao, 2007), our study considers the development and deployment of a GRASS-supported GeoSaaS prototype within a compute cloud as contributing towards closer integration of geospatial and cloud computing.

This section describes the implementation of the prototype GeoSaaS. GRASS is implemented in the C programming language, primarily for the Unix/Linux platform though it has been ported to Cygwin. The software is executable through a Graphical User Interface or alternatively through a command terminal. This means that to interface with GRASS modules, a Java application may either use the Java Native Interface (JNI) or may invoke commands through the exec method of the Java Runtime class. For an application such as GRASS that has interdependent modules, the JNI approach has the potential to invoke a module and ignore other dependent modules thereby crashing the software or even the operating system! The Runtime.exec approach interacts with the application at user interface level therefore interdependent modules are invoked the same way a

Figure 2. An extension of the NIST definition of cloud computing with GIS, interoperability standards and DaaS (adapted from Mell & Grance (2009a))

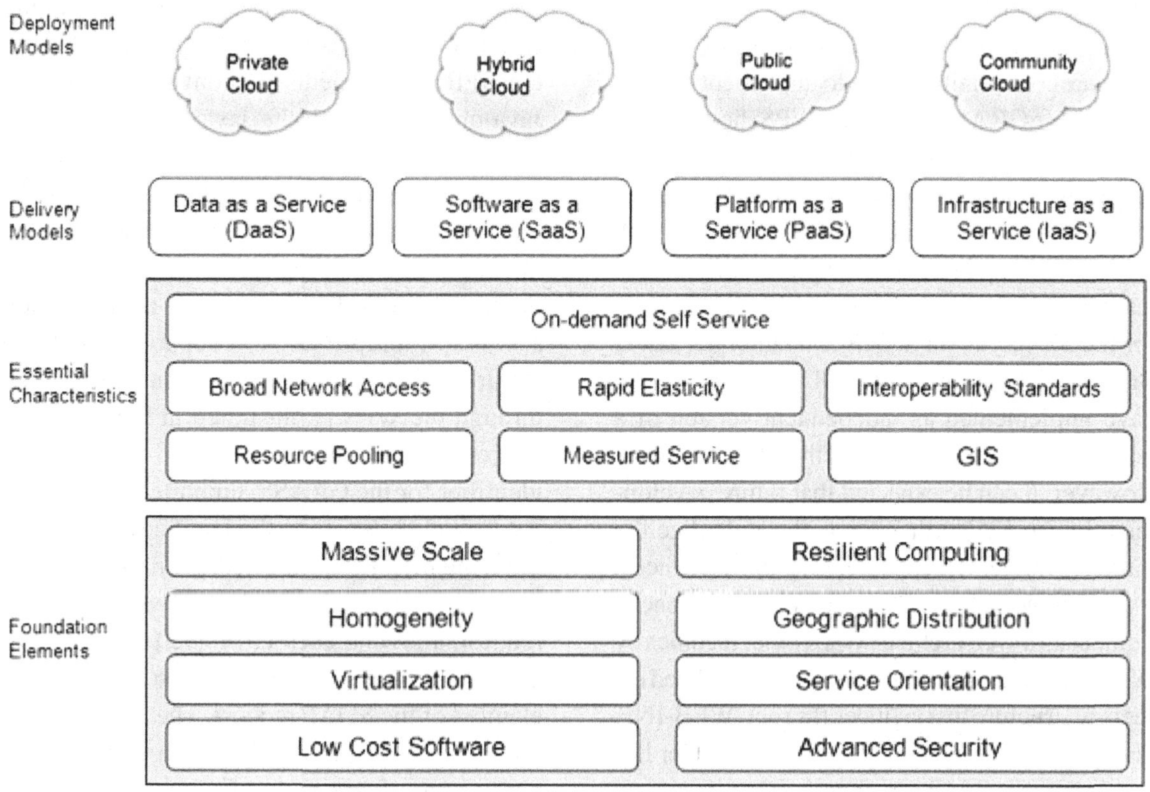

user would manually invoke them. Our geospatial SaaS therefore interfaces with GRASS modules through Java's Runtime class. This approach however, has implications on the asynchronous behavior of the service. GRASS is developed such that only one command can be invoked at a time; even though a batch command can be invoked, the software needs to complete a task before another can be initiated. This means that asynchronous invocation has to be offered and managed by the wrapping service.

Configuration of GRASS requires setting folders for the *location* and *mapset*. The Location folder stores files describing the geographic extent of a project. All datasets in the same Location folder use the coordinate system and geographic extent specified in that Location folder. A Mapset is a folder that organizes maps thematically,

geographically or by project; it is physically a folder within the Location folder. The mapset offers authorization management by allowing only owners of mapsets to select and modify them. The PERMANENT mapset contains read-only base-maps accessible by everyone. Other mapsets can be created and it is necessary to ensure that the WPS has read/write access to these additional mapsets in order to offer GRASS functionality with WPS. A service broker allocates incoming requests to any available GRASS-supported WPS. We refer to the service broker as the GeoProcessing Broker (GPB). The role of the GPB is to mediate between clients and multiple WPS. It is envisioned that mediation through the GPB could benefit compute clouds by enabling applications to distribute processing amongst multiple virtual machines offering the same WPS processes.

Taking the 52°North[4] WPS as a reference implementation, our study developed a WPS wrapper around an installation of GRASS. As already mentioned, the 52°North open source software community intends to implement built-in support for GRASS within the WPS; however, as at March 14th 2010 the capability is still a work-in-progress(52°North, 2010b) and is not yet included in the source code distribution(52°North, 2010a). As explained earlier in this Chapter, multiple studies have implemented their own GRASS interfaces for the 52°North WPS(Bergenheim et al., 2009; Brauner & Schäffer, 2008; Di et al., 2007). We have implemented an independent version of a GRASS-supported instance of the 52°North WPS. However, it can be expected that future development of the 52°North WPS will standardize the multiple implementations of GRASS interfaces.

We deployed the 52°North WPS into Apache Tomcat as a web archive (WAR) file; technically WAR files are zipped files with a standardized directory structure that includes the root, WEB-INF, classes and lib folders. The WEB-INF folder lies inside the root folder and contains the classes and lib folders. Any file outside the WEB-INF folder but inside the root folder or its subfolders can be accessed via URL through the web application. Any file in the classes folder or its subfolders can be retrieved through the getResource method offered by the Java class Class. When the WPS receives a request with a reference to a vector dataset, the service converts the dataset to a shapefile using the GeoTools[5] toolkit. The service then copies the shapefile to the GRASS Location folder and imports it into GRASS. After the GRASS processing has been completed, the service returns the shapefile to the web application to be exported with the WPS response. In contrast, when the WPS receives a raster dataset, the service copies the dataset to the GRASS Location folder without conversion because GRASS uses the GDAL package for reading and writing raster datasets. All of these actions are transparent to the user.

The GPB is accessed through a SOAP-based interface that imports OGC WPS schemas. Figure 3 shows the location of the GPB within a compute cloud. When the SOAP message is received by the GPB, the elements are converted to runtime Java objects through the Java™ API for XML-Based Web Services (JAX-WS). In addition to the Execute complexType offered by the WPS, the GPB introduces a parameter called 'host' for the target service. The host parameter accepts a WPS endpoint reference to offer a single client access to multiple GRASS-supported WPS, as illustrated in Figure 3. The input and output data through the WPS is illustrated in Figure 4. Our implementation accepts URLs of coverages, an identifier for the GRASS-supported process and the formula to apply to the input coverages. The implementation requires URLs of multiple coverages to be separated by hashes (#) within a service request, allowing each coverage to be given an alphabetical identifier for inclusion in the formula element of the SOAP request. The formula illustrated in Figure 4 is simply A-B, a subtraction of one coverage from another. Our prototype applied special characters (i.e. ") to enable the formulae to be forwarded from the service request to the GRASS script via the XML-encoded WPS requests. However, we acknowledge the potential use of the Mathematical Markup Language (MathML)[6] standard of the World Wide Web Consortium (W3C). Future work on OGC web service standards should consider the potential application of MathML for representing formulae.

DEPLOYMENT

We deployed the GeoSaaS prototype in Amazon EC2, a commercial compute cloud. Amazon EC2 offers virtualization infrastructure on which users can select the operating system, web server and applications to create an instance of a virtual machine by. Once the instance has been created, the user interacts with the operating system through

Figure 3.

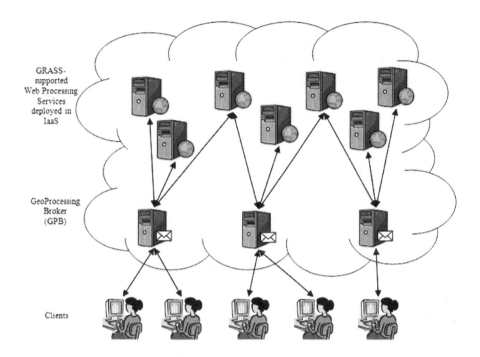

Figure 4. Input and output within the prototype GeoSaaS

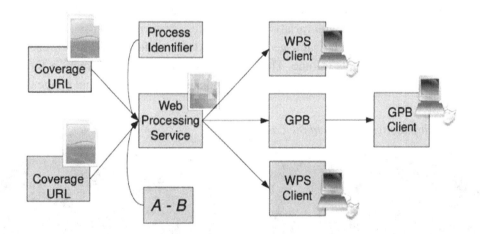

either Remote Desktop, if it is running Microsoft Windows, or Secure Shell (SSH) if it is running Linux. As our implementation is supported by GRASS, we created an instance running Linux. Amazon EC2 charges the user for the time the instance is running and the amount of incoming or outgoing data. The deployment process included

installation of GRASS, Glassfish application server (with the GPB) and Apache Tomcat (with the 52°North WPS). Post installation tasks included configuration of the GRASS mapset and location. Installing GRASS into the basic Fedora Linux image offered by EC2, we found that the pre-installed Rubygems package conflicted with the installation of GRASS. Rubygems is a packaging application used for distributing programs implemented in Ruby. To overcome this, we uninstalled Rubygems and then successfully installed GRASS. All other software required for our prototype was installed without any obstacles. Our study also considered deployment in GAE. However, GAE only offered access to an application server and not an operating system. This means that one is not able to deploy and configure GRASS within GAE. However, we acknowledge that for geoprocesses that are entirely implemented in Java or Python (and executable within its 30-second time limit), GAE would be an alternative platform for deployment.

CASE STUDY: EARTH OBSERVATION IMAGERY ANALYSIS

In order to determine whether our proposed GeoSaaS can be integrated in a service oriented geospatial architecture, a use case was developed that addresses change detection in satellite imagery. Change detection is concerned with variation of reflectance values captured over the same geographic extent but over two points in time. The variation of reflectance values is caused by changes in objects on the ground for example, destruction caused by a forest fire. From an analysis of various image algebra change detection techniques, Lu et al (2004)concluded that image differencing is the most commonly used and thus recommend the technique for digital change detection.

Our case study adopted imagery captured by the Moderate Resolution Imaging Spectroradiometer (MODIS) sensor aboard NASA's Terra satellite. The first image, taken on May 10th 2010, is presented on the left in Figure 5. The second image, taken on May 12th 2010, is presented on the right in Figure 5. Both the images are from the MODIS Aerosol Product which monitors the ambient aerosol optical thickness over oceans and parts of continents. From the images presented in Figure 5, it can be seen that it is almost impossible to visually identify all of the differences between the images. It is in such a situation, where visual detection is constrained, where there is a need for computational change detection. An additional benefit of computational change detection is the possibility of automatically analyzing several images concurrently.

At a basic level there are three steps in image differencing: image subtraction, threshold setting and addition of the original image with the image

Figure 5. The two input coverages used the case study

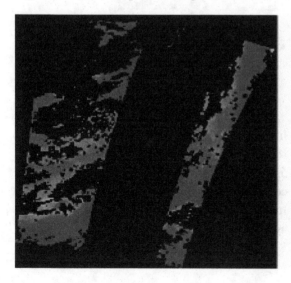 

of detected change. Therefore, the prototype GRASS-supported service had to offer image algebraic capabilities. Multiple WPS requests were transmitted to a group of GRASS-based services through the GPB. Each request was transmitted on a separate thread in order to simulate multiple users accessing the same service group. The successful invocation and operation of the GeoSaaS is evidenced by the output presented in Figure 6. An examination of the output image showed that the pixel values of the output image were equal to the difference between the pixel values of the input images. The output therefore confirmed the successful invocation of the GRASS-based service.

DISCUSSION

In implementing the prototype, the main technologies used were covered by free and open source licenses (i.e. the 52°North WPS and GRASS). Hayes(2008)cautions that the open source movement might find it difficult to adapt to the cloud computing model, as the software is remotely hosted and managed by a third party. However, we contend that the virtualization aspect of cloud computing will be more suited to the open source movement than the commercial community because free and open source software can be installed in as many virtual machines as possible without licensing restrictions. Consequently, within the geospatial community we could see the re-emergence of the free and open source GRASS GIS as a popular solution for geospatial

Figure 6. Image difference of the input coverages

applications. The choice of which compute cloud to deploy the open source GIS in will depend on the limitations of the compute cloud and the budget of the service provider. For example, GAE is limited to Java and Python applications although it offers a free 500MB storage allowance. In contrast, EC2 charges for storage but allows greater freedom of which open source GIS to install in support of a GeoSaaS.

The service brokering of the GPB could facilitate access to WPS deployed in infrastructure such as EC2. However, some of the professional uses of geospatial data are commercially and security sensitive. Therefore, organizations that have traditionally supported the development of GIS may find it difficult to support the development of geospatial compute clouds. There are at least three potential approaches that have been examined by the geospatial community for protecting access to geospatial web services. The techniques examined in the sixth phase of the OGC web service testbed (OWS-6) included OpenID and the eXtensible Access Control Markup Language (XACML)(Gartmann & Leinenweber, 2009). The former is an open and federated framework for providing user authentication. It has been adopted by popular service providers such as Yahoo! and Sourceforge. Both the geospatial extension of the latter (GeoXACML) and the application of spatial obligations with XACML were examined in OWS-6. XACML obligations express actions that must be fulfilled by a policy enforcement point before executing the decision of the policy decision point. Access to a resource is denied if the obligations are not fulfilled. An alternative for cloud computing could be to use the authentication services already offered by a compute cloud, for example, GAE allows applications to authenticate using Google user accounts. However, to ensure interoperability an open framework such as OpenID or GeoXACML is the most appropriate solution. These solutions, however, only address access control to deployed services. Other security-

related issues such as encryption are relevant to compute clouds but out of scope for this Chapter.

Further, releasing location-referenced information to a third-party by storing or computing in compute clouds might have legal implications. To address concerns of privacy, Weiss cautions that "most significantly, the cloud demands a high degree of trust"(Weiss, 2007: pp.25). Therefore, the geospatial community is not alone in having concerns over privacy, trust and security in compute clouds.

However, approaches for anonymising geospatial information before computing in cloud infrastructure might help to address such concerns. Another possible approach for addressing concerns over data storage in the Cloud is to establish private clouds between trusted organizations(Sotomayor, Montero, Llorente, & Foster, 2009). An example of such a cloud is the CARMEN project, a neuroscience initiative involving UK universities and private companies(Watson, Lord, Gibson, Periorellis, & Pitsilis, 2008). The project is investigating how cloud computing and other e-science approaches can help neuroscientists manage the vast quantity of data they use in their research. Sotomayor et al (2009) observe the emergence of hybrid clouds consisting of both private and public aspects. They describe the OpenNebula engine which allows organizations to deploy, use and manage virtual machines, either individually or in groups, by co-scheduling on private or public clouds.

Our study has not examined the billing of users of cloud-based services. However, we observe that services such as Amazon Flexible Payments Service™ (Amazon FPS) and Google Checkout API could be integrated with geospatial applications deployed in compute clouds. Amazon FPS enables developers to charge Amazon's millions of customers through the same payment infrastructure that Amazon uses. The service allows customers to give consent to be charged using their Amazon login credentials, shipping address and payment information. Similarly, the Google Checkout API allows developers to charge customers using their

Google Checkout details. Within a geospatially-enabled compute cloud, services could charge for storage of geospatial data or consumption of resources during data transformation. Such a capability could provide an alternative mechanism for cost-sharing and service sustainability. From our experience of using Amazon EC2, we found that within 9 hours (the duration of a normal working day) and with 250 MB of data transmission, the cost of our instance on Amazon EC2 came up to approximately £1.00. We contend that this is an economic alternative to current hardware costs. However, it raises questions of whether geospatial data transmission can be made more efficient. For example, compression of GML could be made a capability of OGC web services. Further, where alphanumeric attributes change significantly more often than geometric attributes, data handling processes could be modified to allow for geometries to be transmitted only at the beginning of a process; after which, only alphanumeric attributes would then be transmitted into or out of a compute cloud. Such an approach could reduce the size of messages and consequently reduce the cost of using compute clouds. Another approach could be to transmit only features that have changed since the last invocation, although checking currency of features could increase the response time of processes.

A Role for Cloud Computing in Spatial Data Infrastructure

It is necessary to consider cloud computing from the perspective of a Spatial Data Infrastructure (SDI). SDI is a collection of standards, technologies, policies, best practices and institutional arrangements that facilitate the availability of and access to spatial data, services and related resources. Examples of technologies forming part of an SDI include Geospatial-One-Stop (GOS) used by the US national SDI and the INSPIRE geoportal that is used by members of the European Union (Maguire & Longley, 2005). Examples of

policies include the EU INSPIRE directive and the US Executive Order 12906. The former was approved by the European Parliament in 2007 and the latter was signed by former US President Bill Clinton in 1994. These policies provide the legal framework through which government agencies can share geospatial data and are therefore the primary drivers of SDI development in their respective communities. Within each national SDI there are institutional arrangements that enable government agencies to share geospatial data. Examples of standards and best practices include interoperability standards by the OGC and ISO. This list of examples is not exhaustive, but is intended to make the reader aware of the collection of mechanisms that governments put in place to facilitate the sharing of geospatial data resources.

The literature suggests that SDI have evolved over two notable generations. The first generation emerged around the mid-1980s and involved organisations developing data access relationships. Crompvoets et al(Crompvoets, Rajabifard, Bregt, & Williamson, 2004) observed that there was limited knowledge available for countries establishing national SDI within the first generation. Therefore, countries developed SDI based on specific requirements without much previous knowledge and best practices to refer to. They observe that a significant outcome of the first generation of SDI was the documentation of experiences and status reports on SDI initiatives which would eventually inform future developments of SDI. In effect, the first generation resulted in organisations locked to particular vendors in order to gain access to existing databases. The literature suggests that the second generation started around 2000 with a strategy oriented towards a more process-based approach focusing on the creation of infrastructure to facilitate the management of information resources instead of just connectivity to databases(Crompvoets et al., 2004). This second generation included those countries upgrading their existing SDI technologies and those beginning SDI development. Interoperability standards and best practices have played a key role in the development of new SDI. In summary, data was the primary concern of first generation SDI whereas the use and application of data has been the driving force for second generation SDI. Advances in technologies and standards for web applications have led to the extension of second generation SDI to cover the processing of data and not just access to data. Organisations are now able to wrap geospatial algorithms in web applications and offer them on the World Wide Web as applications.

Rajabifard et al (2006) observe that there are indications that a third generation is beginning to emerge, based on virtual jurisdictions and a virtual world. Budhathoki et al (2008) suggest that the third generation of SDI will develop from geographic information volunteered by ordinary citizens through Web 2.0 technologies. We agree with their view and add that not only will ordinary citizens be able to share geographic information through Web 2.0 but scientists will also be able to share geospatial processes in compute clouds within the next generation of SDI. Compute clouds and SDI complement each other well, in that, whereas interoperability is still yet to be addressed in cloud computing(Vaquero et al., 2009), the geospatial community has already established tested protocols and standards in support of interoperability in SDI (OGC, 1999-2010). However, uptake of cloud computing within the wider geospatial community depends on compute clouds leveraging the functionality offered by legacy geospatial software such as GRASS. The complex geospatial algorithms and scientific models that have been fed into GRASS modules over decades of research should be included in future Cloud development in order to ensure uptake within communities that use geospatial data. Failure to consider legacy GIS software in Cloud development would result in cloud computing having to compete with already existing processes and traditions within the spatial data community, potentially leading to slow uptake

of compute clouds or complete rejection. However, a symbiotic growth between geospatial and cloud computing will not only provide additional computational resources but could also lead to cost-sharing between national SDI and capacity building for emerging SDI.

So far, this section has focused on what cloud computing could offer SDI. However, SDI also has much to offer cloud computing beyond just geospatial computing. The second generation of SDI has led to the development of initiatives integrating various aspects of independent national SDI into a seamless infrastructure. Reichardt (2009) observes that initiatives such as OneGeology and GEOSS provide bridges between SDI. OneGeology is an international initiative aiming to create dynamic digital geological map data of the world. Currently 111 geological agencies and surveys participate in OneGeology. GEOSS (Global Earth Observation System of Systems) is an initiative aiming to create a coordinated environmental information system for observing, processing, publishing and discovering earth observation data from space-based satellites, airborne vehicles and *in situ* sensors. Currently 80 countries and 56 organisations participate in the development of GEOSS. These initiatives have established communities, protocols and processes for sharing a common infrastructure. Approaches for best practices and standards provide the enabling mechanisms through which interoperability is achieved through the common infrastructure. The processes involved in SDI-bridging through interoperability standards and consensus building could be applied to cloud computing in order to move towards the vision of a single coordinated Cloud infrastructure. Finally, as compute clouds rely on the economies of scale for sustainability, SDI offer cloud computing a community of users, developers, vendors and interoperability standards with a mature market that can increase revenue for compute clouds.

CONCLUSION

As the case study has demonstrated the GPB and GRASS-supported WPS have the potential to offer geospatial functionality in a compute cloud. We therefore conclude that the OGC's WPS specification could facilitate the provision of geospatial capability in compute clouds. Geospatial processing on compute clouds alone will not provide a complete solution however. It is necessary for GeoSaaS to be complemented by adequate storage in cloud computing as well. This is because some processes within geospatial processing involve a number of steps to arrive at a useful result and each step generates a temporary dataset thereby requiring additional storage. Further, an appropriate user interface that makes the dispatching of requests sent to multiple WPS transparent is necessary to ensure a reasonable level of usability.

Cloud computing has made the unusual step of reaching mainstream popularity. Articles in popular magazines such as the Sunday Times[7] and The Economist(2009) demonstrate the appeal of cloud computing outside the research community. The US and UK governments are also reported to be developing a capability for cloud computing. The Cloud Storefront Apps.gov was announced by the US government's Chief Information Officer, Vivek Kundra, as an initiative to "help to lower the cost of government operations while driving innovation within government by pooling IT resources across organizational boundaries."[8]. The Digital Britain report of the UK government provided justification for establishing a 'G-Cloud', that is a cloud computing infrastructure for government[9]. The UK report observed that a G-Cloud could be established through development of a private cloud to overcome vulnerabilities over data location, security, data recovery, availability and reliability associated with public clouds, such as Amazon EC2.

Future work in geospatial cloud computing should examine the issues of trust and quality of service. Disaster management is a key application area of geospatial technologies. Cloud computing offers disaster management teams an infrastructure ready for collaboration-critical operations. A current project that will help make this possible is GEOSS. Interoperability standards by the OGC are being applied in the development of GEOSS. However, for cloud computing to become a reliable resource for disaster response, the quality of service has to be guaranteed. It is therefore reasonable to assume that services from corporations or government agencies may be favored in comparison to those offered by individuals; this highlights a need for a universally-accepted approach for determining the quality or reliability of services offered within cloud computing. Further, future work should also examine the potential of private cloud between trusted organizations in ensuring security and privacy. Furthermore, with the cost implications of data transmission into and out of compute clouds, future work should consider the efficiency of geospatial data transmission and processing in commercial compute clouds.

ACKNOWLEDGMENT

The research presented in this Chapter is supported by the University of Nottingham through the New Researchers' Fund reference NRF5049.

REFERENCES

Agarwal, P. (2005). Ontological considerations in GIScience. *International Journal of Geographical Information Science*, *19*(5), 501–536. doi:10.1080/13658810500032321

Baranski, B., Schaeffer, B., & Redweik, R. (2009a). Geoprocessing in the Clouds, *FOSS4G*. Sydney.

Baranski, B., Schaeffer, B., & Redweik, R. (2009b). Geoprocessing in the Clouds. *Geoinformatics*, *8*, 24–27.

Bergenheim, W., Sarjakoski, L. T., & Sarjakoski, T. (2009). A Web processing service for GRASS GIS to provide on-line generalisation. In J. Haunert, B. Kieler & J. Milde (Eds.), *Proceedings of the 12th AGILE International Conference on Geographic Information Science (AGILE)*. Hannover, Germany.

Brauner, J., & Schäffer, B. (2008). Integration of GRASS functionality in web based SDI service chains. *Proceedings of the FOSS4G 2008 conference*. Cape Town, South Africa.

Budhathoki, N. R., Bruce, B., & Nedovic-Budic, Z. (2008). Reconceptualizing the role of the user of spatial data infrastructure. *GeoJournal*, *72*(3-4), 149–160. doi:10.1007/s10708-008-9189-x

Crompvoets, J., Rajabifard, A., Bregt, A., & Williamson, I. P. (2004). Assessing the worldwide developments of national spatial data clearinghouses. *International Journal of Geographical Information Science*, *18*(7), 1–25. doi:10.1080/13658810410001702030

data infrastructures. *Computers, Environment and Urban Systems*, *29*(1), 3–14.

Di, L., Zhao, P., Han, W., Wei, Y., & Li, X. (2007). GeoBrain Web service-based Online Analysis System (GeOnAS), *Proceedings of the 2007 NASA Science Technology Conference (NSTC2007)*. Maryland, US.

Douglas, D. H., & Peucker, T. K. (1973). Algorithms for the reduction of the number of points required to represent a line or its caricature. *The Canadian Cartographer*, *10*(2), 112–123.

Fonseca, F. T., Egenhofer, M. J., Agouris, P., & Camara, G. (2002). Using ontologies for integrated Geographic Information Systems. *Transactions in GIS*, *6*(3), 231–257. doi:10.1111/1467-9671.00109

Gartmann, R., & Leinenweber, L. (2009). *OGC 09-035: OWS-6 Security Engineering Report*. Open Geospatial Consortium.

Goran, B., & Finney, D. (1991). GRASS GIS Critical to Army's Land Management Program. *GIS World*, *4*(9), 48–53.

Hayes, B. (2008). Cloud computing. *Communications of the ACM*, *51*(7), 9–11. doi:10.1145/1364782.1364786

Hess, S. (2002). GRASS on the Web, *Proceedings of the Open source GIS – GRASS users conference*. Trento, Italy.

Hobona, G., Fairbairn, D., & James, P. (2007). Semantically-assisted geospatial workflow design. In H. Samet, C. Shahabi & M. Schneider (Eds.), *Proceedings of the ACM international symposium on Advances in geographic information systems (ACMGIS)* (pp. 194-201). Seattle: ACM

Intel Corporation. Canonical Ltd., & Eucalyptus Systems, (Eds.). (2010). *Intel® Cloud Builder Guide to Cloud Design and Deployment on Intel Platforms*. Eucalyptus Systems, Inc.

Kim, W. (2009). Cloud computing: Today and tomorrow. *Journal of Object Technology*, *8*(1), 66–72.

Kurzbach, S., Pasche, E., Lanig, S., & Zipf, A. (2009). Benefits of Grid computing for flood modeling in service-oriented Spatial Data Infrastructures. *GIS. Science*, *3*, 89–96.

Lautenbacher, C. C. (2006). The global Earth observation system of systems: Science serving society. *Space Policy*, *22*(1), 8–11. doi:10.1016/j.spacepol.2005.12.004

Lee, C., & Percivall, G. (2008). Standards-based computing capabilities for distributed geospatial applications. *Computer*, *41*(11), 50–57. doi:10.1109/MC.2008.468

Lee, C., & Percivall, G. (2009). The evolution of geospatial e-infrastructures. *GIS Science, 3,* 68–70.

Lu, D., Mausel, P., Brondízio, E., & Moran, E. (2004). Change detection techniques. *International Journal of Remote Sensing, 25*(12), 2365–2401. doi:10.1080/0143116031000139863

MacEachren, A. M., & Kraak, M. J. (2001). Research challenges in geovisualization. *Cartography and Geographic Information Systems, 28*(1), 3–12. doi:10.1559/152304001782173970

Maguire, D. J., & Longley, P. (2005). The emergence of geoportals and their role in spatial

Mell, P., & Grance, T. (2009a). *Effectively and Securely Using the Cloud Computing Paradigm.* Retrieved from http://csrc.nist.gov/groups/SNS/cloud computing/cloud-computing-v26.ppt

Mell, P., & Grance, T. (2009b). *Definition of cloud computing. National Institute of Standards and Technology.* NIST.

Mitasova, H., & Neteler, M. (2004). GRASS as Open Source Free Software GIS: Accomplishments and Perspectives. *Transactions in GIS, 8*(2), 145–154. doi:10.1111/j.1467-9671.2004.00172.x

NIST. (2009). *Definition of cloud computing (v15).* National Institute of Standards and Technology.

52°North. (2010a). *52°North Geoprocessing Code Repository for GRASS support.* Retrieved from http://52north.org/svn/geoprocessing/main/WPS/trunk/WPS/52n-wps-grass/

52°North. (2010b). *52°North Geoprocessing Community Roadmap 2010.* Retrieved from http://52north.org/maven/project-sites/wps/52n-wps-site/index.html

OGC. (2006). *Discussions, findings, and use of WPS in OWS-4.* Retrieved April 26, 2006, from http://portal.opengeospatial.org/files/?artifact_id=19424

OGC. (1999-2010). *Open Geospatial Consortium standards.* Retrieved on February 12, 2010, from http://www.opengeospatial.org/standards

Raghavan, V., Masumoto, S., Santitamont, P., & Honda, K. (2002). Implementing an online spatial database using the GRASS GIS environment. In M. Ciolli & P. Zatelli (Eds.), *Proceedings of the 2002 Open source GIS - GRASS users conference.* Trento, Italy.

Rajabifard, A., Binns, A., Masser, I., & Williamson, I. (2006). The role of sub-national government and the private sector in future spatial data infrastructures. *International Journal of Geographical Information Science, 20*(7), 727–741. doi:10.1080/13658810500432224

Reichardt, M. (2009). Ocean Science, OneGeology, and GEOSS: Building 'SDI bridges', *Proceedings of the 11th annual conference of the Global Spatial Data Infrastructure Association (GSDI11).* Rotterdam, Netherlands.

Sotomayor, B., Montero, R. S., Llorente, I. M., & Foster, I. (2009). Virtual infrastructure management in private and hybrid clouds. *IEEE Internet Computing, 13*(5), 14–22. doi:10.1109/MIC.2009.119

The Economist. (2009). Clash of the clouds. *The Economist, 392,* 80-82.

Turner, M., Budgen, D., & Brereton, P. (2003). Turning software into a service. *Computer, 36*(10), 38–44. doi:10.1109/MC.2003.1236470

Vaquero, L. M., Rodero-Merino, L., Caceres, J., & Lindner, M. (2009). A break in the clouds: towards a cloud definition. *ACM SIGCOMM Computer Communication Review, 39*(1), 50–55. doi:10.1145/1496091.1496100

Wang, L., Tao, J., Kunze, M., Castellanos, A. C., Kramer, D., & Karl, W. (2008). Scientific cloud computing: early definition and experience. *Proceedings of the 10th IEEE International Conference on High Performance Computing and Communications, 2008. HPCC '08.* (pp. 825-830). IEEE Computer Society.

Watson, P., Lord, P., Gibson, F., Periorellis, P., & Pitsilis, G. (2008). Cloud computing for e-science with CARMEN. In F. Silva, G. Barreira & L. Ribeiro (Eds.), *Proceedings of the 2nd Iberian Grid Infrastructure Conference,* (pp. 3-14). Porto, Portugal.

Weiss, A. (2007). Computing in the clouds. *netWorker, 11*(4), 16–25. doi:10.1145/1327512.1327513

Woolf, A., & Shaon, A. (2009). An approach to encapsulation of Grid processing within an OGC Web processing service. *GIS Science, 3*, 82–88.

Yue, P., Di, L., Yang, W., Yu, G., & Zhao, P. (2007). Semantics-based automatic composition of geospatial Web service chains. *Computers & Geosciences, 33*(5), 649–665. doi:10.1016/j.cageo.2006.09.003

Yue, P., Gong, J., Di, L., Yuan, J., Sun, L., & Wang, Q. (2009). GeoPW: Towards the geospatial processing Web. *Lecture Notes in Computer Science, 5886*, 25–38. doi:10.1007/978-3-642-10601-9_3

Zhu, F., Turner, M., Kotsiopoulos, I., Bennett, K., Russell, M., & Budgen, D. (2006). Dynamic data integration: a service-based broker approach. *International Journal of Business Process Integration and Management, 1*(3), 175–191. doi:10.1504/IJBPIM.2006.010903

ENDNOTES

[1] http://www.oracle.com/technology/products/spatial/index.html

[2] http://portal.opengeospatial.org/files/?artifact_id=35975

[3] http://portal.opengeospatial.org/files/?artifact_id=22873

[4] http://www.52north.org/wps

[5] http://geotools.codehaus.org

[6] http://www.w3.org/TR/2009/CR-MathML3-20091215/

[7] http://technology.timesonline.co.uk/tol/news/tech_and_web/the_web/article6740886.ece

[8] http://www.gsa.gov/Portal/gsa/ep/contentView.do?contentType=GSA_BASIC&contentId=28477

[9] http://www.culture.gov.uk/images/publications/chpt8_digitalbritain-finalreport-jun09.pdf

Section 6
Workflows

Chapter 13
Semantic Web Enabled Intelligent Geoprocessing Service Chaining

Peng Yue
Wuhan University, China

Lianlian He
Hubei University of Education, China

Liping Di
George Mason University, USA

ABSTRACT

In a service-oriented environment, large volumes of geospatial data and diverse geoprocessing functions are accessible as services. An intelligent mechanism is required to facilitate discovery and integration of geospatial data and services so as to enable semi-automated or automated geospatial knowledge discovery. This chapter addresses key research issues for Semantic Web enabled intelligent geoprocessing service chaining. A set of applicable solutions are described, including a common data and service environment, semantic descriptions of geoprocessing services, and a general process for intelligent generation of geoprocessing workflow. Some use cases illustrate the applicability of such solutions. A proof-of-concept prototype system is implemented and some use cases help to demonstrate the applicability of the current approach.

INTRODUCTION

With the advancement of sensor and platform technologies, the capability for collecting geospatial data has significantly increased in recent years. For example, the four satellites of the National Aeronautics and Space Administration (NASA)'s Earth Observing System (EOS) now collect 1000 terabytes annually (Clery and Voss, 2005). The traditional methods of analyzing data by expert analysts fall far short of today's increased demands for geospatial knowledge. As a result, much data may never been analyzed even once after collection. Therefore, technologies for semi-automated

DOI: 10.4018/978-1-60960-192-8.ch013

or automated geospatial knowledge discovery and dissemination are urgently needed for geospatial applications.

Recently, Service-Oriented Architecture (SOA), as a new information infrastructure, is being introduced into scientific research, such as Earth System Grid (ESG), GEONGrid and UK e-science program. In 2005, Ian Foster put forward the concept of Service-Oriented Science (Foster, 2005), referring to the scientific research enabled by the SOA. With this information architecture, large volumes of geospatial data and diverse processing functions are available for worldwide open use. Scientists can use services to contribute their domain knowledge to the community. In such a service-oriented environment, an intelligent mechanism is required to facilitate discovery and integration of geospatial data and services so as to enable semi-automated or automated geospatial knowledge discovery. Semantic Web (Berners-Lee et al., 2001) technologies, which give machine-processable meanings to the documents, allow the semantics of data and services machine-understandable and thus can be processed by machines (reasoning) for more effective discovery, automation, integration, and reuse of geospatial data and services. This chapter addresses the key research issues for Semantic Web enabled intelligent geoprocessing service chaining.

The key research issues include,

1. Developing those syntactically and semantically interoperable geospatial Web Services that can be used to in a distributed environment to discover, request, access, and obtain geospatial data and information;
2. Intelligently orchestrating interoperable geoprocessing services to generate geospatial process models that can transform data into information and information into knowledge for assistance in making decisions;

3. Automatically converting geospatial process models to executable service chains that can be invoked and executed on demand;
4. Management of process models and service chains. The process models and service chains can be archived and catalogued. They can then be advertised as new geospatial services and thus be discovered and used in future geospatial modeling.

A set of applicable solutions are described, including a common data and service environment, semantic descriptions of geoprocessing services, and a general process for intelligent generation of geoprocessing workflow. Some use cases illustrate the applicability of our solutions. A proof-of-concept prototype system is implemented and some use cases help to demonstrate the applicability of our approach.

BACKGROUND

The work described in this chapter builds on and extends work in a variety of domains. In this section, we recapitulate Web Service and the Open Geospatial Consortium (OGC) Web Service technologies relevant to the chapter, briefly introduce Semantic Web Service technologies and current development towards Geospatial Semantic Web, and sketch general approaches to automatic service composition.

Web Service

A Web Service is a software system designed to support interoperable machine-to-machine interaction over a network (Booth et al., 2004). Web Service technologies are a set of technologies for the implementation of SOA. SOA is a way of reorganizing a portfolio of previously siloed software applications and supporting infrastructure into an inter-connected set of services, each accessible through standard interfaces and mes-

Figure 1. The basic SOA operations

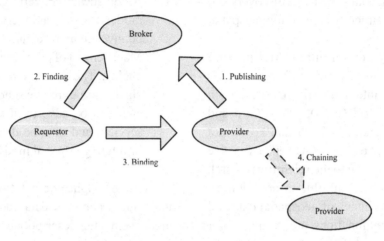

saging protocols (Papazoglou, 2003). There are three key actors in SOA (Figure 1): requestor, provider and broker. The requestor is the user who requires the information services. The provider is the standards-based individual service. The broker is a meta-information repository (e.g., a registry, catalog or clearinghouse). The interactions among these actors involve the operations of publishing, finding and binding. Service composition introduces a new operation into SOA, chaining, which combines services into a dependent series to accomplish a larger task. SOA is the basis for automatic service composition, since services management functions such as registration, discovery, accessing, and execution are well positioned under this structure and these functions are the basic units in the whole automation process.

In order for SOA to work, various standards related to all aspects of service operations are needed. The major international bodies setting the Web Service standards are the World Wide Web Consortium (W3C) and the Organization for the Advancement of Structured Information Standards (OASIS). The major standards related to services are shown in Figure 2. These standards are grouped as five standard stacks: security, service description, service discovery, service binding, and modeling and workflow. The Secure Sockets Layer (SSL) protocol can be combined

with Hypertext Transfer Protocol to provide secure service access and interaction. The Web Services Description Language (WSDL) provides an XML format for describing the exchanged messages, interfaces, and binding protocol of Web Services, thus can be used for service publication. The Universal Discovery Description and Integration (UDDI) is a specification for service registry that can register and discover Web Services. In the service binding stack, the Simple Object Access Protocol (SOAP) provides a lightweight protocol based on XML and HTTP for exchanging structured information when accessing services. The Web Services Business Process Execution Language (WSBPEL), shortly known as BPEL, is an industry-wide standard that specifies the XML-based description of service chains.

In the geospatial Web services area, OGC is the major organization working on developing geospatial Web services standards by adapting or extending the common Web service standards. Through the OGC Web Services (OWS) testbeds, OGC has been developing a series of interface specifications under the OGC Abstract Service Architecture (Percivall, 2002), including Web Feature Service (WFS), Web Map Service (WMS), Web Coverage Service (WCS), Sensor Observation Service (SOS), Catalogue Services for Web (CSW), and Web Processing Service (WPS).

Figure 2. The W3C and OASIS Web service standards

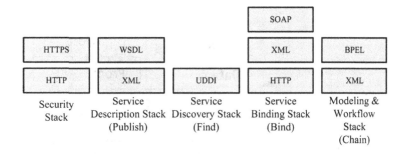

Currently, OGC Web services are not completely interoperable with the W3C SOAP-based Web services. Most of OGC Web service implementations provide access via HTTP GET, HTTP POST and do not support SOAP. The registry service, i.e. CSW, provides the discovery not only on the services, but also on the geospatial data. An Electronic Business Registry Information Model (ebRIM) profile of Catalogue Services for the Web (Martell, 2008) has been developed and approved by OGC for CSW implementation. Conceptually, the OWS also follows the publish-find-bind paradigm in the SOA and has service discovery, description, and binding layers corresponding to UDDI, WSDL, and SOAP in the W3C architecture. In addition, OGC is also experimenting to integrate the W3C Web services standards into the OWS framework by providing support to SOAP/WSDL for OGC Web services.

Semantic Web

Compared to the conventional Web, the Semantic Web excels in two aspects (W3C, 2001): 1) common formats for data interchange (the original Web only had interchange of documents) and 2) a language for recording how the data relates to real world objects. Figure 3 shows the hierarchical architecture of the Semantic Web. At the bottom level, XML provides syntax to represent structured documents with a user-defined vocabulary but does not necessarily guarantee well-defined semantic constraints on these documents. And

XML schema defines the structure of an XML document. The Resource Description Framework (RDF) is a basic data model that identifies objects ("resources") and their relations to allow information to be exchanged between applications without loss of meaning. It is based on a graph model composed of triples. For query of RDF data, there is a W3C recommended query language, namely the SPARQL Protocol And RDF Query Language (SPARQL). RDF Schema (RDFS) is a semantic extension of RDF for describing the properties of generalization-hierarchies and classes of RDF resources. The Web Ontology Language (OWL) adds vocabulary to explicitly represent the meaning of terms and their relationships, such as relations between classes (e.g. disjointness), cardinality (e.g., "exactly one"), equality and enumerated classes. The logic layer represents the facts and derives knowledge, and deductive process and proof validation are deduced by the proof layer. A digital signature can be used to sign and export the derived knowledge. A trust layer provides the trust level or a rating of its quality in order to help users building confidence in the process and quality of information (Antoniou and Harmelen, 2004). Currently there is no consensus on how a rule layer could look like and some proposals exist such as the Rule Interchange Format (RIF) (Kifer, 2008), RuleML (Boley et al, 2001), Notation3 (N3) (Berners-Lee, 2000b) and SWRL (Horrocks, 2004). The top layers providing proof and trust are starting to be addressed by research today.

Figure 3. Semantic Web architecture (Berners-Lee 2000a)

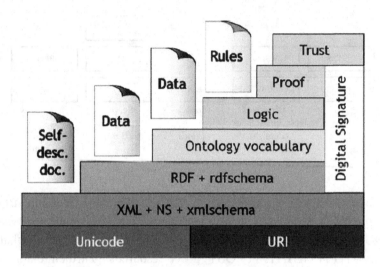

With the emergence of the Semantic Web, there are a number of representative technologies concerning the frameworks for semantics in Web Services. Each of them has its own key concerns and emphasis. Web service ontology (OWL-S) (Martin et al., 2004), which is based on OWL, is primarily concerned with service composition. It models individual services as atomic processes with corresponding operation/functionality, input/output, pre/post-conditions. Service chain is represented as the composite process with control constructs defined based on the workflow pattern such as sequence, parallel split, and choice. Web Service Modeling Ontology (WSMO) (Bruijn et al., 2005) is defined based on the Web Service Modeling Framework (WSMF) (Fensel and Bussler, 2002) which consists of four different main elements for describing Semantic Web services: (1) ontologies that provide the terminology used by other elements, (2) goals that state the intentions that should be solved by Web services, (3) Web service descriptions that define various aspects of a Web service, and (4) mediators which resolve interoperability problems. A more expressive logical language, named Web Service Modeling Language (WSML), is used as the basis

language framework for WSMO, compared with OWL for OWL-S. Semantic Web Services Framework (SWSF) (Battle et al., 2005) is proposed by the Semantic Web Services Initiative (SWSI) and intended to serve as a theoretical and comprehensive framework for semantic specifications of Web services. It also consists of a representational language, called Semantic Web Services Language (SWSL), and an ontology, called Semantic Web Services Ontology (SWSO). Based on the two sublanguages in SWSL, first-order logic (FOL) based SWSL (SWSL-FOL) and logic programming (LP) based SWSL (SWSL-Rules), SWSO has two corresponding types of ontologies, including FLOWS (First-Order Logic Ontology for Web Services) and ROWS (Rules Ontology for Web Services). SWSO also models the Web services as processes, the same as OWL-S does. Yet the process ontology is built on a mature preexisting ontology of process modeling concepts, the Process Specification Language (PSL). Apart from defining a service ontology, Web Service Semantics (WSDL-S) (Akkiraju et al., 2005) and Semantic Annotations for WSDL (SAWSDL) (Farrell and Lausen, 2006) aim to extend existing WSDL elements with semantic annotations. They provide a practical way with less effort to describe the semantics of Web service within the legacy of current Web service standards.

Because geospatial information is heterogeneous, i.e. multi-source, multi-format, multi-scale, and multi-disciplinary, the importance of semantics on accessing and integration of distributed geospatial information has long been recognized (Sheth, 1999). To better support the discovery, retrieval and consumption of geospatial information, the Geospatial Semantic Web is initiated to create and manage geospatial ontologies to capture the semantic network of geospatial world and allow intelligent applications to take advantage of build-in geospatial reasoning capabilities for deriving knowledge. It will do so by incorporating geospatial data semantics and exploiting the semantics of both the processing of geospatial relationships and the description of tightly-coupled service content (Egenhofer, 2002; Lieberman et al., 2005). The Geospatial Semantic Web was identified as an immediately-considered research priority early in 2002 (Fonseca and Sheth, 2002) by University Consortium for Geospatial Information Science (UCGIS). Since 2005, OGC has issued the Geospatial Semantic Web Interoperability Experiment (GSW IE) aiming to develop a method of discovering, querying and collecting geospatial content on the basis of formal semantic specifications (Kolas et al., 2005; Kolas et al, 2006; Kammersell and Dean 2006; Lutz and Kolas, 2007). In this experiment, five types of ontologies are identified, including base geospatial ontology, feature data source ontology, geospatial service ontology, geospatial filter ontology and domain ontology. Based on these ontologies, a user's query can be translated to the data source semantic queries via semantic rules, and then transformed to WFS query through Extensible Stylesheet Language Transformations (XSLT). The query is represented using the SPARQL, and the semantic rules are represented using SWRL.

Automatic Service Composition

Automatic service composition, the intelligent process of creating a service chain, is a hot research topic in the general information technology domain. Available approaches can be categorized from the business perspective and Artificial Intelligence (AI) research area (Srivastava and Koehler, 2003; Rao and Su, 2004; Peer, 2005). Approaches on the service composition from a business perspective focus on workflow-based composition. Workflow is a key technology for automating business processes that involve access to several applications. The Workflow Management Coalition (WfMC) is s a non-profit, global organization of adopters, developers, consultants, analysts and university/research groups engaged in Business Process Management (BPM). The WfMC has been responsible for the creation of a workflow reference model and a glossary of standardized workflow terminology. The WfMC Terminology and Glossary document (WfMC, 1999) defines the Workflow as follows: the automation of a business process, in whole or part, during which documents, information or tasks are passed from one participant to another for action, according to a set of procedural rules. Workflow management is concerned with the declarative definition, enactment, administration and monitoring of business processes. A business process consists of a collection of activities related by data and control flow relationship. An activity is typically performed by executing a program, enacting a human/machine action, or invoking another process (called subprocess). The control flow specifies the locus of control moving through the process. It concerns about the order of (atomic) activities, while data flow focuses on the data exchange among the activities. The traditional workflow systems are ineffective when considering the needs of Web-based applications, with their complex partnerships, possibly among a large number of highly evolving processes. There are some Web service composition languages such as BPEL (OASIS,

2007), Web Service Choreography Interface (WSCI) (W3C, 2002), Web Services Flow Language (WSFL) (IBM, 2001). The control-flow aspect of such languages is comparable to that developed in workflow research (Aalst, 2003) with similar flow control constructs such as sequence, and split. In addition, workflow-based systems are making efforts to support composite Web services (Benatallah et al., 2001; Casati et al., 2001). Business efforts focus mainly on defining standards for composing Web services (Aissi et al., 2002) (e.g., BPEL4WS) and providing platforms to enable B2B interaction on the Web (e.g., IBM WebSphere) (Medjahed et al., 2003).

There is already significant literature addressing the problem of automatic service composition through AI planning. An important representation of planning problems related to the Web service field is using concepts of the state, goal and action from the classical planning domain. The world or a specified domain is modeled as a set of states that can be divided into initial states and goal states. Action is an operation that can change one state to another state. Thus, the assumption for Web service composition as a planning problem is that a Web service can be specified as an action with preconditions and effects. The preconditions are the states that must hold before the action can be executed, and the effects are the state changes when the action is executed (Russel and Norvig, 2003). First, a Web service is a software component that takes input data and produces output data. Thus, the preconditions and effects are the input and the output parameters of the service respectively. Second, the Web service might alter the states of the world after its execution. Then, the world states pre-required for the service execution are the preconditions, and the new states generated after the execution are the effects (Rao and Su, 2004). The semantics for inputs, outputs, preconditions and effects (i.e. IOPE semantics) addressed in the Semantic Web Service technologies are widely used in most AI planning methods for automatic

service composition (Ponnekanti and Fox, 2002; Sirin et al., 2004; Klusch et al., 2005). Peer (2005) summarizes the basic planning paradigms and knowledge-oriented paradigms in available automatic service composition methods from AI planning perspective. The logical representation of services plays an important role in these methods.

Also, there are some geoscience efforts for geospatial Web service composition. Di et al. (2005) introduce a framework for automatic Geospatial Web service composition. OWL-S is adopted as an experimental representation of a geospatial Web service. The other is Geosciences Network (GEON) (Jaeger et al., 2005). Geospatial Web services, including data (GML representation) provider services and customized services with vector data processing functionalities, are sampled to compose a workflow manually in the KEPLER system (Ludäscher et al., 2005), which provides a framework for workflow support in the scientific disciplines. The major feature of the KEPLER system is that it provides high-level workflow design while at the same time hiding the underlying complexity of technologies as much as possible from the user. Both Web service technologies and Grid technologies are wrapped as extensions in the system. For example, individual workflow components (e.g., data movement, database querying, job scheduling, remote execution) are abstracted into a set of generic, reusable tasks in a grid environment (Altintas et al., 2004). More related to the service and data discovery are efforts to add semantically augmented metadata information to annotate data and services (Lutz and Klien, 2006). Template operations are introduced for semantic annotation of services input/output and functionality (Lutz, 2004). WSMO is used to facilitate discovery and invocation of semantically described geospatial Web Services (Roman et al., 2006; Zaharia, R. et al., 2009). Lemmens et al. (2006) experimented with WSDL-S in their use-case implementation.

Figure 4. Landslide susceptibility case

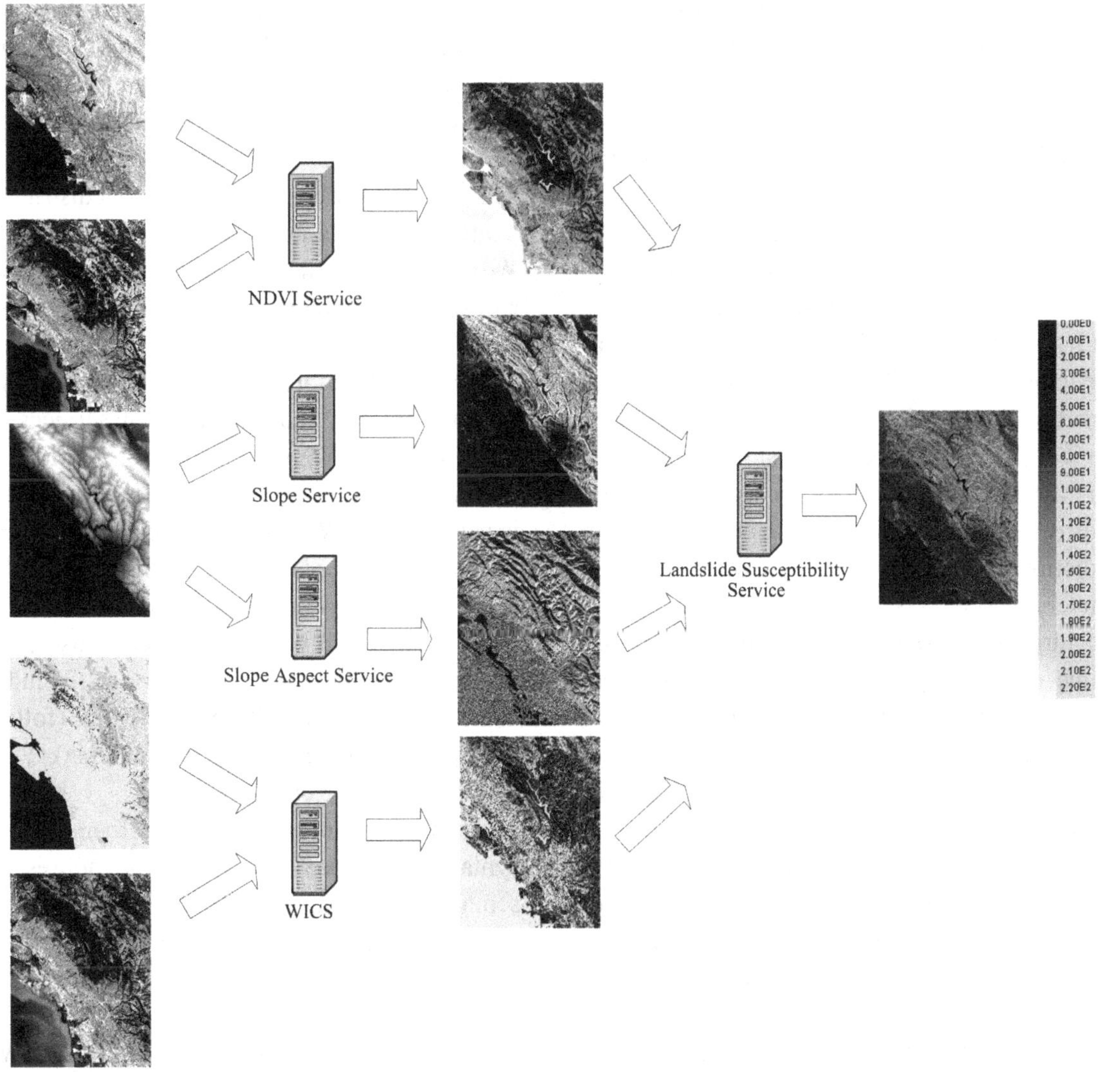

RUNNING EXAMPLES

Two earth science applications are used as examples to help understand the problems that can occur in the Web service based distributed problem solving environment and to illustrate how these problems can be solved using the proposed approach. A short description is given below.

Example 1 (landslide susceptibility case): Assume a geospatial user, John, wants to know: "What is the landslide susceptibility for location L at time T if vegetation were changed?". To as-

sess the landslide susceptibility in a distributed environment, heterogeneous data and various geoprocessing services are needed. As illustrated in Figure 4, the following geoprocessing services are involved to answer the user's question: a geoprocessing service that can derive landslide susceptibility using terrain slope data, slope aspect data, land cover data, and Normalized Difference Vegetation Index (NDVI) data, an NDVI computation service that can derive NDVI from image data, geoprocessing services that can derive terrain slope and aspect data from input

Digital Elevation Model (DEM) data, and a Web Image Classification Service (WICS) that can provide the landcover data. The NDVI service is an important one since the change of vegetation affect the output data of this service.

Example 2 (wildfire prediction case): Assume a geospatial expert, Jack, wants to know: "What is the possibility of having wildfire(s) in Bakersfield, CA and within a 300 kilometer vicinity tomorrow?". As illustrated in Figure 5, various data transformation services, such as Data Format Translation Service (DFTS), Coordinate Transformation Service (CTS), Resolution Conversion Service (RCS), are used to transform input data into the form that can be readily accepted by the wildfire prediction service. To get a wildfire prediction product for the region within 300 kilometers of Bakersfield, a spatial buffer service is required to get the part of the wildfire prediction product provided by the wildfire prediction service by using an Image Cutting Service (IMCS). Geocoder and CTS services are needed to transform the interested geographic address into coordinates that are spatially referenced.

In order to obtain the final answer, aforementioned services and data have to be discovered from the catalogue and chained automatically. The next sections introduce key research issues involved in these cases and how they are solved to enable the automation of intelligent geoprocessing service chaining. It has to be noted that this work, however, is designed to be general and thus is not restricted to only these two examples.

KEY RESEARCH ISSUES TOWARDS SEMANTIC WEB ENABLED INTELLIGENT GEOPROCESSING SERVICE CHAINING

Interoperable Geospatial Web Services

The geoprocessing algorithm provided by geospatial services may handle only a tiny part of the overall geoprocessing or may be a large aggregated processing. In both situations, the service should be well defined, have clear input and output requirements, and can be independently executable. Such service can be reused to construct different geoprocessing workflows for geospatial knowledge discovery. In a distributed data and information environment such as the World Wide Web, there are many independent data and service providers. A complex geoprocessing workflow may be scattered among multiple service providers. Therefore, standards for publishing, finding, binding and execution of services are needed. By following the standards of interfaces, the interoperation of different software systems is achieved and Web services developed by different organizations can be combined to fulfill users' requests. For example, in the landslide susceptibility and wildfire prediction use cases, standards-compliant geospatial services, including WCS, WICS, WCTS, Geocoder Service (following OpenGIS Location Service schema), WPS, and GML, can be employed.

However, current standards focus on the syntactic interoperability and do not address the semantics of geospatial Web services (Percivall, 2002). Semantic Web technologies provide promises for achieving semantic interoperability of geospatial Web services. Semantic Web Services, the combination of Semantic Web and Web Services, aim to provide mechanisms for organizing information and services so that the correct relationships between available data and services can be determined automatically and thus help to build workflows for specific problems. From this point of view, the effort described here shares the same goal as Semantic Web services except that this work will deal with geospatial problems in particular. Thus the work can use Semantic Web Service as the vehicle for the semantic descriptions of geoprocessing Web services.

Figure 5. Wildfire prediction case

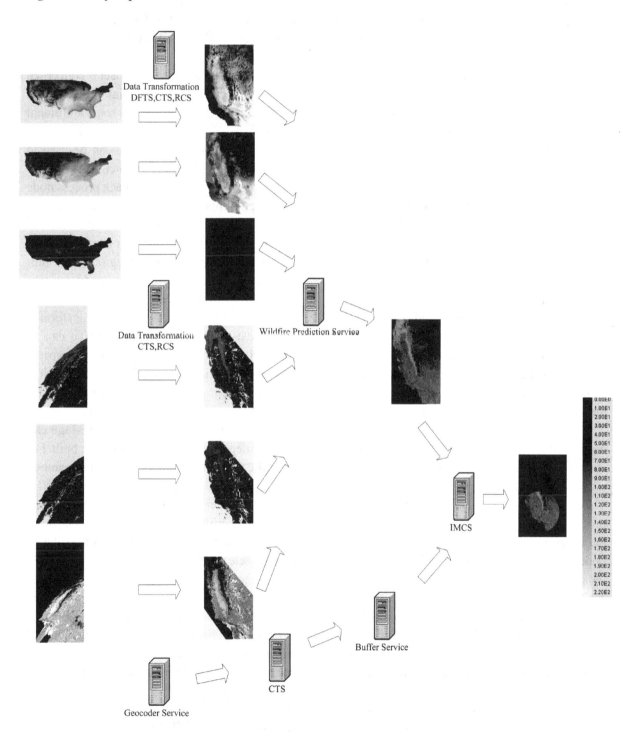

Intelligent Generation of Geospatial Process Models

In the *knowledge discovery* aspect, raw data can be transformed into the knowledge-added data product through the geoprocessing workflow, for example, in the landslide susceptibility case, a landslide susceptibility image, generated from the workflow processing the DEM data and Landsat Enhanced Thematic Mapper (ETM) imagery, is a product from knowledge discovery. The process model of a geoprocessing workflow contains knowledge in a specific application domain. Based on this knowledge, users know how to produce the required data product although the product does not really exist in any archive, therefore a process model produces a *virtual data product*, comparable to those physically archived data product. The virtual data product represents a geospatial data type that it can produce, not an instance (an individual dataset). It can be materialized on demand for users when all required geoprocessing methods and inputs are available.

In a service-oriented science, generation of geospatial process models means generating an abstract composite process model consisting of the control flow and data flow among process nodes. The data flow focuses on the data exchange among process nodes, while control flow concerns about the execution order of process nodes. A process node represents one type of individual services which share the same functional behaviors such as functionality, input and output. Therefore, intelligent generation of geospatial process models can borrow ideas from automatic service composition, combining service models from the semantic descriptions of geospatial Web services with Semantic Web and AI technologies, and exploring semi-automated or automated process modeling methods suitable for geospatial domain.

Automatic Instantiation of Geospatial Process Models into Executable Service Chains

A geospatial data product that a user is concerned with is always subject to spatial and temporal constraints. Users might specify some additional metadata specifications, such as file format, spatial projection. These specifications can be used to materialize the virtual data product. By propagating the specifications down to each process node of a process model, the whole process model is instantiated. Because the required archival data product may be not available in many cases for the user-specified geographic region and conditions, we can tell if a virtual data product can be materialized only by doing the instantiation. After the instantiation, the process model is transformed into an executable service chain which can be executed to produce an instance of the virtual data product. The instantiation process is called *the materialization of the virtual data product*.

Creating an executable service chain requires that correct mappings between the message elements of dependable services should be built. For example, the message elements mapping among a WCS and a WPS process, or different WPS processes. Therefore, service grounding in the semantic descriptions of geospatial Web services, i.e. grounding the semantic types to the syntactic message elements, is important. Message elements mappings between services are indirectly embedded in the mapping of the service message elements to the common semantic types. The correct mappings between the message elements of dependable services can be automatically generated based on data flows in process models and service groundings.

Management of Process Models and Service Chains

In the *knowledge management* aspect, existing process models allow analysts to interactively construct new, complex geospatial process models. The knowledge of modelers has been captured through the construction of process models. After a proper peer-review process, the executable models and service chains will be kept in the system for sharing. Through sharing, reusing and adding geospatial process models and service chains, the capabilities of geospatial knowledge discovery will increase with time. For example, in the wildfire prediction case, the process to create the buffer, which consists of the Geocoder process, CTS and Buffer process, can be reused and shared.

There is a key actor in SOA, i.e. broker. It is used to register and publish metadata information of services, and then provide the functionality of service discovery. Therefore, technologies relating registry services, such as ebRIM, UDDI, can be introduced to provide the registry and discovery of geospatial process models and service chains.

SOLUTIONS FOR IMPLEMENTATION OF SEMANTIC WEB ENABLED INTELLIGENT GEOPROCESSING SERVICE CHAINING

Building Common Data and Service Environment

To facilitate interoperability, two standards-based interoperability environments are needed: the common data environment and the common service environment (Di, 2005). The common data environment is supported by a set of standard interfaces for finding and accessing distributed data. This environment allows geospatial services and value-added applications to access diverse data provided by different providers in a standard way. OGC specifications are widely used by geospatial communities for sharing data and resources and are becoming ISO standards. Therefore, OGC Web services and data specifications, including WCS, WFS, WMS, CSW and GML, are used. The common service environment is built upon

a set of standard interfaces for service declaration, description, discovery, binding, chaining, and execution. The requirements for this set of standards are very similar to the requirements in mainstream Web services technology. Therefore, the standards used in the mainstream Web service arena, such as WSDL, can be adopted. For standards that are not available at OGC, this work adopts standards from W3C and OASIS. In this chapter, we rely on the WSDL for the concrete specification of all geospatial Web services. For those OGC-standards compliant services, WSDL descriptions are created.

Semantic Descriptions of Geoprocessing Services

Existing Semantic Web Services technologies such as OWL-S, WSMO, SWSF, WSDL-S, SAWSDL provides ways to address the semantics of geoprocessing services. These technologies differ in the expressive power of underlying logical representation language and have different focuses. For example, apart from defining a service ontology as OWL-S, WSMO, or SWSF does, WSDL-S and SAWSDL try to describe the semantics of Web service within the legacy of current Web service standards. What they have in common is that all defines the semantics of input, output, precondition and effect (IOPE) of services. When introducing AI planning methods into automatic service composition, a typical feature is that services can be classified into two types: information-providing services and world-altering services (McIlraith et al., 2001; Sirin, et al., 2004). Information-providing services provide the state information of the current world in the planning problem, while world-altering services change the states of the world. The precondition and effect are the key points to apply AI planning methods into automatic service composition.

Usually a geoprocessing service implements a geoprocessing algorithm. Some work (Lutz, 2007) describes geoprocessing services as information-

Figure 6. Semantic description of geoprocessing services

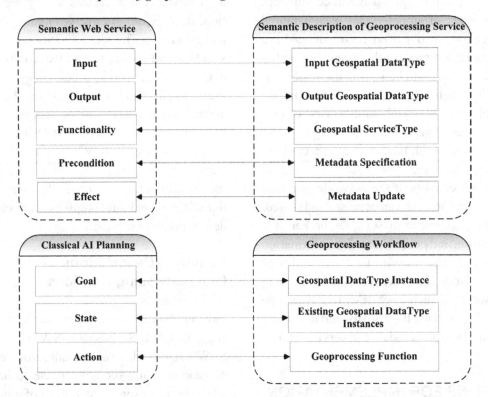

providing services in the sense that they do not change the states of the real world. It is possible to have a different definition if we have a different understand on what is the state of the world. The input data of geoprocessing services are always subject to some metadata specifications such as specific file format, spatial projection. If the states of the world are metadata specifications, then geoprocessing services can be described as world-altering services. Precondition is the metadata specification of input data, and effect is the metadata update of output data. Therefore, the generation of geoprocessing workflow can be dealt with using methods from classical AI planning domain. Figure 6 shows our approach for the semantic description of geoprocessing services. The geospatial domain ontologies play an important role to convey the semantics. To achieve semantic interoperability, the conceptualization of geospatial content should be expressed

formally and explicitly. This can be achieved by using ontologies. An ontology is a formal, explicit specification of a conceptualization that provides a common vocabulary for a knowledge domain and defines the meaning of the terms and the relations between them (Gruber, 1993). Ontologies are crucial to making the semantics of the exchanged content machine-understandable. Thus ontology can make the semantics of the exchanged content machine-understandable. The OWL, a standard Web ontology language recommended by W3C, is used for building ontologies and describing Web resources. Geospatial DataType ontologies can be used to describe the semantics of input and output of geospatial services. To address the semantics of service functionality, geospatial ServiceType ontologies are needed. The creation of geospatial DataType and ServiceType ontologies can refer to existing taxonomies in geospatial domain, such as science and service keywords collection in the

Figure 7. An OWL-S example for a slope calculation service

Global Change Master Directory (GCMD) (Olsen et al., 2004). The precondition and effect can be represented using languages such as SWRL, SPARQL provided by Semantic Web Services technologies (Martin et al., 2004). Figure 7 is an OWL-S description for a slope calculation service. The slope service has an input geospatial DataType, i.e. Terrain_Elevation, and also has a precondition on the input data file format (e.g., GeoTIFF). At output, it generates a specific geospatial DataType, i.e., Terrain_Slope.

A General Process for Intelligent Generation of Geoprocessing Workflow

We propose a general process for intelligent generation of geoprocessing workflow in a service-oriented environment (Figure 8). The proposal is based on previous work, including path planning method for automatic geospatial service composition (Yue et al., 2006) and process planning method for semi-automatic geospatial service composition

(Yue et al., 2009). Three phases are differentiated in the general process:

The *first phase* is the generation of geospatial process models, i.e. an abstract composite process model consisting of the control flow and data flow. Various process modeling methods can be used, assisted by ontologies for geospatial data and services. For example, path finding in a directed graph formulated using semantic relations among multiple geospatial semantic Web services (i.e. path planning method), or action decomposition to make a high-level process model concrete using existing process models (i.e. process planning method). In the path finding approach, a graph with nodes representing services and connection weights representing degrees of semantic matching between nodes is formulated using input/output information from multiple geospatial semantic Web services. The graph is then used to build logical path models, which can be instantiated to a physical service chain for execution in the second phase. In the process planning method, using the available composite processes, an abstract process model can be re-

323

Figure 8. A general process for intelligent generation of geoprocessing workflow

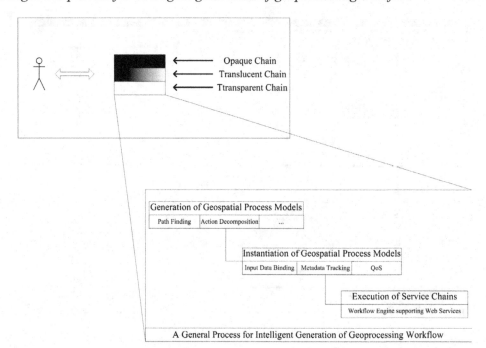

duced to a structured set of subprocesses, which may be further decomposed. The goal is to find a collection of atomic processes for some high-level composite process. In both methods, reasoning based on OWL is used in the generation of geospatial process models.

The logical representation foundation of OWL is Description Logic (DL) (Baader and Nutt, 2003). There are two types of reasoning existed in DL: TBOX reasoning and ABOX reasoning. TBOX reasoning is concerned with relationships between semantic concepts, e.g. subsumption relationship. ABOX reasoning analyses relationships between instances, or between instances and concepts. The semantic match involved in the generation of geospatial process models is limited to the concept level, therefore only TBOX reasoning is used in the phase.

The *second phase* is the instantiation of process models. A geospatial process model is instantiated into an executable service chain. Service grounding, such as XSLT transformation in the service grounding of OWL-S, can be used

to ground the semantic descriptions to syntactic message elements to enable the actual execution. A semantic-augmented registry is used for input data binding during the instantiation process. For example, OGC has recommended an ebRIM profile of Catalogue Services for the Web, therefore the ebRIM profile is extended to record the semantics of geospatial data and services so that a semantic search is supported to improve the recall and precision of data and services discovery. Existing process models and service chains can also be registered in CSW to facilitate the reuse.

When input data are bound to a process model using CSW, each process node will now be grounded to an individual service instance based on the metadata constraints, e.g. it may only support those input data with a certain data file format. Precondition check is required to see whether the service is executable. Since only those data queried from CSW can have detailed metadata information, a simulated metadata propagation process, i.e. metadata tracking, is required before execution to check preconditions of those intermediate services. The precondition check conducts reasoning at the instance level, therefore ABOX reasoning is used. When some preconditions are not satisfied, a certain type of data transformation services, such as DFTS, CTS, RCS, can be inserted automatically into service chains to enable the satisfaction of preconditions. In addition, quality criteria for service selection, i.e. Quality of Service (QoS), also play an important role in locating service instances.

The *third phase* is the execution of service chains. We can use existing workflow engines which support Web services. The execution result can help adjust the output of the first and second phase.

APPLICATIONS OF SEMANTIC WEB ENABLED INTELLIGENT GEOPROCESSING SERVICE CHAINING

A proof-of-concept prototype system is implemented (Yue, 2007). It consists of the following components: Client, Knowledge Base, Catalogue Service, Geospatial Web Services, Process Model Generation, Process Model Instantiation, Service Chain Execution Engine. Client is a Web application. Knowledge Base consists of geospatial DataType ontologies, geospatial ServiceType ontologies and OWL-S descriptions for geospatial Web services. Catalogue Service is based on the extension of OGC ebRIM profile of CSW. Various specifications related to geospatial Web services, including WCS, WICS, WCTS, Geocoder Service (following OpenGIS Location Service schema), WPS, and GML are used. A generation of Dijkstra's algorithm is adopted for path finding modeling. Action decomposition reuses existing process models. Input data binding during process model instantiation is based on the real-time interaction with CSW. A unified interface for the QoS provider is supported so different QoS criteria can be plugged in. Service chains, represented using

OWL-S composite process, can be executed using OWL-S execution engine. They can be converted into Web Services Business Process Execution Language (WSBPEL), a mainstream XML-based service composition language, and sent to a BPEL engine for execution.

The applicability of the proposed approach is demonstrated through its support to both the landslide susceptibility and wildfire prediction examples. In the landslide susceptibility case, related OWL-S descriptions for geospatial services are developed[1]. Using these semantic descriptions of services, path planning method is applied. A process model, composed of NDVI process node and landslide susceptibility computation process node, is created. Through the process instantiation phase, with metadata specification such as spatial (e.g. Dimond Canyon, California, United States) and temporal information (e.g. January 10, 2005), a service chain answering the user's problem is generated. Figure 4 shows that other input data of landslide susceptibility computation service need to be got from the outputs of some services. In the wildfire prediction case[2], a user construct a high-level process model, including an IMCS (with input data: wildfire prediction data and buffer area) and a buffer computation process (with input data: geographic address and buffer radius). Through action decomposition, the buffer computation process can be converted into a concrete process model, which consists of Geocoder, CTS and atomic buffer process. Weather data from National Oceanic & Atmospheric Administration (NOAA) National Digital Forecast Database (NDFD) and MODIS data from NASA EOS are bound to the process model in the instantiation phase. Through metadata tracking, some data transformation services are inserted into the final service chain automatically to satisfy the preconditions of the wildfire prediction service.

In these applications, users are assisted by the ontologies for geospatial data and services and do not need to deal with WSDL descriptions and message element mappings between the dependable services. Our solutions can help the domain expert focus more on the domain knowledge contribution instead of delving into the technical details. Various data processing functions can be shared. The process models can be shared and evolved.

Therefore, the use cases help to demonstrate that

1. interoperable geospatial Web services can be used to discover, request, access, and obtain geospatial data and information in a distributed environment, e.g., we use CSW for searching data, WCS for accessing data and WPS for processing data;
2. such services can be intelligently orchestrated to generate geospatial process model that transform data into knowledge which assists decision makings, e.g., we derive the wildfire prediction image from NOAA NDFD and NASA MODIS data;
3. the geospatial process models can be automatically converted to executable service chains and be invoked and executed on demand, e.g. automatically binding data and service instance to process models, inserting data transformation services automatically using metadata tracking;
4. the process models and service chains can be archived, catalogued, and thus be discovered and used in future geospatial modeling, e.g., reusing the concrete process model for buffer computation using geographic address as input.
5. such intelligent Web service based modeling processes will maximize the potential of individual data and services and significantly advance the geospatial knowledge discovery. Geospatial data and services can be composed intelligently to enable the automated or semi-automated knowledge discovery from large volumes of data in a Web environment.

DISCUSSION

OGC Abstract Service architecture (Percivall, 2002) identifies three types of service chaining: "

1. User-defined (transparent) – the human user defines and manages the chain.
2. Workflow-managed (translucent) – the human user invokes a service that manages and controls the chain. The user is aware of the individual services in the chain.
3. Aggregate (opaque) – the human user invokes a service that carries out the chain. The user has no awareness of the individual services in the chain."

As shown in Figure 8, it is possible to address all of them in the proposed general process for intelligent generation of geoprocessing workflow. For the opaque chaining, users only need to provide the required data product, then process model generation, process model instantiation and service chain execution can be conducted automatically, e.g. path planning method. However, in more sophisticated application such as the wildfire prediction case, human control as the decision support on the generation of process models is more practical and can reduce the uncertainty in the automatic service composition. From this perspective, the process planning approach can be characterized as the translucent chaining. Users can also chain the multiple services manually by themselves, and go to the third phase (i.e. workflow execution) directly (i.e. transparent chain).

The use of Semantic Web technologies bridges the gap between the concepts people use and the data machines interpret. However, the experiment shows that ontology alone is not sufficient for service chaining. Automatic generation of process models must be combined with rules and AI planning to achieve the automation of service chaining. In the path planning method, the connection in the service graph is purely based on the matching of ontology descriptions of the input and output DataTypes, it is suitable only for those geospatial Web services where the semantic concept of a service output can embody the functionality of the service, e.g. a service outputting terrain slope data can be identified as a terrain slope calculation service in most situations. For those services whose functionalities are not conveyed by their output parameters, this approach might cause much uncertainty. There are also different levels of semantic match when locating geospatial services. For example, in the reasoning based on the subsumption relationship, four levels of matches can be defined: EXACT, SUBSUME, RELAXED and FAILED. Choosing different level might cause uncertainty in match. Human intervention might be needed to ensure the higher semantic accuracy for services in the automatically generated models, e.g., users can decide which path is correct in the path planning. Although different process modeling methods might exist, either automatic or semi-automatic, the three-phase process for intelligent generation of geoprocessing workflow is still general.

CONCLUSION

Through proposing a method for semantic descriptions of geospatial Web services and exploring automatic composition of geospatial Web services, the Semantic Web based intelligent geoprocessing service chaining system can provide on-demand geospatial data product tailored to the individual analyst's unique requirements. The general process for intelligent generation of geoprocessing workflow can address all types of service chaining in the OGC abstract service architecture: user-defined, workflow-managed and aggregate. This chapter provides a reference architecture and prototype for sharing and discovery of geospatial knowledge by building geospatial services and geoprocessing models. This community-involved open, accumulated approach will revolutionize the process of geospatial information extraction and knowledge discovery. Therefore, our work will have profound effects on intelligent geospatial knowledge discovery.

ACKNOWLEDGMENT

We are grateful to the anonymous reviewers for their comments. This work was funded jointly by National Basic Research Program of China (2011CB707105), Project 40801153 supported by NSFC, LIESMARS and SKLSE (Wuhan University) Special Research Fundings.

REFERENCES

W3C. (2001). Semantic web. Retrieved February 3, 2007, from http://www.w3.org/2001/sw/

W3C. (2002). *Web service choreography interface (WSCI) 1.0*. Retrieved February 26, 2007, from http://www.w3.org/TR/wsci/

Aalst, W. (2003). Don't go with the flow: web services composition standards exposed. *IEEE Intelligent Systems, 18*(1), 72–76.

Aissi, S., Malu, P., & Srinivasan, K. (2002). E-business process modeling: the next big step. *IEEE Computer, 35*(5), 55–62.

Akkiraju, R., Farell, J., Miller, J. A., Nagarajan, M., Sheth, A., & Verma, K. (2005). *Web service semantics - WSDL-S*. Retrieved March 3, 2007, from http://www.w3.org/2005/04/FSWS/Submissions/17/WSDL-S.htm.

Altintas, I., Birnbaum, A., Baldridge, K., Sudholt, W., Miller, M., Amoreira, C., et al. (2004). A framework for the design and reuse of grid workflows. In *Proceedings of International Workshop on Scientific Applications on Grid Computing, SAG 2004*, LNCS 3458, pp. 119 – 132. Springer.

Antoniou, G., & Harmelen, F. V. (2004). *A semantic web primer* (pp. 17–18). Cambridge, MA: The MIT Press.

Baader, F., & Nutt, W. (2003). Basic description logics. In Baader, F., Calvanese, D., & McGuinness, D. (Eds.), *The description logic handbook: Theory, implementation and applications* (pp. 43–95). Cambridge, UK: Cambridge University Press.

Battle, S., Bernstein, A., Boley, H., et al. (2005). *Semantic web services framework (SWSF) overview*. Retrieved November 17, 2006, from http://www.w3.org/Submission/2005/SUBM-SWSF-20050909/

Benatallah, B., Dumas, M., Fauvet, M.-C., & Abhi, F. A. (2001). *Towards patterns of web service composition. Technical report, UNSWCSE -TR-0111*. University of New South Wales.

Berners-Lee, T. (2000a). *Semantic Web talk*. Invited Talk at XML 2000 Conference. Retrieved May 8, 2006, from http://www.w3.org/2000/Talks/1206-xml2k-tbl/slide10-0.html.

Berners-Lee, T. (2000b). *CWM - closed world machine*. Retrieved June 10, 2007, from http://www.w3.org/2000/10/swap/doc/cwm.html.

Berners-Lee, T., Hendler, J., & Lassila, O. (2001). The semantic web. *Scientific American, 284*(5), 34–43. doi:10.1038/scientificamerican0501-34

Boley, H., Tabet, S., & Wagner, G. (2001, July-August). Design rationale of RuleML: a markup language for semantic web rules, In *Proceedings of SWWS'01*. Stanford, CA.

Booth, D., Haas, H., McCabe, F., Newcomer, E., Champion, M., Ferris, C., & Orchard, D. (2004). *Web services architecture*. W3C working group note. Retrieved October 10, 2009, from http://www.w3.org/TR/ws-arch/

Casati, F., Sayal, M., & Shan, M. (2001, June). Developing e-services for composing e-services. In *Proceedings of 13th International Conference on Advanced Information Systems Engineering(CAiSE)*, Interlaken, Switzerland. Springer-Verlag.

Clery, D., & Voss, D. (2005). All for one and one for all. *Science, 308*(5723), 809. doi:10.1126/science.308.5723.809

de Bruijn, J., Bussler, C., Domingue, J., et al. (2005). *Web service modeling ontology (WSMO)*. Retrieved March 16, 2007, from http://www.w3.org/Submission/WSMO/

Di, L. (2005). A framework for developing web-service-based intelligent geospatial knowledge systems. *Journal of Geographic Information Sciences, 11*(1), 24–28.

Di, L., Zhao, P., Yang, W., Yu, G., & Yue, P. (2005, June). Intelligent geospatial web services. In *Proceedings of Geoscience and Remote Sensing Symposium*. (pp.1229 – 1232).

Egenhofer, M. (2002). Toward the semantic geospatial web. In *Proceedings of 10th ACM International Symposium on Advances in Geographic Information Systems (ACM-GIS)*, McLean, VA.

Farrell, J., & Lausen, H. (2006). *Semantic Annotations for WSDL (SAWSDL)*. Retrieved March 23, 2007, from http://www.w3.org/TR/sawsdl/

Fensel, D., & Bussler, C. (2002). *The web service modeling framework WSMF. Technical report*. Vrije Universiteit Amsterdam.

Fonseca, F., & Sheth, A. (2002). *The geospatial semantic web. Proceedings from UCGIS (University Consortium for Geospatial Information Science)*. USA: Research Priorities.

Foster, I. (2005). Service-oriented science. *Science, 308*(5723), 814–817. doi:10.1126/science.1110411

Gruber, T. R. (1993). A translation approach to portable ontology specification. *Knowledge Acquisition, 5*(2), 199–220. doi:10.1006/knac.1993.1008

Horrocks, I., Patel-Schneider, P. F., Boley, H., Tabet, S., Grosof, B., & Dean, M. (2004). *SWRL: a semantic web rule language combining OWL and RuleML*. W3C Member Submission. Retrieved March 12, 2007, from http://www.w3.org/Submission/SWRL/

IBM. (2001). *Web services flow language (WSFL 1.0)*. Retrieved March 16, 2007, from http://www-4.ibm.com/software/solutions/webservices/pdf/WSFL.pdf

Jaeger, E., Altintas, I., Zhang, J., Ludäscher, B., Pennington, D., & Michener, W. (2005, June). A scientific workflow approach to distributed geospatial data processing using web services. In *Proceedings of 17th International Conference on Scientific and Statistical Database Management (SSDBM'05), Santa Barbara, California*, (pp. 87-90).

Kammersell, W., & Dean, M. (2006, November). Conceptual search: incorporating geospatial data into semantic queries. In *Proceedings of Terra Cognita 2006, Workshop of 5th International Semantic Web Conference. Athens, GA.*

Kifer, M. (2008). Rule interchange format: the framework. In *Proceedings of the 2nd International Conference on Web Reasoning and Rule Systems*. LNCS 5341, (pp. 1–11). Berlin: Springer.

Klusch, M., Gerber, A., & Schmidt, M. (2005, November). Semantic web service composition planning with OWLS-Xplan, In *Proceedings of Agents and the Semantic Web, 2005 AAAI Fall Symposium Series, Arlington, VA.*

Kolas, D., Dean, M., & Hebeler, J. (2006, March). Geospatial semantic web: architecture of ontologies. In *Proceedings of 2006 IEEE Aerospace Conference. Big Sky, MT.*

Kolas, D., Hebeler, J., & Dean, M. (2005). Geospatial semantic web: architecture of ontologies. In *Proceedings of First International Conference on GeoSpatial Semantics (GeoS 2005)*. Mexico City: Springer.

Lemmens, R., Wytzisk, A., By, R. D., Granell, C., Gould, M., & van Oosterom, P. (2006). Integrating semantic and syntactic descriptions to chain geographic services. *IEEE Internet Computing, 10*(5), 42–52. doi:10.1109/MIC.2006.106

Lieberman, J., Pehle, T., & Dean, M. (2005). *Semantic evolution of geospatial web services: use cases and experiments in the geospatial semantic web*. Talk at the W3C Workshop on Frameworks for Semantic in Web Services, Innsbruck, Austria.

Ludäscher, B., Altintas, I., Berkley, C., Higgins, D., Jaeger, E., & Jones, M. (2005). Scientific workflow management and the Kepler system. *Concurrency and Computation, 18*(10), 1039–1065. doi:10.1002/cpe.994

Lutz, M. (2004). Non-taxonomic relations in semantic service discovery and composition. In F. Maurer & G. Ruhe (Eds.), *Proceedings of the First Ontology in Action Workshop, in conjunction with the Sixteenth International Conference on Software Engineering & Knowledge Engineering (SEKE'2004)*. (pp. 482–485).

Lutz, M. (2007). Ontology-based descriptions for semantic discovery and composition of geoprocessing services. *GeoInformatica, 11*(1), 1–36. doi:10.1007/s10707-006-7635-9

Lutz, M., & Klien, E. (2006). Ontology-based retrieval of geographic information. *International Journal of Geographical Information Science, 20*(3), 233–260. doi:10.1080/13658810500287107

Lutz, M., & Kolas, D. (2007). Rule-based discovery in spatial data infrastructures. *Transactions in GIS, 11*(3), 317–336. doi:10.1111/j.1467-9671.2007.01048.x

Martell, R. (Ed.). (2008). *CSW-ebRIM Registry Service - Part 1: ebRIM profile of CSW, (Version 1.0.0)*. Open Geospatial Consortium, Inc.

Martin, D., Burstein, M., Hobbs, J., Lassila, O., McDermott, D., McIlraith, S., et al. (2004). *OWL-based web service ontology (OWL-S)*. Retrieved November 19, 2009, from http://www.daml.org/services/owl-s/1.1/overview/

McIlraith, S. A., Son, T. C., & Zeng, H. (2001). Semantic web services. *IEEE Intelligent Systems, 16*(2), 46–53. doi:10.1109/5254.920599

Medjahed, B., Bouguettaya, A., & Elmagarmid, A. K. (2003). Composing web services on the semantic web. *The VLDB Journal, 12*(4), 333–351. doi:10.1007/s00778-003-0101-5

OASIS (2007). *Web services business process execution language, (version 2.0)*. Web Services Business Process Execution Language(WSBPEL) Technical Committee(TC).

Olsen, L. M., Major, G., Leicester, S., Shein, K., Scialdone, J., Weir, H., et al. (2004). *NASA/Global Change Master Directory (GCMD) Earth Science Keywords (Version 5.1.1)*. Retrieved August 5, 2005, from http://gcmd.nasa.gov/Resources/valids/keyword_list.html

Papazoglou, M. P. (2003). Service-oriented computing: concepts, characteristics and directions. In *Proceedings of Fourth International Conference on Web Information Systems Engineering (WISE 2003)*, Roma, Italy.

Peer, J. (2005). *Web service composition as AI planning - a survey. Technial report*. Gallen, Switzerland: University of St.

Percivall, G. (Ed.). (2002). *The OpenGIS abstact specification, topic 12: OpenGIS Service Architecture, (Version 4.3)*. Open Geospatial Consortium, Inc.

Ponnekanti, S. R., & Fox, A. (2002). SWORD: a developer toolkit for web service composition. In *Proceedings of the International World Wide Web Conference*, Honolulu, HI. (pp. 83-107).

Rao, J., & Su, X. (2004). A survey of automated web service composition methods. In *Proceedings of the First International Workshop on Semantic Web Services and Web Process Composition (SWSWPC 2004)*, San Diego, CA. (pp. 43–54).

Roman, D., Klien, E., & Skogan, D. (2006, November). SWING - A semantic web services framework for the geospatial domain. In *Proceedings of TerraCognita 2006, International Semantic Web Conference ISWC'06 Workshop*. Athens, GA.

Russel, S., & Norvig, P. (2003). *Artificial intelligence: a modern approach* (2nd ed., pp. 375–458). USA: Prentice-Hall Inc.

Sheth, A. (1999). Changing focus on interoperability in information systems: from system, syntax, structure to semantics. In Goodchild, M. F., Egenhofer, M., Fegeas, R., & Kottman, C. A. (Eds.), *The Interoperating Geographic Information Systems* (pp. 5–30). New York: Kluwer.

Sirin, E., Parsia, B., Wu, D., Hendler, J., & Nau, D. (2004). HTN planning for web service composition using SHOP2. *Journal of Web Semantics, 1*(4), 377–396. doi:10.1016/j.websem.2004.06.005

Srivastava, B., & Koehler, J. (2003). Web service composition - current solutions and open problems. In *Proceedings of ICAPS 2003 Workshop on Planning for Web Services*. (pp. 28-35), Trento, Italy.

WFMC. (1999). *Workflow management coalition, terminology & glossary*. Retrieved January 17, 2007, from http://www.wfmc.org/standards/docs/TC-1011_term_glossary_v3.pdf

Yue, P. (2007). *Semantics-enabled intelligent geospatial web service*. (Doctoral dissertation, Wuhan University). State Key Laboratory of Information Engineering in Surveying, Mapping and Remote Sensing. (pp. 72-76).

Yue, P., Di, L., Yang, W., Yu, G., & Zhao, P. (2006). Path planning for chaining geospatial web services, In *Proceedings of the 6th International Symposium on Web and Wireless Geographical Information Systems (W2GIS2006), Hong Kong.* LCNS 4295, (pp. 214-226). Berlin: Springer.

Yue, P., Di, L., Yang, W., Yu, G., Zhao, P., & Gong, J. (2009). Semantic web services based process planning for earth science applications. *International Journal of Geographical Information Science, 23*(9), 1139–1163. doi:10.1080/13658810802032680

Zaharia, R., Vasiliu, L., Hoffman, J., & Klien, E. (2009). Semantic execution meets geospatial web services: A pilot application. *Transactions in GIS, 12*(1), 59–73.

KEY TERMS AND DEFINITIONS

Geoprocessing Workflow: Geoprocessing workflow defines the processing steps including the data flow and control flow among individual geoprocessing functions. The data flow specifies the data exchange between dependent geoprocessing functions, while the control flow defines the execution order among these geoprocessing functions. Geoprocessing functions can be provided by geoprocessing services. Construction of a geoprocessing workflow in a service-oriented environment is regarded as geospatial service chaining.

Geospatial Web Service: A geospatial Web service is a modular Web application that provides services on geospatial data, information, or knowledge. Geospatial Web services can perform any function from a simple geospatial data request to complex geospatial analysis.

OGC Web Service: OGC Web Services are an evolutionary, standards-based framework that enables seamless integration of a variety of online geoprocessing and location services in a distributed environment, regardless of the format, projection, resolution, and the archive location. Currently, most OGC Web service implementations provide access via HTTP GET, HTTP POST and do not support SOAP.

Ontology: From the philosophical perspective, the nature and existence of reality. From the computer science perspective, a shared and common vocabulary for a knowledge domain, definition of its terms, and the relations among them.

Process Instantiation: Dynamic selection and binding of individual Web services with the operators in the process model. The criteria for selection can be based on the QoS (Quality of Service) information.

Process Model: An ordered sequence of cooperative operators. An operator represents a certain type of service which functionality and input/output data are consistent semantically. Two consecutive operators must exchange data with same semantics. Information about an individual service at a particular address is not included.

Semantic Web: A framework for sharing data across boundaries, to serve people more conveniently. Initiated by World Wide Web Consortium (W3C).

Service Composition: The process of creating a service chain that includes service discovery, service selection, composition method and composite service representation.

ENDNOTES

[1] Related OWL-S files are available at http://www.laits.gmu.edu/geo/nga/landslidecase.html

[2] Related OWL-S files are available at http://www.laits.gmu.edu/geo/nga/wildfirecase.html

Chapter 14
Geospatial Service Composition in Grid Environments

Tino Fleuren
University of Kaiserslautern, Germany

Paul Müller
University of Kaiserslautern, Germany

ABSTRACT

The composition of geospatial services (like OGC Web services) allows defining powerful geospatial simulations. In order to benefit from the compute power, parallel execution capabilities, and data management possibilities of a Grid environment (like OGSA), the workflow designer has to meet several challenges including heterogeneous service technologies (like WSRF or REST) large amounts of geospatial data, parallel execution, and instable Grid resources.

The workflow management system enacting these workflows has to support parallelism in an efficient way; it must avoid becoming a bottleneck, which is often the case with classic centralized workflow engines, where all data has to pass through the engines.

This chapter presents a workflow enactment system that maintains the robustness of centralized control (using service orchestration), but is enhanced by distributed components called "proxy services" that can communicate with each other to allow for efficient coupling between parallel tasks and avoiding of unnecessary data transfers (using service choreography).

INTRODUCTION

This chapter discusses the challenges that have to be dealt with when combining existing services to create geospatial service compositions, also known as geospatial workflows that retrieve and process spatial data in a Grid or Cloud environment. Already existing services could be provided by third parties that define the interface, decide

DOI: 10.4018/978-1-60960-192-8.ch014

which service technology is used, own the sources of the service, and deploy the service on their computers. A workflow management system must be able to orchestrate such different services without requiring special service technologies or particular service interfaces. This chapter discusses a workflow management system addressing these challenges.

Web Services originating from Spatial Data Infrastructures (SDI) and Grid services are integrated into workflows to perform geospatial simulations that are large-scale, long-lived, and data-intensive. Since spatial data is highly complex and significantly large, especially if multi-dimensional data is involved, the complexity of algorithms is also affected. These geospatial workflows take advantage of being enacted in a Grid environment, where it is possible to execute tasks on several compute resources in parallel. These compute resources cannot only be the nodes of one compute cluster, but several clusters around the world that are integrated in the Grid environment.

While spatial technology is highly standardized through two international standardization bodies, i.e., the Open Geospatial Consortium (OGC, www.opengeospatial.org) and the ISO (International Standardization Organization), a vital market focusing on spatially aware software has been established within the past ten years. There is a noticeable tendency of most software vendors to integrate interfaces and Web service technologies defined by the OGC (Percivall, 2003).

The Open Grid Forum (OGF, www.ogf.org) is the driving force behind the developments in the field of Grid Computing. Grid computing environments offer impressive promises to overcome problems regarding management of distributed spatial data as well as storage capacity of hitherto unknown degree for spatial data dissemination. Grid infrastructures are typically complex and consist at least of data management services, resource allocation management services and mechanisms providing a high degree of security. Most Grid middleware implementations make use of Web services for communication between resources and use Transport Layer Security (TLS) and its predecessor, Secure Sockets Layer (SSL) for encryption on otherwise insecure communication channels, such as the Internet. Cloud computing is an evolution of Grid computing in that it hides the underlying Grid infrastructure and offers a simpler and more user-centric way of how a customer can access its services. Consequently, geospatial workflows can be made available in a Cloud environment for use as a service on demand (Armbrust et al., 2009).

Because Spatial Data Infrastructures and Grid environments have developed independently of each other, a way to integrate the different technologies needs to be found. OGC and OGF established different technologies and architectures: the abstract geospatial architecture (ISO19119) and the Open Grid Services Architecture (OGSA) (Foster et al., 2005). Both approaches use different types of Web service technology. Services in Grid environments show a great difference to standard Web services, as they are stateful in nature. Therefore, the envisaged geospatial workflows integrate different types of services that must be supported by the workflow engine.

In Fleuren & Müller (2008), we described the proxy-based workflow system we developed within the "Spatial Data Infrastructure Grid" project (GDI-Grid) (von Voigt, 2009). Proxy services were introduced to support the integration of different types of services in geospatial workflows, which we execute in the domain scenarios of the project. These types of services enable us to combine Web services, OGC Web services, Grid services, and Grid jobs directly in workflow descriptions.

In this chapter, we enhance the proxy services in order to improve the performance of parallel execution and to provide efficient data handling. It would be possible to design a new workflow engine that is optimized to cope with these issues. Nevertheless, using an industry standard workflow system as an integral component offers several benefits: they are broadly accepted and have a much larger user community, which leads to greater availability of supported tools and application components. In our work, we focus on OGSA-compliant Grid Services that we deploy inside a Globus Toolkit middleware, which is one implementation of OGSA.

This chapter first discusses the properties of geospatial workflows and the consequential requirements of workflow management systems. A concept of a workflow engine is described that allows executing workflows that comply with common aspects of geospatial requirements in an efficient way and supports the need for scalability and efficient management of data and compute power. The proposed workflow engine enhances the capability of a centralized orchestration engine by offering a middleware composite of proxy services that are able to collaborate by using service choreography.

In detail, we will cover the following research questions:

- What different types of services come into play when combining SDI and Grid technologies? How can these types of services be composed to geospatial workflows?
- How does a combination of service orchestration and service choreography improve workflow performance?
- How can the geospatial workflows take advantage of Grid mechanisms such as the management of large data and integration of several compute clusters?

TECHNICAL BACKGROUND

A Grid environment offers the means for parallel execution and efficient data management. However, several technical issues have to be solved to integrate the geospatial services into the Grid environment. This section introduces the necessary technologies of Spatial Data Infrastructures and Grid environments, and discusses how both worlds can be joined.

Spatial Data Infrastructures and Grid Environments

The Open Geospatial Consortium (OGC) is the driving force behind the developments in the field of Spatial Data Infrastructures, whereas in the field of Grid computing the Open Grid Forum (OGF) embodies this role. Both organizations established different technologies and architectures: the Open Geospatial Consortium Web services (OWS) that comply with the abstract geospatial architecture (ISO19119) and the Open Grid Services Architecture (OGSA) (Foster et al., 2005).

Because of different approaches, the architectures of OWS and OGSA differ in various ways. The major differences encompass service technology, security infrastructure and the stateful nature of Grid services.

Grid environment middleware enable the sharing of heterogeneous resources, and provide a set of services for building a production Grid infrastructure. Major grid middlewares are gLite, UNICORE and Globus Toolkit (EGEE, 2008; Erwin & Snelling, 2002; The Globus Alliance, 2009a).

Geospatial Services

The geospatial community uses Geographic Information Systems (GIS) to solve geographic problems like flood simulation and to collect, manage, and represent geographically referenced information. In order to access GIS in a standardized way, the OGC specified several types of geospatial Web services.

OGC Web services are invoked by using Hypertext Transfer Protocol (HTTP) GET or POST requests. The encoding for the OGC Web service requests can be either XML (HTTP POST/SOAP) or keyword value pairs (HTTP GET/remote procedure call). All OGC Web services are able to describe themselves via the *GetCapabilities* operation, which returns an Extensible Markup Language (XML) document containing the description of the service.

The message format of an OWS depends on the kind of data exchanged. Messages can for example consist of binary data (e.g. images), ASCII-data or of Geographic Markup Language (GML), a XML dialect to handle spatial data.

The OGC specifications include the following services:

- The Web Feature Services (WFS) provide access to stored geographical features, i.e. geographic pieces of interest that can be modeled or represented by using geographic data sets. Examples of geographic features include streets, sewer lines, accidents, etc. WFS provide the *getFeature* function, which is used to query the feature data, and the *describeFeatureType* function, which returns a XML schema allowing the user to parse the returned feature data, i.e. the Geography Markup Language (GML) document. GML is an XML grammar to express geographical features (Vretanos, 2005).
- The Web Coverage Services (WCS) provide raster geospatial data, known as coverages. Coverages are objects within a geographical area. A WCS can be used for discovery, query, or data transformation operations. Data formats supported by a WCS include DTED, GeoTIFF, or NITF (Whiteside & Evans, 2006).
- The Web Map Service (WMS) display and integrate various layers of geographic datasets onto the same map. A WMS provides a standardized access to maps rendered in a format such as PNG, GIF or JPEG by using the operations *getMap* and *getFeatureInfo*. Most of the GIS manufacturers support the WMS interfaces. The optional WMS *getFeatureInfo* operation returns a more detailed description of objects included in the maps (de La Beaujardiére, 2002).
- The Web Processing Services (WPS) perform GIS calculations including processing and analytical functions. WPSs specify any geospatial function including all of its input and output parameters, and execute it. WPS offer the *describeProcess* operation to return a description of a process including inputs and outputs and the *execute* operation that performs the calculations and returns the result (Schut, 2007).

The support of SOAP/WSDL by OGC services has been discussed. WFS and WCS specifications offer guidelines on how to support SOAP/WSDL within an OWS framework. A standardized and uniform wrapping around the exchanged data (SOAP) is possible in the most recently passed standards of OGC (e.g. WPS), which has been demonstrated in OWS-4. However, the GIS community is not yet taking advantage of WSDL/SOAP and most already existing OWS do not offer WSDL/SOAP support (Open Geospatial Consortium, 2004).

WSRF-Based Grid Services

The Grid services comply with the Web Service Resource Framework (WSRF), i.e. a Web service extension for stateful Web services proposed by OASIS (Czajkowski et al., 2005). The WSRF is based on Web services that are described by the standardized and widely used Web Service Description Language (WSDL). Grid services use SOAP as transport protocol.

WSRF defines interfaces to dynamically create a service instance and manage its lifecycle by using a combination of a Web service and a stateful resource, called a WS Resource (Czajkowski et al., 2005). WSRF proposes a factory service pattern for service instantiation: the client calls a service factory that creates the actual service instance, which afterwards stores the state, and assigns a resource key. The resource key is a unique ID that is used in order to identify the resource in later uses and to associate the resource with a Web service. Accordingly, the client accesses the service instance by using an endpoint reference (EPR) containing the URI of the associated Web service and the resource key, which is known as a WS Resource endpoint reference (Sotomayor & Childers, 2006).

Grid Job Execution

Grid environments integrate different resources, for example compute clusters, which run parallel programs by using middlewares like MPI (Message Passing Interface) or PVM (Parallel Virtual Machine). The Grid provides a means to submit Grid jobs to the different cluster batch systems; OGSA specifies Resource Management Services (RMS) that allocate and control resources. For example, the Grid middleware Globus Toolkit 4 implements the WSRF and offers the Web Service Grid Resource Allocation and Management (WS GRAM) component (The Globus Alliance, 2009b). WS GRAM consists of WSRF-based Web services used by computational resources to remotely submit, monitor, and cancel jobs, offering a uniform and flexible interface to batch scheduling systems, such as Portable Batch System (PBS), Condor, and Sun Grid Engine (SGE) (Foster, 2005).

Grid jobs are defined by an XML document, consisting of either a single-job description to start a single execution of an application or a multi-job description used to trigger several jobs simultaneously. Staging activities are applied to transfer all necessary data before or after the job's execution. If staging is requested, suitable delegated security credentials must be passed in order to get the permissions to interact with the data management services that copy input data to the resource node.

Security

Security plays a major role in the OGSA specifications. Every Grid user must meet the terms of the security infrastructure to be able to access any resources within a Grid environment. Security is provided by using certificates for authentication and authorization combined with encrypted communication.

The Grid Security Infrastructure (GSI) (Butler et. al, 2000) provides this basis for the Grid middlewares Globus Toolkit, UNICORE, and gLite. GSI is based on public key cryptography, and extensions of X.509 certificates are used to authenticate users and hosts. A Certificate Authority (CA), i.e. a third party, testifies the ownership of each of the public keys. The owner is responsible to secure his private keys and never to reveal them to the public.

Transport Level Security (TLS) and Message Level Security (WS-Security and WS-SecureConversation) can be applied for signing or encrypting messages. GSI uses several authorization mechanisms, for example, access control lists, a custom authorization handler and access to an authorization service via the Security Assertion Markup Language (SAML) that can be used to describe and to exchange security data.

In a Grid environment, the participating members like individuals and institutions can join groups, known as Virtual Organizations (VO), in order to share knowledge and Grid resources and collaborate to work towards a common goal. Generally, VOs are not limited to computing power but include elements as storage, data sets, sensors, and scientific instruments.

Accessing Data in a Grid Environment

Grid environments provide several solutions for accessing data.

Globus Toolkit offers GridFTP as the basic access technology (The Globus Alliance, 2010a). GridFTP is a high performance data transfer protocol optimized for high bandwidth wide-area networks.

GridFTP is based on the Internet File Transfer protocol, but complies with GSI and is enhanced by features to meet the requirements of Grid environments, for example, striping (extension of the basic protocol for supporting the data transference among multiple servers), and parallelism (using multiple TCP streams in parallel).

The Reliable File Transfer service (RFT) uses standard Web service technology to manage GridFTP file transfers (The Globus Alliance, 2010b). It comprises one control channel and several data channels. The authenticated and authorized user submits a transfer request (consisting of a set of third party GridFTP transfers) to the RFT factory service and thus gets access to a RFT resource.

OGSA-DAI (Open Grid Services Architecture -Data Access and Integration) is a middleware product that allows data resources, such as relational or XML databases, file systems, to be integrated across the network and accessed via Web services, HTTP, FTP or GridFTP (OGSA-DAI, 2010).

Bridging the Gaps

The main approach to bridge the described gaps between the two architectures is to maintain standardized interfaces wherever possible, while simultaneously enhancing functionality to the OGC Web services in order to enable them to communicate or interact with a Grid environment.

An OGC Web service that should be deployed to the Grid needs to be wrapped by a WSRF-compliant Web service. In order to "Grid-enable" the OGC services, they have to be adapted to meet the requirements of the WSRF, especially the concept of dynamic endpoint references (EPR). Furthermore, the service functionality must be enhanced by authentication and authorization mechanisms, such that it can interact with the Grid security infrastructure. Then, the Grid-enabled service can access all Grid resources and for example submit Grid jobs to the underlying compute cluster.

The workflow management system has to allow for integrating both kinds of service technologies. That way, the workflow engine operates from the inside of a Grid environment, i.e. it will act as a Grid client, but it will also need to access already existing OGC Web services that are deployed outside the Grid environment. Hobona, Fairbairn, & James (2007) demonstrate the invocation of Grid-enabled OGC Web services from workflows by using an intermediate SOAP node that intercepts requests and translates them to the appropriate OGC format.

OWS and Grid services use different security standards. The OGC does not provide a service specification to handle security infrastructure-wide yet; however, this topic has been discussed (Elfers & Wagner, 2007). On the other hand, the Grid services comply with the Grid Security Infrastructure, so that only authenticated and authorized users may access them.

Grid service and OGC Web services also differ in the way they can be registered and found. As OGSA again relies on widely known and used standards as Universal Description, Discovery and Integration (UDDI), OWS established the Catalogue Service Web (CS-W). The main difference is again the use of SOAP on the Grid service side and HTTP GET/POST on the OGC Web service side.

In the late 2007, OGF and OGC signed a memorandum of understanding to collaborate with each other (Lee & Percivall, 2009). This collaboration will result in information interchange as well as the development of specifications for spatial applications for Grid environments. One goal is to develop open standards to prevent diverse formats, schemas and algorithms.

The different nature of both infrastructures, result in specific requirements of workflow management systems that try to integrate services of both worlds. The next section discusses the properties of the geospatial workflows and the consequential requirements of workflow management systems.

GEOSPATIAL APPLICATIONS IN GRID ENVIRONMENTS

This section describes basic challenges for the execution of geospatial workflows in a Grid environment. Drawing on the example of a real workflow developed in the Spatial Data Infrastructure Grid project (GDI-Grid), these challenges are discussed and used to derive requirements of workflow management systems. A number of architectures of workflow management systems are presented.

Properties of Geospatial Grid Workflows

The GDI-Grid project focuses on solutions for efficient integration and processing of geo data based on Geo Information Systems (GIS) and Spatial Data Infrastructure (SDI) (von Voigt, 2009). A Grid infrastructure for three sample scenarios is being implemented: flood simulation, disaster routing and noise emission simulation in urban environments.

In all scenarios, the workflows usually commence with accessing specific data sources, for example, public geospatial databases, or sensors, and use one or more geospatial tasks to process this data. For example, LiDAR (Light Detection and Ranging) data is used to create digital elevation models (DEM), which are required in river and coastal engineering applications. In order to handle the high quality LiDAR DEMs, generalization and simplification algorithms are applied that reduce the huge number of data points while simultaneously preserving the structural terrain features such as breaklines.

Lanig & Zipf (2009) describe a workflow that invokes several Geospatial Web services that process LiDAR data. The terrain data may already be copied to the Grid or the first step is to retrieve the data from external suppliers via existing Geospatial Web services (e.g. OGC services). Due to the high measuring point density, LiDAR terrain data can be very large. Therefore, in order to process the terrain data, it is spatially divided into regular tiles using polygons as borders by applying geometric partitioning.

On each tile a sequence of computational steps are performed, which forms a sequential sub workflow or a pipeline. Examples of these steps are triangulation, generating different terrain LODs (Level of Details) and post-processing activities.

The results of each parallel sub workflows have to be merged to the desired TIN (Triangular Irregular Network) or converted to other formats including VRML (Virtual Reality Modeling Language) or KML (Keyhole Markup Language) (Bell, Parisi, & Pesce, 1995; Open Geospatial Consortium, 2009).

This example workflow used in the GDI-Grid project (cf. Figure1), shows several properties that are also common to many other geospatial workflows.

Geospatial workflows do often have an experimental nature: The user performs some transformation on the spatial data, in order to generate a specific map, containing the subject of interest that can be displayed to the user. The structure of the workflow will change, if the user needs new or additional features in the map. Consequently, these workflows are often user-driven, prototypical, and evolutionary.

Geospatial simulations, for example flood simulation, process huge amounts of spatial data, like the LiDAR terrain data of the example, which have to be retrieved by accessing different kind of external sources. OGC Web services are the broadly accepted standard to accessing such data sources; however, other sources like databases are also applicable. Therefore, there is a need

Figure 1. Typical workflow patterns

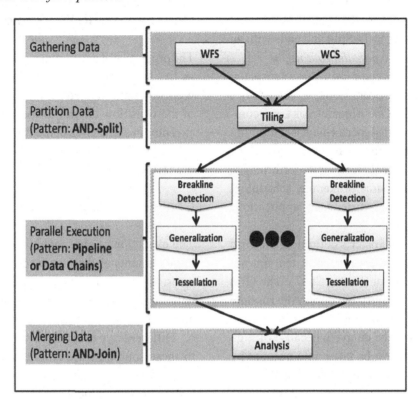

for being able to invoke services implementing different kinds of service technologies.

Parallel computing improves performance of geospatial workflows. To accomplish this, in many scenarios the initial data is divided into tiles, which will then be processed in data transformation chains. A data transformation chain is a sequence of services that are connected by data dependencies. Numerous of these processing chains can be executed concurrently. The data transformation chains can be executed iterative i.e. the next data will be processed not before the first data has processed all stages of the chain; or the chain will act as a pipeline, where all stages run concurrently.

Figure 1 presents basic workflow aspects, which are also common to many data-intensive, large-scale workflows in other research areas and correspond to several classes of workflow patterns, described by the Workflow Management Coali-

tion (WfMC): Pipeline, AND-Split, AND-Join (Workflow Management Coalition, 1999):

- A *pipeline* is a workflow activity that is executed after the completion of a preceding activity in the same workflow; it accepts the output data of its predecessor as input.
- An *AND-split* (or *parallel split*) is a diverging of a branch into several parallel branches each of which execute concurrently. In the geospatial area, the data is often partitioned into area tiles and each branch executes on one tile.
- The *AND-join* (or *synchronization*) activity unites two or more branches into a single subsequent branch, such that each enablement of an incoming branch results in the thread of control being passed to the subsequent branch. Here, the intermediate results are merged into the final result.

In most scenarios, workflows will include all three patterns; the pattern for a sub workflow that commences with an AND-Split and ends with an AND-Join is denoted *parallel routing*.

Further properties common to these geospatial workflows originate from being executed in a Grid environment. One objective of Grid computing is to provide high performance computing power. When executing parallel workflow tasks in a Grid environment, workflow performance is dependent on resource brokerage, scheduling (load balancing), and distributed applications (parallel computing).

According to Ian Foster's definition, the Grid combines many different resources that are not under a central control (Foster, 2002). The Grid environment may be instable during the runtime of the workflow: services may fail, resources go offline, or jobs will be delayed, because of high usage rates. This must be taken into account by advanced workflow fault management techniques (e.g. workflow check pointing and recovery, monitoring).

In a Grid environment, service invocations often consist of short, sporadic method calls (Grid service calls), which launch time- and compute-intensive calculations, thus resulting in long-lived workflows. Typically, data will be pushed to the Grid in bulk data transfers, not pulled, like in other execution environments.

One principle of designing service-oriented architectures is to apply stateful services only when necessary, because the management of state information affects the availability of services and weaken the scalability potential (Erl, 2005). Therefore, workflows, like business workflows are preferably related to the invocation of stateless services (workflow of Web services). In contrast to that, activities of Grid workflows are often related to stateful services (workflow of Grid services).

To process such a workflow efficiently, the workflow engine must support the requirements described in the next section.

Requirements for Enacting Geospatial Grid Workflows

The properties of geospatial workflows, described in the last section, influence the way that the workflows are enacted as well as the architecture of the workflow engines, especially when being executed in a Grid environment. Workflow engines executing these types of workflows face at least the following challenges.

Challenge: Heterogeneity

The execution of geospatial workflows involves huge amounts of data for maps, geographic features, and geographic coverages. Gathering this data from various sources is a main requirement and often the first activity of a geospatial workflow.

Different types of services provide access to these sources, for example, the Web Feature Services and Web Coverage Services that provide access to geographic data. The workflow system must allow for the integration of these services.

One possibility of integrating such a service is to Grid-enable it, i.e. develop a new version of this service that can be deployed in a Grid environment. While numerous implementations of OGC Web services already exist, it becomes strategically necessary to examine which of them should or need to be Grid-enabled. The time-consuming and compute-intensive OGC Web services are best suitable for being executed in the Grid environment. Not every geospatial Web service can be ported to the Grid. There are two reasons for not developing a Grid-enabled version of an existing service. The first reason originates from the requirement of accessing already existing services, including services that are in the hands of third parties that offer no Grid-enabled version of their services. Because the source code is not free, it is not possible to provide a new version that uses the desired service technology. In order to invoke these external services, a wrapper is needed for each individual service that acts as a client.

The second reason for not Grid-enabling a service is to reduce costs. A great number of already existing services such as assisting operations, that are not compute-intensive would not benefit from being executed in a Grid environment. Grid-enabling all of these services would be potentially time-consuming and expensive; therefore, it is more efficient and more flexible to be able to invoke these services directly from a workflow.

When integrating different types of services, a number of technologies, mechanisms, and methods come into play. In order to combine those different approaches, various issues may have to be considered, such as applying different security standards (e.g. providing authentication credentials for remote resources), selecting from multiple execution alternatives, invoking third-party services that demand the usage of certain standards and many others.

Different technologies of Spatial Data Infrastructures (SDI) and Grid environments result in different types of Web services, as well. When designing a geospatial workflow, the workflow system must be capable of invoking the following types of services:

- *WSDL-based Web services* - The standard Web service technology uses WSDL (Web Service Description Language) to describe the interfaces of the services and SOAP to exchange messages between them, independently of the underlying protocol.
- *WSRF-based Grid services* - OASIS specifies Web service extensions for stateful Web services. The Web Services Resource Framework (WSRF) provides a set of operations that Web services may implement to become stateful (Czajkowski et al., 2005). Grid services are WSRF-based services that can be executed in the Globus Toolkit's web service container. In order to Grid-enable the OGC services, they have to be adapted to meet the requirements of the WSRF, especially the concept

of dynamic endpoint references (EPR). Additionally, Grid services comply with the security infrastructure of the Grid, like the Grid Security Infrastructure (GSI) of Globus Toolkit 4.
- *RESTful Web services* - Many Web services follow the paradigm of Representational State Transfer (REST). REST is a design paradigm describing a stateless client-server architecture in which Web services are seen as resources that can be addressed by their URLs. OGC and the wider geospatial community have recently begun to discuss RESTful Web Services. This has happened both internally (Reed, 2006; Turner, 2008; Uslaender, 2007) and externally (Lucchi, Millot, & Elfers, 2008; Mazzetti, Nativi, & Caron, 2009).
- *OGC Web services* – WSDL support of OGC Web services has been discussed, however, it remains optional, and currently most available OGC Web services do not apply WSDL/SOAP. The clients invoke an OGC Web service by using either XML (HTTP POST/SOAP) or keyword-value pairs (HTTP GET/remote procedure call). All OGC Web services are providing an operation to describe themselves by responding with an XML description of their capabilities.
- *Command-line tools and shell scripts* - Several (legacy) geospatial applications can be executed via the command-line or by using shell scripts. These applications can be executed as a Grid job on a compute cluster, so the workflow engine should be capable of submitting such jobs directly, without the need to develop a wrapper service for each job.

Workflows should be independent from the service technology, so that they can easily be executed in a different execution environment. It is unpractical to develop a new workflow management system each time services need to be invoked that comply with a new Grid middleware. For example, BPEL does not support the invocation of WSRF-based Web services. Therefore, the workflow management system should provide a means to integrate new service technology in a straightforward manner.

Already existing services could be provided by third parties that define the interface, decide which service technology is used, own the sources of the service, and deploy the service on their computers. In order to be able to reuse such a service and not having to implement similar service by oneself, the workflow designer needs a workflow management system that is able to orchestrate such different services without requiring special service technologies or particular service interfaces.

Challenge: Data Management

In the first step 'gathering data' of many geospatial workflows like in Figure 1, the data must be acquired. Frequently, in geospatial scenarios, the initial data has to be bought from an institution, for example, a land surveying office that provides certain area maps or LiDAR data. Usually, these institutions offer their data via Web services that comply with the OGC standard.

The volume of spatial data can easily become several terabytes, which have to be processed by the workflow and managed by the workflow engine accordingly. Grid environments provide some mechanisms for data managing and high-speed data transfer; however, some issues must be considered in advance when constructing a geospatial workflow: a classic centralized workflow engine, like a business workflow engine, often becomes a bottleneck and wastes bandwidth, when all data passes through it. For example, when invoking an OGC Web service in order to retrieve raster data, the service's result returns to the service consumer, which would be the workflow engine, no matter how large the raster data is. In the case of a WPS, it could be possible to set the "asReference" at-

tribute in the output element, which then contains the URL to the dataset. However, when integrating already existing services in a workflow, it cannot be guaranteed that the service returns a reference to its output data. In the next step, the workflow engine will forward the data to a processing service, whose output is again passed through the workflow engine.

When workflows need to access Terabyte-size data sets, the limiting factor can be the storage available at the execution sites. Few systems support disk space reservation, so workflows compete with each other for storage space on a first-come-first-serve basis. In general, quotas are only applied at the level of Virtual Organizations (VO), which means, that all members of a VO struggle for storage space. Therefore, the workflow will have to map workflows carefully to the available Grid resources.

It would be desirable, to be able to determine how much storage space is available at the execution site, and estimate the amount of data the workflow activities will need, so that only the resources will be selected that comply with the necessary disk space. In practice, this is often not feasible, because accurate information from the resources is not available, and it is hard to estimate the actual data storage the workflow will need. In addition, the available space on the remote resource may change while transferring data, therefore, the workflow management system would consider a recovery strategy if disk space failures occur and re-schedule the workflow for execution on another resource. The workflow system or the workflow logic need not forget to delete the data that is needed no longer, and thus reduce the workflow footprint (Singh et al., 2007).

Another aspect of data management that has to be considered is caused by data sets that are too large to be transported efficiently. It is necessary for workflow scheduling to consider this when choosing the resources for the computation. The data should be transported directly to the location where it is needed, i.e. where the computation is taking place; unnecessary data transfer should be avoided.

The desired workflow engine should therefore be able to cope with large amount of data.

Challenge: Parallel Computing

In order to take advantage of the powerful resources a Grid environment provides, e.g. access to several clusters anywhere in the world, the workflow processes data in several parallel branches.

This ability of a Grid environment may only be used to its full potential, if a suitable method is found, offering a way to divide the geospatial algorithm into parallel tasks. When constructing the workflow, the designer needs to choose the best parallelism strategy, such as Parallel Execution or Pipelined Execution (Pautasso & Alonso, 2006). A potential means for the parallelization of many geospatial processes is provided by tessellation of an input geometry. While the approach to partition the input data is suitable for transformation algorithms, and simple geometric operations (like buffering or intersection of surfaces where no interdependencies are given), algorithms that are more complex like the creation of climate models, routing or flood-modeling demand more sophisticated parallelization algorithms. There is no generic parallelization algorithm for all different kinds of problems; consequently, a workflow designer has to implement a suitable parallelization algorithm for himself (cf. (Foster, 1995)). It is desirable that the workflow system supports as much parallelism strategies as possible. The following paragraphs present several possibilities of parallelism.

Parallel Execution: Simple Parallelism and Data Parallelism

Invoking several services in parallel that have no data dependencies or interactions is the simplest form of parallel execution (simple parallel execution). The focus is on the algorithms that are to be performed rather than on the processed data.

Disjoint tasks or services will be developed prior to examining their data requirements. For example, if a service invocation in a Grid environment comprises of submitting a job to a computation cluster, the underlying batch system schedules the jobs, determines the available resources, and chooses a suitable one to submit the job to.

Simple parallel execution can be defined from a control-flow perspective or a dataflow perspective. In workflow description languages based on control-flow (e.g. BPEL, Business Process Execution Language) a *flow* construct is a means for simple parallel execution, where different activities are executed concurrently. When using languages that define dataflow (e.g. SCIRun (Johnson & Parker, 1999) or Kepler (Ludäscher et al., 2005)), simple parallelism can be applied in a more straightforward way. The dataflow graph defines data that services will exchange to accomplish their task. When a service A depends on data produced by service B, the execution sequence of A and B are implicitly described. If both services are not linked by data dependencies, they are executed concurrently.

Another form of parallel execution is *data parallelism*, also referred to as *partitioning* or *tiling* in the geospatial domain. First, the data associated with a problem is decomposed. Optimally, the data is divided into pieces (also known as tiles) of approximately equal size, and then the algorithm operating on the data pieces is developed. Each parallel task executes the same code on different data.

Different criteria can be utilized for partitioning spatial data; these include object type (e.g. streets, buildings), operation type (e.g. calculation length, angles), spatial criteria (tiling), geometry type (e.g. area, line, point), and Level of Detail (LoD) (Werder, 2009).

Data parallelism can be static, dynamic, or adaptive. In its static form, the workflow designer knows the number of tiles in advance (i.e., at design-time) and this number is non-varying for all workflow enactments. A dynamic workflow adjusts the number of tiles to the context in which it is executed. For example, a workflow expects the number of tiles as an input parameter, which the workflow client can decide at runtime. Furthermore, when applying adaptive data parallelism, the workflow can even adjust to the current state of the execution environment. The workflow management system determines the number of tiles automatically as a function of available compute resources. However, the workflow system must be able to access monitoring information and to support some sort of reflection on the state of the execution environment.

In both simple parallelism and data parallelism, a synchronizing post-condition can be specified:

- WAIT FOR ANY: the same service is invoked several times on the same data. This can be useful to improve several dependability attributes, for example by calling the same service redundantly, proceeding with the fastest result, while discarding the other results in order to increase availability or performance of the workflow.
- WAIT FOR MAJORITY: multiple service instances will be called and then the workflow proceeds with the results of all successful services and chooses the most appropriate result. This way, the reliability and availability of the workflow improves, however, at the expense of cost and performance.
- WAIT FOR ALL: the workflow will only proceed if all branches finish successfully. This will be the most common approach, when spatial data is divided in several tiles in a geospatial workflow and all results will be needed in further execution of the workflow.

Pipelined Execution

In scientific workflows, data is often streamed through independent processes that consist of several data transformation steps, structured in an application-data-application fashion. We call these processes data transformation chains or pipelines. The data transformation chains run continuously, waiting for input data and producing output. Consequently, in contrast to the sequential execution, where new data is not processed before the previous execution is finished; a pipelined execution can process different data sets at the same time in parallel. In Figure 1, we see k pipelines processing n data sets in parallel. In workflow stage i data set i in $\{1,...,n\}$ is being produced. The services participating in a data transformation chains have the following properties:

- They read a set of input data, process this data, and produce a set of output data. They will continue to operate until they will be destroyed.
- With Grid workflows, the computation could be executed on Grid nodes having the nature of Grid jobs. These jobs execute self-contained applications that can be long-lived.
- When one computation is finished, the output will be the input of the next job.

This way, numerous parallel pipelines are being processed with the goal of an optimal distribution of data and tasks.

Pipeline collision occurs, if new data is available, but the task cannot process the data because it is busy. There are different possibilities how pipeline collisions can be avoided. In the simplest case, new input data for a service is simply discarded, when the service is busy. This could be satisfactory, if it is not necessary that all parallel tasks be fully processed by the pipeline, for example, if the best or fastest result is needed.

In order to avoid loss of data, the execution of a service could be blocked. Then a service can only be invoked, if the predecessor has completed and if its successor is idle. For example, the workflow system Kepler (Ludäscher et al., 2005) and Triana

(Taylor, Shields, Wang, & Rana, 2003) realize the blocking pipeline execution pattern.

Another strategy to avoid pipeline collision is to store the incoming and intermediate data in a queue and let the service process the data, whenever the service is idle. Then the workflow management system has to handle the management of the queue and the storing of the data; it must be guaranteed that enough storage capacity is available.

Another possibility to avoid pipeline collision is to create additional task instances dynamically whenever input data is available for a busy task. Invoking additional service instances may cause data elements to overtake each other, as some may be delayed in the pipeline. The workflow management system must provide efficient mechanism for executing such a pipeline.

Challenge: Robustness

Grid environments enable dynamic composition of distributed resources in order to perform highly compute-intensive tasks. These resources include CPUs, memory and disk storage, data management capabilities, and databases.

However, as many users participate in a Grid environment, execution of services may be delayed. Consequentially, the workflow management system must be able to cope with service timeouts and to re-schedule service invocations. Additionally, if all users submit a Grid job to the resources, large amounts of data will be copied to the worker node that is to process this data. The workflow management system must take into account that disk failures occur, and be able to initiate compensation procedures and re-schedule the execution on another resource.

The dependability of resources cannot be guaranteed in a Grid environment, because it is not under central control; it is always possible for that new resources are added and others go offline. This potential instability of resources affects the execution of geospatial workflows.

Usually, dependability is increased by introducing redundancy. For example, if several service instances or Grid jobs process the same data, the workflow uses the fastest result further and the discards the other results. This practice applies simple parallelism utilizing the Grid job synchronization post-condition WAIT-FOR-ANY as described earlier.

Challenge: Easy Design of Workflows

Workflow description languages eliminate the necessity of having to develop a special middleware to orchestrate services. Now, services can easily be orchestrated to different workflows and third-party services complying with certain standards can rapidly be integrated, too.

Designing and constructing a geospatial workflow should be an easy task. Therefore, workflow designer would like to use a graphical tool for the implementation of a workflow, i.e. orchestrating geospatial services on a graph via drag-and-drop. He is not interested in different service technologies, so the graphical workflow tool should use an abstraction for describing the services. Thus, the user does not need to know, if he is calling a RESTful Web service or a WSRF-based Grid service.

Most workflow systems provide a graphical tool for designing workflows. For example, Kepler's and Triana's tools use a graph or block diagram, where nodes represent workflow activities and edges dataflow dependencies or task orders.

After designing the workflow, it is automatically deployed to the workflow engine, which executes it. Research has been done, on sharing workflows and ensuring their provenance (Davidson & Freire, 2008). Detailed workflow provenance information help scientist to reproduce and validate the results of others, and re-use the knowledge for analyzing, generating, and processing geospatial data. The lack of provenance information may limit the longevity of geospatial data, because without sufficient information about how maps have been generated, their value and utility may be severely diminished.

Efficient portals to distribute existing workflows have been proposed, for example, on the platform *myExperiment* researchers can publish their workflows and share them with others (De Roure et al., 2008). This way, the workflow designer is able to change the workflow rapidly to new requirements. Simultaneously, already existing and validated sub workflow or workflow patterns could be used to create new workflows.

Architecture of a Workflow Engine

Various workflow engine architectures have been proposed, applying different approaches of designing and executing workflows. This section describes several aspects that have the greatest influence on enactment of the envisioned geospatial workflows.

Dataflow or Control-Flow

In a workflow graph, an edge A->B can be interpreted in two ways: B can only start after A has finished, i.e., representing control-flow, or A produces output data that B consumes, when focusing on dataflow.

With the control-flow in mind, the workflow designer defines control-flow dependencies between various services. The workflow description specifies a series of workflow activities like service calls, supporting loops and alternatives in an easy manner. The data paths between the workflow activities are effectively invisible.

On the other hand, designing the dataflow of a geospatial workflow involves the passing of data, scoping of variables, and so on. Dataflow-based workflows promote the data to become the main concept behind any workflow. Services can be plugged together if the output of the first service is equal to the input requirements of the following service. The services execute as soon as all of their input data becomes available. Consequently, the

necessary description comprises input and output data that are specified in terms of data types and their meaning (semantics).

Dataflow allows for building data transformation chains in an easy way; however, defining loops, and alternatives will be more complicated. Then additional services will have to be integrated that implement control functions like alternatives. Moreover, error detection or error compensation can be described more easily from the control-flow perspective.

Generally, workflow description languages mainly focus on either control-flow or dataflow.

Orchestration and Choreography

The two main approaches for service composition are service orchestration and service choreography.

Workflow designer define workflows either from the view of a single centralized participant using orchestration, or from a global perspective using choreography. In service orchestration, each service is invoked sequentially by a centralized workflow control and the input and output data sets are moved to a central location. The large data sets involved in geospatial scenarios, this is not feasible because it results in unnecessary data transfers. Therefore, only handles to the data should pass the workflow management system. Orchestration also encompasses an explicit specification of control-flow and dataflow. A centralized workflow control always acts as a coordinator of the involved services, both control and dataflow messages pass through this centralized server. The services do not know of their participation in a workflow.

Service choreography on the other hand describes collaborative behavior between a set of services in order to achieve a common objective. Choreography is focusing on the interactions between services from a global perspective; all services are aware of their partners and know when to invoke operations. The services are able to communicate directly with each other; no central unit controls the workflow execution. The involved services are aware of their partner services and know when to invoke operations.

Orchestration differs from choreography in that a workflow engine controls the service invocations. The Business Process Execution Language (BPEL) is the dominant orchestration language and it is a standard specified by the OASIS (OASIS, 2007). BPEL can be used to orchestrate Web services based on XML and BPEL offers the means to build workflows with SOAP-based Web services. However, current BPEL engines do not support invocation of Grid services nor OGC Web services. The Web Services Choreography Description Language (WS-CDL) is the leading choreography language (W3C, 2005). WS-CDL choreographies define protocols, whereas BPEL processes can be actually instantiated and executed.

In scientific workflows, where large amounts of intermediate data are transferred between services, a choreography model is a more effective architecture. A service can move its output directly to where it is required as input of the next stage of the workflow, which results in decreasing execution time of a workflow. On the other hand, already existing services that cannot be adjusted may not be able to collaborate and to communicate directly with another service.

In practice however, designing a choreography model is significantly more complex than constructing an orchestration model. That is because in choreography the control-flow cannot be seen directly. This also influences displaying and monitoring the progress of the workflow execution, because it is difficult to get actual information about the state of all peers.

Centralized or De-Centralized Engines

Workflow execution can be controlled by a centralized workflow component or by distributed components. For example, in business workflows usually centralized workflow engines are used,

that control the enactment of the process from a central position in the infrastructure of the business company.

A de-centralized workflow engine should hide the distribution from the workflow designer, such that he does not need to specify, which part of the workflow will be executed on another resource, if he does not wish so. This adds considerable complexity to the workflow management system.

Conclusions

Most scientific workflow systems focus mainly on dataflow models of computation. The design of linear or pipelined workflows can be achieved by a dataflow description in an easy and straightforward manner, however, control-flow modeling often results in more fault-tolerant, robust, and adaptive workflows. Adding control-flow to workflows in such a system, for example, KEPLER (Ludäscher et al., 2005) increases the complexity of the original dataflow-based workflow. The advantage of a centralized orchestration engine like a BPEL engine lies in the easy graphical construction of a workflow description and robustness of control-flow constructs.

Defining the control-flow is simpler for complex workflows containing many loops, or conditional branches. On the other hand, invoking 1000 parallel services or even pipelined sub workflows will result in a complex and huge workflow graph in a language like BPEL. A classical centralized workflow engine would initialize and start all parallel tasks and manage all control and data messages that have to be exchanged. The costs for managing and coordinating all the tasks or services, which operate in parallel, depend on the service granularity. Increasing the number of sub tasks quickly results in more complex workflows and greater expenses for coordination. Nevertheless, scalability is the key requirement in increasing the performance of geospatial simulations.

When integrating an already existing Web service, its result is being returned to the orchestration engine, which results in the orchestration engine being a bottleneck. In a workflow using choreography, the data will be transferred directly to the following service. However, when using existing services it is difficult to make them collaborate. The existing services are self-contained and not aware of the workflow in which they participate. In order to enable services to pass data directly to one another an extra layer of functionality has to be added. In geospatial workflows, where large amounts of intermediate data are transferred between services, a choreography model is a more effective architecture. A service can move its output directly to where it is required as input of the next stage of the workflow, which results in decreasing execution time of a workflow.

A Proxy-Enhanced Orchestration Engine

This section discusses concepts to overcome the issues described earlier. An orchestration engine, in particular a BPEL engine, is presented that controls distributed workflow components, denoted as proxy services that are able to collaborate to allow for choreography.

The hybrid solution combines the benefits of a service orchestration model with the benefits of choreography model. The centralized orchestration model is applied to improve robustness and error handling; the choreography model is used for optimal distributed data transport and efficient parallel or pipelined execution.

Achieving Service Choreography

In order to improve the performance of a workflow, the participating Web services should collaborate by using choreography. This way, the services communicate with each other to allow for efficient coupling between parallel tasks and direct exchange of large amounts of data between each other.

When invoking pre-existing services, it is difficult to make them collaborate. The services are self-contained and not aware of the workflow in which they participate. In order to enable services to pass data directly to one another a supplemental layer of functionality has to be added. This can be achieved by:

- *Enhancing the service interface* - As we aim at a composition of pre-existing services available on the Web in order to provide a new functionality, reprogramming the services and enhancing their interfaces is not a feasible way. Furthermore, this way third-party services could not be integrated, because the owner of the services will only comply with new interfaces, if they can gain advantages from doing so.
- *Developing a wrapper for each service* - A service could be invoked a wrapper service, that provides the necessary interface. For each individual service, such a wrapper would have to be developed.
- *Utilizing proxy services* - Alternatively, the logic can be laid in distributed components, the proxy services that invoke the actual services and provide an additional set of functionality allowing for the desired collaborative behavior. This way, the service interfaces do not need to be altered, which facilitates the desired choreography of services.

Architecture of the Workflow Management System

The workflow management system comprises of a centralized orchestration engine and proxy services.

Centralized Workflow Control
A centralized workflow enactment engine acts as a coordinator between the proxy services initializing the setting and controlling the Web services

and proxy services by sending control-flow messages. In addition, all control-flow constructs of orchestration languages can be used.

Different orchestration languages are imaginable for the centralized control. For example, in the GDI-Grid project an open-source BPEL engine is utilized as the centralized component of the workflow systems, benefiting from the de-facto standard language used for service orchestration.

Proxy Services

The proxy services' main function is to invoke a Web service on behalf of the orchestration engine. This way, the proxy services can invoke services that the orchestration engine does not support. Communication between the Web service and the proxy service can be local, if they are deployed near each other, for example on the same application container or in the same network domain in order to improve performance. A Proxy Creator service is used to instantiate the proxy services. It is also imaginable to install proxy services in advance, so that they exist on all containers.

The proxy services' second function is the distributed execution of workflows and the implementation of choreography functionality in order to improve the performance of a workflow. To this purpose, the proxy services are able to exchange dataflow messages amongst themselves, like in a peer-to-peer network.

Different service technologies could be used to implement the proxy services. For example, in the GDI-Grid project proxy services are implemented as Grid services and deployed on the Globus Toolkit 4 middleware. A prototypical implementation of the Grid job proxy services shows how choreography can be achieved. The data transformation chains are executing Grid jobs that are described by an XML-based document. The proxy services comply with the WSRF, thus, providing a factory service, which can be used to create new instances in an easy way.

The combination of a centralized control with proxy service therefore, maintains the robustness and simplicity of centralized workflow engines being able to detect and handle error, while at the same time improving the workflow performance by using choreography. The workflow management system can be easily deployed and utilized:

- The proxy services can be used without modifications to already existing services and without adding or generating additional code, which would not be possible with pure choreography models, like for example WS-CDL.
- The proxy services can be installed and configured dynamically and remotely. They should be installed as near as possible to the service it will invoke.
- Already existing workflows need only minor changes: instead of calling the service directly, the proxy service is associated with the service and then calls it on behalf of the workflow engine.

Workflows with Standardized Interfaces

Most BPEL workflow engines provide a WSDL/SOAP interface for a workflow, so that Web service clients can invoke the workflow. Geospatial applications can gain flexibility if they offer a standardized interface, for example, an OGC interface, such that the workflow can be accessed by a WPS client.

The proxy-enhanced workflow engine uses a WPS wrapper in order to offer the WPS interface, so that requests sent to the wrapper comply with the OGC WPS specification. The wrapper itself then acts like a workflow client.

Several issues must be solved in order to do so. For example, if the workflow will invoke Grid services, a valid certificate is needed. Therefore, the WPS wrapper receives as parameter some credential information, like login name and passphrase. The wrapper's implementation then uses a MyProxy Credential Management Service to retrieve certificates that can be used for accessing Grid resources (Basney, Humphrey & Welch,

Table 1. Different types of proxy services

Proxy type	Description
Web service proxy	This type of proxy can be used to call a standard WSDL-based Web service.
Grid service proxy	The Grid service proxy is used to invoke a Grid service, i.e. service that complies with the Web Services Resource Framework (WSRF) (Czajkowski et al., 2005).
Grid job proxy	The Grid job proxy can be used to submit a Grid job to a job submission resource, like a compute cluster. A Grid middleware offers a service to submit and monitor such a job. In this manner, legacy applications like executables or scripts can be executed by a proxy service.
OWS proxy	OGC defined the predominant specifications for service interfaces the OGC Web services (OWS). The OWS proxy is able to invoke such an OWS (Percivall, 2003).
RESTful service proxy	This type of proxy service invokes a RESTful service.

2005). MyProxy is an open-source software for managing credentials in an online credential repository.

The implementation of the WPS wrapper is based on the deegree WPS. deegree (http://www.deegree.org/) is an open source project that provides users with implementations for all the major OGC services.

Addressing the Challenge of Heterogeneity

The proxy services invoke the Web service on behalf of the workflow engine; for each service technology, another proxy type is used. Thus, it is possible to enact geospatial Grid workflows using different service technologies. Different versions of proxy services can be used to call different kind of services, like Web services, Grid services, legacy applications via Grid jobs, etc. (cf. Table 1).

The proxy services' interfaces introduce an abstraction layer that eliminates the workflow management engine's dependence from the execution environment of the involved services. A new service technology can be easily integrated to the workflow system by implementing a new proxy type. New proxy services have to comply with the same interface as the other proxy services, and the new service technology is used internally.

As stated earlier, data providers usually provide OWS for data exchange with consumers and thus access to OWS from within Grid jobs must be catered for. This problem has already been tackled by the SeeGEO project (SeeGEO project, 2007) in form of an OGSA-DAI plug-in for OWS access. This plug-in is integrated in the proxy services that can call a WCS or WFS.

Addressing the Challenge of Data Management

By adding data management functionality to the proxy services, wasting of bandwidth can be avoided. The orchestration engine will not become the bottleneck, when huge amounts of data are involved. When invoking a pre-existing service via a proxy service *A*, instead of transferring the service's result unnecessarily to the orchestration engine, the proxy service can store intermediate data in a database. The proxy service *A* then signals the orchestration engine, that the data is available, such that the workflow control can decide to inform the proxy service *B* that is controlling the next service in the workflow. The proxy service *B* then triggers the download of the intermediate data from the database and transfers it directly to service *B*, without service *B* knowing.

The advantage of saving intermediate data in a database, is that, the data would not have to be loaded or even bought from a third party again, when the workflow is executed a second time. For example, the workflow could be constructed only to download geospatial data, if it is not available locally, or if new or more current data is needed. The proxy service can be configured either to delete the intermediate data or to keep it persistent, so that it could be reused if need be.

One possible database that would be perfectly suitable to store the intermediate result is Post-GIS (Strobl, 2008). PostGIS is an open-source geographic information system software that enhances support for geographic objects to the PostgreSQL object-relational database.

The proxy service can be configured such that it does not inform the orchestration engine if data is available, and then the proxy service saves the service's output in a database, or transfers the data directly to another proxy service. This way, it is possible to construct data transformation chains, without sending many control messages to the orchestration engine and thus reducing traffic.

The proxy services are deployed in the Grid environment; therefore, they can use the Grid's data management functionality and protocols. Therefore, exchange of data between proxy services benefits from utilizing the protocols GridFTP or RFT (cf. section Technical Background). As a result, the data transfer will be secure and fast.

OGSA-DAI offers the possibility to store the intermediate data via Web services in any database and could be used to access and integrate PostGIS or other databases.

Addressing the Challenge of Parallel Execution

A combination of an orchestration engine and proxy services provides a means to support all kinds of parallel execution described earlier.

Simple Parallelism

The proxy-enhanced orchestration engine allows several possibilities to make use of parallel execution. For example, workflow description languages like BPEL specify constructs to call Web services asynchronous (one-way) or synchronous (request-response). Additionally, BPEL's construct *flow* allows for creating branches where several activities form a sub workflow that the engine will process concurrently. Using the flow construct, multiple Web services can be called simultaneously.

During the definition of the workflow, the workflow designer needs to identify the services that the workflow needs to interact with and specify the actual communication endpoint in advance. This might be a problem, if the workflow intends to call a particular service, among multiple that implement the same interface (PortType in WSDL Language), the concrete endpoint of which is only known at runtime. In addition, another difficulty occurs when the actual number of services to invoke is not known at design time. Therefore, BPEL allows for assignments of PartnerLinks, thus providing mechanism to change the partner to call.

In addition, the proxy services can be used to call different services in parallel. The proxy services can receive the service's endpoint at runtime, thus, in the workflow description only the endpoints of the proxy service need to be specified at design time or the Proxy Creator service determines and assigns the endpoint to the partner definition at run-time. The description of the service that is assigned to a proxy service could even be an input parameter of the workflow itself, so that it can be set at execution time. This improves the workflow's flexibility. This way, new versions of services can be integrated in the workflow without difficulty.

Data Parallelism

BPEL's flow construct is not the best choice, if the designer of geospatial workflows would like to create parallel tasks for processing a great number of tiles, like 1000, at once in an easy way.

In BPEL 2.0 the *forEach* activity can be applied in a workflow that processes the contained activities in a loop the defined number of times either serially, or in parallel, if the parameter "parallel=true" is set. The number of times the loop executes can be set at runtime, which allows for static and dynamic data parallelism. Therefore, a workflow could divide the input data into sub sets, each of which will be processed in the loop's body.

Furthermore, the proxy service interface provides the means to receive a description of a service and an array of input data in order to carry out as many service invocations in parallel as the length of the array. For example, the Grid job proxy service can be used to start 1000 Grid jobs simultaneously on several clusters. The cluster batch system then determines the available resources and schedules the jobs. This also allows for static and dynamic data parallelism.

Pipelined Execution

When focusing on workflows that operate in a Grid environment, the data transformation chains can be realized by using Grid job proxy service. A Grid job proxy service is able to submit a Grid job to the Grid Resource Allocation and Management (GRAM) (The Globus Alliance, 2009b). The GRAM service provides a uniform interface to job scheduling systems, i.e. the batch operating system like PBS, SGE, Condor, and so on. The Grid accesses this batch system for remote job submission and job execution control.

The following description uses the Grid job proxy services to demonstrate how the proxy services operate, and how a pipelined execution can be applied to make use of parallel execution in a more efficient way. Other proxy services comply with the same interface and operate analogous.

In the beginning of the workflow, the workflow engine creates and configures the Grid job proxy services (see Figure 2). A Grid job proxy is associated with exactly one Grid job description; the proxy service submits the job to the GRAM service, if necessary, several times in parallel with different input data. The Grid job is self-contained and has no understanding of the workflow. The proxy service monitors the execution of its as-

sociated Grid job and checks if its output data is available.

In addition, a proxy service is connected with one or more successor proxy services within the data transformation chain. The proxy service is able to communicate with its successor proxy services, which must be able to process the proxy's output data. This enables the proxy services to coordinate data directly between them, instead of routing all data through the orchestration engine. When the Grid job is finished successfully and the output data is available, it notifies its successor proxy where to find this data. The successor proxy service will use this result as input data for the Grid job it is associated with, and then it will automatically submit this job to the cluster batch system.

If an error occurs and a Grid job fails, the proxy service notifies the workflow engine instead of the successor proxy and the workflow engine can initialize any compensation procedures.

Initializing a Data Transformation Chain

In the first stage of the workflow, the proxy services are created by calling a special service: the *Proxy Creator* (cf. Figure 2) that creates the instances of the requested proxy services and returns the EPRs (dynamic endpoint reference) to the workflow engine, which uses the EPRs to access the proxy services. Each proxy service is then configured according to its function in the data transformation chain. The necessary properties are:

- The Grid job description is set. This includes a detailed job description in the job description language of the Grid middleware like RSL (Resource Specification Language) or an XML-based Job description and the security credential needed to access resources in a Grid environment.
- The proxy is associated with its successor(s) in the data transformation chain. It will receive the necessary details in order to be able to exchange messages with the as-

Figure 2. Initializing data transformation chain

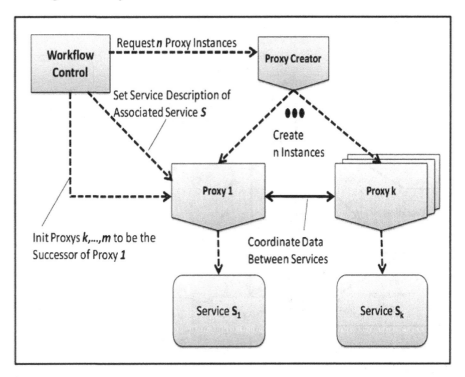

sociated proxy service. For example, this includes the EPR of the successor proxy if they are implemented as WSRF-based Grid services.

- The proxy service knows the name of the output data of the Grid job. It will provide the data in a form that the successor service will accept as input data, for example, it will rename result file(s) to a name the successor proxy service expects. A possible naming schema could demand the number or ID of the data transformation chain and a serial number of the data part.

- One of the proxy services in a data transformation chain is set to be the *End Proxy* service that notifies the workflow engine when the processing of the chain is finished, i.e. the output of the chain is available. This output is further processed in the next stage of the workflow.

This way, each proxy will be associated with its task, i.e. the Grid job and its successor proxy and therefore each data transformation chain will run as long as it is supplied with input data. The chain will terminate, when the End Proxy service detects that the final output data is available. If the Proxy Creator is stateful, it stores the proxy's EPRs, so that it can destroy the proxy service instances if needed.

Executing a Data Transformation Chain

A data transformation chain consisting only of two proxy services A and B (see Figure 3) executes the following steps:

- When input data *InputA_i* is available, proxy service A submits the Grid job *i* to the GRAM, which is then executing application A on the underlying cluster batch system. Application A produces *OutputA_i*.

Figure 3. Executing a data transformation chain

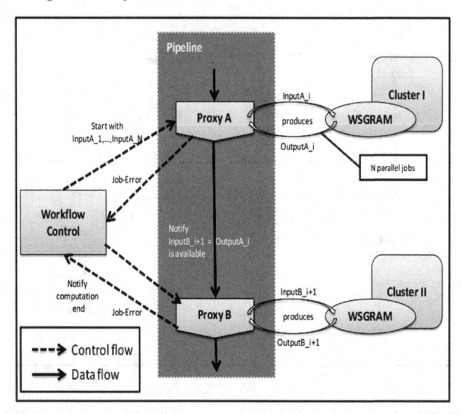

- Grid jobs run several times in parallel with data *InputA_i* in {*InputA_1,...,InputA_N*}.
- After Grid job i is successfully finished, proxy service A renames the *OutputA_i* to *InputB_i+1*. If the job execution fails, the proxy notifies the workflow engine that initializes the failure compensation procedures specified in the workflow description. It is also possible to configure the proxy service to initiate a re-try, and to submit the Grid job for a second time.
- Proxy service A notifies its successor proxy service B, that *InputB_i+1* is available. Because of the proxy services' data management capabilities, proxy service B automatically transfers this data to its execution destination and starts the Grid job that proxy service B is associated with, this means application B is executed on the cluster producing *OutputB_i+1*.

- When proxy service B detects the final data *OutputB_N*, it notifies the workflow engine.

The scenario can be enhanced to n connections between data and applications. For example, proxy services A and B are the predecessor service of a third proxy service C, which only starts the Grid job C, if proxy services A and B are providing the necessary input data *A1,...,AN,B1,...BM*. It is also imaginable for a proxy service to notify several successor proxy services. Therefore, webs of diverse scopes can be woven between the proxy services in an easy way.

In the case of Grid proxy services, the data transformation chain does not process the data in an iterative way, where each data set would have to go through the entire sequence of data transformation services before the next data set of the input vector is processed. Because each participating service and the chain operate continuously, the data processing time will be overlapping. Therefore, the workflow engine is capable of pipelined execution, which would not be possible by using a standard orchestration engine. On the other hand, just using the proxy services to build a pipeline, without involving an orchestration engine would result in a more complex error handling and a less robust workflow execution.

The number of tiles need not be known in advance, because new data elements that may appear while the pipeline is running will be processed automatically. For example, measurements produced in real-time by a sensor or another source of streaming data could be processed.

In the case of the Grid job proxy services, pipeline collision known by other pipeline scenarios (when a task sends data to another task that is busy) will not occur. This is because of its simple way of operating: if a service's data is available, a new Grid job will be submitted. This way, data will pass the chain and the chain will transform it at each stage, until the final output data was generated. If the computation time of each data element varies, this poses no problem, because a new Grid job will be submitted instantly, that also runs in parallel, and the corresponding proxy service will not be blocked for further execution.

One disadvantage of this pipeline poses its dynamic nature, if the progress of its execution should be displayed or monitored. Then the actual state of all participating proxy services and Web services will have to be determined, which is not an easy task.

Because of the different execution times, elements of the data transformation chain may overtake one another within the pipeline while still guaranteeing the ordering of the final results.

If other types of proxy services are used, it may be necessary that the proxy services block execution, manage data buffers between service invocations, or start a new instance of a service in parallel. For example, WSRF-based services comply with a factory pattern. The factory service

is called to instantiate new service instances, which is possible each time new input data is available. This way, the same flexibility like with the Grid job proxy services can be achieved.

Addressing the Challenge of Robustness

When using choreography for executing a data transformation chain, the orchestration engine will only be informed, if the Web service (or Grid job) execution fails and no output has been generated. The error handling and error compensation capabilities of the orchestration are far more effective than a workflow enactment using choreography, i.e. trying to lay such functionality in the proxy services. Combining an orchestration engine with the proxy services yield more robust and stable workflow execution.

Many Grid environments provide powerful data transfer mechanism over wide area, like GridFTP (Allcock et al., 2001), Fast Data Transfer (FDT) (Caltech, 2007), and others. Nonetheless, failures and server timeouts do occur. If the proxy service detects, that its associated service is not responding, for example by receiving a time-out, the proxy service notifies the orchestration engine. If the workflow is designed to react to this problem, it will associate the proxy service with a replacement service, for example an additional service instance deployed to another Grid resource.

The pipelines will be more robust, if the workflow can restart a pipeline, if a proxy service reports an error, if or none of the proxy services answer anymore. On the other hand, the Grid job proxy services could be configured to re-submit a Grid job to another WS GRAM, if the Grid job fails.

Addressing the Challenge of Easy Design of Workflows

Most workflow systems provide graphical tools for the construction of workflows. The workflow designer is an expert in the domain of geospatial application; however, the workflow designer need not be familiar with the different types of services, which he would like combine to service compositions.

The graphical tools of the proposed workflow engine hide the technical details from the workflow designer. Therefore, the graphical tools abstract from the service technology, and hide the fact that actually proxy services are used to invoke these services. When the workflow designer creates a new workflow description, templates are used automatically to add a *Proxy Creator* call that instantiates the proxy services in the beginning of the workflow and destroys them when the workflow finishes. When the designer adds a Web service call to the workflow graph, another template is used to initialize the proxy service with all information needed to invoke the Web service.

In addition, new abstract workflow pattern, like a data transformation chain, can be added to the workflow graph by using drag-and-drop. The corresponding workflow description, e.g. a BPEL document, will contain all necessary configurations, and connections between the proxy services will be generated automatically.

Thus, the workflow designer can concentrate on the actual composition of services.

RELATED WORK

A limited number of research papers identify the problem of centralized approaches to service orchestration, which process large amounts of data. This section provides an overview of different approaches that enact data-centric workflows that use choreography and de-centralized workflow enactments.

Choreography Languages

The Web Services Choreography Description Language (WS-CDL) is the leading choreography language (W3C, 2005); however, WS-CDL has been criticized. The key criticisms include that WS-CDL is bound to specific WSDL interfaces, has no formal foundation and no complete implementations (Barros, Dumas, & Oaks, 2005).

BPEL4Chor adds an additional layer to BPEL in order to allow for choreography (Decker, Kopp, Leymann, & Weske, 2007). BPEL4Chor proposes three artifact types: participant behavior description, participant groundings and participants topology.

Let's Dance is a choreography language that focuses on interaction as the main building block for workflows (Zaha, Barros, Dumas, & ter Hofstede, 2006). Let's Dance allows for different levels of abstraction, interactions are described by an ideal observer who coordinates all interactions between a group of services.

Decentralized Workflow Enactment

The *Flow-based Infrastructure for Composing Autonomous Services* (FICAS) enables distribution of dataflow by using the autonomous service access protocol (ASAP) to be able to separate control-flow from dataflow (Dept David Liu & Liu, 2003). Although FICAS is an architecture for decentralized service orchestration it does not utilize modern standards, like BPEL, and is intrusive to the application code, as each pre-existing service needs to be wrapped with a FICAS interface. In contrast, our approach requires no alteration of pre-existing services, as proxy services invoke the services, which need not be aware that they are interacting with a proxy service.

Barker, Weissman, & Hemert (2009) present the *Circulate* architecture that combines a centralized orchestration engine with proxy services similar to the proposed approach in this chapter, however, they are concentrating on data management and do not contemplate the construction of data transformation chains and the optimization of parallel tasks in Grid environments.

Service Invocation Triggers, address the problem of managing large amounts of data with an orchestration engine (Binder, Constantinescu, & Faltings, 2006). Triggers wait for the required input data before they invoke a service and transfer this data directly to the service. The workflow description will be deconstructed to sequential fragments that do not contain loops or alternatives and then these fragments will be executed in a decentralized manner. This approach also utilizes proxy services; however, their architecture is based on a pure choreography model, which as shown in this chapter has many problems associated with it. In addition, the workflow can become rigid and limited because, it is deconstructed into fragments that cannot contain loops or alternatives. In our approach, all the control flow constructs of an orchestration language, like BPEL, can be used to coordinate the proxy services and the workflow needs not altered.

Hobona, Fairbairn, Hiden, & James (2010) demonstrate the invocation of Grid-enabled OGC Web services from workflows by using an intermediate proxy services (SOAP nodes) that intercepts requests and translates them to the appropriate OGC format. They showed that by using the proxy services they were independent of the workflow language and utilized two different workflow description languages to orchestrate the nodes. These proxy services can store intermediated data in databases. This is similar to our approach; however, the SOAP nodes do not offer orchestration functionality or the construction of pipelines.

Martin, Wutke, & Leymann (2008) present a workflow engine that enacts BPEL workflows in a decentralized and distributed manner. The BPEL process is transformed into a set of individual activities that coordinate themselves by using tokens over shared, distributed tuple spaces.

Triana (Taylor, Shields, Wang, & Rana, 2003) is an open-source problem-solving environment that is able to distribute parts of workflow to remote worker nodes through a peer-to-peer network. It supports the whole workflow life cycle,

i.e. definition, analysis, management, execution, and monitoring of workflows.

Taverna (Oinn, 2004) is an open-source workflow management system that is able to integrate Grid technology. It provides a middleware to support scientists that perform data-intensive experiments on distributed resources. Taverna implements a service-oriented architecture and uses a proprietary language, the Simple Conceptual Unified Flow Language (SCUFL), which is based on dataflow.

CONCLUSION AND FUTURE RESEARCH

This chapter discusses challenges of executing large-scale geospatial workflow in Grid environments. As the Grid offers large amounts of CPU cycles and data storage by accepted standards and implements a common authentication and authorization infrastructure, there is a need to implement components that make the OGC web services interoperable with the Grid environment. In order to achieve this goal, well-accepted standards such as WSRF and OGSA should be used.

The execution of these envisioned geospatial workflows, poses several challenges. External pre-existing services can be re-used and integrated only if the workflows management system is able to cope with heterogeneity. Many pre-existing Web services cannot be altered, or adjusted to comply with a new workflow management system; therefore, the workflow system should be non-invasive to the external Web services.

A significant challenge for workflow system architectures is to integrate control-flow and dataflow seamlessly. Frequently, large amounts of data pass through a classic centralized workflow engine that becomes a bottleneck.

The main goal of executing geospatial simulations in a Grid environment is the expected performance speed-up when exploiting parallelism. Different forms of parallelism may be utilized;

some may be supported by orchestration others benefit from choreography.

Concerning data management and parallel execution, workflow execution can benefit from services that are able to collaborate and to exchange data directly without involvement of the centralized workflow control.

To overcome these challenges and to make use of the Grid environment, this chapter presents a hybrid workflow management system. The proposed workflow management system consists of a centralized orchestration engine, combined with distributed components, the proxy services that allow for service choreography. This way, the workflow management system maintains the robustness and simplicity of a centralized orchestration engine, but the use of proxy services facilitates choreography by allowing services to collaborate. As control-flow is still centralized, this workflow management system has an advantage over systems using choreography in fault detection and error handling. This improves the systems' robustness and aims at the improvement of parallel execution and the implementation of pipelines as well as the optimization of dataflow. New proxy services can be easily implemented to support additional service technologies and infrastructures.

Future directions include the connection of the workflow management system with monitoring agents that deliver information about the current state of the execution environment. The proxy services use this monitoring information to react to the current situation. For example, when the Proxy Creator configures the proxy services, only Grid resources will be chosen that are idle. This way, the workflow management system will support load balancing and will utilize improved scheduling capabilities.

In addition, the logic of the proxy services should be enhanced, such that they support adaptive parallelism. Thus, the proxy services can compensate crashing Grid resources, disk failures etc. For example, if an invoked geospatial Web service does not answer, the proxy services can decide to call a replacement service instead.

In the current version, the workflow designer constructing a data transformation chain must guarantee that the data delivered by one service can be consumed by the next service in the chain. Future implementation should allow for semantically validating service chains.

ACKNOWLEDGMENT

The research described in this chapter is part of the GDI-Grid project (Spatial Data Infrastructure Grid) funded by the BMBF, the German Federal Ministry of Education and Research. The support is gratefully acknowledged.

REFERENCES

W3C. (2005). *Web services choreography description language (version 1.0)*. Retrieved from http://www.w3.org/TR/ws-cdl-10/2005

Allcock, W. E., Bester, J., Bresnahan, J., Chervenak, A. L., Foster, I. T., Kesselman, C., et al. (2001). Secure, efficient data transport and replica management for high-performance data-intensive computing. *CoRR*, cs.DC/0103. Retrieved from http://dblp.uni-trier.de/db/journals/corr/corr0103.html#cs-DC-0103022

Armbrust, M., Fox, A., Griffith, R., Joseph, A. D., Katz, R. H., Konwinski, A., et al. (2009). *Above the clouds: A Berkeley view of cloud computing*. Retrieved from http://www.eecs.berkeley.edu/Pubs/TechRpts/2009/EECS-2009-28.html

Barker, A., Weissman, J. B., & Hemert, J. I. (2009). The circulate architecture: avoiding workflow bottlenecks caused by centralised orchestration. *Cluster Computing, 12*(2), 221–235. doi:10.1007/s10586-009-0072-4

Barros, A., Dumas, M., & Oaks, P. (2005). A critical overview of the web service choreography description language (WS-CDL). *BP Trends Newsletter, 3*(3).

Basney, J., Humphrey, M., & Welch, V. (2005). The MyProxy online credential repository: research articles. *Software, Practice & Experience, 35*(9), 801–816. doi:10.1002/spe.688

Bell, G., Parisi, A., & Pesce, M. (1995). *The virtual reality modeling language (version 1.0) specification.* Retrieved from http://www.web3d.org/technicalinfo/specifications/VRML1.0/index.html

Binder, W., Constantinescu, I., & Faltings, B. (2006). *Decentralized orchestration of Composite Web Services* (pp. 869–876). ICWS.

Butler, R., Welch, V., Engert, D., Foster, I. T., Tuecke, S., Volmer, J., et al. (2000). A national-scale authentication infrastructure. In *IEEE Computer, 33*(12), 60-66.

Caltech. (2007). *Fast Data Transfer (FDT) service.* Retrieved from http://monalisa.cern.ch/FDT/

Czajkowski, K., Ferguson, D. F., Foster, I., Frey, J., Graham, S., Sedukhin, I., et al. (2005). *The WS-Resource Framework.* Retrieved from http://www.globus.org/wsrf/specs/ws-wsrf.pdf

Davidson, S. B., & Freire, J. (2008). Provenance and scientific workflows: challenges and opportunities. *International Conference on Management of Data.* Retrieved from http://portal.acm.org/citation.cfm?id=1376772# Decker, G., Kopp, O., Leymann, F., & Weske, M. (2007). *BPEL4Chor: Extending BPEL for Modeling Choreographies. IEEE International Conference on Web Services (ICWS 2007)* (pp. 296-303). IEEE.

de La Beaujardiére, J. (2002). *Web map service implementation specification.* Open Geospatial Consortium. Retrieved from http://portal.opengeospatial.org/files/?artifact_id=1081&version=1&format=pdf

De Roure, D., Goble, C., Bhagat, J., Cruickshank, D., Goderis, A., Michaelides, D., et al. (2008). myExperiment: Defining the social virtual research environment. *Computer.* IEEE Press. Retrieved from http://eprints.ecs.soton.ac.uk/16560

EGEE. (2008). *gLite 3.0.0 home page.* Retrieved from http://www.glite.org.

Elfers, C., & Wagner, R. M. (2007). GeoDRM engineering viewpoint and supporting architecture. Retrieved from http://portal.opengeospatial.org/files/?artifact_id=21285

Erl, T. (2005). *Service-oriented architecture – concepts, technology, and design.* Prentice Hall.

Erwin, D., & Snelling, D. (2002). UNICORE: A Grid computing environment. *Concurrency and Computation: Practice and Experience, 14*(13-15), 1395–1410. Springer. Retrieved from http://www.springerlink.com/index/AE73FCHPKQENQCE9.pdf

Fleuren, T., & Müller, P. (2008). BPEL workflows combining standard OGC Web services and Grid-enabled OGC Web services. In *Proceeding of 34th Euromicro SEAA.* Parma, Italy: IEEE. Retrieved from http://www.euromicro.org

Foster, I. (1995). *Designing and Building Parallel Programs: Concepts and Tools for Parallel Software Engineering.* Boston: Addison-Wesley Longman Publishing Co., Inc.

Foster, I. (2002). *What is the Grid? A three point checklist.*

Foster, I. (2005). *A globus primer, An Early and Incomplete Draft. Technical report.* Globus Alliance. Retrieved from http://www.globus.org/toolkit/docs/4.0/key/GT4_Primer_0.6.pdf

Foster, I., Von Reich, J., Kishimoto, H., Berry, D., Djaoui, A., A., G., et al. (2005). *The Open Grid Services Architecture, (version 1.0).* Open Grid Forum.

Hobona, G., Fairbairn, D., Hiden, H., & James, P. (2010). Orchestration of Grid-enabled geospatial Web services in geoscientific workflows. *IEEE Transactions on Automation Science and Engineering*, 7(2), 407–411. doi:10.1109/TASE.2008.2010626

Hobona, G., Fairbairn, D., & James, P. (2007). Workflow enactment of Grid-enabled geospatial Web services. In *Proceedings of the 2007 UK e-Science All Hands Meeting*. Retrieved from http://scholar.google.com/scholar?hl=en&btnG=Search&q=intitle:Workflow+Enactment+of+Grid-Enabled+Geospatial+Web+Services#0

Johnson, C. R., & Parker, S. G. (1999). The SCIRun parallel scientific computing problem solving environment. In *Ninth SIAM Conference on Parallel Processing for Scientific Computing*. Retrieved from http://www.sci.utah.edu/publications/siam99/siam99b.ps

Lanig, S., & Zipf, A. (2009). *Towards generalization processes of LiDAR data based on GRID and OGC Web Processing Services (WPS)*. Osnabrück, Germany: Geoinformatik.

Lee, C. A., & Percival, G. (2009). The evolution of geospatial e-infrastructures. In *GIS.Science, 3*.

Liu, D., & Liu, D. (2003). Data-flow distribution in FICAS service composition infrastructure. In *proceedings of the 15th International Conference on Parallel and Distributed Computing Systems*.

Lucchi, R., Millot, M., & Elfers, C. (2008). Resource oriented architecture and REST. *Assessment of impact and advantages on INSPIRE, Ispra: European Communities*.

Ludäscher, B., Altintas, I., Berkley, C., Higgins, D., Jaeger, E., Jones, M., et al. (2005). Scientific workflow management and the Kepler system. *Concurrency Computers: Practice and Experience*.

Martin, D., Wutke, D., & Leymann, F. (2008, September). A novel approach to decentralized workflow enactment. In *Proceedings of the 12th International IEEE Enterprise Distributed Object Computing Conference (EDOC 2008). Munich, Germany,* (pp. 127-136). IEEE Computer Society. Retrieved from http://www.informatik.uni-stuttgart.de/cgi-bin/NCSTRL/NCSTRL_view.pl?id=INPROC-2008-107&engl=0

Mazzetti, P., Nativi, S., & Caron, J. (2009). RESTful implementation of geospatial services for Earth and space science applications. *International Journal of Digital Earth*, 2(1), 40–61. doi:10.1080/17538940902866153

OASIS. (2007). *Web services business process execution language (version 2.0) (WS-BPEL 2.0)*. Retrieved from http://docs.oasis-open.org/wsbpel/2.0/

OGSA-DAI. (2010). *OGSA-DAI*. Retrieved from http://www.ogsadai.org.uk/

Oinn, T., Addis, M., Ferris, J., Marvin, D., Senger M., Greenwood, M., et al. (2004). Taverna: A tool for the composition and enactment of bioinformatics workflows. *Bioinformatics journal, 17*(20), 3045–3054.

Open Geospatial Consortium. (2004). *OWS 2 Common Architecture: WSDL SOAP UDDI (WSDL/SOAP/UDDI)*. Retrieved from https://portal.opengeospatial.org/files/?artifact_id=8348

Open Geospatial Consortium. (2009). *OGC KML standard development best practices*. Retrieved from http://www.opengeospatial.org/standards/kml/

Pautasso, C., & Alonso, G. (2006). Parallel computing patterns for grid workflows. In *Proceedings of the Workshop on Workflows in Support of Large-Scale Science*, 19–23. Retrieved from http://scholar.google.com/scholar?hl=en&btnG=Search&q=intitle:Parallel+computing+patterns+for+grid+workflows#0

Percivall, G. (2003). *OGC reference model.* Retrieved from http://portal.opengeospatial.org/files/?artifact_id=3836

Reed, C. (2006). *An introduction to GeoRSS: A standards based approach for geoenabling RSS feeds.* Open Geospatial Consortium. Retrieved from http://www.opengeospatial.org/pt/06-050r3

Schut, P. (2007). *OpenGIS Web Processing Service.* Open Geospatial Consortium. Retrieved from http://portal.opengeospatial.org/files/?artifact_id=24151

SeeGEO project. (2007). Retrieved from http://edina.ac.uk/projects/ seesaw/seegeo

Singh, G., Vahi, K., Ramakrishnan, A., Mehta, G., Deelman, E., Zhao, H., et al. (2007). Optimizing workflow data footprint. *Scientific Programming, 15*, 249-268. Amsterdam: IOS Press. Retrieved from http://portal.acm.org/citation.cfm?id=1377549.1377553

Sotomayor, B., & Childers, L. (2006). *Globus Toolkit 4 - programming Java services.* The Elsevier Series in Grid Computing. Morgan Kaufmann Publishers.

Strobl, C. (2008). PostGIS. In S. Shekhar & H. Xiong, (Eds.), *Encyclopedia of GIS* (pp. 891-898). Springer. Retrieved from http://dblp.uni-trier.de/db/reference/gis/gis2008.html#Strobl08a

Taylor, I., Shields, M., Wang, I., & Rana, O. (2003). Triana applications within Grid computing and peer to peer environments. *Journal of Grid Computing, 1*, 199-217. Kluwer Academic Publishers. Retrieved from http://journals.kluweronline.com/article.asp?PIPS=5269002

The Globus Alliance. (2009a). *Globus Toolkit 4.* Retrieved from http://www.globus.org

The Globus Alliance. (2009b). *Grid Resource Allocation and Management (GRAM).* Retrieved from http://www.globus.org/toolkit/docs/4.2/4.2.0/developer/globusrun-ws.html

The Globus Alliance. (2010a). *GridFTP.* Retrieved from http://www.globus.org/toolkit/docs/4.2/4.2.1/data/gridftp/

The Globus Alliance. (2010b). *Reliable File Transfer service (RFT).* Retrieved from http://www.globus.org/toolkit/docs/4.2/4.2.1/data/rft/

Turner, A. (2008). *Emerging mass market geo standards.* Retrieved from http://www.slideshare.net/ajturner/mass-market-geo-standards-ogc-technical-committee

Uslaender, T. (2007). *Integration of resource-oriented architecture concepts into OGC Reference Model.* OpenGIS document OGC 07-156.

van der Aalst, W. M., ter Hofstede, A. H., Kiepuszewski, B., & Barros, A. P. (2003). Workflow patterns. *Distributed and Parallel Databases, 14*, 5–51. doi:10.1023/A:1022883727209

von Voigt, G. (2009). *The GDI-Grid project.* Retrieved from http://www.gdi-grid.de

Vretanos, P. A. (2005). *Web feature service implementation specification.* Open Geospatial Consortium. Retrieved from http://portal.opengeospatial.org/files/?artifact_id=8339

Werder, S. (2009, June). Formalization of spatial constraints. *Proceedings of the 12th AGILE International Conference on Geographic Information Science,* Hannover, Germany

Whiteside, A., & Evans, J. (2006). *Web Coverage Service (WCS) Implementation Specifiation.* Open Geospatial Consortium. Retrieved from https://portal.opengeospatial.org/files/?artifact_id=18153

Workflow Management Coalition. (1999). *Terminology and glossary.*

Zaha, J., Barros, A., Dumas, M., & ter Hofstede, A. (2006). *Let's Dance: A language for service behavior modeling. On the move to maningful Internet Systems 2006: CoopIS, DOA, GADA, and ODBASE,* (pp. 145-162). Retrieved from http://dx.doi.org/10.1007/11914853_10

ADDITIONAL READING

Casati, F., Ilnicki, S., Jin, L., Krishnamoorthy, V., & Shan, M. (2000). Adaptive and dynamic service composition in eFlow. *Lecture Notes in Computer Science, 1789*, 13–31. Springer. Retrieved from http://www.springerlink.com/index/56C5X7GQ056C1A9D.pdf

Caverlee, J., Bae, J., Wu, Q., Liu, L., Pu, C., Rouse, W. B., et al. (2007). Workflow management for enterprise transformation. *Informational Knowledge Systems Management, 6*, 61-80. Amsterdam: IOS Press.

Chervenak, A., Deelman, E., Livny, M., Su, M., Schuler, R., Bharathi, S., et al. (2007). Data placement for scientific applications in distributed environments. 8th *IEEE/ACM International Conference on Grid Computing*, 267-274. IEEE.

Deelman, E., & Chervenak, A. (2008). Data management challenges of data-intensive scientific workflows. *Eighth IEEE International Symposium on Cluster Computing and the Grid (CCGRID)*, 687-692. IEEE.

Dörnemann, T., Friese, T., Herdt, S., Juhnke, E., & Freisleben, B. (2007). Grid workflow modelling using grid-specific BPEL extensions. In *German e-Science Conference*, (pp. 1-9). Retrieved from http://scholar.google.com/scholar?hl=en&btnG=Search&q=intitle:Grid+Workflow+Modelling+Using+Grid-Specific+BPEL+Extensions#0

Dörnemann, T., Smith, M., & Freisleben, B. (2008). Composition and execution of secure workflows in WSRF-Grids. *IEEE International Symposium on Cluster Computing and the Grid*, 122-129. Los Alamitos, CA: IEEE Computer Society.

Emmerich, W., Butchart, B., Chen, L., Wassermann, B., & Price, S. L. (2006). Grid service orchestration using the Business Process Execution Language (BPEL). [Springer.]. *Journal of Grid Computing, 3*(3-4), 283–304. doi:10.1007/s10723-005-9015-3

Floros, E., & Cotronis, Y. (2006). Execution and composition of e-science applications using the WS-resource construct. *Proceedings of the 20th IEEE International Parallel & Distributed Processing Symposium*, 1-8. IEEE.

Foster, I. (2005). Service-oriented science. [New York.]. *Science, 308*(5723), 814–817. doi:10.1126/science.1110411

Foster, I., Kesselman, C., Nick, J. M., & Tuecke, S. (2003). The physiology of the grid. *Grid computing: making the global infrastructure.*

James, P., Hobona, G., & Fairbairn, D. (2007). Workflow enactment of Grid-enabled geospatial Web services. In *Proceedings of the 2007 UK e-Science All Hands Meeting*. Retrieved from http://scholar.google.com/scholar?hl=en&btnG=Search&q=intitle:Workflow+Enactment+of+Grid-Enabled+Geospatial+Web+Services#0

Li, P., & Du, Y. (2009). Modeling and design for dynamic workflows based on flexible activities. *Information Technology Journal*, 750-756.

Ludäscher, B., Altintas, I., Bowers, S., Cummings, J., Critchlow, T., Deelman, E., et al. (2009). Scientific process automation and workflow management. In A. Shoshani & D. Rotem (Eds.), *Scientific Data Management, Computational Science Series*. Chapman & Hall. Retrieved from http://daks.ucdavis.edu/~ludaesch/Paper/ch13-preprint.pdf

Menasce, D. (2004). Composing web services: A QoS view. *IEEE Internet Computing, 8*(6), 88–90. doi:10.1109/MIC.2004.57

Ngu, A., Nicholas, N., McPhilips, T., Bowers, S., Ludaescher, B., Critchlow, T., et al. (2007). *Flexible scientific workflows using frames and dynamic embedding*. Retrieved from http://scholar.google.com/scholar?hl=en&btnG=Search&q=intitle:Flexible+Scientific+Workflows+using+Frames+and+Dynamic+Embedding#0.

Padberg, A., & Kiehle, C. (2009). Spatial Data Infrastructures and Grid Computing: the GDI-Grid project. *Geophysical Research Abstracts*, *11*, EGU2009–EGU4242.

Tan, K., & Turner, K. (2006). Orchestrating grid services using BPEL and Globus Toolkit 4. In *Proc. 7th PGNet Symposium,* (p. 31–36). Citeseer. Retrieved from http://scholar.google.com/schol ar?hl=en&btnG=Search&q=intitle:Orchestratin g+Grid+Services+using+BPEL+and+Globus+T oolkit+4#0

Van Der Aalst, W.M.P., Ter Hofstede, A.H.M., Kiepuszewski, A.B. (in press) *Workflow patterns.*

Werder, S., & Krüger, A. (2009). *Parallelizing geospatial tasks in Grid Computing* (pp. 71–76).

KEY TERMS AND DEFINITIONS

Data Transformation Chain: A sequence of services that are connected by data dependencies.

Geospatial Workflow: A geospatial workflow is a composition of geospatial services, either by using orchestration or choreography.

Grid Workflow: A Grid Workflow is a workflow within a Grid Computing environment.

Pipeline: A data transformation chain that is not executed iteratively, but all stages of a pipeline execute in parallel. A pipelined execution of services therefore, performs similar to a pipeline of a CPU.

Proxy Service: A proxy service is able to invoke a service in behalf of the client, e.g. in behalf of the workflow engine by providing a standard interface. This interface also allows for the proxy services to collaborate.

Service Composition or Workflow: Service composition allows defining applications that are more complex by reusing existing services. Workflow description languages can be used to design workflows by using graphical tools. The workflows can be executed by workflow engines instead of developing a program in a language, like C, which has to be compiled and linked.

Section 7
Applications

Chapter 15
Web Services for the Global Earth Observing System of Systems

George Percivall
Open Geospatial Consortium, USA, UK and Australia

ABSTRACT

Web services provide users ever better methods to access and use Earth Observation data. Development of a web services architecture for the Global Earth Observing System of Systems was conducted using an evolutionary development process that depended on standards for geospatial web services. Standards for geospatial web services provide interfaces that can be scaled to global deployment. The GEOSS Architecture Implementation Pilot defined an evolutionary development process and reusable architecting methods for applying web services to a global scale system of systems for Earth observations. ISO/IEC, OGC and other standards are used by the AIP architecture to meet the objectives of GEOSS to enable comprehensive, coordinated and sustained observation of the Earth and also efficient publication and use of the collected information.

INTRODUCTION

Anyone involved in building enterprise information systems might reasonably question the feasibility of the Global Earth Observation System of Systems (GEOSS). The scope and complexity are

DOI: 10.4018/978-1-60960-192-8.ch015

overwhelming: In the highly technical and legacy-heavy domain of Earth observation systems, GEOSS aims to meet information requirements of 80 nations and the European Union as well as the needs of multiple communities of practice in each of nine vast Societal Benefit Areas (SBAs): Agriculture, Biodiversity, Climate, Disasters, Ecosystems, Energy, Health, Water and Weather.

For hundreds of different organizations that provide and/or use geospatial information, GEOSS is supposed to enable comprehensive, coordinated and sustained observation of the Earth and also efficient publication and use of the collected information.

Remarkably, progress has been rapid. Participants in the GEOSS Architecture Implementation Pilot (AIP) have developed and deployed a new development process and they have also deployed working components for the GEOSS Common Infrastructure (GCI) and the broader GEOSS architecture. That is to say, the basic technical foundation of a web services architecture for GEOSS has been established, and it works. The technical foundation has been proven and has undergone continuous improvement in multiple pilot activities based on real-world scenarios and existing national technical resources. And the process for continuous improvement is in place.

Activities similar to GEOSS have been conducted in the past but with less comprehensive approach, e.g., CEOS emphasis on remote sensing, GCOS emphasis on climate, GSDI emphasis on geographic information:

- The Committee on Earth Observations (CEOS) was established in 1984 to coordinates civil space-borne observations of the Earth. CEOS agencies strive to enhance international coordination and data exchange and to optimize societal benefit. CEOS is a participating organization in GEO to provide the space component for GEOSS.
- The Global Climate Observing System (GCOS) is a joint undertaking of several agencies of the United Nations. The goal of GCOS is to provide comprehensive information on the total climate system. As a system of climate-relevant observing systems, it constitutes, in aggregate, the climate-observing component of GEOSS.
- The Global Spatial Data Infrastructure (GSDI) Association promotes international collaboration in support of local, national and international spatial data infrastructure developments that allow nations to better address social, economic, and environmental issues. GSDI emphasizes common conventions and technical agreements to make it easy for communities, nations and regional decision-makers to discover, acquire, exploit and share geographic information vital to the decision process.

GEOSS builds on these previous efforts with characteristic unique to GEOSS including: emphasis on quantifiable societal benefits; inclusion of remote sensed and in-situ data and data from spatial data infrastructures; identification of international standards as the means to coordinate a system-of-systems; and the establishment of GEO through a series of ministerial-level summits.

BACKGROUND

The Global Earth Observation System of Systems (GEOSS) will provide comprehensive, coordinated and sustained observations of the Earth system, in order to improve monitoring of the state of the Earth, increase understanding of Earth processes, and enhance prediction of the behaviour of the Earth system. GEOSS will meet the need for timely, quality long- term global information as a basis for sound decision making, and will enhance delivery of benefits to society. As with the Internet, GEOSS will be a global and flexible network of content providers allowing decision makers to access an extraordinary range of information at their desk. [GEO 2009]

The Group on Earth Observations (GEO) is coordinating efforts to build GEOSS. GEO is a voluntary partnership of governments and international organizations. It provides a framework within which these partners can develop new projects and coordinate their strategies and investments. As of September 2009, GEO's Members include 80 Governments and the European Commission. In addition, 58 intergovernmental, international, and regional organizations with a mandate in Earth observation or related issues have been recognized as Participating Organizations.

GEO is constructing GEOSS on the basis of a 10-Year Implementation Plan for the period 2005 to 2015. The Plan defines a vision statement for GEOSS, its purpose and scope, expected benefits, and the nine "Societal Benefit Areas" of disasters, health, energy, climate, water, weather, ecosystems, agriculture and biodiversity. The GEO Work Plan is a "living" document, updated annually, containing some 70 overarching Tasks. Each Task supports one of the nine societal-benefit or four transverse areas and is carried out by interested Members and Participating Organizations. The GEO Secretariat is responsible for coordinating the Tasks and other activities that are driving the 10-Year Implementation Plan for GEOSS.

The GEOSS Architecture Implementation Pilot (AIP) is a core task (GEO Task AR-09-01b) of the GEO Architecture and Data Committee (ADC). AIP supports the elaboration of the GEOSS Architecture (See Figure 1). The requirements for AIP are based on meeting user needs and com-

munity scenario requirements as recommended by the other tasks of GEO and the User Interface Committee (UIC). One of the main outcomes of the pilot is to augment the operational capability of the GEOSS Common Infrastructure, which in turn supports the operational needs of the users. The Results of the AIP are transitioned to GEO Task AR-09-01a and the GEOSS Common Infrastructure.

GEO Members and Participating Organizations conducted the second phase of AIP (AIP-2) from June 2008 to September 2009. The main achievements of AIP-2 included:

- Developed and demonstrated six SBA scenarios in close collaboration with other GEO Tasks. AIP-2 used an evolutionary development process tailored to the technology of GEOSS and considering the globally distributed nature of the GEO participants.

- Defined and refined a reusable process to implement SBA scenarios in a Service oriented Architecture (SoA) tailored to GEOSS based upon international standards for software development including UML

Figure 1. Elaboration of GEOSS architecture

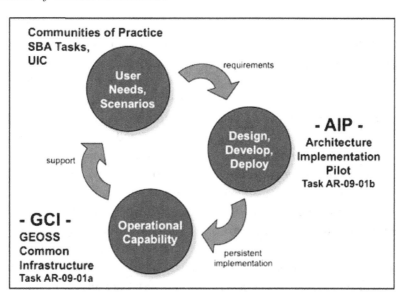

and RM-ODP. An element of the process was the definition of ten general use cases for a web services architecture that transversely support all SBAs.

- Augmented GEOSS deployment through identification of engineering components types to be contributed by GEO Members and Participating Organizations. The number of registered components and services instances was increased in the GEOSS Components and Services Registry (CSR) with an emphasis on "persistent exemplar services" committed to providing relevant services for an extended duration, with high availability through GEOSS Interoperability Arrangements.

The full results of AIP-2 are documented in 12 Engineering Reports and 10 Demonstration Videos [AIP 2009]. Much of this chapter is derived from the *AIP-2 Summary Engineering Report* [Percivall 2009].

DEVELOPMENT OF WEB SERVICES ARCHITECTURE FOR GEOSS

Interoperability Arrangements Based on Standards

The GEOSS 10 Year Plan clearly identifies the role of standards in the development of the GEOSS information system architecture:

"The success of GEOSS will depend on data and information providers accepting and implementing a set of interoperability arrangements, including technical specifications for collecting, processing, storing, and disseminating shared data, metadata and products. GEOSS interoperability will be based on non-proprietary standards, with preference given to formal international standards. Interoperability will be focused on interfaces, defining only how system components
interface with each other and thereby minimizing any impact on affected systems other than where such systems have interfaces to the shared architecture." [GEO 2005]

Standards are the basis for the success of the Internet and the World Wide Web. A standard describes a set of rules that have been agreed to in some industry consensus forum, such as the Internet Engineering Task Force (IETF), the International Organization for Standardization (ISO), or the Open Geospatial Consortium (OGC). As described in The Importance of Going Open, [OGC, 2005] "non-interoperability causes organizations to spend much more than necessary on geospatial information technology development". Organizations like the OGC, the World Wide Web Consortium (W3C), the IETF, and others are open organizations as any individual or organization can participate, the topics of debate are largely public, decisions are democratic (usually by consensus), and specifications are free and readily available. An "open" process is necessary to arrive at an "open" standard. The openness that OGC promotes is part of this general progress.

Certainties in the GEOSS Technical Architecture

One key certainty in the GEOSS technical architecture is that it is "service-oriented". This means that network-resident software components interact in a client/server fashion with other network-resident software components. Internet-resident geoprocessing clients send instructions to Web servers, and those servers respond by providing processing services or data.

Another key certainty is that these client/server communications will use interfaces and encodings that implement open, not proprietary, standards. Because GEOSS clients and services implement open standard interfaces, anyone can write software that takes advantage of those clients and services (subject in many cases, of course, to access restrictions). This adheres to the basic paradigm of openness on the World Wide Web: Open standard interfaces such as HTTP and open standard encodings such as HTML enable diverse developers to write software components that reliably interoperate with countless other components on the Web.

As a "system of systems", GEOSS is composed of contributed Earth Observation systems, ranging from primary data collection systems to systems for the creation and distribution of information products. Although all GEOSS systems continue to operate within their own mandates, GEOSS systems can leverage each other so that the overall GEOSS becomes much more than the sum of its component systems. This synergy develops as each contributor supports common arrangements designed to make shared observations and products more accessible, comparable, and understandable.

The GEOSS architecture is defined using standards from many organizations. The full list of standards is contained in the GEOSS Standards Registry that is maintained by the GEO Standards and Interoperability Forum (SIF) [SIF 2009]. Many of the standards in the SIF related to web services are standards from the OGC.

Open Geospatial Consortium Standards

The Open Geospatial Consortium (OGC) is an international not-for-profit voluntary industry consensus standards organization that provides a forum and proven processes for the collaborative development of free and publicly available interface specifications [OGC, 2009a]. OGC open standards have been implemented broadly in the marketplace and are helping to foster distributed and component technology solutions that geo-enable web, wireless, and location based services as well as broader government and business IT enterprises worldwide. OGC works closely with standards organizations and consortia in the technology community. For example, OGC maintains

alliances for coordination with IEEE, IETF, W3C, ISO and other organizations.

OGC standards are used in the AIP web services architecture. The OGC standards are grouped in the following categories: OGC Web Services (OWS), Sensor Web Enablement (SWE), and Geo-Processing Workflow (GPW). All OGC standards are available on the Web for no charge [OGC, 2009b].

OWS standards provide access, discovery and encoding of Earth Observation information. The OWS standards are defined using open Internet standards; in particular HTTP, URL, MIME and XML. SOAP and WSDL bindings for OWS standards are also available. OWS specifications include:

- OGC Web Map Service (WMS)
- OGC Web Feature Service (WFS)
- OGC Web Coverage Service (WCS)
- OGC Catalogue Service for the Web (CSW).
- OGC Geography Markup Language (GML)

SWE Standards are focused on discovery, exchange, and processing of sensors and corresponding observations, as well as the tasking of sensors and sensor systems. SWE specifications include:

- OGC Sensor Model Language (SensorML)
- OGC Observations & Measurements (O&M)
- OGC Sensor Observation Service (SOS)
- OGC Sensor Planning Service (SPS)
- OGC Sensor Alert Service (SAS)
- OGC Web Notification Service (WNS)

Geoprocessing Workflow (GPW) Standards enable the automation of spatial process/models, in whole or part, during which information is passed from one distributed Geoprocessing Service to another according to a set of procedural rules using standardized interfaces. The most robust approach OGC has implemented for GPW utilizes:

- OGC Web Processing Service (WPS)
- OASIS Business Process Execution Language for Web Services (BPEL)

The OGC standards are mature baseline of specifications that define interfaces in a web services environment. As the OGC standards define interfaces, they may be deployed in many different system architecture variations. The OGC Reference Model describes several example deployments, but these deployments are not normative. Individual programs and projects define architectures suited to their community objectives, development process and architecture styles. The following sections define these choices and how the choices were made for the GEOSS AIP.

Evolutionary Development Process

No system of systems as large as GEOSS could be planned and built in a linear fashion. The GEOSS was necessarily conceived to evolve to meet changing needs and to take advantage of rapidly evolving information technologies. The AIP Task employs an "evolutionary development process" whereby the architecture, the delivered systems, and the stakeholders co-evolve. To meet this situation the AIP development process has been informed by the approach of Leonardo da Vinci:

"First I shall do some experiments before I proceed farther, because my intention is to cite experience first and then with reasoning show why such experience is bound to operate in such a way."

The AIP process provides a structure for experimenting with prototypes that are adapted to user needs, while simultaneously capturing, increasing and sharing knowledge about GEOSS. Each phase of AIP involves extensive prototyping, testing, documentation and demonstration of

interoperability arrangements. Stakeholder needs are reassessed with each iteration of the development process; the architecture is used to guide each system as it moves through development, and appropriate versions are used to evaluate each system on delivery. Architectures developed under this approach emphasize flexibility and adaptability. This approach is well suited to software system development in cases where it is impossible to postulate all of the requirements and the system development can proceed iteratively.

Figure 2 shows the steps for a single phase of the AIP development process. The main result of the Concept Development phase is a Call for Participation (CFP) that is released to the GEO community and the public. Organizations that respond to the CFP then gather for a Kickoff workshop for the phase that begins the development process. The Development Phase includes design development, design review and testing activities. A phase of AIP is completed with the delivery of demonstrations, Engineering Reports, and the transition of new functionality to persistent operations. The AIP process is an application of the process previously defined and used in the OGC Interoperability Program. The OGC process has been used and refined in 35 testbeds and pilot initiatives, mostly notably for the development of the OGC Web Services Standards (OWS) baseline.

Reusable Architecting Process

An objective for GEOSS is to provide decision-support tools to a wide variety of users. As with the Internet, GEOSS will be a global and flexible network of content providers allowing decision makers to access an extraordinary range of information at their desk. To achieve this goal, the GEOSS Architecture must provide an easy process to integrate the GEOSS components in support of many SBA communities. This section describes an architecting process for implementing the needs of an SBA community into the GEOSS architecture.

Figure 2. AIP development approach

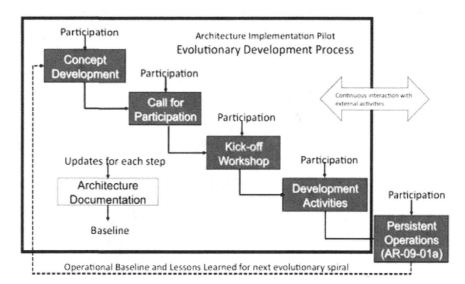

The process developed in the AIP is called a "reusable process" because implementing the GEOSS Service oriented Architecture for the various Societal Benefit Areas (SBAs) will involve many players over time, and those players will benefit from a proven formal process for implementation. Later players will benefit from the experiments and documentation that has gone before. The process begins with a scenario defined by the SBA community and then employs GEOSS resources to make a variety of Earth observation information assets available for researchers and decision makers in that SBA community.

The core of the reusable process are community *Scenarios* and transverse *Use Cases*. (Definitions for terms in *italic* typeface are listed below) *Scenarios* are narrative description of the activities of the SBA communities with minimal discussion of the implementation architecture. *Scenarios* provide an end user view of the value of GEOSS. *Scenarios* are implemented in the GEOSS architecture by *use cases*. *Use cases* describe reusable functionality of the GEOSS service oriented architecture implemented through *Interoperability Arrangements*. This process builds on these core concepts using a system modeling process based

on international standards tailored to the GEOSS environment.

Development of architecture models is a step towards a mature GEOSS: "Creating explicit models of a system's design is the step leading from art to practice" [Alexander, 1964]. AIP begins with the typical architecture practice of describing a system from multiple viewpoints. The AIP process tailors international standards for system architecture by considering the environment of GEOSS, in particular: 1) GEOSS is a system-of-system development that does not begin with a "blank sheet" but rather requires iteration of design synthesis with existing implementations, and 2) Contributions are made by GEO Members with no central procurement authority.

The Reusable Process

The reusable process for deploying SBA Scenarios into the GEOSS Architecture is shown in Figure 3 and described in Table 1. This process is iterative with the main flow of activities as shown in the Figure, but the process is not accomplished in one pass. It is important that the SBA communities are considering the SoA technology when conceiving

Figure 3. Reusable SBA to SoA process

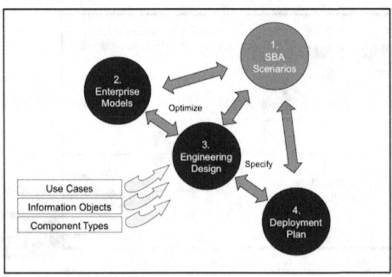

Table 1. SBA to SoA process steps

Step	Activities	Artifacts
1. Scenarios	SBA community experts develop narrative descriptions of *processes* for the desired behavior of decision makers using Earth Observations in the context of GEOSS Scenario development occurs with a general understanding of GEOSS. The SBA community experts develop the narrative with an understanding of the basic GEOSS architecture, e.g. the *generalized use cases*.	• Objectives • *Scenarios* • *Processes*
2. Enterprise Models	AIP system engineers - working with SBA community experts - elaborate and specify the scenarios into enterprise models. Steps in the *processes* are detailed in *activity* actions.	• *Activity diagram* • *Enterprise objects* • Context diagram
3. Engineering Design	AIP architects - working with the SBA Community experts and AIP system engineers - develop optimized designs for the enterprise models by applying and refining SoA *use cases, information objects,* and *component types*. Each *activity* action is assigned to a pre-existing *generalized use case* or a *specialized use case* is developed.	• Refinement of *Generalized use cases* • *Specialized use cases* • *Information objects* • *Component Types* • *Interoperability Arrangements*
4. Deployment	Component providers – working with AIP architects and Community Moderators – identify, develop (as necessary) and register a set of *component instances* based upon the engineering design. Components include those provided by the community and discovered in the wider GEOSS. Deployment includes testing that the components meet the community objectives. Demonstrations are developed to communicate the system operation to users.	• *Component Instances* • *Persistent Exemplars* • *Demonstrations*

of their objectives as SoA provides capabilities that not previously available.

An Appendix provides the terminology used in modeling the architecture as part the AIP process.

Architecture Artifacts

The preceding section described the process used to develop the AIP architecture. The resulting AIP architecture is organized and documented using

Table 2. RM-ODP viewpoints and AIP-2 architecture artifacts

Enterprise Viewpoint	• GEO Community objectives • SBA Scenarios • GEOSS Users
Information Viewpoint	• Information Objects
Computational Viewpoint	• Web Service Standards
Engineering Viewpoint	• SoA Use Cases • Engineering Components
Technology Viewpoint	• Component Instances registry • Persistent Exemplars

the approach of the ISO RM-ODP standard. The key element of RM-ODP is the organization of an architecture into a set of viewpoints. The table below shows how the following sections are organized in an RM ODP architecture.

A set of reports documenting the results of AIP-2 are available [AIP, 2009].

SBA Scenarios

GEOSS is simultaneously addressing nine areas of critical importance to people and society. It aims to empower the international community to protect itself against natural and human-induced disasters, understand the environmental sources of health hazards, manage energy resources, respond to climate change and its impacts, safeguard water resources, improve weather forecasts, manage ecosystems, promote sustainable agriculture and conserve biodiversity. GEOSS coordinates a multitude of complex and interrelated issues simultaneously. This crosscutting approach avoids unnecessary duplication, encourages synergies between systems and ensures substantial economic, societal and environmental benefits.

AIP-2 established "operational, research and technical exemplars" in six scenarios representing four SBAs:

- Health SBA: Air Quality & Health: Smoke Event: AIP-2 participants focused on Air Quality with a scenario entitled, "Southern California Smoke" which describes how air quality event managers would use data available through GEOSS to predict and analyze the effect of smoke plumes on air. [See also Robinson 2009]

- Biodiversity SBA: Pika Distribution -- GEOSS was used to predict how the distribution of Pika will change with climate change in the Great Basin of North America. [See also Nativi, 2009]

- Biodiversity SBA: Arctic Food Chain -- GEOSS was used to assess the impact of climate change on the species of a simple food chain in the Arctic region.

- Biodiversity SBA: Polar Ecosystems -- GEOSS was used to identify the extent and degree of vegetation changes in response to climate change in arctic ecosystems, and in particular, the boreal-tundra ecotone.

- Disaster Management SBA: AIP-2 participants used GEOSS components and standard services to supply forecasts, a stream of satellite and in-situ observations, and derived maps integrated with local and regional data sets to support all phases of the disaster cycle. The scenario is applied to flooding disasters caused by tropical storms, hurricanes, cyclones, and tsunamis in particular, but can be easily re-cast to cover other disaster types such as earthquakes, wildfires, landslides, volcanoes, tornadoes, and many more.

- Energy SBA: Renewable Energy: AIP-2 participants developed an end-to-end scenario between a data provider on the one hand and a consulting company looking for the best place to site a solar power plant on the other hand. Both benefit from GEOSS as a centralized point of access. The needs of the data providers looking for an efficient dissemination of his databases are expressed. [See also Menard, 2009]

These scenarios provided a structure for extensive prototyping, testing, documentation and demonstration.

GEOSS Users

At the beginning of AIP-2, the GEOSS users were minimally characterized into two categories: GEOSS Service Consumers and GEOSS Service Providers. As AIP-2 development progressed, it became clear that a more comprehensive description of the GEOSS users is needed. The AIP-2 Use Case ER provides a further elaboration of the actors in the use cases based upon examining the use cases. Further description of the GEOSS Users will be required in AIP-3 based upon the AIP-2 results along with definitions from the GCI Task Force and the User Interface Committee.

The GCI Concept of Operations document provides definitions of users

- Publisher – Individual(s) authorized by Member and Participating Organizations to commit GEOSS Components and/or Services

- Operator – The agency/organization responsible for the operation and maintenance of a committed service and related data

- Approver – Acts to approve or disapprove an entry or update in one of the GEOSS Registries and the GEO Web Portals.

- Software and services integrator (Integrator) – A class of user typically engaged in support of one or more application areas who is able to use GEOSS to locate suitable services, data, and related resources, and to develop and deploy integrating software solutions that cater to a specific context or subject area.

- GEOSS-Experienced users – Users who understand the concepts of GEOSS and seek registered resources through the GEO Web Portal interface or desktop applications.

- Issue-Oriented Users - Researchers and science-to-policy analysts who work on specific issues that fall within one or more Societal Benefit Areas.

Figure 4. Use cases for the AIP service-oriented architecture

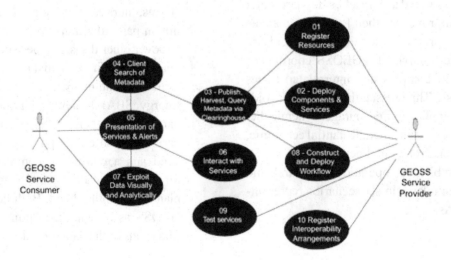

SoA Use Cases

To coordinate development across the SBA Scenarios a set of generalized use cases (Figure 4 and Table 3) were developed. The generalized use cases show the reuse of GEOSS service oriented architecture for a narrow action, e.g., discovery, data access. (The use cases were also titled transverse technology use cases.) Use cases are specific to interoperability arrangements. A use case template for was provided early in AIP-2 enabling consistent development of AIP-2 use cases. Each of the steps in a scenario process are implemented through a use case. For some steps, the use case needs to be tailored to the SBA thereby creating a specialized use case.

Table 3. AIP-2 use case summaries

Use Case	Title	Actors and Interfaces
Registration and Harvesting Use Cases		
1. Register Resources	Register resources in GEOSS Components and Services Registry (CSR) or Community Catalog	• # Service Provider • # Components and Services Registry • # Community Catalog Provider
10. Register New Interop-erability Arrangements	Register, in the GEOSS Standards and Interoperability Registry (SIR), new and recommended interoperability arrangements) as well as utilized standards.	• # Service Provider • # Components and Services Registry • # Standards & Interoperability Registry • # SIF Moderator
3. Harvest & Query via Clearinghouse	This use case describes the steps for harvesting and/or query-ing service or content metadata from community catalogs or services via a GEOSS Clearinghouse	• # Service Provider • # GCI Registry • # GEOSS Clearinghouse • # Client Application
Clients and Portals Use Cases		
4. Search for Resources	Steps for portals and application clients to support the GEOSS user in searching for resources of interest via the GEOSS Clearinghouse or Community Catalogs	• # GEOSS User • # Portals and Client Applications • # GEOSS Clearinghouse • # Community Catalog
5. Present Services and Alerts	Present GEOSS User with services and alerts as returned per the user's search criteria	• # GEOSS User • # Portals and Client Applications • # GEOSS Service Providers
7. Exploit Data Visually and Analytically	Steps for exploitation in Client Applications of datasets served through Web Services and online protocols as used within GEOSS.	• # GEOSS User • # Components and Services Registry • # GEOSS Service Providers • # Portals and Client Applications
Deployment and Access Use Cases		
2. Deploy Resources	Deploy Resources for use in GEOSS	• # Service Provider • # Components and Services Registry
6. Interact with Services	Interact with Services	• # Service Provider • # Portals and Client Applications
Service Testing Use Cases		
9. Test Services	Service Provider tests its service using a proper Test tool discovered in the GEOSS CSR.	• # Service Provider • # Components and Services Registry # Test Facility/Tool • # Relevant Standards Authority
Workflow Use Cases		
8. Construct and Deploy Workflow	Design, deploy and execute a workflow. described in Business Execution Language (BPEL) or any other script language.	• # GEOSS Integrator • # Client Application • # Service Provider

The AIP-2 Use Cases Engineering Report describes the use cases in detail. The report contains the generalized use cases that were specialized to implement the specific SBA scenarios. The SBA Scenarios and specialized use cases are defined in separate AIP-2 ERs. The Use Case ER contains a mapping of the use cases to the GEOSS AIP Components Types.

Engineering Components

The systems and components that comprise GEOSS are contributed by GEO members and participating organizations. As a result of AIP-1 and several other GEO tasks, a set of engineering components were established in May 2008 as the GEOSS Common Infrastructure (GCI) Initial Operating Capability (IOC). One objective of AIP-2 was to augment the GCI beyond the level of IOC. AIP-2 defined a several types of components beyond the GCI components that are needed to accomplish the SBA scenarios. Figure 5 shows the GCI augmented by a set of additional GEOSS-relevant engineering components.

From an SoA point of view, a *component* represents a modular part of a system that encapsulates its contents and whose manifestation is replaceable within its environment. A *component* is modeled throughout the development life cycle and successively refined into deployment and run-time. For AIP-2, *component types* are design concepts that encapsulate *information objects* and provide *services* on the information through *interfaces. Component instances* are developments that have been deployed and are accessible at a network address. *Component instances* are registered in the GEOSS CSR. Business functions are offered for use by other components as services.

The components shown in Figure 5 are organized using a three-tier model that is typical in SoA. The tiers help to categorize the components but it is does not constrain the component interactions, e.g., client tier components need not go only to the middle tier, they may directly access the bottom tier.

Figure 5. AIP-2 engineering components augment the GCI IOC

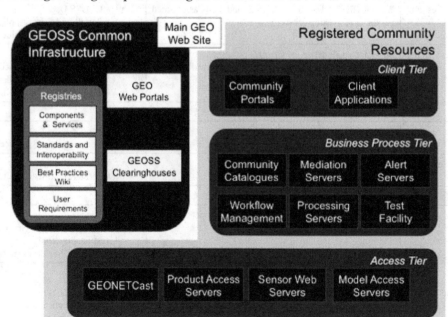

- The top tier is the only one with which people deal directly. The Clients and Portals in this layer provide users access to the other components;
- The middle tier embodies business processes to aid clients in achieving tasks in the SoA. The services in general embody everything from discovery to complex geoprocessing on sets of data from various repositories and from generation of map views to statistical charts that the client gets back at the end of the process;
- The lower tier provides read and/or write access to data, whether its geospatial data, accounting records, or sensor data.

A description of each component type and some example interoperability arrangements are listed in Table 4.

Table 4. GEOSS engineering component types

Component	Description	Example Interoperability Arrangements
Main GEO Web Site	Earthobservations.org	http
GEO Web Portals	A single point of access to information, internal or external to GEOSS, relevant to all SBAs and is of interest to various types of users	http, CSW, WMS, KML
GEOSS Registries	Component and Service Registry (CSR) Standards and Interoperability Registry (SIR) GEOSS Best Practices Wiki GEOSS User Requirements Registry	
GEOSS Clearinghouse	Provides search access to high-level metadata from all catalogs registered in the CSR through remote harvest of metadata or provision of distributed search. Indexes all CSR entries.	CSW, ISO 23950
Community Portals	A community-focused portal (website) that provides a human user interface to identified content	CSW, ISO23950, KML, WMS
Client Applications	Application hosted on users computer to access remote services and provide manipulation of the data in the client application. Clients may be specific to a user community or may be more generic geospatial data applications.	CSW, ISO23950, WMS, WFS, WCS, SOS, SPS, WPS, CAP, KML, RSS, GeoRSS
Community Catalogues	Collection of community-organized information descriptions (metadata) exposed through standard catalog service interfaces	CSW, ISO 23950
Mediation Servers	federates several catalogue services with differing vocabulary and offers results through a catalogue service.	CSW, ISO 23950
Alert Servers	Component provides feeds of alerts.	CAP, RSS, GeoRSS
Workflow Management	Encapsulates an engine capable of managing workflows, services, activities, and workflow execution instances.	BPEL
Processing Servers	Components that accepts requests to process data using an algorithm hosted in the component. The data is accessed from a remote service.	WPS
Test Facility	Provides persistent services to support the service registration and operational monitoring of services.	WMS, WFS, WCS, CSW
Product Access Servers	Services to access Earth Observation data. Typically hosted by a facility that provides redundant resources for both high availability and high performance.	WMS, WFS, WCS, ftp, OpenDAP
Sensor Web Servers	Services to access sensors and sensors networks: e.g.; ground station and associated satellites; and in-situ networks of sensors.	SOS, SPS, SAS
Model Access Servers	Services to access outputs of predictive models of geospatial information, hosted by a simulation and modeling center.	WMS, WCS, WFS, SOS
GEONETCast	Global network of satellite-based data dissemination systems to distribute data via broadcast.	DVB-S

Lessons Learned from AIP-2

The approaches, techniques and artifacts described in the preceding sections were developed in the second phase of the GEOSS Architecture Implementation Pilot (AIP-2) that was completed in 2009. The following items are areas where AIP can continue to optimize the process and results towards meeting the objectives of GEOSS:

- User involvement: Although user involvement has been a focus since inception of AIP, it is important to continue to increase engagement with the GEO User Interface Committee and GEOSS users generally in the definition and elaboration of the GEOSS Architecture.
- Stability of services: Many components and services utilized in AIP-2 were prototypes of persistent exemplar data services dependent upon the developers winning a proposal. Funding needs to be allocated to support data delivery infrastructure capacity for integration of satellite data and value added services for local use in addition to funding the local utilization and capacity building activities.
- Data and Information are lesser-developed areas of the architecture in comparison to services, for example. Development is needed of an information architecture for GEOSS based upon international standards for geospatial information. Data Sharing Principles Task Force outcomes may require AIP to focus on the topics of GeoDRM, User Registration and Authentication.
- GEOSS should anticipate heterogeneous metadata but promote minimum documentation for specific purposes, e.g. GEOSSRecord for discovery.
- GEOSS should aim to use existing standards/specifications and work through the proper channels where modifications to these standards/specifications are deemed appropriate.
- Distributed search and metadata. Further work is needed on the functions of the clearinghouse including coordination with the registries, harvest and searching of community catalogues and refinement of search metadata for GEOSS.
- AIP-2 involved both "development through prototyping scenarios" along with development of "UML system engineering models". The prototyping approach tends to discount the value of abstract, requirements-oriented modeling of UML. The UML process is typical of a system development process focused on robust definition of requirements prior to synthesis and implementation. A balance of the two activities was the focus of AIP-2: the software development was accomplished in parallel with modeling and so they are not in direct alignment. Continued refinement during iteration of AIP-3 will progress to a mature architecture.

FUTURE RESEARCH DIRECTIONS

In the AIP, projects are being defined that link together satellite providers and value added services with national partners and regional/international agencies in a many-to-many relationship under pilot programs. These pilot programs are local in nature, but supported on a global scale with orbital, aerial, and in-situ sensors and analytical models. The data, when they are combined with underlying socio-economic data and infrastructure, can be used to predict risk and assess effective mitigation strategies.

But such resources will not be utilized unless institutional arrangements are in place. In addition to providing institutional support for the technical interoperability work described above, GEO assists in establishing framework agreements that cross country and agency lines to enable societal benefit through open data sharing principles.

The next iteration of AIP Evolutionary Development (AIP-3) has begun as of December 2009. The baseline for AIP-3 will be AIP-2. This baseline includes both process and products. The AIP-2 process for development and architecting will be refined further. The SBA-to-SOA process began with a focus on "scenarios and use cases" and has become a rich set of concepts shared across the AIP development community. This architecting process will need to be further refined and simplified to be more efficient in the AIP-3 and for use by others not deeply involved in AIPs. The AIP-2 products of deployed components and services will be a basis for AIP-3 development. A key objective for AIP-3 is a focus on data content. AIP-1 and AIP-2 have developed a robust service architecture for serving EO data. There is still the need for EO data providers to adopt web services as effective way to deliver EO data to large communities in a loosely coupled fashion building on the success of the broader Internet.

CONCLUSION

The challenge of defining a web services architecture to meet the needs for GEOSS has been met, and yet, there is much work to be done to propagate this architecture. As the author William Gibson has said, "the future is already here, it's just not evenly distributed" [NPR 2009]. The architecture and process developed in AIP will certainly evolve as it is implemented for further societal benefit area applications and the technology including standards is advance to be ever more efficient. The participants in the Architecture Implementation Pilot and in GEOSS more generally will undertake this future development in order that Earth observations can be made available for humanities critical decisions.

REFERENCES

AIP. (2009). *AIP-2 Engineering Reports, OGC Network*. Retrieved December 21, 2009, from http://www.ogcnetwork.net/AIP2ERs

Alexander, C. (1964). *Notes on the Synthesis of Form*. Cambridge, MA: Harvard Press.

GEO. (2005, February). *Global Earth Observation Systems of Systems – GEOSS – 10-Year implementation plan, GEO 1000 / ESA BR-240*. Amsterdam: ESA.

Menard, L., Wald, L., Blanc, P., & Mines, T. R. (2009, May). Sitting of a solar power plant: Development of Web service based on GEOSS data and guidance. *Proceedings from the 33rd International Symposium on Remote Sensing of the Environment*, Stresa, Italy.

Nativi, S., Mazzetti, P., Saarenmaa, H., Kerr, J., & Tuama, O. E. (2009). Biodiversity and climate change use scenarios framework for the GEOSS Interoperability Pilot Process. *Ecological Informatics*, *4*(1), 23–33. doi:10.1016/j. ecoinf.2008.11.002

NPR. (2009, November). *The Science in Science Fiction*, William Gibson speaking at 11:55 in Talk of the Nation, National Public Radio. Retrieved from http://www.npr.org/templates/story/story. php?storyId=1067220

OGC. (2005, July). The importance of going open-an OGC White Paper. *The Open Geospatial Consortium*. Retrieved from http:// portal.opengeospatial.org/files/?artifact_ id=6211&version=2&format=pdf

Robinson, E. (2009, May). Air quality and GEOSS: status, issues and panel discussion. *Technical Session 34, 33rd International Symposium on Remote Sensing of the Environment*, Stresa, Italy. Retrieved from http://wiki.esipfed. org/index.php/AQ_&_GEOSS_Session_during_ISRSE_May_2009

ADDITIONAL READING

GEO. (2009). *GEO - Group on Earth Observations, Home*. Retrieved December 21, 2009, from http://www.earthobservations.org/

GEOSS. (2007). *Strategic Guidance for Current and Potential Contributors to GEOSS*. The Group on Earth Observations. Retrieved from http://www.earthobservations.org/documents/portal/25_Strategic%20Guidance%20Document.pdf

http://www.rm-odp.net/files/resources/LON-040_UML4ODP_IS/LON-040_UML4ODP_IS.pdf

IEEE. (1998). *IEEE standard for application and management of the systems engineering process - description (IEEE Std 1220-1998)*, IEEE Standards Association. Retrieved from http://standards.ieee.org/reading/ieee/std_public/description/se/1220-1998_desc.html

IEEE. (2008). *IEEE Systems Journal, 2*(3).

ISO 19119. (2005). *Geographic information – services*. Retrieved from http://www.iso.org/iso/catalogue_detail.htm?csnumber=39890

OGC. (2009a). *Welcome to the OGC Website*. Retrieved December 21, 2009, from http://www.opengeospatial.org/

OGC. (2009b). *OpenGIS® Standards and Related OGC documents*. Retrieved December 21, 2009, from http://www.opengeospatial.org/standards

OGC. (2009c). *OGC Interoperability Program Policies and Procedures*. The Open Geospatial Consortium, Retrieved December 21, 2009, from http://www.opengeospatial.org/ogc/policies/ippp

Percivall. (2009). *AIP-2 Summary Engineering Report*. GEOSS architecture implementation pilot (phase 2, version 1.1).

Rechtin, E. (1991). *Systems Architecting*. Prentice Hall.

RM-ODP. (1996). *Information technology-Open Distributed Processing-Reference Model: Foundations(RM-ODP, Part 2)*. Retrieved from http://standards.iso.org/ittf/PubliclyAvailableStandards/index.html

SIF. (2009). *GEOSS Standards Registry Home*. Retrieved December 21, 2009, from http://seabass.ieee.org/groups/geoss/

UML4ODP. (2008). *Information technology-Open Distributed Processing-Use of UML for ODP system specifications*. Retrieved from http://www.iso.org/iso/catalogue_detail.htm?csnumber=52089

UML. (2007). *Unified Modeling Language: Superstructure*. Object Management Group (version 2.1.1). Retrieved from http://www.omg.org/cgi-bin/doc?formal/07-02-05

APPENDIX: MODELING TERMINOLOGY

This appendix lists terminology used in the AIP Modeling process. The terms are taken from several standards. Some terms are unique to the AIP process. Figure 6 shows relationships between some of the terms.

Figure 6. AIP system modeling terminology

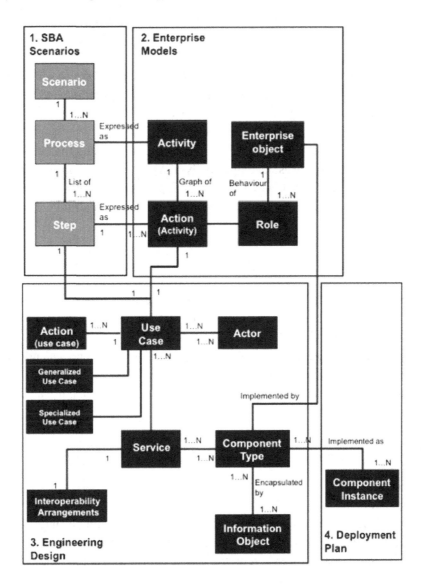

The following references are used in this section. The references in order of precedence:

1.   UML4ODP (2008)
2.   RM-ODP (1996)
3.   UML (2007)

Several additional references are also mentioned for specific terms.

Scenario (as used in AIP-2, scenario can be best understood considering the term Process from [UML4ODP])

- The modelling of *behaviour* may be structured into one or more *processes*, each of which is a graph of *steps* taking place in a prescribed manner and which contributes to the fulfillment of an objective. In this approach, a *step* is an abstraction of an *action* in which the *enterprise objects* that participate in that *action* may be unspecified. [UML4ODP])
- Scenario defines the "business" objectives of the Community in using the GEOSS architecture.
- A template for SBA Scenarios was developed early in AIP-2 process implicitly defining concepts. Refinement of the template based upon the preceding paragraph results in these concepts: A *scenario* may contain one or more *processes*. A *process* is defined in narrative form as a set of *steps* in a table.

Activity (Diagram):

- An *activity* is a single-headed directed acyclic graph of *actions*, where occurrence of each *action* in the graph is made possible by the occurrence of all immediately preceding actions (i.e. by all adjacent actions which are closer to the head). [RM-ODP]
- The notation for an *activity* is a combination of the notations of the nodes and edges it contains, plus a border and name displayed in the upper left corner. [UML]
- *Activity* replaces ActivityGraph in UML 1.5. *Activities* are redesigned to use a Petri-like semantics instead of state machines. [UML]

Enterprise object

Community object

- Each *enterprise object* models some entity (abstract or concrete thing of interest) in the Universe of Discourse. A particular kind of *enterprise object* is a *community object*, which models, as a single object, an entity that is elsewhere in the model refined as a community. [UML4ODP]

Role: Identifies a specific behaviour of an enterprise object in a community. [UML4ODP]

Action: Something that happens [RM-ODP]

Use Cases:

Generalized Use Case

Specialized Use Case

- A *use case* is the specification of a set of actions performed by a system, which yields an observable result that is, typically, of value for one or more *actors* or other stakeholders of the system. [UML]
- Each *use case* specifies a unit of useful functionality that the subject provides to its users (i.e., a specific way of interacting with the subject). [UML]
- AIP defines both *generalized use cases* and *specialized use cases*. A *generalized use case* specifies *actions* of value to GEOSS in general. A *specialized use case* refines a *generalized use case* as needed for a specific SBA community's requirements.
- *Use cases* for AIP focus on *services* and *interoperability arrangements*.

Actor

- An *actor* specifies a role played by a user or any other system that interacts with the subject. (The term "role" is used informally here and does not necessarily imply the technical definition of that term found elsewhere in this specification.) [UML]
- *Actors* may represent roles played by human users, external hardware, or other subjects. [UML]
- *Actors* are external to the subject of the use case. [UML paraphrased]

Service

- A *service* is a distinct part of the functionality that is provided by an entity through *interfaces* [ISO 19119:2005]
- In AIP-2, *services* are types of computational objects as defined in [RM-ODP].

Interface

- An *interface* is an abstraction of the behaviour of an object that consists of a subset of the interactions of that object together with a set of constraints on when they can occur.
- RM-ODP defines three types of *interfaces*: 1) A signal interface is an interface in which all the interactions are signals; 2) An operation interface is an interface in which all the interactions are operations; 3) A stream interface is an interface in which all the interactions are flows.
- For SoA: an *interface* is a named set of operations that characterize the behaviour of an entity [ISO 19119]
- In GEOSS, agreements about interfaces are termed *interoperability arrangements*.

Interoperability arrangements

- GEOSS *interoperability arrangements* are to be based on the view of complex systems as assemblies of components that interoperate primarily by passing structured messages over network communication services. [GEOSS Strategic Guidance Document, October 2007]
- By expressing interface interoperability specifications as standard service definitions, GEOSS system interfaces assure verifiable and scalable interoperability, whether among components within a complex system or among discrete systems. [GEOSS Strategic Guidance Document, October 2007]

Information object

Information held by the ODP system about entities in the real world, including the ODP system itself, is modeled in an information specification in terms of *information objects*, and their relationships and behaviour. [UML4ODP]

Component type

Component instance

A *component* represents a modular part of a system that encapsulates its contents and whose manifestation is replaceable within its environment. [UML]

A *component* is modeled throughout the development life cycle and successively refined into deployment and run-time. [UML]

For AIP-2, *component types* are design concepts that encapsulate *information objects* and provides *services* on the information through *interfaces*. *Component instances* are developments that have been deployed and are accessible at a network address. *Component instances* are registered in the GEOSS CSR.

Chapter 16

Operational Delivery of Customized Earth Observation Data Using Web Coverage Service

Wenli Yang
George Mason University, USA

ABSTRACT

Global long term Earth Observation (EO) provides valuable information about the land, ocean, and atmosphere of the Earth. EO data are often archived in specialized data systems managed by the data collector's system. For the data to be fully utilized, one of the most important aspects is to adopt technologies that will enable users to easily find and obtain needed data in a form that can be readily used with little or no manipulation. Many efforts have been made in this direction but few, if any, data providers can deliver on-demand and operational data to users in customized form. Geospatial Web Service has been considered a promising solution to this problem. This chapter discusses the potential for operational and scalable delivery of on-demand personalized EO data using the interoperable Web Coverage Service (WCS) developed by the Open Geospatial Consortium (OGC).

INTRODUCTION

Earth observation (EO) data are routinely collected by hundreds of instruments on board various plat-

DOI: 10.4018/978-1-60960-192-8.ch016

forms, especially the several dozens of spacecraft operated by the world's major space agencies. The EO data are precious resources and are obtained with huge investments from both governments and the private sector. The data and their derived products are potentially useful to a very wide range of user communities from specific domain scientists to the general public. There are, however, many challenges in utilizing all the EO data fully, not only because of their high heterogeneity and very diverse archival forms but also because of their massive and rapidly increasing volumes. This chapter discusses the perspective of providing an operational and scalable interoperable Web Service, OGC's WCS, to allow easy and customized access to EO data. The chapter is structured in the following way. First, a background on interoperable Web Services for EO data access is provided and the OGC WCS data models and specifications are introduced. Second, the current status of WCS usage is reviewed and the potential problems in using WCS in a production environment are discussed. Finally, a summary is provided and the perspective of broad adoption of this technology across EO communities is analyzed.

GEOSPATIAL WEB SERVICE FOR EO DATA ACCESS

Geospatial Web Services and Standards

Geospatial Web Services are Web-based geospatial applications that are modular, self-contained, and self-described with standard interfaces and thus support application-to-application interaction across different systems. Geospatial Web Services can be used to search for, access, and process geospatial data and information. The primary advantage of adopting Web Services is that they are standards-based and thus potentially fully interoperable among different applications and systems. There is a rich literature on Web Services and comprehensive reviews of Geospatial Web Services can be found (e.g., Zhao et al, 2007; Kralidis, 2007; Dietz, 2010). In addition to standards used in general Web Services such as

the extensible markup language (XML) and the Simple Object Access Protocol (SOAP), most geospatial Web Services are developed using two suites of standards, namely those developed by the Technical Committee for Geographic information/Geomatics of the International Organization for Standardization (ISO/TC211) and those by the Open Geospatial Consortium (OGC). The TC/211 standards are mainly on the theoretical, conceptual, framework, or content levels, although some also specify implementation encodings such as ISO 19139:2007, which provides an XML schema implementation for TC/211's metadata (ISO 19115:2003) and service standards (ISO 19119:2005). TC/211 standards "specify methods, tools and services for data management (including definitions and description), acquiring, processing, analyzing, accessing, presenting and transferring such data in digital/electronic form between different users, systems and locations."[1] OGC standards are focused on detailed protocols, interfaces, and encodings for geospatial Web Services so that "software developers use these documents to build support for the interfaces or encodings into their products and services."[2] Such implementable standards are called OGC implementation specifications and are developed based on OGC abstract specifications where the conceptual foundations are defined. The two standards bodies, ISO/TC211 and OGC, have collaborated closely in the past few years. Some OGC standards have been adopted by ISO/TC211 as international standards, such as the Web Map Service standard (as ISO 19128:2005) and Web Feature Service standard (now ISO 19142). Many geospatial Web Services have been developed and deployed in the past decade. The most relevant geospatial Web Service for EO data access is the Web Coverage Service because it deals primarily with data modeled as multi-dimensional arrays, which is the predominant EO data model.

Geospatial Coverage Model and OGC WCS Implementation Specification

Definition of a Geospatial Coverage

The design of the WCS implementation specification is based on the coverage models defined in the OGC Abstract Specification Topic 6, The Coverage Type and its Subtypes (OGC, 2000), and ISO 19123:2005, Schema for coverage geometry and functions (ISO/TC211, 2005). In the Abstract Specification Topic 6, geospatial coverages are described as "two- (and sometimes higher-) dimensional metaphors for phenomena found on or near a portion of the Earth's surface." They fundamentally provide "humans with an n-dimensional (where n is usually 2, and occasionally 3 or higher) "view" of some (usually more complex) space of geographic features". ISO 19123 (ISO/TC211, 2005) states, "a coverage is a function from a spatial, temporal or spatiotemporal domain to an attribute range. A coverage associates a position within its domain to a record of values of defined data types." Yang and Di (2008) describe a geospatial coverage as providing "a representation of a phenomenon or phenomena within a bounded spatiotemporal region by assigning a value or a set of values to each position within the spatiotemporal domain". An example of a coverage is a two-dimensional floating-point array whose element values represent the land surface temperature of an area. Essentially, a geospatial coverage consists of three primary elements: a domain defined by a geometry in a spatiotemporal coordinate reference system (CRS), a range including one or more value sets, and a mapping function or a set of mapping functions from the domain to the range that produces value(s) representing certain phenomenon/phenomena in the domain.

The Quadrilateral Grid Coverage

Several coverage subtypes are defined in both OGC Abstract Specification Topic 6 and ISO 19123, among which the quadrilateral grid coverage, including the image subtype in Topic 6, is most relevant to EO data, which are usually encoded as n-dimensional (n-D) arrays (n≥2). A quadrilateral grid coverage is a coverage that its domain is defined by "a network composed of two or more sets of curves in which the members of each set intersect the members of the other sets in a systematic way" (ISO/TC211, 2005), with each set of curves representing one dimension in the coverage's domain. Because a coverage's domain is defined in a spatiotemporal coordinate system, there can be no more than four sets of "curves" in the above definition, i.e., one time dimension and up to three spatial dimensions. The two published stable versions of the WCS specification, version 1.0.0 and version 1.1.2[3], are limited to this coverage subtype[4]. For brevity, "quadrilateral grid coverage" is referred to as "grid", "grid coverage", or "coverage" thereafter in this chapter.

Figures 1(a) through 1(d) show examples of a 2-D grid coverage and the relationships between grid dimensions (U, V) and Earth CRS dimensions (X, Y) The grid's dimensions, (U, V), represent two horizontal spatial dimensions. Figure 1(a) represents a 2-D grid with dimensions U and V, respectively, and an origin at O. There are five grid points along each of the two dimensions, i.e., two sets of five "curves" as defined in ISO19123, although the "curves" in this figure are actually straight lines. In fact, in the grid's own CRS, (UOV), the "curves" will always be straight lines because they represent nothing but $u=0$, $u=1$, ..., $u=m$, and $v=0$, $v=1$, ..., $v=n$, where m and n are number of grid point at the grid's horizontal and vertical directions. The valid range of the grid shown in figure 1(a) includes only the 25 grid points where two sets of lines intersect. As a result, the grid coverage's range values are only definable at positions corresponding to these 25 points. Figures 1(b) and 1(c) illustrate the relationship between the grid coverage's CRS and an Earth CRS ($XO'Y$). In Figure 1(b), the grid's CRS (UOV) aligns with the Earth CRS ($XO'Y$)

except for an offset shift, while in Figure 1(c), the grid's CRS (UOV) has an angle with the Earth CRS ($XO'Y$) in addition to an offset shift. In both cases, the distances between any two neighboring grid points, or grid spacing, as indicated by offset vectors V_1 and V_2, are uniform in the Earth CRS. The coordinate values (x,y) in the (XY) space for each grid point (u,v) in the (U,V) space can be derived using an affine transformation based on the offsets vectors, V_1 and V_2, and particular (u,v) values. ISO 19123 defines such grid coverage as being georectified. In Figure 1(d), the grid points are located irregularly in the Earth CRS ($XO'Y$). The position of a grid point (u,v) in the (XY) space cannot be determined based on an affine relationship. Other methods, such as polynomial fitting functions, are needed to related the coordinate values (u,v) in the grid CRS to the corresponding coordinate values (x,y) in the Earth CRS. Such grid coverage is defined as georeferenced, but not georectified. Most spectral radiance measurement data products in the NASA EOSDIS are provided in georeferenced grid coverage where the two dimensions in grid CRS are usually along and across the satellite's track direction.

The OGC WCS Implementation Specification

Two stable versions of the WCS specification are available: version 1.0.0 and version 1.1.0 (OGC, 2005; OGC, 2008). The latter was followed by two corrigendum releases: 1.1.1 and 1.1.2. These corrigenda are minor improvements such as fixing inconsistencies, making clarifications, and editorial polishing. The two versions of the specification will be referred to as WCS v1.0 and v1.1 thereafter in this chapter. WCS v1.0 and v1.1 are not compatible, although they are designed based on the same coverage model—ISO19123 and OGC Topic 6—and have the same overall structure. Some of the differences between the two versions have significant impacts on WCS capability to serve EO data. A discussion on the

main v1.0 and v1.1 differences and their consequences on WCS server implementation will be provided later in this section after the main WCS functionalities have been reviewed.

WCS provides three operations: GetCapabilities, DescribeCoverage, and GetCoverage. The GetCapabilities operation allows clients to obtain metadata information about a WCS service instance. These metadata include general service information, such as service identification and server provider information, and the content information of a specific server. The content information either contains or provides reference to brief descriptions of the coverage(s) available from the server, including available coverage identification, description, bounding box (i.e., domain), supported format, and CRS. With such content information, clients can either request further detailed information on a coverage or directly request coverage data, using the other two operations. The GetCapabilities response is encoded in XML, following the appropriate WCS version's schema. WCS v1.1 also permits encoding using SOAP. The DescribeCoverage operation allows a client to further request, usually after receiving the GetCapabilities response, a full description of one or more coverages offered by a WCS server. The main additional information provided in the DescribeCoverage response, as compared to that from the GetCapabilities response, is on the coverage's range. For n-D EO data arrays, the DescribeCoverage response provides three particular pieces of information in addition to that from the GetCapabilities response: the n-D data array's dimension sizes, the non-spatiotemporal axis (or axes) for higher than 2-D data such as the name and size of the array axis that representing spectral wavelength bands, and the available interpolation method. In WCS v1.0, the DescribeCoverage operation for all coverage offered can be requested by not specifying any coverage name. In WCS v1.1, individual coverage names must be provided. The DescribeCoverage response is also encoded in XML (either with or without SOAP for v1.1).

Figure 1.(a) A two-dimensional quadrilateral grid; (b) A georectified quadrilateral grid in an Earth CRS; (c) A georectified quadrilateral grid in an Earth CRS with a rotation; (d) A un-georectified quadrilateral grid in an Earth CRS

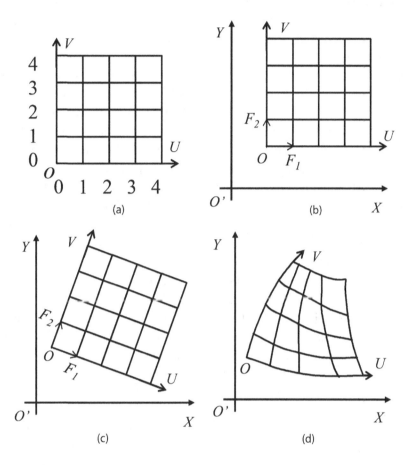

After receiving a DescribeCoverage response, a client should be able to actually obtain coverage data, in his/her customized form, by sending a GetCoverage request, in which the customization parameters for the returned data are defined. These parameters include output coverage's format and CRS, temporal range and resolution, spatial extent and resolution, subsetting along any n-D array, and method of interpolation if needed. In WCS v1.0, the response, i.e., output coverage data, must be sent to the client in a binary encoding appropriate to the format specified by the client. In v1.1, binary encoding alone is not allowed. An XML component, either with or without SOAP, must be included in the response. The XML can

either be packed with binary-encoded coverage data and sent to the client or be sent to the client without the binary-encoded coverage data. In the latter case, the binary-encoded coverage data are temporarily stored at the server side for the client to retrieve asynchronously.

The Main Differences between WCS v1.0 and v1.1 and Their Implications

The main changes introduced in v1.1, as compared to v1.0, include (OGC, 2008):

a)   Use of GridCRS in specifying a coverage's domain,

b) Allowing nested hierarchical description for related coverages in a service offering,

c) Allowing multiple range fields (or variables, parameters) to be included in a coverage,

d) Different response encoding methods for the GetCoverage request, and

e) Using a format profile to specify the output coverage format.

Although any of the above changes alone is enough to make v1.1 incompatible with v1.0 (in addition to syntax/data structure changes), items (c) and (d) are particularly important to EO data users and deserve to be discussed here. Many variables[5] in EO data are best (sometimes required to be) used in connection with other variables. For example, the measured spectral radiance values must be interpreted together with the viewing and illumination geometries during the observation, and use of retrieved atmospheric aerosol values may be based on quality assurance confidence flags. Thus, data encoded in some widely used EO data formats, such as the HDF-EOS (Hierarchical Data Format for EOS) format in the NASA EOS-DIS community and the CF-netCDF (Network Common Data Format for Climate and Forecast) format in the atmospheric and oceanography communities, often include more than one variable in a single physical file. In WCS v1.0, only one variable is allowed at the range side and a client must send multiple requests to obtain more than one variable, even though the variables are originally stored in one single physical file at the server side. The need to make multiple requests unnecessarily increases, often significantly, server side process load, because a server needs to perform the same spatiotemporal subsetting and CRS transformation (e.g., reprojecting between two map projections) multiple times for multiple variables. It also causes inconvenience at the client side by not only the requirement for multiple requests (and thus longer total interaction time with the server) but also the need either to use multiple returned files, rather than just one, or to combine multiple files before

use. Allowing multi-variable requests in WCS v1.1 represents a substantial improvement over v1.0 for the EO users.

There are two options for coverage output format in v1.1 (not differentiating XML from SOAP). One is the asynchronous method in which a coverage XML document (may or may not be in SOAP) is sent to the client synchrounously. The XML document contains the output coverage's metadata, including mandatory spatial bounding box information and optional CRS transformation information, and references from which coverage data can be retrieved. A server may provide multiple references that may include not only coverage data but also additional information such as a user's guide for that data. After receiving the XML response, a client then retrieves the actual coverage data asynchronously. The other output method is synchronous response with coverage data being sent to client immediately after the data is generated at the server side. The synchronous method is similar to that used in v1.0. However, v1.1 requires that the synchronous output must include the coverage XML metadata and the metadata must be packed in the response together with the binary encoding of coverage data as a multipart message. While this requirement provides standard coverage metadata, it may cause a problem in some user communities (as discussed later in this chapter). The asynchronous output method is a useful extension to v1.0, especially when a user request involves large data volume and/or long server side processing. A server may choose to send client the reference(s) to coverage data before the data are actually generated in the server side. A server may also pack a large coverage data in several smaller coverage files to avoid possible time-out during when client retrieves the data. One potential problem is that information regarding when the references to coverage data and other metadata remain valid is not defined. A client may try to retrieve the data prematurely, using the references in the synchronously returned coverage XML document, or may wait too long when the references are not available. The former problem can be avoided if a server always sends the XML response after the output coverage data are actually produced, but doing so means that a server does not take advantage of being able to prevent potential server-side time-out error when dealing with requests involving long processing time. An optional availability element could have been included in the XML response scheme in the v1.1 specification to allow a server to define time period for which output coverage data are available.

In addition to the support for multiple range fields and the output coverage format, the adoption of format profiles for WCS v1.1, rather than just the data format names, is also worth describing. WCS v1.1 still supports any data encoding format that can adequately describe a coverage's domain and range information, such as the widely-used and self-contained CF-netCDF and HDF-EOS formats. However, use of more formal format encoding profiles defined by OGC is encouraged. Such format profiles provide standard descriptions of the format in which a coverage is encoded, including pointers to documentation for the encoding format used, data model mapping to the OGC's coverage model, and coverage metadata (OGC, 2008). The use of OGC adopted format profiles will improve data interoperability, especially among those user communities where one prescribed format is now often privileged. Currently, only the WCS application profile for netCDF format extension has been developed. The profile is currently limited to encoding of a quadrilateral grid in alignment with the WCS coverage model (OGC, 2009).

The WCS v2.0 Implementation Specification

In addition to the two published stable versions, the OGC WCS Specification Working Group (WCS/SWG) is developing a newer version, v2.0. Because of the many possibilities for a coverage being offered and requested, it has been recognized

that it is unlikely for one coverage server to implement all possible WCS functionalities. A solution to this is to make many parameters optional. However, a specification with too many options may introduce difficulties in interoperability and may be especially hard for client implementation. Given these problems, the WCS/SWG adopted a new approach in developing WCS v2.0. The new approach is to use a core plus extension model. The core of WCS v2.0 defines only a minimal set of requirements. Multiple extensions can be added at any time to extend the functionalities/capabilities not defined by the core specification. Example extensions include providing CRS transformations, support for a specific data-encoding format profile, and support for additional protocols (e.g., Representational State Transfer, or REST). The core still defines the three operations GetCapabilities, DescribeCoverage, and GetCoverage, but the actual functionalities of a service instance are dependent upon the extensions it supports. The core specification alone is not implementable and a minimum set of extension standards is needed. These minimum extensions include a format extension and a protocol extension. Most implementations are expected to support more than one protocol such as GET/KVP, POST/XML, or SOAP. Support for format extensions depends more on the user community. The WCS v1.1 extension for netCDF encoding application profile, after necessary revision and enhancement, e.g., enabling more general grid types, is expected to be adopted as a v2.0 format extension (OGC, 2009). WCS 2.0 is again not backward compatible with the previous versions.

Current Implementation Status and Potential Issues for Operational Adoption

WCS Implementations

The first WCS draft specification was released in early 2001 as version 0.0.3 (OGC, 2001). Several revised versions were released in the same year and a number of testbed demonstrations and prototypical deployments were implemented, especially after a relatively stable version 0.7 was released in early 2002 during Open Web Service initiative 1 (OGC, 2002). WCS adoption has increased rapidly since version 1.0 was published in 2005. Today many WCS server/client products have been developed and a number of EO data providers are supporting operational WCS access to their data holdings, most based on version 1.0, with some on version 1.1 and a few on earlier versions. Several dozen WCS-related implementing/implemented software products, including servers, clients, and software containing WCS compliant components, are registered in the OGC's product Web site by about 30 companies[6]. Many EO data products are accessible though WCS. For example, more than 100 WCS or WCS-related service instances are registered in the NASA's Global Climate Change Master Directory[7] (GCMD) data service registry. Several hundred data products or files with WCS access are available from the catalog[8] of the Federation of Earth Science Information Partners (DataFed), an infrastructure for real-time integration and web-based delivery of distributed monitoring data (Husar and Poirot, 2005). A search on "WCS" in the Geospatial One Stop[9] data products returned about 160 entries. Third-party WCS support for data from major EO agencies has also been reported (e.g., Li et al, 2008). Nevertheless, WCS is observed to be underused in the EO community for both the EO data product types/volumes and their delivery methods. Operational and searchable WCS servers are few in OGC-compatible registries. For instance, a search on WCS service in the Global Earth Observation System of Systems (GEOSS) catalogue[10], a registry compliant with the OGC Catalogue Service for Web (CSW), returned only about a dozen entries, and a significant percentage (>40%) of the entries are either not accessible/functional or not compliant with WCS specifications. Among the several dozen WCS-related components in the

OGC product registry, only about 20% are labeled as "Certified OGC compliant". A random check on the Datafed and GCMD catalogues indicates that many of the data entries and/or WCS access points are for accessing individual variables or just a few related variables in a very small number of product types or model outputs. This makes the number of WCS in DataFed and GCMD insignificant as compared with, for example, thousands of unique data product types, many of which may each include dozens or hundreds of single variables, distributed by EOSDIS each year and with the more than twenty thousand single variables in the Moderate-resolution Imaging Spectroradiometer (MODIS) Adaptive Processing System[11] (MODAPS) which archives the land product for the NASA EOSDIS' MODIS sensor. A number of factors may have contributed to the limited operational use of WCS in delivering data in major EO data/information systems such as EOSDIS. A discussion of these factors and potential solutions are presented in the rest of this section.

Virtual Coverage Offering

Early implementations of WCS servers were based mostly on physical data files at the server provider's system, e.g., the first WCS server capable of performing on-the-fly georectification for HDF-EOS swath data set up by the Center for Spatial Information Science and Systems (CSISS) of George Mason University (GMU) (Yang & Di, 2003). In such implementations, a coverage offered by a WCS server corresponds to a physical file. A client can request a subset of the file together with other transformations, such as interpolation and reprojection. This works well in cases when a physical file has a large spatial extent, e.g., global coverage. For EO data with small spatial extent, a single data file may not cover a user's region of interest (ROI) and thus multiple requests are needed to get a full coverage for a ROI. Because the WCS coverage model allows flexible description and offering of a coverage, a WCS server can hide physical file properties and offer a virtual (i.e., physically non-existing) coverage which can be mosaicked from multiple files on-the-fly. A client will then be able to request a coverage at any spatial location and granularity without knowing the actual spatial coverage of a data file at the server side. Recent implementations have shown an increasing trend to decouple a data file from the coverage offered. For example, the global Digital Elevation Model data download portal[12] supported by CSISS/GMU allows clients to define any spatial region on the entire Earth surface although there it extends over many DEM data files at the server's database. Virtual coverages along the temporal dimension are more frequently offered as time series data for products already having global coverage, usually having relatively coarse spatial resolution, e.g., the global atmospheric time series coverage derived from the OMI (Ozone Mapping Instrument) observations supported by the NASA GES DISC[13] (Goddard Space Flight Center Earth Science Data and Information Service Center). It is, on the other hand, sometimes difficult, or not the best choice, to offer virtual coverages when the process of generating an output coverage involves more steps than a simple spatial or temporal assembly process does. For example, when two or more overlapping Landsat ETM+ (Enhanced Thematic Mapper Plus) images are to be mosaicked, several different methods may be used to handle overlapping pixels, such as simple distance based buffer zone averaging, ground feature based merging (e.g., following linear features), and including pixel quality related weights (e.g., viewing angle, atmospheric conditions). The multiple mosaicking options and potentially sophisticated processing methods will affect not only the server's on-the-fly mosaicking performance but also make it difficult for a server to describe the nature of the coverage offered and for a client to get enough information on the output coverage values. Thus, in such cases, file-based coverage offering may be a better approach for the server and may also

be desirable for the clients. Although a client needs to send multiple requests and to deal with multiple returned coverages, the client will have more control on how to derive the final coverage data values. Because the multiple output coverages are already georectified, client side mosaicking may not be very difficult, compared to mosaicking from un-georectified satellite swath data.

Catalogue of Coverage Offered

The coverages offered by a WCS server are provided in its response to a GetCapabilities operation. The content metadata in the response lists a summary of coverages the server provides, such as names/identifiers, descriptions, and approximate spatial bounding boxes. A user can search the information included in the content metadata and select coverages of interest. If a server serves a very large number of coverages, thousands, or even millions, a client may find it difficult to retrieve and/or search the GetCapabilities response XML. The issue is more obvious in v1.0 because v1.0 does not support multiple fields, i.e., multiple variables, offering in one coverage. Although both v1.0 and v1.1 allow a reference to an external catalogue to be cited to avoid the server listing the coverages in the GetCapabilities response XML, few, if any, deployed servers use an external catalogue. This is mainly because doing so requires that a client be interoperable with the external catalogue service, preferably an OGC compliant one, i.e., a server compliant with OGC CSW. Presently, the most common implementations are either to list all coverages in one GetCapabilities response or to provide one server instance for each coverage (or each physical data file containing one or a few coverages). For example, the NASA GES DISC's Giovanni WCS server[14] lists thousands of coverages it can serve while the Unidata THREDDS (Thematic Realtime Environmental Distributed Data Services) WCS server[15] provides each of its dataset entries with a unique WCS access point (as well as other access URLs). The Unidata strategy is very appropriate for data users starting a search in data product registries, either OGC compliant or not. Once data of interest is found, the data catalogue can point the user to the WCS server access point. All the WCS access points can be registered as server instances in a service catalog. Between the single server for all coverages and the unique server for each single coverage, another choice can be to classify coverages into different groups each sharing some similar/same properties and provide one service instance for each group which contains, for example, no more than a few hundred coverages. In v1.0, coverage summaries can be hierarchically structured and the common properties of grouped coverages can be shared/inherited, thus making the catalogue in the GetCapabilities response XML much smaller and easy to handle.

Performance and Scalability

Performance and scalability are among main considerations for WCS providers, especially those who support large data archives in a production environment. A well- performing WCS server is expected to produce a correct response for any request within the server's advertised capability and a highly scalable server should be able to serve its clients at any load level. Performance and scalability are closely tied with each other. Very high client demands may affect a server's performance. The performance and scalability of a WCS are related to many factors, for example, hardware infrastructure (e.g., CPU, memory, bandwidth), software systems/tools (e.g., database, job scheduler), and the coding of the WCS server. Only the potential impacts of different strategies for offering coverages on performance and scalability are discussed here. Either as mentioned earlier, a WCS provider may offer "real" coverages in the granularities of physical files in its data archive or "virtual" ones that must be assembled on the fly from a potentially large number of data files. When file-based coverages are offered, each request

from a client usually does not require significant resources (CPU, memory, disk, etc) and can be quickly fulfilled. The main performance and scalability considerations come when many clients send requests at the same time, perhaps hundreds, or thousands of requests simultaneously. In such a case the machine hosting the service may be flooded and may not respond correctly. Limits on allowed requests, (e.g., no more than 10 per minute per client/IP) may be needed to maintain the server's performance. It is expected that such a scalability limit should not cause major concern in most user communities except those where very high temporal frequency data are persistently required. Virtual coverage offering is in most cases a desirable option from the clients' point of view but a server runs a greater risk of performance and scalability problems. For most EO data acquired or derived from orbital platforms, a truly virtual coverage usually means no limit in the spatial dimensions (i.e., global extent) and a maximum extent (years to dozens of years) in the temporal dimension. Delivery of such a coverage in its entirety is usually impossible except when the spatial resolution (grid spacing) of data is very coarse. For example, a one-day MODIS spectral radiance coverage will involve on-the-fly georectification and mosaicking of 288 files, each being several hundred megabytes in size. Finer resolution EO data, such as Landsat ETM+, will require dealing with much larger data volumes. Thus, an appropriate balance between coverage spatiotemporal extent and server performance/scalability must be reached. In addition to spatiotemporal extent, the data volume of an output grid depends more on output grid point's spacing (or cell size, if one considers a grid point value representing a cell). A server provider needs to design a granularity scheme, based on the property of data and use scenarios, that maximizes the coverage's spatiotemporal extent but at the same time ensures the server's performance. In many cases, scalability is dependent on client request behavior. For example, the DescribeCoverage response tells the grid spacing of an offered coverage but it does not provide information on the finest and coarsest grid spacing that may be requested for a coverage. Small grid spacing for a large spatial extent may cause significant load to a server. Interactions with potential user communities are very important in designing an optimum offering method. A configurable offering scheme that can be periodically adjusted based on client access patterns will help to improve performance and scalability.

Lineage Information

WCS was designed to deliver data, usually transformed (i.e., subsetted, reprojected, etc), with the original semantics of the input coverage(s) kept unchanged, so that the output coverage data can be used for numerical analysis such as scientific modeling with the same meaning as its input coverage(s). Although the semantics of an output coverage is usually maintained in most coverage servers, significant modification may have been applied to the original data, at the server provider's will. For example, different levels of quality screening can be applied to an atmospheric parameter coverage; thus, the output data can have varying degrees of quality. The classes of the original land surface classification data may be reassigned on-the-fly if a server offers additional classification schemes other than the one on which the original classification was based (e.g., from a scheme at a more detailed level to one of a coarser level). When a server offers virtual coverages, many more operations may be applied to the original coverage data from which the output coverage is generated, such as the mosaicked coverage described earlier in this chapter and the vegetation index coverage derived from red and near infrared spectral reflectance. In many cases, lineage information on the process of deriving an output coverage and on the input coverage or coverages are important because an end user, in case of any concern or uncertainty, may want to trace back to the original source

data and the WCS process in order to get a better understanding of the output data. The WCS specifications provide standard ways for specifying some parameters, such as the interpolation method and the CRS transformation method (the latter being determined by input and output CRS URNs/codes). WCS v1.1 requires that the output include a coverage metadata element, which contains a mandatory bounding box and optional CRS and CRS transformation information. This information is far from enough for a user to fully understand the coverage values generated from a process other than simple spatial and temporal subsetting. Currently, the content and syntax of coverage metadata are largely dependent on the format encoding profile used for the output, but most encoding formats, including CF-netCDF and HDF-EOS, do not contain lineage information. More standardized and comprehensive metadata, such as the ISO data content metadata and service metadata (ISO 19115:2003, ISO 19119:2005) may need to be required.

The Swath and Vertical Profile EO Data

A satellite swath dataset is a data array in a satellite coordinate system whose axes are usually called along-track and cross-track (*Track/XTrack*). For scan sensors, e.g., whiskbroom and pushbroom sensors, time values for data points at different locations in the *Track/XTtrack* space change continuously as sensors scan (there is no *XTrack*-direction change for a pushbroom sensor). The quadrilateral grid-coverage model supported by WCS v1.0 and v1.1 implicitly requires that, for such swath data, either the time dimension not be explicitly defined or the time values be grouped into a certain fixed granularity within which time values are not differentiated. This is because each single data value, or one row of along track data values, must be declared as one coverage if not doing so. Thus, a 5-minute swath granule for MODIS radiance data, for example, must be offered as having only one time value whose resolution is 5-minute. This works fine when a single or a few granules are concerned; the coverage can be viewed as having a temporal in the order of minutes. When a longer time period, e.g., a few hours, is covered, such treatment may not be appropriate for data representing time-variant parameters such as temperature and moisture. In such cases, the data can only be offered without the time dimension defined. When needed, the time values can be offered as a separate coverage or as a separate field in the same coverage. When the time dimension is not defined, the swath can either be offered in an image or engineering CRS (e.g., the *Track/XTrack* CRS), or an Earth CRS. On-the-fly georectification is required when swath data are offered in an Earth CRS. Profile data are common from sensors measuring atmospheric properties (e.g., the Cloud Profiling Radar, CPR, on board NASA's CloudSat). Many profile data are two-dimensional coverages with one dimension being vertical and the other being the satellite track. The same time issue exists for profile data. In addition, offering profile data in Earth CRS in WCS is difficult, because WCS requires 2D horizontal bounding boxes while the profile data's horizontal dimension is a curve on the Earth's surface. Nevertheless, profile data can be offered in image or engineering CRSs.

Connection with Existing Community-adopted Application Software

Different EO communities usually have their own conventional application software, such as the tools for analyzing/visualizing the HDF/HDF-EOS files in NASA EOS community and the netCDF/CF-netCDF files in the atmospheric and oceanographic community. Direct connectivity of such software to WCS servers can be an important consideration for the tool users in using data products delivered through WCS. Most such tools allow accessing a HTTP URL-referenced remote file, including a WCS GetCoverage request. Thus, data offered in WCS v1.0 protocol are directly readable

by the tools, while those offered in WCS v1.1 are not because of the MIME multipart encoding in its output, which limits the user base of the service to a certain degree. A WCS server provider may need to consult the target user community when selecting a version to support.

Connection with Other Interoperable Standards

The OGC community has its roots in geographic information systems. It thus initially focused more on geographic data or data on and near the surface of the solid Earth rather than those on the fluid parts of the Earth, i.e., the ocean and atmosphere. It was recognized later that it would be beneficial to bring together standards and technologies from different communities. Several such efforts have been attempted in connecting OGC Web Services with services used in the fluid Earth community, in which OPeNDAP (Open-source Project for a Network Data Access Protocol) and THREDDS are widely used. The GALEON (Geo-interface to Atmosphere, Land, Earth, Ocean, NetCDF) project[16] successfully harmonized the development in the two communities. The WCS netCDF application profile was part of the GALEON achievements. Experiments were also carried out with a direct cross community data/information model and service interconnection. Direct cross protocol message exchange between client/server seems difficult but it is possible to develop handlers for a server provider to connect others servers using that use different protocols.

WCS Software Maturity and Stability

The availability of mature and stable WCS software, especially server software, is one of the main constraints on the adoption of WCS. Because the standard is evolving, many WCS servers set up during testbed demonstration and prototypical implementation stages have become unavailable, either unreachable or nonfunctional, yet many server URLs are still available at various Web sites and through other online resources (e.g., downloadable documents). This is true even at the time this chapter is written, almost five years after the release of the stable version 1.0 specification. Such a situation may make those unfamiliar with OGC reluctant to adopt or implement the WCS server for operational use. Stability is more a concern for major EO data providers who are less likely, as compared to small data store operators, to risk using or buying evolving open-source or commercial software in their daily production environment. This issue will ease as stable servers are more widely set up and more clients or client components are included in proprietary software packages of major Geographical Information System (GIS), remote sensing, and/or image processing vendors.

WCS Version Compatibility

Version incompatibility is another concern for WCS adoption. When incompatible newer versions of the specification are being developed, potential users of the specification are likely to wait for the newer version instead of using/implementing the older ones. WCS v1.1 provides several advantages over v1.0, yet there are fewer compatible clients, which may mean fewer customers from the data provider's point of view. The core plus extension approach used in the current v2.0 specification design will ease this problem by reducing the need for developing yet newer versions. The modular design leaves much more room for accommodating different extensions, yet still makes them compliant with the same core version.

SUMMARY AND FUTURE DIRECTIONS

The immense and exponentially increasing volume of EO data requires that advanced tools be used so that end users in a wide spectrum of communities can fully explore and easily obtain the data. OGC Web Services give data suppliers the technologies to provide on-demand delivery of tailored data, which are not only in the right granularity and format defined by users but in most cases also at substantially reduced volumes, thus significantly facilitating online transferring. Among the many OGC Web Services, WCS is particularly suitable for EO data archived in the form of multidimensional arrays. WCS servers can be made not only to perform spatiotemporal subsetting, reformatting, and coordinate reference system transformation, but, when designed and implemented appropriately, also to deliver virtual coverage data assembled (e.g., merged, mosaicked, fused, and modeled) on-the-fly from multiple, possibly a large number of, physical data files. On the other hand, the great potential of WCS, like a double-edged sword, also brings significant challenges to service providers in such aspects as performance, scalability, quality assurance, and provenance information. At present, WCS service is still limited in the EO communities, especially in the production environments of major space agencies. Most deployed servers exploit only a subset of the possible WCS capabilities, such as one specific CRS transformation and one particular output format support. Some service instances are targeted only for specific user communities. Adoption of the OGC WCS service has been steady but modest. This status of progression is likely to continue in the near term, considering the potential complexity of the service. With sufficient interactions between providers and users in focused communities, WCS servers equipped with full utilization of the functionalities and capabilities enabled and allowed by the WCS data model and interface protocols are expected to be widely deployed and used in the EO communities.

REFERENCES

Dietz, C. (2010). *Geospatial Web services, open standards, and advances in interoperability: A selected, annotated bibliography.* Retrieved March 15, 2010 from http://purl.oclc.org/coordinates/a8.htm.

Husar, R., & Poirot, R. (2005). DataFed and Fastnet: Tools for agile air quality analysis. *Environmental Manager,* 39-41. Retrieved from http://datafedwiki.wustl.edu/images/c/c4/EM_DataFed_FASTNET_050720.pdf

ISO/TC211. (2005). *Schema for coverage geometry and functions.* Retrieved June 22, 2006, from http://www.isotc211.org/

Kralidis, A. (2007). Geospatial Web services: The evolution of Geospatial Data Infrastructure. In Scharl, A., & Tochtermann, K. (Eds.), *The Geospatial Web: How Geobrowsers, Social Software and the Web 2.0 Are Shaping the Network Society* (pp. 223–228). London: Springer-Verlag.

Li, P., Di, L., & Yu, G. (2008). Serving Aura HIRDLS Level 2 data through OGC WCS. In *Proceedings of 28th IEEE International Geoscience & Remote Sensing Symposium (Vol. II),* (pp.1333-1336).

NOAA. (2007). *Environmental data management at NOAA: Archiving, stewardship, and access.* National Academy of Sciences, Washington DC. Retrieved from http://www.nap.edu/catalog/12017.html.

OGC. (2000). *The OpenGIS abstract specification topic 6: The coverage type and its subtypes (OGC-00-106).* Retrieved March 01, 2010, from http://portal.opengeospatial.org/files/?artifact_id=985&version=1

OGC/J. Evans (Ed.). (2001). *Web coverage service (version 0.0.3), OGC 01-010.* Retrieved March 1, 2010 from http://portal.opengeospatial.org/files/?artifact_id=1000&version=1

OGC/J. Evans (Ed.). (2002). *OWS1 Web coverage service, (version 0.7), OGC 02-024.* Retrieved March 1, 2010 from http://portal.opengeospatial.org/files/?artifact_id=2669&version=1

OGC/J. Evans (Ed.). (2005). *Web coverage service, (version 1.0.0), OGC-05-076.* Retrieved March 01, 2010 from http://portal.opengeospatial.org/files/?artifact_id=12582&version=2

OGC/J. Evans and A. Whiteside (Ed.). (2008). *Web coverage service implementation standard (version 1.1.2), OGC-07-067r5.* Retrieved March 01, 2010 from http://portal.opengeospatial.org/files/?artifact_id=27297&version=2

OGC/S. Nativi & B. Domenico (Ed.). (2009). *Web coverage service 1.1.2 extension for CF-netCDF 3.0 encoding (version 3.0), OGC-09-018r01.* Retrieved March 1, 2010 from http://portal.opengeospatial.org/files/?artifact_id=35296&version=1

Yang, W., & Di, L. (2003). Subsetting, georectifying, and reformatting of NASA EOS data through the Web, in image processing and pattern recognition in remote sensing. S. Ungar, S. Mao, & Y. Yasuoka (Eds). *Proceedings of the SPIE, 4898,* pp. 239-246.

Yang, W., & Di, L. (2008). Geographic coverage standards and services. S. Shekhar and H. Xiong (Eds.), *Encyclopedia of GIS.* (pp. 355-358). Springer.

Zhao, P., Yu, G., & Di, L. (2007). Geospatial Web services. In Hilton, B. (Ed.), *Emerging Spatial Information Systems and Applications* (pp. 1–35). Hershey, PA: Idea Group.

KEY TERMS AND DEFINITIONS

Coordinate Reference System: A system that unambiguously defines the space and/or temporal position of a point. A coordinate system is a system that uses one or more scalar values, each of which represents a coordinate in the system and defines the position of a point along the coordinate. A coordinate system contains the origin, where all coordinate values are zero, and direction, which points from a smaller coordinate value to a larger value. A geospatial coordinate reference system is a coordinate system with a geo-datum, which ties the origin of the coordinate system to a location on the Earth and defines the orientation of the coordinate system.

Data Customization: The generation of data according to specific requirements of individual data customers so that data can be directly used is user-side systems without involving any kind of conversion.

Earth Observation: The observing and recording of data about planet Earth, including its atmosphere, biosphere, hydrosphere, and lithosphere, as well as the interactions of the physical, chemical, and biological processes among different spheres. Theoretically, Earth observation data range an extremely broad level of scales, including data collected from microscopic observations of mineral structures and those obtained from satellite observations of global atmospheric circulations. More commonly, Earth observation refers to the gathering of the Earth's information using scientific instruments on board moving platforms, particularly the airborne and space-borne platforms.

Interoperability: The ability of exchange information and work together among different systems. There are different levels of interoperability. At the syntactic level, different systems communicate by following protocols defined using standardized vocabularies encoded in standardized schemes. At the semantic level, different systems can understand the meaning, not just the syntax, of information. The WCS protocol discussion in this chapter achieves syntactic interoperability.

Web Coverage Service: A web-based service for delivering customized geospatial data but without changing the physical meaning of the original data values. For example, if the original coverage data represent the value of soil moisture measurement, the service's output data are expected to be still the moisture value in the same unit of measurement but not something like color index values representing different level of soil moisture. This characteristic of delivering "untainted" data distinguishes the WCS service from some other geospatial Web services, such as portrayal services where input and output data values are not numerically comparable.

ENDNOTES

[1] http://www.isotc211.org/

[2] http://www.opengeospatial.org/

[3] Version 1.1.2 is a corrigendum 2 release of version 1.1.

[4] A newer version, WCS version 2.0, which is currently under development, will allow extensions to more coverage types.

[5] In different EO communities, an observed measurement or a retrieved biophysical value for a phenomenon may be referred to as variable, parameter, measurement, etc. These terms are used interchangeably in the context of this chapter.

[6] http://www.opengeospatial.org/resource/products

[7] http://gcmd.nasa.gov/Keyword-Search/Home.do?Portal=GCMD_Services&MetadataType=1

[8] http://webapps.datafed.net/datafed_catalog.aspx

[9] http://www.geodata.gov/

[10] http://geossregistries.info/

[11] http://modaps.nascom.nasa.gov/services/

[12] http://ws.csiss.gmu.edu/DEMExplorer/

[13] http://acdisc.sci.gsfc.nasa.gov/daac-bin/
     wcsL3?

[14] http://gdata1.sci.gsfc.nasa.gov/daac-bin/G3/
     giovanni-wcs.cgi?

[15] http://motherlode.ucar.edu:8080/thredds/
     catalog.html

[16] https://sites.google.com/site/galeonteam/
     Home

Chapter 17
Using Geospatial Web Services Holistically in Emergency Management

Ning An
Oracle America, Inc., USA

Gang Liu
Lanzhou University, China

Baris Kazar
Oracle America, Inc., USA

ABSTRACT

To confront the ever-growing volume and complexity of disasters, development should begin on a highly interoperable, loosely coupled, dynamic, geospatially-enabled information platform with comprehensive situational awareness. This chapter argues that geospatial Web services are a crucial building component for the emergency management community to develop this desired information platform because geospatial Web services, along with other non-spatial Web services, can provide interoperability. In addition to discussing how geospatial Web services, especially the ones standardized by the Open Geospatial Consortium, have been used in different phases of emergency management, the chapter contends that a holistic approach with geospatial Web services will create more value for emergency management. It concludes by pointing out some future work that is worth exploring in order to cope with the ever-changing nature of emergency management.

INTRODUCTION

Natural disasters, including earthquakes, tsunamis, floods and droughts, have always posed tremendous obstacles to the survival and development of society. With rapid population growth and expanding urbanization, these disasters have become an even bigger threat to humanity. Around the world, many governmental, public and private organizations have steadily invested in emergency management to minimize the social and economic damage, especially the loss of life,

DOI: 10.4018/978-1-60960-192-8.ch017

caused by natural disasters. The United Nations General Assembly even designated the 1990s as the International Decade for Natural Disaster Reduction (United Nations General Assembly, 1989).

The terrorist attack on the World Trade Center on September 11, 2001 and subsequent high profile terrorist attacks in other countries highlighted the devastating impacts of another kind of disasters, i.e., human-caused disasters. This type of disaster is caused by human negligence, error, malicious action or the failure of a man-made system. The 1986 Chernobyl nuclear disaster in Ukraine is another high profile example of human-caused disaster.

The increased complexity and growing frequency of recent natural and human-caused disasters clearly indicate that society as a whole is heading toward what Beck referred to as a "Risk Society" (1992). Managing emergency to minimize the loss in a "Risk Society" is a daunting task, and requires collaboration from various constituencies within the whole society, especially government agencies, international humanitarian organizations and at times governments of multiple countries.

Over the years, the emergency management community has used different information technologies to improve its effectiveness, capacity and ability to collaborate. Since location information is an inherent attribute of disasters and emergencies, people have used spatial information technologies in different phases of emergency management. However, this critical information has been used separately in various organizations, and a cohesive and collaborative usage is rare (if there is any at all).

The popularity of Google Map, Google Earth, Microsoft Virtual Earth and other related applications has drawn significant attention to the underlying geospatial Web services. Researchers and practitioners in various domains, and, more importantly, ordinary Web users have

enthusiastically embraced these geospatial Web services because of their strong interoperability and flexibility. This rapid adoption in turn pushes organizations in the public and private sectors to leverage these technologies to enable and enhance the interoperability in their business applications, and emergency management is one such application. The collaborative nature of emergency management fits well with the strength of geospatial Web services that emphasize the interoperability of loosely coupled systems and integration of information from different sources.

By reviewing the historical and recent advances in this area, we hope to convey the potential for using existing and emerging geospatial Web services, especially the standardized ones established by the Open Geospatial Consortium (OGC), in emergency management. After discussing in detail how to use OGC geospatial Web services in different phases of the classic four-phase model of emergency management – mitigation, preparedness, response and recovery (Waugh, 1994) – we argue that the strength of geospatial Web services can only be fully utilized in a holistic approach. We further discuss the direction of future work that is needed to improve the usage of geospatial Web services in emergency management. While most of the discussion in this chapter is geared toward the United States, the basic concepts and ideas are also applicable globally.

BACKGROUND

In this section, we first discuss the key concept: interoperability. We will then study why interoperability is important in emergency management system. Service-Oriented Architecture (SOA) is the state-of-the-art technical approach to provide interoperability; and the use of Web services, including geospatial Web services, is the most standard way to implement SOA.

Interoperability

Interoperability is the focal concept that will be discussed throughout this chapter. According to (Canadian Geospatial Data Infrastructure Architecture Working Group, 2005), "interoperability is the ability of a system or component of a system to access a variety of heterogeneous resources by means of a single, unchanging operational interface." Interoperability allows different systems to interoperate even though they are developed using different technologies and operate independently in diverse environments. An interoperability agreement among systems should include business process and technical specifications for collecting, processing, storing and disseminating shared data and metadata.

High interoperability increases the economic value of owning and sharing information, which in turn dramatically speeds up the availability of information. It will facilitate the long-term collaborative effort to increase knowledge and awareness of risks and hazards that surround us. To realize the full value of interoperability, many international standardization bodies, including the International Organization for Standardization (ISO) and the Open Geospatial Consortium (OGC), define standards to encourage interoperability.

Interoperability in Emergency Management

Emergency management aims to protect life, property and the environment in the event of disasters, and it requires the efforts of many parties: Federal and State agencies; public, nonprofit and private organizations; and individual citizens. For example, there are 12 Emergency Support Functions (ESFs) in the US government: Transportation, Communications, Accounting and Budget Controls, Firefighting, Information and Planning, Mass Care, Resources Support, Health & Medical Services, Urban Search and Rescue, Hazardous Materials, Food and Energy (United States, Federal Emergency Management Agency, 2001). Led by FEMA, 28 Federal agencies support State and local organizations through one or more of the ESFs. Many private critical infrastructure partners, including utilities, telecommunications, transportation and financial firms, and numerous nonprofit organizations, including the Red Cross and other humanitarian organizations, are also required to forge partnerships and information sharing arrangements with public authorities.

All of these organizations have their own individual hardware platforms, software systems, and often proprietary applications to manage their information. To ensure and enhance the effectiveness of the emergency management effort, they need an interoperable mechanism to share critical information including geospatial information with other parties in the emergency management community.

The negative impact of poor interoperability was apparent in the aftermath of the September 11th Terrorist Attack (ERDAS, 2008). Within 24 hours of the attack, the City of New York swiftly used the Emergency Management Data Committee (EMDC) and created a crisis center equipped with dedicated geospatial resources including machines and personnel. In total, this center served 2,600 specific requests made by teams in the field. The NY/NJ Port Authority, the City of New York and the utility (Con Edison) that provided electric service in New York City, however, all used different vendor platforms, and therefore there was no cohesive interoperable platform in place. The EMDC could have served more field requests promptly, but the poor interoperability seriously hindered information access, exchange, dissemination, and the possibility of creating an immediate and comprehensive view of the affected area.

We should move from a "need-to-know" culture toward a "need-to-share" culture. In the next section, we will discuss the best technology paradigm available that can facilitate progress toward greater interoperability.

Service-Oriented Architecture in Emergency Management

Service-Oriented Computing is a new-generation distributed computing paradigm that consists of many primary components, including Services, Service-Oriented Architecture (SOA), Service-Oriented Solution Logic, Service Composition and Service Inventory. Service-Oriented Computing applies service-orientation principles to realize interoperability across its paradigm. Some key service-orientation principles include loose coupling, autonomy, reusability, composability and discoverability.

While SOA only addresses the architectural model aspect of Service-Oriented Computing, the media and the industry have broadly used it as synonymous with Service-Oriented Computing itself. To respect this tradition and make our references more consistent, we will use SOA as a synonym of Service-Oriented Computing throughout this chapter.

Legacy IT systems are dominant in the existing government infrastructure, and they are quite different from one government organization to another. While many government organizations have started working on major modernization efforts, it is impractical and financially impossible to move everyone to a homogenous platform. One major reason is that operating and maintenance (O&M) costs of these legacy IT systems consume an increasing amount of the IT budget, and the average split between O&M and new initiatives reached 80% and 20% in 2006 (Leganza, 2006). These government organizations have begun to realize that SOA is a critical component of their e-government strategies. First of all, SOA clearly provides them the best opportunity to integrate processes across departments and encourage resource sharing while maximizing benefits

from their investment in their legacy systems. Secondly, the SOA methodology encourages strong collaboration, and it fosters a close working relationship between IT organizations and subject-matter experts to build interoperable services that aim to meet business requirements from the very beginning. Finally, SOA approach is highly iterative, and it enables government organizations to utilize small initial budgets to develop desired services in phrases without committing to risky, expensive and long-running projects. Leganza (2006) stated that government agencies had been more aggressive in adopting SOA than their counterparts in the private sector: "43% of government decision-makers respond that their organizations were either using SOA selectively or that they had an enterprise-level strategy and commitment to SOA as opposed to 39% of non-government respondents."

This trend of adopting SOA in government agencies pushes the adoption of SOA in emergency management as well. Besides being compatible with the organizational environment, SOA is indeed the best technical approach currently available to implement the interoperability needed for effective emergency management. The European Commission attested to this by funding ORCHESTRA (Open ARCHitEcture and Spatial Data InfrasTRucture For Risk Management) to "design and implement an open service oriented software architecture that will improve the interoperability among actors involved in multi-risk management" (Annoni et al., 2005). More specifically, the SOA effort in ORCHESTRA was to integrate both geospatial and non-geospatial Web services to facilitate the information flow in emergency management.

While SOA is an architectural model that is not restricted to individual technology platforms, the most formidable technology platform associated with the realization of SOA is Web services. We will discuss Web services, specifically geospatial Web services, in a later section.

Geospatial Information in Emergency Management

Every emergency or disaster has an inherent geospatial footprint that identifies the location of its occurrence and delineates the extent of its impact. Ryan Cast, the geospatial information officer at the US Department of Homeland Security's (DHS) CIO office stated that "We were able to identify 67 out of 77 homeland security business activities that have a geospatial context" (Miller, 2004). We can use this ubiquitous presence of geospatial information to connect related events, entities and objects to form a comprehensive view of one particular crisis or multiple crises. First responders and other support services can utilize this comprehensive view to address emergency planning, resource allocation during the emergency response, as well as the post-emergency recovery.

Many organizations have recognized the crucial role that geospatial information plays in emergency management. They have collected relevant geospatial information in their systems and acquired the tools to process and analyze this information. Different organizations, however, maintain their geospatial information in their individual software systems and hardware platforms. This isolation makes it very difficult to access any geospatial information outside any one particular system. To break this isolation and access geospatial information across different platforms, we currently must build special tools for the targeted proprietary library and acquire daunting knowledge about the underlying targeted environment.

The extra work currently required could undermine the quality and the integrity of the geospatial information (ERDAS, 2008). Moreover, this ad hoc integration could prevent geospatial information being shared in a timely manner. Under the extreme pressure of the emergency management process, especially during the emergency response phase, first responders and decision makers have

to estimate without adequate information and make hasty decisions.

Terms

To facilitate the discussion in this chapter, we define the following terms:

1. **EMP** stands for Emergency Management Personnel, and broadly refers to first responder, mitigation planner, scientific/technical supporter, data/service provider, decision maker and other people involved in emergency management. If needed, we will refer to different group of EMP explicitly.
2. **EMCC** stands for Emergency Management Control Center. Organizations performing this function have many different names, but we use EMCC consistently in this chapter to simplify the discussion.

OGC GEOSPATIAL WEB SERVICES

Earlier we made it clear that SOA is the most capable technology paradigm to deliver the interoperability required by emergency management. Through its standardization process and rapidly growing deployment, Web services technology has become the most mature technology platform in the current marketplace for implementing SOA. Using open standards, Web services are web-based applications that dynamically interact with other web-based applications to achieve interoperability. Web services are platform neutral, and have been widely deployed to facilitate interoperability across different hardware platforms, software architectures and programming languages.

Geospatial Web services are simply Web services that deliver fundamental geospatial information in an interoperable fashion. They can provide users with a feasible approach to integrate many different geospatial applications in the context of legacy geospatial platforms. For example, the

Global Disaster Alert and Coordination System (http://www.gdacs.org/) uses Web services offered by Google Earth to enable regular users and professional analysts to access, process and visualize real-time geospatial information via the Web.

One example of Open Standards for geospatial Web services is the Open Web Services (OWS) specifications formulated by the Open Geospatial Consortium (OGC). The OGC is an international standardization organization focused on developing open standards to integrate electronic location resources, and in turn to advance geospatial interoperability. Its mission on geospatial interoperability squarely matches the dire needs of emergency management (Open Geospatial Consortium, 2006). OGC Geospatial Web Services will reduce the total cost of system ownership while providing comprehensive visibility to distributed geospatial resources. They provide many tangible technical benefits to the emergency management community: 1) no data conversion needed if all data is in GML format; 2) no unnecessary redundancy of geospatial data at different organizations; 3) native Web access to the geospatial data; and 4) use of the existing standards-based Web service security infrastructure. Government agencies have recognized that geospatial information, especially standards-based geospatial information, is essential in emergency management. The DHS Geospatial Enterprise Architecture (GEA) has comprehensively adopted the OGC Web Services (OWS) suite of interoperability standards. To be more involved in OGC standardization activities, the DHS became a Principal Member of OGC in 2005 (Open Geospatial Consortium, 2007).

OGC also recognizes that emergency management is an area where its Web service-related standards will have broader impact. It established the Risk and Crisis Management Working Group (RCM WG) to create and promote interoperable geospatial products for the Emergency Management community through changes and extensions to OpenGIS® specifications. For its flagship Interoperability Program ("rapidly develop, test

and deliver proven candidate specifications into OGC Specification Program"), emergency response has been used in demonstration scenarios for prototyping in the past several years.

Formulated by the OGC, OpenGIS® Specifications clearly specify interfaces, encoding and protocols that enable interoperable geoprocessing services, data and applications. We can utilize many of OpenGIS® Specifications in emergency management. The following table provides a brief summary of some OpenGIS® standards that can be used in emergency management. We will cover their scope and potential usage in emergency management.

HOLISITICALLY USING OGC WEB SERVICES IN EMERGENCY MANAGEMENT

In this section, we first describe how geospatial Web services, especially the ones formulated by OGC, can be utilized in four phases of emergency management: mitigation, preparedness, response and recovery. We then argue that a holistic approach will create more value for the emergency management community.

Mitigation

Mitigation encompasses activities that assess various types of vulnerability, and that design and take measures to avoid or reduce the possibility of disasters and the impact of their consequences (Waugh, 1994). Clearly, mitigation is proactive rather than reactive, and it starts with identifying potential threats and risks.

Vulnerability Assessment

Some of these vulnerabilities or threats are easy to identify. For example, if information from an OGC WCS server reveals that a fault line is close to a coastal city, we know immediately that

Table 1. OGC geospatial web services and their usage in emergency management

	Scope	Usage
Catalog Service for Web (CS-W)	CS-W defines an open service API to publish, access and search the collection of metadata on geospatial data, services and other related resources. Geospatial Web services use CS-W to register their descriptive metadata for other services or clients to consume.	As long as there are multiple geospatial resources being used in emergency management activities, CS-W can be useful to maintain their metadata and facilitate their usage.
Geo Decision Support Service (GeoDSS)	GeoDSS utilizes workflow management to engage distributed geospatial Web services in multiple domains, GeoDSS enables interoperable mechanism to produce context aware information or knowledge, and hence aid decision making in forming, analyzing and selecting alternatives.	In the emergency response phase, GeoDSS can orchestrate other functional OGC geospatial Web services into a workflow to provide insightful support for decision-making.
Geo Processing Workflow (GPW)	GPW interconnects geo-processing through service chaining to meet specific workflow requirements.	Similar in usage to GeoDSS.
GeoRSS	GeoRSS is a lightweight mechanism to extend existing web RSS feeds with geographic information. Although it is created outside the OGC, GeoRSS is supported and sponsored by the OGC, and might become an OGC standard.	GeoRSS can dynamically and selectively share the latest geospatial information with EMP in the field.
Sensor Alert Service (SAS)	SAS defines an open service API to publish deliverable alerts from sensors and to subscribe to these alerts.	SAS can provide alerts information from a radioactivity sensor to the EMCC.
Sensor Observation Service (SOS)	SOS defines an open service API for obtaining sensor data, specifically "observation" data and platform descriptions from one or more deployed sensors. SOS belongs to the OGC Sensor Web Enablement (SWE) suite of standards.	SOS can provide real time measurements from water level sensors to be used in early warning systems for storms or floods.
Sensor Planning Service (SPS)	SPS defines an open service API to determine the capabilities of a sensor and the feasibility of collecting data from it, and how to task this sensor. SPS belongs to the OGC SWE suite of standards.	It can be used in tsunami and earthquake warning system, severe weather forecasting and tracking, flood warnings, and environmental catastrophes.
Symbology Encoding (SE)	SE defines an XML encoded styling language to style feature and coverage data. It is independent of any service specification. Both the service provider and the service consumer can understand this styling language.	To minimize map-reading errors, information should be presented in symbols familiar to EMP from different domains. The OGC SE and related Styled Layer Descriptor (SLD) specification can satisfy the needs of diverse emergency management teams who share different data sources, but require conformity to map styles that are designed for a particular task.
Web Coverage Service (WCS)	WCS defines an open service API that describes, accesses and delivers multidimensional "grid coverage" data over the Web. The "grid coverage" generally refers to phenomena that can be represented by values at each measurement point, including satellite images and digital aerial photos.	WCS can be instrumental in establishing the "ground truth" by sharing satellite images of the affected area by an emergency event. For example, to mitigate the risk posed by a wildfire, WCS can help identify homes located on a specific slope and close to certain species of flammable vegetation.
Web Feature Service (WFS)	WFS standard defines an open service API to manipulate and query discrete geospatial features, and possibly within a transaction.	WFS is a common service that can be used in many different emergency management scenarios. For example, it can report damaged properties in a given geospatial area.
Web Map Service (WMS)	WMS defines an open service API to render and return spatial data as static maps, and to overlay images from multiple sources.	WMS can provide simple raster maps in the emergency response phase, and provide a background map for routing the EMP to the scene.
Web Notification Services (WNS)	WNS defines an open service API for asynchronous delivery of messages or alerts from Web services participating in a service workflow. WNS belongs to the OGC SWE suite of standards.	WNS enables the asynchronous dialogue between Web services and their clients for long durations. It could be useful in coping with unreliable communication channels during certain emergencies.
Web Processing Service (WPS)	WPS defines an interface with which a client can discover a published geospatial process, bind to this process, request this process to complete a specific geospatial task and deliver the process result to a desired location. The current version of WPS is 1.0.0.	During the emergency response phase, a first responder can use WPS to perform complex terrain analysis on the emergency location and return only the desired result back.

earthquake, flood and tsunami are among the main threats to the city.

Many of these threats, however, are obscure at the initial stage. To have complete visibility of potential exposures and threats, the EMCC needs information from various geospatial data sources, including the land survey agency, utility companies and common citizens. Ülgen (2005) outlined their pilot "Neighborhood Geographic Information Sharing System" that provided volunteers with skills and geospatial tools to identify seismic risks in their own neighborhood and to create multiple mitigation measures. Mobilizing local communities in the mitigation effort has at least two immediate benefits: 1) residents are naturally very motivated and their participation is very active; 2) each community has its own unique set of skills and talents. Recognizing this uniqueness and empowering the local community in the mitigation effort will make this effort more effective.

These neighborhood volunteers have effectively used low-cost mobile devices to collect and compile data before sending it to a remote geospatial server via the Internet. With this field information, interactive thematic maps can be created to facilitate the formation of the mitigation measures and possible alternatives. We can use geospatial Web services to improve the interoperability of this pilot project. First of all, a WFS-T client can be developed for the mobile devices to interact with the central WFS-T server. Secondly, WMS can be used to generate thematic maps for designing the mitigation measures.

During this assessment phase, we need to identify the most vulnerable communities in the entire system. Often these communities consist of underprivileged populations, and they will be least likely to be able to recover on their own from disasters. Special kinds of mitigation programs need to be developed to remedy this.

Vulnerability Discovery

To further discover the relationships between potential threats, known exposures and historic emergency events require more advanced analytical technologies. Utilizing real-time information from multiple sources provided by geospatial Web services, geospatial visualization technologies can provide desired analytical capabilities. Using geospatial information provided by WFS and WCS, EMP can pinpoint hazards on the digital maps provided by WMS and evaluate the consequences of potential emergencies.

Vulnerability Reduction

When designing mitigation measures to reduce vulnerability, EMP can use geospatial Web services to integrate underlying information from multiple sources to model, analyze and visualize dynamic and interdependent communities. When evaluating alternative mitigation measures, the geospatial contingency model and underlying information provided by geospatial Web services are able to respond to what-if analysis that evaluate the potential consequences, impact and effectiveness of these measures.

One key mechanism for vulnerability reduction is to communicate the mitigation messages clearly with all stakeholders. Geospatial Web services provide a mechanism to disseminate this information to the public. For example, we need to educate real estate developers about the existence of hazards in the planned area, and about the existing mitigation techniques for these hazards in this geospatial area. The public also needs to be notified of the existence of hazards in this area, and of the potential consequences of purchasing properties there.

Once we choose mitigation measures and put them into action, we can utilize geospatial Web services to monitor and track the vulnerability reduction effort. EMP would collect, update, analyze, and publish regularly a detailed vulnerability report that maps potential hazards, their probable impacts, measures to reduce the vulnerability and the progress of vulnerability reduction for each community. This task will be carried out in a very distributed environment and involves many community-based organizations. Guided by the SOA principles, geospatial Web services fit this requirement very well. Authorities would set annual vulnerability reduction targets, and would allocate budget and personnel resources to meet these targets.

All in all, geospatial Web services can be a powerful tool to implement a systematic approach of risk mitigation as discussed in (Rajabalinejad, 2009).

Preparedness

Because mitigation measures cannot prevent all emergencies, preparedness measures are required for the planning, training, and inter-agency collaboration that must take place before an emergency strikes (Waugh, 1994). The failure in emergency preparedness can be costly, and even deadly. Horswell & Hegstrom (2005) reported that the evacuations of New Orleans and Houston in advance of the 2005 hurricanes Katrina and Rita were especially disastrous: hundreds of thousands of people were unable to leave despite many hours of advance warning. The roads out of both cities were heavily congested, while roads into them were almost empty and were failing to be utilized. It was disturbing that many deaths from Hurricane Rita were directly caused by the evacuation itself. Apparently the road network and other spatial information were neglected during the preparedness phase. Otherwise, the direction of some roads should have been reversed to facilitate the evacuation (Kim, Shekhar, & Min, 2008). Unfortunately, there seem to be little, if any, collaboration on this among highway transportation authorities, police and the EMCC.

Early Warning System

Geospatial Web services can offer real-time monitoring for emergency early warning. Several organizations in Taiwan extensively used OGC Sensor Web Enablement standards to develop their Debris Flow Monitoring System (Yu, Lee, Ye, Chung & Fang, 2009). Figure 1 offers an architectural sketch of this monitoring system based on Figure 9 and Figure 13 in (Yu, Lee, Ye, Chung & Fang, 2009). This monitoring system used OGC Web services in the following three major activities. First, implementing domain-specific business logic, system administrators employed SPS services to task various sensors deployed in debris flow monitoring stations to make desired observations and raise appropriate alerts under anticipated circumstances. Secondly, users used SOS services to obtain observation data, and filter out the information they deemed unimportant. Thirdly, users used SAS services to subscribe to alerts that they were concerned about; when anticipated events happened, they would get alerts sent by WNS services. Their experience demonstrated that OGC Web services could help us integrate real-time information from heterogeneous sources. This important real-time information can be delivered over the Internet to relevant agencies, while it could selectively be used for public consumption as well. In addition to traditional communication channels, government agencies can use the Web to disseminate critical information to the public. Geospatial web services and social network can be used to achieve this.

Training Program

Training is essential both for emergency management professionals and for the general public.

Professional Training
To effectively prepare for emergency situations, "scenario planning" based on real-world information is critical. It will provide the practical

Figure 1. UML deployment diagram of taiwan debris flow monitoring system

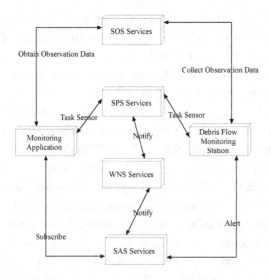

analysis of potential consequences, and evaluate the effectiveness of the measures in place. A logging service (to be discussed in the "Holistic Approach" section) can provide analysis of the information flow that occurred during the actual emergency response and recovery process. This will help improve the existing emergency plan, and make the training more concrete and closer to the real world.

To provide hands-on training for professional EMP, geospatial information can provide detailed geospatial reference data to create the most realistic emergency scenario possible. Training can include: 1) manipulating key features retrieved through the interaction with WFS servers; 2) visualizing key features through the interaction with WMS server and Symbology encoding; and 3) performing emergency management related analysis through interaction with advanced geospatial Web services. Since multiple training organizations can share this information via geospatial Web services, the training overhead can be reduced while the efficiency can be improved. We can also selectively offer certain features of operational Web services to allow the trainee to access the real emergency management system.

Public Training

For the general public, we should lower technical barriers and enable the public to easily access emergency preparedness information. The public has embraced popular geospatial Web services, including Google Map, Google Earth and Microsoft Virtual Earth, and gained good knowledge of how to use them. Leveraging their knowledge and resourcefulness, we could develop intuitive user interface tools to help them understand potential hazards on the online map in their geospatial proximity and how to cope with them. Another Web technology tool that can be incorporated is the maturing online social network. With essential and dynamic spatial information from geospatial Web services, we can develop the content and format of emergency education tools based on the participant's location or interest. Social network can also help forge self-reliant networks at work, home, churches and other locations.

Spatial Statistics for Training Programs

For people using training that incorporates OGC geospatial Web Services, we can easily collect training statistics, including the home location of trainees and whether they are emergency management professionals or not. To gain a more complete understanding, information about trainees who are not using the automatic system can be compiled and input into the system, so that we can dynamically see the rates of population penetration and the spatial diffusion of various training programs. Collecting this statistical information can serve multiple purposes: 1) increased accountability: the dissemination of emergency preparedness information can be easily tracked and monitored by EMP at different levels; 2) measured effectiveness: these statistics and the statistics collected after emergencies could provide some quantitative measurement of the effectiveness of various emergency training programs.

RESPONSE

Response refers to activities following an emergency; to some extent, it is the actual activation of an emergency response plan if there is one (Waugh, 1994). It includes the activities that provide immediate emergency assistance for victims, stabilize the situation, mitigate concomitant incidents and initiate the recovery operations.

One of first tasks in the response phase is to establish an Emergency Management Control Center (EMCC). An EMCC usually needs a military-style "Common Operation Picture" (COP) to harness a wide range of diverse data sources including geospatial data sources. This COP should provide the integrated capability to receive, correlate, and present a comprehensive view on key reference points, deployment of planned operations, multilevel overlays and projections of properties that are already damaged or are in danger. By design, geospatial Web services enable EMCC to build the COP and utilize it in response operations as follows: a) display the current location of emergency responder units; b) assign tasks based on overall situation; c) route different emergency responder units to the best suitable location. Working with the maturing online social network, geospatial Web services can also be used to publish important emergency information to the public, and to collect real-time information from the field. This transparency will help avoid chaos and improve the efficiency of emergency response.

Geospatial Web services can be instrumental in field operations as well. When first responders arrive at the scene, they need to have an accurate understanding of the surroundings. They immediately need to have dynamic information on their current location and adjacent areas, and to be able to display this information on their mobile devices. Their access to computing resources, however, is very limited. Geospatial Web services can help them leverage powerful computing resources at the EMCC. OGC Web Processing Service, for example, is an excellent tool for first responders

to perform geo-processing by utilizing computing resources at the EMCC. For WPS, its input data could also be stored on the server, requiring the client only to specify the path to input data that is desired. This alleviates both the limited computing power and scarcity of reference data at EMP's mobile devices. This capability could be particularly useful for processes requiring real-time data such as weather observations or live traffic information close to the emergency scene. On the ground, first responders from different organizations often need to communicate with each other. They can deploy lightweight geospatial Web services to enable them to communicate in an interoperable manner.

While a simple geospatial Web service, such as WFS-T, can be easily used in responding to a crisis situation (Reznik and Hynek, 2009), more meaningful work has been done on how to map existing emergency response workflow onto a service chain of basic OGC Web Services (Weiser and Zipf 2007).

Within the OGC itself, OGC Web Services (OWS) testbeds have been the major initiative of the OGC Interoperability Program to collaboratively experiment and demonstrate OGC Web services technologies for geospatial interoperability. These OWS testbeds have consistently used emergency response scenarios in their demonstrations.

OWS-4 (Open Geospatial Consortium, 2007b) used a Homeland Security scenario in which multiple government agencies respond to a "dirty bomb" that exploded at a shipping terminal in Newark airport. The collaborative efforts of these agencies in different functional areas were heavily dependent on the interoperability among multiple services. One of the major response tasks was to select a suitable building in Newark airport to set up a field hospital. It required collaboration using the following OGC geospatial Web services: a modified WFS-T serving features from Building Information Model (BIM), another WFS serving features from CityGML, a WMS serving imagery

Figure 2. UML deployment diagram of environmental impact evaluation

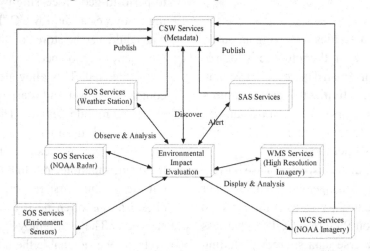

and two-dimensional map, and a CS-W maintaining the repository of WFS services for different BIMs. Another task was to evaluate how the environmental conditions would affect the dispersion of the radioactive plume emitted by the "dirty bomb". As illustrated in Figure 2, environment analysts utilized the following OGC geospatial Web services to accomplish this goal: one WMS service providing high resolution images, one WCS service providing satellite images collected by the National Oceanic and Atmospheric Administration (NOAA), one SOS offering Doppler Radar Images generated by NOAA, one SOS offering weather information, one SOS offering the information from environmental sensors, one SAS providing alert information from radioactive sensor, and one CS-W maintaining the meta information for all these involved OGC Web services.

One of OWS-5 demonstrations was the "NASA EO Wildfire Scenario". In this scenario, image data, provided by an OGC SOS service, was processed in a workflow to identify areas where more detailed data needed to be collected. An OGC SPS service then initiated this additional collection process and an OGC SOS actually performed this collection. In addition to SOS and SPS, other OGC geospatial Web services including WFS, CS-W and WPS were used in this workflow.

OWS-6 (Open Geospatial Consortium, 2009) used the response to a hostage crisis in a government building as a scenario to demonstrate how OGC geospatial Web services could be used for decision Support Services (DSS). Here, they used OGC SOS to provide camera video images of the armed intrusion, and helped identify the room in which the hostages were kept. OGC WMS was then used in both outdoor and indoor 3D routing for the rescue team. This demonstration also utilized OGC Symbol Encoding (SE) and Styled Layer Descriptor (SLD) for rendering maps and images.

RECOVERY

In the context of emergency management, recovery aims to return normal or better quality of life to a community after it responds to an emergency. Waugh (1994) referred to recovery as the actions taken to restore order and vital systems, including electric, water and medical systems, to minimum operating standards, and to provide assistance to victims in the way of temporary housing, food and other basic necessities. Johnson (2000) categorized Waugh's definition as one phase of recovery: "short-term recovery." He pointed out there is an additional "long-term recovery" phase that restores and even improves all affected services, including schools and all streets, to their full capacities.

Accomplishing an efficient and coordinated recovery is not an easy task. Hsu (2006) reported that nearly eight months after Hurricane Katrina, out of a hastily improvised $10 billion aid package from US federal government, as much as $1 billion and perhaps much more were wasted and misspent. Frances Fragos Townsend, then President Bush's homeland security and counterterrorism adviser, was quoted in Hsu's report saying that the federal effort "foundered due to inadequate planning and poor coordination."

The dire need for effective coordination and collaboration has also been shown in other countries. Diehl & Heide (2005) claimed that every year in the Netherlands, several disaster recovery efforts call for the involvement from multiple municipal agencies, provincial agencies and other parties that use a variety of data systems. Their practical experience showed that high-quality geospatial information is required for the adequate recovery of disasters. However, the wide range of diverse data systems at different agencies limits the usage of the geospatial information to individual organizations, thus diminishing the effectiveness of disaster recovery.

The timely integration of different types of geospatial data from diverse sources can improve the efficiency of recovery operation, reduce the loss of lives and property, and ease the pain of the affected population. Maiyo, Köbben & Kerle (2009) argued that geospatial Web services are the right fundamental technology to create a collaborative post-disaster information platform to achieve this integration, and help improve the coordination and effectiveness of the recovery effort. Geospatial technologies can play a crucial role in both short-term recovery and long-term recovery, as we will discuss below.

Using Geospatial Web Services in Short-Term Recovery

Geospatial Web services can be used in setting up the initial recovery and displaying the progress during its course until the short-term recovery is complete. For short-term recovery, they are instrumental in at least three key areas: 1) assessing damage; 2) allocating resources; 3) reporting status.

EMP can use geospatial Web services, along with Sensing technologies, GPS and other related technologies, to spot damaged properties and determine the type and severity of the damage. WCS and SOS will provide accurate damage information in the field, especially for areas that are difficult for humans to access. The speed and precision that geospatial Web services bring to assessing disaster damages will enhance EMP's capabilities to plan and prioritize recovery tasks, and to allocate resources (medicine, food, clothing and personnel, for example) accordingly.

Once the recovery effort is in progress, Geospatial Web services can work in concert with telecommunication technologies to determine and display areas where vital short-term services have been restored so that critical resources can be dynamically channeled to other needed areas. WMS can help provide important mapping information to display damage assessment for the overall disaster area, or for specific locations. For large-scale emergencies that involve ongoing work in multiple locations, this can be extremely useful.

Using Geospatial Web Services in Long-Term Recovery

Long-term recovery often involves rebuilding the entire infrastructure, including streets, utility networks, schools and hospitals. It can take many organizations multiple years to complete, and the cost can easily rise dramatically for large-scale emergencies. Monitoring the progress of multiple recovery sites, accounting for recovery fund usage, and keeping communication among multiple organizations for such a long period of time are challenging. Since geospatial Web services can link schedule, status, accounting and other crucial information to each location, they can provide real-time information visually to each party because of the interoperability. Using this real-time information judiciously, EMP can dynamically prioritize recovery tasks and align key investments.

In essence, using geospatial Web services along with other functional web services to integrate various types of data and information for diverse sources will strengthen analytical capabilities, functional efficiencies and overall decision making for emergency and disaster recovery. Furthermore, different organizations at different times during the recovery process need different kind of geospatial information, mapping functions and analytical capabilities. Web Services Business Process Execution Language (WS-BPEL) can express Web services composition logic, and can dynamically orchestrate geospatial Web services to deliver desired information and functionality to specific users.

HOLISTIC APPROACH

It is clear from the discussions in the previous sections that all phases of emergency management need to access and use critical geospatial information, and that geospatial Web services provide a robust interoperable platform for emergency management community to achieve this. However, most existing work focuses on one or two of emergency management phases. While modeling the emergency management into four phases brings clarity and focus to a group of related activities, it can run the risk of not seeing the forest for the trees. We should understand that there is no clear line between each phase of emergency

management. For example, authorities engaged in the recovery phase must continue the effort on mitigation and response to concomitant events.

For different types of emergencies, Annoni et al. (2005) also argued that an integrated approach is needed. They reiterated that all phases of emergency management usually involve a vast range of individual organizations at various administrative levels with different information systems performing analysis, monitoring, dissemination and other functions. Complex administrative boundaries and poor interoperability of technical systems seriously impede the overall emergency management efforts. Holistically handling both natural disasters and human-caused disasters requires that the underlying technical platform have high flexibility, openness and adaptability. Geospatial Web services and their embodied SOA paradigm have these desired characteristics.

Not having a comprehensive awareness of the information in the system can have major consequence as demonstrated by real events. Commenting on the attempted 2009 Christmas Day attack, President Barack Obama said "The U.S. government had sufficient information to have uncovered this plot and potentially disrupt the Christmas Day attack. But our intelligence community failed to connect those dots, which would have placed the suspect on the 'no fly' list. In other words, this was not a failure to collect intelligence; it was a failure to integrate and understand the intelligence that we already had" (The White House Blog, 2010). Failing to connect the dots implied failures in at least two areas: 1) while a mechanism for sharing information across multiple government agencies appeared to exist, it failed to share information in an efficient and effective manner; 2) collected and shared information was not properly analyzed: it was not analyzed by different agencies collaboratively and the underlying relationships between collected information were not utilized. If we take an isolated view of emergency management based on phases, agen-

Figure 3. A holistic approach to using geospatial web services in emergency management

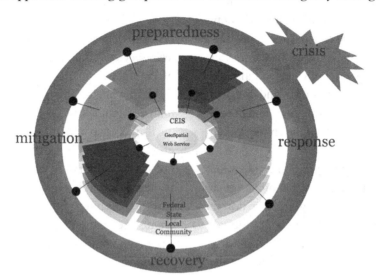

cies, or geography areas, we will repeat the failure in not being able to connect the dots.

We should always recognize that different emergency management activities are dynamically intertwined, and they can affect each other positively or negatively. Actors at different level of different organizations also need to be interconnected at times. Once we have a better understanding of the dynamic and complex nature of emergency management, it will become feasible to build a system of services that create, manage and orchestrate various services to manage emergencies.

In the rest of this section, we will take a holistic and integrated approach to evaluate how to utilize geospatial Web services in the entire emergency management system. By holistic, we mean that we will consider the entire emergency management system as a whole: 1) addressing the four phases of emergency management together as a whole; 2) dealing with both natural disasters and human-caused disasters; 3) simultaneously serving actors in different functional areas and at different levels. This approach (as shown in Figure 3) will clearly improve the overall situational awareness of and insight into the emergencies. More importantly, it

will lead to a better interoperability not only for different entities at different levels but also across different phases of emergency management.

Figure 3 is an extension to a diagram developed in the National Information Exchange Model (NIEM Program Management Office, 2007), and it shows conceptually how we utilize Web services including geospatial Web services to address emergency management with a holistic approach. In this Figure, CEIS stands for Collaboration Emergency Information System. Clearly, we are far away from the customary post disaster "war-room" Geographic Information System (GIS) implementation. We propose to build and operate an SOA-based open system that has multipurpose, multilevel, and multiuser characteristics.

Multipurpose means that we address four phases of emergency management including mitigation, preparedness, response and recovery simultaneously as a whole. *Multilevel* means that we enable actors at the federal, state, local, community, and at times even individual household (not depicted in Figure 3) levels to participate in emergency management. *Multiuser* highlights the fact that we have multiple stakeholders from a wide range of domains, including government agencies and humanitarian organizations. Organizations currently involved in emergency management all have their own structures and there are few or no system-level links connecting them. Our open system will support both horizontal (i.e., across different functional areas) and vertical (i.e., different levels of the same functional area) information sharing throughout the entire system and across multiple phases.

This system has a dynamic communication infrastructure with a variety of channels (each simplified as a line emanating from a dot in Figure 3) to reach all levels from community all the way to federal organizations. We could use this communication infrastructure for emergency public announcements, emergency response plan review, information exchange and hazard mitigation programs. Since geospatial Web services are an inherent component of our system, as long as this information has a location component, the communication will enable the effective sharing of this geospatial information. For example, a hazard mitigation program will come with maps of hazard areas.

Because of the open and participatory nature of this emergency management system, it will have an extremely wide range of data generated from numerous sources, including satellite images and in-site sensors. To have a global understanding of what services are available and where, we need to deploy OGC CS-W compliant services to multiple locations at multiple levels. Although we strive to provide every stakeholder with a global view of a geospatial data source that might be interesting, and although we enable them to access these data sources via a standard interface, we will limit their capabilities based on their specific roles. In addition, the core geospatial information must be provided and maintained by the authoritative data providers since this fundamental data needs to be accurate, dynamically updated and shared across the entire emergency management community.

Crowdsourcing

As a part of broad Web 2.0 technologies, geospatial Web services could expand the scope and capacity of emergency management by enabling people from all walks of life to participate in emergency management activities.

Raw geospatial information, especially satellite images, offers little if any value to non-geospatial experts in emergency management. It takes thorough processing, detailed analysis, careful mapping and accurate interpretation to create the required geospatial information that can be understood and used by regular users. To respond to the emergencies promptly, we often do not have enough spatial experts and computing resources at hand. Using geospatial Web services, domain experts across the world can provide high quality processing and analysis, and therefore participate in emergency management effort. For example, led by ImageCat Inc., an international consortium developed a "social networking tool" within Microsoft Virtual Earth, called Virtual Disaster Viewer (http://www.virtualdisasterviewer.com/), to enable dozens or even hundreds of earthquake experts to participate in evaluating the earthquake's impact and damage swiftly. Virtual Disaster Viewer uses User Generated Content (UGC) tool geotagging, along with the geospatial Web services offered by Virtual Earth, to associate damaged buildings with their locations in Microsoft Virtual Earth so that the experts can visually inspect them.

Immediately after a disaster, the victims often find that they themselves are the only resource available to respond to and recover from this disaster. We can use geospatial Web services along with popular User Generated Content (UGC) tools, including geotagging, GeoWIKI and GeoRSS, to enable and assist people with varying geospatial backgrounds in reporting emergencies, assessing damages, and validating information in the field. This greatly improves their ability to cope with disasters.

Crowdsourcing allows ordinary citizens and emergency management experts to share detailed information about various aspects of particular event, such as destroyed road surfaces and contaminated wells.

Incorporating user-generated content into the dynamic emergency management system is also an important component of our holistic approach. User-generated content can appear in multiple phases of emergency management: as a source of early warning information, real-time reports and feedback. The question is how to take advantage of user-generated content.

In summary, geospatial Web services will help establish a robust infrastructure to enable the secure, effective and rapid sharing of information among agencies across geographical boundaries, political jurisdictions and different phases of emergency management.

Information Flow

Geospatial Web services can help us build a distributed and collaborative platform that enables multi-directional information flow within the entire emergency management system. Many real deployments have demonstrated that geospatial Web services can reliably disseminate information without compromising quality or speed. The OGC Sensor Web Enablement (SWE) suite of standards provides a solid mechanism to provide critical information from the field to the EMCC.

When the infrastructure is heavily damaged by disasters, the information flow between the field and the EMCC can be very challenging. The sharing of information in the field among first responders from different organizations, and sometimes with organizations themselves affected by disasters, becomes crucial. Currently these organizations are often on different underlying hardware and software systems. Rapid progress in mobile computing makes it feasible to host lightweight geospatial Web services on first responders' mobile computing platforms. How-

ever, how to leverage geospatial Web services to facilitate communication among first responders and affected organizations and individuals is an interesting area to be further explored.

System of Services

Considering emergency management holistically favors a top-down approach for creating service inventories. This means that when we define and build individual services, we will ensure these services will be highly normalized, standardized and aligned with each other, and more importantly with the goal of the overall system.

Service Modeling

We need to recruit people with a high degree of expertise in emergency management to design and analyze business services to ensure that the scope and specification of the service accurately represent the business logic of the service and its reusability. For example, the subject matter experts can model different disasters, such as tsunami, chemical cloud dispersion, and terrorist attack, as different services. For each individual disaster, EMP can use its modeled service for training, deployment during an emergency and analysis of the consequences.

Functionality of Geospatial Web Services

In terms of functionality, there are three types that exist in emergency management systems: 1) Reference Services that provide their clients with fundamental geospatial information, including base maps, satellite images and demographic information; 2) Situational Services that dynamically provide information on the ground (for example, a bridge was just blocked by debris ten minutes ago); 3) Geoprocessing and Analysis Services that perform geospatial analysis on the collected data and provide insights to decision makers.

Core Services vs. Peripheral Services

To manage multiple incidents simultaneously and across geospatial and temporal spaces, we need to have numerous services with different functionality in the emergency management system. Broadly, they can be categorized into two types: core and peripheral services.

On the one hand, core services have global scope and actively interact with many other services. Core services need to be centrally and securely managed by the appropriate government agencies, as they provide the key core information to the entire emergency community. For example, a core service can be an OGC CS-W geospatial Web service keeping the catalog information for services offered by all utilities in one particular state.

On the other hand, peripheral services have local scope and only actively exchange information with partners within the proximity in terms of geography and administrative hierarchy. The mobile Web services deployed in the field are often peripheral services.

Service Inventory

To increase emergency management agility through wide-scale service composition and to enable increasingly high efficiency by repeatedly utilizing delivered services, we need to create a service inventory with a high percentage of services with strong reusability. The service inventory should have mechanisms to manage registration and repository of various services. It should also enable EMP to quickly discover desired off-the-shelf services, select them, and compose these services into a customized Service-Oriented emergency management solution.

Because of the complex and diversified nature of emergency management, this service inventory should contain a wide spectrum of services, including real-time monitoring, logging and advanced analytic services.

1. Real-time Monitoring Services: to gain comprehensive situational awareness, decision makers and first responders often need to access, process and visualize real time information. Only a fully integrated framework can maximize benefits from the real-time flow of information. Critical infrastructure players, including utility and telecommunication firms, have developed strong capacity in processing constantly changing business data sets, and they can share them with other partners in the emergency management community. For example, Supervisory Control and Data Acquisition (SCADA) systems offer real-time status information about a utility network, and this information has tremendous value for decision makers and first responders during and after an emergency. Any attempt to statically extract this kind of dynamic information could break the relationship between the spatiotemporal data and business data. This lost/broken relationship could seriously limit our ability to "connect the dots". To avoid this pitfall, we could encapsulate a SCADA system with OGC SOS services and participate in the collaboration with other services in the system in a real-time manner.

2. Logging Services: these services capture the information flow among stakeholders during the emergency response and recovery phases. A logging service can serve multiple purposes: 1) it will help establish accountability for participating organizations, and help in later evaluation of these organizations' performance during these two phases; 2) it can analyze the pattern of information flow and help identify gaps in the information flow and improve the effectiveness of the overall system; 3) it will provide a rich source of real-world material for training and education institutes, including the FEMA Emergency Management Institute (http://training.fema.gov/). To implement this, we

need to create detailed log information from geospatial Web services and non-geospatial Web services that participate in emergency management.

3. Analytic Services: these services perform advanced analysis on the information collected from other services. With the involvement from subject matter experts, these services will help us "connect the dots" and thus provide critical support for decision-making.

4. Mobile Web Services: there are two practical usages of mobile Web services (Hirsch, Kemp, & Ilkka, 2006, p. 2). First, mobile devices can act as Web service clients. In an emergency management context, EMP can use mobile device to access geospatial Web services and gain situational awareness. Secondly, mobile devices can offer Web services to other service consumers, including a Web service client running on another mobile device. This is the case when a first responder provides information collected in the field to the EMCC or exchanges situational data with another first responder from a different organization.

5. Portal Services: these services dynamically bring information from other services together, and present relevant information coherently to other services or clients. Depending on the system needs and the performance requirement, these portal services can be flexibly reconfigured on the fly.

Service Composition

Web services, including geospatial Web services, are often designed to perform one particular set of tasks. Based on the nature of individual emergency and available emergency management services, we need to identify suitable Web services and use service composition to create a feasible solution. The capabilities of different services would be published and broadcasted so that all appropriate service consumers can dynamically find them and bind them into their overall solutions if needed.

This standard publish-find-bind model is instrumental in enabling an individual EMCC to build a customized Web services-centric emergency management solution based on the nature of the individual emergencies. Note that the severity and scope of emergencies can dictate the number and the scope of services available to one particular EMCC.

When we consider service composition, we should ensure that the entire system must operate independently of information sources. This will improve the viability of the system in the event that a key data source becomes unavailable.

Service composition often calls for a chain of services to implement certain functionality. The length and complexity of the service chain could impede the timely delivery of critical information; hence, these two aspects need to be evaluated during the service composition design.

Service Deployment

Due to the scale and complexity of emergency management, we should develop automatic tools that facilitate service deployments. In addition, the environment for emergency management is complex and often not stable. We could deploy the same service to different locations simultaneously. This designed redundancy would help increase the robustness of the overall system, and also improve information availability during emergencies.

Service Evolution

The designed interoperability will enable service developers to readily replace one service implementation with another for technical or business reasons.

Workflow Considerations

We need to analyze the existing business processes in various emergency management organizations and derive a generic process model from them. With this model in place, we could develop tools capable of establishing an end-to-end information flow with Web services for emergency management in the most automatic fashion possible. For example, once a certain predefined threshold is reached or a certain event occurs, the workflow of a planned action plan could be launched automatically, including electronically requesting data, automatically monitoring key measurements and notifying key stakeholders.

We need to provide tools to incorporate emergency management practices into the everyday workflow of related professionals, including EMP, city planners, land developers and others. Establishing a holistic end-to-end service management workflow will certainly increase the depth and overall effectiveness of services.

We need to incorporate the emergency management mechanism into the day-to-day work process, especially in the key organizations in emergency management. Currently, complex relationships exist among emergency management organizations, but they only become active during the extraordinary circumstances of an emergency. During the emergency response and recovery phases, an enormous information flow occurs among the multiple organizations involved. The scale of this information flow far exceeds the normal flow. However, the communication platform and process should be tightly incorporated into the normal daily work process; otherwise, it will become impossible to communicate and coordinate at the critical time of an emergency.

For long-term purposes, it becomes possible to create an application by incorporating multiple services into a single workflow. This will make it easy to adjust application functionality based on needs because services can be added to or removed from the workflow dynamically.

Security

While we have been arguing for an open platform for emergency management, we do recognize the strong need to protect information and business processes for individual organizations, especially

government agencies. While each organization has its own security infrastructure and mechanisms, we need a system-wide multi-level security mechanism to enable each organization to control how to share sensitive information with different partners.

Using geospatial Web services as building blocks for the proposed emergency management system provides us with a comprehensive yet generic security model – the Web Services Security framework that aims to utilize existing security mechanisms. Established by the Organization for the Advancement of Structured Information Standards (OASIS), this framework consists of several international standards: WS-Security, WS-Policy, WS-Trust, WS-Privacy, WS-Authorization, WS-Federation and WS-SecureConversation.

Our task becomes how to model our security framework based on these standards and how to ensure that information will be displayed securely based on role and security clearance requirements. OGC (ERDAS, 2008) has worked with its sponsors to ensure that its geospatial Web services standards can be deployed within the most stringent of security paradigms, including the Department of Defense PKI security framework. If extra security and higher performance are required, our system is also capable of providing dedicated Web services on the dedicated communication network.

FUTURE WORK

As we have discussed in the previous sections, geospatial Web services have great potential for emergency management. However, there are still some issues that need to be carefully addressed in order to improve the effectiveness of geospatial Web services in emergency management. In this section, we will briefly discuss some of these issues.

Using SOA governance to align geospatial Web services with the underlying business processes is a major issue. Organizational and technological factors are vital and intertwined in developing a successful emergency management system. Organizational factors often provide the purpose for technological factors, and to some extent they dictate the effectiveness of the emergency management effort; on the other hand, technological factors delineate the scope of organizational factors, and to some extent they determine the efficiency of the emergency management effort.

It is apparent that technological advances, such as geospatial Web services, are in themselves insufficient to overcome many obstacles, including endemic organizational problems, which have held back past efforts. As discussed in (Alegre, Sassier, Pierotti & Lazaridis, 2005), key stakeholders, including government agencies, infrastructure service providers and end users, need to work in concert to develop a shared vision of an organizational model that is valid for multiple thematic issues of emergency management.

Once this model is in place, we need to develop SOA governance that consists of policies and procedures to enable relevant organizations to manage and monitor service creation and usage, and then ensure that these services operate within the appropriate organizational and architectural constraints. Under the guidance of SOA governance, reusable Web services, including geospatial Web services, could be shared effectively across different processes, organizations and areas to realize their full value for emergency management. The loosely coupled nature of geospatial Web services will not only make them easier to be deployed into an emergency system, but this could also be instrumental in facilitating the evolution of this shared operational model.

We need to adopt a standardized approach across the board in emergency management. While the underlying Web services and particularly geospatial Web services are standards-centric, most business process and protocols have not been fully developed. The lack of standards can hinder collaboration across levels from community, local, state, federal to international. Political leaders at all levels should support the International Organiza-tion for Standardization (ISO), along with other regional and national organizations, in initiatives on standardization. Of course, these standards need to be refined continuously to counter the ever-changing landscape of emergencies.

In addition, there is a need for a standards-based Ontology. Having common terminology is essential to ensuring efficient and clear communication. Since people and organizations participating in emergency management come from very different backgrounds, establishing a standards-based common ontology can enhance effective and efficient communication for EMP from various organizations. This ontology will bring the interoperability of an emergency management system from a syntactical level to a semantic level. It will also help geospatial Web services realize their potential in emergency management.

While many research works, prototype systems and pilot programs have proven the effectiveness of using geospatial Web services in emergency management systems (Open Geospatial Consortium, 2007b), we still need a large-scale deployment to verify fundamental benefits discussed earlier and to identify shortcomings that need to be further addressed.

Although geospatial Web services are mainly infrastructure technologies, client-side usability is essential to any successful implementation. This has been demonstrated by the great success of Google Map and Google Earth. When we work on usability, we simply cannot assume EMP to be traditional GIS experts with deep knowledge about spatial information. We need to assist system usability designers in analyzing user needs for displaying and processing information, and to provide underlying generic Web services to facilitate easier and more intuitive operations for end users. Emerging geo-annotation tools, including GeoNote, can be used for this purpose.

The last issue we want to discuss here is data authenticity, which is critical to emergency management. Authentic data leads to knowledge that is vital for decision-making, problem-solving and planning. This becomes a major issue when we incorporate user-generated content into the system. While this kind of data brings real-time and rich (and sometimes the only available) information to emergency management, verifying the accuracy of the information will be a challenging task. One possible approach is to use data from different sources to either mutually confirm or deny. For example, for a particular event, different organizations often have similar observations to support each other; but their observations are significantly different, this will create doubts about the authenticity of the observations. Another approach is to develop a model to dynamically adjust authenticity for each data source. For example, the initial authenticity value of one particular data source may be very low or zero when it first starts to provide data, but when its data is verified over the time, the authenticity value of that data source can increase. However, if its data is proven to be wrong, its authenticity value can decrease.

CONCLUSION

As we move toward a "Risk Society" (Beck, 1992), managing various emergencies to minimize human, social and economic loss becomes one basic function of our society that requires great collaboration across the board from regular citizens to international organizations. Information technologies have been crucial in managing emergencies. Geospatial technologies, in particular, have been proven to be one of cornerstones of emergency information management.

The advancements in geospatial technologies, geospatial Web services and its embodied Service-Oriented Architecture methodology deliver the interoperability that is sorely needed by emergency management professionals. Geospatial Web services, especially ones standardized by the Open Geospatial Consortium (OGC), are state-of-the-art, platform independent and language neutral. They are poised to be powerful tools to greatly improve the efficiency and effectiveness of emergency management. In this chapter, we have discussed how geospatial Web services can be used in all phases of emergency management: mitigation, preparedness, response and recovery. We have especially argued that only through a holistic approach can the full potential of geospatial Web services be realized in emergency management.

In reality, the use of geospatial Web services in emergency management has only begun to be explored. While small-scale pilot projects and prototype systems have shown great promise, achieving the full potential of geospatial Web services requires continuous involvement and dedicated work from the research community, practitioners and especially government agencies. There are many issues that need to be addressed before we can see the large-scale deployment of geospatial Web services in emergency management. We need to develop practical utility tools and best practices to enable the emergency management community to reap the benefits provided by geospatial Web services.

We also need to recognize that technological advancement, including in geospatial Web services, is by itself alone is far from sufficient. There are many organizations participating in emergency management, and different organizations have different motivations, such as government mandate, humanitarian need or commercial interests. These different perspectives directly lead to a variety of possibly competing or even conflicting interests. The control and ownership of shared Web services might become an issue. Without clear policies and agreement about cooperation, the interoperability provided by geospatial Web services is at risk of not being used properly or not being used at all.

ACKNOWLEDGMENT

This work was supported in part by the National Natural Science Foundation of China under Grant no. 90924025. We wish to thank Chuck Murray for his wonderful work and attention to detail in editing our chapter. The authors also appreciate the encouragement and helpful comments from the editor of this book, Professor Peisheng Zhao, and anonymous reviewers.

REFERENCES

Alegre, C., Sassier, H., Pierotti, S., & Lazaridis, P. (2005). A new geo-information architecture of risk management. In Oosterom, P., Zlatanove, S., & Fendel, E. M. (Eds.), *Geo-Information for Disaster Management* (pp. 543–550). Berlin: Springer. doi:10.1007/3-540-27468-5_38

Annoni, A., Bernard, L., Douglas, J., Greenwood, J., Laiz, I., & Lloyd, M. (2005). Orchestra: Developing a unified open architecture for risk management applications. In Oosterom, P., Zlatanove, S., & Fendel, E. M. (Eds.), *Geo-Information for Disaster Management* (pp. 1–17). Berlin: Springer. doi:10.1007/3-540-27468-5_1

Beck, U. (1992). *Risk society: Towards a new modernity*. London: Sage Publications Ltd.

Canadian Geospatial Data Infrastructure Architecture Working Group. (2005). *The Canadian Geospatial Data Infrastructure Architecture Description Version 2.0*. Retrieved Dec. 11, 2009, from http://www.geoconnections.org/publications/tvip/arch_E/CGDI_Architecture_final_E.html

Diehl, S., & Heide, J. (2005). Geo Information Breaks through sector think. In Oosterom, P., Zlatanove, S., & Fendel, E. M. (Eds.), *Geo-Information for Disaster Management* (pp. 85–108). Berlin: Springer. doi:10.1007/3-540-27468-5_7

ERDAS, Inc. (2008). *Open Geospatial Consortium (OGC) interoperability: A requirement for critical infrastructure protection and homeland security*. White Paper. Retrieved from http://www.erdas.com/LinkClick.aspx?fileticket=TUGcmFQTFBg%3d&tabid=132&mid=540

Hirsch, F., Kemp, J., & Ilkka, J. (2006). *Mobile Web services: Architecture and implementation*. West Sussex, UK: John Wiley & Sons Ltd. doi:10.1002/9780470017982

Horswell, C., & Hegstrom, E. (2005, Sep. 29). Evacuation lessons come at high cost: 107 lives. *Houston Chronicle*. Retrieved from http://www.chron.com/disp/story.mpl/front/3374468.html

Hsu, S. S. (2006, April 14). Waste in Katrina response is cited: Housing aid called inefficient in audits. *Washington Post*. Retrieved from http://www.washingtonpost.com/wp-dyn/content/article/2006/04/13/AR2006041302159.html

Johnson, R. (2000). GIS Technology for disasters and emergency management. *An ESRI White Paper*. Retrieved November 1, 2009, from http://www/esri.com/library/whitepapers/pdfs/disaster-mgmt.pdf

Kim, S., Shekhar, S., & Min, M. (2008). Contraflow transportation network reconfiguration for evacuation route planning. *IEEE Transactions on Knowledge and Data Engineering*, 20(8), 1–15. doi:10.1109/TKDE.2007.190722

Leganza, G. (2006, Dec. 12). Why Is SOA hot in government? *Forrester Inc.* Retrieved from http://www.forrester.com/rb/Research/why_is_soa_hot_in_government/q/id/40673/t/2

Maiyo, L., Köbben, B., & Kerle, N. (2009). Collaborative post-disaster damage mapping via Geo Web Services. In Konecny, M., Zlatanova, S., Bandrova, T., & Friedmannova, L. (Eds.), *Cartography and Geoinformatics for early warning and emergency management: towards better Solutions (Joint symposium of ICA working group on CEWaCM and JBGIS Gi4DM)* (pp. 386–395). Brno, Czech Republic: Masaryk University.

Miller, J. (2004, July 02). *DHS weaves geospatial data into its enterprise architecture*. Retrieved from http://gcn.com/articles/2004/07/02/dhs-weaves-geospatial-data-into-its-enterprise-architecture.aspx

NIEM Program Management Office. (2007). *Introduction to the National Information Exchange Model*. Retrieved from http://www.niem.gov/files/NIEM_Introduction.pdf

Open Geospatial Consortium, Inc. (2006). *OGC vision, mission, & goals*. Retrieved on December 1, 2009 from http://www.opengeospatial.org/ogc/vision

Open Geospatial Consortium, Inc. (2007a). *How OGC membership helps organizations involved in homeland security*. Retrieved from http://www.opengeospatial.org/ogc/markets-technologies/homeland-security

Open Geospatial Consortium, Inc. (2007b). *OGC Web services phase 4 demonstration*. Retrieved from http://www.opengeospatial.org/pub/www/ows4/index.html

Open Geospatial Consortium, Inc. (2009). *OGC Web services phase 6 demonstration*. Retrieved from http://www.opengeospatial.org/pub/www/ows6/web_files/ows6.html

Rajabalinejad, M. (2009). A systematic approach to risk mitigation. In Konecny, M., Zlatanova, S., Bandrova, T., & Friedmannova, L. (Eds.), *Cartography and Geoinformatics for early warning and emergency management: towards better solutions (Joint symposium of ICA working group on CEWaCM and JBGIS Gi4DM)* (pp. 386–395). Brno, Czech Republic: Masaryk University.

Reznik, T., & Hynek, Z. (2009). Data management in crisis situations through WFS-T Client. In Konecny, M., Zlatanova, S., Bandrova, T., & Friedmannova, L. (Eds.), *Cartography and Geoinformatics for early warning and emergency management: towards better solutions (Joint symposium of ICA working group on CEWaCM and JBGIS Gi4DM)* (pp. 386–395). Brno, Czech Republic: Masaryk University.

The White House Blog. (2010, January 5). *The urgency of getting this right*. Retrieved from http://www.whitehouse.gov/blog/2010/01/05/urgency-getting-right

Ülgen, S. (2005). Public participation Geographic Information Sharing systems for community based urban disaster mitigation. In Oosterom, P., Zlatanove, S., & Fendel, E. M. (Eds.), *Geo-Information for Disaster Management* (pp. 1427–1434). Berlin: Springer. doi:10.1007/3-540-27468-5_98

United Nations General Assembly. (1989, December 22). *Resolution 236 session 44*. Retrieved Nov 15, 2009, from http://www.un.org/Docs/journal/asp/ws.asp?m=A/RES/44/236

United States, Federal Emergency Management Agency. (May, 2001). *Information Technology Architecture Version 2.0: The Road to e-FEMA, Volume 1*. Retrieved from http://www.fema.gov/pdf/library/it_vol1.pdf

Waugh, W. L. Jr. (1994). Regionalizing emergency management: Counties as state and local Government. *Public Administration Review, 54*, 253–258. doi:10.2307/976728

Weiser, A., & Zipf, A. (2007). *Web service orchestration of OGC Web services for disaster management. Geomatics Solutions for Disaster Management* (pp. 239–254). Berlin: Springer.

Yu, H.-J., Lee, Z.-H., Ye, C.-F., Chung, L.-K., & Fang, Y.-M. (2009) *OGC®: sensor Web enablement application for debris flow monitoring system in Taiwan*. Retrieved Nov 1, 2009, from OGC website http://portal.opengeospatial.org/files/?artifact_id=34126

KEY TERMS AND DEFINITIONS

Emergency Management: It is the continuous process by all related government agencies, communities, groups and individuals to minimize the impact of natural and human-caused disasters. It generally consists of four phases: mitigation, preparedness, response and recovery.

Holistic Emergency Management: Using interoperable Web Services technologies, including Geospatial Web Services standardized by OGC, this proposed approach aims to create a comprehensive understanding of various aspects of emergency information across the four phases of emergency management so that individuals, communities and government agencies in different functional areas and at different levels can more effectively manage both natural and human-caused disasters as a whole.

Mitigation: In Emergency Management, mitigation encompasses proactive activities that assess vulnerabilities and that design and implement measures to avoid, or reduce the severity of, emergencies.

OGC Geospatial Web Services: These are a set of Web Services formulated and standardized by Open Geospatial Consortium to provide geospatial related services; they include Catalog Service for Web (CS-W), Web Coverage Service (WCS), Web Feature Service (WFS), WMS (Web Map Service) and more.

Preparedness: In Emergency Management, preparedness refers to measures and activities in planning, training, inter-agency collaboration and community education before emergencies strike.

Response: In Emergency Management, response encompasses activities that provide immediate emergency assistance for victims, stabilize the situation, mitigate concomitant incidents and initiate the recovery operations right after an emergency occurs.

Recovery: In Emergency Management, recovery refers to activities that return the community to a normal or better quality of life after an emergency.

SOA: It stands for Service-Oriented Architecture. For historical reasons, it is used here as synonymous with Service-Oriented Computing, which applies various service-orientation principles to realize interoperability across its paradigm.

Web Services: Web Services are web-based applications that use open standards to dynamically interact with other web-based applications to achieve interoperability. Web Services are platform neutral, and have been widely deployed to facilitate interoperability across different hardware platforms, software architectures and programming languages.

Chapter 18
A SOA–Based System for Territory Monitoring

Elena Roglia
Turin University, Italy

Rosa Meo
Turin University, Italy

ABSTRACT

This chapter outlines the functionalities of a system that integrates sensor data transmitted by a fleet of unmanned aircrafts for territorial surveillance and protection from natural disasters.

Some functions of the system are based on the Service Oriented Architecture paradigm (Erl, 2005) and follow Open Geospatial Consortium (OGC) standards (Open Geospatial Consortium) in the representation of geographical data in a multidimensional, spatiotemporal view.

Next is a presentation of the complete system architecture, followed by a discussion of the details of the various services. Amongst these services, management and simulation of tactical planning, management of data and streaming video, the system also presents a service for the annotation of the interested spatial objects. Annotation deploys the web services (Alonso, Casati, Kuno, & Machiraju, 2004) exported by OpenStreetMap (OpenStreetMap) with the purpose to exploit the on-line information sources continuously updated by the social networks communities.

INTRODUCTION

In the last ten years the Piedmont region, as like many other regions in Italy and in the world, have been subjected to an increased rate of natural

DOI: 10.4018/978-1-60960-192-8.ch018

disasters due to frequent episodes of extreme and severe weather conditions that cause floods, landslides, windstorms, fires, earthquakes and tidal waves. In these circumstances, agencies that deal with civil protection need to react promptly and therefore must continuously monitor for just such emergencies and the environment conditions. Furthermore, in regions in which industrial and agricultural activities take place there is a strong need of environmental surveillance to guarantee protection against occurrences of water pollution, unauthorized waste disposal and dumping of dangerous materials.

The case study addresses the geo-spatial services provided by the central station of the SMAT project[1]. SMAT is a distributed system that applies advanced monitoring of the territory for the prevention and control of a wide range of natural events (floods, landslides, fires) and also for environment protection against human intervention (traffic, urban planning, pollution and cultivation). The system will operate within the integrated organizational structures already in place (institutional or commercial) and will provide information in real time to the authorities responsible for civil protection and intervention in case of an emergency. Examples of these organizations are the government bodies of the Piedmont Region, Provinces, Civil Protection, municipality and ARPA (the Regional Agency for the Prevention and the Environment).

SMAT has the aim to perform territory surveillance by means of Unmanned Aircraft Systems (UAS). SMAT is a *system of systems* since it controls and coordinates at least three different platforms, each responsible of a fleet composed by specific typology of Unmanned Aircraft Vehicle (UAV). A UAV is equipped with different payload sensors (radar, hyper-spectral, EO, infrared) that will download streaming video of the target territory. Each UAV will operate at different altitudes and thus obtain different benefits in terms of speed and persistence. The operative centers of each UAS (known as Control Station, CS), are already present on the territory and will exchange information with a Supervision and Coordination Station (SS&C).

Figure 1 shows the main components involved in the SMAT project. The aerial components are constituted by three different UAVs. The ground components are constituted by three control stations that are responsible for each UAV tactical

Figure 1. The SMAT architecture

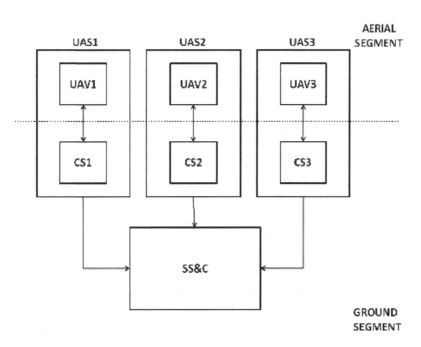

control (flight operations, sensor activities), data gathering and data transmission to the SS&C station.

The requirements that the system is called to satisfy are numerous and must respond to different problems and needs.

The goal of the system will be to perform a surveillance of areas subject to natural disasters and a more general surveillance of areas subject to human intervention. These goals require establishing a system able to manage a variety of missions that differ in topics and scenarios. According to the action lines foreseen by the mission (floods, landslides, pollution and aeronautics) the system operator will be able to retrieve, quickly and accurately, relevant data for the mission goal from separate sources (images, video, files, and web). The system should be able to support the integration of various sources of information coming from the different CS. Each UAV, equipped with a set of sensors specific for the singular mission, downloads to its ground control station a large set of information: telemetry data on vehicle position and asset, the sensor images and video of the territory. In turn, each CS communicates to the SS&C the received data (see Figure 1). As regards to data communication links, each ground control station will connect to SS&C with a high performance, dedicated and very efficient link due to the large volume of data that should be provided in near-real-time to the SS&C operators.

The system in general should provide its operators the information necessary to manage and coordinate the mission plans of multiple UAVs making them coexist and collaborate. To this purpose the system should interface with multiple UAS. At the same time, the operative modes of the different UAV platforms should be left independent and autonomous. In fact, each UAS consists of an already existing and complex system that differs from the others by proprietary implementation choices such as, flight control mode, sensor activation during the flight, sensor

configuration, data storage and the data transmission mode to the ground, etc.

The SS&C system should support the work of multiple operators. There are operators that prepare the mission of each single UAV and generate a mission plan, operators that control the mission execution by monitoring in near-real-time the mission video and images, operators that post-process the data from the mission and generate mission reports and final users from the civil protection force who elaborate the history of the data and plan the next missions goals.

The operators can provide additional maps with annotations, metadata and accompanying files extracted from external sources (such as the web). For these purposes the system must perform data storage, guarantee data persistence and be able to provide both a geo-spatial and a temporal reference to the stored information. The requirements that show the presence of a spatiotemporal reference in the data, images and video downloaded by the sensors answer the need of data integration and near-real-time data fusion in a multi-dimensional context. Furthermore, the system must be able to present to all operators multimedia data both in 2D and 3D formats.

In conclusion the system operations have been categorized as follows:

Operations before mission start: SS&C is involved in the overall mission planning, in the allocation of the operational tasks to the UAS and in setting up communication links with relevant Authorities.

Operations during mission execution: SS&C is involved in monitoring the mission progress, in receiving collected data from UAS, in the communication with end users and in the update of the information stored. Additionally it must support the SS&C operator in his/her interaction with the system.

Operations after mission conclusion: After mission execution, SS&C will complete the second level exploitation of data that involves operations like image processing, orthorectification, image mosaiking, geospatial referencing, annotation and cartography metadata retrieval. It will disseminate its results and will issue a conclusive mission report.

POSSIBLE ROADMAPS TO ACHIEVE THE PROJECT OBJECTIVES

At a first look, in order to accomplish the project goals, a Service Oriented Architecture (SOA) (Erl, 2005) seems the perfect system architectural choice. Indeed, the project needs to integrate different independent systems, existing platforms and respond with a variety of services to different users' needs.

A SOA architecture is based on web services which are software components that can be called on demand. It can integrate different, autonomous systems for which interoperability is guaranteed. The single software applications become the components of a more complex system but at the same time the user requirements of the different applications are satisfied and integrated in a transparent way. Furthermore, a SOA approach to system development can produce a system that can be flexibly adapted to changing requirements and technologies. It offers easier maintenance and allows integrating a large number of functionalities that can be distributed.

Although software based on web services has all these desirable qualities, often these qualities come at the expense of a final system whose overall performance is not suitable to treat a large volume of data. This is due to the latency in communication over the web for the high volume of data that would be exchanged by the web services (using eXtensible Markup Language –XML (W3C XML)). These facts result in an unacceptable situation for a system dedicated to disaster monitoring that works in conditions in which data must be transmitted almost in real-time. Section on system implementation discusses web services that have been adopted in SMAT in post-mission activities.

They perform geospatial data annotation that does not have strict time requirements.

In the context of the system post-mission activity, geospatial web services have been largely adopted in SMAT for which SS&C has the role of a client application. Indeed, geospatial web services are self-contained, self–described applications that the client can publish, locate and invoke dynamically across the web. Geospatial web services allow an easy distribution of geospatial data and applications across platforms, operating systems and computer languages. Developers can easily integrate geospatial functionality and data into their custom applications. Geospatial web services are an immediate way to provide interoperability between applications and functionalities: thus are the corner stones in building modular and distributed GIS applications.

There are many Geospatial web services available on the web. Probably the best known are Google Maps (Google Maps) /Earth (Google Earth) and OpenStreetMap (OpenStreetMap).

These and other examples such as Yahoo Maps (Yahoo Maps) or MultiMap (MultiMap) can be used by any application that interfaces with the web. Although their interfaces are publicly available, their data, formats, and services are proprietary. In other words, they are defined, developed and owned by a commercial company. An apparent disadvantage is that if in the future the company decides to discontinue the service or obfuscate portions of data, external applications relying on them, would merely adapt to their decision.

Alternatively, Open Standards are created in an open, participatory process, where everyone interested can influence the standard. There is a set of such well-defined Open Standards for Geospatial Web services: the Open Web Services (OWS) of the Open Geospatial Consortium (Open Geospatial Consortium). For the above reasons, whenever possible, we use open source software components that adopt open standards in the implementation of the system. Examples include Geoserver (Geoserver) used for map visualization and feature rendering, OpenLayers (OpenLayers) used for dynamic map development and visualization, GeoExt (GeoExt) that enriches the map layout on the web, ExtJS (ExtJS) used to compose rich web applications. OpenGL (OpenGL), originally developed by Silicon-Graphics Inc is a de-facto multi-platform standard for computer graphics and provides a powerful processing environment to present images in 2D and 3D.

The remainder of this chapter is structured as follows.

Firstly an overview of the fundamental concepts behind geospatial web services is presented.

Secondly the architecture of the system followed by its implementation is described. Successively, existing problems in metadata integration for geospatial annotation are discussed. The same section presents our solution. It is based on the adoption of ontology for semantic data attribution and a categorization of the geospatial target areas based on mission action lines. The presentation of maps and features in a case study that monitors floods using WMS (OGC WMS) and WFS (OGC WFS) standards is discussed.

Finally we outline future research directions in which we present the emerging trends in the development of GIS services and SOA architectures. From this we can draw-out the conclusions in which we summarize the key benefits of the proposed architecture.

BACKGROUND

This section summarizes a few basic concepts of the Service Oriented Architecture (SOA) and includes some well-known projects in the UAS community which are related to our work. However, it should be noted that it is not possible to give a comprehensive description of SOA nor to mention all related projects given the limited available space of a chapter.

A Service Oriented Architecture (SOA) is an architectural model for building systems that focuses on the concept of service. A system built using the SOA philosophy consists of well-defined and independent services that reside on multiple processors within a network (e.g. the internal network of a company or a network between multiple companies or internet). Each service provides certain functionalities and can use other services made available, creating applications of greater complexity. The abstraction of SOA is not tied to any specific technology, but simply defines some properties, oriented to reuse and integration in a heterogeneous environment. Each service must be defined by an interface which is independent from the service implementation. It must therefore be defined in terms of its operations, regardless of the methods and technologies used to implement the operations. This makes the service platform- and operating system- independent. There are several benefits of this architecture.

From the users' perspective, a SOA setting is an open and interoperable environment, which is based on reusability and standardized components. Basically a SOA creates an infrastructure for application development. Furthermore, this architecture allows to increment interoperability between services and the system extensibility.

The SOA paradigm is based on loosely-coupled modules. These modules can be Web services that are orchestrated together by means of standard communication protocols, Web Service Description Language –WSDL (W3C WSDL), Simple Object Access Protocol –SOAP (W3C SOAP) and Universal Description Discovery and Integration –UDDI (Uddi XML). This Web Service technology communicates to its parties regardless of the platform and language implementation. It uses standard XML schemas, which provide well-formed data packages and conformity to consensus standards. In turn this provides a form of automatic information extraction and verification. The benefits of using Web services is that the user does not need to know how the services are built, but she/he only needs to know how to access them.

A Web Service communicates with Simple Object Access Protocol messages (SOAP) (Scribner & Stiver, 2000) which describe the packaging, encoding and exchange of structured information in a decentralized, distributed environment. In addition, it uses XML and HTTP (Berners-Lee, Fielding, & Frystyk, 1996) technologies to define a messaging framework.

Web Services are defined by four major elements of WSDL: *portType*, *message*, *types* and *binding*. *PortType* defines the operations provided by the Web Services and the involved messages. *Message* defines the operations data elements. *Types* are data types used by the Web Service. *Binding* defines the communication protocols. A Web Service is identified by an URI (Uniform Resource Identifier) (W3C URI) whose public interfaces and connections are defined and described by XML documents.

In recent years, there has been a growing diffusion of Web Services based on *Representational State Transfer* (REST) architecture. The term *Representational State Transfer* was introduced and defined in 2000 by Roy Fielding in his doctoral dissertation (Fielding, 2000). This architectural style was developed in parallel with the HTTP/1.1 protocol.

A RESTful web service (also called a RESTful web API) is a simple web service implemented using HTTP and the principles of REST.

A REST web service requires the following constraints:

1. Interfaces are limited to HTTP.
2. The set of operations supported by web services are defined by the HTTP methods: GET, DELETE, POST and PUT.
3. Messages can be encoded with URL encoding.
4. Service and service providers must be resources while a consumer can be a resource.

REST web services require little infrastructure support apart from standard HTTP and XML

processing technologies, which are now well supported by most programming languages and platforms. REST web services are simple and effective because HTTP is the most widely available interface, and it is good enough for most applications. In many cases, the simplicity of HTTP simply outweighs the complexity of introducing an additional transport layer (He, 2003).

The concept of Web Service implies an architectural model made of distributed objects (or applications), which are located in different parts of the network and platforms. By taking advantage of the Web Services technology, the obtained system is implemented according to SOA. To date, Web Services represent the best solution for the realization of a SOA on a large scale or on the Internet.

Within the proposed architecture we aim at the extraction and management of information (cartography, video and image data produced by each platform, free repository available on line) from the different, available data sources using standard based on web services. Basic principles are derived from the *Open Geospatial Consortium* (OGC) standardized OGC Web Services (OWS) such as Web Map Service (WMS) (OGC WMS), Web Feature Service (WFS) (OGC WFS) and Web Coverage Service (WCF) (OGC WFS). The use of open standards and distributed computing technologies in the proposed architecture enables heterogeneous resources (data, processing and computing power) interoperability, real-time data access and customized data delivery.

To be complete, hereinafter the main Web Services and main encoding specifications defined by the Open Geospatial Consortium are described. They are the key components for the proposed implementation. We must note that the use of Web Services is also widely used in the development of Spatial Data Infrastructure (SDI).

The term *Spatial Data Infrastructure* is often used to denote the relevant base collection of technologies, policies and institutional arrangements that facilitate the availability and access to spatial data. SDI provides a basis for spatial data discovery, evaluation, and application for users and providers. Due to the size of the organizations, one of the principles is that data and metadata are not managed centrally, but managed by the data originator/owner. Usually it is adopted at a government level to manage and share geospatial data via computer networks. The SDI provides a basis for users and providers within all levels of government, the commercial sector, the non-profit sector, academia and citizens (Global Spatial Data Infrastructure, 2004). OGC is active in the preparation of technical specifications for the construction of standard components in the implementation of a SDI. In this context, SMAT system could act the role of a single actor in an SDI.

Web Map Service (WMS)

This OGC specification defines the interactions between client and server applications for the delivery of maps from geographical data over HTTP. WMS provides different functions such as: *GetCapabilities* that allows to negotiate the protocol level for the client-server communication, *GetMap* that allows to obtain a map (typically in PNG, GIF or JPEG image format) specifying layers to display, styles, the spatial area to be displayed, image size and background color. It supports different file formats: raster data, vector data and Google Earth data. *GetFeatureInfo* is useful to discover which object is placed in a given location point and its spatial properties. WMS operations are invoked by submitting requests in the form of Uniform Resource Locators (URLs) (W3C URL). The content of these URLs depends on the operations and the parameters of the requests.

Web Feature Service (WFS)

This service operates at a level of *source code* of the geographical information. It allows the user to add, delete, update and retrieve features from a map,

find a feature definition (feature proper name and type) and lock features to prevent modification.

In WFS, objects are called spatial WFS Features. They have an identifier, one or more geometry types and attributes (Simple Features). WFS provides a *GetCapabilities* function analogous to the *GetCapabilities* in WMS, a *DescribeFeatureType* function that describes the FeatureType structure and a *GetFeature* function that extracts features of one or more FeatureTypes.

In addition it optionally carries out transactional operations on features like insertions, updates and deletions.

WFS returns original geographic data semantics in an XML notation called Geography Markup Language (GML) (OGC GML). GML provides encodings for many concepts including features, geometry, coordinate reference systems, topology, time and metrics.

Web Coverage Service (WCS)

This service defines a standard interface and operations that enable interoperable access to geospatial objects covering a geographical area or *coverage* (*GetCoverage*). It uses parameters directly related to the spatial and/or temporal dimensions of coverage. Furthermore this service shall implement the *DescribeCoverge* operation, in order to get the coverage descriptive information.

Geography Mark-Up Language (GML)

This is an XML standard language defined by OGC. It is used to exchange geographic data on the web and to store the semantics that a software application associates to the geometry representing some geographic object. Put simply, it can be expressed by a tag, a line representing a highway or a polygon representing a building. It is an encoding language of the responses provided by WMS, WFS and WFS-G (OGC WFS-G). Certain parts of the schema (Filter) are also used to set filters in the requests of WFS services. It is the standard format for Spatial Data Infrastructures (SDI).

Sensor Web Enablement (SWE)

This service enables the discovery, exchange and processing of sensor observations, as well as, tasking of the sensor systems (OGC SWE).

The functionality includes: discovery of sensor systems, determination of sensors capabilities and quality of measurements, access to sensor parameters that automatically allow software to process and georeference observations, retrieval in standard encodings of real-time or time-series observations and coverage, tasking of sensors to acquire observations of interest, subscription and publishing of alerts to be issued by sensors or sensor services based upon certain criteria.

Several standard interface and encodings for describing sensors and sensor observations have been built and prototyped. *Sensor Model Language* (SensorML), is a set of standard models and XML schemas for describing sensor systems and processes associated with sensor observations. *Observations & Measurements* (O&M) consists in general models and XML encodings for observations and measurements obtained by sensors. *Transducer Model Language* (TML) is a conceptual approach and XML encoding for supporting real-time streaming of observations and tasking commands from and to sensor systems. *Sensor Observation Service* (SOS) is an open interface for a service by which a client can obtain observations from a sensor and platform descriptions from one or more sensors. *Sensor Planning Service* (SPS) is an open interface for a service by which a client can determine the feasibility of collecting data from one or more sensors and submit a collection of requests to the sensors and configurable processes. *Sensor Alert Service* (SAS) is an open interface for a web service for publishing and subscribing to alerts from sensors or simulation systems. *Web Notification Service* (WNS) is an open interface

for a service by which a client may conduct asynchronous dialogues; message interchanges with one or more other services. Each UAS does not implement the communication with SS&C using this sensor web standard infrastructure. As previously mentioned, this decision is due to the high volume of exchanged data and the requirements of near real-time response of the SS&C to mission events (see Section entitled Possible Roadmaps to Achieve the Project Goals). As a consequence, SS&C does not implement web services related to sensor activity and does not use directly the above specifications.

Keyhole Markup Language (KML)

KML is largely inspired by GML. The difference is that GML is a pure data description language, leaving styling to SLDs and context documents. KML merges both data and portrayal instructions into a single file.

KML provides a way to link the existing geospatial information stored in a geographic database directly to Google Earth. By means of KML (OGC KML), users are allowed to use both a set of predefined tags, proper of KML, or to define custom tags as the attributes of the objects. Once described, the objects can be uniformly interpreted. This is an opportunity for the annotation of spatial objects and the addition of semantics to locations. This functionality, however, is in contrast with Geographic Markup Language (GML).

KML uses a tag-based structure with nested elements and attributes encoded using XML.

KML has a large number of features, from simple geometry markup, to 3-D models, image pyramids, camera views, and so on. One of the features of Google Earth is the possibility to record specific places or points of interest and give them appropriate symbols and labels. This allows the users to create and share maps with their own point of interests (called *placemarks)*. Each placemark is described by its name, a description (provided by a hypertext), the style, view (the desired place-mark location), altitude and a customizable icon.

Sharing information and data helps to provide near real time situational awareness and collect/display assessment data for operations. With this service, originally ideated with the purpose to transfer knowledge within a community, the SS&C user can evaluate and monitor changes in a situation.

KML allows sharing placemarks, shapes and folder data with other people; then, information can be saved to a web server or a network server. This allows a better accessibility to the data, an ease of distribution and automatic updates and a backup.

Volunteered Geographic Information (VGI)

VGI is a collection of tools that have the purpose to create, assemble, and disseminate geographic data provided voluntarily by individuals (Goodchild, 2007). An example of this phenomenon, also used in the SMAT project, is OpenStreet-Map. OpenStreetMap web site comes out from an open community project. It provides general map information and allows users to create online their own maps or contribute to edit and tag geographic information created by other users. VGI is a special case of the larger Web phenomenon known as user-generated content.

Semantic Interoperability and Metadata

Web services can communicate with each other via a platform-independent messaging protocol. When an enterprise begins using an SOA to integrate processes across diverse functional areas, a clear requirement is that service consumers must convert their local definitions to the definitions of the service provider to be able to interoperate with each other. Addressing these semantic concerns involves discovery how information is used

differently by each of the members in a trading partnership (or community), and how that information maps to the normative community view.

Currently, semantic interoperability solutions use a common ontology as a mediation layer in order to abstract data terms, vocabularies and information into a shareable distributed model. Mapping to ontology preserves the native semantics of the data and eliminates the need for custom-developed code.

However, any solution to semantic interoperability must accommodate the fact that the same data item may mean different things from different semantic viewpoint. The core element that is needed to support any semantic-based interoperability solution is metadata (Papazoglou, 2007). Over the last few years, different works on semantics and geo-ontologies have focused on semantic interoperability. These works include the role of ontology for spatiotemporal databases (Frank, 2003), the notion of semantic reference systems and the grounding of geographical categories (Kurhn, 2003), (Scheider, Janowicz, & Kuhn, 2009), semantics-based and context aware retrieval of geographic information (Lutz & Klien, 2006) and Semantic Geospatial Web services (Roman & Klien, 2007).

Ontologies are central to realizing the Semantic Web and Semantic Geospatial Web, as they formally specify concepts and their relationships and provide the means to create semantic metadata for objects (under the form of documents, data files, databases, etc.) (Perry, Sheth, & Arpinar, 2007). Metadata for geospatial web services can describe basic sources and simple authorship information. In addition metadata can describe the structure of geospatial data (vector or raster data) and their functional types (data conversion format). Furthermore, semantic metadata can describe the domain of geospatial data and geospatial services such as for example the thematic type for data (like for the population distribution) and functional domain types (like for land surface temperature estimation).

W3C has adopted Resource Description Framework (RDF) (W3C RDF) as the standard for the representation of semantic metadata. Metadata in RDF is encoded as statements about resources. A resource is identifiable by a Uniform Resource Identifier (URI) and described by attributes under the form of literals, i.e., values (e.g. Strings, Integers). Relationships in RDF, known as Properties, are binary relationships between two resources or between a resource and a literal, which take on the roles of Subject and Object, respectively. The Subject, Predicate and Object compose an RDF statement. It can be represented as a directed graph with typed edges and nodes. A directed edge labeled with the Property name connects the Subject to the Object.

RDF Schema (RDFS) (W3C RDFS) provides a standard vocabulary for schema-level constructs such as Class, SubClassOf, Domain, and Range. In addition, the Web Ontology Language (OWL) (W3C OWL) further extends RDFS by defining additional vocabulary for describing classes and properties (e.g. cardinality, disjointness property, etc). Other standards for the representation of ontologies are OWL-S (W3C OWL-S) and Semantic Web Service Language (SWRL) (W3C SWRL), (Peisheng, Yu, & Di, 2007)

The Web is becoming an increasingly important tool for data retrieval and information integration. To this purpose, vocabularies and comprehensive ontology datasets are required because they enable the disambiguation and alignment of other data and information.

LinkedGeoData (Auer, Lehmann, & Hellmann, 2009) is an effort to add a spatial dimension to the Web of Data/Semantic Web. LinkedGeoData uses the information collected by the OpenStreetMap project and makes it available as an RDF knowledge base according to the Linked Data principles.

The transformation and publication of the OpenStreetMap data according to these principles adds a new dimension to the Data Web. Thanks to this new dimension, spatial data can be retrieved and linked at a finer level of granularity. This enhancement enables a variety of Linked Data applications such as geo-data syndication or semantic-spatial searches.

Related Work on UAS Applications

In this section we review some projects that are the state of the art in UAS applications.

- ERAST - Environmental Research Aircraft and Sensor Technology (NASA Erast): a NASA Project, for the development and flight-demonstration of UAS for cost effective science missions (NASA). The project focuses primarily in the construction of an aircraft capable of operating in the rarefied stratosphere. The project also attempts to reduce the technical risks associated with developing avionics, structures, science payloads, solar cells and heat exchangers for piston engines that must operate at extreme altitudes.

- WRAP - Wildfire Research and Applications Partnership (NASA Wrap): a NASA project for the management of missions over the USA west coast for real-time fire monitoring. The project evolved a highly-integrated air-to-ground system of sensors, data systems and platforms for monitoring, processing and feeding meaningful, highly-intelligible data to wildfire incident commanders. WRAP project is focused on the evaluation and the improvement of data delivery (telemetry) to facilitate a rapid decision support mechanism for wildfire analysis.

The above two projects are more focused on developing materials and technologies for an efficient sensor data delivery rather than on defining a system architecture.

- SKY-EYE: a project for the design and the development of a prototype system that will support the operations of the Spanish regional fire-fighters (Pastor, Royo, Lopez, Barrado, Santamaria, & Prats, 2007). The project system architecture is a communication architecture oriented to mission management and information flow.

- DISMAR: a project for the development of a distributed system for monitoring and forecast of the marine environment and the integration of data from various observation platforms and modelling systems (Hamre & Éamonn, 2005). DISMAR is a web-based system designed to integrate and visualize a variety of data types, including satellite images, model fields and in situ data to monitor pollution events and harmful algal blooms. The next stage of this pan-European project is called InterRisk and will address the need to provide better access to information concerning the management of the natural and anthropogenic risk activities in Europe (Depledge, 2009).

Cited projects have similar goals to SMAT project but are less interested in an intensive use of the geospatial services provided by external sources.

Other projects, that involve the usage of UAS, represent new scientific fronts of application.

- The United Nations Peace-keeping activity: it had its first experience with UAS in Western Congo, with the purpose to help MONUC during the election period from June to November 2006. These UAS helped to spot and track illegal fire-arms transfer nearby the city by the two main parties (Roux).
- A SOA-based debris flow monitoring system was proposed by Lan and Kun (Lan-Kun, Yao-Min, Tien-Yin, Bing, & Bastian, 2009) to demonstrate how SOA helps debris flow disaster management and illustrates its performance when grid

computing is integrated into the software architecture.

- The Software Architecture of the Berkeley UAV Platform (Tisdale, 2006) was proposed as an effective architecture that allowed a team of UAS to collaboratively perform a set of missions. Proposed architecture consists of several independent processes that send UAV information (sensor data, telemetry, aircraft commands, payload tasks and command, etc.) to the ground station.

In addition we must mention a project that is not immediately related to SMAT but must be highlighted for the project scope of environment protection: Global Earth Observation System of Systems – GEOSS – launched by GEO (Group on Earth Observations) at G8 Summit in 2002. GEO is coordinating international efforts to build a public infrastructure based on an Internet portal. The purpose is to build a *system of systems* that provides the results on the monitoring of the changes in the global environment by several independent systems. It promotes also common technical standards to integrate into a coherent data set the measurements of the different instruments. This "system of systems" is aimed to support policymakers, resource managers, science researchers and many other experts and decision-makers.

All cited projects, similarly to the SMAT project, require a loose coupling between different components realized by the use of a SOA architecture. Some of them present also a real time data acquisition and distribution function and a system architecture oriented to mission management.

More generally the distinguishing issue in SMAT is that the goal of the mission could be very variable. As a consequence the operator could have the need to retrieve a variety of different information that is used in the annotation of the spatial objects of interest. Thus, the search of this kind of information on the web is justified because the web is kept in constant evolution by external organisms such as OpenStreetMap project and GoogleMaps. As we will see in Section on metadata integration for geospatial annotation, the information structure and its semantic are controlled through the usage of XML languages and ontologies over the tags.

ARCHITECTURE FOR THE SS&C

The architecture developed for the SMAT project is a high performance, high broad bandwidth architecture to support coupling archive and real-time geospatial data with scientific applications such as simulation, visualization and analytical software.

SS&C software components are designed around and deploy the services provided by a Geographical Information System (GIS). Web Services couple data assimilation tools with archived geospatial data.

Major Components of the Architecture

The architecture is constituted by a multi-tier system. It contains a client, a middleware and a data layer. Each layer has the role to control a specific category of software components: database services (GIS and DBMS), geo-processing services and user applications.

Data storage layer: The data storage layer answers the requests coming from the other layers. It prepares the multimedia content from metadata provided by the content repositories. The data tier provides all the actual data: both geo-spatial (vector, raster, relational) and other (e.g. documents, multimedia). In addition it can provide general, statistical and descriptive information on all the data by means of metadata.

The DBMS and GIS provide storage and persistence to the data: documents, images, multi-media files, maps, processed video, frames, reports, etc.

Geo-processing layer: The middleware tier provides the various computational services. This includes video and image processing, metadata search and update, retrieval of both data and services, retrieval of transformed data, maps and other content through a multi-dimensional reasoning and querying paradigm. In particular, the SS&C operator will explore and query the information in a multidimensional model whose principal dimensions are: time (at which the information such as images, video, etc, are gathered), space (which is the object of interest represented in the images), UAV, sensor (filming the spatial objects) and mission. Each of these dimensions is represented with descriptive characteristics.

For instance, time with the temporal hierarchy (day, month, year, etc); UAV with its type; Mission with the details on the various mission plans, such as the tasks by which it is composed and the relative constraints; Sensor with the operative mode, type, and applicable parameters; Space with its geospatial description.

The middleware tier provides services for data integration and data analysis to the user application layer.

In the context of the SMAT project this software layer essentially consists in the Supervision and Control Station of the system (SS&C).

User layer: It provides the GUI of the system. It is web-based and provides a range of functionalities such as querying the catalogues and viewing results (e.g., metadata and maps), performing spatial visualization, or system administration.

Figure 2 shows the main components involved in the proposed architecture. It explains in greater detail the services exposed by the different layers.

- The **Data Storage Layer** provides services for the centralized Database Storage, the File System Storage and a GIS database. The Services allow to archive, retrieve and manage all the data received, processed and generated in the SS&C (e.g. mission data, simulation and historical data). In ad-

Figure 2. System architecture

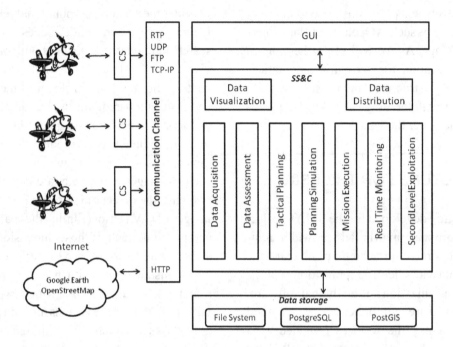

dition, it provides the capability for cataloguing images and data in terms of spatial data indexing using a GIS database. The data storage services are a neutral data interface for the exchange of information between the various components of the SS&C. These services provide a view on the data which simplifies the task of data retrieval and storage and is less prone to errors.

The Data storage contains a Common Data Model that defines a singular common representation of the content of the Data Storage Layer. A simplified UML schema of the Common Data Model relative to the tactical planning is described in Figure 3 in the Section on System Implementation. The data model provides all the definitions and relationships among the relevant objects in SMAT including the products of post mission processing such as videos, frames, annotated maps, mission reports, etc.

The **SS&C** offers different services which need to receive and provide data to the data storage services. They are described in the following.

- The **Data Acquisition function** implements the capabilities to manage the simultaneous reception of the data sent by the UAS through the associated network connections. This function exchanges information with the Communication Channel and the Data Storage Function. Data received through the Communication Channel are sent, in parallel, to the Data Storage Layer and to the Real Time Monitoring Function of the SS&C. This function is crucial also for the annotation process because through it data from the web is retrieved.

- The **Data Assessment function** provides the capabilities to perform detailed post mission analysis and mission report generation of the received and processed data, retrieving them from the SS&C archive.

Figure 3. The essential components of the data model for the tactical planning

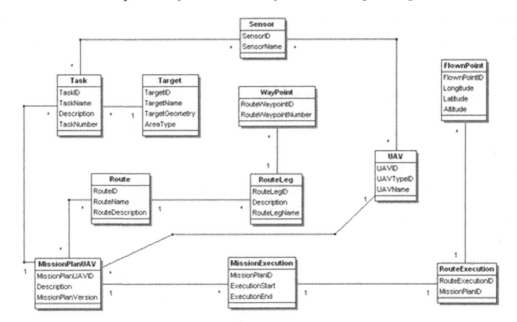

- The **Tactical Planning** function supports the SS&C user to develop the mission plan which in turn, is the overall strategic plan of multiple UAS working together. This function includes: a *MissionPlan manager* involved in the mission plan preparation, validation, transmission, import and modification during the negotiation between the SS&C and the single CS; a *TaskEditor* that graphically supports the user in the definition, preparation and allocation of the necessary resources for the task; a *Scheduler* that provides graphical capabilities to support the user in the monitoring, creating, allocating and the insertion of a task in the context of the whole mission plan; a *Decisional Support* block that contains all the software, file and data that are required for the planning process and the required consistency checks, an *Operations Coordination Function* that provides the capabilities necessary to support all the coordinated activities (i.e. Voice Coordination Capabilities, Time Management Systems displays and events countdown, Anomaly Reporting and Tracking System and Console log system).

- The **Planning Simulation Function** provides the capabilities to simulate the mission plans in order to present to the operator, the results of the planned monitoring task and perform if necessary additional checks for its validation against the mission objectives. The Planning Simulation provides support for the preparation, analysis and/or modification, for the operations team training and users' analysis and visualization.

- The **Mission execution function** communicates with the Data Storage and the Data Acquisition functions to find all the necessary information to be sent to the function of Data Visualization in order to perform a monitoring of the current mission.

- The **Real Time Monitoring** provides computational capabilities, i.e. algorithms used to process the received data, and generate additional data products that enhance the information level of the acquired data for the users benefit. In particular, through the use of openGL library (OpenGL), a cartographic overlay on video images with data from sensor is performed.

- The **Second Level Exploitation Function** provides functionality for data comparison and correlation, data conversion, data representation, Digital Terrain Model (DTM) generation and annotation. All second level exploitation algorithms are developed in such a way to allow re-processing of the data under operator request. The new generated data products must be independent from the initial product, in the sense that they are stored and managed independently. The algorithms that provide the computational capabilities for image processing and the sensor data processing steps include for example a different post processing activity like image mosaiking, refined footprint computation and mission coverage area computation. All second level exploitation algorithms, when applicable, shall provide the capability to the operator to monitor the progress and execution of the processing, providing messages and notification on its status.

- The **Data Distribution Function** provides the data collection (i.e. mission major events, failures and problems occurred, operational area description, mission plan data, recorded video and images, etc.) and report generation functionalities.

- The **Data Visualization Services** provide to the operator all the Graphical User Interface (GUI) capabilities necessary to perform the assigned task, namely Real Time Mission Monitoring, Post Mission Data Processing and Mission Planning. A Navigator Panel drives the operator in selecting the proper data visualization applications. Data Visualization services allow a certain number of functionalities: *2D or 3D Tactical Map* provide the capability to present in a geographical map the mission evolution in terms of the UAV real time position, planned trajectory and mission targets. Furthermore the 3D Tactical Map provides 3D visualization of the environment characterized by the following layered information: realistic morphologic terrain description, main buildings, rivers, streets, electrical grid, railways, trees and airports.

The **Communication Channel** is used to manage the interchange of information between the CSs and SS&C and between SS&C and the Web.

In particular, telemetry data is transmitted in synchronous mode from the CSs to the SS&C through a TCP/IP port that communicates with a Telemetry Acquisition Functions. Files are exchanged in asynchronous mode between CSs and SS&C using a FTP manager. Video is transmitted in synchronous mode using a RTP/UDP port that communicates with a Video Data acquisition Function.

All data collected from these three functions are sent to the data storage functions.

In addition the Video data acquisition function sends data also to the real time monitoring function.

The following describes the **user layer** (GUI) components.

Data presentation: A single access point provides, via a web portal, the information provided by Data Visualization and Data Distribution services. The portal is the front-end of the system providing access to all its features through the facilities of a web browser. The key components of the portal are:

- The *map viewer* provides the interface for the interaction with GIS.
- The *notes viewer* displays user interpretation notes and abstracts (including legend graphics) of the map layers.

- The *updates viewer* displays abstracts of the most recent data sets available for a geographic area of interest (definable by the user).
- The *profile client* allows the user to set preferences for geographic bounding boxes, map projection, and layer groups; furthermore, it allows the users to bookmark their selection for future and easy access.
- The *metadata browser* provides an interface to the metadata catalogue which in turn also provides links for downloading data (when available).

Data visualization and dashboard: The engine assigned for the representation of the analysis results on geographical maps is created with dynamic data navigation capabilities. Among other things, the engine will give the possibility of displaying several business indicators on the same map, in order to dynamically aggregate data according to different dimensions at the chosen hierarchical levels, and browse by drill-down into the dimension hierarchies or cross navigation in order to expose details or to compare data from a statistical viewpoint.

System Implementation

The following details the implementation of the SMAT system.

The database layer uses PostgreSQL (PostgreSQL Global Development Group) DBMS with the PostGIS (PostGIS) extension that natively supports GIS data types and operations.

The Common Data Model that we have designed should provide all the relationships among the relevant objects for the SMAT project. This should allow the management and storage of the data generated by the tactical planning function (mission plan for a single UAV, sensors, tasks, the composition of the route in terms of segments, Way-points, etc.), by SS&C (processed video, reports, GIS referenced objects) and received from each UAS or the SS&C system (images, files, videos, data on mission execution, data on the effective route execution, etc.).

Figure 3 exemplifies the UML schema of the main concepts of the data model stored in the SS&C, in particular regarding the mission of the UAS. For each of the data model concepts, the data storage layer offers services for creation, access and update.

The *MissionPlanUAV* entity contains the details of the mission for a single UAV. Each individual *MissionPlanUAV* contributes to the overall mission plan which is contained in the entity *MissionPlan* that contains the details of the overall Mission.

The SS&C data model includes the definition of *Task* as the specific activity to be performed for each *Target* area, the specific object of interest for the surveillance activity. A *MissionPlanUAV* contains different tasks that span the entire route covered by each UAV. *Tasks* are ordered from the take-off to the landing and different sensors may be required to accomplish a task.

The *Route* entity details the proposed planned route to be flown during the mission execution.

Way-points, *Flown-points* and *Target* areas are the objects that constitute the spatial dimension of the proposed data model. These objects could be located at the different levels of the spatial hierarchy that describes the spatial dimension. In the following sections a spatial hierarchy derived from the digital cartography and adopted for the present project will be described. Furthermore, way-points, flown-points and target areas are the main spatial objects whose neighbourhood constitutes the goal of the query capabilities of a GIS and of the annotation by means of the web services of OpenStreetMap.

Figure 4 presents the main activity diagram. It explains how the SOA architecture works at run-time.

After the mission start the tactical planning service is called.

Figure 4. The main activity diagram of the SS&C

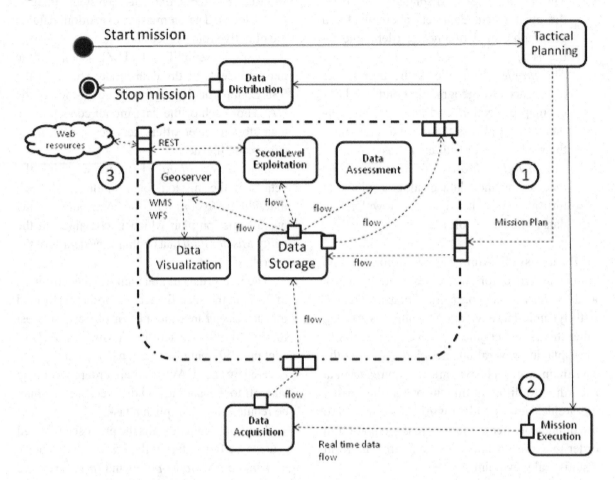

Tactical planning hides a more complex series of activities such as the mission task constraints checking and the negotiation with the UASs, which finally allows reaching a consistent and shared plan. The result is a final mission plan that is stored in the data storage layer.

When mission plan is ready and the authorization for take-off has been received from the competent authorities, mission execution is triggered. During mission execution payload sensors mounted on the UAV are activated. Streaming sensor data and telemetry data starts to flow from UAV to CS and in turn towards the data acquisition function. The data flow is stored in the data storage layer and later sent to the other components of the system: data assessment, second level exploitation

and data visualization. As regards data visualization, an external component is adopted to allow a powerful visualization of geographical maps. This is Geoserver that will be described briefly in the following.

Geoserver: To enhance the spatial information about a particular target area *Geoserver* is used (GEOSERVER). Geoserver is an open source project, fully featured by Web Map Service (WMS) and Web Feature Service (WFS). It is focused on the WFS side of geo-web services, with emphasis on optimising the delivery of geographic features and attributes, rather than just images. However it is still a competent WMS. Furthermore it delivers data in a variety of other geo-standardized interfaces (e.g. GML or KML), and in custom formats (e.g. SVG (W3C SVG), PDF or geoRSS (GeoRSS)). Figure 7 shows an example of map rendering through a WMS request. Features are shown and obtained by a WFS request.

All the above functionalities are performed primarily through the use of GeoServer technology. As previously mentioned, KML is used as the output file format because it has the advantage of displaying geographic data in an Earth browser, such as Google Earth. The output is overlayed (always correctly geo-referenced with the reference coordinate system) to the portion of the terrestrial globe indicated by spatial coordinates in the output file from the server. This allows also displaying the users' notes and metadata. An example is shown in Figure 8, which is a portion of the same map that is presented in Figure 7.

The core functionality of Geoserver is delivered through Java servlets.

It is capable to extract data from PostGIS database and to return it as a KML file. KML files constitute a common format for further data integration with annotations posted by social networks users on Google Earth. In fact, the KML files can be imported into Google Earth for visualization and are ready for further analyses. Geoserver delivers KML using a Styled Layer Descriptors (SLD), an XML-based schema specified by the OGC for describing the appearance of map layers. SLD tells the server how the map should be rendered; whether to draw lines in black, or to color them in blue with a nice outline and text labels. The style of the map is specified in the SLD file as a series of rules. Then, the data matching those rules is styled appropriately in the KML output.

As already said, a KML file contains a basic description of a place, associated longitude, latitude, tilt and other positional information (such as a specified camera view) that support Google Earth functionality. It encodes the various placemarks, ground overlays, paths and polygons within in the Google Earth client. In particular, the core modules that would be expected for any implementation are the following:

```
<kml> - the root element
<Document> - the container for fea-
tures, styles, and schemas
<atom> - tags used for attribution
<Folder> - used to hierarchically
accomodate other Features (Folders,
Placemarks, NetworkLinks)
<Placemark> - an element with a geo-
metrical description
<Link> and <NetworkLink> - basic
linking to other files should be sup-
ported in core
<ScreenOverlay> - draws an image
overlay fixed to the screen, such as
for a compass, logo or legend
<TimeStamp> and <TimeSpan> - A moment
or span in time
<Geometry> - Same as Simple Features
for GML.
```

Features can be labeled, associated with descriptive text (which can include hyperlinks to other KML or HTML resources) and associated with 'TimeSpan' elements for specifying the time period for which they are valid. This is an important element for the correct representation of the temporal dimension of the stored information. Placemark elements contain one or more geometries, including points, lines, polygons and 3D models. Together these features provide considerable flexibility in the specification of interactive, abstract geographic graphics.

In case of flooding, bridges and highways are constantly monitored by the civil protection. In such a scenario it is useful to have information about previous floods.

An Example of a possible annotation: We report here as an exemplifying case, an excerpt of a KML file regarding the bridge named Dora Baltea, located near the Turin-Milan motorway. It was generated adding new information to an original description file. In this case, the added information, available on the web, is the image of the bridge during the flood in the year 2000 in Piedmont.

The addition of the picture is an example of annotation. It occurs through the description tag. The problem here is that the semantic of the annotation is not validated. In the next section we show how this problem has been solved.

```
<Placemark>
<name>Dora Baltea bridge - TO-MI </
name>
<description>Dora Baltea bridge,
flood scenario, Piedmont 2000
http:// www.provincia.torino.it/
emergenza/dopoallu/ 12_to_mi.htm/ de-
scription>
<LookAt>
<longitude>7.981971764790663</longi-
tude>
<latitude>45.24556348140584</lati-
tude>
<altitude>0</altitude>
<range> 750.9200000009473 </range>
<tilt>0</tilt>
<heading> -0.01999999999998257 </
heading>
<altitudeMode> relativeToGround </
altitudeMode>
<gx:altitudeMode> relativeToSeaFloor
</gx:altitudeMode>
</LookAt>
<styleUrl> #msn_ylw-pushpin </
styleUrl>
<Point>
<coordinates> 7.981971764790663,
45.24556348140584,0 </coordinates>
</Point>
</Placemark>
```

Metadata Integration and Geospatial Annotation

The geospatial description of the target area provides essential information for the SS&C operator; in regards to consistency and integrity checks during the mission plan preparation. For instance, the altitude of a UAV on a route waypoint must be higher than the altitude of the underlying mountain location, or of the energy transportation lines.

For this reason the integration of different sources and the annotation of the interested characteristic of the area became crucial in the proposed project.

Piedmont Region provides the cartography of the territory in raster and shape format. This is a very helpful source of information but it is 'time-invariant'. To make it dynamic, the existing maps are integrated with additional information obtained from the web. We call this phase annotation by metadata.

A popular VGI system is used for this purpose: OpenStreetMap (OpenStreetMap) since it is constantly being updated by the subscribed users. In addition it can have volunteer users from all over the world including the less developed regions, where obtaining data can be difficult for most commercial mapping companies.

The features are created by contributors using GPS or survey devices and are combined through wiki-style (Wikipedia) collaborative software.

This type of integration involves the resolution of problems of syntactic and semantic heterogeneity.

Syntactic heterogeneity arises from the fact that shape files follow a relational paradigm to represent information while OSM files follow an XML-schema. Semantic heterogeneity arises for the different meaning, interpretation or intended use of data derived by OSM tags. A tag in OSM takes the form of a (key-value) pair in which the key is a label describing a cartography entity while value is a further specification of the key.

OSM data comprises three basic types – *nodes, ways and relations*. Nodes represent any spatial object. Ways represent streets. Relations allow expressing complex concepts by introducing relationships between them. Each individual element can have a number of arbitrary tags. Users can create arbitrary attributes and attribute values.

In general we can observe that key-value pairs represent a class-subclass specification of a geographic element: (i.e. key=highway, value =motorway). Additional tags can represent properties, accessories and restrictions that refer to a spatial object but for the purposes of this argumentation they will not be considered.

It occurs that the ontology model of OSM does not correspond to the ontology usually adopted in cartography.

The cartographic ontology usually is built using two types of objects: *Element* and *Entity*. *Element* represents the unit that appears in an image of a spatial area. The representation occurs in terms of topological primitives and does not have a logical level structure in the common GIS systems. *Entity* refers to a class of objects existing in the real world, logically structured in a set of Elements. An entity is often described as a composition of elements. Both of them represent sub-concepts that specify in a greater level of detail a more general Geographic Concept. For instance, the element that stands for '*limit of tree cultivation*' can represent the Entity '*row of trees*' and both fall under the more general concept of '*vegetation*'.

Our Solution to the Syntactic and Semantic Heterogeneity

Syntactic heterogeneity between two annotations has been solved using osm2pgsql (OpenStreetMap Osm2pgsql). It is a utility program that converts OpenStreetMap (OSM) data into a format that can be loaded into PostgreSQL.

Semantic heterogeneity has been solved considering that the two hierarchies are similar because both are created for annotation of maps but differ for the fact that OSM ontology is richer than the cartographic ontology and includes information that for the specific purposes of the SMAT project are not always relevant. For this reason we tackled the problem by merging the top-level classes (OSM key and cartographic Entity) and adding as elements of the cartographic ontol-

ogy the OSM value that are meaningful for the mission operative scenarios. This leads to a new enriched ontology that contains all the elements of the cartography and that can handle tags placed online by users of the web. The merge operation has been performed as follows.

There are three cases:

1) If an OpenStreetMap key represents the same spatial object of a cartographic Entity with the same name no operation is done (i.e. railways).

2) If an OpenStreetMap key represents the same spatial object of a cartographic Entity but appears with a different name (a synonym), in the concept description of the final ontology we include as a synonym the OSM key for the purposes of a translation operation. The class in the final ontology remains represented by the *Entity* name.

3) If an OpenStreetMap key is not represented by any cartographic *Entity* name, the key is added as a new concept of the final ontology.

A Categorization of Entities According to the Action Lines

We must take note that the SMAT final users often have different needs and in particular the mission intervention might be motivated by different lines of action belonging to four categories: Floods, Landslides, Pollutions and Aeronautics.

This suggests to speed-up the search of spatial objects according to the different emergency scenarios in which they could be monitored. With this purpose we categorize the spatial objects of the proposed ontology according to the lines of actions of the UAVs missions. The table shown in Figure 5 shows a schematic representation of the ontology obtained after the merge process with the categorization of spatial entities.

The ontology has the form of taxonomy with classes at two levels.

Figure 5. The ontology on the annotation tags and a categorization according to the mission action lines

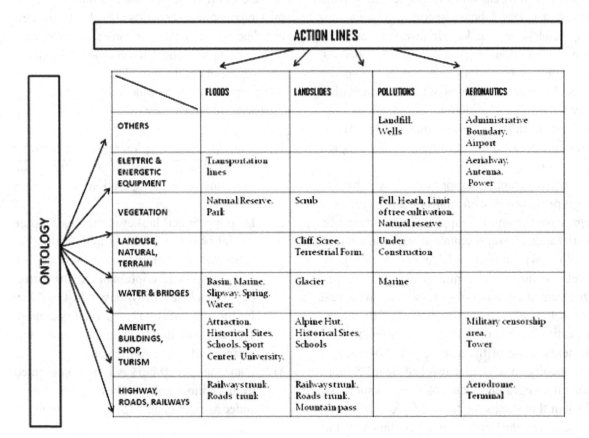

	FLOODS	LANDSLIDES	POLLUTIONS	AERONAUTICS
OTHERS			Landfill, Wells	Administrative Boundary, Airport
ELETTRIC & ENERGETIC EQUIPMENT	Transportation lines			Aerialway, Antenna, Power
VEGETATION	Natural Reserve, Park	Scrub	Fell, Heath, Limit of tree cultivation, Natural reserve	
LANDUSE, NATURAL, TERRAIN		Cliff, Scree, Terrestrial Form	Under Construction	
WATER & BRIDGES	Basin, Marine, Slipway, Spring, Water	Glacier	Marine	
AMENITY, BUILDINGS, SHOP, TURISM	Attraction, Historical Sites, Schools, Sport Center, University	Alpine Hut, Historical Sites, Schools		Military censorship area, Tower
HIGHWAY, ROADS, RAILWAYS	Railways trunk, Roads trunk	Railways trunk, Roads trunk, Mountain pass		Aerodrome, Terminal

The first row of the table represents the four action lines considered for the categorization process of the classes. In the first cell of the other rows (first column) one of the classes at the first level of the taxonomy is shown. In the other cells of the same row, the subclasses are presented. In this way all the subclasses have been categorized according to the action lines.

When a cell in the table is not empty it means that the subclass of the hierarchy represents spatial objects that are relevant to that action line. For example, *Road Trunk* is a subclass of the primary class *Roads and Railways* (with synonymous *Highway*). Moreover, it represents a common entity of interest for two action lines categories: *Floods* and *Landslides*. Therefore, in the table you can find the subclass *Road Trunk* placed under the specific column for the two action lines.

Figure 6 shows in detail the activity diagram related to the process of metadata extraction from OpenStreetMap.

At first the user interacts with the system by means of the GUI. She/he starts by requesting to the GeoAnnotation service of the SS&C the spatial area of interest and the action line of the mission (*MetadataSearch*). The GeoAnnotation service requests to Geoserver the coordinates of the area (bounding box - bbox). This request if performed via web service call to Geoserver. In fact, Geoserver exposes the WCS service to extract the coordinates for the four vertices of the bbox. It is the *DescribeCoverage* request.

Figure 6. Sequence activity diagram for the retrieval of metadata and the annotation of maps

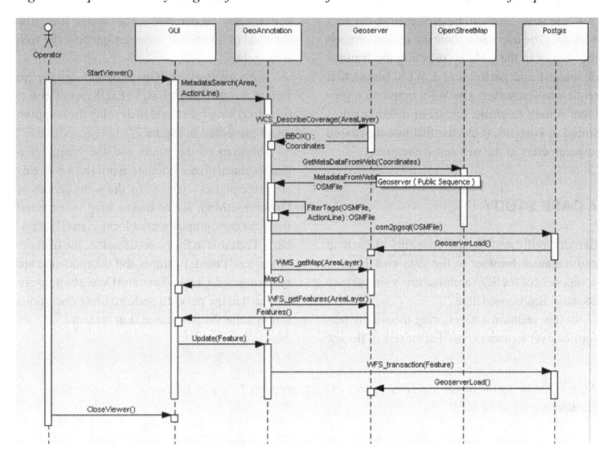

Extracted coordinates are used as parameters to perform a further web service request (*Get-MetaDataFromWeb*). This request is addressed to OpenstreetMap. Requests to OpenstreetMap web services are based on the ideas of the Restful API (OpenStreetMapAPI). These web services are the server components to which REST requests are addressed. The REST requests take the form of HTTP GET, PUT, POST, and DELETE messages. In this way OpenStreetMap exposes services for fetching raw geospatial data from its database or for storing data in it. In OpenStreetMap, the bbox of the selected area (the AreaLayer) is used to retrieve all nodes, any relations that refer to the nodes and all ways that refer to at least one node inside the bbox. This information is returned with an OSM file by *MetaDataFromWeb*.

The mission action lines, initially provided by the user in the first request (*MetadataSearch*) with parameter *ActionLine,* are used by *FilterTags* to filter the nodes in the OSM file. This filtering process is carried out by *FilterTags* according to the taxonomy of spatial objects presented in Figure 5. *FilterTags* returns the modified OSM file.

osm2pgsql is then used to load up the content of this latter file into the PostGIS database. Here data are stored as shape files.

To generate a map and a features table of the retrieved data a WMS service request (*getMap*) and a WFS service request (*getFeatures*) are directed to Geoserver.

These requests allow the user to analyze both graphically and in tabular format the extracted information.

Figure 7 shows an example of this rendering in a case study that will be presented in the next Section. The user can update the information on the map or in the table by selecting the features of interest and performing a WFS-Transaction request to Geoserver. The WFS transaction protocol is used to create, update or delete features stored in PostGIS. (Selected features are passed as parameters in the web service request).

A CASE STUDY

In order to illustrate the functionality of the map and metadata browser in the data visualization component of the SOA architecture, a simple user scenario is proposed here.

In this scenario a monitoring mission is performed over an area exposed at the risk of floods.

In addition to the information extracted from the cartography (raster maps and shape files) the retrieval of additional information from the web is launched.

The OpenLayers (OpenLayers) JavaScript library, together with ExtJS (ExtJS) and GeoExt (GeoExt) have been used to develop the mapping client presented in Figure 7.

The map of the roads and the basins of a geographical area in Piedmont are shown. Roads are presented as retrieved by the web services of OpenStreetMap. River basins map is retrieved from the cartography stored locally, in GIS database. The table in the panel describes the features of the roads map. Features and the road map are synchronized. Create, Save and Delete buttons are included in the panel to perform these operations through the WFS – transaction protocol.

Figure 7. Map of the roads and river basins of a geographical area in Piedmont. The table shows the features retrieved by WFS

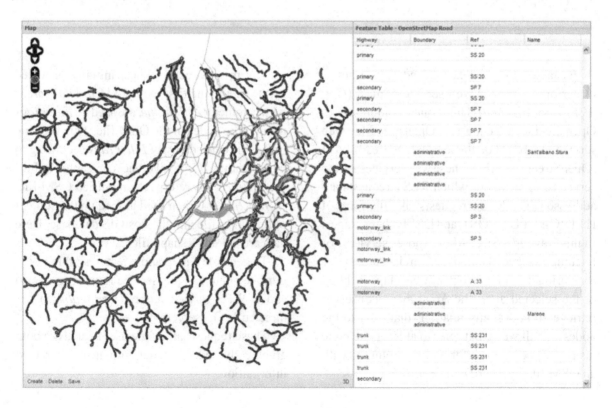

The "3D" button delivers data in 3D by means of GoogleEarth. GeoServer supports Google Earth by providing KML as a WMS output format. This means that adding data published by GeoServer is as simple as constructing a standard WMS request and specifying "format=application/vnd.google-earth.kml+XML" as the outputFormat. Figure 8 shows the resulting 3D map of a portion of the above area.

FUTURE RESEARCH DIRECTIONS

We believe that the future research directions for this kind of projects on geospatial web services are fully related to the users' activity in social networks on the web and the always growing in rich open source software implementations. In fact, the projects that consist in the integration of resources related to the geospatial information fully benefit for the growing and update information that is posted by the geo community.

A further interesting point for research is the necessity of recognizing related annotations that appear as different. For instance, because the annotation makes use of different nouns or synonymous referred to the same concept. Here the integration of geo annotation with the rich research on Natural Language Processing could be extremely useful and could help to alleviate the problem.

Further research direction could be the study of user preferences and profiles related to the locations by application of data mining functionalities. This study can also be connected to the integration of recommendation systems to the geospatial projects and could give further impact to the available geospatial services.

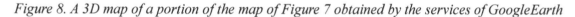

Figure 8. A 3D map of a portion of the map of Figure 7 obtained by the services of GoogleEarth

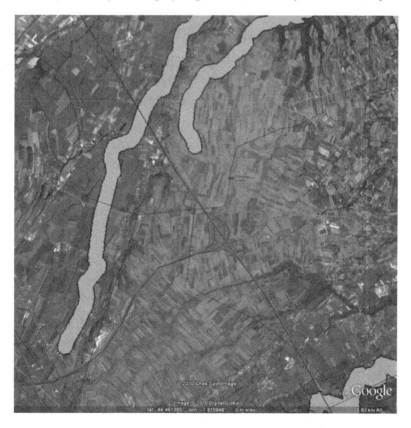

However, it is essential that these studies be conducted in a privacy-preserving fashion (Privacy Enhancing Technologies, 2009). Indeed, it must be recognized that the geospatial projects and the availability of images and information on locations could constitute at the same time a big help to the users but could also become a risk for personal and private information. We must be aware of these risks and must conduct appropriate research directives. First of all, the new research directions should aim to conceive the systems implementations in a secure way such that the risk of inappropriate usage of the information is reduced and recognized. Secondarily, applications implementations that make use of web services have been recently recognized as a new security threat to systems (Bertino, Martino, Paci, Squicciarini, 2010). We expect to see in the near future an appropriate solution in this field.

CONCLUSION

This chapter provides a summary of the SMAT project. It is a geospatial project whose aim is to collect data by payload sensors mounted on a flood of UAS for the territorial protection against natural disasters or monitoring on illegal human activity related to pollution and cultivation. We described the three-tier software architecture and the functionalities of its software components. In this context we highlighted and distinguished the connections on the components based on web services. In some specific cases, such as the link between the ground components that must exchange a large volume of sensor data, communication is not based on web services. In other cases, such as in the retrieval of metadata for the annotation of maps, geospatial web services are used based on WMS and WFS open standards.

Within the project, a geospatial system has been constructed which largely makes use of open source software like Geoserver, open community projects like Google Earth and adopts KML lan-

guage and OGC standards for the spatial objects representation, annotation, retrieval and exchange. In particular, we discussed in detail the activity and sequence diagrams for a specific functionality whose implementation is based on geospatial web services: it consists of the metadata retrieval functionality and the map annotation of target spatial areas. Finally, we showed the obtained results in the annotation of a map for a case study of a mission for floods monitoring and prevention.

REFERENCES

W3C OWL. (2010). *OWL Web Ontology Language*. Retrieved from http:// www.w3.org / TR /owl-features/

W3C OWL-S. (2010). *OWL-S: Semantic Markup for Web Services*. Retrieved from http:// www.w3.org/ Submission/OWL-S/

W3C RDF. (2010). *Resource Description Framework (RDF)*. Retrieved from http://www.w3.org/ RDF/

W3C RDFS. (2010). *RDF Vocabulary Description Language 1.0: RDF Schema*. Retrieved from http:// www.w3.org / TR /owl-features/

W3C SOAP. (2010). *Simple Object Access Protocol (SOAP) 1.1*. Retrieved from http:// www.w3.org/ TR/2000/ NOTE- SOAP-20000508/

W3C SVG. (2010). *Scalable Vector Graphics (SVG)*. Retrieved from http:// www.w3.org/ Graphics/ SVG/

W3C SWRL. (2010). *Semantic Web Services Language (SWSL)*. Retrieved from http:// www.w3.org/ Submission/ SWSF- SWSL/

W3C URI. (2010). *URIs, URLs, and URNs: Clarifications and recommendations 1.0*. Retrieved from http://www.w3.org/ TR/uri-clarification/

W3C URL. (2010). *Addressing URL: Overview* Retrieved from http:// www.w3.org/ Addressing/ URL/ Overview.html

W3C WSDL. (2010). *Web Services Description Language (WSDL) 1.1*. Retrieved from http:// www.w3.org/ TR/wsdl

W3C XML. (2010). *Extensible Markup Language (XML)*. Retrieved from http://www.w3.org/ XML/

Alonso, G., Casati, F., Kuno, H., & Machiraju, V. (2004). *Web services: concepts, architectures and applications*. Springer-Verlag.

Auer, S., Lehmann, J., & Hellmann, S. (2009). LinkedGeoData adding a spatial dimension to the Web of data. *International Semantic Web Conference (ISCW 2009)*. Washington.

Berners-Lee, T., Fielding, R., & Frystyk, H. (1996). *Hypertext Transfer Protocol -- HTTP/1.0*. USA: RFC Editor.

Depledge, M. (2009). Novel approaches and technologies in pollution assessment and monitoring. *Ocean and Coastal Management*, *52*, 336–341. doi:10.1016/j.ocecoaman.2009.04.001

Erast, N. A. S. A. (2010). *Environmental Research Aircraft and Sensor Technology*. Retrieved from http:// www.nasa.gov/ centers/dryden/ history/ past projects/Erast/ index.html

Erl, T. (2005). *Service-oriented architecture: Concepts, technology, and design*. Upper Saddle River, NJ, USA: Prentice Hall PTR.

Ext, J. S. (2010). *ExtJS- Javascript Framework and RIA Platform*. Retrieved May 4, 2010, from http://www.extjs.com/

Fielding, R. (2000). *Architectural styles and the design of network-based software architectures*. Unpublished doctoral dissertation, University of California, Irvine

Frank, A. (2003). Ontology for spatio-temporal databases. *LNCS*, *2520*, 9–77.

GeoExt. (2010). *JavaScript toolkit for rich Web mapping applications*. Retrieved from http:// www.geoext.org/

GeoRSS. (2010). *GeoRSS*. Retrieved May 4, 2010, http://www.georss.org/ Main_Page

Geoserver. *Welcome to Geoserver*. Retrieved 05 04, 2010, from http://geoserver.org/ display/ GEOS/ Welcome

Global Spatial Data Infrastructure. (2004). *SDI cookbook*. Retrieved from www.gsdi.org/ docs2004/ Cookbook/ cookbookV2.0.pdf

Goodchild, M. (2007). Citizens as sensors: the world of volunteered geography. *GeoJournal*, *69*(4), 211–221.doi:10.1007/s10708-007-9111-y

Google Earth. (2010). *Google Earth Home page*. Retrieved from http:// earth.google. com/intl/it/

Google Maps. (2010). *Google maps italia*. Retrieved from http://maps.google.it/

Group on Earth Observations. (2010). *What is GEOSS? The Global Earth Observation System of Systems*. Retrieved from http://www.earth observations.org/ geoss.shtml

Hamre, T. S., & Éamonn, Ó. T. (2005). DISMAR - Data Integration System for Marine Pollution and Water Quality. *31st International Symposium on Remote Sensing of Environment*.

He, H. (2003). *What is Service-Oriented Architecture*. Retrieved from http:// pesona.mmu. edu.my /~wruslan/ SE2/ Readings/ detail/Reading -28.pdf

Kurhn, W. (2003). Semantic reference systems. *International Journal of Geographic*, *17*(5), 405–409.doi:10.1080/1365881031000114116

Lan-Kun, C., Yao-Min, F., Tien-Yin, C., Bing, J., & Bastian, B. (2009). A SOA based debris flow monitoring system architecture and proof-of-concept implementation. *17th International Conference on Geoinformatics*, (pp. 1-6).

Lutz, M., & Klien, E. (2006). Ontology-based retrieval of geographic information. *International Journal of Geographical Information Science*, *20*(3), 233–260. doi:10.1080/13658810500287107

MultiMap. (2010). *MultiMap from Bing*. Retrieved from http://www.multimap.com/

Object Manager Group-UML. (2010). *UML Resource Page*. Retrieved from http://www.uml.org/

OGC GML. (2010). *OpenGIS Geography Markup Language (GML) Encoding Standard*. Retrieved from http://www.open geospatial.org/ standards/ gml

OGC KML. (2010). *KML*. Retrieved from http://www.open geospatial.org/ standards/kml/

OGC SWE. (2010). *Sensor Web Enablement WG*. Retrieved from http://www.open geospatial.org / projects/groups/ sensorweb

OGC WCS. (2010). *Web Coverage Service*. Retrieved from http://www.open geospatial.org/ standards/wcs

OGC WFS. (2010). *Web Feature Service*. Retrieved from http://www.open geospatial.org/ standards/wfs

OGC WFS-G. (2010). *WFS Gazetteer Profile 1.0 SWG*. Retrieved from http://www.open geospatial. org/ projects/groups/ wfsgaz1.0swg

OGC WMS. (2010). *Web Map Service*. Retrieved from http://www.open geospatial.org/ standards/ wms

Open, G. L. (2010). *OpenGL The Industry's Foundation for High Performance Graphics*. Retrieved from http://www.opengl.org/

Open Geospatial Consortium. (2010). *Open Geospatial Consortium*. Retrieved from www. open geospatial.org

OpenLayers. (2010). *OpenLayers Home*. Retrieved from http://openlayers.org/

OpenStreetMap. (2010). *Osm2pgsql*. Retrieved from http://wiki.open streetmap.org/ wiki/Osm 2pgsql

OpenStreetMap. (2010). *OpenStreetMap*. Retrieved from www.openstreetmap.org

Papazoglou, M. P. (2007). *Web Services: Principles and Technology*. England: Pearson Prentice Hall.

Pastor, E., Royo, P., Lopez, J., Barrado, C., Santamaria, E., & Prats, X. (2007). Project SKY-EYE: Applying UAVs to Forest Fire Fighter Support and Monitoring. *2007 UAV Conference*, Paris.

Peisheng, Z., Yu, G., & Di, L. (2007). Geospatial Web Services. In Hilton, B. N. (Ed.), *Emerging spatial Information Systems and applications* (pp. 1–35). Hershey: Idea Group, Inc.

Perry, M., Sheth, A., & Arpinar, I. (2007). Geospatial and temporal semantic analytics. In Karimi, H. A. (Ed.), *Encyclopedia of Geoinformatics*.

PostGIS. (2010). *PostGIS: Home*. Retrieved from http:// postgis.refractions.net/

PostgreSQL Global Development Group. (2010). *PostgreSQL*. Retrieved from http:// www.postgresql.org/

Roman, D., & Klien, E. (2007). SWING - A semantic framework for geospatial services. In Scharl, A., & Tochtermann, K. (Eds.), *The Geospatial Web: How geo-browsers, social software and the Web 2.0 are shaping the network society* (pp. 229–234). Berlin: Springer.

Roux, A. (2010). *Intelligence and peacekeeping-are we winning?* Retrieved from http:// se1.isn. ch/ serviceengine /Files/ ISN/101775/ ichaptersection_ singledocument/ 3D21E3F5- BF86-4429-B9F7-A2DB571 BA19A/en/ Chapter+3.pdf

Scheider, S., Janowicz, K., & Kuhn, W. (2009). *Grounding geographic categories in the meaningful environment. LNCS* (pp. 69-87). COSIT 2009. Berlin/Heidelberg: Springer.

Scribner, K., & Stiver, M. C. (2000). *Understanding Soap: Simple Object Access Protocol.* Indianapolis, IN: Sams.

Tisdale, J. R. (2006). The software architecture of the Berkeley UAV platform. *Proceedings of the IEEE Conference on Control Applications.* Munich.

Uddi, X. M. L. (2010). *Uddi.XML.org.* Retrieved from http:// uddi.xml.org/ uddi-org

Wrap, N. A. S. A. (2010). *Wildfire Research and Applications Partnership (WRAP) project.* Retrieved from http:// geo.arc.nasa.gov/ sge/ WRAP/

Yahoo Maps. (2010). *Yahoo local maps.* Retrieved from http:// maps.yahoo.com/

ADDITIONAL READING

Barnachi, P., Moessner, K., Presser, M., & Meissner, S. (Eds.). (2009). *Smart sensing and context* (4th ed.).

Berendt, B., Mladenic, D., de Gemmis, M., Semeraro, G., Spiliopoulou, M., & Stumme, G. (Eds.). (2009). *Knowledge discovery enhanced with semantic and social information.* Springer.

Bertino, E., Martino, L., Paci, F., Squicciarini, A. (2010). *Security for Web services and service-oriented architectures, 12.*

Gal, C., Kantor, P., & Lesk, M. (Eds.). (2009). *Protecting persons while protecting the people.*

Goldberg, I., & Atallah, M. (Eds.). (2009). *Privacy enhancing technologies.* Springer.

Hadzic, M., Chang, E., & Wongthongtham, P. Dillon, T. (2009). *Ontology-based multi-agent systems.* Springer.

Jasani, B., Pesaresi, M., Schneiderbauer, S., & Zeug, G. (Eds.). (2009). *Remote sensing from space.* Springer. doi:10.1007/978-1-4020-8484-3

Markowitch, O., Bilas, A., Hopeman, J. H., Mitchell, C. J., & Quisquater, J. J. (Eds.). (2009). *Information security theory and practice: Smart devices, pervasive systems, and ubiquitous networks.* Springer.

Ozok, A. A., & Zaphiris, P. (Eds.). (2009). *Online communities and social computing.* Springer.

KEY TERMS AND DEFINITIONS

GIS: Is an information system that captures, stores, analyzes, manages and presents data that is linked to a geographic location.

OGC: Is an international organization with the objective of developing and implement standards for content, services and exchange of geographic data.

Ontology: Is a formal representation of a set of concepts in a particular domain. It is used also to express the relationship between the concepts.

SOA: Is a software architecture design to support communication between services.

SS&C: Supervision and Coordination Station; it receives information from each UAV and provides support to store and process the sensor data received by the UAVs communication channel.

UAV: Unmanned Aerial Vehicles are spatial vehicles with not a human pilot.

UAS: Unmanned Aircraft Systems are systems consisting of an uninhabited airplane, piloted by embedded avionics and supervised by an operator on ground.

Waypoints: Are sets of coordinates that identify a point in physical space.

Web Service: Is a software system design to support the interoperability between different computers on the same network.

WFS: Is a standard interface that allows the request and the import by a client of geographic object through the web using a platform-independent call.

WMS: Is an OGC technical specification that dynamically produces maps of spatially- related data from geographic information

ENDNOTE

[1]   SMAT F1 working group is a consortium composed of Universities and Research centres (Università di Torino, Politecnico di Torino, ISMB), three Industries (Alenia Aeronautica, which is also Project Leader, Selex Galileo and Altec) and eleven Small Medium Enterprises (Auconel, Axis, Blue Group, Carcerano, DigiSky, Envisens, Nautilus, Nimbus, Sepa, Spaic, Synarea), all operating in the Regione Piemonte.

Chapter 19
GeoBrain Online Analysis System:
An SOA–Based Geospatial Web Portal

Weiguo Han
George Mason University, USA

Liping Di
George Mason University, USA

Peisheng Zhao
George Mason University, USA

Xiaoyan Li
George Mason University, USA

ABSTRACT

The geospatial Web portal is the gateway to combining news, information, data, and applications from the geosciences community. Service Oriented Architecture (SOA), Software as a Service, Rich Internet Application, and other emerging Web standards and technologies have revolutionized the implementation of Web portals. The GeoBrain project is developing a comprehensive Web service-oriented geospatial portal, the GeoBrain Online Analysis System (GeOnAS). This data-rich and service-centric geospatial portal provides easy, fast, and federated Web access to geospatial data, information, and services compliant with Open Geospatial Consortium standards from multiple sources. It offers standards-based geospatial data discovery, retrieval, visualization and analysis to facilitate geosciences research and education around the world, and to help decision-makers and analysts work more efficiently and effectively within an SOA runtime environment. Asynchronous JavaScript and XML (Ajax) also brings more responsive, interactive, and dynamic features to this Web portal and creates a better Web experience to its end users in the confines of a modern browser.

DOI: 10.4018/978-1-60960-192-8.ch019

1. INTRODUCTION

Service Oriented Architecture (SOA) provides a modern computing infrastructure for integrating data, services, and applications in a flexible and loosely coupled manner. This evolving technology offers an adaptive architecture for the construction of Web geospatial applications. As a collection of techniques, the growing popularity of Ajax leads to the delivery of appealing Web geospatial applications in a completely new way.

To make geospatial information and services from distributed sources accessible, the Open Geospatial Consortium (OGC) has led the development and implementation of a series of standards for geospatial contexts and services since its founding in 1994 (Nativi et al, 2006). Many organizations have published their geospatial data and services adhering to these standards. How to search, discover, download, visualize and analyze these resources in a comprehensive geospatial Web portal utilizing the full potential of emerging technologies is a challenging and meaning task.

To achieve this challenging goal, the GeoBrain project funded by NASA aims to make geospatial data, information, and services from distributed sources publicly reusable and consumable across the Web (Di et al., 2007). A comprehensive Web service-oriented online geospatial analysis system, the GeoBrain Online Analysis System (GeOnAS, http://geobrain.laits.gmu.edu/OnAS/), has been built to make petabytes of geospatial data and information from multiple providers easily accessible through a compelling interface, and provide powerful geospatial analysis service and modeling capabilities to the public and the wider geospatial user community in SOA environment.

This chapter mainly introduces the architecture and implementation of GeOnAS. The reminder of this chapter is organized as follows. Section 2 reviews the progress in the development of the geospatial Web portal and the related technologies. Section 3 presents the system general architecture, design and implementation in details. In section 4, stream extraction is used as a demonstration of system functionality. Finally, section 5 summarizes the conclusions and directions for future work.

2. OVERVIEW

This section reviews the progress and applications of SOA, OGC Web services, Ajax, and the Geospatial Web portal.

2.1 SOA

SOA is an architecture that organizes discrete software functionality in a uniform way as discoverable and reusable Web services over the Internet. It offers an innovative and flexible approach for the design and development of Web applications across organizations to meet business or mission needs. This technology is designed to improve interoperability between diverse applications and support seamless business integration with a set of linked Web services (Nezhad et al, 2006).

Web Services empower software functionality with standards-based Web interfaces. They should be self-contained, self-describing, reusable, and application-based units of work. To comply with these principles, providers of these services publish information about them in service registries through the Universal Description, Discovery and Integration (UDDI) service, and describe them in Web Services Description Language (WSDL) for consumers to discover those services they need dynamically and retrieve the required information for service composition and invocation (Christiensen et al, 2001), as shown in Figure 1. Simple Object Access Protocol (SOAP) is adopted to communicate among these services on the network (Box et al, 2000).

The development of various standards, products, and tools for supporting SOA is advancing at a rapid pace. SOA has been widely adopted to design and build composite applications for achieving desired business processes and col-

Figure 1. SOA paradigm

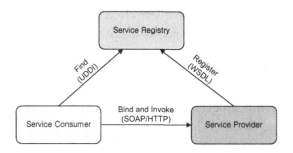

laborations in highly distributed and continuously evolving environments. It is chosen because of its advantage in better reuse of existing applications, legacy systems, and software components through service wrapping, faster and cost-effective development, and integration through service composition and aggregation, and easier adaptation to the complex and changing business environment through service replacement and updating (Josuttis, 2007).

To keep up with technology trend to SOA and meet the high demands from the geospatial community, SOA has been utilized to provide the integrated system service offerings by which different geospatial Web applications communicate and collaborate with each other in a multi-party and heterogeneous environment. SOA offers a global, national, local and organizational spatial data infrastructure (SDI) framework with catalog, discovery, management and governance of geospatial services to share geospatial information on the Web (Kiehle et al, 2007).

Using SOA and spatial Web services, the Earth Science Gateway (ESG) of NASA streamlines access to Earth observations, simulation models, and decision support tools through open and standard web protocols. By organizing detailed metadata about online resources into a flexible and searchable registry, ESG helps researchers, decision-makers, and others access a wide variety of observations and predictions of natural and human phenomena related to Earth Science (Bambacus et al, 2007). ESG provides an easy,

efficient, and useful approach to integrate different geospatial systems and components through open and standards-based interfaces (Birk et al, 2006).

SOA promotes geospatial Web services management, discovery and utilization among the geospatial community and common users and delivers more shortcut solutions to decision making.

2.2 OGC Web Services

OGC has been creating a series of standards or specifications for Web services to execute tasks such as geospatial data discovery, access, portrayal, and processing (Nash et al, 2008). Like international standards, these services facilitate the interoperability and accessibility of geospatial information and services from distributed sources and are actively and widely supported by commercial software and open-source geospatial software.

Geospatial catalog services support the registry, description, discovery, and access to information resources within geospatial community. The Catalog Service for the Web (CSW) specifies the standard interfaces for publishing and searching in catalogues of metadata for geospatial data, information services and other resources (Voges & Senkler, 2005). Some general query criteria are spatial extent, temporal extent, keywords, and data source. OGC/CSW has been implemented in many systems, for example, CSW by Center for Spatial Information Science and Systems (CSISS) (Bai et al, 2007), ESG by the NASA Geosciences Interoperability Office and Compusult Ltd. (Birk et al, 2006), and the Geonetwork open source geospatial catalogue (http://geonetwork-opensource.org/software), deegree Catalogue Service (http://www.deegree.org/).

Geospatial data services customize different kinds of geospatial data sets according to user-specified parameters. Web Coverage Service (WCS) provides access to geographical coverage across the Web via a standard interface and operations. Clients can request coverage data that is clipped, re-projected, re-sampled, and returned in some raster data format (Whiteside & Evans, 2008). Web Map Service (WMS) handles map data rendering and manipulation (de la Beaujardière, 2006). The images are generally portrayed in formats (e.g. png, gif or jpeg) which can be displayed by the common browsers. Styled Layer Descriptor (SLD) is the styling language for WMS map servers. Pre-defined and user-defined styles are allowed to extend WMS service, and the legend symbols for them can be acquired (Lupp, 2007). As a client side specification, Web Map Context (WMC) is used to exchange or save the view of one or more maps generated from WMS (Sonnet, 2005). The Web Feature Service (WFS) supports queries of vector data repositories (Vretanos, 2002). Geography Markup Language (GML) is an XML grammar for the modeling, transport, and storage of geographic information, including both spatial and non-spatial attributes of features.

Geospatial processing services provide operations for processing or transforming geospatial data. The Web Processing Service (WPS) defines the standard interface for discovery, publishing, and binding to geospatial process, and plays an important role in automating workflow that involves geospatial data and geo-processing services (Schut, 2007). These data and processing services can be accessed across a network, or available at the server. The standardized geo-processing services can be generated from any algorithm, calculation, or model (e.g. buffer analysis, shortest path, and color composition) that operates on geospatial data. An open source framework written in Java has been developed by 52° North to deploy WPS services (Foerster, 2006). It offers two plug-ins for uDig and JUMP. Python Web Processing Service (pyWPS) is another open source framework that implements the OGC WPS specification; it supports Geographic Resources Analysis Support System (GRASS) functions (Neteler & Mitasova, 2007) and the R Project for Statistical Computing (Cepický & Becchi, 2007).

These OGC specifications make complex geospatial information and services accessible and useful to Web geospatial applications across the globe. They also have been effectively implemented and adopted in geospatial SOA frameworks.

2.3 Ajax

Rich Internet Applications (RIAs) are replacing traditional HTML because of their more-interactive user experience and deployment across browsers and desktops (Han et al, 2009). Lawton (2008) discusses RIA development methods, including Ajax, Flash, Silverlight, and JavaFX. So far, Ajax has been more stable, viable, and flourishing than other alternatives. Its use has presented fewer problems for clients.

Ajax is really several familiar technologies bundled together in powerful new ways (Garret, 2005). They are the Document Object Model (DOM), Cascading Style Sheets (CSS), Dynamic HyperText Markup Language (DHTML), Extensible Markup Language (XML), and JavaScript. DOM represents the structure of XML and HTML documents, and DOM Application Program Interfaces (APIs) provide a way to handle the returned document from the server and update the displayed page. DTHML and CSS are adopted to create the interactive and dynamic web pages. XML is for data manipulation and conversion. JavaScript is the client-side script for dynamically caching and displaying information that has been received using XML. The *XMLHttpRequest* object in the JavaScript programming language is utilized to perform asynchronous interaction with the back-end server via standard HTTP *GET/POST* requests.

Ajax based applications bring the user interface and its functionality with of rich, responsive, intuitive, interactive, and dynamic features entirely inside the browser without a plug-in or other software required (Paulson, 2005). Besides rendering HTML and executing script blocks, the browser plays a more active role in processing HTTP requests and responses in these applications. Instead of traditional "click, wait, and refresh" user interaction, these Web applications show better performance and web experience since they can add or retrieve users' requests asynchronously without reloading web pages.

The browser-side Ajax frameworks provide a set of prepackaged controls, components, utilities, and JavaScript APIs that help developers to build web sites and applications more easily and flexibly. Many Ajax frameworks are available for free download and use. The favorite ones are ExtJS, Prototype/Script.aculo.us, jQuery, Dojo Toolkit and Yahoo User Interface (YUI). These frameworks make the development of RIA much more akin to that of desktop applications. The selection criteria for the Ajax framework for the implementation of dynamic Web applications should include widget availability, file size to browser, ease of maintenance and quality of documentation (Turner et al., 2007). In addition, quality of community support, popularity, and performance are also important factors to be considered. Moreover, Ajax-enabled open source Web mapping frameworks like OpenLayers (http://openlayers.org/) and MapBuilder (http://www.mapbuilder.net/) are widely used to build rich Web-based geographic applications. These promising geospatial frameworks are compliant with the OGC standards for WMS, WFS, WMC, and GML. They also support layers from Google, Yahoo, and Microsoft Bing Map.

Ajax provides a strong foundation for developing a SOA Web portal. Because of its advantages and tremendous industry momentum, Ajax is utilized in the GeoBrain project to create a more intuitive and responsive geospatial Web portal within an SOA environment.

2.5 Geospatial Web Portals

A Web portal acts as an entry point that integrates information from multiple sources into a single Web site, and provides users more reliable, up-to-date, and user-friendly information within it. The Geospatial Web portal usually functions as a Web-based gateway to discover, and manage, and

view distributed geospatial resources (Maguire & Longley, 2005). OGC also develops Geospatial Portal Reference Architecture to guide the geospatial community in implementing standards-based portals (Rose, 2004). The techniques and standards mentioned described above have led to profound changes in the delivery of interoperable and comprehensive geospatial Web portals (Goodchild et al, 2007).

According to Maguire and Longley (2005), geospatial portals can be classified as catalog portals and application portals. Enterprise portals are another type of geospatial portal (Tang & Selwood, 2005). A typical geospatial portal should include geospatial resources and services, catalog service, and applications that can be customized by users (Yang et al., 2006). The geoportal also should provide tools to search metadata, retrieve geospatial data, and even store metadata documents.

The geospatial Web portal is one of the key components and important tools of the National Spatial Data Infrastructure (NSDI). The basic requirement for this kind of geospatial portal is support for recognized standards of the World Wide Web Consortium (W3C), the International Organization for Standardization (ISO), the Organization for the Advancement of Structured Information Standards (OASIS), OGC, and other organizations. These standards play an important role in solving the interoperability issue between different sub nodes and systems. As part of an e-government initiative of the United States, Geospatial One-Stop (GOS, http://www.geodata.gov), a geoportal links users to different levels (local, regional, state, and federal) of data sets that have been registered in a centralized metadata catalog database, and provides them scientific knowledge in reports, maps, models and applications, as shown in Figure 2. Within the Infrastructure for Spatial Information in Europe (INSPIRE), the European community also launches their geoportals of NSDI, like Norway (http://www.geonorge.no/

Figure 2. Website of geospatial one-stop

Portal/ptk), Sweden (http://www.eulis.eu/), and Spain (http://www.idee.es)

In recent years, there also has been a proliferation of geospatial Web portals for sharing of geospatial information based on theme. For example, The NATional CARBon Sequestration Database and Geographic Information System (NatCarb, http://www.natcarb.org/) provides geographic information concerning carbon sequestration (Carr et al, 2008).

The Global Earth Observation System of Systems (GEOSS) provides decision-makers, managers, and other users of Earth observations three GEO Web Portals (GWPs) for searching and exploring the data, information, imagery, services, and applications which have been registered in GEOSS Registries or harvested by GEOSS Clearinghouses(Mandl et al, 2007). These three portals are ESRI GWP, ESA/FAO GWP, and Compusult GWP. These portals greatly improve the efficiency and effectiveness of geospatial activities within and across organizations, connect the existing geospatial resources of service providers seamlessly throughout the web, and reduce the time and cost users spend finding relevant and usable geospatial resources. And their open source software could be utilized by the GEOSS community to create their own portals contributing to the establishment of an interoperable

GEOSS. Geonetwork and deegree also provide open source frameworks to build integrated and standards-based geospatial Web portals. Zhang et al (2006) discuss the possibility of combining Grid computing, Web services, OGC specifications and the Semantic Web together to construct comprehensive geospatial portals that are capable of performing advanced analytical services.

Although the current geospatial portals are very popular in the geospatial community, most of them still remain weak in on-the-fly analytical and modeling functions. Accessing, retrieving, and visualizing geospatial data is just a point of departure for geoportals; analyzing these data is the highest level of their core capabilities. Through composition of two interfaces that are tailored to address the specific requirements from different fields of the Earth science community, NASA Giovanni acts as an integrated Web doorway to access, visualize, and analyze huge volumes of remote sensing data and also offers a platform for peers to share, verify, and investigate results (Acker & Leptoukh, 2007). But it does not support standardized outer Web service invocation because of the limitation in system capability. GeOnAS aims at being a comprehensive geospatial Web portal with intuitive geospatial data discovery, management, and visualization capabilities, as

Figure 3. System architecture

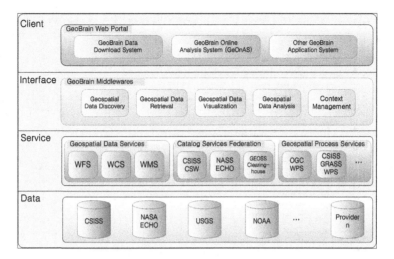

well as analysis functionality within the SOA run time environment.

3. SYSTEM IMPLEMENTATION

The modern computing infrastructure and emerging Web technologies formulate an essential SOA to supply the framework for the development of GeOnAS. The interoperability and flexibility of GeOnAS is ensured through adoption of recognized standards (e.g. W3C, ISO, OASIS and OGC) and Java, XSD, XML, JSP, Ajax, J2EE (Zhao et al, 2005). This geospatial Web portal offers an interactive entry point to search, retrieve, visualize, and analyze geospatial data in the context of location and time, and to leverage geospatial resources across the network to foster new insights and better decision making. The general system architecture is shown as Figure 3.

GeOnAS provides users with the ability to find the appropriate resources from different online repositories, preview data images for an area of interest, obtain metadata information about a source, customize data with specified parameters, visualize the data in different styles, download data which meets research needs, analyze data through locating and invoking geospatial Web

services, and save the context information for future use or exchange without any browser plug-in or client software. The process is shown in Figure 4. All operations can be performed with a few mouse clicks and several keyboard inputs.

3.1 Online Geospatial Repository Access

Via SOA and Web services, GeOnAS provides direct access to geospatial information and data from multiple repositories across data center environments in a federated framework. The GeoBrain development team has implemented CSISS Catalog Service Federation (CSF) to provide an integrated and unified access to the GMU CSISS Server, the National Aeronautics and Space Administration (NASA) Earth Observing System Clearinghouse (ECHO), the United States Geological Survey (USGS) Landsat Archive, the National Oceanic and Atmospheric Administration (NOAA) Geostationary Operational Environmental Satellite (GOES), and other data services compliant with OGC standards over the web. These integrated data are especially valuable in geospatial education and research because they provide a variety of data sources,

Figure 4. Sequence diagram

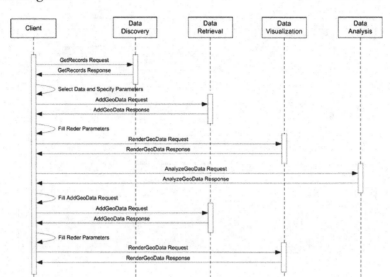

multi-disciplinary coverage and science-oriented data collections (Deng & Di, 2009).

The GMU CSISS Server provides nearly 16 terabytes of geospatial data, including Landsat, SRTM, ASTER, BlueMarble, EO1, Earth's City Lights, WindSat, and GOES, which are obtained from NASA, USGS and other organizations to provide faster and easier access than access to data in the original archives. Using the OGC CSW specification, the ebRIM (Electronic business Registry Information Model) profile and the ISO 19115:2003/19119:2005 standards, CSISS CSW supports registration, publication, and discovery of both geospatial data and services in an OGC and ISO interoperable form. Metadata on the CSISS server and CSISS GRASS WPS that describes the spatial extent, temporal extent, data quality, keywords, and other characteristics of Earth observation data are extracted and registered in CSISS CSW and exposed through a CSW ebRIM web interface. And additionally, important and popular geospatial datasets are being collected and stored in this server.

As a spatial and temporal metadata registry, ECHO provides a uniform view for terabytes of NASA's data from distributed archive centers.

These metadata cover multiple science disciplines and domains. ECHO also offers a service registry for data services and search services from other organizations. Accessing ECHO through its published APIs not only allows broader use of NASA's data, but also helps users search, retrieve, customize, and use these data efficiently. A CSW adapter for ECHO has been developed using ECHO's public API. This adapter is registered and integrated within CSISS CSF as a virtual CSW. It acts as a broker between ECHO and CSF: it translates standard CSW requests transferred by CSF to parameters required by ECHO for search, wraps the search results from ECHO in a standard CSW response, and then transfers them to CSF. A user can select the data of interest from the response. This data can also be downloaded and cached on GeoBrain servers, then processed, visualized and analyzed in GeOnAS.

The Landsat Archive is the valuable collection of continuously acquired global imagery from Landsat 1 through Landsat 7, dating back to 1972. These Landsat images have been frequently downloaded from USGS website since its release in 2009. Users around the world can browse and request this available collection at no charge via

EarthExplorer or Global Visualization Viewer (GloVis). Another CSW adapter for the USGS Landsat archive also has been developed to easily access and retrieve multiple land scenes. The plug-in hides the tedious human interactions. Similar to the ECHO adapter, the Landsat adapter wraps the metadata information in a CSW schema, and exchanges it with CSISS CSF. In addition, it stores and indexes the downloaded data on GeoBrain servers to avoid the repetitive download of the same data sets. Seamless integrating access to this full archive with GeOnAS saves the user's time in finding, retrieving, and processing Landsat data on-demand, especially that imagery with an "Online" tag.

Through backend interaction with the NOAA Comprehensive Large Array-data Stewardship System (CLASS) in the CSW adapter for GOES, GOES data can be found and obtained through a series of processes in GeOnAS. And integration with the CLASS Simple NOAA Archive Access Portal (SNAAP) within the adapter is in progress to make it possible to order and discover appropriate environmental data from multiple archives by such properties as time, location, and type.

Any OGC compliant third-party catalogues like ESRI Clearinghouse also are supported by GeOnAS to retrieve data content directly.

More adapters will be built to turn non-standard data sources and corresponding metadata information consistently into services that are callable by CSISS CSF and easily integrated into the productive and flexible environment of GeOnAS; CSISS CSF will become a service level clearinghouse and a central point of data publishing and discovery.

3.2 OGC Web Services Integration

Along with geospatial catalog services, SOA enables GeOnAS to support the extensibility of other OGC standards, including geospatial data services (WCS, WFS, and WMS) and geospatial processing services (OGC WPS and GRASS WPS). Support for these specifications enables this geospatial Web portal to interoperate with Web services from other vendors across the globe conveniently, and interact smoothly with any GIS or RS application supporting these standards.

3.2.1 Geospatial Data Services Support

Geospatial data from other providers using data services compliant with OGC specifications also can be imported and used directly in GeOnAS via middleware of geospatial data retrieval.

GeoBrain WCS supports both version 1.1.0 and 1.0.0 of the OGC WCS specification, as well as WCS-T, and provides three operations (i.e. *GetCapabilities*, *DescribeCoverage*, and *GetCoverage*) to serve coverage data in multiple formats (e.g. GeoTIFF, HDF-EOS, netCDF). Common Coordinate Reference Systems (CRSs) are supported by both input and output data. This service is registered as an associated WCS service in CSISS CSW to serve all coverage data stored in the CSISS server or obtained and cached from other sources. The processing time depends on the size of the results file.

GeoBrain WFS supports the interchange of geographic vector data as features. The outputs of a *GetFeature* request are encoded in GML or stored in an ESRI Shapefile that contains the required vector data and serves as the input for complex vector or raster analysis. A WFS resources link registered in CSW or clearinghouse also can be served as the feature data sources. GeoBrain WMS is deployed to render spatially referenced pictorial images dynamically from the vector, imagery, and terrain data layers for geospatial data display and result verification in GeOnAS workbench.

The URL of a known OGC data service also could be supported to load and process data from that service in the workbench. Integrating these OGC-compliant data sources into the GeOnAS SOA framework not only would improve GeOnAS's productivity and enhance its flexibility, but would also promote distribution and application of these data sources.

Figure 5. Web services tree

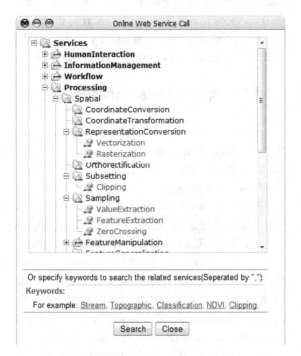

3.2.2 Geospatial Processing Services Support

The GeoBrain project develops a suite of WPS from GRASS to perform geographical operation and analysis. The detailed description of these services, including operations, input and output parameters, service location, WSDL, etc, can be got at http://geobrain.laits.gmu.edu/grassweb/manuals/index.html. All these processing services are standards-compliant, self-contained, and loosely coupled with each other, so they can be composed into a workflow to construct more complicated geospatial models. And these services are registered and organized in the hierarchical structure in CSISS CSW (as displayed in Figure 5) so that they can be managed, discovered, and invoked effectively. The tree structure derives from the semantic types of computations defined in ISO 19119:2005 standard. This structure can be easily browsed to locate the service of interest.

GeOnAS also offers the ability to discover, negotiate with, integrate, and invoke external

OGC WPS. The data mining algorithms in Algorithm Development and Mining (ADaM) from the University of Alabama in Huntsville (UAH) Information Technology and Systems Center (ITSC) are packaged as Web services for deployment and use. These services include image processing, pattern recognition, texture, and utilities, and provide the scientific community a powerful data mining capability to build a high-level product from Earth observation data (Graves et al, 2007). This Web service suite has been tested and validated using georeferenced raster data in GeOnAS.

In conclusion, GeOnAS offers an easier and more cost-effective way to integrate with existing OGC-compliant Web services within the SOA runtime environment.

3.3 Middleware

The middleware in GeOnAS carry out geospatial data discovery, geospatial data retrieval, geospatial data visualization, geospatial data analysis, and context management. These middleware connect geospatial applications to SOA together, and integrate and mange a variety of geospatial applications, services and data on the back end. They are implemented as Web services to be accessed through open and callable interfaces and invoked by XML messages in the SOA context.

3.3.1 Geospatial Data Discovery

GeOnAS provides several means to discover geospatial data by searching the CSISS CSF servers or inputting the OGC data services URL directly.

To search for data information in selected CSW servers, the requests encoded in XML contain one or more filter constraints like spatial extent, temporal range, keywords, and platform name. The standard CSW *GetRecords* requests are sent to CSISS CSF which transfers the requests to the specified CSW or clearinghouse using the corresponding plug-in. Metadata information

Figure 6. Metadata information

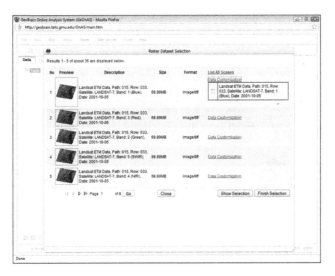

(e.g. identifier, bounding coordinates, thumbnail, size, format, and description) about geospatial data meeting the query criteria are retrieved and wrapped in *GetRecordsResponse*, and then returned to the client via CSISS CSF. All information will be listed and viewed in the Web page to help users choose those datasets that are pertinent to their specific research needs, as shown in Figure 6. Through the thumbnails, users can easily learn the relation between the spatial extent of the data and the spatial bounding box specified and select the data of interest. The available browse images derived from source data also can be retrieved as a quick view. To avoid parsing a large size xml file, the numbers of records returned by one query is specified. Then, the response can be returned in batches, and displayed as Web pages.

Standard OGC WCS and WFS access components are developed via the corresponding *Get-Capabilities* request to retrieve identifier, name, description, spatial extent, provider, and other attributes about available geospatial data from the whole XML Capabilities document.

3.3.2 Geospatial Data Retrieval

GeOnAS retrieves geospatial data by processing the *AddGeoDataRequest* request listed, as seen in Figure 7, and returning the full response in XML in the middleware of geospatial data retrieval. And this middleware also processes *RemoveG-eoDataRequest* request to remove those cached temporary files when they are not needed.

The raster data involved in the *AddGeoData-Request* request can be obtained by a WCS *Get-Coverage* request. The *GetCoverage* request includes parameters like coverage identifier, projection, user-defined spatial extent, resolution, width, height, and format. GeoBrain WCS will deal with this request and return the actual raster data or their location URLs in XML. The returned raster data will be stored with a UUID file name for geospatial visualization and analysis.

The vector data (points, lines, and polygons) contained in the *AddGeoDataRequest* request also could be retrieved through WFS *GetFeature* request. Among the *GetFeature* request parameters are type name, bounding box, filter, and output format. A GML document or ESRI Shapefile containing the real feature data returned by WFS also is saved as a file with UUID name. All cached

Figure 7. AddGeoDataRequest in XML

```
<?xml version="1.0" encoding="UTF-8"?>
<AddGeoDataRequest xmlns="http://geobrain.laits.gmu.edu" xmlns:xsi="http://www.w3.org/2001/XMLSchema-instance"
xsi:schemaLocation="http://geobrain.laits.gmu.edu http://geobrain.laits.gmu.edu/yaxing/schemas/geobrain/GeoPortalManager.xsd">
    <GeoDataInfo>
        <geoDataType>Raster</geoDataType>
        <geoDataName>
/Volumes/RAIDL1/LANDSAT/WRS2/ETM/p015/p015r033_7x20011005.ETM-EarthSat-Orthorectified/p015r033_7i20011005_z18_n
n30.tif</geoDataName>
        <geoDataDescription>Landsat ETM Data, Path: 015, Row: 033, Satellite: LANDSAT-7, Band: 3 (Red), Date: 2001-10-05</
geoDataDescription>
        <geoDataFormat>GTiff</geoDataFormat>
        <geoDataURL>
http://geobrain.laits.gmu.edu:81/cgi-bin/wcs110?service=WCS&amp;version=1.0.0&amp;request=getCoverage&amp;coverage=GEOTI
FF:"/Volumes/RAIDL1/LANDSAT/WRS2/ETM/p015/p015r033_7x20011005.ETM-EarthSat-Orthorectified/p015r033_7i20011005_z1
8_nn30.tif":Band&amp;crs=EPSG:4326&amp;bbox=-77.1199,38.791513,-76.909395,38.99511&amp;format=GTiff&amp;width=629&amp;
height=775</geoDataURL>
        <geoServiceURL> </geoServiceURL>
        <BBOX>
            <crs>EPSG:4326</crs>
            <minx>-77.1199</minx>
            <miny>38.791513</miny>
            <maxx>-76.909395</maxx>
            <maxy>38.99511</maxy>
        </BBOX>
    </GeoDataInfo>
</AddGeoDataRequest>
```

Figure 8. RenderRequest in XML

```
<?xml version="1.0" encoding="UTF-8"?>
<RenderRequest xmlns="http://geobrain.laits.gmu.edu" xmlns:xsi="http://www.w3.org/2001/XMLSchema-instance"
xsi:schemaLocation="http://geobrain.laits.gmu.edu http://geobrain.laits.gmu.edu/yaxing/schemas/geobrain/GeoPortalManager.xsd">
    <RenderInfo>
        <imageid>img206293250428416840</imageid>
        <dataid>9c2c3429-9c34-43b0-bc95-3f41c0f02925</dataid>
        <gdsname>/Volumes/RAIDL1/GEOPORTAL_DATA_CACHE/data/4e54120f-362c-4560-bcc9-92817db28cc2.tif</gdsname>
        <bandno>1</bandno>
        <sizex>696</sizex>
        <sizey>582</sizey>
        <BBOX>
            <crs>EPSG:4326</crs>
            <minx>-77.13638591237113</minx>
            <miny>38.791513</miny>
            <maxx>-76.89290908762888</maxx>
            <maxy>38.99511</maxy>
        </BBOX>
        <format>PNG</format>
        <bScale>false</bScale>
        <palette>Gray</palette>
    </RenderInfo>
</RenderRequest>
```

temporary raster or vector files can be exported to the local machine in multiple formats and projection coordinates, so the user can work with them using GIS or RS desktop software.

The georeferenced image data (JPG, PNG, GIF or TIF) returned by a WMS *GetMap* request or WPS output also is kept in the cache directory with a temporary unique file name. The image can be directly loaded to the workbench.

3.3.3 Geospatial Data Visualization

Data visualization renders both raster and vector geospatial objects on the fly when processing a *RenderRequest* request, as shown in Figure 8. It also offers a set of configurable styles from which to choose.

To support map operations like Zoom In/Out, Pan, Full Extent, and Previous/Next View in the workbench, the portrayal middleware generates user specified maps quickly from cached geospatial data in the specified project, format, and style.

For raster data, besides the predefined styles *Gray, GrayWave, Rainbow, Nature,* and *Wave,* data visualization also supports scale-dependent styling as well as customized styling. By default, the selected color palette matches the min-max range of the data granule. When contrast enhancement is needed, the color palette will be mapped to the specified value range. A Classified color palette to render the data flexibly in a series of classes also is supported and allows for faster identification of important categories. Thus, the raster data can be visualized in many different

Figure 9. SOAP request and response

```
<?xml version="1.0" encoding="utf-8"?>
<soapenv:Envelope xmlns:soapenv="http://schemas.xmlsoap.org/soap/envelope/" xmlns:xsi="
http://www.w3.org/2001/XMLSchema-instance" xmlns:xsd="http://www.w3.org/2001/XMLSchema">
   <soapenv:Body>
      <ns1:ndvi xmlns:ns1="http://Grass_Raster_NDVI.grass.ws.laits.gmu.edu">
         <ns1:nirImageURL>
http://geobrain.laits.gmu.edu/geoportal_data_cache/data/eeaad060-6bc4-4117-95f1-f034d13b8171.tif</ns1:nirImageURL>
         <ns1:redImageURL>
http://geobrain.laits.gmu.edu/geoportal_data_cache/data/490ad4e3-cc10-4f02-a5f3-da04337a9f87.tif</ns1:redImageURL>
         <ns1:outputGeoTiffType>Float32</ns1:outputGeoTiffType>
      </ns1:ndvi>
   </soapenv:Body>
</soapenv:Envelope>
```

ways in GeOnAS. The contextual rendering of feature data is provided through a WMS *GetMap* request with SLD support.

3.3.4 Geospatial Data Analysis

Data analysis is the capability of performing advanced raster and vector analysis on the retrieved geospatial data. It offers the end-users a powerful Web service client to invoke GRASS WPS services and third party OGC-compliant WPS services within the SOA environment of GeOnAS. This function features the special characteristic of GeOnAS comparing to other geospatial Web portals.

One middleware, named the Web Service Caller Client, is implemented based on Axis2 Java APIs and deployed to discover, select, and invoke either inner or outer processing services asynchronously. The HTTP request and response messages are exchanged in SOAP format between the middleware and services. Consider invoking the Web Normalized Difference Vegetation Index (NDVI) service, the SOAP request and response are listed in Figure 9. The output link and format will be extracted from the SOAP response by the middleware. Next, the output will be cached as introduced in the section of Geospatial Data Retrieval, and then the visualized results will be returned to the browser client.

In consideration of the significant overhead in calling the geospatial Web service, E-mail notification is added in the middleware to inform of the invocation status if the working context is closed.

The useful geospatial analysis functions (for raster and vector data) are available through the graphic user interface (GUI) of the GeOnAS client. The client provides these functions with intuitive forms to input map data, select an operation and specify required parameters. Some raster analysis functions integrated in the client are image algebra, image stretching, clipping, mosaicking, spatial profiling, spatial filtering, classification, color composition, and statistics. Vector analysis functions include buffer analysis, shortest path and feature extraction. These common functions are very helpful and useful for users to quickly analyze those data retrieved from different source in GeOnAS environment.

3.3.5 Map Context Management

Map context management is creating and configuring new context, saving current context, and exporting context as a Keyhole Markup Language (KML) file, so the context can be integrated in Google Earth or other software supporting OGC WMC file to share geospatial data, visualize visualizing the analysis result and even validate the result of processing service.

When creating new context, the user can specify the context bounding box by location name, inputting coordinate values, or dragging the box in the integrated Google Map interface. The context file contains the information about the layers and the view window extent in use. This helps set up the work environment for next time. The saved context file also can be used for data sharing and publishing.

Figure 10. GeOnAS Web portal

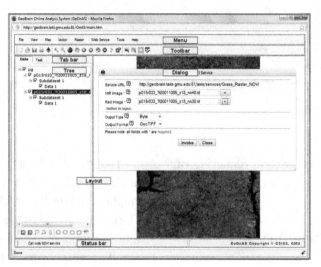

3.4 Desktop-Like Geospatial Portal

The browser client of GeOnAS is an SOA-enabled and Ajax-based rich internet application. This desktop-like geospatial portal allows processing of all presentation logic and user interaction flows in the common browsers.

The GUI components, Layout, Menu, Toolbar, Dialog, Tree, Tab, etc are integrated in the GeOnAS client so it looks and behaves more like traditional desktop applications, as shown in Figure 10. The appearance parameters including caption, color, font, position, images, and tip of these components are loaded from the configuration xml files.

Like the components of desktop software, the Layout component helps define the user interface structure, and specify web page elements along with their sizes programmatically. The classic layout of desktop GIS or RS software is adopted for convenience and consistency. By clicking on text and/or a symbol, a Menu/Toolbar component offers a quick, direct, and flexible shortcut for execution of each function or command. In response to the click event of an HTML element, associated callback functions are used to perform an operation. The Tree component allows users to show or hide the selected layer and control

display order. The tree list is updated dynamically when geospatial dataset is added or removed, and dataset information is presented in a hierarchical view. When the associated HTML element is selected, popup modeless or modal dialog with the content of user choice enables the user to input parameter values or specify other attributes for next operation. The Status Bar display has three sections: current state of user operation, mouse position, and copyright information. The Tab component is used to switch between the map layers tree list and the tasks list. The Tooltip component provides helpful information regarding the element over which the mouse cursor hovers.

4. DEMONSTRATION

GeOnAS is currently running in a cluster environment. In this SOA environment, it provides online access to heterogeneous geospatial data and powerful geospatial services to users worldwide and helps them discover and retrieve the right geospatial data for input to analytical services. The following demonstration using hydrologic analysis as an example shows GeOnAS's capa-

Figure 11. Stream extraction procedure

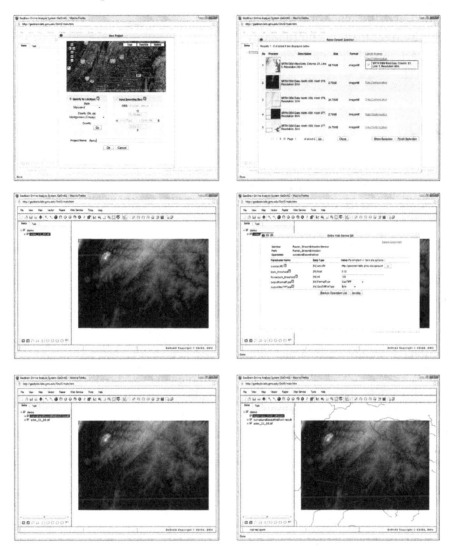

bilities for geospatial data accessing, retrieving, visualization and analysis.

Stream extraction is one of the common hydrologic modeling and geomorphologic analysis functions. Luo et al. (2009) introduce the implementation of wrapping a morphology-based method as a Web Service in GeOnAS to extract a stream network from Digital Elevation Model (DEM) data and to compare this method with others from GRASS and TauDEM which also have been wrapped as Web services and incorporated in GeOnAS. Figure 11 illustrates the stream extrac-

tion process in GeOnAS, using the SRTM 90m DEM dataset as an example. Figure 11a shows new context creation; the specified bounding box is that of Montgomery County, Maryland. In Figure 11b, metadata information of SRTM 90m DEM and preview images are displayed for choosing the waveband data. Figure 11c displays the subset of raster data covering the example area. Map data and other parameters required by the Web stream extraction service are specified in the form shown in Figure 11d. Figure 11e represents the output image of this service invocation. After adding USA River and Stream layer from WFS to the current context, the differences between the streams extracted by Web stream for morphology based stream extraction and the actual ones are shown as Figure 11f.

5. CONCLUSION

Since GeOnAS was released to the project partners for public testing on August 2007, nearly 6,000 users from around the world have visited its Web site. Figure 12 gives a specific overview map of the site visitors' distribution in the USA during the year of 2009. GeOnAS has demonstrated its cutting-edge capabilities in geospatial data publishing and accessing, information processing and retrieving, and knowledge building and sharing at several professional conferences(Deng & Di, 2009), among them, the AccessData 2008 Workshop, the ESIP 2008 Winter meeting, and W2GIS 2008. Furthermore, GeOnAS has been used in the research and classroom teaching of project partners and users, like Northern Illinois University, George Mason University, and Appalachian State University. Following the suggestions and feedback from users and project partners, the GeoBrain development team has improved system stability and reliability through clustering, optimized the source code to make the system faster and more responsive, and enriched system functions with a more intuitive interface and Web geospatial processing services that are more powerful.

GeOnAS will continue to exploit new features within the SOA environment. Cloud computing, reusable components, and toolkit development will be considered in the future development of GeOnAS. Cloud computing will help GeOnAS leverage more computing resources, which are needed in complex geospatial analysis. Reusable components and toolkits from GeOnAS will help the geosciences community establish their own cost effective portals to administer and operate

Figure 12. Visitors distribution

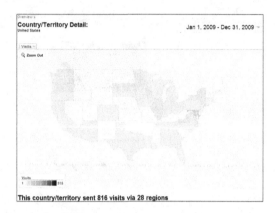

common services. In particular, these components will be useful and helpful to promote compatible service architectures and integrated Web portals. An authorization system also will be added to define and check users and their saved contexts. In addition, the *Canvas* object defined in HTML 5 will be used to render data with different styles in the client and reduce the support from server side.

In conclusion, GeOnAS provides an SOA-based learning and research environment to capture, load, and act upon distributed geospatial data in an efficient and effective manner. This consistent and comprehensive portal offers an effective user experience with nothing more than a web browser. It not only improves discovery, retrieval, and integration of geospatial data and information from multiple sources to address unique research needs, but also employs distributed Web geospatial services to perform specific tasks in a platform-independent fashion. It has great potential for impact on the work of Geosciences researchers around the world, and will help them migrate from desktop GIS or RS software to online data-rich and service-centric geospatial applications.

REFERENCES

Acker, J. G., & Leptoukh, G. (2007). Online analysis enhances use of NASA Earth science data. *Eos, Transactions, American Geophysical Union, 88*(2), 14–17. doi:10.1029/2007EO020003

Bai, Y., Di, L., Chen, A., Liu, Y., & Wei, Y. (2007). Towards a geospatial catalogue federation Service. *Photogrammetric Engineering and Remote Sensing, 73*(6), 699–708.

Bambacus, M., Yang, C., Evans, J., Cole, M., Alameh, N., & Marley, S. (2007). An interoperable portal supporting prototyping geospatial applications. *URISA Journal, 19*(2), 15–21.

Birk, R., Frederick, M., Dewayne, L. C., & Lapenta, M. W. (2006). NASA's applied sciences program: transforming research results into operational success. *Earth Imaging Journal, 3*(3), 18–23.

Box, D., Ehnebuske, D., Kakivaya, G., Layman, A., Mendelsohn, N., Nielsen, H. F., et al. (2000). *Simple Object Access Protocol (SOAP) Version 1.1*, W3C Note May 8, 2000. Retrieved October 13, 2007, from http://www.w3.org/TR/2000/NOTE-SOAP-20000508/

Carr, T. R., Rich, P. M., & Bartley, J. D. (2008). Linking distributed data from the carbon sequestration regional partnerships. *Journal of Map & Geography Libraries, 4*(1), 131–147. doi:10.1300/J230v04n01_08

Cepický, J., & Becchi, L. (2007). Geospatial processing via Internet on remote servers – PyWPS. *OSGeo Journal, 1*, 1-5.

Christiensen, E., Curbera, F., Meredith, G., & Weerawarana, S. (2001). *Web Service Description Language (WSDL) 1.1*, W3C Note March 15, 2001. Retrieved October 13, 2007, from http://www.w3.org/TR/wsdl

Deng, M., & Di, L. (2009). Building an online learning and research environment to enhance use of geospatial data. *International Journal of Spatial Data Infrastructures Research, 4*, 77–95.

Di, L., & Zhao, P. Han. W., Wei, Y., & Li X. (2007). GeoBrain Web Service-based Online Analysis System (GeOnAS). *Proceedings of NASA Earth Science Technology Conference 2007*, College Park, MD.

Foerster, T. (2006). An open software framework for web service-based geo-processing. *Proceedings of the Free and Open Source Software for Geospatial (FOSS4G 2006)*, Lausanne, Switzerland.

Foster, I. (2005). Service-Oriented science. *Science, 308*(5723), 814–817. doi:10.1126/science.1110411

Garret, J. J. (2005). *Ajax: A new approach to Web applications*. Retrieved December 18, 2009, from http://www.adaptivepath.com/publications/essays/archives/000385.php

Goodchild, M. F., Fu, P., & Rich, P. M. (2007). Geographic information sharing: the case of the Geospatial One-Stop portal. *Annals of the Association of American Geographers. Association of American Geographers, 97*(2), 250–266. doi:10.1111/j.1467-8306.2007.00534.x

Graves, S., Ramachandran, R., Keiser, K., Maskey, M., Lynnes, C., & Pham, L. (2007). Deployable suite of data mining Web services for online science data repositories. *Proceedings of the 87th AMS Annual meeting*, San Antonio, TX.

Han, W., Di, L., & Zhao, P. (2009). Using AJAX for desktop-like Geospatial Web application development. *Proceedings of the 17th International Conference on Geoinformatics*, Fairfax, VA.

Josuttis, N. M. (2007). *SOA in Practice*. Sebastopol, CA: O'Reilly.

Kiehle, C., Greve, K., & Heier, C. (2007). Requirements for next generation spatial data infrastructures-standardized Web based geoprocessing and Web service orchestration. *Transactions in GIS, 11*(6), 819–834. doi:10.1111/j.1467-9671.2007.01076.x

la Beaujardiere, D. J. (Ed.). (2006). *OGC Web map server implementation specification.* Wayland, MA: Open Geospatial Consortium Inc.

Lawton, G. (2008). New ways to build rich Internet applications. *Computer, 41*(8), 10–12. doi:10.1109/MC.2008.302

Luo, W., Li, X., Molloy, I., & Stepinski, T. (2009). Web service for extracting stream networks from DEM data. *Proceedings of the 17th International Conference on Geoinformatics*, Fairfax, VA.

Lupp, M. (Ed.). (2007). *OGC Styled Layer Descriptor profile of the Web map service implementation specification.* Wayland, MA: Open Geospatial Consortium Inc.

Maguire, D. J., & Longley, P. A. (2005). The emergence of geoportals and their role in spatial data infrastructures. *Computers, Environment and Urban Systems, 29*, 3–14.

Mandl, D., Sohlberg, R., Justice, C., Ungar, S., Ames, T., Frye, S., et al. (2007). Experiments with user centric GEOSS architectures. *Proceedings of IEEE International Geoscience and Remote Sensing Symposium 2007*, Barcelona, Spain.

Nash, E., Korduan, P., Abele, S., & Hobona, G. (2008). Design requirements for an AJAX and Web-Service based generic Internet GIS client. *The 11th AGILE International Conference on Geographic Information Science*, Girona, Spain.

Nativi, S. H. M., Domenico, B., Caron, J., Davis, E., & Bigagli, L. (2006). Extending THREDDS middleware to serve OGC community. *Advances in Geosciences, 8*, 57–62. doi:10.5194/adgeo-8-57-2006

Neteler, M., & Mitasova, H. (2007). *Open Source GIS: A GRASS GIS Approach.* New York: Springer.

Nezhad, H., Benatallah, B., Casati, F., & Toumani, F. (2006). Web services interoperability specifications. *Computer, 39*(5), 24–32. doi:10.1109/MC.2006.181

Paulson, L. D. (2005). Building rich Web applications with AJAX. *Computer, 38*(10), 14–17. doi:10.1109/MC.2005.330

Rose, L. (Ed.). (2004). *Geospatial Portal Reference Architecture, A Community Guide to Implementing Standards-Based Geospatial Portals.* Wayland, MA: Open Geospatial Consortium Inc.

Schut, P. (Ed.). (2007). *OpenGIS® Web Processing Service.* Wayland, MA: Open Geospatial Consortium Inc.

Sonnet, J. (Ed.). (2005). *OGC Web Map Context Documents.* Wayland, MA: Open Geospatial Consortium Inc.

Tang, W., & Selwood, J. (2005). *Spatial Portals: Gateways to Geographic Information.* Redlands, CA: ESRI Press.

Turner, A., Wang, C., & Journal, D. (2007). *Ajax: Selecting the framework that fits.* Retrieved October 13, 2009, from http://www.ddj.com/web-development/199203087

Voges, U., & Senkler, K. (Eds.). (2005). *OGC Catalogue Services specification 2.0 - ISO 19115/ISO 19119 application profile for CSW 2.0.* Wayland, MA: Open Geospatial Consortium Inc.

Vretanos, P. A. (Ed.). (2002). *OGC Web Feature Service implementation specification.* Wayland, MA: Open Geospatial Consortium Inc.

Whiteside, A., & Evans, J. D. (Eds.). (2008). *OGC Web Coverage Service implementation standard.* Wayland, MA: Open Geospatial Consortium Inc.

Yang, C., Cao, Y., Evans, J., Kafatos, M., & Bambacus, M. (2006). Spatial Web portal for building spatial data infrastructure. *Journal of Geographic Information Sciences, 12*(1), 38–43.

Zhang, T., & Tsou, M. (2009). Developing a grid-enabled spatial Web portal for Internet GIServices and geospatial cyberinfrastructure. *International Journal of Geographical Information Science, 23*(5), 605–630. doi:10.1080/13658810802698571

Zhao, P., Deng, D., & Di, L. (2005). Geospatial Web Service Client. *Proceedings of ASPRS 2005 Annual conference*, Baltimore.

ADDITIONAL READING

Agarwal, P. (2005). Ontological considerations in GIScience. *International Journal of Geographical Information Science, 19*(5), 501–536. doi:10.1080/13658810500032321

Alameh, N. (2003). Chaining Geographic Information Web Services. *IEEE Internet Computing, 6*(18), 22–29. doi:10.1109/MIC.2003.1232514

Atay, M., Chebotko, A., Liu, D., Lu, S., & Fotouhi, F. (2007). Efficient schema-based XML-to-Relational data mapping. *Information Systems, 32*(3), 458–476. doi:10.1016/j.is.2005.12.008

Baker, J. C., Lachman, B. E., Frelinger, D. R., O'Connell, K. M., Hou, A., & Tseng, M. S. (2004). *Assessing the homeland security implications of publicly available geospatial information*. Washington, DC: NGA.

Busby, J. R., & Kelly, P. (2004, February). Australian spatial data infrastructures. In *Proceedings of the 7th international global spatial data infrastructure conference*, Bangalore, India.

Craglia, M., & Masser, I. (2002). Geographic information and the enlargement of the European Union: four national case studies. [URISA]. *Journal of the Urban and Regional Information Systems Association, 14*(2), 43–52.

Curtain, G. G., Sommer, M. H., & Vis-Sommer, V. (Eds.). (2004). *The world of e-government*. Haworth, UK: Haworth Press.

Di, L., & Ramapriyan, H. K. (Eds.). (2010). *Standard-based data and Information Systems for Earth observation*. Berlin/Heidelberg, Germany: Springer-Verlag.

FGDC. (2004). *Geospatial one-stop: encouraging partnerships to enhance access to geospatial information*. Retrieved from http://www.fgdc.gov/publications/documents/geninfo/gos.pdf

Groot, R., & McLaughlin, J. (Eds.). (2000). *Geospatial data infrastructure: concepts, cases, and good practice*. New York: Oxford University Press.

Lemmens, R., Wytzisk, A., By, R. D., Granell, C., Gould, M., & Van Oosterom, P. (2006). Integrating semantic and syntactic descriptions to chain geographic services. *IEEE Internet Computing, 10*(5), 42–52. doi:10.1109/MIC.2006.106

Longley, P. A., Goodchild, M. F., Maguire, D. J., & Rhind, D. W. (2001). *Geographic information systems and science*. Chichester, UK: Wiley.

Masser, I. (1999). All shapes and sizes: the first generation of national spatial data infrastructures. *International Journal of Geographical Information Science, 13*(1), 67–84. doi:10.1080/136588199241463

Smith, B., & Mark, D. M. (2001). Geographical categories: an ontological investigation. *International Journal of Geographical Information Science, 15*(7), 591–621. doi:10.1080/13658810110061199

Stal, M. (2002). Web services: Beyond component based computing. *Journal of Communication ACM.*, *45*(10), 71–76.

Swan, J., Foerster, T., Lemmens, R., Hobona, G., Anand, S. & Jackson, M. (2008). Discovery and invocation of schematization services: a use case for OGC-EuroSDRAGILE persistent test bed for Europe. *GEOconnexion International magazine, 7*(10): 24-27.

Tait, M. G. (2005). Implementing geoportals: applications of distributed GIS. *Computers, Environment and Urban Systems, 29*(1), 33–47.

Van Loenen, B., & Kok, B. C. (Eds.). (2004). *Spatial data infrastructure and policy development in Europe and the United States*. Delft, UK: DUP Science.

Williamson, I. P., Rajabifard, A., & Feeney, M. E. (Eds.). (2003). *Developing spatial data infrastructures: from concept to reality*. New York: Taylor & Francis. doi:10.1201/9780203485774

Zhao, P., Di, L., Yue, P., Yu, G., & Yang, W. (2009). Semantic web based geospatial knowledge transformation. *Computers & Geosciences, 35*(4), 798–808. doi:10.1016/j.cageo.2008.03.013

KEY TERMS AND DEFINITIONS

Ajax: Stands for Asynchronous JavaScript and XML, which bundles several familiar technologies together in new ways, including Document Object Model, Cascading Style Sheets, Dynamic HyperText Markup Language, Extensible Markup Language, and JavaScript.

GeoBrain: A comprehensive cyberinfrastructure that provides advanced, specialized, value-added, and well-integrated Earth observation data, information and knowledge services to worldwide users. It is supported by NASA's Research, Education and Applications Solution Network (REASoN) program (No. NNG04GE61A).

GeOnAS: Abbreviation of GeoBrain Online Analysis System, it offers multisource geospatial data discovery, heterogeneous geospatial data retrieval, simultaneous geospatial data visualization, and powerful geospatial data analysis.

OGC: Abbreviation of Open Geospatial Consortium, an international standards organization, which has developed a series of standards for geospatial contexts and services.

SOA: Stands for Service Oriented Architecture, which is an architecture that organizes discrete software functionality in a uniform way as discoverable and reusable Web services over the network.

Web Portal: An entry point that offers more reliable, multisource, up-to-date, and user-friendly information.

Web Service: A standard based Web interface to software functionality, it should be self-contained, self-describing, reusable, and application-based units of work.

Compilation of References

°North. (2010a). *52°North Geoprocessing Code Repository for GRASS support.* Retrieved from http://52north. org/svn/geoprocessing/main/WPS/trunk/WPS/52n-wps-grass/

°North. (2010b). *52°North Geoprocessing Community Roadmap 2010.* Retrieved from http://52north.org/maven/ project-sites/wps/52n-wps-site/index.html

Aalst, W. (2003). Don't go with the flow: web services composition standards exposed. *IEEE Intelligent Systems, 18*(1), 72–76.

Acker, J. G., & Leptoukh, G. (2007). Online analysis enhances use of NASA Earth science data. *Eos, Transactions, American Geophysical Union, 88*(2), 14–17. doi:10.1029/2007EO020003

Ackland, R. (2009). Social network services as data sources and platforms for e-researching social Networks. *Social Science Computer Review, 27*, 481–492. doi:10.1177/0894439309332291

Ackoff, R. (1989). From data to wisdom. *Journal of Applied System Analysis, 16*, 3–9.

Adleman, L., Rivest, R. L., & Shamir, A. (1978). A method for obtaining digital signature and public-key cryptosystems. *Communications of the ACM, 21*(2), 120–126. doi:10.1145/359340.359342

Agarwal, P. (2005). Ontological considerations in GIScience. *International Journal of Geographical Information Science, 19*(5), 501–536. doi:10.1080/13658810500032321

Agumya, A., & Hunter, G. J. (1997). Determining fitness for use of geographic information. *ITC Journal, 2*(4), 109–113.

AIP. (2009). *AIP-2 Engineering Reports, OGC Network.* Retrieved December 21, 2009, from http://www.ogcnetwork.net/AIP2ERs

Aissi, S., Malu, P., & Srinivasan, K. (2002). E-business process modeling: the next big step. *IEEE Computer, 35*(5), 55–62.

Akkiraju, R., Farell, J., Miller, J. A., Nagarajan, M., Sheth, A., & Verma, K. (2005). *Web service semantics - WSDL-S.* Retrieved March 3, 2007, from http://www. w3.org/2005/04/FSWS/Submissions/17/WSDL-S.htm.

Alameh, N. (2003). Chaining geographic information Web Services. *IEEE Internet Computing, 07*(5), 22–29. doi:10.1109/MIC.2003.1232514

Alegre, C., Sassier, H., Pierotti, S., & Lazaridis, P. (2005). A new geo-information architecture of risk management . In Oosterom, P., Zlatanove, S., & Fendel, E. M. (Eds.), *Geo-Information for Disaster Management* (pp. 543–550). Berlin: Springer. doi:10.1007/3-540-27468-5_38

Alexander, C. (1964). *Notes on the Synthesis of Form.* Cambridge, MA: Harvard Press.

Allcock, W. E., Bester, J., Bresnahan, J., Chervenak, A. L., Foster, I. T., Kesselman, C., et al. (2001). Secure, efficient data transport and replica management for high-performance data-intensive computing. *CoRR, cs. DC/0103.* Retrieved from http://dblp.uni-trier.de/db/ journals/corr/corr0103.html#cs-DC-0103022

Alonso, G., Casati, F., Kuno, H., & Machiraju, V. (2004). *Web services: concepts, architectures and applications*. Berlin: Springer Verlag.

Altintas, I., Birnbaum, A., Baldridge, K., Sudholt, W., Miller, M., Amoreira, C., et al. (2004). A framework for the design and reuse of grid workflows. In *Proceedings of International Workshop on Scientific Applications on Grid Computing, SAG 2004*, LNCS 3458, pp. 119–132. Springer.

Andrei, M., Berre, A., Costa, L., Duchesne, P., Fitzner, D., Grcar, M., et al. (2008). *SWING: A Geospatial Semantic Web service environment*. Paper given at the Workshop on Semantic Web meets Geospatial Applications, and AGILE 2008.

Andrews, T., Curbera, F., Dholakia, H., Goland, Y., Klein, J., Leymann, F., et al. (2003). *Business process execution language for Web Services (version 1.1)*. 136. OASIS. Retrieved from http://download.boulder.ibm.com/ibmdl/pub/ software/dw/ specs/ws-bpel/ ws-bpel.pdf

Anjomashoaa, A., Brisard, F., Drescher, M., Fellows, D., Ly, A., & McGough, S. (2005). *Job Submission Description Language (JSDL) (Specification No. GFD-R.056)*. Global Grid Forum.

Ankolekar, A., Burstein, M. H., Hobbs, J. R., Lassila, O., Martin, D. L., McIlraith, S. A., et al. (2001). DAML-S: Semantic Markup for Web Services. In I. Cruz, F. Decker, S. Euzenat, & J. McGuinness (Ed.), *First Semantic Web Working Symposium, Vol. 75. SWWS* (pp. 411-430). IOS Press.

Annoni, A., Bernard, L., Douglas, J., Greenwood, J., Laiz, I., & Lloyd, M. (2005). Orchestra: Developing a unified open architecture for risk management applications . In Oosterom, P., Zlatanove, S., & Fendel, E. M. (Eds.), *Geo-Information for Disaster Management* (pp. 1–17). Berlin: Springer. doi:10.1007/3-540-27468-5_1

Antoniou, G., & Harmelen, F. V. (2004). *A semantic web primer* (pp. 17–18). Cambridge, MA: The MIT Press.

ANZLIC Spatial Information Council. (2010). *Australian Spatial Data Infrastructure*. Retrieved July 9, 2010 from http://www.anzlic.org.au/ASDI_quick.html

Arbia, G., Griffith, D., & Haining, R. (1998). Error propagation modelling in raster GIS: overlay operations. *International Journal of Geographical Information Science, 12*(2), 145–167. doi:10.1080/136588198241932

Arbia, G., Griffith, D., & Haining, R. (1999). Error propagation modelling in raster GIS: adding and ratioing operations. *Cartography and Geographic Information Science, 26*(4), 297–315. doi:10.1559/152304099782294159

Armbrust, M., Fox, A., Griffith, R., Joseph, A. D., Katz, R. H., Konwinski, A., et al. (2009). *Above the clouds: A Berkeley view of cloud computing*. Retrieved from http://www.eecs.berkeley.edu/Pubs/TechRpts/2009/ EECS-2009-28.html

Arroyo, S., Lara, R., Gómez, J., Berka, D., Ding, Y., & Fensel, D. (2004). Semantic aspects of Web services . In Singh, M. (Ed.), *Practical Handbook of Internet Computing*. Baton Rouge, LA and New York, NY: Chapman & Hall and CRC Press. doi:10.1201/9780203507223.ch31

Athanasis, N., Kalabokidis, K., Vaitis, M., & Soulakellis, N. (2009). Towards a semantics-based approach in the development of geographic portals. *Computers & Geosciences, 35*(2), 301–308. doi:10.1016/j.cageo.2008.01.014

Auer, S., Lehmann, J., & Hellmann, S. (2009). LinkedGeoData: adding a spatial dimension to the Web of data. In *Proceedings of the ISWC 2009*, LNCS 5823, 731-746.

Axelrod, R. (1997). *The complexity of cooperation: agent-based models of competition and collaboration*. Princeton, NJ: Princeton University Press.

Baader, F., & Nutt, W. (2003). Basic description logics . In Baader, F., Calvanese, D., & McGuinness, D. (Eds.), *The description logic handbook: Theory, implementation and applications* (pp. 43–95). Cambridge, UK: Cambridge University Press.

Bai, Y., Di, L., & Wei, Y. (2009). A taxonomy of geospatial services for global service discovery and interoperability. *Computers & Geosciences, 35*, 783–790. doi:10.1016/j.cageo.2007.12.018

Bai, Y., Di, L., Chen, A., Liu, Y., & Wei, Y. (2007). Towards a geospatial catalogue federation Service. *Photogrammetric Engineering and Remote Sensing, 73*(6), 699–708.

Bai, Y., Di, L., & Keiser, K. (2007a). *Review of NASA ECHO (version 8) Web service registration process*, Technical Whitepaper submitted to the Earth Science Data Systems' Technology Infusion Working Group.

Bambacus, M., Yang, C., Evans, J., Cole, M., Alameh, N., & Marley, S. (2007). An interoperable portal supporting prototyping geospatial applications. *URISA Journal, 19*(2), 15–21.

Baranski, B. (2008). Grid computing enabled Web processing service. In E. Pebesma, M. Bishr, & T. Bartoschek (Eds.), *Proceedings of the 6th Geographic Information Days*, IfGI prints (Vol. 32, pp. 243-256). Presented at the GI-days 2008, Muenster, Germany: Institute for Geoinformatics. Retrieved from http://www.gi-tage. de/ archive/2008/ downloads/accepted Papers/Papers/ Baranski.pdf

Baranski, B. (2009). *OWS-6 WPS Grid Processing Profile Engineering Report* (OGC Public Engineering Report No. 09-041r3) (p. 101). OGC.

Baranski, B. (Ed.). (2009). *OGC OWS-6 WPS grid processing profile engineering report*. (Version 1.0.0, 09-041r3).

Baranski, B., Schaeffer, B., & Redweik, R. (2009). Geoprocessing in the clouds. In *Proceedings of Free and Open Source Software for Geospatial Conference*. Presented at the Foss4g 2009, Sydney: OSGeo.

Barker, A., Weissman, J. B., & Hemert, J. I. (2009). The circulate architecture: avoiding workflow bottlenecks caused by centralised orchestration. *Cluster Computing, 12*(2), 221–235. doi:10.1007/s10586-009-0072-4

Barros, A., Dumas, M., & Oaks, P. (2005). A critical overview of the web service choreography description language (WS-CDL). *BPTrends Newsletter, 3*(3).

Basney, J., Humphrey, M., & Welch, V. (2005). The MyProxy online credential repository: research articles. *Software, Practice & Experience, 35*(9), 801–816. doi:10.1002/spe.688

Battle, S., Bernstein, A., Boley, H., et al. (2005). *Semantic web services framework (SWSF) overview*. Retrieved November 17, 2006, from http://www.w3.org/Submission/2005/SUBM-SWSF-20050909/

Bechhofer, S., van Harmelen, F., Hendler, J., Horrocks, I., McGuinness, D. L., Patel-Schneider, P. F., et al. (2003). *OWL Web ontology language reference*. Retrieved November 18, 2009, from http://www.w3.org/TR/owl-ref/

Beck, U. (1992). *Risk society: Towards a new modernity*. London: Sage Publications Ltd.

Becker, C., & Bizer, C. (2009). Exploring the Geospatial Semantic Web with DBpedia Mobile. *Journal of Web Semantics: Science . Services and Agents on the World Wide Web, 7*(4), 278–286. doi:10.1016/j.websem.2009.09.004

Bell, M. (2008). *Introduction to service-oriented modeling. Service-oriented modeling: service analysis, design, and architecture*. Wiley & Sons.

Bell, M. (2008). *Service-Oriented Modeling (SOA): service analysis, design, and architecture*. Hoboken, New Jersey: Wiley & Sons.

Bell, D., & Lapadula, J. (1973). *Secure computer systems: A mathematical model (Microfiche ed.)*.

Bell, G., Parisi, A., & Pesce, M. (1995). *The virtual reality modeling language (version 1.0) specification*. Retrieved from http://www.web3d.org/technicalinfo/specifications/ VRML1.0/index.html

Benatallah, B., Dumas, M., Fauvet, M.-C., & Abhi, F. A. (2001). *Towards patterns of web service composition. Technical report, UNSWCSE -TR-0111*. University of New South Wales.

Bennett, K., Layzell, P., Budgen, D., Brereton, P., Macaulay, L., & Munro, M. (2000). Service-based software: the future for flexible software. *APSEC, 2000*, 214–221.

Bergenheim, W., Sarjakoski, L. T., & Sarjakoski, T. (2009). A Web processing service for GRASS GIS to provide on-line generalisation. In J. Haunert, B. Kieler & J. Milde (Eds.), *Proceedings of the 12th AGILE International Conference on Geographic Information Science (AGILE)*. Hannover, Germany.

Bernard, L., & Craglia, M. (2005). *SDI—from spatial data infrastructure to service-driven infrastructure, research workshop on cross-learning between SDI and II. First research workshop on cross-learning on spatial data infrastructures (SDI) and information infrastructures (II).* International Institute for Geo-Information Science and Earth Observation.

Bernard, L., Kanellopoulos, L., Annoni, A., & Smits, P. (2005). The European Geoportal—one step towards the establishment of a European spatial data infrastructure. *Computers, Environment and Urban Systems, 29*(1), 15–31.

Bernard, L., Craglia, M., Gould, M., & Kuhn, W. (2005). Towards an SDI research agenda. In *Proceedings of the 11th EC GIS Conference* (pp. 147-151). Presented at the 11th EC GIS & GIS Workshop and ESDI: Setting the Framework, Sardinia, Italy.

Berners-Lee, T., Hendler, J., & Lassila, O. (2001). The Semantic Web. *Scientific American Magazine, 284*(5), 34–43. doi:10.1038/scientificamerican0501-34

Berners-Lee, T., Fielding, R., & Frystyk, H. (1996). *Hypertext Transfer Protocol -- HTTP/1.0.* USA: RFC Editor.

Berners-Lee, T. (2000a). *Semantic Web talk.* Invited Talk at XML 2000 Conference. Retrieved May 8, 2006, from http://www.w3.org/2000/Talks/1206-xml2k-tbl/slide10-0.html.

Berners-Lee, T. (2000b). *CWM - closed world machine.* Retrieved June 10, 2007, from http://www.w3.org/2000/10/swap/doc/cwm.html.

Berners-Lee, T., Fielding, R., & Masinter, L. (1998). Uniform Resource Identifiers (URI): Generic syntax. *Internet Engineering Task Force (IETF) Memo – RFC 2396.*

Berners-Lee, T., Hendler, J., & Lassila, O. (2001). The Semantic Web. *Scientific American,* Retrieved July 9, 2010, from http://www.scientificamerican.com/article.cfm?id=the-semantic-web

Bernstein, A., & Klein, M. (2002). Towards high-precision service retrieval. In I. Horrocks and J. Hendler (Eds.), *Proceedings from The First International Semantic Web Conference (ISWC 2002),* (pp. 84-101). Sardinia, Italy: Springer.

Bertolotto, M., & Egenhofer, M. J. (2001). Progressive transmission of vector map data over the World Wide Web. *GeoInformatica, 5*(4), 345–373. doi:10.1023/A:1012745819426

Binder, W., Constantinescu, I., & Faltings, B. (2006). *Decentralized orchestration of Composite Web Services* (pp. 869–876). ICWS.

Birk, R., Frederick, M., Dewayne, L. C., & Lapenta, M. W. (2006). NASA's applied sciences program: transforming research results into operational success. *Earth Imaging Journal, 3*(3), 18–23.

Bishop, M. (2005). *Introduction to computer security.* Boston: Addison-Wesley.

Bishop, B., & Fischer, F. (2008). IRIS - Integrated Rule Inference System. *Proceedings from the 1st Workshop on Advancing Reasoning on the Web: Scalability and Commonsense (ARea2008) at the 5th European Semantic Web Conference (ESWC'08), Tenerife, Spain.*

Bishr, Y. (1998). Overcoming the semantic and other barriers to GIS interoperability. *International Journal of Geographical Information Science, 12,* 299–314. doi:10.1080/136588198241806

Bishr, M., & Mantelas, L. (2008). A trust and reputation model for filtering and classifying knowledge about urban growth. *GeoJournal, 72*(3-4), 229–237. doi:10.1007/s10708-008-9182-4

Bishr, Y. (1998). Overcoming the semantic and other barriers to GIS interoperability. *International Journal of Geographical Information Science, 12*(4), 299–314. doi:10.1080/136588198241806

Bishr, Y., Pundt, H., Kuhn, W., Molenaar, M., & Radwan, M. (1997). Probing the concept of information communities-a first step toward semantic interoperability. M.F. Goodchild, et al (Eds.), *Proceedings of Interop'97-Interoperating Geographic Information Systems*, 55-71. Kluwer.

Bittner, T. (1997). A qualitative coordinate language of location of figures within the ground. *Proceedings from the International Conference on Spatial Information Theory: A Theoretical Basis for GIS table of contents.* Laurel Highlands, PEN.

Bizer, C. (2009). The emerging Web of linked data. *IEEE Intelligent Systems, 24*(5), 87–92. doi:10.1109/MIS.2009.102

Bizer, C., Heath, T., & Berners-Lee, T. (2009a). Linked data - the story so far. *International Journal on Semantic Web and Information Systems, 5*(3), 1–22.

Bizer, C., Lehmann, J., Kobilarov, G., Auer, S., Becker, C., & Cyganiak, R. (2009b). DBpedia - A crystallization point for the Web of data. *Web Semantics: Science . Services and Agents on the World Wide Web, 7*(3), 154–165. doi:10.1016/j.websem.2009.07.002

Bizer, C., Heath, T., & Berners-Lee, T. (2008). Linked data: principles and state of the art. *Proceedings from the World Wide Web Conference, 2008.*

Boley, H., Tabet, S., & Wagner, G. (2001, July-August). Design rationale of RuleML: a markup language for semantic web rules, In *Proceedings of SWWS'01*. Stanford, CA.

Booth, D., Haas, H., McCabe, F., Newcomer, E., Champion, M., Ferris, C., & Orchard, D. (2004). *Web services architecture*. W3C working group note. Retrieved October 10, 2009, from http://www.w3.org/TR/ws-arch/

Borodin, A., Roberts, G. O., Rosenthal, J. S., & Tsaparas, P. (2005). Link analysis ranking: algorithms, theory, and experiments. *ACM Transactions on Internet Technology, 5*(1), 231–297. doi:10.1145/1052934.1052942

Box, D., Ehnebuske, D., Kakivaya, G., Layman, A., Mendelsohn, N., Nielsen, H. F., et al. (2000). *Simple Object Access Protocol (SOAP) Version 1.1*, W3C Note May 8, 2000. Retrieved October 13, 2007, from http://www.w3.org/TR/2000/NOTE-SOAP-20000508/

Boyd, D., & Ellison, N. (2007). Social network sites: definition, history, and scholarship. *Journal of Computer-Mediated Communication, 13*(1).

Brauner, J. (2008). Providing GRASS with a Web processing service interface. In E. Pebesma, M. Bishr, & T. Bartoschek (Eds.), *Proceedings of the 6th Geographic Information Days*, IfGI prints (Vol. 32, pp. 91-116). Presented at the GI-days 2008, Muenster, Germany: Institute for Geoinformatics.

Brauner, J., & Schaeffer, B. (2008). *Integration of GRASS functionality in Web based SDI service chains.* (pp. 420-429). Presented at the FOSS4G 2008, Cape Town, South Africa. Retrieved from http://www.osgeo.org/ocs/index.php/foss4g/2008/paper/view/133

Brauner, J., Foerster, T., Schaeffer, B., & Baranski, B. (2009). Towards a research agenda for geoprocessing services. In J. Haunert, B. Kieler, & J. Milde (Eds.), *12th AGILE International Conference on Geographic Information Science.* Presented at the AGILE 2009, Hanover, Germany: IKG, Leibniz University of Hanover. Retrieved from http://www.ikg.uni-hannover.de/agile/file admin/agile/paper/124.pdf

Brickley, D., & Guha, R.V. (2004). *RDF vocabulary description language 1.0.*

Brin, S., & Page, L. (1998). The anatomy of a large-scale hypertextual Web search engine, *7th International World Wide Web Conference, 30*, 107-117.

Bröring, A., Janowicz, K., Stasch, C., & Kuhn, W. (2009). Semantic challenges for sensor plug and play. In: *Web & Wireless Geographical Information Systems, 7 & 8.* Maynooth, Ireland.

Brujin, J., Bussler, C., Fensel, D., Hepp, M., Keller, U., Kifer, M., et al. (2005). Web Service Modelling Ontology (WSMO). *World Wide Web Consortium*, Retrieved July 9, 2010, from http://www.w3.org/Submission/WSMO/

Bucher, B., & Jolivet, L. (2008). Acquiring service oriented descriptions of GI processing software from experts. In Bernard, L., Friis-Christensen, A., Pundt, H., & Compte, I. (Eds.), *AGILE 2008*.

Budhathoki, N. R., Bruce, B., & Nedovic-Budic, Z. (2008). Reconceptualizing the role of the user of spatial data infrastructure. *GeoJournal, 72*(3-4), 149–160. doi:10.1007/s10708-008-9189-x

Buehler, K., & McKee, L. (Eds.). (1996). *The OpenGIS Guide: introduction to interoperable geoprocessing and the OpenGIS specification*. OGIS TC Document 96-001, OGIS Project 6 Technical Committee of the OpenGIS Consortium, Inc.

Burnett, M., Weinstein, B., & Mitchell, A. (2007). ECHO – enabling interoperability with NASA earth science data and services. *Proceedings from Geoscience and Remote Sensing Symposium and IGARSS 2007*.

Butler, R., Welch, V., Engert, D., Foster, I. T., Tuecke, S., Volmer, J., et al. (2000). A national-scale authentication infrastructure. In *IEEE Computer, 33*(12), 60-66.

Cai, C., Schade, S., & Gudiyangada, T. (2010). Schema mapping in INSPIRE - extensible components for translating geospatial data. *Proceedings from the 13th AGILE Conference on GIScience*.

Callahan, K. M. (1985). Social science research in the information age: online databases for social scientists. *Social Science Computer Review, 3*, 28–44. doi:10.1177/089443938500300104

Caltech. (2007). *Fast Data Transfer (FDT) service*. Retrieved from http://monalisa.cern.ch/FDT/

Canadian Geospatial Data Infrastructure Architecture Working Group. (2005). *The Canadian Geospatial Data Infrastructure Architecture Description Version 2.0*. Retrieved Dec. 11, 2009, from http://www.geoconnections.org/publications/tvip/arch_E/CGDI_Architecture_final_E.html

Cardoso, J., Miller, J., Sheth, A., Arnold, J., & Kochut, K. (2004). Modeling quality of service for workflows and web service processes. *Web Semantics: Science, Services, and Agents on the World Wide Web, 1*(3), 281–308. doi:10.1016/j.websem.2004.03.001

Cardoso, J., & Sheth, A. (2003). Semantic e-workflow composition. *Journal of Intelligent Information Systems, 21*(3), 191–225. doi:10.1023/A:1025542915514

Carr, T. R., Rich, P. M., & Bartley, J. D. (2008). Linking distributed data from the carbon sequestration regional partnerships. *Journal of Map & Geography Libraries, 4*(1), 131–147. doi:10.1300/J230v04n01_08

Casati, R., & Varzi, A. C. (1999). *Parts and places. The Structures of Spatial Representation*. Cambridge, MA: MIT Press.

Casati, F., Ilnicki, S., Jin, L., & Krishnamoorthy, V. (2000). *Adaptive and dynamic service composition in eFlow*. Technical Report HPL-2000-39, HP Laboratories, Palo Alto.

Casati, F., Sayal, M., & Shan, M. (2001, June). Developing e-services for composing e-services. In *Proceedings of 13th International Conference on Advanced Information Systems Engineering(CAiSE)*, Interlaken, Switzerland. Springer-Verlag.

Caspary, W., & Scheuring, R. (1993). Positional accuracy in spatial databases. *Computers, Environment and Urban Systems, 17*, 103–110. doi:10.1016/0198-9715(93)90040-C

Cepický, J., & Becchi, L. (2007). Geospatial processing via Internet on remote servers – PyWPS. *OSGeo Journal, 1*, 1-5.

Chandrasekaran, S., Miller, J. A., Silver, G. S., Arpinar, B., & Sheth, A. P. (2003). Performance analysis and simulation of composite web services. *EM – . Electronic Markets, 13*(2), 120–132. doi:10.1080/1019678032000067217

Chappell, D. (2008). *A short introduction to cloud platforms: an enterprise-oriented view*. Retrieved November 18, 2009, from http://www.davidchappell.com/CloudPlatforms-Chappell.pdf

Chen, N., Di, L., Yu, G., & Wei, Y. (2009). Use of ebRIM-based CSW with sensor observation services for registry and discovery of remote-sensing observations. *Computers & Geosciences, 35,* 360–372. doi:10.1016/j.cageo.2008.08.003

Chen, M., Ebert, D., Hagen, H., Laramee, R., van Liere, R., & Ma, K. (2009). Data, information, and knowledge in visualization. *Computer Graphics and Applications, IEEE, 29*(1), 12–19. doi:10.1109/MCG.2009.6

Chen, R., & Xie, J. (2008). Open source databases and their spatial extensions . In Hall, G. B., & Leahy, M. G. (Eds.), *Open Source Approaches in Spatial Data Handling* (pp. 105–129). Berlin: Springer-Verlag. doi:10.1007/978-3-540-74831-1_6

Christiensen, E., Curbera, F., Meredith, G., & Weerawarana, S. (2001). *Web Service Description Language (WSDL) 1.1,* W3C Note March 15, 2001. Retrieved October 13, 2007, from http://www.w3.org/TR/wsdl

Chung, L., Fang, Y., Chou, T., Lee, B., & Baranski, B. (2009). A SOA based debris flow monitoring system. Architecture and proof-of-concept implementation. In *17th International Conference on Geoinformatics* (pp. 1-6). Presented at the Geoinformatics 2009, Washington, USA: IEEE.

Clayberg, E., & Rubel, D. (2008). *Eclipse Plug-ins* (3rd ed.). Addison-Wesley Professional.

Clery, D., & Voss, D. (2005). All for one and one for all. *Science, 308*(5723), 809. doi:10.1126/science.308.5723.809

Compliance, O.G.C. (2010). Retrieved from http://www.opengeospatial.org/compliance

Compliant, O. G. C. (2010). Retrieved from http://www.opengeospatial.org/resource/products/compliant

Conover, H., Goodman, H., Zavodsky, B., Regner, K., Maskey, M., Lu, J., et al. (2008). *Intelligent Assimilation of Satellite Data into a Forecast Model Using Sensor Web Processes and Protocols.*

Cox, S. (2007). OGC implementation specification 07-022r1: observations and measurements, part 1 – observation schema.

Craglia, M., Goodchild, M., Annoni, A., Camara, G., Gould, M., & Kuhn, W. (2008). Next-generation digital Earth. *International Journal of Spatial Data Infrastructure Research, 3*(1), 146–167.

Critchell-Ward, A., & Landsborough-McDonald, K. (2007). Data protection law in the European Union and the United Kingdom. In D. Campbell, & A. Alibekova (Eds.), *The comparative law yearbook of international business* (pp. 515-578). Alphen uan den Rhin: Kluwer Law International.

Crompvoets, J., Rajabifard, A., Bregt, A., & Williamson, I. P. (2004). Assessing the worldwide developments of national spatial data clearinghouses. *International Journal of Geographical Information Science, 18*(7), 1–25. doi:10.1080/13658810410001702030

Crompvoets, J., & Bregt, A. (2007). National spatial data clearinghouses, 2000–2005 . In Onsrud, H. (Ed.), *Research and theory in advancing spatial data infrastructure* (pp. 133–146). Redlands, CA: ESRI Press.

Cruz, I., & Sunna, W. (2008). Structural alignment methods with applications to geospatial ontologies. *Transactions in GIS, 12*(6), 683–711. doi:10.1111/j.1467-9671.2008.01126.x

Curbera, F., Duftler, M., Khalaf, R., Nagy, W., Mukhi, N., & Weerawarana, S. (2002). Unravelling the Web services web: an introduction to SOAP, WSDL, and UDDI. *IEEE Internet Computing, 6*(2), 86–93. doi:10.1109/4236.991449

Czajkowski, K., Ferguson, D. F., Foster, I., Frey, J., Graham, S., Sedukhin, I., et al. (2005). *The WS-Resource Framework.* Retrieved from http://www.globus.org/wsrf/specs/ws-wsrf.pdf

Daemen, J., & Rijmen, V. (2002). *The design of rijndael: AES - the advanced encryption standard with 17 tables.* Berlin: Springer.

Davidson, S. B., & Freire, J. (2008). Provenance and scientific workflows: challenges and opportunities. *International Conference on Management of Data*. Retrieved from http://portal.acm.org/citation.cfm?id=1376772#

Decker, G., Kopp, O., Leymann, F., & Weske, M. (2007). *BPEL4Chor: Extending BPEL for Modeling Choreographies. IEEE International Conference on Web Services (ICWS 2007)* (pp. 296-303). IEEE.

De Bruijn, J., Lausen, H., Polleres, A., & Fensel, D. (2006). *The Web Service Modelling Language - WSML: An overview*. Berlin and Heidelberg, Germany: Springer.

de Bruijn, J., Bussler, C., Domingue, J., et al. (2005). *Web service modeling ontology (WSMO)*. Retrieved March 16, 2007, from http://www.w3.org/Submission/WSMO/

de Jesus, J., Hiemstra, P., & Dubois, G. (2008). Web-based geostatistics using WPS. In *Proceedings of GI-days 2008*. Institute for Geoinformatics.

de La Beaujardiére, J. (2002). *Web map service implementation specification*. Open Geospatial Consortium. Retrieved from http://portal.opengeospatial.org/files/?artifact_id=1081&version=1&format=pdf

de la Beaujardière, J. (2006). *Web Map Server Implementation Specification (Version 1.3.0)*. Retrieved March 1, 2010, from http://portal.opengeospatial.org/files/index.php?artifact_id=14416.

De Roure, D. (2006). Vision and research directions 2010 and beyond - future for European Grids: Grids and service-oriented knowledge utilities. *Next Generation Grids Expert Group Report 3*.

De Roure, D., Goble, C., Bhagat, J., Cruickshank, D., Goderis, A., Michaelides, D., et al. (2008). myExperiment: Defining the social virtual research environment. *Computer*. IEEE Press. Retrieved from http://eprints.ecs.soton.ac.uk/16560

Deng, M., & Di, L. (2009). Building an online learning and research environment to enhance use of geospatial data. *International Journal of Spatial Data Infrastructures Research, 4*, 77–95.

Densham, P. J. (1991). *Spatial decision support systems. Geographical Information Systems: Principles and Applications*. London: Longman.

Depledge, M. (2009). Novel approaches and technologies in pollution assessment and monitoring. *Ocean and Coastal Management, 52*, 336–341. doi:10.1016/j.ocecoaman.2009.04.001

Devillers, R., Bedard, Y., & Jeansoulin, R. (2005). Multidimensional management of geospatial data quality information for its dynamic use within GIS. *Photogrammetric Engineering and Remote Sensing, 71*(2), 205–215.

Di, L. (2005). A framework for developing web-service-based intelligent geospatial knowledge systems. *Journal of Geographic Information Sciences, 11*(1), 24–28.

Di, L., & Zhao, P. (2008). Geospatial Semantic Web interoperability . In Shekhar, S., & Xiong, H. (Eds.), *Encyclopedia of GIS* (pp. 70–77). Springer. doi:10.1007/978-0-387-35973-1_119

Di, L., & Zhao, P. Han. W., Wei, Y., & Li X. (2007). GeoBrain Web Service-based Online Analysis System (GeOnAS). *Proceedings of NASA Earth Science Technology Conference 2007*, College Park, MD.

Di, L., Chen, A., Yang, W., & Zhao, P. (2003). *The integration of Grid technology with OGC Web Services (OWS) in NWGISS for NASA EOS Data*. (pp. 24-27). Presented at the GGF8 & HPDC12 2003. Seattle: Science Press.

Di, L., Zhao, P., Yang, W., Yu, G., & Yue, P. (2005, June). Intelligent geospatial web services. In *Proceedings of Geoscience and Remote Sensing Symposium*. (pp.1229 – 1232).

Diaz, L., Costa, S., Granell, C., & Gould, M. (2007). Migrating geoprocessing routines to Web services for water resource management applications. In M. Wachowicz & L. Bodum (Eds.), *10th AGILE International Conference on Geographic Information Science*. Aalborg University, Denmark.

Diehl, S., & Heide, J. (2005). Geo Information Breaks through sector think . In Oosterom, P., Zlatanove, S., & Fendel, E. M. (Eds.), *Geo-Information for Disaster Management* (pp. 85–108). Berlin: Springer. doi:10.1007/3-540-27468-5_7

Dietz, C. (2010). *Geospatial Web services, open standards, and advances in interoperability: A selected, annotated bibliography.* Retrieved March 15, 2010 from http://purl.oclc.org/coordinates/a8.htm.

Dimitrakos, T. (2003). A service-oriented trust management framework. In R. Falcone, S. Barber, L. Korba & M. Singh (Eds.), *Trust, Reputation, and Security: Theories and Practice*, (53-72). Bologne, Italy: AAMAS Selected papers.

Douglas, D. H., & Peucker, T. K. (1973). Algorithms for the reduction of the number of points required to represent a digitized line or its caricature. *Cartographica: The International Journal for Geographic Information and Geovisualization, 10*(2), 112–122. doi:10.3138/FM57-6770-U75U-7727

Doyle, A. (1997). *WWW Mapping Framework.* OGC Project Document.

Doyle, A., & Reed, C. (May 2001). *Introduction to OGC Web Services.* OGC® White Paper. Retrieved from http://portal.opengeospatial.org/files/?artifact_id=14973&version=1&format=pdf

Duke, A., Davies, J., & Richardson, M. (2005). Enabling a scalable service-oriented architecture with semantic web services. *BT Technology Journal, 23*(33), 191–201. doi:10.1007/s10550-005-0041-2

Eastlake, D., Reagle, J., Solo, D., Bartel, M., Boyer, J., Fox, B., et al. (2002). *XML-signature syntax and processing.* W3C Recommendation.

EC (2007). Directive 2007/60/EC of the European Parliament and of the Council of 23 October 2007 on the assessment and management of flood risks. *Official Journal of the European Union.*

EC. (2002). *Directive 2002/49/EC of the European Parliament and of the Council of 25 June 2002 relating to the assessment and management of environmental noise.* Official Journal of the European Communities.

EGEE. (2008). *gLite 3.0.0 home page.* Retrieved from http://www.glite.org.

Egenhofer, M. (2002). Towards the geospatial semantic Web. In Voisard, A., & Chen, S. (Ed.), *ACM International Symposium on Advances in Geographic Information Systems, Vol. 1. ACM 2002* (pp. 1-4). McLaen, CM Press.

Egenhofer, M. (2002). Toward the Semantic Geospatial Web. *Proceedings from the Tenth ACM International Symposium on Advances in Geographic Information Systems,* 1-4. ACM Press.

Elfers, C., & Wagner, R. M. (2007). GeoDRM engineering viewpoint and supporting architecture. Retrieved from http://portal.opengeospatial.org/files/?artifact_id=21285

Erast, N. A. S. A. (2010). *Environmental Research Aircraft and Sensor Technology.* Retrieved from http://www.nasa.gov/ centers/dryden/ history/past projects/ Erast/ index.html

ERDAS, Inc. (2008). *Open Geospatial Consortium (OGC) interoperability: A requirement for critical infrastructure protection and homeland security.* White Paper. Retrieved from http://www.erdas.com/LinkClick.aspx?fileticket=TUGcmFQTFBg%3d&tabid=132&mid=540

Erl, T. (2005). *Service-oriented architecture: Concepts, technology, and design.* Upper Saddle River, NJ, USA: Prentice Hall PTR.

Erwin, D., & Snelling, D. (2002). UNICORE: A Grid computing environment. *Concurrency and Computation: Practice and Experience, 14*(13-15), 1395–1410. Springer. Retrieved from http://www.springerlink.com/index/AE73FCHPKQENQCE9.pdf

ESRI. (2007). *ESRI geospatial portal technology.* Retrieved July 13, 2010, from http://www.esri.com/library/whitepapers/pdfs/geospatial-portal-technology.pdf

EU. (2007). Directive 2007/2/EC of the European parliament and of the council of 14 March, 2007 establishing an infrastructure for spatial information in the European community (INSPIRE). *Official Journal of the European Union.*

European Parliament and Council. (2007). *Directive 2007/2/EC of the European Parliament and of the Council of 14, March 2007, establishing an Infrastructure for Spatial Information in the European Community (INSPIRE).* Official Journal on the European Parliament and of the Council.

Euzenatand, J., & Shvaiko, P. (2007). *Ontology matching.* Heidelberg, Germany: Springer.

Executive Office of the President. (1994). Coordinating geographic data acquisition and access: the national spatial data infrastructure. *Executive order 12906 . Federal Register, 59.*

Ext, J. S. (2010). *ExtJS- Javascript Framework and RIA Platform.* Retrieved May 4, 2010, from http://www.extjs.com/

Fabrikant, S. I., & Buttenfield, B. P. (2001). Formalizing semantic spaces for information access. *Annals of the Association of American Geographers. Association of American Geographers, 91*, 263–280. doi:10.1111/0004-5608.00242

Farrell, J., & Lausen, H. (Eds.). (2007). *Semantic Annotations for WSDL and XML Schema, W3C Candidate Recommendation.* Retrieved May 21, 2010, from http://www.w3.org/TR/sawsdl/

Farrell, J., & Lausen, H. (2006). *Semantic Annotations for WSDL (SAWSDL).* Retrieved March 23, 2007, from http://www.w3.org/TR/sawsdl/

Federal Geographic Data Committee. (2000). *Content standard for digital geospatial metadata.* Metadata ad hoc working group. Retrieved July 9, 2010, from http://www.fgdc.gov/metadata/csdgm/

Federal Geographic Data Committee. (2010). *National Spatial Data Infrastructure.* Retrieved July 9, 2010, from http://www.fgdc.gov/nsdi/nsdi.html

Feng, C., & Flewelling, D. M. (2004). Assessment of semantic similarity between land use/land cover classification systems. *Computers, Environment and Urban Systems, 28*, 229–246. doi:10.1016/S0198-9715(03)00020-6

Fensel, D., Bussler, C., Ding, Y., & Omelayenko, B. (2002). The Web Service Modeling Framework (WSMF). *Electronic Commerce Research and Applications, 1*, 113–137. doi:10.1016/S1567-4223(02)00015-7

Fensel, D., & Bussler, C. (2002). *The web service modeling framework WSMF. Technical report.* Vrije Universiteit Amsterdam.

Ferraiolo, D. F. (2007). *Role-based access control* (2nd ed.). London: Artech House.

Fielding, R. (2000). *Architectural styles and the design of network-based software architectures.* Unpublished doctoral dissertation, University of California, Irvine

Fitzner, D., Hoffmann, J., & Klien, E. (2009). Functional description of geoprocessing services as conjunctive datalog queries. *GeoInformatica*, (October): 2009.

Fleuren, T., & Müller, P. (2008). BPEL workflows combining standard OGC Web services and Grid-enabled OGC Web services. In *Proceeding of 34th Euromicro SEAA.* Parma, Italy: IEEE. Retrieved from http://www.euromicro.org

Florczyk, A., Lopez-Pellicer, F. J., Béjar, R., Nogueras-Iso, J., & Zarazaga-Soria, F. J. (2010). *Applying semantic linkage in the Geospatial Web.* M. Painho, et al (Eds.), *Geospatial Thinking, 201-220. Springer.*

Foerster, T. (2006). An open software framework for web service-based geo-processing. *Proceedings of the Free and Open Source Software for Geospatial (FOSS4G 2006),* Lausanne, Switzerland.

Foerster, T., & Schaeffer, B. (2007). A client for distributed geo-processing on the web. In G. Tayler & M. Ware (Eds.), *W2GIS.* LCNS 4857, 252-263. Springer.

Foerster, T., & Stoter, J. E. (2006). Establishing an OGC Web processing service for generalization processes. In *Proceedings from ICA workshop on Generalization and Multiple Representation*, Portland, OR. Retrieved from http://aci.ign.fr/ Portland/paper/ ICA2006-foerster_stoter.pdf

Foerster, T., Burghardt, D., Neun, M., Regnauld, N., Swan, J., & Weibel, R. (2008). Towards an interoperable Web generalisation services framework. In *Proceedings of the 11th ICA Workshop on Generalization and Multiple Representation*. Montpellier, France.

Fonseca, F., Egenhofer, M., Davis, C., & Camara, G. (2002). Semantic granularity in ontology-driven geographic information systems. *Annals of Mathematics and Artificial Intelligence, 36*, 121–151. doi:10.1023/A:1015808104769

Fonseca, F. T., Egenhofer, M. J., Agouris, P., & Camara, G. (2002). Using ontologies for integrated Geographic Information Systems. *Transactions in GIS, 6*(3), 231–257. doi:10.1111/1467-9671.00109

Fonseca, F., & Sheth, A. (2002). *The geospatial semantic web. Proceedings from UCGIS (University Consortium for Geospatial Information Science)*. USA: Research Priorities.

Fonsenka, F., & Sheth, A. (2002). *The Geospatial Semantic Web, UCGIS White Paper*. Retrieved May 21, 2010, from http://www.personal.psu.edu/faculty/f/u/fuf1/Fonseca-Sheth.pdf

Foster, I., & Kesselman, C. (2003). *The Grid 2: Blueprint for a New Computing Infrastructure*. Morgan Kaufmann Publishers.

Foster, I. (2005). Service-oriented science. *Science, 308*(5723), 814–817. doi:10.1126/science.1110411

Foster, I. (1995). *Designing and Building Parallel Programs: Concepts and Tools for Parallel Software Engineering*. Boston: Addison-Wesley Longman Publishing Co., Inc.

Foster, I. (2002). *What is the Grid? A three point checklist.*

Foster, I. (2005). *A globus primer, An Early and Incomplete Draft. Technical report*. Globus Alliance. Retrieved from http://www.globus.org/toolkit/docs/4.0/key/GT4_Primer_0.6.pdf

Foster, I., Von Reich, J., Kishimoto, H., Berry, D., Djaoui, A., A., G., et al. (2005). *The Open Grid Services Architecture, (version 1.0)*. Open Grid Forum.

Frank, A. U. (2003). *Ontology for spatio-temporal databases*. LCNS 2520, 9-77. Heidelberg, Germany: Springer.

Friis-Christensen, A., Lucchi, R., Lutz, M., & Ostlaender, N. (2009). Service chaining architectures for applications implementing distributed geographic information processing. *International Journal of Geographical Information Science, 23*(5), 561–580. doi:10.1080/13658810802665570

Friis-Christensen, A., Ostlander, N., Lutz, M., & Bernard, L. (2007). Designing service architectures for distributed geoprocessing: challenges and future directions. *Transactions in GIS, 11*(6), 799–818. doi:10.1111/j.1467-9671.2007.01075.x

Friis-Christensen, A., Bernard, L., Kanellopoulos, I., Nogueras-Iso, J., & Peedell, S. Schade, S.et al. (2006). Building service oriented application on top of a Spatial Data Infrastructure - a forest fire assessment example. In *Proceedings of the 9th Agile Conference on Geographic Information Science* (pp. 119-127). Visegrad, Hungary.

Gahegan, M., Luo, J., Weaver, S. D., Pike, W., & Banchuen, T. (2009). Connecting GEON: making sense of the myriad resources, researchers and concepts that comprise a geoscience cyberinfrastructure. *Computers & Geosciences, 35*(4), 836–854. doi:10.1016/j.cageo.2008.09.006

Gao, S., Mioc, D., Yi, X., Anton, F., and Oldfield, E. (2008), Geospatial services for decision support on public health. *The International Archives of the Photogrammetry, Remote Sensing and Spatial Information Sciences, 37*(B8).

Gardels, K. (1998). *A Web Mapping Scenario*. OGC Project document 98-068.

Garret, J. J. (2005). *Ajax: A new approach to Web applications*. Retrieved December 18, 2009, from http://www.adaptivepath.com/publications/essays/archives/000385.php

Gartmann, R., & Leinenweber, L. (2009). *OGC 09-035: OWS-6 Security Engineering Report*. Open Geospatial Consortium.

Geller, G. N., & Melton, F. (2008). Looking forward: applying an ecological model Web to assess impacts of climate change. *Biodiversity, 9*(3 & 4), 79–83.

Geller, G. N., & Turner, W. (2007). The model Web: A concept for ecological forecasting. *IEEE International Geoscience and Remote Sensing Symposium*. (pp. 2469-2472), Barcelona, Spain.

GEO. (2005, February). *Global Earth Observation Systems of Systems – GEOSS – 10-Year implementation plan, GEO 1000 / ESA BR-240*. Amsterdam: ESA.

GeoExt. (2010). *JavaScript toolkit for rich Web mapping applications*. Retrieved from http://www.geoext.org/

GeoNetwork. (2009). *GeoNetwork OpenSource community website*. Retrieved from http://geonetwork-opensource.org/

GeoRSS. (2010). *GeoRSS*. Retrieved May 4, 2010, http://www.georss.org/ Main_Page

Geoserver. *Welcome to Geoserver*. Retrieved 05 04, 2010, from http://geoserver.org/ display/GEOS/ Welcome

GeoSpatial One-Stop. Retrieved July 13, 2010, from http://gos2.geodata.gov/wps/portal/gos

Geraci, A. (1991). *IEEE standard computer dictionary: compilation of IEEE standard computer glossaries* (Katki, F., McMonegal, L., Meyer, B., Lane, J., Wilson, P., & Radatz, J., Eds.). The Institute of Electrical and Electronics Engineers, Inc.

Giannecchini, S., Spina, F., Nordgren, B., & Desruisseaux, M. (2006). Supporting interoperable geospatial data fusion by adopting OGC and ISO TC 211 standards. *From proceedings at FUSION 2006*. Florence, Italy.

Global Spatial Data Infrastructure Association. (2010). *Global Spatial Data Infrastructure*, Retrieved July 9, 2010, from http://www.gsdi.org/

Global Spatial Data Infrastructure. (2004). *SDI cookbook*. Retrieved from www.gsdi.org/ docs2004/ Cookbook/ cookbookV2.0.pdf

Goguen (2005). Data, schema ontology and logic integration. *Logic Journal of the IGPL 13*(6), 685-715.

Gollmann, D. (1999). *Computer security*. New York: Wiley.

Goodchild, M. (2007). Citizens as voluntary sensors: Spatial Data Infrastructure in the world of Web 2.0. *International Journal of Spatial Data Infrastructures Research, 2*(1), 24–32.

Goodchild, M. F., Egenhofer, M. J., Fegeas, R., & Kottman, C. A. (Eds.). (1999). *Interoperating Geographic Information Systems*. New York: Kluwer.

Goodchild, M. F. (2009). NeoGeography and the nature of geographic expertise. *Journal of Location Based Services, 3*(2), 82–96. doi:10.1080/17489720902950374

Goodchild, M. F., Egenhofer, M., Fegeas, R., & Kottman, C. (1999). *Interoperating Geographic Information Systems*. Norwell, MA: Kluwer Academic Publishers.

Goodchild, M., Fu, P., & Rich, P. (2007). Sharing geographic information: an assessment of the Geospatial One-Stop. *Annals of the Association of American Geographers. Association of American Geographers, 97*(2), 250–266. doi:10.1111/j.1467-8306.2007.00534.x

Goodchild, M. (2007). Citizens as sensors: the world of volunteered geography. *GeoJournal, 69*(4), 211–221. doi:10.1007/s10708-007-9111-y

Goodchild, M. F., Fu, P., & Rich, P. M. (2007). Geographic information sharing: the case of the Geospatial One-Stop portal. *Annals of the Association of American Geographers. Association of American Geographers, 97*(2), 250–266. doi:10.1111/j.1467-8306.2007.00534.x

Goodwin, J., Dolbear, C., & Hart, G. (2008). Geographical linked data: the administrative geography of Great Britain on the Semantic Web. *Transactions in GIS*, *12*(1), 19–30. doi:10.1111/j.1467-9671.2008.01133.x

Google Earth. (2010). *Google Earth Home page*. Retrieved from http:// earth.google. com/intl/it/

Google Maps. (2010). *Google maps italia*. Retrieved from http://maps.google.it/

Goran, B., & Finney, D. (1991). GRASS GIS Critical to Army's Land Management Program. *GIS World*, *4*(9), 48–53.

Grandison, T., & Sloman, M. (2000). A survey of trust in internet applications. *IEEE Communications Surveys and Tutorials*, *3*(4), 2–16. doi:10.1109/COMST.2000.5340804

Granell, C., Díaz, L., & Gould, M. (2010). Service-oriented applications for environmental models: reusable geospatial services. *Environmental Modelling & Software*, *25*(2), 182–198. doi:10.1016/j.envsoft.2009.08.005

Granell, C., Diaz, L., & Gould, M. (2007). Managing Earth observation data with distributed geoprocessing services. In *Proceedings from Geoscience and Remote Sensing Symposium* (pp. 4777 - 4780). Presented at the IGARSS 2007, IEEE.

Granell, C., Gould, M., & Ramos, F. (2005). Service composition for SDIs: integrated components creation. In *Proceedings of Sixteenth International Workshop on Database and Expert Systems Applications* (pp. 475-479). Presented at the Workshop on Geographic Information Management (DEXXA 05), Copenhagen: IEEE.

Graves, S., Ramachandran, R., Keiser, K., Maskey, M., Lynnes, C., & Pham, L. (2007). Deployable suite of data mining Web services for online science data repositories. *Proceedings of the 87th AMS Annual meeting*, San Antonio, TX.

Grenon, P., & Smith, B. (2004). SNAP and SPAN: towards dynamic spatial ontology. *Spatial Cognition and Computation*, *4*(1), 69–103. doi:10.1207/s15427633scc0401_5

Groot, R., & McLaughlin, J. (2000). *Geospatial data infrastructure: Concepts, cases, and good practice*. Oxford: Oxford University Press.

Group on Earth Observations. (2010). *What is GEOSS? The Global Earth Observation System of Systems*. Retrieved from http://www.earth observations.org/ geoss. shtml

Gruber, T. R. (1995). Towards principles for the design of ontologies used for knowledge sharing. *International Journal of Human-Computer Studies*, *43*(5), 907–928. doi:10.1006/ijhc.1995.1081

Gruber, T. R. (1993). A translation approach to portable ontology specification . *Knowledge Acquisition*, *5*(2), 199–220. doi:10.1006/knac.1993.1008

Guarino, N. (1995). Formal ontology, conceptual analysis and knowledge representation. *International Journal of Human-Computer Studies*, *43*(5), 625–640. doi:10.1006/ijhc.1995.1066

Guarino, N. (1998). Formal ontology and information systems . In Guarino, N. (Ed.), *Formal ontology in information systems* (pp. 3–15). Amsterdam: IOS Press.

Guercke, R. Brenner & Sester, M. (2008). Data integration and generalization for SDI in a Grid Computing Framework. *In proceedings from 2008 ISPRS Congress*. Beijing.

Hafner, M., & Breu, R. (2009). *Security engineering for service-oriented architectures*. Berlin: Springer.

Haklay, M., & Weber, P. (2008). OpenStreetMap: User-Generated Street Maps. *IEEE Pervasive Computing/ IEEE Computer Society [and] IEEE Communications Society*, *7*(4), 12–18. doi:10.1109/MPRV.2008.80

Hamre, T. S., & Éamonn, Ó. T. (2005). DISMAR - Data Integration System for Marine Pollution and Water Quality. *31st International Symposium on Remote Sensing of Environment*.

Han, W., Di, L., & Zhao, P. (2009). Using AJAX for desktop-like Geospatial Web application development. *Proceedings of the 17th International Conference on Geoinformatics*, Fairfax, VA.

Harnad, S. (1990). The Symbol Grounding Problem. *Physica D. Nonlinear Phenomena, 42,* 335–346. doi:10.1016/0167-2789(90)90087-6

Harrison, M. A., Ruzzo, W. L., & Ullman, J. D. (1976). Protection in operating systems. *Communications of the ACM, 19*(8), 461–471. doi:10.1145/360303.360333

Hartig, K. (2009). *What is cloud computing? Cloud Computing Journal.* SYS-CON Media Inc.

Harvey, F., Kuhn, W., Pundt, H., Bisher, Y., & Riedemann, C. (1999). Semantic interoperability: a central issue for sharing geographic information. *The Annals of Regional Science, 33,* 213–232. doi:10.1007/s001680050102

Havlik, D., Bleier, T., & Schimak, G. (2009). Sharing sensor data with SensorSA and Cascading Sensor Observation Service. *Sensors (Basel, Switzerland), 9*(7), 5493–5502. doi:10.3390/s90705493

Havlik, D., & Schimak, G. (2009). Sensors anywhere – sensor Web enablement in risk management applications. *Ercim News*. Retrieved July 9, 2010, from http://ercim-news.ercim.eu/

Hayes, B. (2008). Cloud computing. *Communications of the ACM, 51*(7), 9–11. doi:10.1145/1364782.1364786

He, H. (2003). *What is Service-Oriented Architecture.* Retrieved from http:// pesona.mmu. edu.my /~wruslan/ SE2/ Readings/ detail/Reading -28.pdf

Henneboehl, K., & Pebesma, E. (2008). *Providing R functionality through the OGC Web Processing Service.* Paper presented at the The R user conference, Technische Universitaet Dortmund.

Henson, C. A., Pschorr, J. K., Sheth, A. P., & Thirunarayan, K. (2009). SemSOS: Semantic Sensor Observation Service. *International Symposium on Collaborative Technologies and Systems (CTS 2009).*

Herring, J. (2001). Quality is the future of geoprocessing. *GeoInformatica, 5*(4), 323–325. doi:10.1023/A:1012711401679

Herring, J. (Ed.). (2009). *The specification model: A standard for modular specifications.* OGC Document 08-131r3. Retrieved from https://portal.opengeospatial. org/files/?artifact_id=34762

Hess, S. (2002). GRASS on the Web, *Proceedings of the Open source GIS – GRASS users conference.* Trento, Italy.

Heuvelink, G. B. M. (1998). *Error propagation in environmental modelling with GIS.* London: Taylor & Francis.

Hill, L. L. (2006). *Georeferencing: The Geographic Associations of information: digital libraries and electronic publishing.* Cambridge, MA: The MIT Press.

Hipkiss, R. (1995). *Semantics: defining the discipline.* Mahwah, NJ: Lawrence Erlbaum Associates.

Hirsch, F., Kemp, J., & Ilkka, J. (2006). *Mobile Web services: Architecture and implementation.* West Sussex, UK: John Wiley & Sons Ltd. doi:10.1002/9780470017982

Hobona, G., Fairbairn, D., Hiden, H., & James, P. (2010). Orchestration of Grid-enabled geospatial Web services in geoscientific workflows. *IEEE Transactions on Automation Science and Engineering, 7*(2), 407–411. doi:10.1109/TASE.2008.2010626

Hobona, G., Fairbairn, D., & James, P. (2007). Semantically-assisted geospatial workflow design. In H. Samet, C. Shahabi & M. Schneider (Eds.), *Proceedings of the ACM international symposium on Advances in geographic information systems (ACMGIS)* (pp. 194-201). Seattle: ACM

Hobona, G., Fairbairn, D., & James, P. (2007). Workflow enactment of Grid-enabled geospatial Web services. In *Proceedings of the 2007 UK e-Science All Hands Meeting.* Retrieved from http://scholar.google.com/scholar?hl=en &btnG=Search&q=intitle:Workflow+Enactment+of+Grid-Enabled+Geospatial+Web+Services#0

Holtman, K., & Mutz, A. (1998). Transparent content negotiation in HTTP. *Internet Engineering Task Force (IETF) Memo – RFC 2295.*

Homburg, V. (2008). *Understanding e-government: Information systems in public administration.* New York, NY: Routledge.

Horrocks, I., Patel-Schneider, P. F., Boley, H., Tabet, S., Grosof, B., & Dean, M. (2004). *SWRL: a semantic web rule language combining OWL and RuleML*. W3C Member Submission. Retrieved March 12, 2007, from http://www.w3.org/Submission/SWRL/

Horswell, C., & Hegstrom, E. (2005, Sep. 29). Evacuation lessons come at high cost: 107 lives. *Houston Chronicle*. Retrieved from http://www.chron.com/disp/story.mpl/front/3374468.html

Hsu, S. S. (2006, April 14). Waste in Katrina response is cited: Housing aid called inefficient in audits. *Washington Post*. Retrieved from http://www.washingtonpost.com/wp-dyn/content/article/2006/04/13/AR2006041302159.html

Huber, V. (2001). UNICORE: A Grid computing environment for distributed and parallel computing. In V. Malyshkin (Ed.), *Proceedings of the 6th International Conference on Parallel Computing Technologies* (Vol. 2127, pp. 258-265). Presented at the PaCT 01, Novosibirsk, Russia: Springer.

Hubmann-Haidvogel, A., Scharl, A., & Weichselbraun, A. (2009). Multiple coordinated views for searching and navigating Web content repositories. *Information Sciences*, *179*, 1813–1021. doi:10.1016/j.ins.2009.01.030

Husar, R., & Poirot, R. (2005). DataFed and Fastnet: Tools for agile air quality analysis. *Environmental Manager,* 39-41. Retrieved from http://datafedwiki.wustl.edu/images/c/c4/EM_DataFed_FASTNET_050720.pdf

IBM. (2001). *Web services flow language (WSFL 1.0)*. Retrieved March 16, 2007, from http://www-4.ibm.com/software/solutions/webservices/pdf/WSFL.pdf

IEEE GEOSS. (2009). *IEEE Standards Association – GEOSS standards registry*. Retrieved from http://seabass.ieee.org/groups/geoss/

IETF (2000). *RFC 2828- internet security glossary*.

IETF (2007). *Security preconditions for session description protocol (SDP) media streams*. (RFC 5027).

Imamura, T., Dillaway, B., & Simon, E. (2002). *XML encryption syntax and processing*. W3C Recommendation.

Infraestrutura Nacional de Dados Espaciais. (2010). *Infraestrutura Nacional de Dados Espaciais*. Retrieved July 9, 2010, from: http://www.inde.gov.br/

INSPIRE. (2007a). Directive 2007/2/EC of the European Parliament and of the Council of 14 March 2007 establishing an infrastructure for spatial information in the European community. *Official Journal of the European Union. L&C*, 18.

INSPIRE. (2007b). *INSPIRE Network Services Performance Guidelines* (p. 22). INSPIRE Consolidation Team.

INSPIRE. (2008). *INSPIRE Network Services Architecture* (p. 30). European Commission.

INSPIRE. (2009). *INSPIRE data specification transport networks (Version 3.0)*. INSPIRE Thematic Working Group on Transport Networks.

INSPIRE. (2004). *INSPIRE scoping paper*. Retrieved November 18, 2009, from http://www.ec-gis.org/inspire/reports/inspire scoping24mar04.pdf.

Intel Corporation. Canonical Ltd., & Eucalyptus Systems, (Eds.). (2010). *Intel® Cloud Builder Guide to Cloud Design and Deployment on Intel Platforms*. Eucalyptus Systems, Inc.

International Organization for Standardization. (2003). *Geographic information – metadata*. Technical Committee 211. Retrieved July 9, 2010, from http://www.iso.org/iso/catalogue_detail.htm?csnumber=26020

International Organization for Standardization. (2007). *Geographic information: Metadata and XML schema implementation*. Technical Committee 211. Retrieved July 9, 2010, from http://www.iso.org/iso/catalogue_detail.htm?csnumber=32557

ISO (1996). Information technology-open systems interconnection-security frameworks in open systems: access control framework.

ISO (2003). 19115 Geographic information - metadata. *ISO/TC211 standard*.

ISO (2004). *MPEG-21 rights expression language (REL)*, ISO/IEC JTC - 21000-5.

ISO (2005). 19119 Geographic information - services. *ISO/TC211 standard.*

ISO (2007). 19139 Geographic information - metadata - XML schema implementation. *ISO/TC211 standard.*

ISO 19107. (2003). *Geographic Information – spatial schema.* International Organization for Standards. Retrieved from http://www.iso.org/iso/catalogue_detail.htm?csnumber=26012

ISO 19119. (2005). *Geographic information – services.* International Organization for Standards. Retrieved from http://www.iso.org/iso/iso_catalogue/catalogue_tc/catalogue_detail.htm?csnumber=39890

ISO 23950. (2003). Information Retrieval (Z39.50): Application Service Definition and Protocol Specification.

ISO 7498-1. (1994). *Information technology–open systems interconnection–basic reference model.*

ISO TC 211. (2009) *Terms and definitions.* Retrieved from http://www.isotc211.org/Terminology.htm

ISO/IEC. (2002). *ISO/IEC 13250 topic maps.* Information Technology Document Description and Processing Languages.

ISO/TC 211. (2005). *Geographic information - Services (ISO Standard 19119).* 67. International Organization for Standardization.

ISO/TC211 (2001). *19101 Geographic information - Reference model.* ISO/TC211 standard.

ISO/TC211. (2002). *ISO 19113 Geographic information - quality principles.* Geneva: ISO.

ISO/TC211. (2003a). *ISO 19114 Geographic information - quality evaluation procedures.* Geneva: ISO.

ISO/TC211. (2003b). *ISO 19115 Geographic information – metadata.* Geneva: ISO.

ISO/TC211. (2005). *ISO 19119 Geographic information – services.* Geneva: ISO.

ISO/TC211. (2005). *Schema for coverage geometry and functions.* Retrieved June 22, 2006, from http://www.isotc211.org/

ISO/TS19139. (2007). *Geographic information -- Metadata -- XML schema implementation.* Retrieved from: http://www.iso.org/iso/catalogue_detail.htm?csnumber=32557

ITU-T. (2005)... . *ITU-T RECOMMENDATION, X,* 509.

ITU-T. (1994). *Telephone network and ISDN - quality of service, network management and traffic engineering.* International Telecommunication Union. ITU.

ITU-T. (2001). *Transmission systems and media, digital systems and networks.* International Telecommunication Union. ITU.

Jaeger, E., Altintas, I., Zhang, J., Ludäscher, B., Pennington, D., & Michener, W. (2005, June). A scientific workflow approach to distributed geospatial data processing using web services. In *Proceedings of 17th International Conference on Scientific and Statistical Database Management (SSDBM'05), Santa Barbara, California,* (pp. 87-90).

Janowicz, K., & Keßler, C. (2008). The Role of ontology in improving gazetteer interaction. *International Journal of Geographical Information Science, 22*(10), 1129–1157. doi:10.1080/13658810701851461

Janowicz, K., Schade, S., Bröring, A., Keßler, C., Maue, P., & Stasch, C. (2010). Semantic Enablement for Spatial Data Infrastructures. *Transactions in GIS, 14*(2), 111–129. doi:10.1111/j.1467-9671.2010.01186.x

Janowicz, K. Schade, S., Bröring, A., Keßler, C., & Stasch, C. (2009, October). A transparent semantic enablement layer for the Geospatial Web. *In proceedings from the Terra Cognita 2009 Workshop, in conjunction with the 8th International Semantic Web Conference (ISWC2009).*

Janowicz, K., Keßler, C., Schwarz, M., Wilkes, M., Panov, I., Espeter, M., et al. (2007). Algorithm, implementation and application of the SIM-DL similarity server. In F.T. Fonseca, A. Rodriguez, & S. Levashkin (Eds.), *Second International Conference on GeoSpatial Semantics (GeoS 2007).* LCNS 4853, (pp. 128-145).

Janowicz, K., Schade, S., Bröring, A., Keßler, C., Maué, P. & Stasch, C. (2010). *Semantic enablement for Spatial Data Infrastructures.* Transactions in GIS 14(2).

Jirka, S., & Bröring, A. (2009). *OGC discussion paper 09-112 – sensor observable registry*. Technical report, Open Geospatial Consortium.

Johnson, C. R., & Parker, S. G. (1999). The SCIRun parallel scientific computing problem solving environment. In *Ninth SIAM Conference on Parallel Processing for Scientific Computing*. Retrieved from http://www.sci.utah.edu/publications/siam99/siam99b.ps

Johnson, R. (2000). GIS Technology for disasters and emergency management. *An ESRI White Paper*. Retrieved November 1, 2009, from http://www/esri.com/library/whitepapers/pdfs/disastermgmt.pdf

Joint Centre Research. (2010). *Infrastructure for spatial information in the European community*. Retrieved July 9, 2010, from http://inspire.jrc.ec.europa.eu/

Jones, S., & Morris, P. (1999). *TRUST-EC: Requirements for trust and confidence in e-commerce. Technical Report EUR 18749 EN*. European Commission Joint Research Centre.

Josuttis, N. M. (2007). *SOA in Practice*. Sebastopol, CA: O'Reilly.

Kalfoglou, Y., Hu, B., Reynolds, D., & Shadbolt, N. (2005). *Semantic integration technologies survey. Technical report, e-print #10842*. University of Southampton.

Kammersell, W., & Dean, M. (2006, November). Conceptual search: incorporating geospatial data into semantic queries. In *Proceedings of Terra Cognita 2006, Workshop of 5th International Semantic Web Conference. Athens, GA*.

Kanneganti, R., & Chodavarapu, P. (2008). *SOA security*. Greenwich, CT: Manning.

Katikaneni, U., Ladner, R., & Petry, F. (2004). Internet delivery of meteorological and oceanographic data in wide area naval usage environments. In *Proceedings of the 13th international World Wide Web Conference Alternate* (pp. 84-88). New York: ACM.

Keens, S. (2007). *OWS-4 Workflow IPR (OGC IPR No. 06-187)*. OGC.

Keßler, C., Raubal, M., & Wosniok, C. (2009). Semantic rules for context-aware geographical information retrieval. In P. Barnaghi (Ed.), *European Conference on Smart Sensing and Context, EuroSSC 2009*. LNCS 5741, (pp. 77–92).

Kiehle, C., Heier, C., & Greve, K. (2007). Requirements for next generation Spatial Data Infrastructures-standardized Web Based geoprocessing and Web Service orchestration. *Transactions in GIS, 11*(6), 819–834. doi:10.1111/j.1467-9671.2007.01076.x

Kiehle, C., Greve, K., & Heier, C. (2006). Standardized geoprocessing - taking spatial data infrastructures one step further. In *9th AGILE International Conference on Geographic Information Science* (pp. 273-282). Visegrad, Hungary.

Kifer, M. (2008). Rule interchange format: the framework. In *Proceedings of the 2nd International Conference on Web Reasoning and Rule Systems*. LNCS 5341, (pp. 1–11). Berlin: Springer.

Kim, W. (2009). Cloud computing: Today and tomorrow. *Journal of Object Technology, 8*(1), 66–72.

Kim, S., Shekhar, S., & Min, M. (2008). Contraflow transportation network reconfiguration for evacuation route planning. *IEEE Transactions on Knowledge and Data Engineering, 20*(8), 1–15. doi:10.1109/TKDE.2007.190722

Klien, E. (2007). A rule-based strategy for the semantic annotation of geodata. *Transactions in GIS, 11*(3), 437–452. doi:10.1111/j.1467-9671.2007.01054.x

Klopfer, M., & Kanellopoulos, I. (Eds.). (2008). *ORCHESTRA-an open service architecture for risk management*.

Klopfer, M., & Simonis, I. (Eds.). (2009). *SANY-an open service architecture for sensors*.

Klusch, M., Gerber, A., & Schmidt, M. (2005, November). Semantic web service composition planning with OWLS-Xplan, In *Proceedings of Agents and the Semantic Web, 2005 AAAI Fall Symposium Series, Arlington, VA*.

Klyne, G., & Carroll, J.J. (2004). *Resource Description Framework (RDF): concepts and abstract syntax*.

Kolas, D., Dean, M., & Hebeler, J. (2006, March). Geospatial semantic web: architecture of ontologies. In *Proceedings of 2006 IEEE Aerospace Conference. Big Sky, MT.*

Kolas, D., Hebeler, J., & Dean, M. (2005). Geospatial semantic web: architecture of ontologies. In *Proceedings of First International Conference on GeoSpatial Semantics (GeoS 2005)*. Mexico City: Springer.

Kralidis, A. (2007). Geospatial Web services: The evolution of Geospatial Data Infrastructure . In Scharl, A., & Tochtermann, K. (Eds.), *The Geospatial Web: How Geobrowsers, Social Software and the Web 2.0 Are Shaping the Network Society* (pp. 223–228). London: Springer-Verlag.

Krüger, A., & Kolbe, T. H. (2008). Mapping Spatial Data Infrastructures to a GRID environment for optimised processing of large amounts of spatial data. In *Proceedings from the 2008 ISPRS Congress Beijing*.

Kuhn, W. (2003). Semantic Reference Systems. *International Journal of Geographical Information Science, 17*(5), 405–409. doi:10.1080/1365881031000114116

Kuhn, W. (2005). Geospatial semantics: why, of what, and how? In Spaccapietra, S., & Zimányi, E. (Eds.), *Journal of Data Semantics* (pp. 1–24). Berlin: Springer. doi:10.1007/11496168_1

Kuhn, W. (2009). Semantic Engineering. In G. Navratil (Ed.), *Research Trends in Geographic Information Science*. LNGC, 63-74.

Kurhn, W. (2003). Semantic reference systems. *International Journal of Geographic, 17*(5), 405–409. doi:10.1080/1365881031000114116

Kurzbach, S., Pasche, E., Lanig, S., & Zipf, A. (2009). Benefits of Grid computing for flood modeling in service-oriented Spatial Data Infrastructures. *GIS. Science, 3*, 89–96.

Kurzbach, S., & Pasche, E. (2009). A 3D terrain discretization grid service for hydrodynamic modeling. *Proceedings of the 8th International Conference on Hydroinformatics (HEIC)*, Concepción, Chile.

la Beaujardiere, D. J. (Ed.). (2006). *OGC Web map server implementation specification*. Wayland, MA: Open Geospatial Consortium Inc.

Lake, R., & Farley, J. (2007). Infrastructure for the geospatial Web . In Scharl, A., & Tochtermann, K. (Eds.), *The Geospatial Web, Advanced Information and Knowledge Processing Series* (pp. 15–26). London, UK: Springer.

Lanig, S. & Zipf, A. (2009): Towards generalization processes of LiDAR data based on GRID and OGC Web Processing Services (WPS). From *Proceedings in Geoinformatik 2009*, Osnabrück, Germany.

Lanig, S., Schilling, A., Stollberg, B., & Zipf, A. (2008). Towards standards-based processing of digital elevation models for Grid computing through Web Processing Service (WPS). In *ICCSA*, LCNS 5073. (pp. 191-203). Presented at the Computational Science and Its Applications (ICCSA 2008), Perugia, Italy: Springer Verlag.

Lan-Kun, C., Yao-Min, F., Tien-Yin, C., Bing, J., & Bastian, B. (2009). A SOA based debris flow monitoring system architecture and proof-of-concept implementation. *17th International Conference on Geoinformatics*, (pp. 1-6).

Lassila, O., & Swick, R. (1999). *Resource Description Framework (RDF) model and syntax specification*. Retrieved from http://www.w3.org/TR/PR-rdf-syntax/

Lassoued, Y., Wright, D., Bermudez, L., & Boucelma, O. (2008). Ontology-based mediation of OGC catalogue service for the Web – a virtual solution for integrating coastal Web atlases. In J. Cordeiro, S. Shishkov, A. Ranchordas, & M. Hrlfert (Eds.), *Third International Conference on Software and Data Technologies, Vol. I* (pp. 192-197). Porto, Portugal: INSTICC Press.

Lausen, H., Polleres, A., & Roman, D. (2005). *Web Service Modeling Ontology (WSMO)*. Retrieved May 21, 2010, from http://www.w3.org/Submission/WSMO/

Lautenbacher, C. C. (2006). The global Earth observation system of systems: Science serving society. *Space Policy, 22*(1), 8–11. doi:10.1016/j.spacepol.2005.12.004

Lawton, G. (2008). New ways to build rich Internet applications. *Computer*, *41*(8), 10–12. doi:10.1109/MC.2008.302

Lee, C., & Percivall, G. (2008). Standards-based computing capabilities for distributed geospatial applications. *Computer*, *41*(11), 50–57. doi:10.1109/MC.2008.468

Lee, C., & Percivall, G. (2009). The evolution of geospatial e-infrastructures. *GIS Science*, *3*, 68–70.

Lee, C. A. (2001, November). Grid computing. *GRID 2001, Second International Workshop*. Denver, CO: Springer.

Lee, C. A., & Percival, G. (2009). The evolution of geospatial e-infrastructures. In *GIS.Science, 3.*

Lee, K., Jeon, J., Lee, W., Jeong, S.-H., & Park, S.-W. (2003). *QoS for Web services: requirements and possible approaches. W3C Working Group Note.* Retrieved on March 15, 2010, from http://www.w3c.or.kr/kr-office/TR/2003/ws-qos/

Leganza, G. (2006, Dec. 12). Why Is SOA hot in government? *Forrester Inc.* Retrieved from http://www.forrester.com/rb/Research/why_is_soa_hot_in_government/q/id/40673/t/2

Lehto, L. (2007). Schema translations in a Web service based SDI. In M. Wachowicz & L. Bodum (Eds.), *10th Agile International Conference on Geographic Information Science 2007*. Aalborg University, Denmark.

Leite, F. L. Jr, Baptista, C. S., Silva, P. A., & Silva, E. R. (2007). WS-GIS: towards a SOA-based SDI federation . In Davis, C. A. Jr, & Monteiro, V. M. (Eds.), *Advances in Geoinformatics* (pp. 199–214). Heidelberg, Germany: Springer.

Lemmens, R., Wytzisk, A., de By, R., Grannel, C., Gould, M., & van Oosterom, P. (2006). Integrating semantic and syntactic descriptions to chain geographic services. *IEEE Internet Computing*, *10*(5), 42–52. doi:10.1109/MIC.2006.106

Lemmens, R., de By, R. A., Gould, M., Wytzisk, A., Grannell, C., & van Oosterom, P. (2007). Enhancing geo-service chaining through deep service descriptions. *Transactions in GIS*, *11*(6), 849–871. doi:10.1111/j.1467-9671.2007.01079.x

Lemmens, R. (2006). *Semantic interoperability of distributed geo-services* (Doctoral dissertation, Delft University of Technology). Retrieved from http://www.ncg.knaw.nl/Publicaties/Geodesy/ pdf/63Lem mens.pdf

Lewis, P. M., Bernstein, A., & Kifer, M. (2001). *Database systems: an application oriented approach*. Boston: Addison-Wesley.

Li, P., Di, L., & Yu, G. (2008). Serving Aura HIRDLS Level 2 data through OGC WCS. In *Proceedings of 28th IEEE International Geoscience & Remote Sensing Symposium (Vol. II)*, (pp.1333-1336).

Li, W., Li, Y., Liang, Z., Huang, C. & Wen, Y. (2005). *The design and implementation of GIS Grid Services*. LNCS 3795.

Li, W., Yang, C., & Raskin, R. (2008). A semantic enhanced model for searching in spatial web portals. In: *AAAI Spring Symposium semantic scientific knowledge integration technical report SS-08-05,* 47-50. Palo Alto, CA.

Lieberman, J., Pehle, T., Morris, C.,Kolas, D., Dean, M., Lutz, M., et al. (2006). *Geospatial Semantic Web interoperability experiment report.*

Lieberman, J., Pehle, T., & Dean, M. (2005). *Semantic evolution of geospatial web services: use cases and experiments in the geospatial semantic web*. Talk at the W3C Workshop on Frameworks for Semantic in Web Services, Innsbruck, Austria.

Lime, S. (2008). Map server. In Hall, G. B., & Leahy, M. G. (Eds.), *Open Source Approaches in Spatial Data Handling* (pp. 65–85). Berlin: Springer-Verlag. doi:10.1007/978-3-540-74831-1_4

Liu, D., & Liu, D. (2003). Data-flow distribution in FICAS service composition infrastructure. In *proceedings of the 15th International Conference on Parallel and Distributed Computing Systems.*

Lu, D., Mausel, P., Brondízio, E., & Moran, E. (2004). Change detection techniques. *International Journal of Remote Sensing, 25*(12), 2365–2401. doi:10.1080/0143116031000139863

Lucchi, R., Millot, M., & Elfers, C. (2008). Resource oriented architecture and REST: Assessment of impact and advantages on INSPIRE. *JCR Scientific and Technical Report.* EUR 23397.

Ludäscher, B., Altintas, I., Berkley, C., Higgins, D., Jaeger, E., & Jones, M. (2005). Scientific workflow management and the Kepler system . *Concurrency and Computation, 18*(10), 1039–1065. doi:10.1002/cpe.994

Luo, W., Li, X., Molloy, I., & Stepinski, T. (2009). Web service for extracting stream networks from DEM data. *Proceedings of the 17th International Conference on Geoinformatics,* Fairfax, VA.

Lupp, M. (Ed.). (2007). *OGC Styled Layer Descriptor profile of the Web map service implementation specification.* Wayland, MA: Open Geospatial Consortium Inc.

Lutz, M., & Kolas, D. (2007). Rule-based in Spatial Data Infrastructure. *Transactions in GIS, 11*(1), 317–336. doi:10.1111/j.1467-9671.2007.01048.x

Lutz, M., Sprado, J., Klien, E., Schubert, C., & Christ, I. (2008). Overcoming semantic heterogeneity in Spatial Data Infrastructures. *Computers & Geosciences, 35*(4), 739–752. doi:10.1016/j.cageo.2007.09.017

Lutz, M. (2007). Ontology-based descriptions for semantic discovery and composition of geoprocessing services . *GeoInformatica, 11*(1), 1–36. doi:10.1007/s10707-006-7635-9

Lutz, M., & Kolas, D. (2007). Rule-based discovery in spatial data infrastructures. *Transactions in GIS, 11*(3), 317–336. doi:10.1111/j.1467-9671.2007.01048.x

Lutz, M., & Klien, E. (2006). Ontology-based retrieval of geographic information. *International Journal of Geographical Information Science, 20*(3), 233–260. doi:10.1080/13658810500287107

Lutz, M. (2004). Non-taxonomic relations in semantic service discovery and composition. In F. Maurer & G. Ruhe (Eds.), *Proceedings of the First Ontology in Action Workshop, in conjunction with the Sixteenth International Conference on Software Engineering & Knowledge Engineering (SEKE'2004).* (pp. 482–485).

Lutz, M., Riedemann, C., & Probst, F. (2003). A classification framework for approaches to achieving semantic interoperability between GI Web services. In *Proceedings from COSIT 2003.* 186-203.

MacEachren, A. M., & Kraak, M. J. (2001). Research challenges in geovisualization. *Cartography and Geographic Information Systems, 28*(1), 3–12. doi:10.1559/152304001782173970

Maguire, D. J., & Longley, P. A. (2005). The emergence of geoportals and their role in spatial data infrastructures. *Computers, Environment and Urban Systems, 29,* 3–14.

Maiyo, L., Köbben, B., & Kerle, N. (2009). Collaborative post-disaster damage mapping via Geo Web Services . In Konecny, M., Zlatanova, S., Bandrova, T., & Friedmannova, L. (Eds.), *Cartography and Geoinformatics for early warning and emergency management: towards better Solutions (Joint symposium of ICA working group on CEWaCM and JBGIS Gi4DM)* (pp. 386–395). Brno, Czech Republic: Masaryk University.

Mandl, D., Sohlberg, R., Justice, C., Ungar, S., Ames, T., Frye, S., et al. (2007). Experiments with user centric GEOSS architectures. *Proceedings of IEEE International Geoscience and Remote Sensing Symposium 2007,* Barcelona, Spain.

Manning, C. D., Prabhakar, R., & Schütze, H. (2008). *Introduction to information retrieval.* Cambridge, UK: Cambridge University press.

Manso, M. A., & Wachowicz, M. (2009). GIS design: A review of current issues in interoperability. *Geography Compass, 3*(3), 1105–1124. doi:10.1111/j.1749-8198.2009.00241.x

Martell, R. (Ed.). (2008). *CSW-ebRIM Registry Service - Part 1: ebRIM profile of CSW, (Version 1.0.0).* Open Geospatial Consortium, Inc.

Martell, R. (2009). *CSW-ebRIM Registry Service - part 1: ebRIM profile of CSW.* Retrieved from http://portal.opengeospatial.org/modules/admin/license_agreement.php?suppressHeaders=0&access_license_id=3&target=http://portal.opengeospatial.org/files/index.php?artifact_id=31137

Martin, D., Paolucci, M., McIlraith, S., Burstein, M., McDermott, D., & McGuinness, D. (2005). Bringing semantics to Web services: The OWL-S Approach . In Cardoso, J., & Sheth, A. (Eds.), *Semantic Web services and Web process composition* (pp. 26–42). Berlin: Springer. doi:10.1007/978-3-540-30581-1_4

Martin, D., Burstein, M., Hobbs, J., Lassila, O., McDermott, D., McIlraith, S., et al. (2004). *OWL-based web service ontology (OWL-S).* Retrieved November 19, 2009, from http://www.daml.org/services/owl-s/1.1/overview/

Martin, D., Paolucci, M., & Wagner, M. (2007) *Toward semantic annotations of Web services: OWL-S from the SAWSDL Perspective.* Retrieved May 21, 2010, from http://www.ai.sri.com/OWL-S-2007/final-versions/OWL-S-2007-Martin-Final.pdf

Martin, D., Wutke, D., & Leymann, F. (2008, September). A novel approach to decentralized workflow enactment. In *Proceedings of the 12th International IEEE Enterprise Distributed Object Computing Conference (EDOC 2008). Munich, Germany,* (pp. 127-136). IEEE Computer Society. Retrieved from http://www.informatik.uni-stuttgart.de/cgi-bin/NCSTRL/NCSTRL_view.pl?id=INPROC-2008-107&engl=0

Masolo, C., Borgo, S., Gangemi, A., Guarino, N., & Oltramari, A. (2003). *D18-ontology library.* Deliverable of the WonderWeb Project.

Masser, I. (2005). *GIS worlds: Creating Spatial Data Infrastructures.* Redlands, California: ESRI PRESS.

Masser, I. (1999). All shapes and sizes: The first generation of national spatial data infrastructures. *International Journal of Geographical Information Science, 13*(1), 67–84. doi:10.1080/136588199241463

Masser, I. (2007). *Building European spatial data infrastructures.* Redlands, CA: ESRI Press.

Maué, P., & Schade, S. (2009). *Data integrations in the Geospatial Semantic Web. Cases on semantic interoperability for Information Systems Integration: Practices and Applications* (pp. 100–122). Hershey, PA: IGI Global.

Maué, P., Schade, S., & Duchesne, P. (2008). *OGC discussion paper 08-167r1: semantic annotations in OGC standards.*

Maué, P., Schade, S., & Duchesne, P. (2009). OGC discussion paper 08-167r1: semantic annotations in OGC standards. *Technical report, OGC, 2009.*

Mayer-Schonberger, V., & Lazer, D. (Eds.). (2007). *Governance and information technology: from electronic government to information government.* Cambridge, MA: MIT Press.

Mazzetti, P., Nativi, S., & Caron, J. (2009). RESTful implementation of geospatial services for Earth and Space Science applications. *International Journal of Digital Earth, 2*(1), 40–61. doi:10.1080/17538940902866153

Mazzetti, P., Nativi, S., & Caron, J. (2009). RESTful implementation of geospatial services for Earth and space science applications. *International Journal of Digital Earth, 2*(1), 40–61. doi:10.1080/17538940902866153

MBARI. (2009). *Marine plug-and-work consortium.* Retrieved from http://www.mbari.org/pw/puck.htm

McIlraith, S. A., Son, T. C., & Zeng, H. (2001). Semantic web services. *IEEE Intelligent Systems, 16*(2), 46–53. doi:10.1109/5254.920599

Medjahed, B., Bouguettaya, A., & Elmagarmid, A. K. (2003). Composing web services on the semantic web. *The VLDB Journal, 12*(4), 333–351. doi:10.1007/s00778-003-0101-5

Mell, P., & Grance, T. (2009b). *Definition of cloud computing. National Institute of Standards and Technology.* NIST.

Mell, P., & Grance, T. (2009a). *Effectively and Securely Using the Cloud Computing Paradigm.* Retrieved from http://csrc.nist.gov/groups/SNS/cloud-computing/cloud-computing-v26.ppt

Menard, L., Wald, L., Blanc, P., & Mines, T. R. (2009, May). Sitting of a solar power plant: Development of Web service based on GEOSS data and guidance. *Proceedings from the 33rd International Symposium on Remote Sensing of the Environment*, Stresa, Italy.

Menasce, A. D., & Almeida, A. F. V. (2000). *Scaling for e-business - technologies, models, performance, and capacity*. Upper Saddle River, NJ: Prentice Hall.

Menasce, A. D., & Almeida, A. F. V. (2002). *Capacity planning for Web Services: metrics, models, and methods*. Upper Saddle River, NJ: Prentice Hall.

Microsoft. (2006). *UBR Shutdown FAQ*. Retrieved from http://uddi.microsoft.com/about/FAQshutdown.htm

Mika, P. (2005). Ontologies are us: A unified model of social networks and semantics. In *Proceedings of the 4th International Semantic Web Conference (ISWC 2005)*.

Miles, A., & Bechhofer, S. (2009). *SKOS Simple Knowledge Organization System Namespace Document - HTML Variant*.

Miller, J. (2004, July 02). *DHS weaves geospatial data into its enterprise architecture*. Retrieved from http://gcn.com/articles/2004/07/02/dhs-weaves-geospatial-data-into-its-enterprise-architecture.aspx

Mitasova, H., & Neteler, M. (2004). GRASS as Open Source Free Software GIS: Accomplishments and Perspectives. *Transactions in GIS, 8*(2), 145–154. doi:10.1111/j.1467-9671.2004.00172.x

Mitchell, T. (2005). *Web Mapping Illustrated*. Sebastopol, CA: O'Reilly.

Müller, M., Vogel, R., & Bernard, L. (2009). Multi-criteria evaluation for emergency management in a Web service environment. In M. Konecny, S. Zlatanova, T. Bandrova, & L. Friedmannova (Eds.), *Cartography and Geoinformatics for early warning and emergency management: towards better solutions* (pp. 439-446). Presented at the Joint Symposium of ICA Working Group on CEWaCM and JBGIS Gi4DM, Prague: Masaryk University Brno.

MultiMap. (2010). *MultiMap from Bing*. Retrieved from http://www.multimap.com/

Murray, D. (2009). True spatial data interoperability: new tools are turning a dream into reality. *GeoWorld*. March 2009, 24-26.

Myerson, J. (2008). *Cloud computing versus grid computing* (p. 9). IBM Corporation. Retrieved from http://www.ibm.com/ developer works/web/ library/wa- cloudgrid/

Na, A. & Priest, M. (2007). *OGC implementation specification 06-009r6: OpenGIS Sensor Observation Service (SOS)*.

NASA. (2009). WCS for accessing Atmospheric Infrared Sounder (AIRS) Data. Retrieved from http://idn.ceos.org/KeywordSearch/Metadata.do?Portal=webservices&KeywordPath=(Project%3A+Short_Name%3D%27EOS%27]&EntryId=NASA_GES_DISC_AIRS_Atmosphere_Data_Web_Coverage_Service&MetadataView=Full&MetadataType=1&lbnode=mdlb1

Nash, E. (2008). WPS application profiles for generic and specialised processes. In E. Pebesma, M. Bishr, & T. Bartoschek (Eds.), *Proceedings of the 6th Geographic Information Days*, IfGI prints (Vol. 32, pp. 69-79). Presented at the GI-days 2008, Muenster, Germany: Institute for Geoinformatics.

Nash, E., Korduan, P., Abele, S., & Hobona, G. (2008). Design requirements for an AJAX and Web-Service based generic Internet GIS client. *The 11th AGILE International Conference on Geographic Information Science*, Girona, Spain.

National Center for Geographic Information and Analysis. (2004). *Specialist meeting on Spatial Webs and Data Integration*. December 2-4, Santa Barbara, CA.

National Institute of Standards and Technology (NIST). (2009). *Cloud computing*. Retrieved November 27, 2009, from http://csrc.nist.gov/groups/SNS/cloud-computing/cloud-def-v15.doc

National Research Council. (2003). *IT Roadmap to a geospatial future*. Washington, D.C.: National Academies Press.

National Science Foundation (NSF). (2007). *Cyberinfrastructure vision for 21ˢᵗ century discovery*. Retrieved July 13, 2010, from http://www.nsf.gov/pubs/2007/nsf0728/nsf0728.pdf

Nativi, S., Bigagli, L., Mazzetti, P., Mattia, U., & Boldrini, E. (2007). Discovery, query and access services for imagery, gridded and coverage data a clearinghouse solution. *Proceedings from Geoscience and Remote Sensing Symposium and IGARSS, 2007*, 4021–4024.

Nativi, S., Mazzetti, P., Saarenmaa, H., Kerr, J., & Tuama, O. E. (2009). Biodiversity and climate change use scenarios framework for the GEOSS Interoperability Pilot Process. *Ecological Informatics*, *4*(1), 23–33. doi:10.1016/j.ecoinf.2008.11.002

Nativi, S. H. M., Domenico, B., Caron, J., Davis, E., & Bigagli, L. (2006). Extending THREDDS middleware to serve OGC community. *Advances in Geosciences*, *8*, 57–62. doi:10.5194/adgeo-8-57-2006

NC OneMap. (2008). *NC OneMap*. Retrieved from http://www.nconemap.com/Default.aspx?tabid=287

Nebert, D. (Ed.). (2004). *Developing Spatial Data Infrastructures: The SDI Cookbook*. Global Spatial Data Infrastructure.

Nebert, D. (2004). The SDI Cookbook, Version 2.0. *Global Spatial Data Infrastructure Association, Technical Working Group Report*.

Nebert, D., Whiteside, A., & Vretanos, P. (2007). *OpenGIS catalogue services specification*, (Version 2.0.2). Retrieved March 1, 2010 from http://portal.opengeospatial.org/files/?artifact_id=20555

Nebert, D., Whiteside, A. & Vretanos, P. (2007). *OGC implementation specification 07-006r1: OpenGIS catalogue services specification*.

Neteler, M., & Mitasova, H. (2007). *Open Source GIS: A GRASS GIS Approach*. New York: Springer.

Neteler, M., & Mitasova, H. (2008). Open source GIS: A GRASS GIS approach (3ʳᵈ ed.). *The International Series in Engineering and Computer Science, 773*. New York: Springer.

Neuman, B., & Ts'o, T. (1994). Kerberos: An authentication service for computer networks. *IEEE Communications Magazine*, *32*(9), 33–38. doi:10.1109/35.312841

Neun, M., Burghardt, D., & Weibel, R. (2008). Automated processing for map generalization using web services. *GeoInformatica*.

Nezhad, H., Benatallah, B., Casati, F., & Toumani, F. (2006). Web services interoperability specifications. *Computer*, *39*(5), 24–32. doi:10.1109/MC.2006.181

NIEM Program Management Office. (2007). *Introduction to the National Information Exchange Model*. Retrieved from http://www.niem.gov/files/NIEM_Introduction.pdf

NIST. (2009). *Definition of cloud computing (v15)*. National Institute of Standards and Technology.

NOAA WCS. (2009). *HF radar Web Coverage Service (WCS)*. Retrieved from http://hfradar.ndbc.noaa.gov/

NOAA. (2007). *Environmental data management at NOAA: Archiving, stewardship, and access*. National Academy of Sciences, Washington DC. Retrieved from http://www.nap.edu/catalog/12017.html.

Nogueras-Iso, J., Zarazaga-Soria, F., Bejar, R., Alvarez, P., & Muro-Medrano, P. (2005). OGC Catalog Services: a key element for the development of Spatial Data Infrastructures. *Computers & Geosciences*, *31*, 199–209. doi:10.1016/j.cageo.2004.05.015

NPR. (2009, November). *The Science in Science Fiction*, William Gibson speaking at 11:55 in Talk of the Nation, National Public Radio. Retrieved from http://www.npr.org/templates/story/story.php?storyId=1067220

OASIS(2005b). Profiles for the OASIS security assertion markup language (SAML) V2.0.

OASIS(2007). Security Assertion Markup Language(v2.0) technical overview.

OASIS (2002a). UDDI version 3.0.

OASIS (2005a). *eXtensible access control markup language 2.0*.

OASIS (2005c). *Web services trust standard (WS-trust)*.

OASIS. (2002b). *Web services security policy language*. WS-SecurityPolicy.

OASIS. (2006). *Web Service Resource 1.2 (WS-Resource)*. OASIS Standard.

OASIS. (2007). *Web services business process execution language (version 2.0) (WS-BPEL 2.0)*. Retrieved from http://docs.oasis-open.org/wsbpel/2.0/

OASIS. (2009). *Service oriented architecture*.

OASIS. (2010). *Online community for the universal description, discovery, and integration*. Retrieved from http://uddi.xml.org/.

Object Manager Group-UML. (2010). *UML Resource Page*. Retrieved from http://www.uml.org/

OGC(2006a). Geospatial Digital Rights Mangement Reference Model (GeoDRM RM).

OGC(2006b). OpenGIS Web Service common implementation specification (OWS-common).

OGC(2007). OpenGIS catalog service implementation specification.

OGC (2002). *Web map service implementation specification*.

OGC (2003). *OpenGIS reference model*.

OGC (2008). *License broker engineering report*.

OGC. (2003). Open Geospatial Consortium Inc. Web Mapping Service Implementation Specification 1.1.

OGC. (2005). Open Geospatial Consortium Inc. Web Feature Service Implementation Specification 1.1.

OGC. (2005b). OpenGIS® filter encoding implementation specification (version 1.1).

OGC. (2006a). Open Geospatial Consortium Inc. Web map service implementation specification (version 1.3.0).

OGC. (2007). OpenGIS Geography Markup Language (GML) Encoding Standard 3.2.1.

OGC. (2007a). OpenGIS® Geography Markup Language (GML) encoding standard (version 3.2.1).

OGC. (2007b). OpenGIS® catalogue service implementation specification (version 2.0.2).

OGC. (2008). Open Geospatial Consortium Inc. Web coverage service implementation specification (version 1.1.2).

OGC. (2010). OpenGIS® table joining service implementation standard (10-070).

OGC.(2006). Open Geospatial Consortium Inc. Web Coverage Service Implementation Specification 1.0.

OGC CSW ebRIM. (2009). *CSW-ebRIM Registry Service - part 1: ebRIM profile of CSW*. Retrieved from http://portal.opengeospatial.org/files/?artifact_id=31137

OGC CSW ISO 19115 (2007), *Catalogue services specification 2.0.2 - ISO metadata application profile*. Retrieved from http://portal.opengeospatial.org/files/?artifact_id=21460

OGC document 03-065r6. (2003). *Web coverage service (ver. 1.0.0)*. Retrieved May 21, 2010, from http://www.opengeospatial.org/standards/wcs

OGC document 04-021r2. (2004). *OpenGIS catalogue service specification*, Retrieved May 21, 2010, from http://www.opengeospatial.org/standards/cat

OGC document 04-024. (2004). *Web map service (ver. 1.3)*. Retrieved May 21, 2010, from http://www.opengeospatial.org/standards/wms

OGC document 04-094. (2005). *Web feature service implementation specification, version 1.1.0*. Retrieved May 21, 2010, from http://www.opengeospatial.org/standards/wfs

OGC document 05-007r7. (2005). *Web processing service*, Retrieved May 21, 2010, from http://www.opengeospatial.org/standards/wps

OGC GML. (2010). *OpenGIS Geography Markup Language (GML) Encoding Standard*. Retrieved from http://www.open geospatial.org/ standards/gml

OGC KML. (2010). *KML*. Retrieved from http://www.open geospatial.org/ standards/kml/

OGC SWE. (2010). *Sensor Web Enablement WG*. Retrieved from http://www.open geospatial.org /projects/ groups/ sensorweb

OGC WCS. (2010). *Web Coverage Service*. Retrieved from http://www.open geospatial.org/ standards/wcs

OGC WFS. (2010). *Web Feature Service*. Retrieved from http://www.open geospatial.org/ standards/wfs

OGC WFS-G. (2010). *WFS Gazetteer Profile 1.0 SWG*. Retrieved from http://www.open geospatial.org/ projects/ groups/ wfsgaz1.0swg

OGC WMS. (2010). *Web Map Service*. Retrieved from http://www.open geospatial.org/ standards/wms

OGC. (1999-2010). *Open Geospatial Consortium standards*. Retrieved on February 12, 2010, from http://www. opengeospatial.org/standards

OGC. (2000). *The OpenGIS abstract specification topic 6: The coverage type and its subtypes (OGC-00-106)*. Retrieved March 01, 2010, from http://portal.opengeospatial.org/files/?artifact_id=985&version=1

OGC. (2000). *Web map service interface specification*, (version 1.0 Project Document 00-028). Retrieved from http://www.opengeospatial.org/standards/wms

OGC. (2005, July). The importance of going open-an OGC White Paper. *The Open Geospatial Consortium*. Retrieved from http://portal.opengeospatial.org/files/?artifact_id=6211&version=2&format=pdf

OGC. (2006). *Discussions, findings, and use of WPS in OWS-4*. Retrieved April 26, 2006, from http://portal.opengeospatial.org/files/?artifact_id=19424

OGC. *(2006b)*. OGC White Paper - an introduction to GeoRSS: a standards based approach for geo-enabling RSS feeds.

OGC. (2007). *OGC Glossary*. Retrieved from http://www.opengeospatial.org/ogc/glossary

OGC. (2007). *OpenGIS Web Processing Service* (OGC implementation specification No. OGC 05-007r7). Open Geospatial Consortium. Retrieved from http://www.open geospatial.org/ standards/wps

OGC. (2007c). *OGC® KML (version 2.2)*.

OGC. (2008). *OGC KML* (specification No. OGC 07-147r2). OGC Standard (p. 251). Open Geospatial Consortium. Retrieved from https://portal.open geospatial. org/ files/?artifact_id=27810

OGC. (2008). *Open GIS Reference Model*. Retrieved July 13, 2010, from http://www.opengeospatial.org/ standards/orm

OGC. (2009) *Catalogue service*. Retrieved from http:// www.opengeospatial.org/standards/cat

OGC. (2009). Open Geospatial Consortium Inc. *OWS-6 Geoprocessing Workflow Architecture Engineering Report*.

OGC. (2010). *Implementing Products*. Retrieved from http://www.opengeospatial.org/resource/products

OGC/J. Evans (Ed.). (2001). *Web coverage service (version 0.0.3), OGC 01-010*. Retrieved March 1, 2010 from http://portal.opengeospatial.org/files/?artifact_id=1000&version=1

OGC/J. Evans (Ed.). (2002). *OWS1 Web coverage service, (version 0.7), OGC 02-024*. Retrieved March 1, 2010 from http://portal.opengeospatial.org/files/?artifact_id=2669&version=1

OGC/J. Evans (Ed.). (2005). *Web coverage service, (version 1.0.0), OGC-05-076*. Retrieved March 01, 2010 from http://portal.opengeospatial.org/files/?artifact_id=12582&version=2

OGC/J. Evans and A. Whiteside (Ed.). (2008). *Web coverage service implementation standard (version 1.1.2), OGC-07-067r5*. Retrieved March 01, 2010 from http://portal.opengeospatial.org/files/?artifact_id=27297&version=2

OGC/S. Nativi & B. Domenico (Ed.). (2009). *Web coverage service 1.1.2 extension for CF-netCDF 3.0 encoding (version 3.0), OGC-09-018r01*. Retrieved March 1, 2010 from http://portal.opengeospatial.org/files/?artifact_id=35296&version=1

OGSA-DAI. (2010). *OGSA-DAI*. Retrieved from http://www.ogsadai.org.uk/

Oinn, T., Addis, M., Ferris, J., Marvin, D., Senger M., Greenwood, M., et al. (2004). Taverna: A tool for the composition and enactment of bioinformatics workflows. *Bioinformatics journal, 17*(20), 3045–3054.

Olsen, L. M., Major, G., Leicester, S., Shein, K., Scialdone, J., Weir, H., et al. (2004). *NASA/Global Change Master Directory (GCMD) Earth Science Keywords (Version 5.1.1)*. Retrieved August 5, 2005, from http://gcmd.nasa. gov/Resources/valids/keyword_list.html

Olsen, L., & Stevens, T. (2008). *Service Entry Resource Format (SERF) standard.* (ESDS-RFC-013v0.1). Retrieved from http://www.esdswg.org/spg/rfc/esds-rfc-013/ESDS-RFC-013v0.1.pdf

Omran, E. L. E., & van Etten, J. (2007). Spatial-data sharing: applying social-network analysis to study individual and collective behaviour. *International Journal of Geographical Information Science, 21*(6), 699–714. doi:10.1080/13658810601135726

Onchaga, R. (2006). Quality of service management framework for dynamic chaining of geographic information services. *International Journal of Applied Earth Observation and Geoinformation, 8*(2), 137–148. doi:10.1016/j.jag.2005.06.012

Onchaga, R. (2005). *On quality of service and geo-service compositions.* Paper presented at the AGILE Conference on Geographic Information Science, Estoril, Portugal.

Onchaga, R., Widya, I., Morales, J., & Nieuwenhuis, L. J. M. (2008, November). *An ontology framework for quality of geographical information services.* Paper presented at the ACM GIS conference, Irvine, CA.

O'Neill, M. (2003). *Web services security.* McGraw-Hill Osborne Media.

Onsrud, H., Poore, B., Rugg, R. T., & Wiggins, L. (2004). The future of the spatial information infrastructure . In McMaster, R. B., & Usery, E. L. (Eds.), *A research agenda for Geographic Information Science* (pp. 225–255). Boca Raton: CRC Press. doi:10.1201/9781420038330.ch8

Open Geospatial Consortium. (2010). *Open Geospatial Consortium.* Retrieved March 1, 2010, from http://www.opengeospatial.org/.

Open Geospatial Consortium. (2004). *Web map service interface.* Retrieved July 9, 2010, from http://www.opengeospatialorg./standards/wms

Open Geospatial Consortium. (2007). *Open GIS catalogue services specification.* Retrieved July 9, 2010, from http://www.opengeospatialorg./standards/csw

Open Geospatial Consortium. (2008). *Web coverage service implementation standard.* Retrieved July 9, 2010, from http://www.opengeospatialorg/standards/wcs

Open Geospatial Consortium. (2008). *Web feature service implementation specification.* Retrieved July 9, 2010, from http://www.opengeospatialorg./standards/wfs

Open Geospatial Consortium. (2004). *OWS 2 Common Architecture: WSDL SOAP UDDI (WSDL/SOAP/ UDDI).* Retrieved from https://portal.opengeospatial.org/files/?artifact_id=8348

Open Geospatial Consortium. (2009). *OGC KML standard development best practices.* Retrieved from http://www.opengeospatial.org/standards/kml/

Open Geospatial Consortium, Inc. (2006). *OGC vision, mission, & goals.* Retrieved on December 1, 2009 from http://www.opengeospatial.org/ogc/vision

Open Geospatial Consortium, Inc. (2007a). *How OGC membership helps organizations involved in homeland security.* Retrieved from http://www.opengeospatial.org/ogc/markets-technologies/homeland-security

Open Geospatial Consortium, Inc. (2007b). *OGC Web services phase 4 demonstration.* Retrieved from http://www.opengeospatial.org/pub/www/ows4/index.html

Open Geospatial Consortium, Inc. (2009). *OGC Web services phase 6 demonstration.* Retrieved from http://www.opengeospatial.org/pub/www/ows6/web_files/ows6.html

Open Geospatial Consortium. (2010). *Open Geospatial Consortium.* Retrieved from www.open geospatial.org

Open, G. L. (2010). *OpenGL The Industry's Foundation for High Performance Graphics*. Retrieved from http://www.opengl.org/

OpenIOOS. (2010). Retrieved from http://www.openioos.org/real_time_data/gm_sos.html

OpenLayers. (2010). *OpenLayers Home*. Retrieved from http://openlayers.org/

OpenStreetMap. (2010). *OpenStreetMap FAQ*. Retrieved March 1, 2010, from http://wiki.openstreetmap.org/wiki/FAQ.

OpenStreetMap. (2010). *Osm2pgsql*. Retrieved from http://wiki.open streetmap.org/ wiki/Osm 2pgsql

OpenStreetMap. (2010). *OpenStreetMap*. Retrieved from www.openstreetmap.org

Oracle Corporation. (2010). *Oracle spatial datasheet*. Retrieved March 1, 2010, from http://www.oracle.com/technology/products/spatial/htdocs/data_sheet_9i/9iR2_spatial_ds.html

Ostlaender, N. (2009). *Creating specific spatial decision support Systems in Spatial Data Infrastructures*. Unpublished doctoral dissertation, University of Muenster, Germany.

OWS-7. (2010). *OGC Web Service Test Bed 7*. Retrieved from http://www.opengeospatial.org/projects/initiatives/ows-7

Papazoglou, M. P., & Heuvel, W. (2007). Service oriented architectures: approaches, technologies and research issues. *The International Journal on Very Large Data Bases, 16*(3), 389–415. doi:10.1007/s00778-007-0044-3

Papazoglou, M. P. (2007). *Web Services:Principles and Technology*. England: Pearson Prentice Hall.

Papazoglou, M. P. (2003). Service-oriented computing: concepts, characteristics and directions. In *Proceedings of Fourth International Conference on Web Information Systems Engineering (WISE 2003)*, Roma, Italy.

Pastor, E., Royo, P., Lopez, J., Barrado, C., Santamaria, E., & Prats, X. (2007). Project SKY-EYE: Applying UAVs to Forest Fire Fighter Support and Monitoring. *2007 UAV Conference*, Paris.

Paulson, L. D. (2005). Building rich Web applications with AJAX. *Computer, 38*(10), 14–17. doi:10.1109/MC.2005.330

Pautasso, C., & Alonso, G. (2006). Parallel computing patterns for grid workflows. In *Proceedings of the Workshop on Workflows in Support of Large-Scale Science*, 19–23. Retrieved from http://scholar.google.com/scholar?hl=en&btnG=Search&q=intitle:Parallel+computing+patterns+for+grid+workflows#0

Payne, T., Paolucci, M., Kawmura, T., & Sycara, K. (2002). Semantic matching of Web service capabilities. *Proceedings of the International Semantic Web Conference*.

Peer, J. (2005). *Web service composition as AI planning - a survey. Technial report*. Gallen, Switzerland: University of St.

Peisheng, Z., Yu, G., & Di, L. (2007). Geospatial Web Services . In Hilton, B. N. (Ed.), *Emerging spatial Information Systems and applications* (pp. 1–35). Hershey: Idea Group, Inc.

Peltz, C. (2003). Web services orchestration and choreography. *Computer, 36*(10), 46–52. doi:10.1109/MC.2003.1236471

Peng, Z. R. (2005). A proposed framework for feature level geospatial data sharing: a case study for transportation network data. *International Journal of Geographical Information Science, 19*(4), 459–481. doi:10.1080/13658810512331319127

Peng, Z.-R., & Kim, E. (2008). A standard-based integration framework of distributed transit trip planning systems. *Journal of the Intelligent Transportation Systems, 12*(1), 13–19. doi:10.1080/15472450701849642

Peng, Z.-R., & Tsou, M.-H. (2003). *Internet GIS: distributed Geographic Information Services for the internet and wireless networks*. Hoboken, NJ: John Wiley & Sons.

Percivall, G. (Ed.). (2002). *The OpenGIS abstact specification, topic 12: OpenGIS Service Architecture, (Version 4.3)*. Open Geospatial Consortium, Inc.

Percivall, G. (2002). *ISO 19119 and OGC Service Architecture*. Presented at FIG XXII International Congress, Washington, D.C.

Percivall, G. (2003). *OGC reference model*. Retrieved from http://portal.opengeospatial.org/files/?artifact_id=3836

Percivall, G. (2009). *OGC Interoperability Program*. Retrieved from http://www.opengeospatial.org/ogc/programs/ip

Percivall, G., Reed, C., Leinenweber, L., Tucker, C., and Cary, T. (2008). *The OGC Reference Model (ORM)*. OGC Document OGC 08-062r4.

Perry, M., Sheth, A., & Arpinar, I. (2007). Geospatial and temporal semantic analytics . In Karimi, H. A. (Ed.), *Encyclopedia of Geoinformatics*.

Platt, M. (2007). Geospatial Data and Web 2.0 - a MapMart perspective. *Directions Magazine*, July 26, 2007.

Ponnekanti, S. R., & Fox, A. (2002). SWORD: a developer toolkit for web service composition. In *Proceedings of the International World Wide Web Conference*, Honolulu, HI. (pp. 83-107).

PostGIS. (2010). *PostGIS: Home*. Retrieved from http://postgis.refractions.net/

PostgreSQL Global Development Group. (2010). *PostgreSQL*. Retrieved from http:// www.postgresql.org/

Poveda, J., Gould, M., & Grannell, C. (2004, April). *ACE GIS project overview: adaptable and composable e-commerce and geographic information services*. Paper presented at the AGILE Conference on Geographic Information Science, Heraklion, Greece.

Raghavan, V., Masumoto, S., Santitamont, P., & Honda, K. (2002). Implementing an online spatial database using the GRASS GIS environment. In M. Ciolli & P. Zatelli (Eds.), *Proceedings of the 2002 Open source GIS - GRASS users conference*. Trento, Italy.

Rajabalinejad, M. (2009). A systematic approach to risk mitigation . In Konecny, M., Zlatanova, S., Bandrova, T., & Friedmannova, L. (Eds.), *Cartography and Geoinformatics for early warning and emergency management: towards better solutions (Joint symposium of ICA working group on CEWaCM and JBGIS Gi4DM)* (pp. 386–395). Brno, Czech Republic: Masaryk University.

Rajabifard, A., Binns, A., Masser, I., & Williamson, I. (2006). The role of sub-national government and the private sector in future spatial data infrastructures. *International Journal of Geographical Information Science, 20*(7), 727–741. doi:10.1080/13658810500432224

Rajabifard, A., Kalantari, M., & Binns, A. (2009). SDI and metadata entry and updating tools . In van Loenen, B., Besemer, J. W. J., & Zevenbergen, J. A. (Eds.), *SDI convergence: research, emerging tools, and critical assessment* (pp. 121–135). Rotterdam: Netherlands Geodetic Commission.

Ramakrishnan, R., & Gehrke, J. (2003). *Database management systems*. New York: McGraw Hill.

Ran, S. (2003). A model for web services discovery with QoS. *SIGecom Exchanges, 4*(1), 1–10. doi:10.1145/844357.844360

Rao, J., & Su, X. (2004). A survey of automated web service composition methods. In *Proceedings of the First International Workshop on Semantic Web Services and Web Process Composition (SWSWPC 2004)*, San Diego, CA. (pp. 43–54).

Raskin, R. G., & Pan, M. J. (2005). Knowledge representation in the Semantic Web for Earth and Environmental Terminology (SWEET). *Computers & Geosciences, 31*(9), 1119–1125. doi:10.1016/j.cageo.2004.12.004

Rath, S. (2007): *Model discretization in 2D hydroinformatics based on high resolution remote sensing data and the feasibility of automated model parameterisation*. Unpublished doctoral dissertation, Hamburg University of Technology, Hamburg, Germany.

Reed, C. (2006). *An introduction to GeoRSS: A standards based approach for geoenabling RSS feeds*. Open Geospatial Consortium. Retrieved from http://www.opengeospatial.org/pt/06-050r3

Reed, C. (Ed.). (2009). *OGC technical committee policies and procedures*. OGC Document 09-020r14.

Reeves, A. C., & Bednar, D. A. (1994). Defining quality: alternatives and implications. *Academy of Management Review, 19*(3), 419–445. doi:10.2307/258934

Reichardt, M. (2009). Ocean Science, OneGeology, and GEOSS: Building 'SDI bridges', *Proceedings of the 11th annual conference of the Global Spatial Data Infrastructure Association (GSDI11)*. Rotterdam, Netherlands.

Reznik, T., & Hynek, Z. (2009). Data management in crisis situations through WFS-T Client . In Konecny, M., Zlatanova, S., Bandrova, T., & Friedmannova, L. (Eds.), *Cartography and Geoinformatics for early warning and emergency management: towards better solutions (Joint symposium of ICA working group on CEWaCM and JBGIS Gi4DM)* (pp. 386–395). Brno, Czech Republic: Masaryk University.

Richardson, R., & Smeaton, A. (1995). *Using WordNet in a knowledge-based approach to information retrieval, technical, CA-0395*. Dublin, Ireland: Dublin City University, School of Computer Applications.

Richardson, L., & Ruby, S. (2007). *RESTful Web Services*. Sebastopol, CA: O'Reilly Media.

Riehle, D. (2007). The economic motivation of open source software: stakeholder perspectives. *IEEE Computer, 40*(4), 25–32.

Robinson, A. H., Morrison, J. L., Muehrcke, P. C., Kimerling, A. J., & Guptill, S. C. (1995). *Elements of Cartography* (6th ed.). New York: Wiley.

Robinson, E. (2009, May). Air quality and GEOSS: status, issues and panel discussion. *Technical Session 34, 33rd International Symposium on Remote Sensing of the Environment*, Stresa, Italy. Retrieved from http://wiki.esipfed.org/index.php/AQ_&_GEOSS_Session_during_ISRSE_May_2009

Rodriguez, M., Egenhofer, M., & Rugg, R. (2004). Comparing geospatial entity classes: an asymmetric and context-dependent similarity measure. *International Journal of Geographical Information Science, 18*, 229–256. doi:10.1080/13658810310001629592

Roman, D., & Klien, E. (2007). SWING – a semantic framework for geospatial Web services . In Scharl, A., & Tochtermann, K. (Eds.), *The Geospatial Web: how GeoBrowsers, social software and the Web 2.0 are shaping the network society* (pp. 229–234). London: Springer.

Roman, D., Klien, E., & Skogan, D. (2006, November). SWING - A semantic web services framework for the geospatial domain. In *Proceedings of Terra Cognita 2006, International Semantic Web Conference ISWC'06 Workshop*. Athens, GA.

Roman, D., Schade, S., Berre, A. J., Rune Bodsberg, N., & Langlois, J. (2009). Environmental services infrastructure with ontologies – a decision support framework. *EnviroInfo 2009*, Berlin, Germany.

Roman, D., Schade, S., Berre, A. J., Rune Bodsberg, N., & Langlois, J. (2009b): Model as a Service (MaaS). *Proceedings from AGILE Workshop, Grid Technologies for Geospatial Applications*, Hannover, Germany.

Rose, L. (Ed.). (2004). *Geospatial Portal Reference Architecture, A Community Guide to Implementing Standards-Based Geospatial Portals*. Wayland, MA: Open Geospatial Consortium Inc.

Rosenblatt, W. (2002). *Digital rights management business and technology*. New York: M & T Books.

Roux, A. (2010). *Intelligence and peacekeeping-are we winning?* Retrieved from http://se1.isn.ch/serviceengine/Files/ ISN/101775/ ichaptersection_ singledocument/ 3D21E3F5- BF86-4429- B9F7-A2DB571 BA19A/en/ Chapter+3.pdf

Rumbaugh, J., Jacobson, I., & Booch, G. (1999). *UML Reference Manual*. Boston, MA: Addison-Wesley.

Russel, S., & Norvig, P. (2003). *Artificial intelligence: a modern approach* (2nd ed., pp. 375–458). USA: Prentice-Hall Inc.

Sandhu, R. S., & Samarati, P. (1994). Access control: Principle and practice. *IEEE Communications Magazine*, *32*(9), 40–48. doi:10.1109/35.312842

Schade, S. (2008). *Semantic reference systems accounting for uncertainty. Quality aspects in Spatial Data Mining*. Boca Raton, FL: CRC Press.

Schade, S. (2010). *Ontology-driven translation of geospatial data. GISDIS*. Amsterdam: IOS Press BV.

Schade, S., & Cox, S. (2010). Linked data in SDI or how GML is not about trees. M. Painho et al. (Eds), *Proceedings of AGILE Conference 2010*.

Schade, S., Klien, E., Maué, P., Fitzner, D., & Kuhn, W. (2008b). Report on modelling approach and guideline. *Deliverable D3.2 of the SWING Project*. Retrieved November 18, 2009, from http://swing-project.org/deliverables.

Schade, S., Maué, P., & Langlois, J. (2008). Ontology engineering with domain experts-a field report. *Proceedings of the European Geosciences Union - General Assembly*, Vienna, Austria.

Schaeffer, B., & Foerster, T. (2008). A client for distributed geo-processing and workflow design. *Journal for Location Based Services*, *2*(3), 194–210. doi:10.1080/17489720802558491

Schaeffer, B. (2009). *OGC® OWS-6 geoprocessing workflow architecture engineering Report* (OGC Public Engineering Report No. 09-053r5) (p. 78). OGC.

Scharl, A. (2007). Towards the geospatial Web: media platforms for managing geotagged knowledge repositories . In Scharl, A., & Tochtermann, K. (Eds.), *The Geospatial Web: how geobrowsers, social software and the Web 2.0 are shaping the network society* (pp. 3–14). London: Springer.

Scharl, A., Stern, H., & Weichselbraun, A. (2008) Annotating and visualizing location data in geospatial Web applications. In S. Boll, C. Jones, E. Kansa, P. Kishor, M. Naaman, R. Purvers, et al. (Eds.), *International Workshop on Location and the Web, ACM, New York, Vol. 1* (pp. 65-68). New York: ACM Press.

Scheider, S., Janowicz, K., & Kuhn, W. (2009). *Grounding geographic categories in the meaningful environment. LNCS* (pp. 69-87). COSIT 2009. Berlin/Heidelberg: Springer.

Schmeh, K. (2009). *Kryptografie (4th ed.)*. Heidelberg: dpunkt-Verl.

Schneier, B. (1999). *The twofish encryption algorithm: A 128-bit block cipher*. New York: Wiley.

Scholten, M., Klamma, R., & Kiehle, C. (2006). Evaluating performance in spatial data infrastructures for geoprocessing. *IEEE Internet Computing*, *10*(5), 34–41. doi:10.1109/MIC.2006.97

Schuster, G., & Stuckenschmidt, H. (2001). Building shared ontologies for terminology integration. Paper presented in *KI-01 Workshop on Ontologies*, Vienna, Austria.

Schut, P. (Ed.). (2007). *OpenGIS® Web Processing Service*. Wayland, MA: Open Geospatial Consortium Inc.

Schut, P. (2007). *OGC Implementation Specification 05-007r7: OpenGIS Web Processing Service*.

Schut, P. (2007). *OpenGIS Web Processing Service*. Open Geospatial Consortium. Retrieved from http://portal.opengeospatial.org/files/?artifact_id=24151

Science, G. I. S. (2009). *SDI and the GRID special issue*. Retrieved from http://portal.opengeospatial.org/files/?artifact_id=35975

Scribner, K., & Stiver, M. C. (2000). *Understanding Soap: Simple Object Access Protocol*. Indianapolis, IN: Sams.

SeeGEO project. (2007). Retrieved from http://edina.ac.uk/projects/ seesaw/seegeo

Senkler, K., Voges, U., & Remke, A. (2004). *An ISO 19115/19119 profile for OGC catalogue services CSW 2.0*. Presented at the 10th EC GI & GIS Workshop, ESDI State of the Art, Warsaw, Poland.

Senkler, K., Voges, U., Einspainer, U., Kanellopoulos, I., Millot, M., Luraschi, G., et al. (2006). *Software for distributed metadata catalogue services to support the EU portal*. Europe Commission – Joint Research Centre. Retrieved July 9, 2010, from http://inspire.jrc.ec.europa.eu

Shan, C., Lin, C., Marinescu, D. C., & Yang, Y. (2002). Modeling and performance analysis of QoS-aware load balancing of Web-server clusters. *Computer Networks, 40*, 235–256. doi:10.1016/S1389-1286(02)00253-0

Shen, Z., Luo, J., Zhou, C., Cai, S., Zheng, J., & Chen, Q. (2004). Architecture design of Grid GIS and its applications of Image Processing based on LAN. *Information Sciences, 166*, 1–17. doi:10.1016/j.ins.2003.10.004

Sheth, A. (1999). Changing focus on interoperability in information systems: from system, syntax, structure to semantics. In Goodchild, M. F., Egenhofer, M., Fegeas, R., & Kottman, C. A. (Eds.), *The Interoperating Geographic Information Systems* (pp. 5–30). New York: Kluwer.

Shi, X. (2005). Removing syntactic barriers for Semantic Geospatial Web services. *UCGIS 2005*.

Singh, G., Vahi, K., Ramakrishnan, A., Mehta, G., Deelman, E., Zhao, H., et al. (2007). Optimizing workflow data footprint. *Scientific Program*ming, *15*, 249-268. Amsterdam: IOS Press. Retrieved from http://portal.acm.org/citation.cfm?id=1377549.1377553

Singh, R. (Ed.). (2008). *Loosely coupled synchronization of geographic databases in the Canadian geospatial data infrastructure.* OGC. Retrieved from http://portal.opengeospatial.org/files/?artifact_id=26609

Sirin, E., Parsia, B., Wu, D., Hendler, J., & Nau, D. (2004). HTN planning for web service composition using SHOP2. *Journal of Web Semantics, 1*(4), 377–396. doi:10.1016/j.websem.2004.06.005

Smith, B. (1995). Formal ontology, common sense and cognitive science. *International Journal of Human-Computer Studies, 43*, 641–667. doi:10.1006/ijhc.1995.1067

Smits, P., & Friis-Christensen, A. (2007). Resource discovery in a European Spatial Data Infrastructure. *IEEE Transactions on Knowledge and Data Engineering, 19*(1), 85–95. doi:10.1109/TKDE.2007.250587

Sonnet, J. (Ed.). (2005). *OGC Web Map Context Documents*. Wayland, MA: Open Geospatial Consortium Inc.

Sotomayor, B., Montero, R. S., Llorente, I. M., & Foster, I. (2009). Virtual infrastructure management in private and hybrid clouds. *IEEE Internet Computing, 13*(5), 14–22. doi:10.1109/MIC.2009.119

Sotomayor, B., & Childers, L. (2006). *Globus Toolkit 4 - programming Java services.* The Elsevier Series in Grid Computing. Morgan Kaufmann Publishers.

Srivastava, B., & Koehler, J. (2003). Web service composition - current solutions and open problems. In *Proceedings of ICAPS 2003 Workshop on Planning for Web Services.* (pp. 28-35), Trento, Italy.

Staab, S., van der Aalst, W., Benjamins, R., Sheth, A., Miller, J., & Bussler, C. (2003). Web Services: been there, done that? *IEEE Intelligent Systems, 18*(1), 72–85. doi:10.1109/MIS.2003.1179197

Stevens, S. S. (1946). On the theory of measurement. *Science, 103*(2684), 677–680. doi:10.1126/science.103.2684.677

Stock, K. M., Atkinson, R., Higgins, C., Small, M., Woolf, A., & Millard, K. (2010). A semantic registry using a feature type catalogue instead of ontologies to support Spatial Data Infrastructures. *International Journal of Geographical Information Science, 24*(2), 231–252. doi:10.1080/13658810802570291

Stock, K., Small, M., Ou, Y., & Reitsma, F. (2009). *OGC discussion paper 09-010 – OWL application profile of CSW.*

Stollberg, B., & Zipf, A. (2007). OGC Web processing service interface for Web service orchestration - aggregating geo-processing services in a bomb threat scenario . In *Proceedings of Web and Wireless Geographical Information Systems, LNCS* (pp. 239–251). Heidelberg, Germany: Springer-Verlag. doi:10.1007/978-3-540-76925-5_18

Stollberg, B., & Zipf, A. (2008). *Geoprocessing services for spatial decision support in the domain of housing market analyses - experiences from applying the OGC Web processing service interface in practice.* Paper presented at the AGILE 2008, Girona, Spain.

Strobl, C. (2008). PostGIS. In S. Shekhar & H. Xiong, (Eds.), *Encyclopedia of GIS* (pp. 891-898). Springer. Retrieved from http://dblp.uni-trier.de/db/reference/gis/gis2008.html#Strobl08a

Strong, D. M., Lee, Y. W., & Wang, R. Y. (1997). Data quality in context. *Communications of the ACM, 40*(5), 103–110. doi:10.1145/253769.253804

Su, Y., Jin, Z., & Peng, J. (2010). Building service oriented sharing platform for emergency management – an earthquake damage assessment example . In Luo, Q. (Ed.), *Advancing computing, communication, control and management, lecture notes in electrical engineering* (*Vol. 56*, pp. 247–255). London: Springer. doi:10.1007/978-3-642-05173-9_32

Subbiah, G., Alam, A., Khan, L., & Thuraisingham, B. (2007, November). *Geospatial data qualities as web services performance metrics*. Paper presented at the ACM GIS conference, Seattle, Washington.

Suda, B. (2006). *Using microformats*. Sebastopol, CA: O'Reilly Media.

Tait, M. (2005). Implementing geoportals: applications of distributed GIS. *Computers, Environment and Urban Systems, 29*, 33–47.

Tang, W., & Selwood, J. (2005). *Spatial Portals: Gateways to Geographic Information*. Redlands, CA: ESRI Press.

Taylor, I., Shields, M., Wang, I., & Rana, O. (2003). Triana applications within Grid computing and peer to peer environments. *Journal of Grid Computing, 1*, 199-217. Kluwer Academic Publishers. Retrieved from http://journals.kluweronline.com/article.asp?PIPS=5269002

The Economist. (2009). Clash of the clouds. *The Economist, 392*, 80-82.

The Globus Alliance. (2009a). *Globus Toolkit 4*. Retrieved from http://www.globus.org

The Globus Alliance. (2009b). *Grid Resource Allocation and Management (GRAM)*. Retrieved from http://www.globus.org/toolkit/docs/4.2/4.2.0/developer/globusrun-ws.html

The Globus Alliance. (2010a). *GridFTP*. Retrieved from http://www.globus.org/toolkit/docs/4.2/4.2.1/data/gridftp/

The Globus Alliance. (2010b). *Reliable File Transfer service (RFT)*. Retrieved from http://www.globus.org/toolkit/docs/4.2/4.2.1/data/rft/

The White House Blog. (2010, January 5). *The urgency of getting this right*. Retrieved from http://www.whitehouse.gov/blog/2010/01/05/urgency-getting-right

Tisdale, J. R. (2006). The software architecture of the Berkeley UAV platform. *Proceedings of the IEEE Conference on Control Applications*. Munich.

Tr'epanier, M., Chapleau, R., & Allard, B. (2002). Transit user information system for transit itinerary calculation on the Web. *Journal of Public Transportation, 5*(3), 13–32.

Tu, S., Flanagin, M., Wu, Y., Abdelguerfi, A., Normand, E., Mahadevan, V., et al. (2004). Design strategies to improve performance of GIS Web services. *Proceedings of the International Conference on Information Technology: Coding and Computing (ITCC 04), 2*.

Turhan, A., Bechhofer, S., Kaplunova, A., Liebig, T., Luther, M., Möller, et al. (2006, November). DIG 2.0 — towards a flexible interface for description logic reasoners. *Second international workshop OWL: Experiences and Directions*.

Turner, M., Budgen, D., & Brereton, P. (2003). Turning software into a service. *Computer, 36*(10), 38–44. doi:10.1109/MC.2003.1236470

Turner, A. (2008). *Emerging mass market geo standards*. Retrieved from http://www.slideshare.net/ajturner/mass-market-geo-standards-ogc-technical-committee

Turner, A., Wang, C., & Journal, D. (2007). *Ajax: Selecting the framework that fits*. Retrieved October 13, 2009, from http://www.ddj.com/web-development/199203087

Turton, I. (2008). GeoTools . In Hall, G. B., & Leahy, M. G. (Eds.), *Open source approaches in spatial data handling, advances in geographic information* (pp. 153–167). Berlin: Springer Verlag. doi:10.1007/978-3-540-74831-1_8

Tzitzikas, Y., Spyratos, N., & Constantopoulos, P. (2005). Mediators over taxonomy-based information sources. *The International Journal on Very Large Data Bases*, *14*(1), 112–136. doi:10.1007/s00778-003-0119-8

U.S. Executive Order 12906. (1994). Coordinating geographic data acquisition and access: the national Spatial Data Infrastructure. Retrieved July 11, 2010, from http://www.fgdc.gov/nsdi/policyandplanning/executive_order

Uddi, X. M. L. (2010). *Uddi.XML.org*. Retrieved from http:// uddi.xml.org/ uddi-org

Ülgen, S. (2005). Public participation Geographic Information Sharing systems for community based urban disaster mitigation . In Oosterom, P., Zlatanove, S., & Fendel, E. M. (Eds.), *Geo-Information for Disaster Management* (pp. 1427–1434). Berlin: Springer. doi:10.1007/3-540-27468-5_98

Umuhoza, D., Agbinya, J. I., Moodley, D., & Vahed, A. (2008). *A reputation based trust model for geospatial web services*. Paper presented at the 1st WSEAS International Conference on Environmental and Geological Science and Engineering, Malta.

United Nations General Assembly. (1989, December 22). *Resolution 236 session 44*. Retrieved Nov 15, 2009, from http://www.un.org/Docs/journal/asp/ws.asp?m=A/RES/44/236

United States, Federal Emergency Management Agency. (May, 2001). *Information Technology Architecture Version 2.0: The Road to e-FEMA, Volume 1*. Retrieved from http://www.fema.gov/pdf/library/it_vol1.pdf

Uschold, M., & Gruninger, M. (1996). Ontologies: principles, methods and applications. *The Knowledge Engineering Review*, *11*(2), 95–155. doi:10.1017/S0269888900007797

USGS WFS. (2009). *USGS Framework Web Feature Services*. Retrieved from http://frameworkwfs.usgs.gov/

Uslaender, T. (2007). *Integration of resource-oriented architecture concepts into OGC Reference Model*. OpenGIS document OGC 07-156.

Uslander, T. (Ed.). (2007). *Reference Model for the ORCHESTRA Architecture (RM-OA) V2 (Rev 2.1)*. Retrieved from http://portal.opengeospatial.org/files/?artifact_id=23286.

van de Sompel, H., Nelson, M. L., Sanderson, R., Balakireva, L. L., Ainsworth, S., & Shankar, H. (2009). *Memento: Time travel for the Web*. Retrieved from http://www.arXiv.org

van der Aalst, W. M., ter Hofstede, A. H., Kiepuszewski, B., & Barros, A. P. (2003). Workflow patterns. *Distributed and Parallel Databases*, *14*, 5–51. doi:10.1023/A:1022883727209

van der Aalst, W., Dumas, M., Hofstede, A. T., Russell, N., Verbeek, H., & Wohed, P. (2005). Life after BPEL? In *Formal Techniques for Computer Systems and Business Processes*, LCNS 3670, 35-50. Berlin: Springer.

van Oort, P. A. J., Hazeu, G. W., Kramer, H., Bregt, A. K., & Rip, F. I. (2010). Social networks in spatial data infrastructures. *GeoJournal*, *75*(1), 105–118. doi:10.1007/s10708-009-9294-5

Vaquero, L. M., Rodero-Merino, L., Caceres, J., & Lindner, M. (2009). A break in the clouds: towards a cloud definition. *ACM SIGCOMM Computer Communication Review*, *39*(1), 50–55. doi:10.1145/1496091.1496100

Vasudevan, V. (April 2001). *A Web Services Primer*. Retrieved from http://webservices.xml.com/pub/a/ws/2001/04/04/webservices/index.html

Vaughan-Nichols, S. (2002). Web services: Beyond the hype. *IEEE Computer*, *35*(2), 18–21.

Veregin, H. (1995). Developing and testing of an error propagation model for GIS overlay operations. *International Journal Geographical Information Systems*, *9*(6), 595–619. doi:10.1080/02693799508902059

Veregin, H. (1996). Error propagation through the buffer operation for probability surfaces. *Photogrammetric Engineering and Remote Sensing*, *62*(4), 419–428.

Voges, U., & Senkler, K. (Eds.). (2005). *OGC Catalogue Services specification 2.0 - ISO 19115/ISO 19119 application profile for CSW 2.0*. Wayland, MA: Open Geospatial Consortium Inc.

von Voigt, G. (2009). *The GDI-Grid project*. Retrieved from http://www.gdi-grid.de

Vretanos, P. A. (Ed.). (2002). *OGC Web Feature Service implementation specification*. Wayland, MA: Open Geospatial Consortium Inc.

Vretanos, P. A. (2005). *Web feature service implementation specification*. Open Geospatial Consortium. Retrieved from http://portal.opengeospatial.org/files/?artifact_id=8339

W3C OWL. (2010). *OWL Web Ontology Language*. Retrieved from http:// www.w3.org / TR /owl-features/

W3C OWL-S. (2010). *OWL-S: Semantic Markup for Web Services*. Retrieved from http:// www.w3. org/ Submission/OWL-S/

W3C RDF. (2010). *Resource Description Framework (RDF)*. Retrieved from http://www.w3.org/RDF/

W3C RDFS. (2010). *RDF Vocabulary Description Language 1.0: RDF Schema*. Retrieved from http:// www.w3.org / TR /owl-features/

W3C SOAP. (2010). *Simple Object Access Protocol (SOAP) 1.1*. Retrieved from http:// www.w3.org/ TR/2000/NOTE- SOAP-20000508/

W3C SVG. (2010). *Scalable Vector Graphics (SVG)*. Retrieved from http:// www.w3.org/ Graphics/ SVG/

W3C SWRL. (2010). *Semantic Web Services Language (SWSL)*. Retrieved from http:// www.w3.org/ Submission/SWSF- SWSL/

W3C URI. (2010). *URIs, URLs, and URNs: Clarifications and recommendations 1.0*. Retrieved from http://www.w3.org/ TR/uri-clarification/

W3C URL. (2010). *Addressing URL: Overview* Retrieved from http:// www.w3.org/ Addressing/URL/ Overview.html

W3C WSDL. (2010). *Web Services Description Language (WSDL) 1.1*. Retrieved from http://www.w3.org/ TR/wsdl

W3C XML. (2010). *Extensible Markup Language (XML)*. Retrieved from http://www.w3.org/ XML/

W3C. (2001). Semantic web. Retrieved February 3, 2007, from http://www.w3.org/2001/sw/

W3C. (2001). *Web Services Description Language (WSDL 1.1)*. Retrieved from http://www.w3schools.com/xsl/

W3C. (2001). *XML Schema Part 0: Primer*. Retrieved from http://www.w3.org/TR/ xmlschema-0/

W3C. (2001b). *URIs, URLs, and URNs: Clarifications and Recommendations 1.0*. Retrieved from http://www.w3.org/TR/uri-clarification/

W3C. (2002). *Web service choreography interface (WSCI) 1.0*. Retrieved February 26, 2007, from http://www.w3.org/TR/wsci/

W3C. (2003). *Web services federation language (WS-federation)*.

W3C. (2004). *OWL Web ontology language overview*. Retrieved on May 21, 2010, from http://www.w3.org/TR/owl-features/

W3C. (2004). *W3C working group note: Web service architecture*. Retrieved November 18, 2009, from http://www.w3.org/TR/ws-arch/

W3C. (2004). *Web services addressing (WS-addressing)*.

W3C. (2005). *Web services choreography description language (version 1.0)*. Retrieved from http://www.w3.org/TR/ws-cdl-10/2005

W3C. (2006a). *Web service policy*.

W3C. (2006b). *Web services policy attachment (WS-Policy Attachment)*. W3C member submission.

W3C. (2008). *SPARQL query language for RDF*. Retrieved from http://www.w3.org/TR/ xmlschema-0/

W3C. (2009a). *OWL 2 Web ontology language document overview-W3C recommendation*. Retrieved November 18, 2009, from http://www.w3.org/TR/owl2-overview/

W3C. (2009b). *SKOS Simple Knowledge Organization System reference - W3C OWL Working Group Recommendation.* Retrieved November 18, 2009, from http://www.w3.org/TR/2009/REC-skos-reference-20090818/

W3Schools. (2010). *XSLT Tutorial.* Retrieved from http://www.w3schools.com/xsl/

Wache, H., Vögele, T., Visser, U., Stuckenschmidt, H., Schuster, G., Neumann, H., et al. (2001). Ontology-based integration of information - a survey of existing approaches. *Proceedings from IJCAI-01 Workshop: Ontologies and Information Sharing, Seattle, WA.*

Wang, D. Y., & Strong, D. M. (1996). Beyond accuracy: what quality means to data consumers. *Journal of Management Information Systems, 12*(4), 5–34.

Wang, R. Y. (1998). A product perspective on total data quality management. *Communications of the ACM, 41*(2), 58–65. doi:10.1145/269012.269022

Wang, L., Tao, J., Kunze, M., Castellanos, A. C., Kramer, D., & Karl, W. (2008). Scientific cloud computing: early definition and experience. *Proceedings of the 10th IEEE International Conference on High Performance Computing and Communications, 2008. HPCC '08.* (pp. 825-830). IEEE Computer Society.

Wang, X., Lao, G., DeMartini, T., Reddy, H., Nguyen, M., & Valenzuela, E. (2002). XrML--eXtensible rights markup language. *Proceedings of the 2002 ACM Workshop on XML Security.* (pp. 71-79).

Watson, P., Lord, P., Gibson, F., Periorellis, P., & Pitsilis, G. (2008). Cloud computing for e-science with CARMEN. In F. Silva, G. Barreira & L. Ribeiro (Eds.), *Proceedings of the 2nd Iberian Grid Infrastructure Conference,* (pp. 3-14). Porto, Portugal.

Waugh, W. L. Jr. (1994). Regionalizing emergency management: Counties as state and local Government. *Public Administration Review, 54,* 253–258. doi:10.2307/976728

Weerawarana, S. (2006). *Web services platform architecture: SOAP, WSDL, WS-policy, WS-addressing, WS-BPEL, WS-reliable messaging and more* (4th ed.). Upper Saddle River, NJ: Prentice Hall/PTR.

Weerawarana, S., Curbera, F., Leymann, F., Storey, T., & Ferguson, D. (2005). *Web services platform architecture: SOAP, WSDL, WS-policy, WS-addressing, WS-BPEL, WS-reliable messaging, and more.* Prentice Hall PTR.

Weiser, A., & Zipf, A. (2007). Web service orchestration of OGC Web services for disaster management . In Li, J., Zlatanova, S., & Fabbri, A. (Eds.), *Geomatics Solutions for Disaster Management, LNGC* (pp. 239–254). Berlin: Springer Verlag. doi:10.1007/978-3-540-72108-6_16

Weiss, A. (2007). Computing in the clouds. *netWorker, 11*(4), 16–25. doi:10.1145/1327512.1327513

Werder, S. (2009, June). Formalization of spatial constraints. *Proceedings of the 12th AGILE International Conference on Geographic Information Science,* Hannover, Germany

Werthner, H., Hepp, M., Fensel, D., & Dorn, J. (2006, June 14-16). Semantically-enabled service-oriented architectures: a catalyst for smart business networks. *Proceedings of the Smart Business Networks Initiative Discovery Session,* Rotterdam, *The Netherlands.*

WFMC. (1999). *Workflow management coalition, terminology & glossary.* Retrieved January 17, 2007, from http://www.wfmc.org/standards/docs/TC-1011_term_glossary_v3.pdf

White Paper, O. G. C. (2001). *Introduction to OGC Web Services.* Retrieved May 21, 2010, from http://www.opengeospatial.org/pressroom/papers

Whiteside, A., & Evans, J. D. (Eds.). (2008). *OGC Web Coverage Service implementation standard.* Wayland, MA: Open Geospatial Consortium Inc.

Whiteside, A., & Evans, J. (2008). *Web Coverage Service Implementation Standard (Version 1.1.2).* Retrieved March 1, 2020 from http://portal.opengeospatial.org/files/?artifact_id=27297

Whiteside, A., & Evans, J. (2006). *Web Coverage Service (WCS) Implementation Specification.* Open Geospatial Consortium. Retrieved from https://portal.opengeospatial.org/files/?artifact_id=18153

Wiederhold, G. (1992). Mediators in the architecture of future Information Systems. *IEEE Computer Magazine, 25*(3), 38–49.

Wiegand, N., & García, C. (2007). A task-based ontology approach to automated Geospatial Data Retrieval. *Transactions in GIS, 11*(3), 355–376. doi:10.1111/j.1467-9671.2007.01050.x

Williamson, I., Rajabifard, A., & Feeney, M. F. (2003). *Developing Spatial Data Infrastructures: from concept to reality.* London: Taylor & Francis. doi:10.1201/9780203485774

WMS. (2008, 2009). *iPhone and Android WMS apps.* Retrieved from http://androidgps.blogspot.com/2008/09/simple-wms-client-for-android.html http://www.app-storehq.com/mapprowms-iphone-61560/app

Woolf, A., & Shaon, A. (2009). An approach to encapsulation of Grid processing within an OGC Web processing service. *GIS Science, 3*, 82–88.

Workflow Management Coalition. (1999). *Terminology and glossary.*

World Wide Web Consortium. (2004). *OWL Web Ontology Language Guide.* Retrieved July 9, 2010, from http://www.w3.org/TR/owl-guide/

Wrap, N. A. S. A. (2010). *Wildfire Research and Applications Partnership (WRAP) project.* Retrieved from http://geo.arc.nasa.gov/ sge/ WRAP/

WSMO working group. (2004). *WSMO.* Retrieved on May 21, 2010, from http://www.wsmo.org/

Yahalom, R., Klein, B., & Beth, T. (1993). Trust relationships in secure systems-a distributed authentication perspective. *Proceedings from 1993 OEEE Computer Society Symposium on Research in Security and Privacy.* (pp. 150-164).

Yahoo Maps. (2010). *Yahoo local maps.* Retrieved from http:// maps.yahoo.com/

Yang, C., Wong, D. W., Yang, R., Kafatos, M., & Li, Q. (2005). Performance-improving techniques in web-based GIS. *International Journal of Geographical Information Science, 19*(3), 319–342. doi:10.1080/13658810412331280202

Yang, C., Li, W., Xie, J., & Zhou, B. (2008). Distributed geospatial information processing: sharing distributed geospatial resources to support Digital Earth. *International Journal of Digital Earth, 1*, 259–278. doi:10.1080/17538940802037954

Yang, C., Evans, J., Cole, M., Marley, S., Alameh, N., & Bambacus, M. (2007). The emerging concepts and applications of the spatial Web portal. *Photogrammetric Engineering and Remote Sensing, 73*(6), 691–698.

Yang, C., Cao, Y., Evans, J., Kafatos, M., & Bambacus, M. (2006). Spatial Web portal for building spatial data infrastructure. *Journal of Geographic Information Sciences, 12*(1), 38–43.

Yang, W., & Di, L. (2003). Subsetting, georectifying, and reformatting of NASA EOS data through the Web, in image processing and pattern recognition in remote sensing. S. Ungar, S. Mao, & Y. Yasuoka (Eds). *Proceedings of the SPIE, 4898*, pp. 239-246.

Yang, W., & Di, L. (2008). Geographic coverage standards and services. S. Shekhar and H. Xiong (Eds.), *Encyclopedia of GIS.* (pp. 355-358). Springer.

Yu, H.-J., Lee, Z.-H., Ye, C.-F., Chung, L.-K., & Fang, Y.-M. (2009) *OGC®: sensor Web enablement application for debris flow monitoring system in Taiwan.* Retrieved Nov 1, 2009, from OGC website http://portal.opengeospatial.org/files/?artifact_id=34126

Yue, P., Di, L., Yang, W., Yu, G., & Zhao, P. (2007). Semantics-based automatic composition of geospatial Web service chains. *Computers & Geosciences, 33*(5), 649–665. doi:10.1016/j.cageo.2006.09.003

Yue, P., Di, L., Yang, W., Yu, G., Zhao, P., & Gong, J. (2009). Semantic web services based process planning for earth science applications. *International Journal of Geographical Information Science, 23*(9), 1139–1163. doi:10.1080/13658810802032680

Yue, P. (2007). *Semantics-enabled intelligent geospatial web service*. (Doctoral dissertation, Wuhan University). State Key Laboratory of Information Engineering in Surveying, Mapping and Remote Sensing. (pp. 72-76).

Yue, P., Di, L., Yang, W., Yu, G., & Zhao, P. (2006). Path planning for chaining geospatial web services, In *Proceedings of the 6th International Symposium on Web and Wireless Geographical Information Systems (W2GIS2006), Hong Kong*. LCNS 4295, (pp. 214-226). Berlin: Springer.

Zaha, J., Barros, A., Dumas, M., & ter Hofstede, A. (2006). *Let's Dance: A language for service behavior modeling. On the move to maningful Internet Systems 2006: CoopIS, DOA, GADA, and ODBASE*, (pp. 145-162). Retrieved from http://dx.doi.org/10.1007/11914853_10

Zaharia, R., Vasiliu, L., Hoffman, J., & Klien, E. (2009). Semantic execution meets geospatial web services: A pilot application. *Transactions in GIS, 12*(1), 59–73.

Zeng, L., Benatallah, B., Ngu, A. H. H., Dumas, M., Kalagnanam, J., & Chang, H. (2004). Qos-aware middleware for web services composition. *IEEE Transactions on Software Engineering, 30*(5), 311–327. doi:10.1109/TSE.2004.11

Zeng, L., Benatallah, B., Dumas, M., Kalagnanam, J., & Sheng, Z. (2003). *Quality driven web services composition*. Paper presented at 12th international conference on World Wide Web, Budapest, Hungary.

Zhang, C., Li, W., & Zhao, T. (2007). Geospatial data sharing based on geospatial semantic web technologies. *Journal of Spatial Science, 52*(2), 35–49.

Zhang, C., Zhao, T., & Li, W. (2010b). A framework for Geospatial Semantic Web-based spatial decision support system. *International Journal of Digital Earth, 3*, 111–134. doi:10.1080/17538940903373803

Zhang, C., Zhao, T., Li, W., & Osleeb, J. (2010a). Towards logic-based geospatial feature discovery and integration using web feature service and Geospatial Semantic Web. *International Journal of Geographical Information Science, 24*, 903–923. doi:10.1080/13658810903240687

Zhang, T., & Tsou, M. (2009). Developing a grid-enabled spatial Web portal for Internet GIServices and geospatial cyberinfrastructure. *International Journal of Geographical Information Science, 23*(5), 605–630. doi:10.1080/13658810802698571

Zhao, P., Di, L., Yue, P., Wei, Y., & Yang, W. (2009). Semantic Web-based geospatial knowledge transformation. *Computers & Geosciences, 35*, 798–808. doi:10.1016/j.cageo.2008.03.013

Zhao, P., Yu, G., & Di, L. (2007). Geospatial Web services . In Hilton, B. (Ed.), *Emerging Spatial Information Systems and Applications* (pp. 1–35). Hershey, PA: Idea Group.

Zhao, P., Deng, D., & Di, L. (2005). Geospatial Web Service Client. *Proceedings of ASPRS 2005 Annual conference*, Baltimore.

Zhao, P., Di, L., Han, W., Wei, Y., & Li, X. (2008, June). *Building service-oriented architecture based geospatial web portal*. Paper presented at the 2008 Geoinformatics Conference, Potsdam, Germany.

Zhao, T., Zhang, C., Wei, M., & Peng, Z.-R. (2008). Ontology-based geospatial data query and integration. In: Cova, T. J., Miller H. J, Beard K., Frank, A. U., and Goodchild, M. F. (Eds.), *Lecture Notes in Computer Science: Geographic Information Science, 370-392*. Springer.

Zhou, N. (2003). A study on automatic ontology mapping of categorical information. In *Proceedings of national conference on digital government research. 401-404*.

Zhou, N. (2008). Geospatial semantic integration. In S. Shekhar, & H. Xiong (Eds.), *Encyclopedia of GIS*. 386-388. New York: Springer.

Zhou, N., & Wei, H. (2008). Semantic integration and visualization for geospatial data portals. In *Proceedings of the 2008 international Conference on Digital Government Research. 417-418*. Digital Government Society of North America.

Zhu, F., Turner, M., Kotsiopoulos, I., Bennett, K., Russell, M., & Budgen, D. (2006). Dynamic data integration: a service-based broker approach. *International Journal of Business Process Integration and Management, 1*(3), 175–191. doi:10.1504/IJBPIM.2006.010903

About the Contributors

Peisheng Zhao is a Research Associate Professor in Center for Spatial Information Science and Systems at George Mason University. Dr. Zhao received his Ph. D. in Geographic Information System and Cartography from China Academy of Sciences, China in 2000. His research interests include geospatial information interoperability, and geospatial data mining and knowledge discovery. He is known for his contributions to geospatial Web services and workflow. He has published more than 30 peer-reviewed papers in these areas. Dr. Zhao is a co-investigator of several NASA, NGA, FGDC and OGC funded projects. He is an active OGC member to involve the development of standards for geospatial and location based services. In addition, he acts as a reviewer for several journals and participates in various conference and workshop program committees.

Liping Di holds a Ph.D. in Remote Sensing and GIS from the University of Nebraska-Lincoln. He is currently the professor and director of the Center for Spatial Information Science and Systems (CSISS), George Mason University. His research interest is in the area of GIS, remote sensing, interoperability, Semantic Web, global climate and environmental changes. Contact him at ldi@gmu.edu.

* * *

Suchith Anand is an Ordnance Survey Research Fellow at the Centre for Geospatial Science, University of Nottingham. He holds a PhD in Computer Science from the University of Glamorgan, Wales. He also holds an MSc in Geographic Information from City University, London. His research interests are in open source GIS, automated map generalization, geohydroinformatics, mobileGIS, location based services, optimization techniques and asset management. He is a member of the International Cartographic Association (ICA) and chairs the ICA Working Group on Open Source Geospatial Technologies.

Ning An has a Ph. D. in Computer Science and Engineering from the Pennsylvania State University, U.S.A., and has been an active researcher and developer in the spatial information systems for many years. Dr. An has published more than 15 papers in leading international journals and conferences including The VLDB Journal, IEEE Transactions on Knowledge and Data Engineering, International Conference on Data Engineering, and International Conference on World Wide Web. His research interests are in spatial information management, web computing, mobile computing and crisis management. Currently, Dr. An works in the spatial development team at New England Development Center, Oracle Corporation and servers as Cui Ying Professor at Lanzhou University, P. R. China. He is member of IEEE.

Fabio Gomes de Andrade is an adjunct professor at the Computer Science Department of Federal Institute of Education, Science and Technology of Paraiba, Brazil, where he has been since 2002. He received his Master degree in Computer Science from University of Campina Grande in 2006. Actually, Mr. Andrade is a PhD student at the Computer Science Department of University of Campina Grande, under supervision of Dr. Cláudio de Souza Baptista, and his thesis focuses on the use of semantics to enhance geographic data discovery on spatial data infrastructures. Besides, his research interests include spatial data integration, web semantic, distributed databases and information retrieval.

Cláudio de Souza Baptista is an Associate Professor at the Computer Science Department of University of Campina Grande, Brazil, where he has been since 1994. He is also the Coordinator of the Information Systems Laboratory at the same university. He received his PhD degree in Computer Science from University of Kent at Canterbury, United Kingdom, in 2000. From 1991-1993 he worked as a Software Engineer at the Vale Company in Brazil. His research interests include database, distributed databases, digital libraries, geographical information systems, information retrieval, data warehouses, and multimedia databases. He has authored more than 40 papers in international conferences, book chapters and journals.

Bastian Baranski is a research associate at the Institute for Geoinformatics (IfGI) and besides, he works for the company con terra GmbH as a Software Engineer. He obtained his Master's degree in Informatics from the University of Dortmund (Germany) and currently writes his Ph.D. thesis. In this context, he focuses on the integration of Service Level Agreements (SLA) in open standards based Spatial Data Infrastructures (SDIs) and the active enforcement of Quality of Service (QoS) goals by means of Grid and Cloud Computing technologies. In his position at the company con terra GmbH, he is also the internal project manager for the SLA4D-Grid research project that is funded by the German Federal Ministry of Education and Research.

Luis E. Bermudez has a Ph.D. and M.S. in Hydroinformatics from Drexel University, and an M.S. in Industrial Engineering from the Andes University in Bogota, Colombia. He has 15 years of experience in software development, GIS, knowledge representation and semantic web, data integration and international project management. His work has advanced the cyberinfrastructure of hydrologic and marine observatories in the US and abroad. As the Coastal Research Technical Manager at the Southeastern University Research Association he works on advancing the cyberinfrastructure to support improvement of models in research communities and integration of observing systems. He lectures a course in Geospatial Web Services and Interoperability at the University of Maryland. He specializes and has co-authored multiple publications in geospatial web services, integration of observing systems, semantic web and integration and workflow of numerical models. He is also a member of the Open Geospatial Consortium (OGC) and W3C working groups.

Geoinf. Johannes Brauner joined the scientific staff of the Professorship for Geoinformation Systems at Technische Universität Dresden after he finished his Diploma in Geoinformatics at the Institute for Geoinformatics at University of Münster in 2008 about wrapping legacy Geinformation Systems with a WPS interface. He formerly worked for the Institute of Geoinformatics and con terra GmbH in Münster in various research and development projects. Currently, he is a PhD candidate, works for the

EU-funded GIGAS and EO2HEAVEN projects and is chair of the AGILE/EuroSDR/OGC Persistent Spatial Data Infrastructure Testbed for Research and Teaching in Europe (PTB). As part of his ongoing PhD research, he is interested in the formalization and the semantics of geoprocesses. Additionally, he is member of the 52°North Geoprocessing Community.

Helen Conover is technical lead for the Information Technology and Systems Center at the University of Alabama in Huntsville, where she oversees a variety of research projects. Ms. Conover has specialized in data systems interoperability since helping develop NASA's distributed Information Management System working prototype for the Earth Observing System Data and Information System (EOSDIS) in the early 1990's. Current data systems projects include the NASA AMSR-E Science Investigator-led Processing System (SIPS), Land and Atmosphere Near-real-time Capability for EOS (LANCE) for AMSR-E, as well as Information Technology for the Genesis and Rapid Intensification Processes (GRIP) airborne field experiment in the summer and fall of 2010. Currently, Ms. Conover serves in the Standards Process Group of NASA Earth Science Data Systems Working Groups, and on the Data Management and Communications (DMAC) Metadata Expert Team for the multi-agency Integrated Ocean Observing System (IOOS).

Tino Fleuren is a research assistant at the University of Kaiserslautern, Germany and is doing his PhD under the supervision of Prof. Dr. Paul Müller at Integrated Communication Systems Lab (ICSY). His research interests lie in the area of service-oriented computing, and scientific workflows. He focuses on efficient execution of large scale, data intensive science applications especially geospatial workflows on current and emerging distributed platforms like clusters, Grids and Clouds. This includes aspects of advanced data management – storage, movement, and discovery – as well as integration of diverse service technologies like OGC Web services and Grid services. He received his diploma in computer science from the University of Kaiserslautern, Germany. Contact him at fleuren@informatik.uni-kl.de; P.O. Box 3049, D-67653 Kaiserslautern

Theodor Foerster (1980) is a research associate at the Institute for Geoinformatics (IFGI) and is a member of the Sensor web, web-based geoprocessing and simulation lab (SWSL). He has 5+ years of job experience with a strong focus on design and development of web-based architectures for geographic applications. Until November 2009, he was a PhD candidate at the International Institute for Geoinformation Science and Earth Observation (ITC) in Enschede, the Netherlands, where he received his PhD degree from the University of Twente for his research about Web-based Architecture for On-demand Maps - Integrating Meaningful Generalization Processing. Before that he worked at IFGI as a researcher. In 2004 he obtained a Diploma degree in Geoinformatics from the University of Muenster. He is active member of the 52°North open source initiative (www.52north.org) and is leading the development of the 52°North Web Processing Service (52n WPS) at the 52°North Geoprocessing Community. Besides that he is participating in the standardization of Geoprocessing Services at OGC.

Rüdiger Gartmann is employed as a Senior Consultant at con terra GmbH, which is the professional services branch of ESRI Germany. There he acts as product manager for security and rights management-related products, and as a project manager for SDI projects with a special focus on geospatial rights management (GeoRM). In this field, Rüdiger Gartmann also represents con terra at standards organizations such as OGC, chairing the GeoRM Standards Working Group and editing the GeoRM Common specification. Rüdiger Gartmann has a Master's degree in Business Computer Science from the University of Essen, Germany, and has a strong research background in the field of distributed computing from more than 10 years working for the Fraunhofer Societey and the University of Münster.

Carlos Granell is a postdoctoral researcher at the Institute of New Imaging Technologies, Universitat Jaume I (Spain), where he graduated in Computer Engineering (2000) and received his doctorate in Computer Science (2006). His lines of research are centred on Geographic Information Systems (GIS), Spatial Data Infrastructures (SDI), interoperability, geoprocessing services, workflow, and the composition and reuse of geographic services. He has taken part in several public funded research projects, both at national and European level, the most important of which are the European projects ACE-GIS, AWARE and recently EuroGEOSS. He has carried out research stages at SINTEF (Norway), at the Faculty of Geo-Information Science and Earth Observation of the University of Twente (The Netherlands), and the University of Nottingham (UK).

Sara James Graves is the Director of the Information Technology and Systems Center, the University of Alabama System Board of Trustees University Professor and Professor of Computer Science at the University of Alabama in Huntsville. Her current service includes membership on the National Academy of Sciences Board on Research Data and Information, the Executive Committee of CODATA, the International Council for Science: Committee on Data for Science and Technology; the Oak Ridge National Laboratory Climate Change Science Institute Science Advisory Board; the Board of Trustees for the Southeastern Universities Research Association (SURA), and is a Founding Member, National Oceanic and Atmospheric Administration Science Advisory Board Data Archiving and Access Requirements Working Group. Dr. Graves directs research and development in large-scale distributed information systems, data mining and knowledge discovery, high performance computing and networking, semantic web and grid technologies and services, geospatial data analysis and visualization. She has been the Principal Investigator on many research projects with DOD, DOE, NASA, NOAA, NSF, and other entities. Her degrees are in Computer Science and Mathematical Sciences, and she has served as chair or member of over 100 Ph.D. and M.S. committees.

Weiguo Han received the B.Sc. degree in applied mathematics from Tianjin University, China, in 1996, the M.Sc. degree in computer science from Huazhong University of Science and Technology, Wuhan, China, in 2002, and the Ph.D. degree in geoinformatics from the Institute of Geographic Sciences and Natural Resources Research, Chinese Academy of Sciences, Beijing, China, in 2005. He is currently a Research Assistant Professor with the Center for Spatial Information Science and Systems, George Mason University, Fairfax, USA. His research interests include Geospatial information services, remote sensing data analysis, Semantic Web, SOA based Web information system, spatial and temporal data mining, and spatial analysis.

Lianlian He holds a B.Sc. degree in Informatics and Computational Sciences (2002) and a M.Sc. degree in Computational Mathematics from the Wuhan University (2005). She is currently working as a lecturer in the department of Mathematics, Hubei University of Education, China. Her research interest is on the applications of computational mathematic methods in Geoinformatics and Bioinformatics. Contact her at gonewithhll@163.com.

Gobe Hobona is a postdoctoral researcher in the Centre for Geospatial Science (CGS) at the University of Nottingham. He holds a PhD in Geomatics from Newcastle University. His research interests are on the integration of geospatial web services with e-science approaches such as ontologies, grid and cloud computing. Within the SAW-GEO project he led the development of a workflow management system for orchestrating grid and geospatial web services based on the international standard ISO19119, Open Grid Services Architecture (OGSA) and the Business Process Execution Language (BPEL). He has participated in several projects relating to Spatial Data Infrastructure, for example, GIS4EU, GIGAS and the Global Earth Observation System of Systems (GEOSS).

Elias Ioup is currently a computer scientist with the Naval Research Laboratory Geospatial Sciences and Technology Branch and a doctoral student in Engineering and Applied Science at the University of New Orleans. Elias Ioup has authored several publications on spatial databases and machine learning. He holds a B.S. with honors in mathematics and a B.S. in computer science from the University of Chicago.

Mike Jackson has over 30 years research experience in the location-based services, mapping and remote sensing sectors within government, industry and academia. His previous posts include CEO of Laser-Scan and Director of Space Division at QinetiQ. He is currently the Director of the Centre for Geospatial Science at the University of Nottingham and is a non-executive Director of the Open Geospatial Consortium Inc. (OGC). He is a member of the recently formed GEOSS Common Infrastructure Coordinating Team and the UK Location Council Interoperability Board. Professor Jackson is a management board member of the European Centre for Innovation in Geospatial and Location Based Services (an industry consortium involving Oracle, TeleAtlas, Capgemini, EBN etc.). He has published widely in the area of geospatial science and is a frequent key-note speaker at conferences worldwide.

Baris M. Kazar got his undergraduate degree from the Electrical and Electronics Engineering Department of the Middle East Technical University in 1996. Dr. Kazar got his Master of Science degree from the Electrical and Computer Engineering department of the University of Minnesota, Twin Cities in 2000, whose focus was on Computer Engineering. Dr. Kazar received his doctorate degree from the Electrical and Computer Engineering department of the University of Minnesota, Twin Cities in 2005. Since 2005, Dr. Kazar has been working in Oracle Spatial Group of Oracle America Inc. Dr. Kazar has been on Program Committees of various GIS and Data Mining conferences. He was UCGIS Young Scholars' Committee Student Representative for the year 2004-05. He got travel awards from NSF TeraGrid Workshop on Cyber-GIS 2010, GIScience 2004, and the 2003 ACM Federated Computing Research Conferences: Principles and Practice of Parallel Programming (PPoPP'03) Conference. He is member of IEEE Computer Society.

Ken Keiser is a researcher at the Information Technology and Systems Center, located at the University of Alabama in Huntsville. He is actively involved in projects to improve the distributed access, visualization and analysis of geospatial data. Ken participates in Earth science data systems forums and working groups across various agencies and science disciplines.

Fábio Luiz Leite Júnior is an Adjunct professor at the Computing and Mathematics Department of State University of Paraíba, Campina Grande, Brazil, where he has been since 2010. He received Master in Computer Science degree from Federal University of Campina Grande in 2007.Since 2008, He has been worked on Research, Development and Innovation projects concerning to GIS, Power Systems, Systems Integration and Interoperability. Also, He is CIO in Inteligis Soluções em Sistemas, where he coordinates systems development. Currently, his research interests include web semantic, database, distributed databases, digital libraries, geographical information systems and information retrieval. He has authored more than 10 papers in international conferences, book chapters and journals.

Xiaoyan Li received the B.Eng. degree and the M.Eng. degree in power mechanical engineering from Inner Mongolia University of Technology, Hohhot, China, respectively in 1993 and in 2000, and the Ph.D. degree in thermophysics engineering from University of Science and Technology of China, Hefei, China, in 2004.

Gang Liu got his Bachelor of Science degree from the Department of Applied Mathematics at Chengdu University of Technology, P. R. China in 2000. Subsequently, Mr. Liu got his Master of Science degree from the same department at Chengdu University of Technology in 2003 with a focus on designing nonlinear algorithms. Since then, he has been a lecturer in School of Information Science & Engineering at Lanzhou University. Currently, he is also a Ph. D. candidate in School of Mathematics and Statistics at Lanzhou University, and his research interests are in spatial information management, especially how to utilize geospatial information in public crisis management.

Manil Maskey is pursuing PhD in Computer Science at the University of Alabama in Huntsville, where he is also a Research Scientist for the Information Technology & Systems Center. His research spans the fields of geospatial web services, visualization, data mining, and visual analytics. He is a member of the IEEE. He has Bachelor of Science degree in Mathematics and Computer science from the Fairmont State University and Master of Science degree in Computer Science from the University of Alabama in Huntsville. His prior industry experiences include designing and developing customer analysis, market basket analysis, and personalization software for customer relationship technology. His current projects include science collaboration framework development and science workflow tools development.

Paul Müller is a professor in the computer science department and the director of the central computing department of the University of Kaiserslautern, Germany. His research interests include distributed applications, Grid computing, and service-oriented architectures, with a special focus on how the SOA-concepts can be applied to the next generation of the Internet. His Integrated Communications Systems Lab (ICSY) is aiming at the development of services to implement integrated communication within heterogeneous environments especially in the context of the emerging discussion about Future Internet. This is achieved by using service-oriented architectures (SOA), Grid technology, and communication middleware within a variety of application scenarios ranging from personal communication (multimedia) to ubiquitous computing. He is member of the Euro-NF network of excellence for Future Internet. Prof. Müller received his PhD in mathematics at the University of Ulm, Germany. Contact him at pmueller@ informatik.uni-kl.de; P.O. Box 3049, D-67653 Kaiserslautern

George Percivall is an accomplished leader in the development of information systems and international standards for geospatial information. As OGC's Chief Architect, he is responsible for the overall vision for the OGC baseline and its evolution through developments by OGC members. As Executive Director of OGC's Interoperability Program, he is responsible for managing OGC's Interoperability Program, which involves planning and executing testbeds, pilot projects, interoperability experiments etc., and for OGC's compliance testing program. Prior to joining OGC, Mr. Percivall had leadership roles on several NASA projects. He was Chief Engineer of the Earth Observing System Data and Information System (EOSDIS) for the Landsat/Terra release; Principal engineer for NASA's Geospatial Interoperability Office; and, represented NASA in OGC, ISO TC211, and CEOS. He was the Director of the Geospatial Interoperability Group of GST, Inc. Previously, he led developments in Intelligent Transportation Systems with the US Automated Highway Consortium and General Motors Systems Engineering. He holds a BS in Physics and an MS in Electrical Engineering from the University of Illinois - Urbana.

Carl Reed is currently the Chief Technology Officer of the Open Geospatial Consortium, Inc. (OGC). In his role as CTO, Dr. Reed also participates in and collaborates with other standards organizations, including OASIS, NENA, ISO, and the IETF, to insure harmonization of geospatial standards across information communities. In a 2006 collaboration, Dr. Reed helped define the initial GeoRSS specification. Prior to the OGC, Reed was the vice president of geospatial marketing at Intergraph. This was after a long tenure at GIS software company Genasys II, where he served as chief technology officer for Genasys II worldwide. From 1989 to 1996, Dr. Reed was president of the Genasys Americas operation. Dr. Reed received his PhD in Geography, specializing in systems architectures for GIS technology, from the State University of New York at Buffalo in 1980. For his contributions to the geospatial industry, in 2009 Reed was inducted into the URISA GIS Hall of Fame.

Elena Roglia took her degree in mathematics science at Mathematics Science Department of Turin University. Her thesis focuses on Hopfield neural networks and Boltzmann machine. She is a PhD student in Computer science and High technology at Department of Computer Science of Turin University. Her research topics include machine learning techniques for classification and regression with particular emphasis on neural networks, data mining techniques for features selection and geographical information systems. Currently, she holds a contract for project collaboration with the Department of Computer Science of Turin University, where she is involved in the design and implementation of the SSC control station for the project SMAT-F1 promoted by Piedmont Region for the development of innovative technologies for territorial monitoring by means of Unmanned Aerial Vehicle.

Rosa Meo took her Master degree in Electronic Engineering in 1993 and her Ph.D. in Computer Science and Systems Engineering in 1997, both at the Politecnico di Torino, Italy. From 2005 she is associate professor at the Department of Computer Science in the University of Turin, where she works in the Database and Data Mining research field. From 2000 to 2003 she was responsible for the University of Torino the cInQ Project (consortium on knowledge discovery by Inductive Queries) funded by the V EU Funding Framework. She is active in the scientific activity in the field of Database and Data Mining in which she published more than 40 papers. She served in the Programme Committee of many International and National Conferences on Databases and Data Mining, among which VLDB, ACM KDD, IEEE ICDM, SIAM DM, ACM CIKM, ECML/PKDD, ACM SAC, DEXA, DaWak.

Richard Onchaga Moses is a lecturer in the department of Geospatial Science and Engineering at the Kenya Polytechnic University College, Nairobi, Kenya. He is currently a PhD candidate at the University of Twente, Enschede. Richard holds a Master of Science degree in Geoinformatics degree from ITC, Enschede, The Netherlands and a Bachelor of Science degree in Surveying from the University of Nairobi, Kenya. His research interests include quality in distributed geographic information systems, architecture and middleware support for geospatial web services and optimization of geoinformation production processes.

Zhong-Ren Peng is Professor and Chair of the Department of Urban and Regional Planning at the University of Florida, Gainesville, FL, USA, and Cheung Kong Chair Professor of the College of Transportation Engineering at Tongji University, Shanghai, P.R. China. His major research interests are in the areas of geographic information science; Internet GIS; transportation and land use planning, modeling and policy; information technology for planning; international planning. Dr. Peng has worked as a principal investigator or Co-PI on numerous research projects. Funding for his research has been provided by the National Science Foundation (NSF), the Federal Transit Administration, Federal Geographic Data Committee, and the Wisconsin and Florida Departments of Transportation (DOT). Dr. Peng has published over 30 peer-reviewed articles in academic journals and is the principle author of the book "Internet GIS: Distributed geographic information services for the Internet and wireless networks" (Co-author Ming Hsiang Tsou) which was published in March 2003 by Wiley & Sons.

John Sample has been a computer scientist with the Naval Research Laboratory since 1998 and is currently the lead for NRL's geospatial intelligence (GEOINT) research and development activities. Dr. Sample has authored several book chapters, conference proceedings and journal articles related to geospatial and environmental data dissemination. He holds a B.S. in mathematics from the University of Southern Mississippi and a Ph.D. in computer science from Louisiana State University.

Sven Schade holds a diploma and PhD in Geoinformatics; both from the University of Muenster (Germany). He worked at the Institute for Geoinformatics of the University of Muenster for more than seven years, where he was involved in teaching and in numerous national and European research projects relating to Spatial Data Infrastructures (SDI) and Semantic Web technology. In October 2009, he became postdoctoral researcher at the SDI group of the Joint Research Centre (JRC) of the European Commission. His research is focusing on the translation of geospatial data and interoperable service architectures. He specifically addresses the use of Linked Data in the Sensor Web and possible contributions to the Digital Earth vision.

Bastian Schäffer is a research assistant at the Institute for Geoinformatics (IfGI) at the University of Münster, where he also obtained his Master's degree from in 2008. Additionally, B. Schäffer is currently in the process of writing his Ph.D. thesis at IfGI. Besides, he is the head of the 52°North Open Source initiative's Geoprocessing Community. In this context, B. Schäffer is interested in interoperable web service architectures, standards, spatial data infrastructures, geoprocessing workflows, virtual organizations, cloud computing and security aspects of those topics. He is also a member of several OGC standards working groups and leading the specification of the WPS 2.0 SWG.

Wenli Yang is with the Center for Spatial Information Science and Systems, George Mason University, in Fairfax Virginia. His work mainly involves Earth observing remote sensing data and information systems, including data and information models, standardization, services, and system design and implementation. Some of the recent projects he involved include service interoperability among different Earth science research communities, intelligent Web services for automated geospatial knowledge discovery, intelligent archives in the context of knowledge building systems, and large scale data mining. He also teaches under graduate and graduate courses, including remote sensing application, earth image analysis, and digital processing of remote sensing imagery.

Peng Yue holds a Ph.D. in GIS from the Wuhan University. He is currently an associate professor at State Key Laboratory of Information Engineering in Surveying Mapping and Remote Sensing at Wuhan University, China. His research interest is on GIS interoperability, Web GIS, and Geospatial Semantic Web. He has been involved in many related research projects, including Choreographed Intelligent Web Services for Automated Geospatial Knowledge Discovery funded by U.S. NGA NURI, GeoBrain project funded by U.S. NASA REASoN program, Metadata Tracking in Geospatial Service Chaining and Geospatial Data Provenance funded by NSF of China, Grid GIS and Semantic Web-based Intelligent Geospatial Web Service funded by Ministry of Science and Technology of China. . Contact him at geopyue@gmail.com.

Chuanrong Zhang is an assistant professor at the University of Connecticut. She got her PhD degree in GIS from University of Wisconsin, Milwaukee in 2004. She has several years of working experience in computer companies. She holds a joint appointment at department of Geography and Center for Environmental Sciences and Engineering in the University of Connecticut. She has interests in GIS, Geostatistics and their applications in natural resource management and environmental evaluation. Her current research concentrates on Geospatial Semantic Web and development of Markov Chain Geostatistics. Dr. Zhang has published over 50 peer-reviewed articles in academic journals, book chapters, and conference proceedings.

Tian Zhao is an associate professor in computer science at the University of Wisconsin – Milwaukee. His research areas are programming languages, type systems, type inference, software engineering, and Geospatial Semantic Web.

Naijun Zhou received his Ph.D. in GIScience from the University of Wisconsin – Madison in 2005, and two Masters degrees in computer science and GIS respectively. He is currently an assistant professor in the Department of Geography at the University of Maryland at College Park, where he teaches both undergraduate and graduate courses of GIS, spatial databases and statistics. His current research interests include geospatial interoperability using ontological and semantic technologies, developing automated algorithms for data integration, and their applications in Internet GIS and geospatial portals. He has published numerous research articles in journals, referred conferences and books, and served as a reviewer or a committee member for journals, books and conferences. His research program has been supported by federal and state agencies such as National Science Foundation, USGS and the State of Maryland.

Index

X

XML format design 18
XML Schema Document (XSD) 32, 33

Y

Yahoo Maps 429, 453
YouTube 195